PHILIP'S

STREETS East Sussex

Bexhill, Brighton, Eastbourne, Hastings, Hove, Lewes, Uckfield

www.philips-maps.co.uk
First published in 1994 by
Philip's, a division of
Octopus Publishing Group Ltd
www.octopusbooks.co.uk
Endeavour House, 189 Shaftesbury Avenue
London WC2H 8JY
An Hachette UK Company
www.hachette.co.uk

Fourth colour edition 2008
Second impression 2012
ESUDA

ISBN 978-1-84907-244-1 (spiral)

© Philip's 2008

os Ordnance Survey®

This product includes mapping data licensed
from Ordnance Survey® with the permission
of the Controller of Her Majesty's Stationery
Office. © Crown copyright 2008. All rights
reserved. Licence number 100011710.

Speed camera data provided by
PocketGPSWorld.com Ltd

Post Office is a trade mark of Post Office Ltd in
the UK and other countries.

Printed in China

Contents

II Mobile safety cameras

III **Key to map symbols**

IV **Key to map pages**

VI **Route planning**

VIII Administrative and Postcode boundaries

1 **Street maps** at 3½ inches to 1 mile

189 **Street maps of Brighton and Lewes town centres** at 7 inches to 1 mile

191 **Index** of towns, villages, streets, hospitals, industrial estates, railway stations, schools, shopping centres, universities and places of interest

Digital Data

The exceptionally high-quality mapping found in this atlas is available as digital data in TIFF format, which is easily convertible to other bitmapped (raster) image formats.

The index is also available in digital form as a standard database table. It contains all the details found in the printed index together with the National Grid reference for the map square in which each entry is named.

For further information and to discuss your requirements, please contact
philips@mapsinternational.co.uk

Information Centre   0871 6630031

Mobile safety cameras

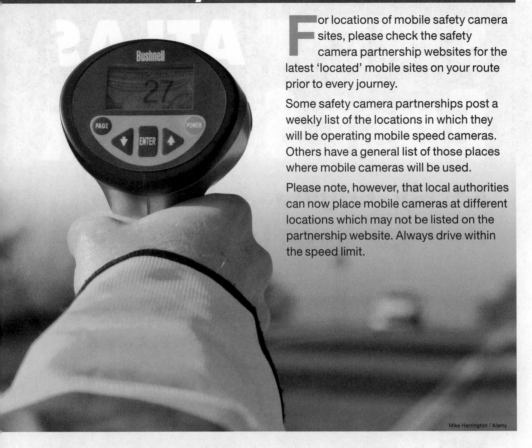

Mike Harrington / Alamy

For locations of mobile safety camera sites, please check the safety camera partnership websites for the latest 'located' mobile sites on your route prior to every journey.

Some safety camera partnerships post a weekly list of the locations in which they will be operating mobile speed cameras. Others have a general list of those places where mobile cameras will be used.

Please note, however, that local authorities can now place mobile cameras at different locations which may not be listed on the partnership website. Always drive within the speed limit.

Useful websites

Sussex Safer Roads Partnership
www.sussexsaferroads.gov.uk

Kent and Medway Safety Camera Partnership
www.kmscp.org

Further information
www.dvla.gov.uk

www.thinkroadsafety.gov.uk

www.dft.gov.uk

www.road-safe.org

Symbol	Description
(22a)	**Motorway** with junction number
	Primary route – dual/single carriageway
	A road – dual/single carriageway
	B road – dual/single carriageway
	Minor road – dual/single carriageway
	Other minor road – dual/single carriageway
	Road under construction
	Tunnel, covered road
(30) (30)	**Speed cameras - single, multiple**
	Rural track, private road or narrow road in urban area
	Gate or obstruction to traffic (restrictions may not apply at all times or to all vehicles)
	Path, bridleway, byway open to all traffic, restricted byway
	Pedestrianised area
DY7	**Postcode boundaries**
	County and unitary authority boundaries
	Railway, tunnel, railway under construction
	Tramway, tramway under construction
	Miniature railway
Walsall	**Railway station**
	Private railway station
South Shields	**Metro station**
	Tram stop, tram stop under construction
	Bus, coach station

Symbol	Description
◆	**Ambulance station**
◆	**Coastguard station**
◆	**Fire station**
◆	**Police station**
✚	**Accident and Emergency entrance to hospital**
H	**Hospital**
+	**Place of worship**
i	**Information Centre** (open all year)
🛒	**Shopping Centre**
P P&R	**Parking, Park and Ride**
PO	**Post Office**
⛺ 🚐	**Camping site, caravan site**
▶ ✗	**Golf course, picnic site**
Prim Sch	**Important buildings, schools, colleges, universities and hospitals**
	Built up area
	Woods
River Ouse	**Tidal water, water name**
	Non-tidal water – lake, river, canal or stream
	Lock, weir, tunnel
Church	**Non-Roman antiquity**
ROMAN FORT	**Roman antiquity**
87 190	**Adjoining page indicators and overlap bands** The colour of the arrow and the band indicates the scale of the adjoining or overlapping page (see scales below)

Enlarged mapping only

Symbol	Description
	Railway or bus station building
	Place of interest
	Parkland

■ The small numbers around the edges of the maps identify the 1 kilometre National Grid lines ■ The dark grey border on the inside edge of some pages indicates that the mapping does not continue onto the adjacent page

Acad	Academy	Inst	Institute	Recn Gd	Recreation Ground	
Allot Gdns	Allotments	Ct	Law Court			
Cemy	Cemetery	L Ctr	Leisure Centre	Resr	Reservoir	
C Ctr	Civic Centre	LC	Level Crossing	Ret Pk	Retail Park	
CH	Club House	Liby	Library	Sch	School	
Coll	College	Mkt	Market	Sh Ctr	Shopping Centre	
Crem	Crematorium	Meml	Memorial	TH	Town Hall/House	
Ent	Enterprise	Mon	Monument	Trad Est	Trading Estate	
Ex H	Exhibition Hall	Mus	Museum	Univ	University	
Ind Est	Industrial Estate	Obsy	Observatory	W Twr	Water Tower	
IRB Sta	Inshore Rescue Boat Station	Pal	Royal Palace	Wks	Works	
		PH	Public House	YH	Youth Hostel	

The scale of the maps on the pages numbered in blue is 5.52 cm to 1 km • 3½ inches to 1 mile • 1: 18103

0	¼	½	¾	1 mile
0	250m 500m	750m 1 kilometre		

The scale of the maps on pages numbered in red is 11.04 cm to 1 km • 7 inches to 1 mile • 1: 9051

0	220 yards	440 yards	660 yards	½ mile
0	125m 250m	375m ½ kilometre		

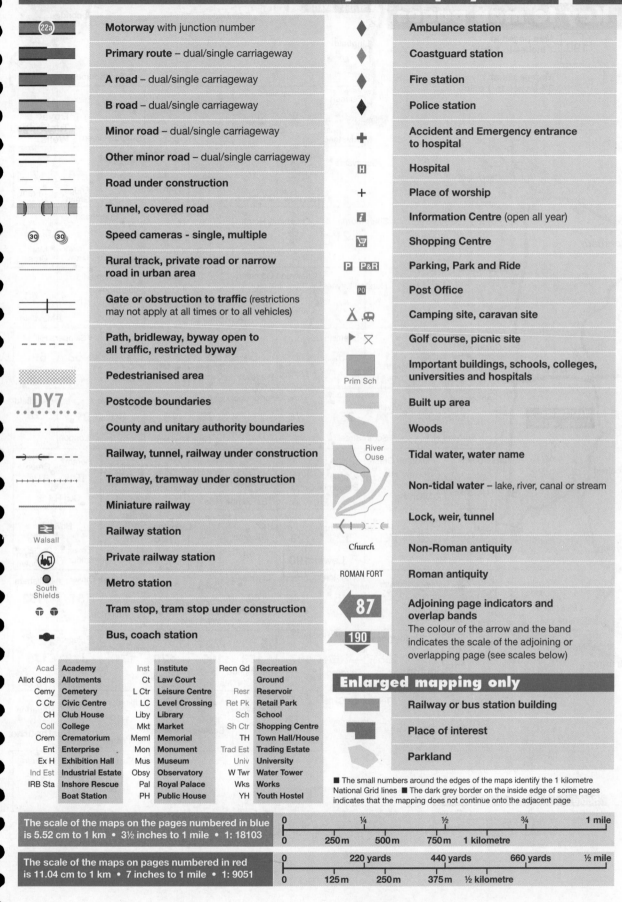

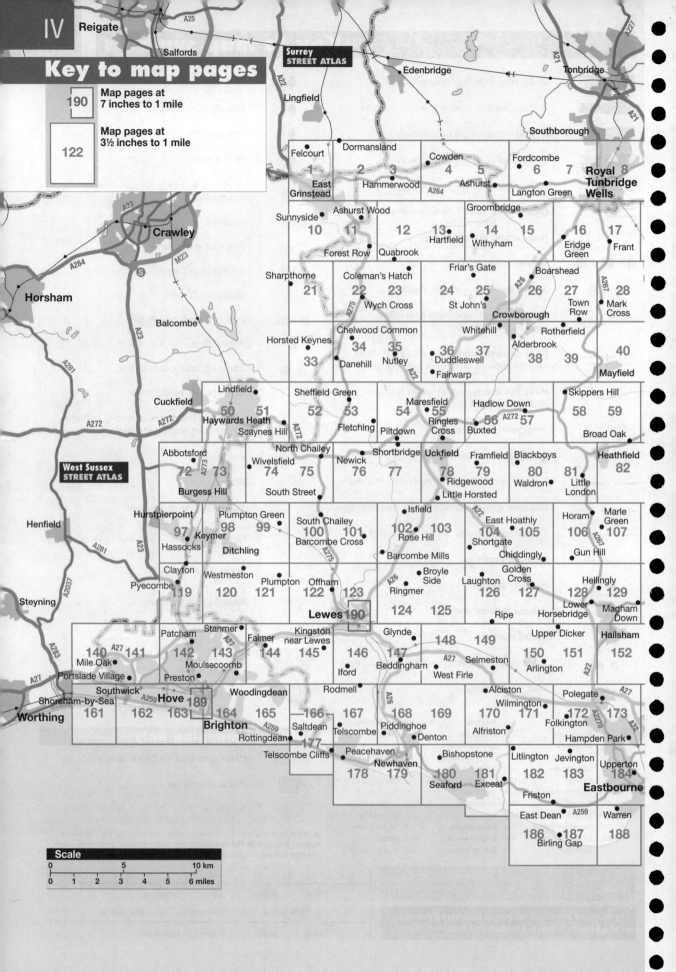

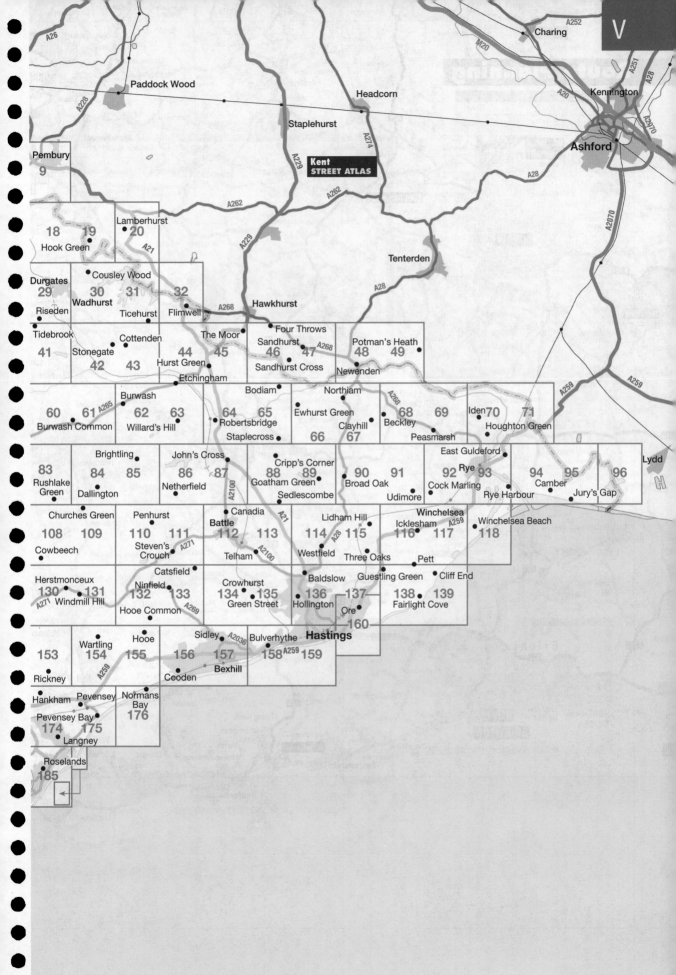

Route Planning

Scale

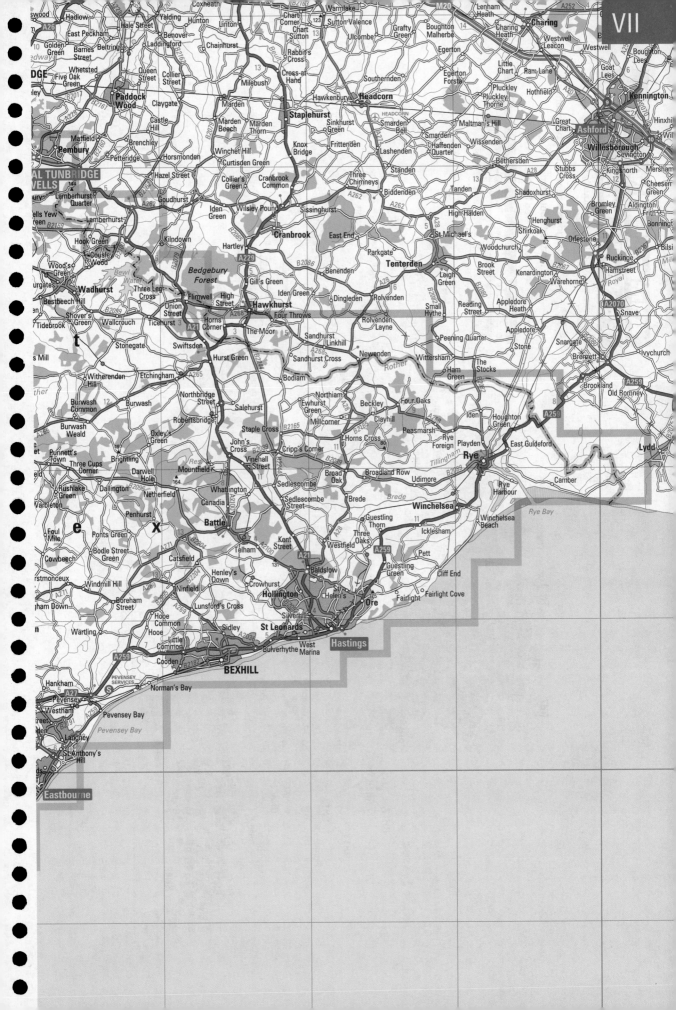

Administrative and Postcode boundaries

Scale

County and county borough boundaries

Local government district boundaries

Postcode boundaries

Area covered by this atlas

0   5   10   15 km

0   5   10 miles

Surrey

West Sussex

Kent

East Sussex

Rother

Wealden

Lewes

City of Brighton & Hove

Brighton

Hastings

Eastbourne

TQ TR
TV

TN29
Camber
TN29
Peasmarsh Iden
Rye
Northiam TN31
TN30
Winchelsea
TN36
TN17
Newenden
Sandhurst
Broad Oak
Westfield TN35
Baldslow
Pett
TN18 Salehurst
Robertsbridge
TN32
Hurst Green
TN19
Burwash
TN17
Ticehurst
Lamberhurst
Wadhurst
Stonegate
TN5
TN3
Frant
Royal Tunbridge Wells
TN4 TN2
TN1
TN2
Mayfield
TN20
Groombridge
TN3
Crowborough
TN6
Langton Green
Cowden
Hartfield
TN7
TN8
East Grinstead
Forest Row
RH19
RH18
RH17
Horsted Keynes
Haywards Heath
RH16
Keymer
BN6
RH15
Burgess Hill
Pyecombe
BN45
Patcham
BN1
Portslade-by-Sea
BN41
Southwick
BN43
Shoreham-by-Sea
BN42
Hove
BN3
Brighton
BN2
Woodingdean
Saltdean
Peacehaven
BN10
Newhaven
BN9
Seaford
BN25
Newick
Barcombe Cross
Ringmer
Lewes
BN7
BN8
Glynde
Laughton
East Hoathly
Framfield
Uckfield
TN22
Maresfield
Nutley
Buxted
Heathfield
TN21
Rushlake Green
Herstmonceux
Hailsham
BN27
Berwick
Polegate
BN26
Alfriston
East Dean
BN20
Eastbourne
BN21 BN22
BN22
BN23
Langney
BN24
Pevensey Bay
TN39
Pebsham
Bexhill
TN40
Crowhurst
TN33
Battle
TN38
St Leonards
TN37
Hastings
TN34

RH7
RH17
TN11
TN2
TN17

Kent

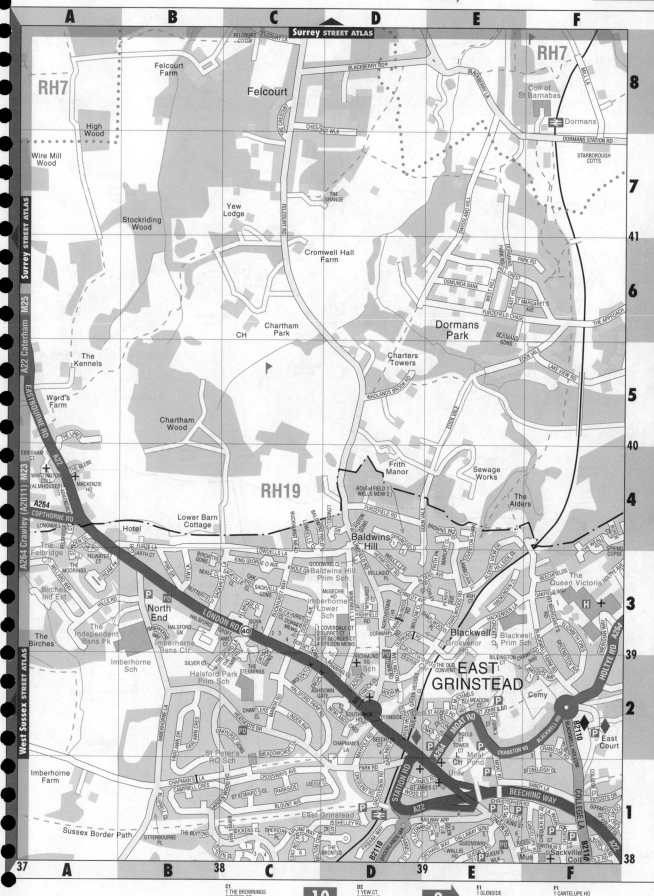

C1
1 THE BROWNINGS
2 BYRON GR
3 CHAUCER AVE
4 TENNYSON RISE
5 THE SAYERS
6 WORDSWORTH RISE

D2
1 YEW CT
2 BEECH CL
3 ELM CT
4 ST CATHERINE'S CT

E1
1 GLENSIDE
2 GREGORY CT
3 WARELAND HO
4 OVERTON CT
5 BROOKLAND HO
6 INSTITUTE WLK
7 CANTELUPE MEWS

F1
1 CANTELUPE HO
2 RUDGE HO
F2
1 ROBIN CL
2 EARLE HO
3 EASTCOURT VILLAS
4 THE OLD SURGERY
5 ST JULIAN
6 DRURY LO

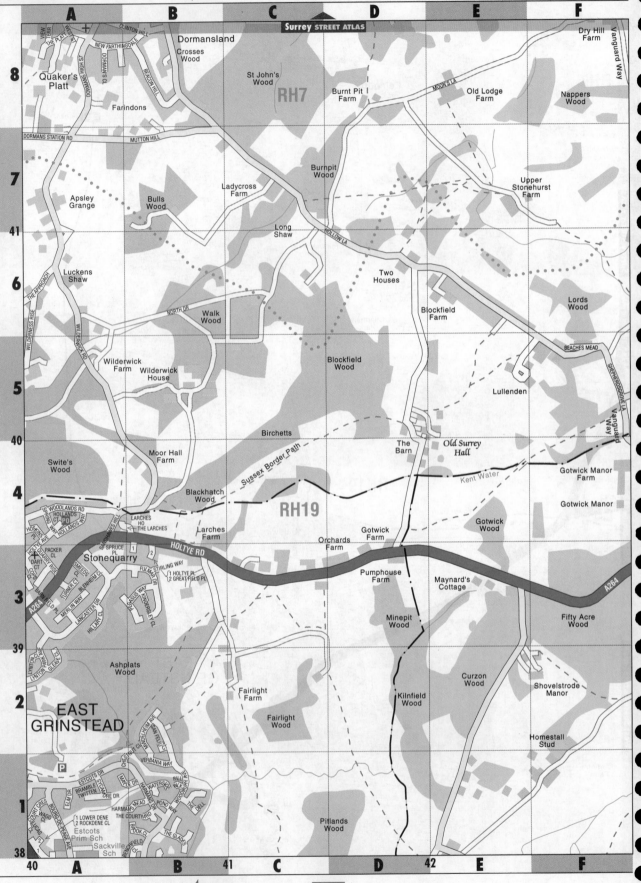

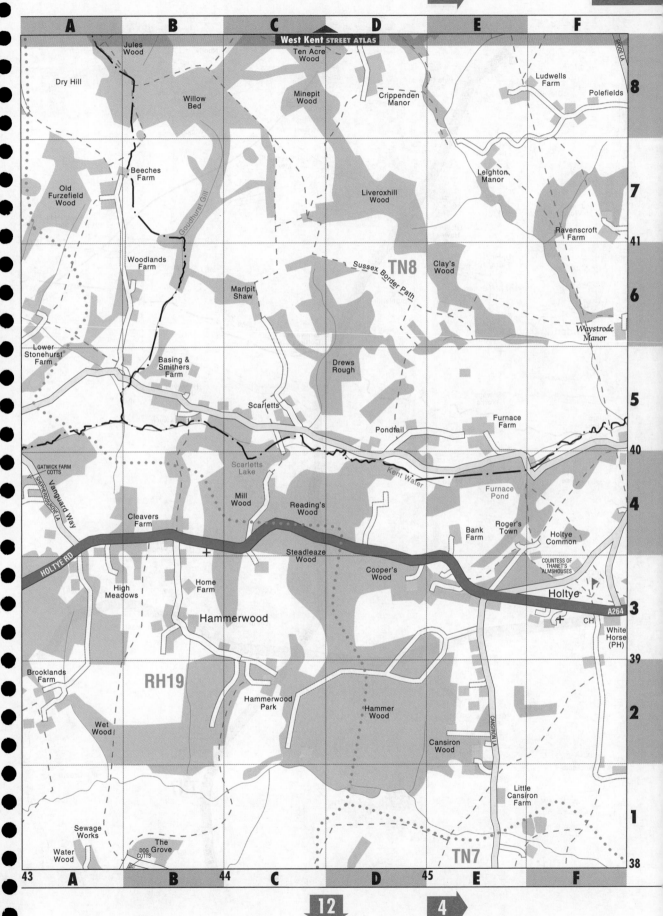

West Kent STREET ATLAS

A   B   C   D   E   F

SPODE LA

Jules Wood

Dry Hill

Ten Acre Wood

Minepit Wood

Crippenden Manor

Ludwells Farm

Polefields

8

Willow Bed

Beeches Farm

Leighton Manor

7

Old Furzefield Wood

Goudhurst Gill

Woodlands Farm

Liveroxhill Wood

Ravenscroft Farm

41

Sussex Border Path

TN8

Clay's Wood

6

Marlpit Shaw

Waystrode Manor

Lower Stonehurst Farm

Basing & Smithers Farm

Drews Rough

5

Scarletts

Furnace Farm

Pondtail

40

GATWICK FARM COTTS

Scarletts Lake

Kent Water

Vanguard Way

SHEPHERDSGROVE LA

Mill Wood

Reading's Wood

Furnace Pond

4

Cleavers Farm

Steadleaze Wood

Bank Farm

Roger's Town

Holtye Common

COUNTESS OF THANET'S ALMSHOUSES

HOLTYE RD

High Meadows

Home Farm

Cooper's Wood

Holtye

Hammerwood

A264

3

CH

White Horse (PH)

39

Brooklands Farm

RH19

Hammerwood Park

Hammer Wood

CANSIRON LA

2

Wet Wood

Cansiron Wood

Sewage Works

The Grove

DOG GROVE COTTS

Little Cansiron Farm

1

Water Wood

TN7

38

43   A   B   44   C   D   45   E   F

A B C D E F

8
7
41
6

5
40
4

3
39
2

1
38
46 47 48

A B C D E F

Mount Noddy
Claydene
Pyle Gate Farm
B2026
PO
BLOWERS HILL
Cowden
Rickwoods Farm
RAILWAY COTTS
Wickens
Saxbys Mead
Jones's Wood
THE PADDOCKS
COWDEN CROSS
Glover's Hawes
Saxbys
Sandfields Farm
Uphill Farm
MOAT LA
Butterwell Bridge
Southlands
Moat Farm
Cowden
CHESTNUT PL
NORTH ST
PRIOR'S WAY
Crown Inn (PH)
TN8
Kentwater Cottages
Sussex Border Path
CHANTLERS MEAD
THE SQUARE
CHURCH ST
HIGH ST
COWDEN MEWS
Sewage Works
Kent Water
Holywych House
Kitford Bridge
Sussex House Farm
Holywych Farm
Holtye House
Heathersome's Wood
Langley Farm
Peter's Wood
Cullinghurst Farm
Hethe House
Great Wood
TN3
Sussex Oak (PH)
A264
Cullinghurst Wood
Mast
B2026
A264
39
Broomland Wood
Scragg's Farm
GOODTREES LA
Chantlers Farm
EDENBRIDGE RD
Tye Farm
Lower Brockshill Farm
Coomb Wood
TN7
Beech Green Park
BEECH GREEN LA
Puckstye Farm
SPADE LA
B2026

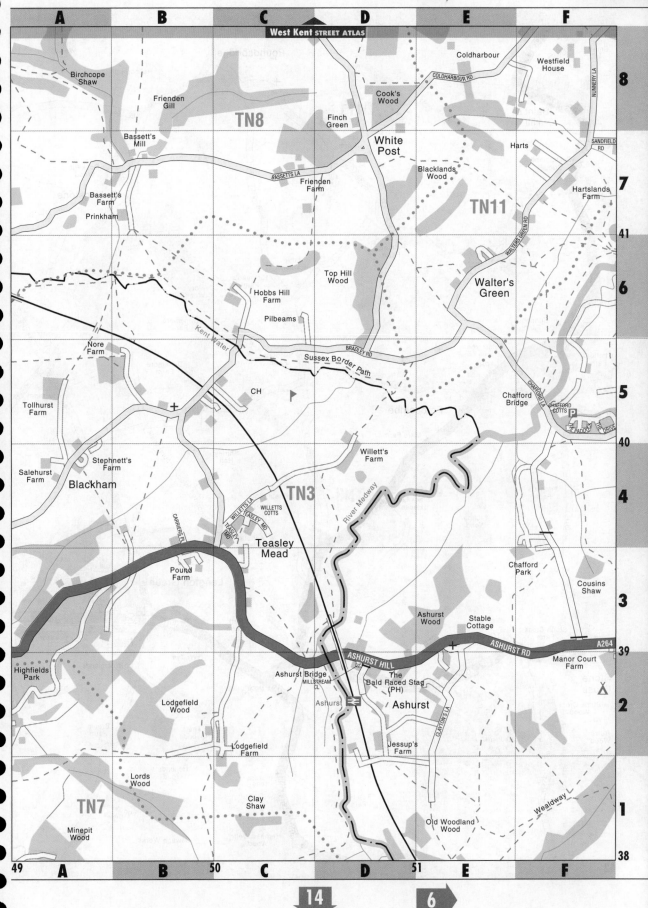

West Kent STREET ATLAS

A B C D E F

8

Birchcope Shaw

Coldharbour

Westfield House

COLDHARBOUR RD

Frienden Gill

TN8

Cook's Wood

Finch Green

White Post

Harts

SANDFIELD RD

Bassett's Mill

Blacklands Wood

Hartslands Farm

7

BASSETTS LA

Frienden Farm

TN11

41

Bassett's Farm

Prinkham

Top Hill Wood

Walter's Green

6

Hobbs Hill Farm

Kent Water

Pilbeams

BRADLEY RD

Sussex Border Path

Chafford Bridge

CHAFFORD LA

Chafford Cotts

5

Nore Farm

CH

PADDOCK DRIVE

40

Tollhurst Farm

Willett's Farm

River Medway

4

Salehurst Farm

Stephnett's Farm

Blackham

TN3

WILLETTS LA

WILLETTS COTTS

TEASLEY MD

Chafford Park

Cousins Shaw

3

CARRIERS PL

TEASLEY MD

Teasley Mead

Pound Farm

Ashurst Wood

Stable Cottage

ASHURST RD

A264

39

Highfields Park

ASHURST HILL

Ashurst Bridge

MILLSTREAM CL

The Bald Faced Stag (PH)

Ashurst

Manor Court Farm

2

Lodgefield Wood

Ashurst

CLAYTON'S LA

Lodgefield Farm

Jessup's Farm

Lords Wood

Wealdway

1

TN7

Clay Shaw

Old Woodland Wood

Minepit Wood

38

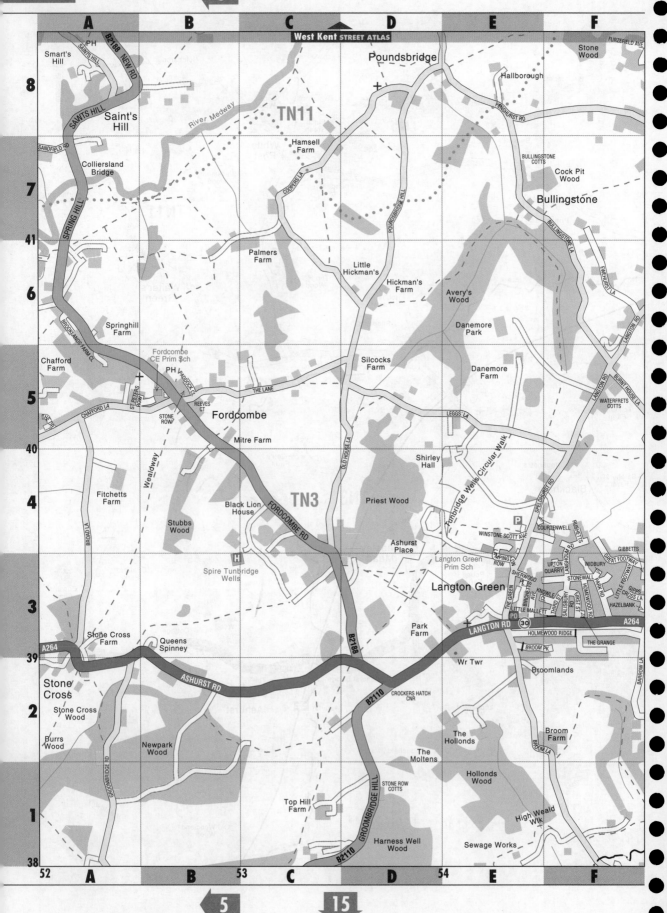

West Kent STREET ATLAS

A B C D E F

8
7
41
6
5
40
4
3
39
2
1
38

TN3

TN4

Speldhurst
George & Dragon Inn (PH)
Speldhurst CE Prim Sch

Stockland Green
Broomhill Farm
Salomons Mus
Caen Farm
Southborough CE Prim Sch

Caenwood Farm
Tunbridge Wells Girls Gram Sch

Shadwell Wood

Mill Farm

Smockham Farm

Went Farm

Harwarton Farm
Broomhill Bank Sch

Bennett Memorial Diocesan School

Hurst Wood

Bishops Down Prim Sch
Rose Hill School

Peacock Farm

Lower Green

Cemy

Jockeys Farm

Burnt House La

Farnham House

St Pauls CE Prim Sch

Denny Bottom

Mount Ephraim

Rusthall

Rusthall Common

Bishop's Down

Hotel

Wellington Rocks

Bishops Down

Cricket Ground

Rusthall House

Orchard Lea

Holmewood House School

Rusthall Farm

Nevill Park

ROYAL TUNBRIDGE WELLS

Tunbridge Wells Common

Hungershall Park

Tunbridge Wells Circular Wlk
River Grom
Spa Valley Rly

High Rocks Inn (PH)
High Rocks

High Rocks

Friezland Wood

Three Acre Wood

Ramslye

St Marks CE Prim Sch

Tunbridge Wells West

TN2

LANGTON RD

BISHOP'S DOWN

8

A4
1 SUFFOLK MEWS

A5
1 HAMILTON HO
2 WOODBURY CL
3 ST GEORGES CT
4 EXCHANGE MEWS

← 7

West Kent STREET ATLAS

TN4

TN1

TN2

ROYAL TUNBRIDGE WELLS

TN3

High Brooms

Sherwood

Blackhurst

Ferndale

Camden Park

Banner Farm

Hawkenbury

Mount Sion

Madeira Park

St John's

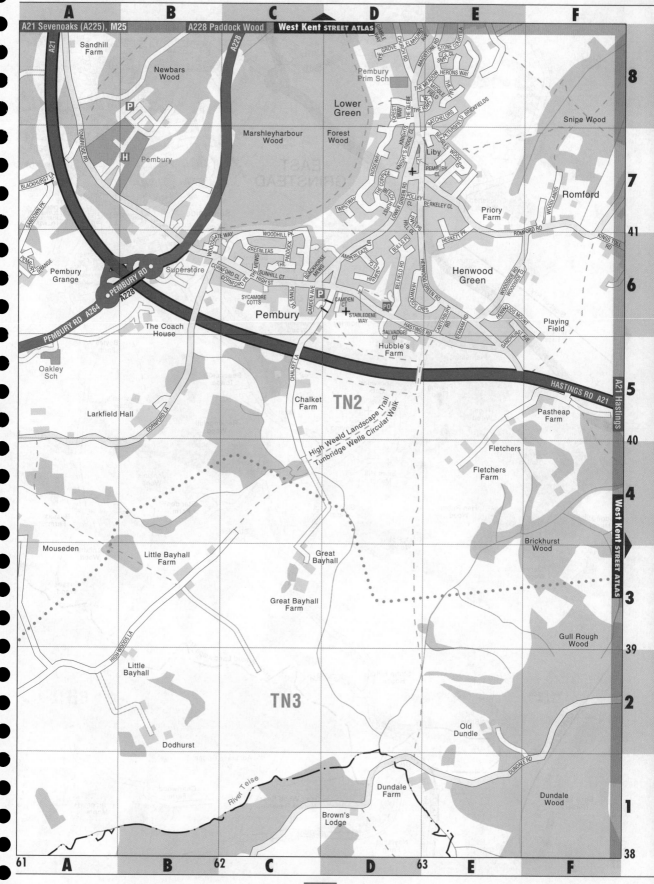

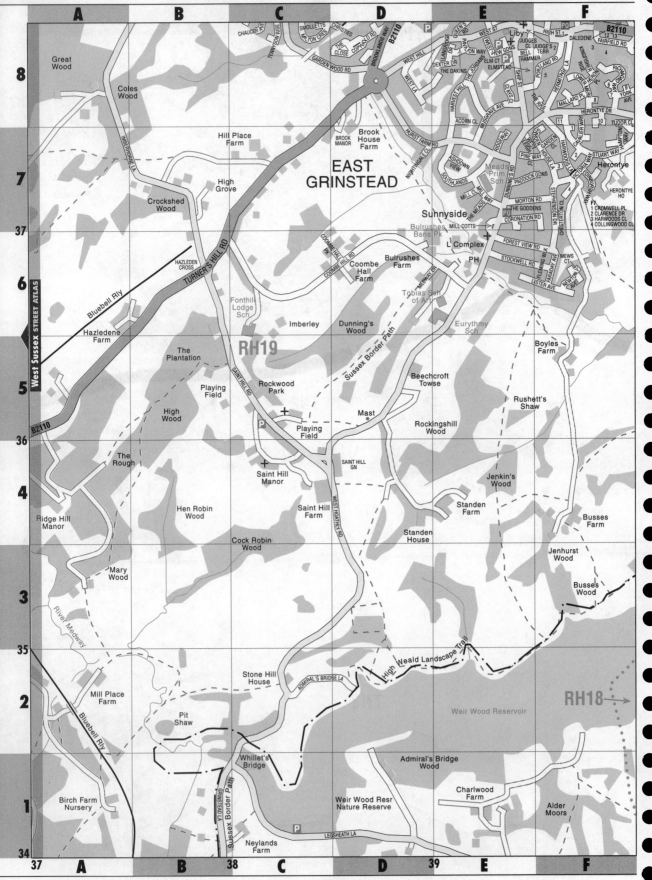

F8
1 MIDDLE ROW
2 FOREST LODGE
3 SACKVILLE CT
4 GREAT HOUSE CT
5 PORTLAND HO
6 CORNWALL GDNS

7 NORMANDY CL
8 WILLOW MEAD
9 KINGS COPSE
10 REGAL DR
11 BECKETT WAY
12 TOLLGATE PL
13 FAIRVIEW CT

EAST GRINSTEAD

RH19

RH18

West Sussex STREET ATLAS

RH19

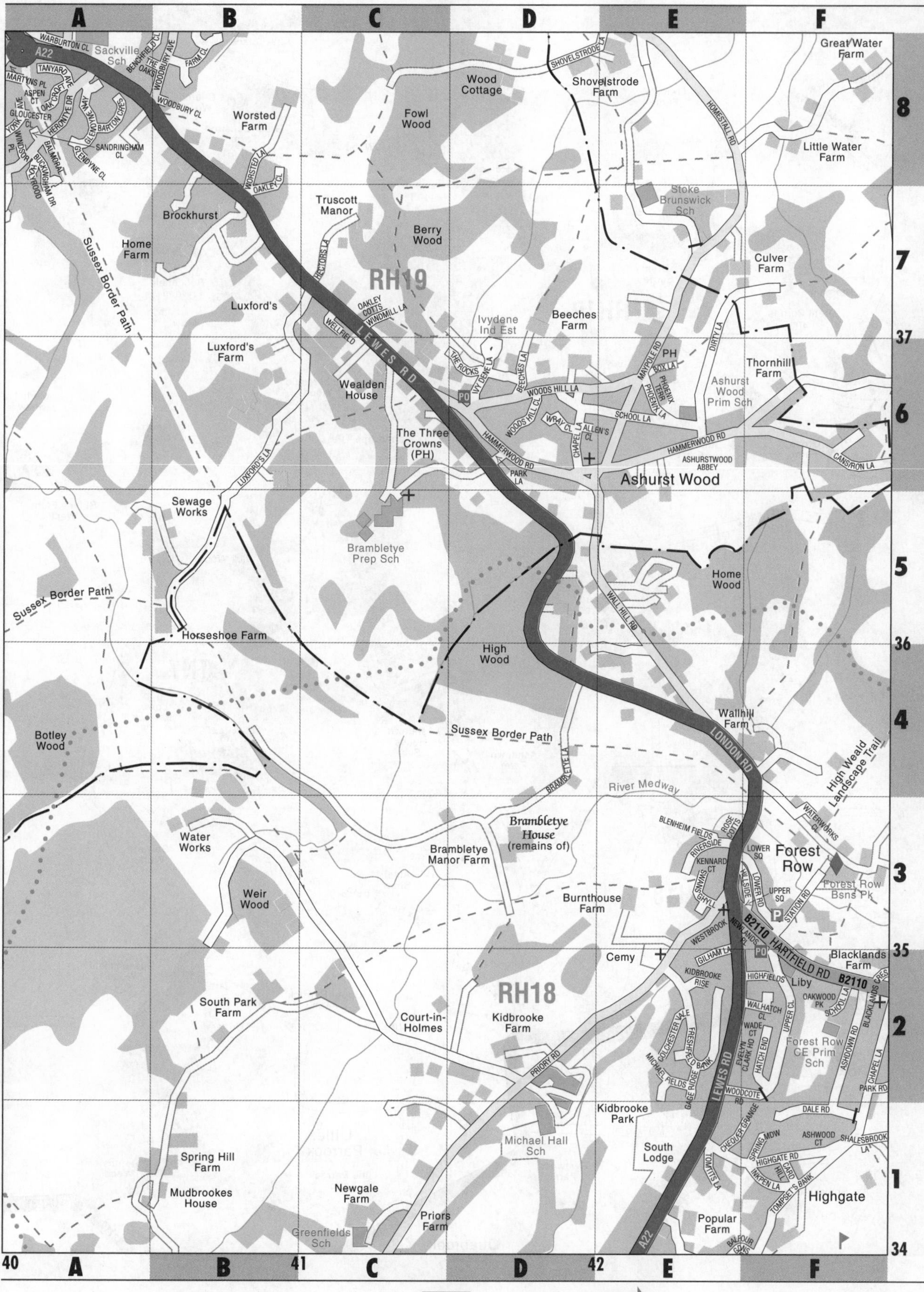

RH18

Ashurst Wood

Forest Row

Highgate

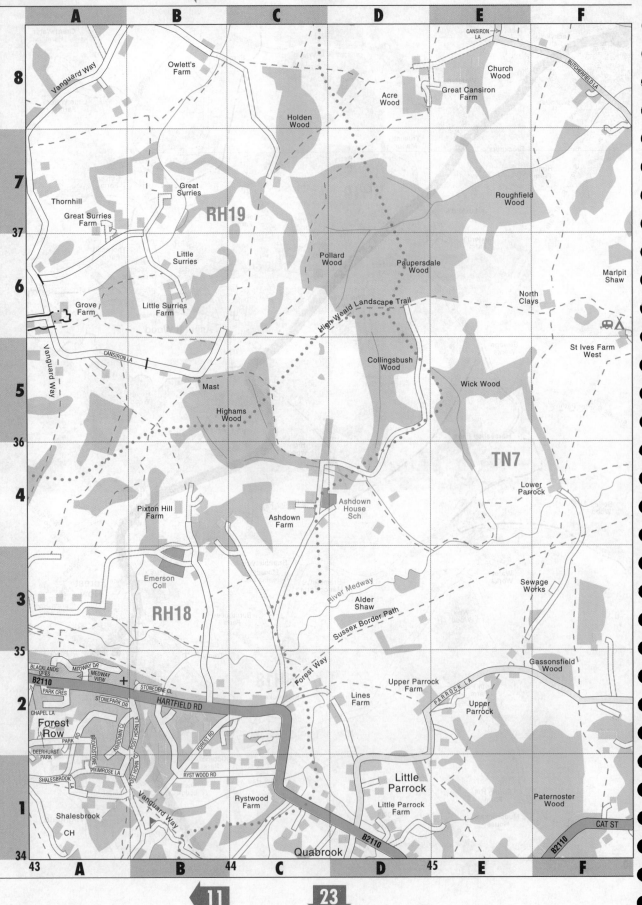

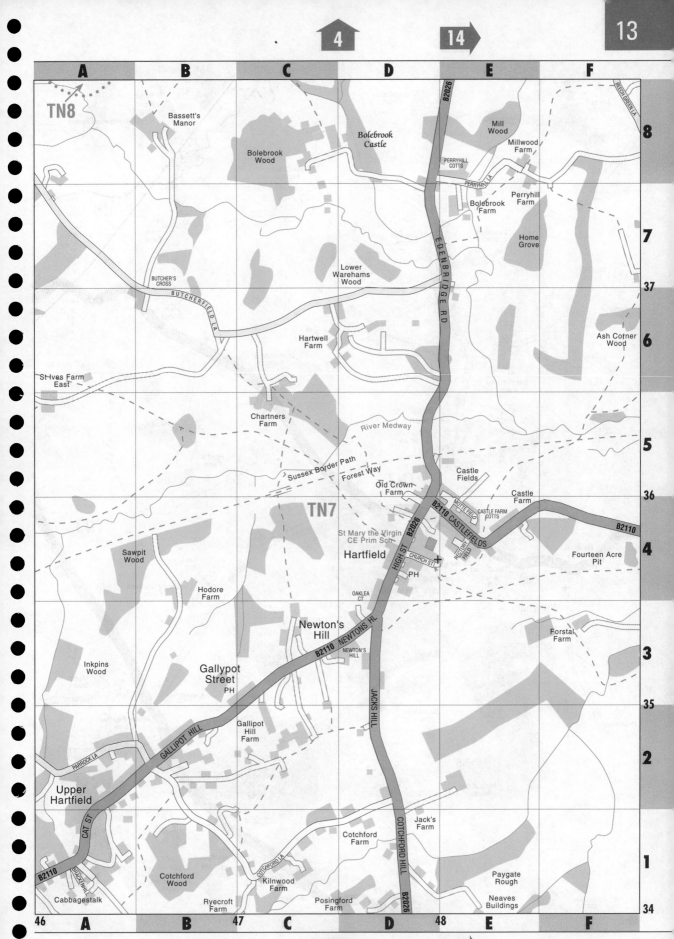

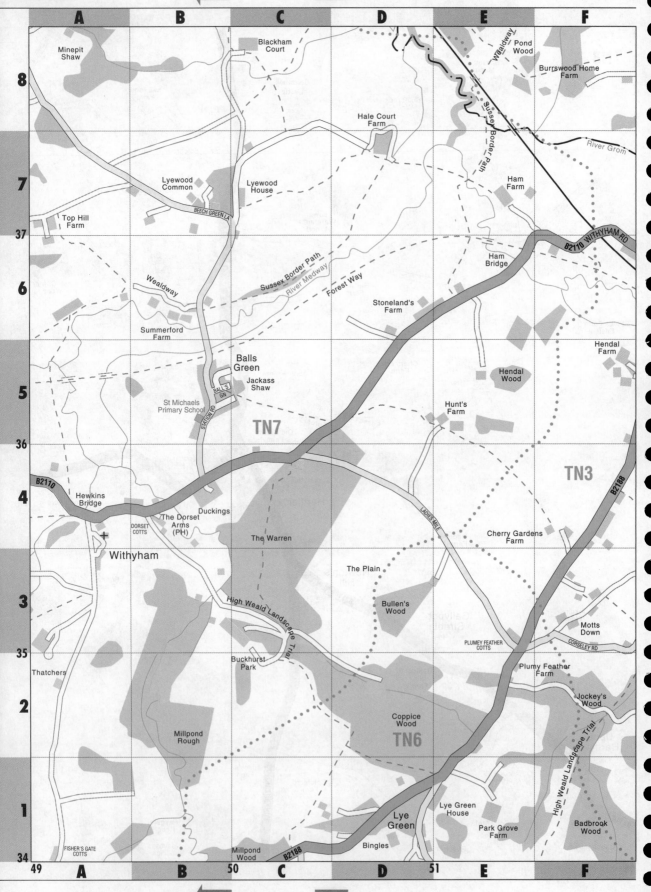

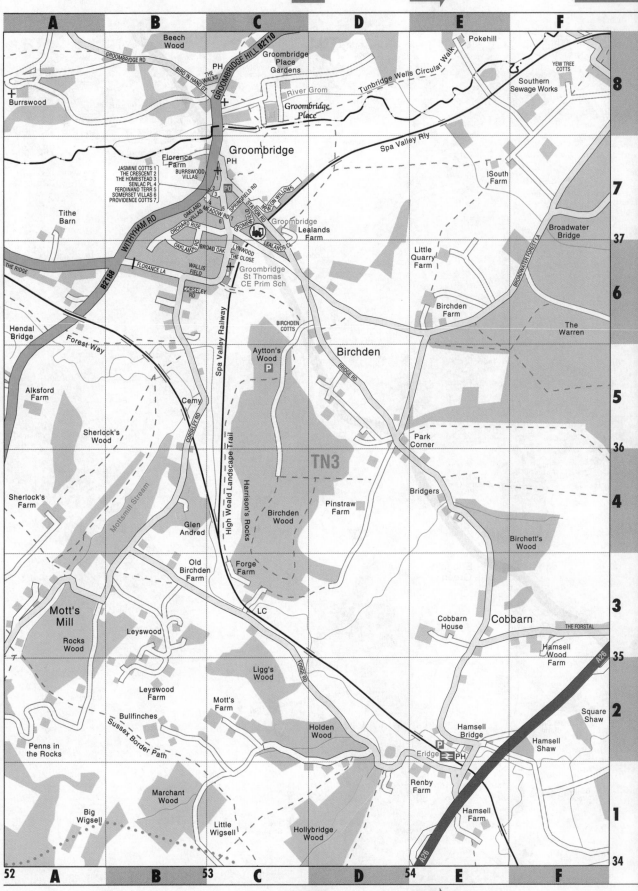

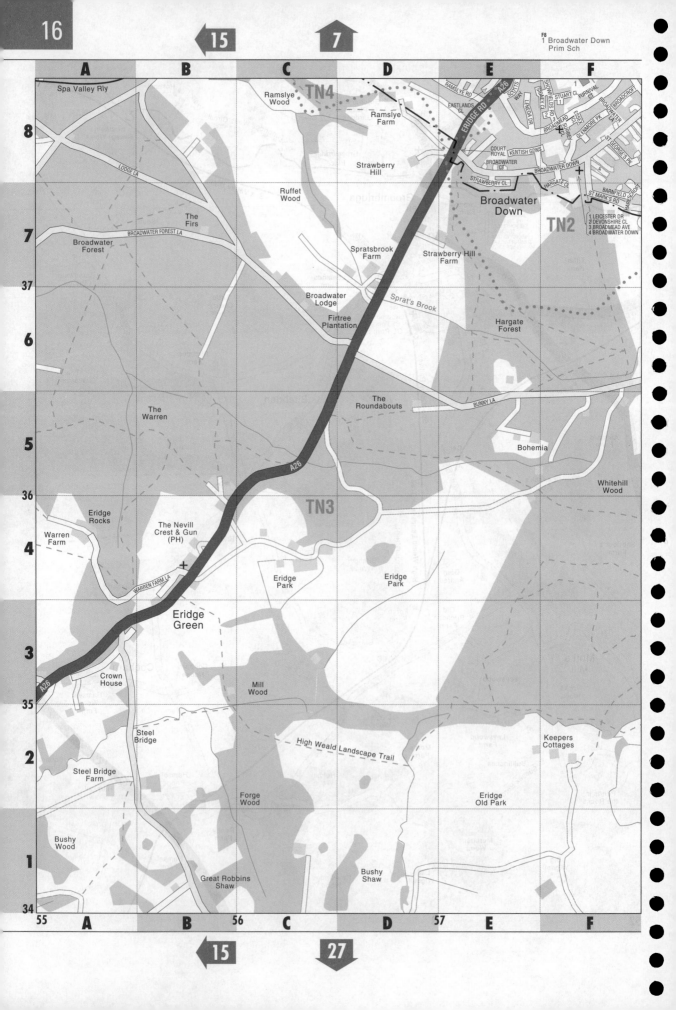

A   B   C   D   E   F

Spa Valley Rly

Ramslye
Wood

TN4

Ramsbye RD

A26

SCOTTS
WAY

EASTLANDS
CL

ERIDGE RD

Ramslye
Farm

SHOWFIELDS RD
SUSSEX DR

STUART CL
LENEDA DR

FURNIVAL
CT

BROADCROFT
BROADWATER
GLENMORE PK

ST GEORGE'S PK

8

Lodge La

Strawberry
Hill

COURT
ROYAL
BROADWATER
CT

KENTISH GDNS

BROADWATER DOWN

BROADMEAD

ESSEX CL

TN2

1 LEICESTER DR
2 DEVONSHIRE CL
3 BROADMEAD AVE
4 BROADWATER DOWN

Ruffet
Wood

STRAWBERRY CL

STRAWBERRY CL

HARGATE CL

ST MARK'S RD

BARNFIELD CL

HAREWOOD CROFT

Broadwater
Down

The Firs

7

Broadwater Forest La

Broadwater
Forest

Sprats Brook
Farm

Strawberry Hill
Farm

37

Broadwater
Lodge

Sprat's Brook

Firtree
Plantation

Hargate
Forest

6

The
Warren

The
Roundabouts

BUNNY LA

Bohemia

5

Whitehill
Wood

36

Eridge
Rocks

A26

TN3

Warren
Farm

The Nevill
Crest & Gun
(PH)

4

WARREN FARM LA

Eridge
Park

Eridge
Park

Eridge
Green

3

Crown
House

A26

Mill
Wood

35

Steel
Bridge

High Weald Landscape Trail

Keepers
Cottages

2

Steel Bridge
Farm

Forge
Wood

Eridge
Old Park

Bushy
Wood

1

Great Robbins
Shaw

Bushy
Shaw

34

55   A   B   56   C   D   57   E   F

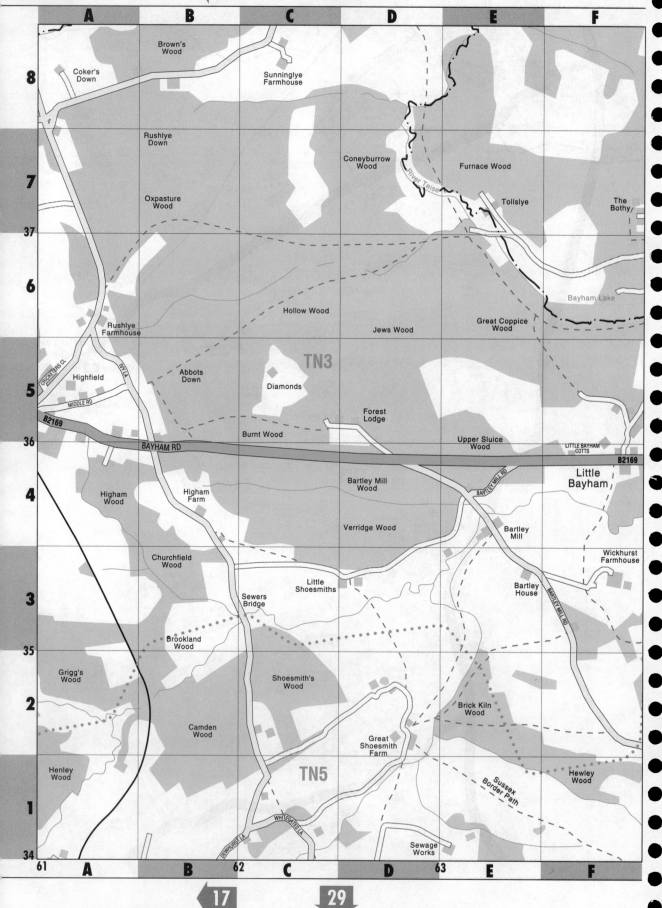

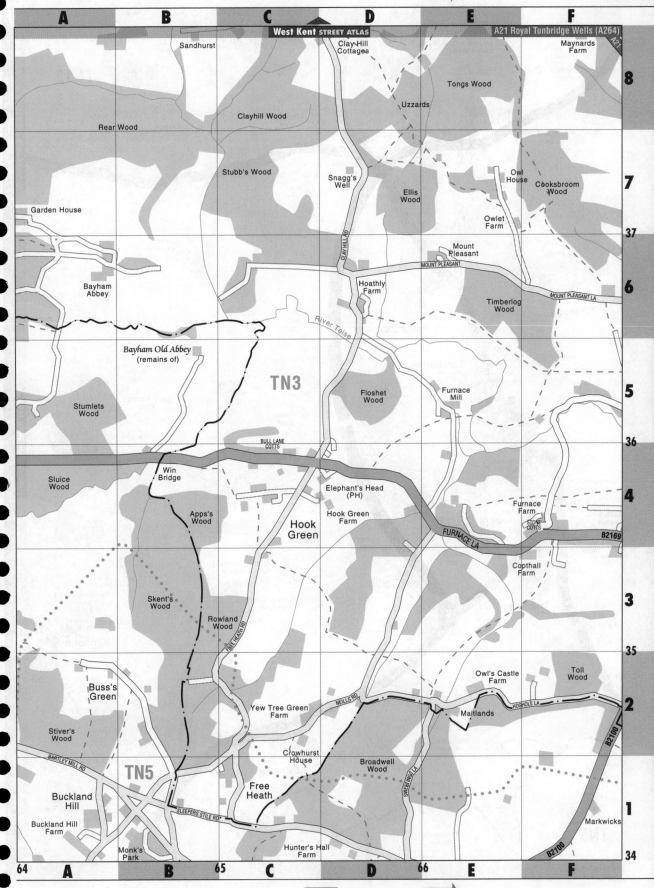

Maynards Farm

Sandhurst

Clay Hill Cottages

Tongs Wood

8

Clayhill Wood

Uzzards

Rear Wood

Owl House

Cooksbroom Wood

7

Stubb's Wood

Snagg's Well

Ellis Wood

Owlet Farm

37

Garden House

Mount Pleasant

MOUNT PLEASANT

6

Bayham Abbey

Hoathly Farm

MOUNT PLEASANT LA

Timberlog Wood

River Teise

Bayham Old Abbey
(remains of)

TN3

Floshet Wood

Furnace Mill

5

Stumlets Wood

BULL LANE COTTS

36

Sluice Wood

Win Bridge

Elephant's Head (PH)

Furnace Farm

STONE COTTS

4

Apps's Wood

Hook Green Farm

FURNACE LA

B2169

Hook Green

Copthall Farm

Skent's Wood

3

Rowland Wood

FREE HEATH RD

35

Buss's Green

Owl's Castle Farm

Toll Wood

Yew Tree Green Farm

NEILLS RD

HOGHOLE LA

2

Maitlands

Stiver's Wood

B2100

BARTLEY MILL RD

TN5

Crowhurst House

Broadwell Wood

SWEETINGS LA

Buckland Hill

Free Heath

Markwicks

Buckland Hill Farm

SLEEPERS STILE RD

B2100

Monk's Park

Hunter's Hall Farm

34

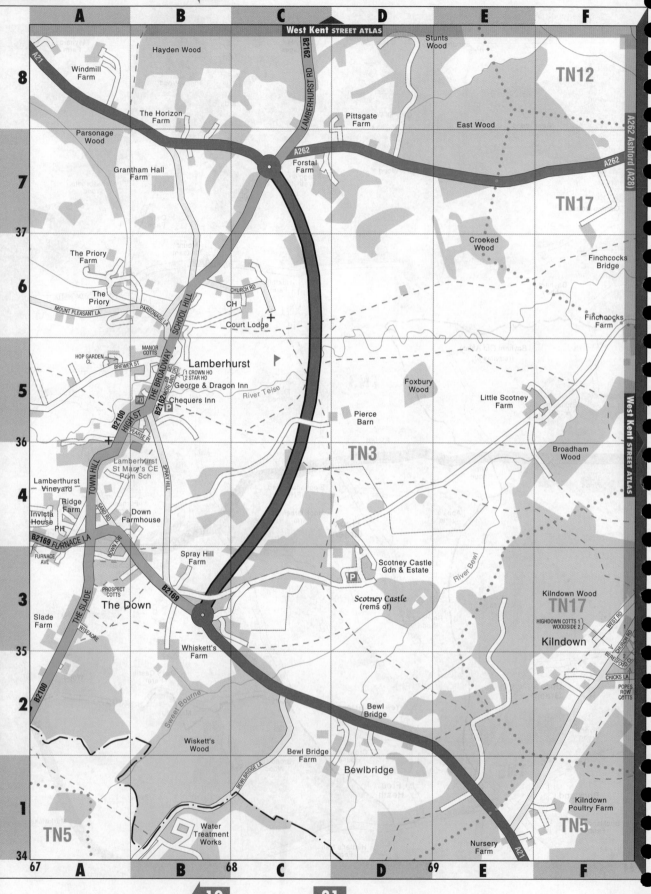

West Kent STREET ATLAS

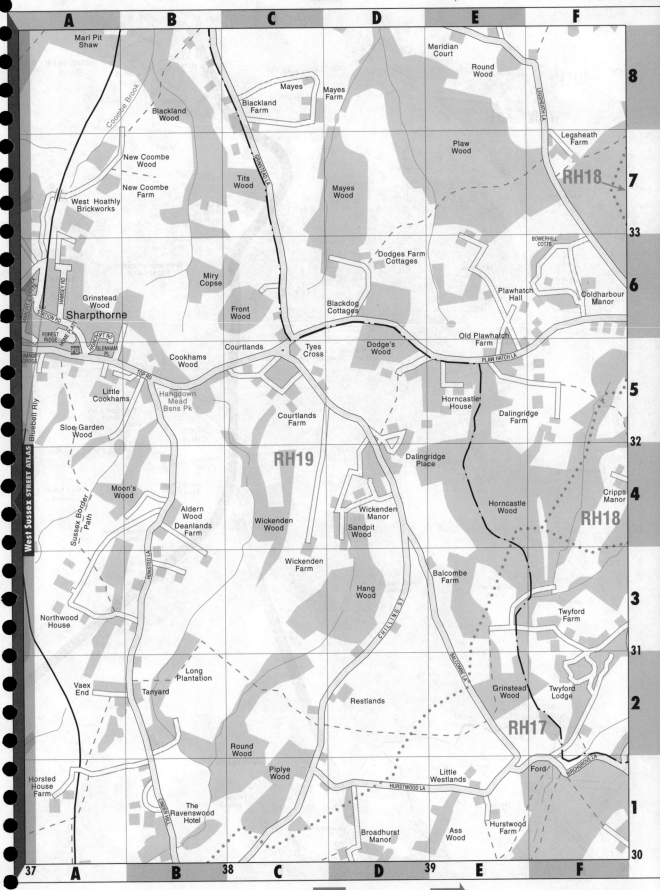

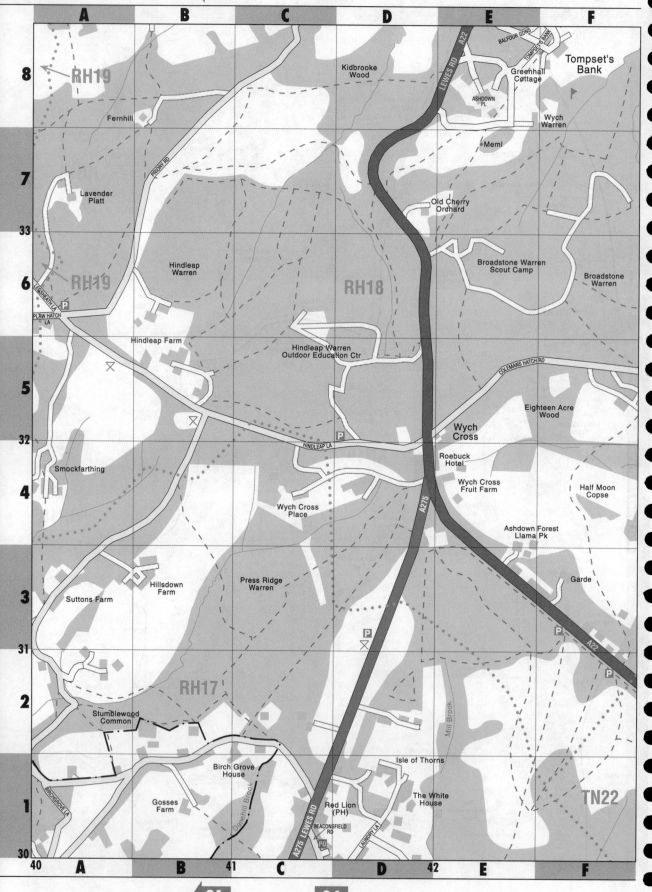

RH19

Fernhill

Lavender
Platt

33

RH19

Hindleap
Warren

PLAW HATCH
LA

Hindleap Farm

Smockfarthing

Suttons Farm

Hillsdown
Farm

Stumblewood
Common

RH17

Gosses
Farm

Birch Grove
House

Kidbrooke
Wood

RH18

Hindleap Warren
Outdoor Education Ctr

HINDLEAP LA

Wych Cross
Place

Press Ridge
Warren

Old Cherry
Orchard

Broadstone Warren
Scout Camp

COLEMANS HATCH RD

Wych
Cross

Roebuck
Hotel

Wych Cross
Fruit Farm

Eighteen Acre
Wood

Ashdown Forest
Llama Pk

BALFOUR GDNS

TOMPSET'S BANK

Greenhall
Cottage

ASHDOWN
PL

Tompset's
Bank

Wych
Warren

Meml

Broadstone
Warren

Half Moon
Copse

Garde

TN22

Red Lion
(PH)

BEACONSFIELD
RD

Isle of Thorns

The White
House

Mill Brook

LEWES RD

A22

A275

LEWES RD

LESWEATH LA

BIRCHGROVE LA

PRIORY RD

Danehill Brook

LAUNDRY LA

8

7

6

5

4

32

3

31

2

30

1

40   A   41   B   C   41   D   42   E   F

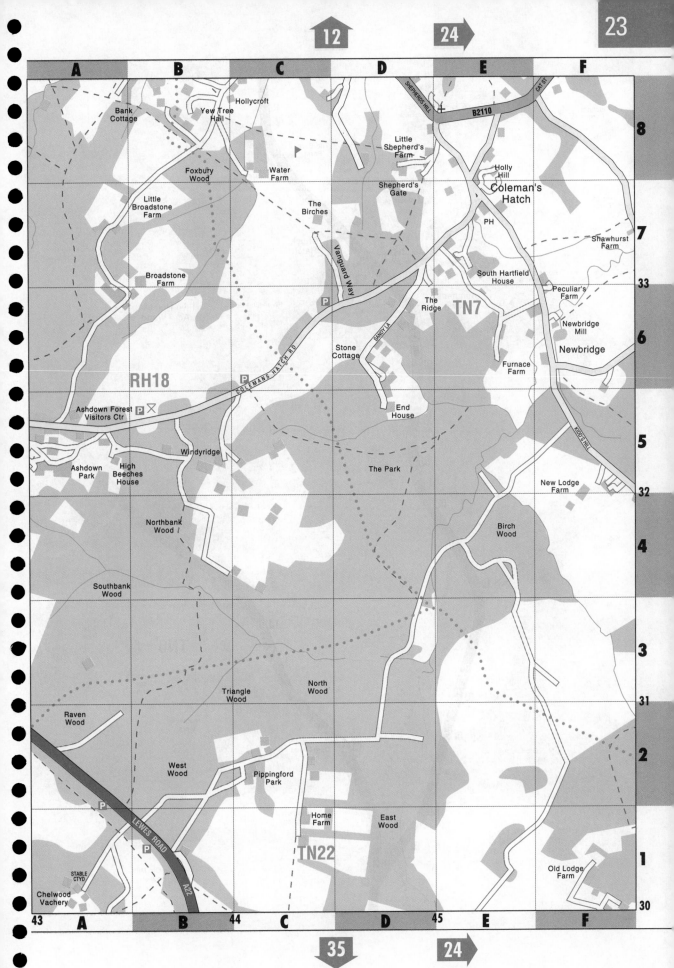

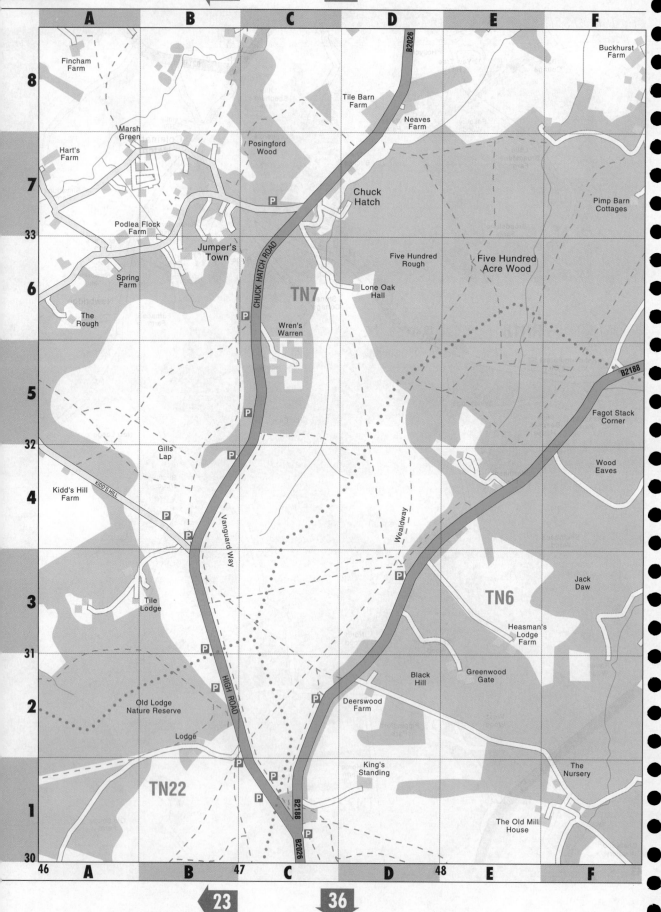

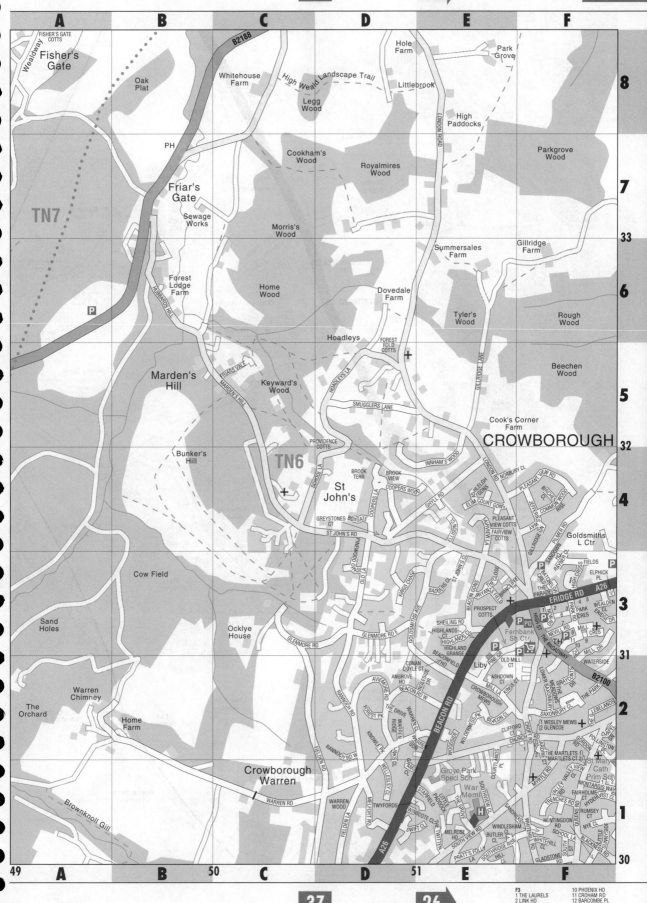

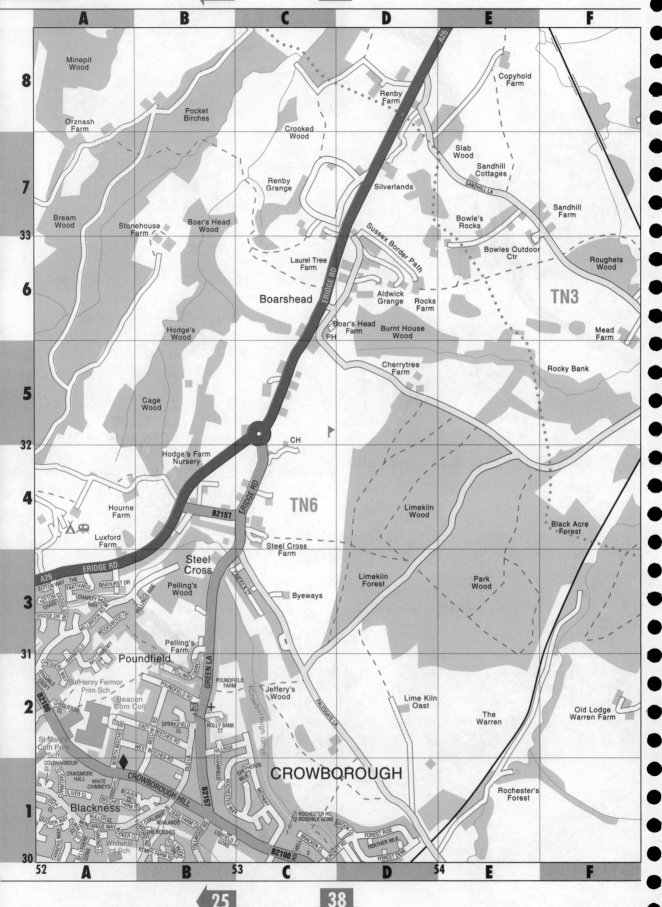

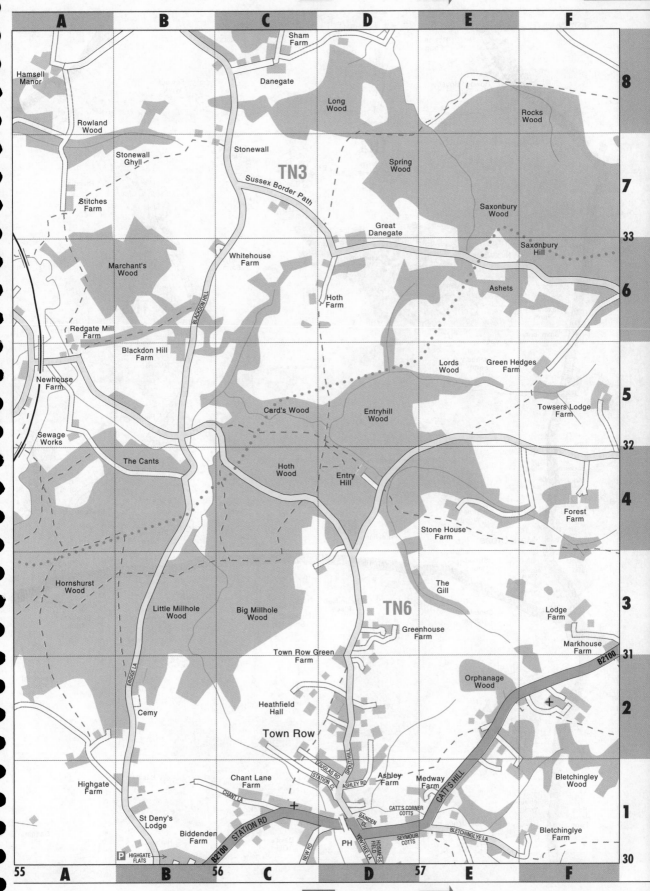

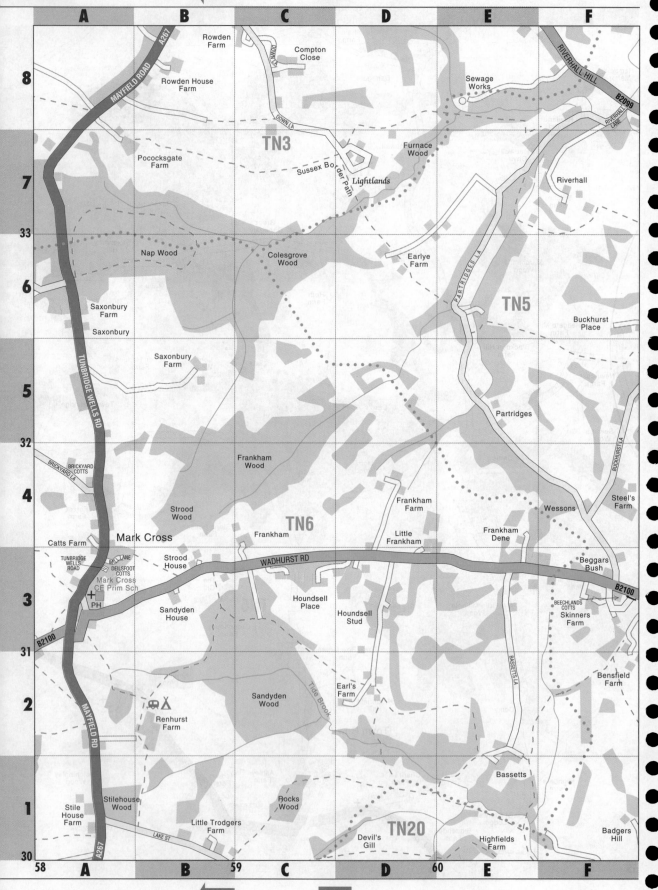

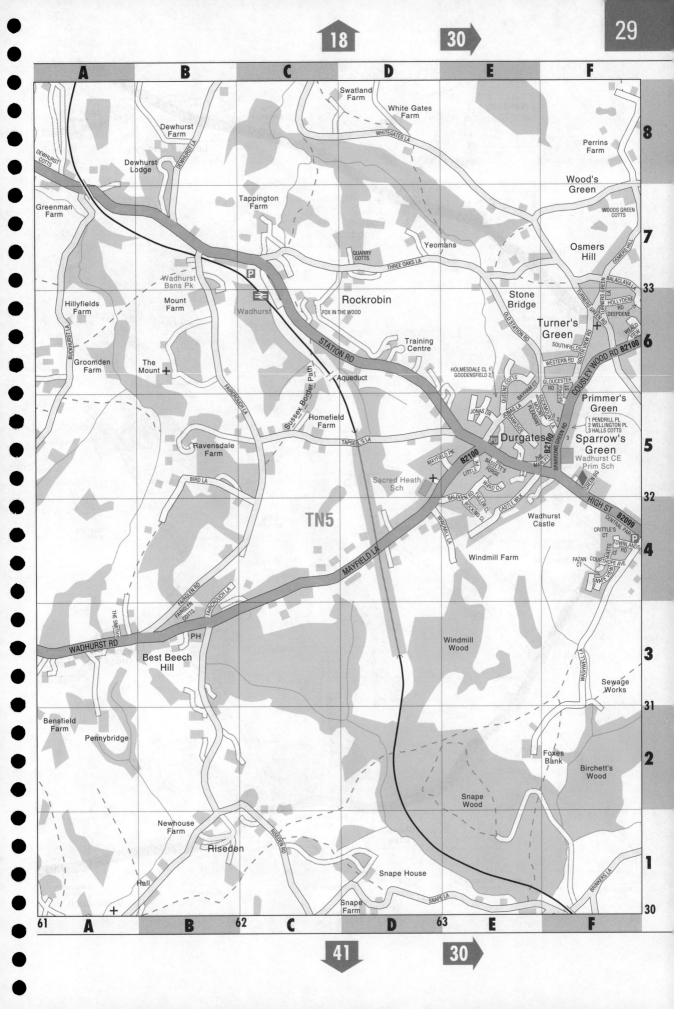

A B C D E F

8

7

33

6

5

32

4

3

31

2

1

30

Swatland Farm

White Gates Farm

WHITEGATES LA

Perrins Farm

Wood's Green

WOODS GREEN COTTS

Dewhurst Farm

DEWHURST LA

Osmers Hill

OSMERS HILL

DEWHURST COTTS

Dewhurst Lodge

Tappington Farm

Yeomans

Stone Bridge

BALACLAVA LA

Greenman Farm

Wadhurst Bsns Pk

QUARRY COTTS

THREE OAKS LA

OLD STATION RD

TURNERS GREEN RD

SOUTH VIEW RD

HOLLYDENE RD

DEEPDENE

Hillyfields Farm

HILLYFIELDS LA

Mount Farm

Rockrobin

FOX IN THE WOOD

Turner's Green

SOUTHFIELDS

WESTERN RD

COUSLEY WOOD RD

WEALD VIEW

B2100

Wadhurst

STATION RD

Training Centre

HOLMESDALE CL 1
GOODENSFIELD 2

QUEENS COTTS

GLOUCESTER RD

GEORGE ST

Primmer's Green

Groomden Farm

The Mount

FAIRCROUCH LA

Aqueduct

Sussex Border Path

BAYHAM CT

JONAS LA

MOUNT PLEASANT

JONAS DR

COCKMOUNT LA

1 PENDRILL PL
2 WELLINGTON PL
3 HALLS COTTS

Sparrow's Green

Homefield Farm

TAPSEL'S LA

PO

Durgates

SPARROWS GREEN RD

Wadhurst CE Prim Sch

Ravensdale Farm

BIRD LA

MAYFIELD PK

B2100

LITTLE PK

BASSETT'S FORGE

MAYFIELD

GREEN SQ

Sacred Heath Sch

BALDOCK RD

FULLER CL

WARD CL

CASTLE WLK

HIGH ST

CENTRAL PAR

B2099

TN5

MAYFIELD LA

BOCKING CL

Wadhurst Castle

CRITTLE'S CT

TOWNLANDS RD

FAIRGLEN RD

FAIRGLEN COTTS

FAIRCROUCH LA

WINDMILL LA

Windmill Farm

FAZAN CT

COURTHOPE AVE

WATTS CL

SNAPE VIEW

THE SMITHY

WADHURST RD

PH

Best Beech Hill

Windmill Wood

WASHWELL LA

Sewage Works

Bensfield Farm

Pennybridge

Foxes Bank

Birchett's Wood

RISEDEN RD

Snape Wood

Newhouse Farm

Riseden

Snape House

BRINKERS LA

Hall

Snape Farm

SNAPE LA

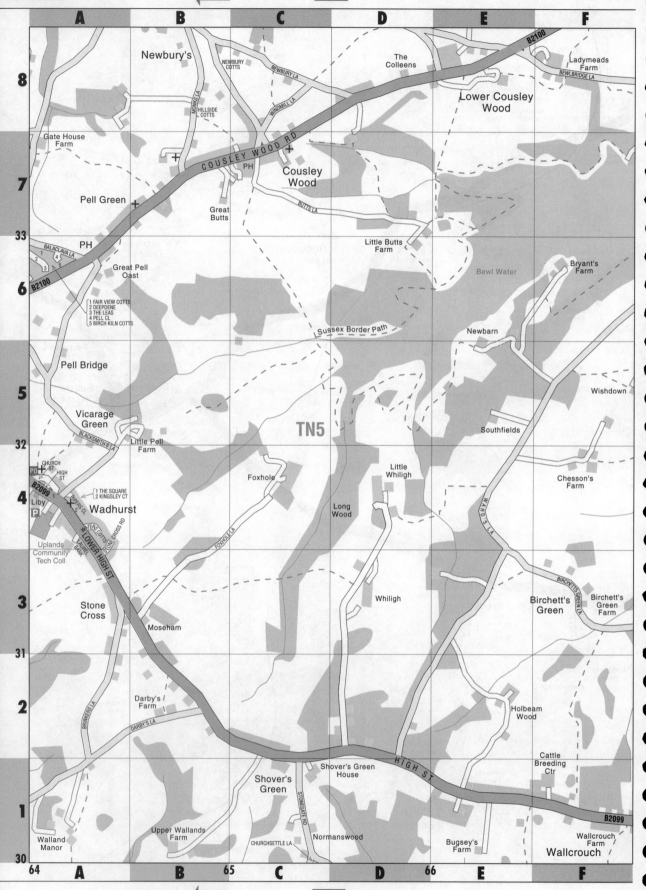

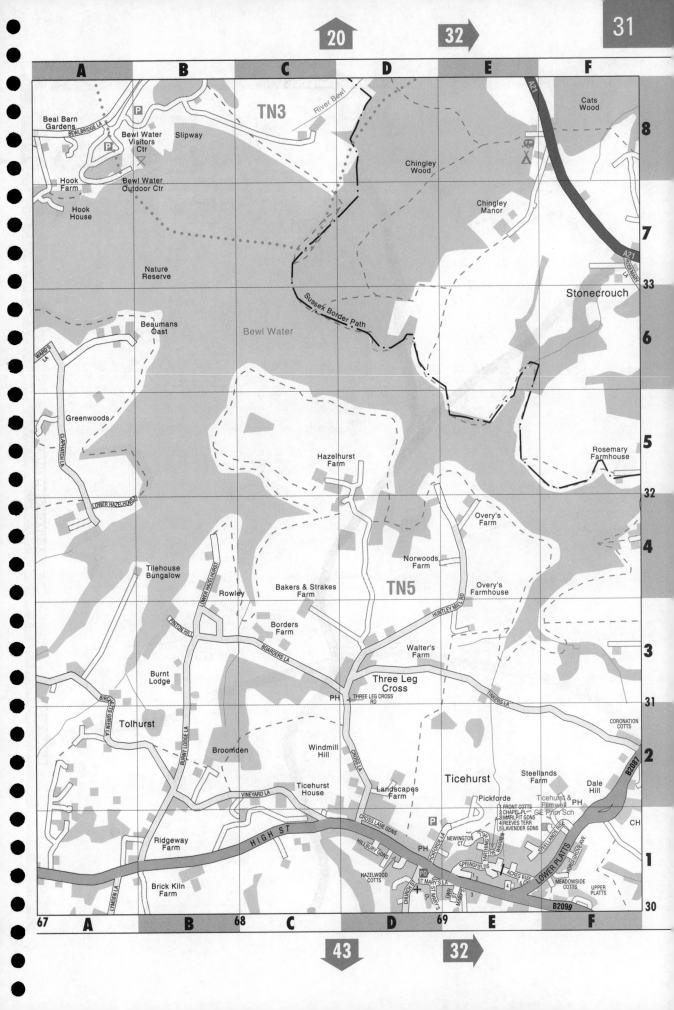

West Kent STREET ATLAS

Combwell
Wood

Bedgebury
National Pinetum

B2079

PARK LANE

Park
House

Springwood
Lodge

Bedgebury Park
Woods

Combwell Priory
Farm

TN17

LADY OAK LA

Stonecrouch
Farm House

A21

33

Starvegoose
Bank

6

Windmill Down

Flimwell
Grange

B2079

Windy
Ridge

Mast

Radio
Station

5

ROSEMARY LA

P

32

TN5

FLIMWELL CL

TN18

Ketley
Farm

Sussex Border Path

4

FRUITFIELDS

RED OAST
COTTS

BLENHEIM WAY

LONDON RD

PH

1 2

DOWNASH HO 1
DOWNASH CT 2

OLD WARDSDOWN
NURSERY
BEWL BRIDGE CL

UNION
ST

High St

B2087

A268

PH

3

Flimwell

SUNNYBANK

UNION
STREET

BROOM HILL
COTTS

HAWKHURST RD

Mount Pleasant
Farm

GINGERBREAD LA

A268 Hawkhurst

31

Berner's
Hill

CLARKS YD

MEADOW VIEW

A268

B2087

Seacox
Heath

2

Quedley

West
Lodge

Ringden
Wood

Keeper's
Cottage

Saw Mill

1

Ringden
Farm

A21

Sewage Works

TN19

30

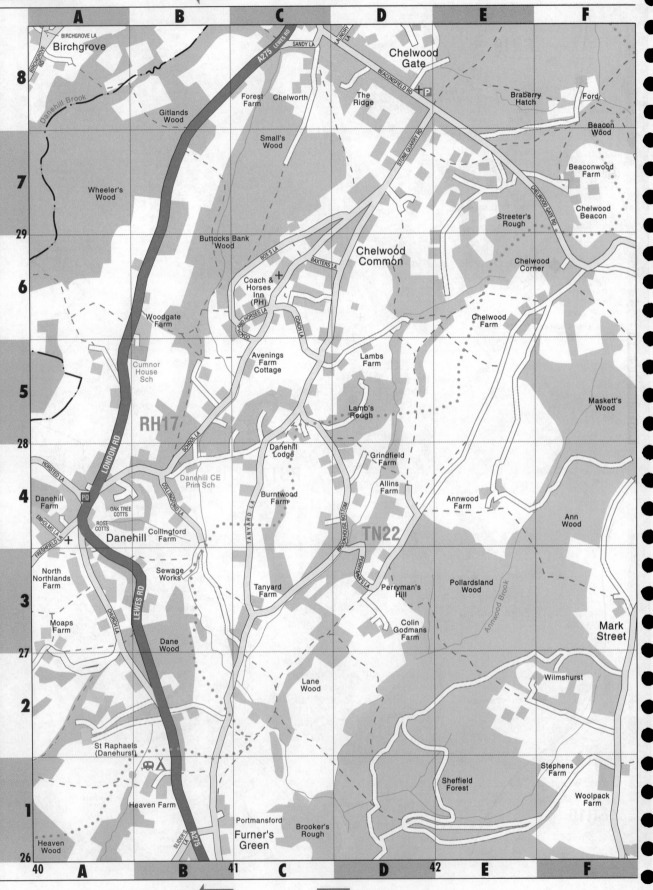

Birchgrove
BIRCHGROVE LA
BIRCHGROVE RD
Danehill Brook
Gitlands Wood
Wheeler's Wood
A275 LEWES RD
SANDY LA
Forest Farm
Chelworth
Small's Wood
LADBURY LA
Chelwood Gate
The Ridge
BEACONSFIELD RD
P
STONE QUARRY RD
Braberry Hatch
Ford
Beacon Wood
Beaconwood Farm
CHELWOOD GATE RD
Chelwood Beacon
Streeter's Rough
Buttocks Bank Wood
BOX'S LA
BAXTERS LA
Chelwood Common
Chelwood Corner
Coach & Horses Inn (PH)
COACH AND HORSES LA
COACH LA
Woodgate Farm
Cumnor House Sch
LONDON RD
Avenings Farm Cottage
Lambs Farm
Chelwood Farm
Maskett's Wood
RH17
SCHOOL LA
Lamb's Rough
Danehill Lodge
Grindfield Farm
Allins Farm
Annwood Farm
Ann Wood
Danehill CE Prim Sch
Burntwood Farm
TANYARD LA
TN22
BROOKHOUSE BOTTOM
HORSTED LA
PO
Danehill Farm
OAK TREE COTTS
ROSE COTTS
COLLINGFORD LA
Danehill
Collingford Farm
ENHOLMS LA
FRESHFIELD LA
North Northlands Farm
Sewage Works
PERRYMAN'S LA
Perryman's Hill
Pollardsland Wood
Annwood Brook
Mark Street
Moaps Farm
CHURCH LA
LEWES RD
Dane Wood
Tanyard Farm
Colin Godmans Farm
Lane Wood
Wilmshurst
St Raphaels (Danehurst)
Heaven Farm
Sheffield Forest
Stephens Farm
Woolpack Farm
Heaven Wood
SLUGEY'S LA
A275
Portmansford
Furner's Green
Brooker's Rough

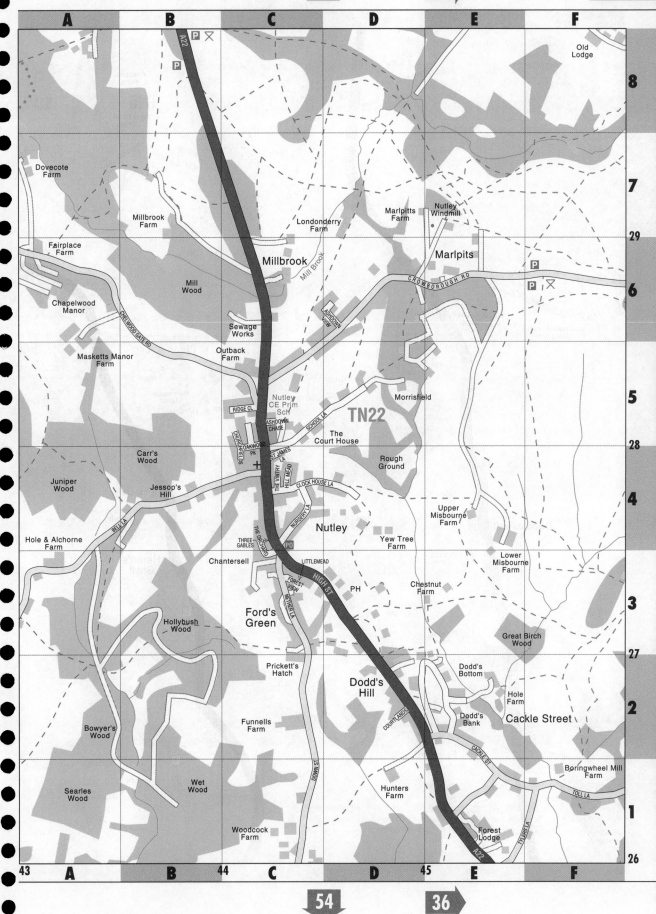

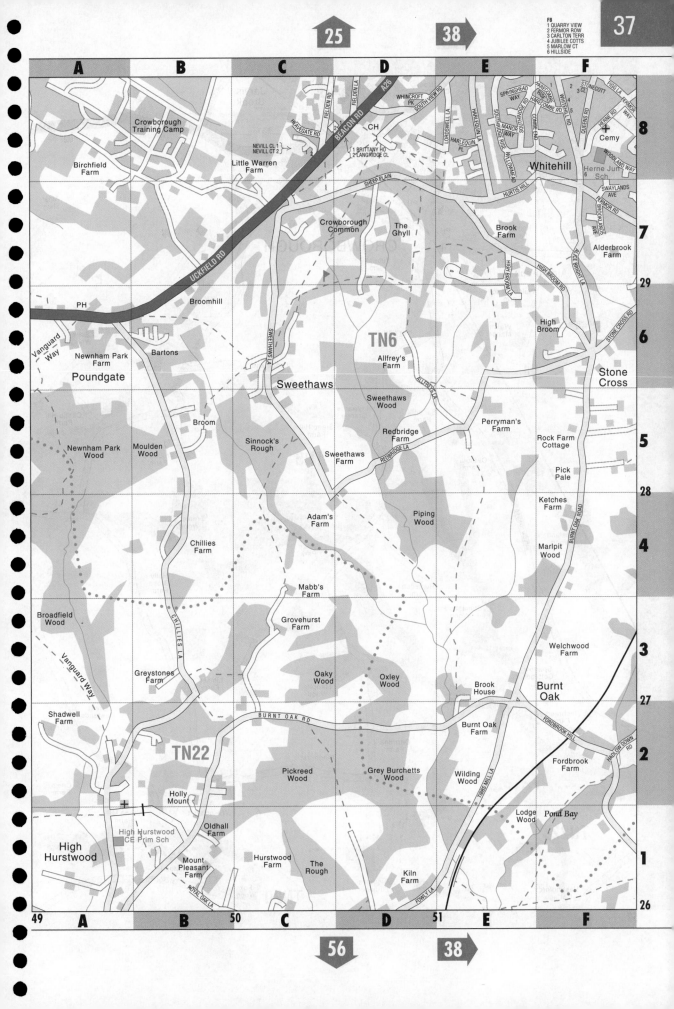

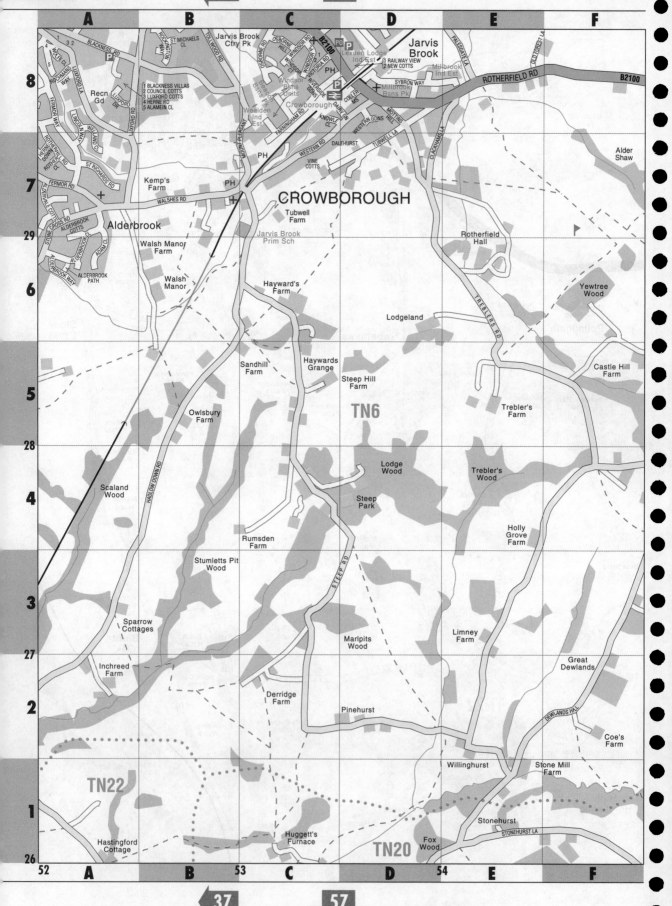

CROWBOROUGH

Jarvis Brook

Alderbrook

TN6

TN22

TN20

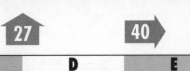

A **B** **C** **D** **E** **F**

TN6

Frenches Farm

Stunt's Wood

Newlands Farm

Lakestreet Wood

8

Brick Kiln Wood

Tompsett's Wood

Wet Wood

Mousehall

LAKE ST

TN5

Long Gill

Longham Wood

Lakestreet Manor

Tidebrook House

7

Great Trodgers Farm

Harewood Farm

TIDEBROOK

Coldharbour Wood

29

Rusher's Cross Farm

BASSETTS LA

6

Heronry Wood

Rusher's Cross

Cinderhill Wood

Great Wallis Farm

Furnace Wood

Sharnden

Ashurst Wood

Banky Wood

Pennybridge Farm

PENNYBRIDGE LA

RUSHERS CROSS

5

A267

Rose Garth

Clay's Wood

Vicarage Wood

New House Farm

Sandpit Wood

28

TN20

Coggins Mill

Old Palace Farm

LITTLE TRODGERS LA

Old Place

Glebe Farm

Sharnden Old Manor Farm

4

COGGINS MILL LA

TUNBRIDGE WELLS RD

Heron's Folly

Hole Wood

Merrieweathers

3

St Leonards Mayfield Sch and remains of *Archbishop's Palace*

Recn Gd

Mayfield CE Prim Sch

ALEXANDRA RD

PIPERS YD

PH

2

SOUTHMEAD CL

A267

Liby

FLETCHING ST

1 ALEXANDRA TERR
2 DUNSTANS CROFT
3 WARREN COTTS

EAST ST

Luckhurst Crouch Farm

27

ROTHERFIELD LA

VIC'A RD

THE GLN

THE GR

PO

HIGH ST

3 4

SOUTH ST

THE AVENUE

1 ST MARY-IN-THE-FIELDS
2 BREWERS GR
3 STAR MEWS
4 STAR LA
5 SUNNYBANK CL
6 HILLSIDE

THE WARREN

STATION RD

OLD LA

THE HOLLIES

ST THOMAS OF CANTERBURY CT

VALE RD

P

5

6

SN'S

2

Hooper's Farm

Versyns Farm

Red House Farm

Winters Farm

ASHLEY GDNS

WEST ST

Mayfield

SCOTSFORD HILL

KNOWLE PK

2

Old Sandalls

PICCADILLY LA

WITHERENDEN RD

Little Bainden Farm

Knowle Hill

Cranesden

Great Bainden

1

KNOWLE HILL

NEWICK LA

26

58 **A** **B** 59 **C** **D** 60 **E** **F**

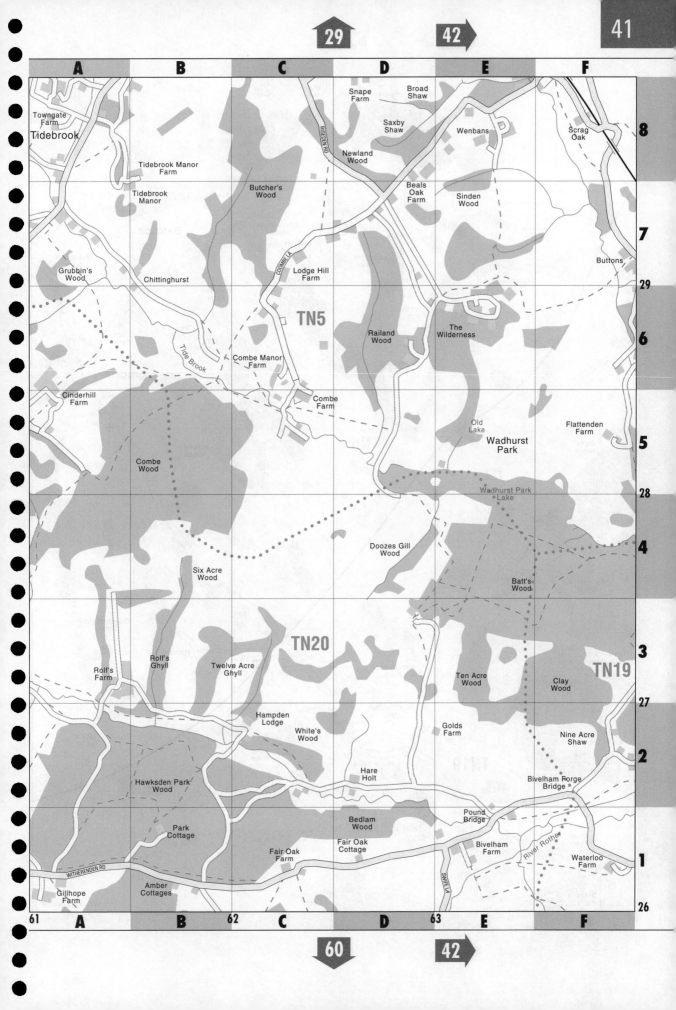

A B C D E F

8

Middle
Wood

Slidingfield
Wood

River Limden

The
Olives

7

CHURCHSETTLE LA

Bricklehurst
Manor

Bardown

Longfield
Shaw

Bricklehurst
Farm

BARDOWN RD

Mabb's Hill
Farm

29

Churchsettle
Farm

Bardown
Farm

Peartree
Wood

Maplesden
Farm

Cooper's
Farm

Cock
Farm

MABB'S HILL

THE ACORNS

6

Maplesden

Stonegate

LIMDEN LA

LIMDEN CL

FORGE
FIELD

Coalpit
Wood

COTTENDEN RD

STONEGATE
CT

OWLS
GDNS

Stonegate
CE Prim Sch

5

TN5

Dens
Wood

Hoadley
Wood

STATION RD

Dens
Farm

28

4

Dens Bridge

Tide Brook

Marchant's
Wood

PEARTREE HILL

Church Wood
Shaws

3

Batt's Wood
Cottages

Stonegate

Hammerden

Newbridge
Wood

27

Witherenden
Farm

Cock's
Wood

2

Witherenden
Mill

PEARTREE HILL

Alder
Wood

Orchard
Shaw

Bivelham Forge
Farm

TN19

Witherenden
Bridge

River Rother

High
Wood

Witherenden Hill

Bines
Farm

Round
Wood

1

Bines
Farm

Great
Bines

Woodknowle
Farm

Wreckery Bridge

26

64 A B 65 C D 66 E F

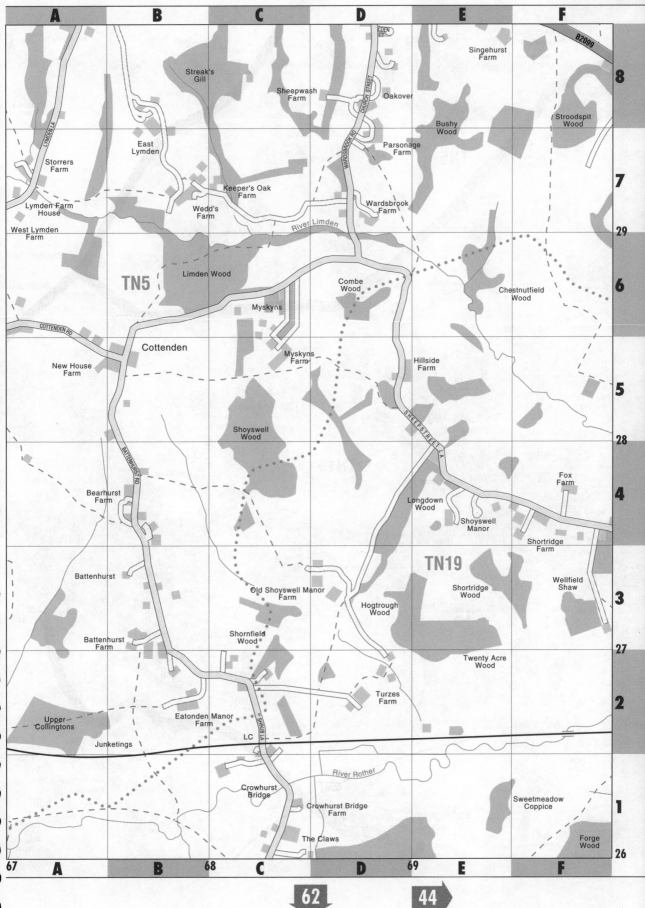

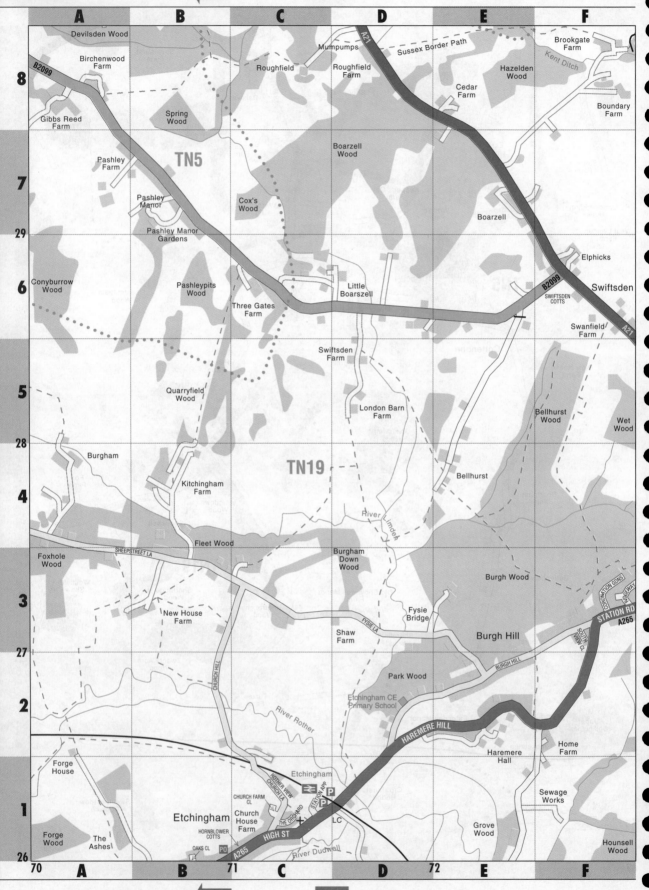

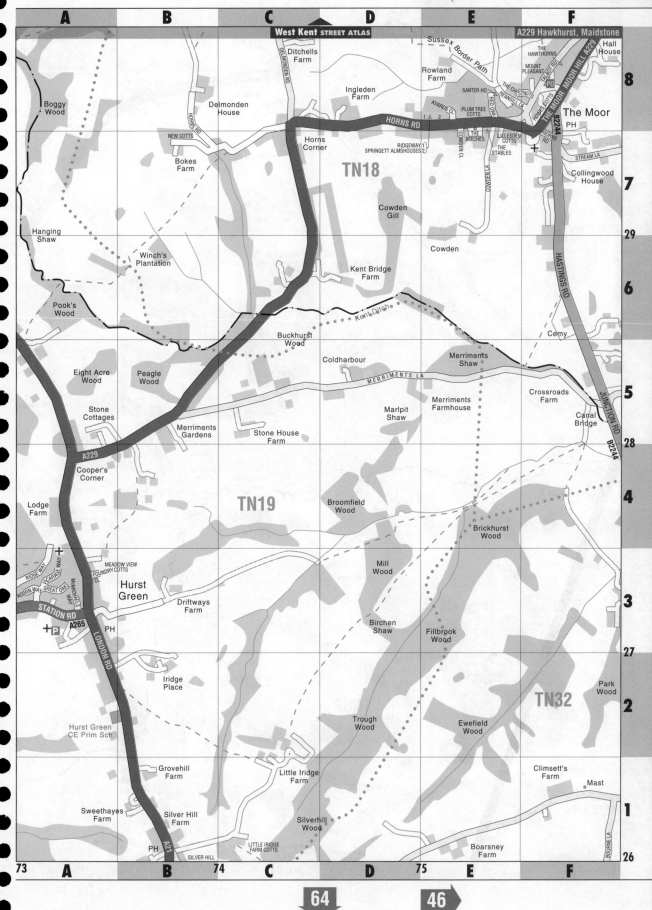

West Kent STREET ATLAS

A229 Hawkhurst, Maidstone

8

Boggy Wood

Ditchells Farm

Sussex Border Path

Rowland Farm

THE HAWTHORNS

MOUNT PLEASANT

Hall House

Delmonden House

Ingleden Farm

SANTER HO

THE CHESTNUTS

THE MOOR MOOR HILL A229

Delmonden House

NEW COTTS

Horns Corner

AVARDS CL

PLUM TREE COTTS

THE BEECHES

The Moor

Bokes Farm

HORNS RD

RIDGEWAY

SPRINGETT ALMSHOUSES

THE STABLES

LILLESDEN COTTS

PH

Collingwood House

7

TN18

Kent Bridge Farm

Cowden Gill

Cowden

STREAM LA

29

Hanging Shaw

COWDEN LA

6

Winch's Plantation

Kent Bridge Farm

Kent Ditch

HASTINGS RD

Pook's Wood

Buckhurst Wood

Coldharbour

Merriments Shaw

Cemy

5

Eight Acre Wood

Peagle Wood

MERRIMENTS LA

Merriments Farmhouse

Crossroads Farm

Stone Cottages

Marlpit Shaw

Canal Bridge

JUNCTION RD

Merriments Gardens

Stone House Farm

28

A229

B2244

Cooper's Corner

4

Lodge Farm

TN19

Broomfield Wood

Brickhurst Wood

RIDGE WAY

MEADOW VIEW CL

FOUNDRY COTTS

Mill Wood

ACORN WAY

V CARTERS WAY

GREAT ONE WAY

MICHAELS WAY

Hurst Green

Driftways Farm

3

STATION RD

A265

PH

Birchen Shaw

Fillbrook Wood

27

LONDON RD

Iridge Place

TN32

Park Wood

2

Hurst Green CE Prim Sch

Trough Wood

Ewefield Wood

Grovehill Farm

Little Iridge Farm

Climsett's Farm

Mast

Sweethayes Farm

Silver Hill Farm

Silverhill Wood

1

PH

A21

LITTLE IRIDGE FARM COTTS

Boarsney Farm

BOURNE LA

SILVER HILL

26

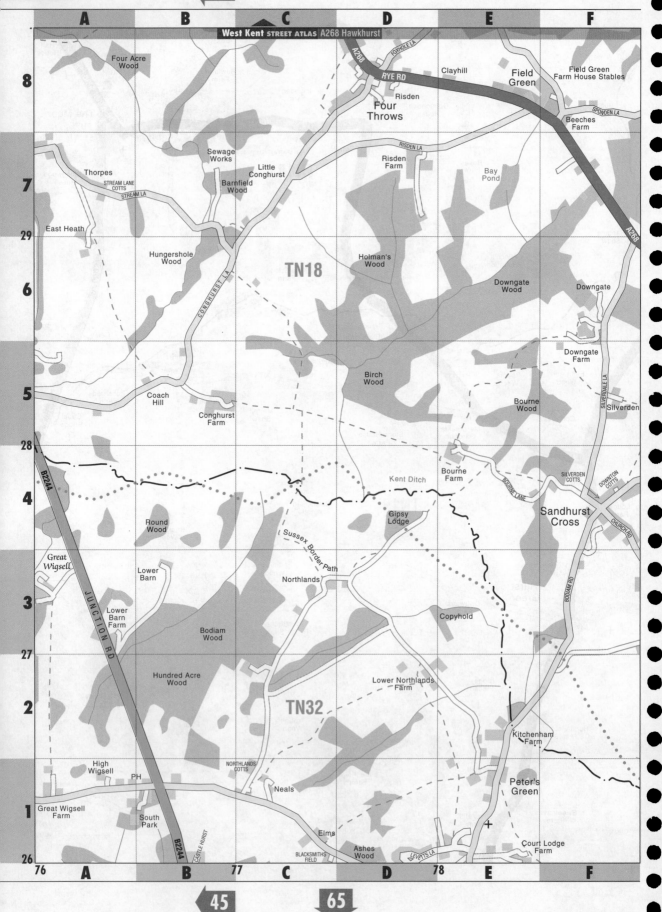

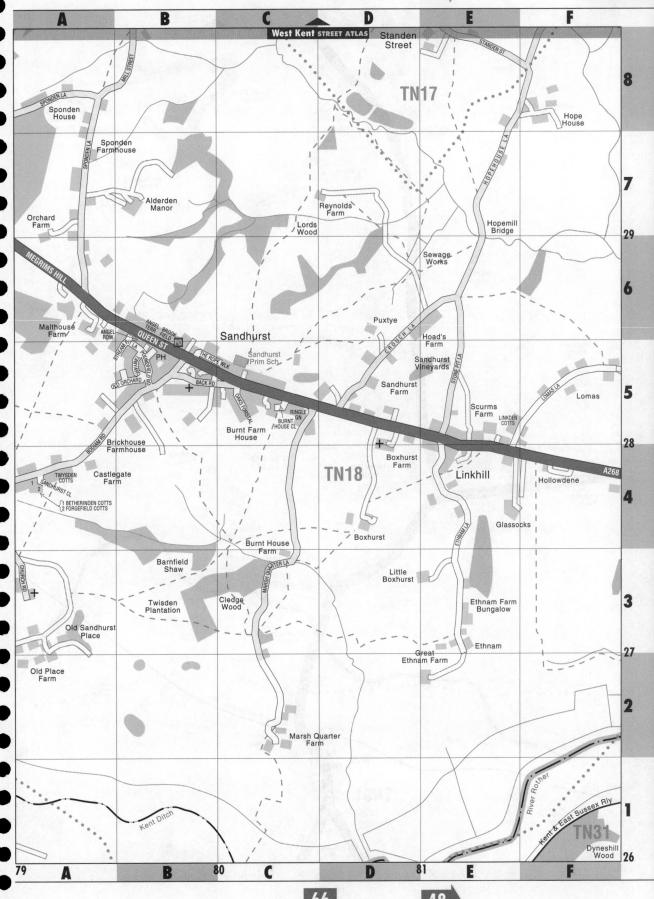

48

West Kent STREET ATLAS

Standen
Street

TN17

Hope
House

STANDEN ST

HOPEHOUSE LA

Hopemill
Bridge

Sewage
Works

29

SPONDEN LA

MILL STREET

Sponden
House

Sponden
Farmhouse

Alderden
Manor

Reynolds
Farm

Lords
Wood

8

7

6

Orchard
Farm

MEGRIMS HILL

Malthouse
Farm

ANGEL BROOK
TERR FIELD
ANGEL
ROW
QUEEN ST
PO

Sandhurst

Puxtye

CROUCH LA

Hoad's
Farm

Sandhurst
Vineyards

STONE PITT LA

LOMAS LA

Lomas

5

STREAM LA
POUNDFIELD RD
VANYARD

PH

THE ROPE WLK

Sandhurst
Prim Sch

Sandhurst
Farm

Scurms
Farm

LINKDEN
COTTS

OLD ORCHARD

BACK RD

OAKS TONSTAL

RINGLE
GN
BURNT
HOUSE CL

Burnt Farm
House

28

Boxhurst
Farm

Linkhill

Hollowdene

A268

BODIAM RD

Brickhouse
Farmhouse

TWYSDEN
COTTS

Castlegate
Farm

TN18

Boxhurst

ETHNAM LA

Glassocks

4

1
2
SANDHURST CL
1 BETHERINDEN COTTS
2 FORGEFIELD COTTS

Burnt House
Farm

Little
Boxhurst

Ethnam Farm
Bungalow

3

CHURCH RD

Barnfield
Shaw

Twisden
Plantation

Cledge
Wood

MARSH QUARTER LA

Ethnam

27

Old Sandhurst
Place

Great
Ethnam Farm

Old Place
Farm

2

Marsh Quarter
Farm

River Rother

Kent & East Sussex Rly

TN31

1

Kent Ditch

Dyneshill
Wood

26

A   B   C   D   E   F

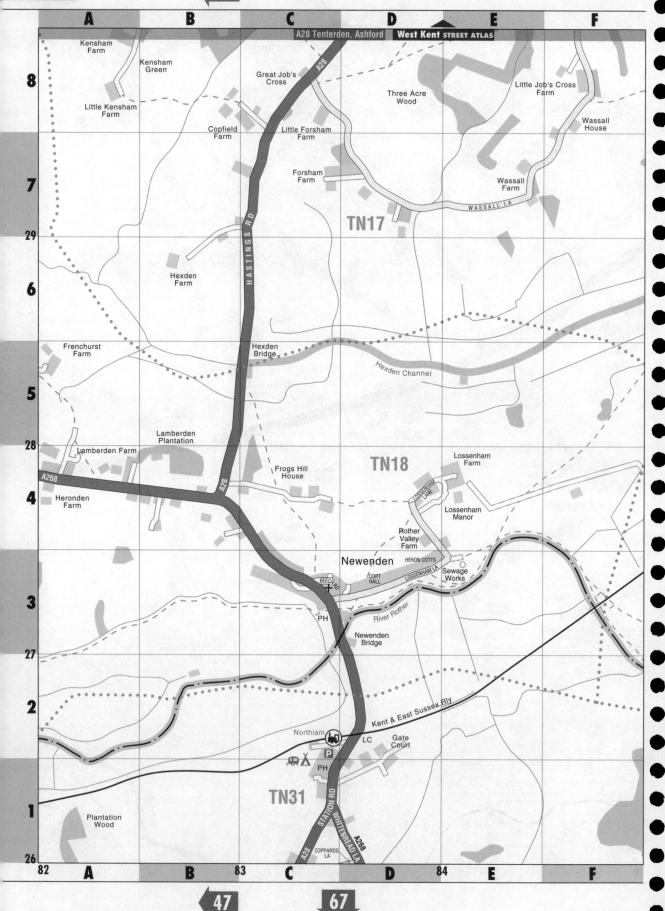

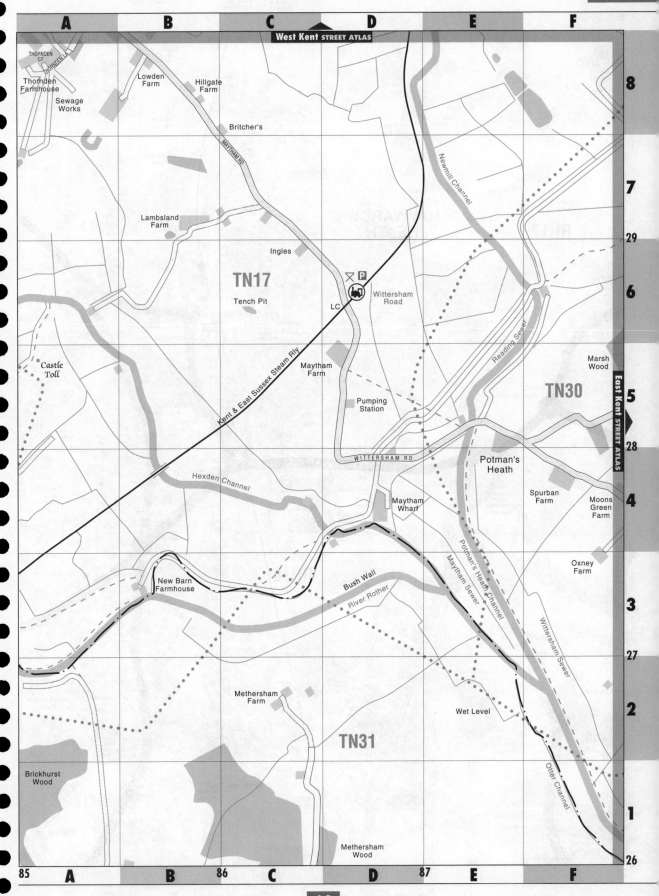

East Kent STREET ATLAS

Thornden Ct
THORNDEN LA
Thornden Farmhouse
Sewage Works
Lowden Farm
Hillgate Farm
Britcher's
Lambsland Farm
Ingles
TN17
Tench Pit
Castle Toll
Maytham Farm
Pumping Station
Wittersham Road
LC
Kent & East Sussex Steam Rly
Hexden Channel
WITTERSHAM RD
Maytham Wharf
New Barn Farmhouse
Bush Wall
River Rother
Methersham Farm
TN31
Brickhurst Wood
Methersham Wood
Newmill Channel
Reading Sewer
Marsh Wood
TN30
Potman's Heath
Spurban Farm
Moons Green Farm
Oxney Farm
Potman's Heath Channel
Maytham Sewer
Wittersham Sewer
Wet Level
Otter Channel

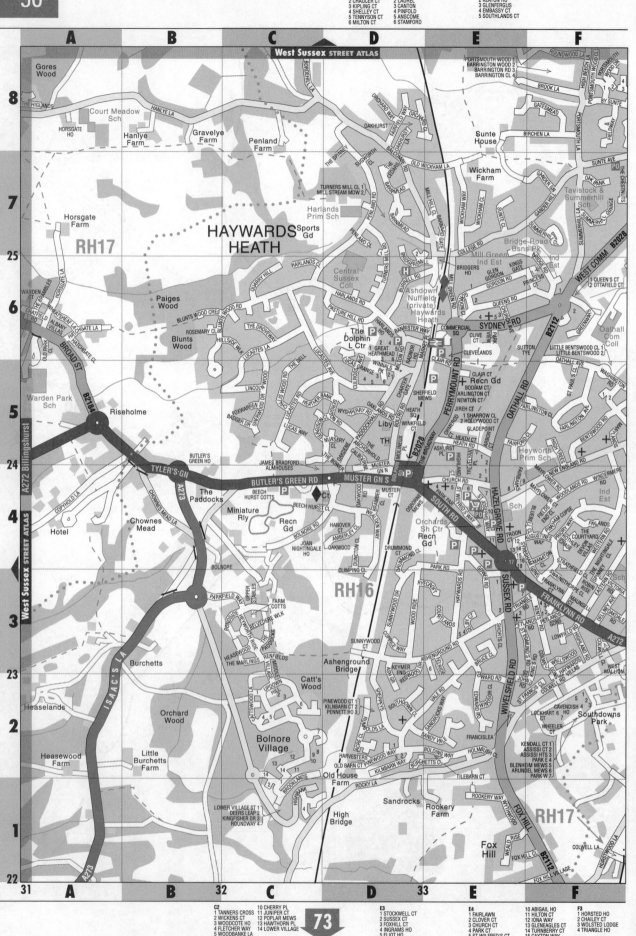

D5
1 BYRON CT
2 CHAUCER CT
3 KIPLING CT
4 SHELLEY CT
5 TENNYSON CT
6 MILTON CT

D6
1 WILTON
2 LAUREL
3 CANTON
4 PINFOLD
5 ANSCOME
6 STAMFORD

E6
1 COPYTHORNE HO
2 KEATON HO
3 GLENFERGUS
4 EMBASSY CT
5 SOUTHLANDS CT

HAYWARDS HEATH

RH17

RH16

RH17

73

C2
1 TANNERS CROSS
2 WICKENS CT
3 WOODCOTE HO
4 FLETCHER WAY
5 WOODBANKE LA
6 WEAVERS MEAD
7 PIERCES LA
8 WHITEBEAM MEWS
9 WHITEBEAM CT
10 CHERRY PL
11 JUNIPER CT
12 POPLAR MEWS
13 HAWTHORN PL
14 LOWER VILLAGE

E3
1 STOCKWELL CT
2 SUSSEX CT
3 FOXHILL CT
4 INGRAMS HO
5 ELIOT HO
6 ASHENGROUND CL
7 PRIORY CT

E4
1 FAIRLAWN
2 CLOVER CT
3 CHURCH CT
4 PARK CT
5 ST WILFRED'S CT
6 THE HEIGHTS
7 HIGHFIELD CT
8 HAZELGROVE GDNS
9 HEATH CL
10 ABIGAIL HO
11 HILTON CT
12 IONA WAY
13 GLENEAGLES CT
14 TURNBERRY CT
15 CAXTON WAY
16 MUIRFIELD CT
17 SUSSEX SQ
18 CARNOUSTIE CT

F3
1 HORSTED HO
2 CHAILEY CT
3 WOLSTED LODGE
4 TRIANGLE HO

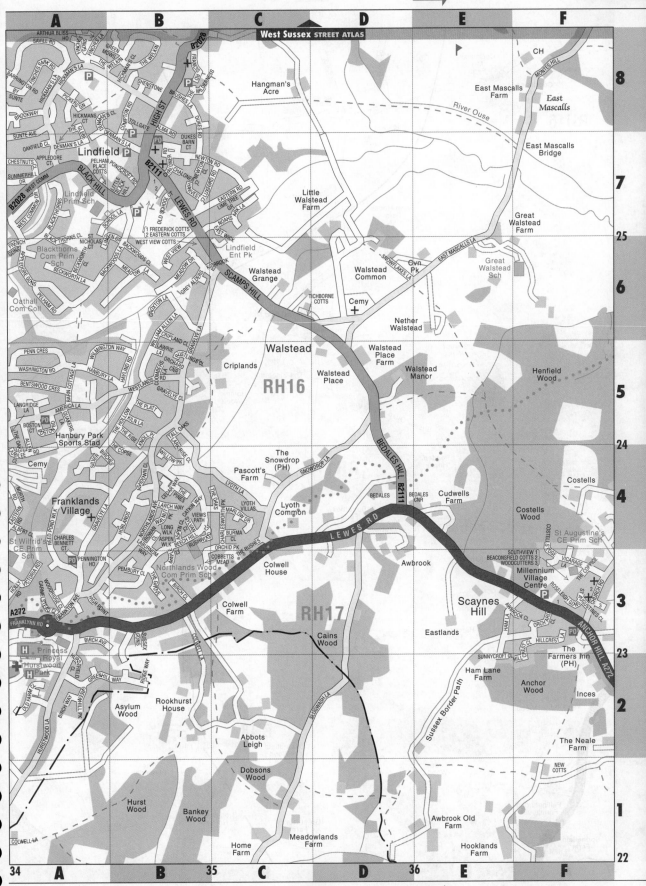

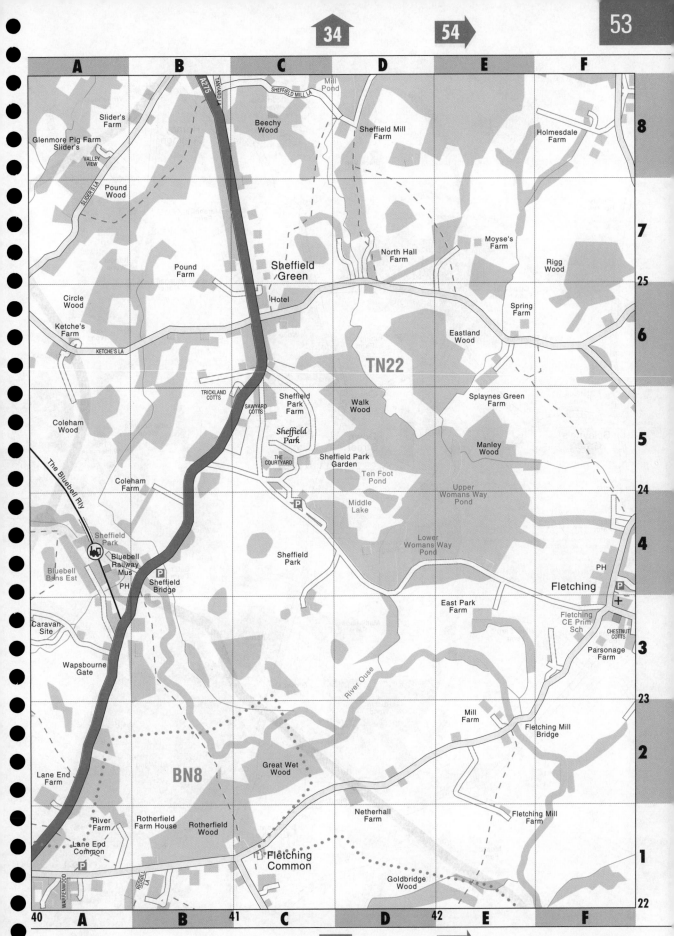

53
35

A
B
C
D
E
F
8
7
25
6
5
24
4
3
23
2
1
22
43
44
45
Searles
Searles Lake
Courtland Wood
Whitehouse Farm
Horney Common
PICKETTS LA
OLD FORGE LA
A22
Black Ven Farm
Poultry Houses
Marshall's Farm
St Clears Farm
Spring Wood
Kennel Wood
Clapwater Farm House
Marshall's Manor
High Wood
Lower Flitteridge Wood
Ruttingham Farm
Cave Wood
Flitterbanks
Flitteridge Farm
DOWN ST
Little Brown's Wood
Splayne's Green
Down Street
The Wilderness
TN22
Downstreet Farmhouse
Knabb Farm
FOREST PK
QUEENS DR
Atherall's Farm
Forge Wood
A272
Downstreet Rough
CHERRY COTTS
Fletching
Batt's Farm
Mallingdown Farm
Parsonage Farm
White Barn Farm
Batt's Wood
Batt's Bridge Stream
Sewage Works
Grover's Farm
Ruston Wood
Hungry Hatch
Oak Ferrars Farm
CH
Park Wood
Pilt Down
Piltdown Golf Club
Moses Farm
Piltdown Pond
Fairhazel Wood
Piltdown
PH
A272
53
77

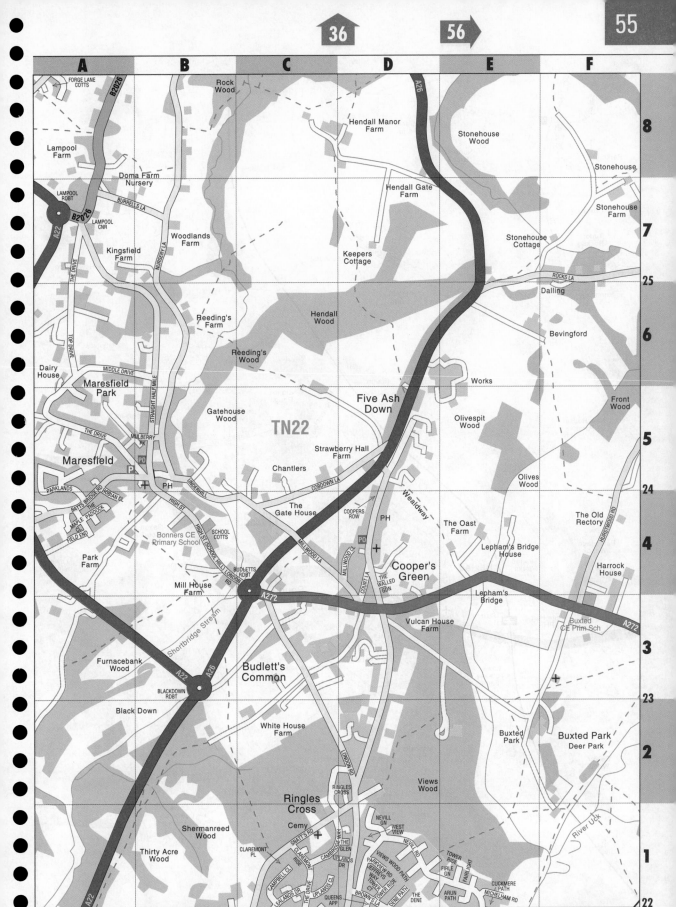

55 37

A B C D E F

8

Perrymans La
Challies La
PO
Royal Oak La
Maypole Drive
Cherry Gdns
PH
Parkhurst
Nordens Green
Holders Farm
Sleeches
Buxted Wood

7
Coxbrook
Tudor Rocks
Rocks La
Fowly La
Greenhurst
Grove Wood
Howbourne Farm

25
The Hermitage
Huggett's Farm

6
Hurstwood Rd
Foxhole Farm

New House Farm
River Uck
Coes Rough
Stones Rough
Buxted Wood La
Rosemount

5
Vanguard Way
Howbourne La

24
Church La
Redbrook La
TN22
Dolloways Bank House
A272

4
Parsonage Wood
Sewage Works
Buxted
St Mary's Garth
Park View
Littlewood La
Eight Bells
Nursery Field
Spotted Cow La
Saxon Court
Toll Farm
Lower Wood

St Marys Mead
High St
Broad Oak
Britts Farm Rd
Britts Orch
Pound Green
Popeswood Farm
Stone's Wood

3
White Hart (PH)
Buxted
Buxted Ct
Gordon Rd
Higglers Cl
Potter's Green
Limes La
Abbotswood House
A272

Lower Totease Farm
Framfield Rd

23
Nan Tucks La

2
Culver Wood
Mascalls Farm
Bish Wood

Tanyard Cotts
Tanyard Farm
Lower Lowlands Farm

1
Shepherd's Hill

22
Streele La
Etchingwood
Pound La

49 A B 50 C D 51 E F

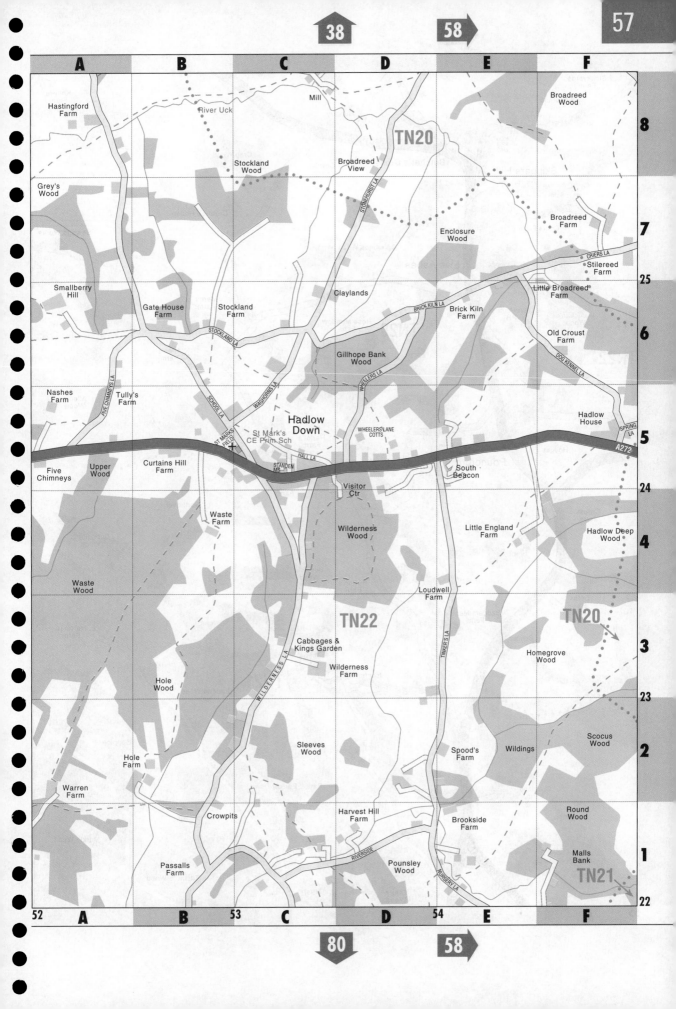

A B C D E F

8

Hastingford Farm

River Uck

Mill

Broadreed Wood

TN20

7

Grey's Wood

Stockland Wood

Broadreed View

Broadreed Farm

STONEHURST LA

Enclosure Wood

CRIERS LA

Stilereed Farm

25

Smallberry Hill

Gate House Farm

Stockland Farm

STOCKLAND LA

Claylands

BRICK KILN LA

Brick Kiln Farm

Little Broadreed Farm

Old Croust Farm

6

FIVE CHIMNEYS LA

Nashes Farm

Tully's Farm

SCHOOL LA

WAGHORNS LA

Gillhope Bank Wood

WHEELERS LA

DOG KENNEL LA

Hadlow House

SPRING LA

5

ST MARKS FIELD

St Mark's CE Prim Sch

Hadlow Down

WHEELERS LANE COTTS

A272

Five Chimneys

Upper Wood

Curtains Hill Farm

HALL LA

STANDEN MS

South Beacon

24

Waste Farm

Visitor Ctr

Little England Farm

Hadlow Deep Wood

4

Waste Wood

Wilderness Wood

Loudwell Farm

TN22

TN20

3

Hole Wood

WILDERNESS LA

Cabbages & Kings Garden

Wilderness Farm

TINKER'S LA

Homegrove Wood

23

Hole Farm

Sleeves Wood

Spood's Farm

Wildings

Scocus Wood

2

Warren Farm

Crowpits

Harvest Hill Farm

Brookside Farm

Round Wood

1

Passalls Farm

RIVERSIDE

Pounsley Wood

NURSERY LA

Malls Bank

TN21

22

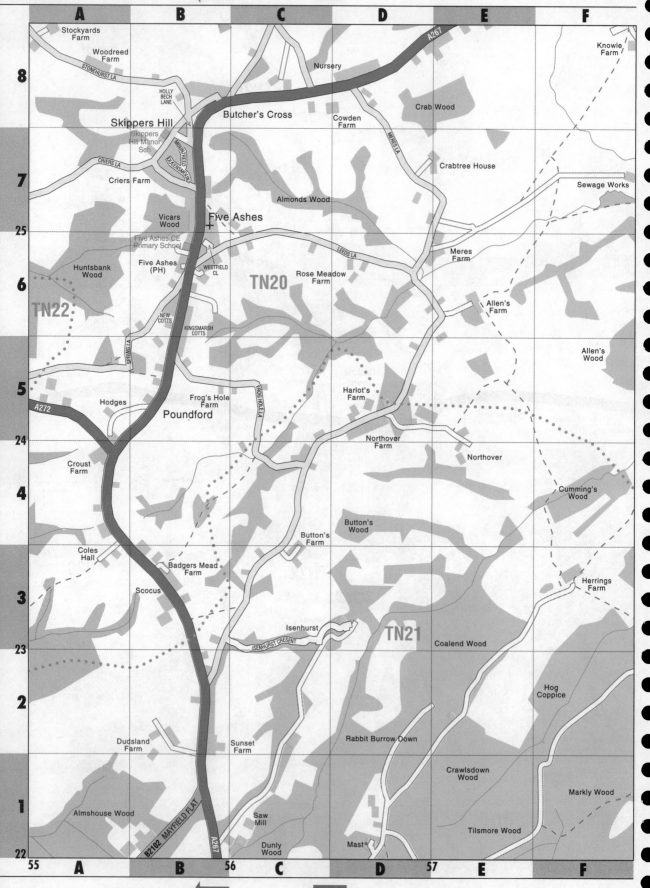

A B C D E F

8

Stockyards Farm
Woodreed Farm
STONEHURST LA
HOLLY BECH LANE
Skippers Hill
Skippers Hill Manor Sch
Butcher's Cross
Nursery
A267
Cowden Farm
Crab Wood
Knowle Farm

7
CRIERS LA
Criers Farm
MOUNTFIELD
QUEENSMOR
MERES LA
Crabtree House
Sewage Works

25
Vicars Wood
Five Ashes CE Primary School
Five Ashes
Almonds Wood
LEEDS LA
Meres Farm

6
Huntsbank Wood
Five Ashes (PH)
WESTFIELD CL
TN20
Rose Meadow Farm
Allen's Farm

TN22
NEW COTTS
KINGSMARSH COTTS
SPRING LA
Allen's Wood

5
A272
Hodges
Frog's Hole Farm
FROG HOLE LA
WOOD
Harlot's Farm

24
Croust Farm
Poundford
Northover Farm
Northover
Cumming's Wood

4

Coles Hall
Badgers Mead Farm
Button's Wood
Button's Farm
Herrings Farm

3
Scocus
Isenhurst
ISENHURST CRESENT
TN21
Coalend Wood

23

2
Dudsland Farm
Sunset Farm
Rabbit Burrow Down
Hog Coppice

Crawlsdown Wood
Markly Wood

1
Almshouse Wood
B2102 MAYFIELD FLAT
A267
Saw Mill
Tilsmore Wood

22
Dunly Wood
Mast

55 A B 56 C D 57 E F

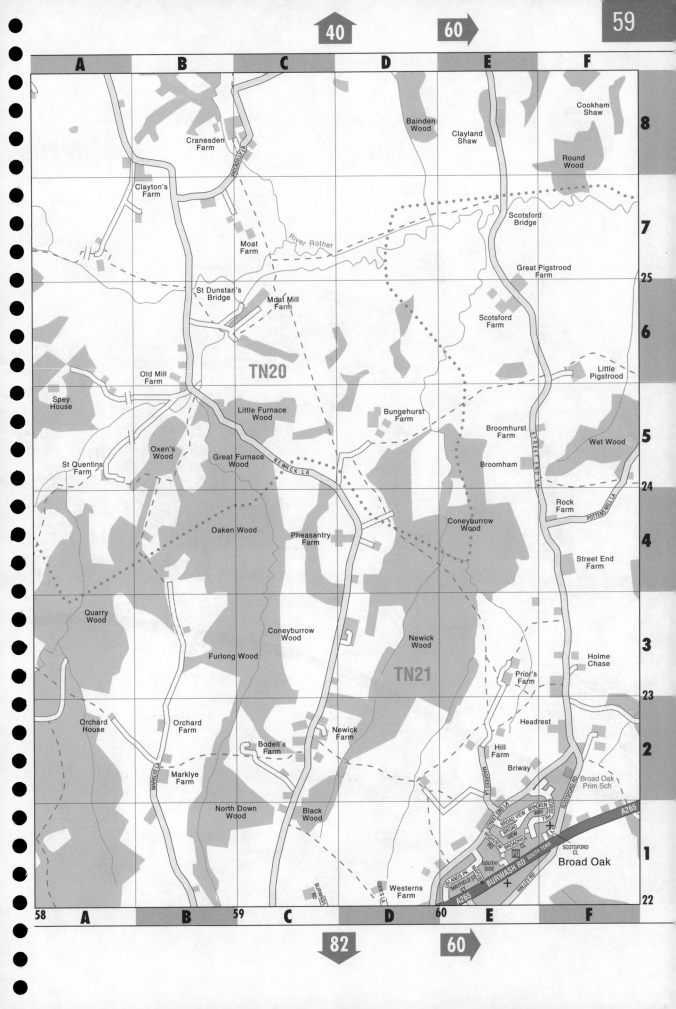

A B C D E F

8

Great Calem Wood

Little Calem Wood

Froghole Farm

TN20

River Rother

Froghole Bridge

Turk's Bridge

7

Turk's Farm

Holmshurst Manor Farm

Great Broadhurst Farm

Little Broadhurst Farm

Oaken Wood

25

Coxdown Farm

6

Little Stonehurst Farm

Great Stonehurst Farm

Lakedown Farm

Nursements Farm

Great Bigknowle Farm

Shovels Wood

Ashen Wood

POTTENS MILL LA

Pottens Mill Farm

Limberlost Farm

Marlpit Shaw

Climshurst Wood

TN19

5

Taylor's Farm

Knowle Farm

Broadhurst

Blackdown Wood

SWIFE LA

24

Corner Farm

Foxhole Wood

Oakdown Farm

4

TN21

PAINE'S CNR

Foxhole Farm

Baltham Wood

Little Park Hill Farm

Doel's Farm

A265

Barklye Farm

Mill House Farm

THE MARTLETTS

3

Olives Farm

Burralands

Holban's Farm

Black Sand Wood

23

Swife Wood

Cedar Swiffe Farm

Kingsdown Farm

Poundsford

2

Swiffes Farm

Home Farm

Poundsford Farm

A265

Spinney Farm House

Tottingworth Park

Oak Hall

Milkhurst Wood

Applebrook Farm

Stonehole Wood

1

Limekiln Wood

22

61 A B 62 C D 63 E F

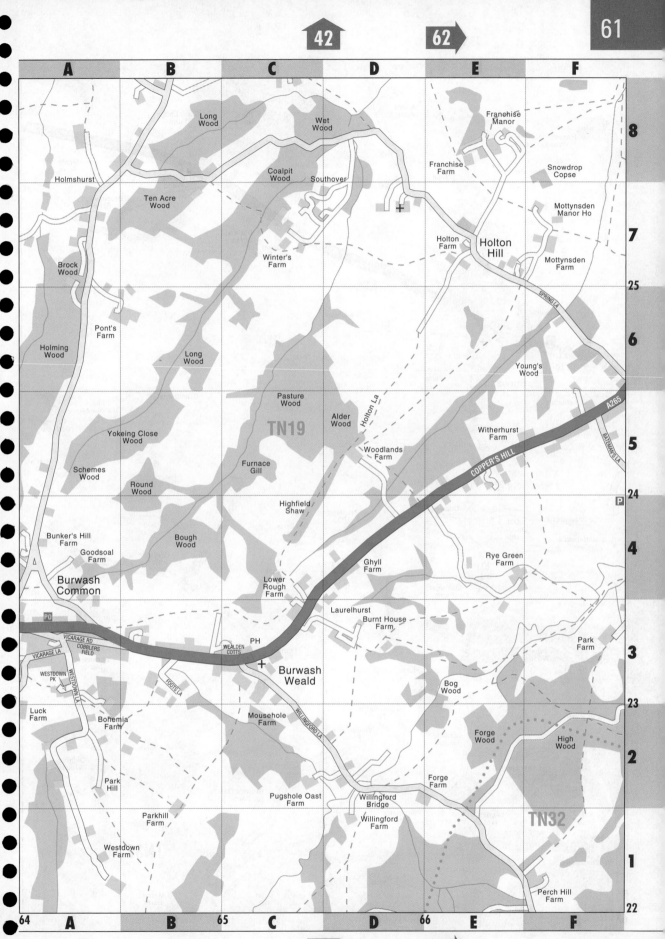

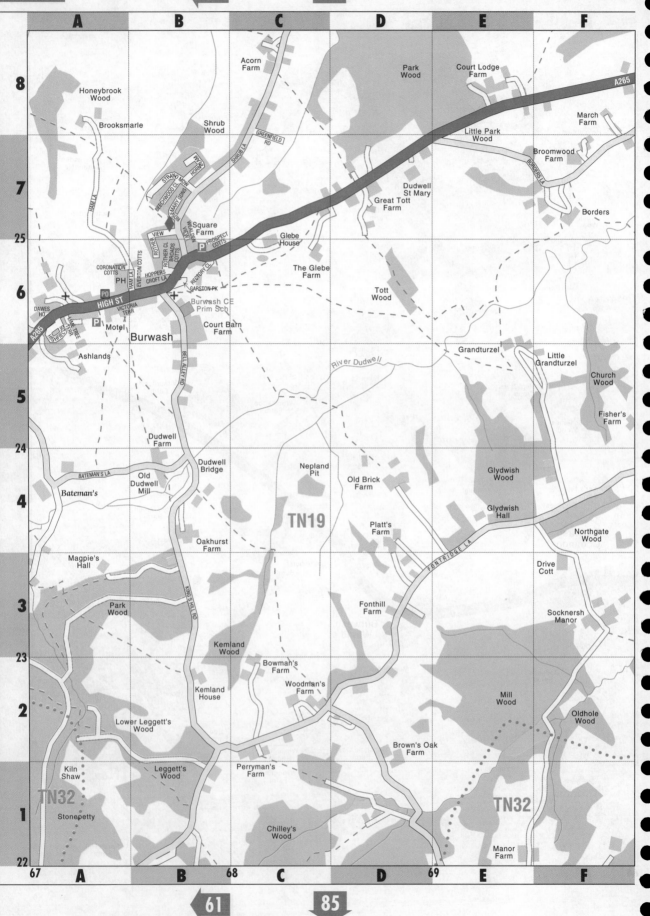

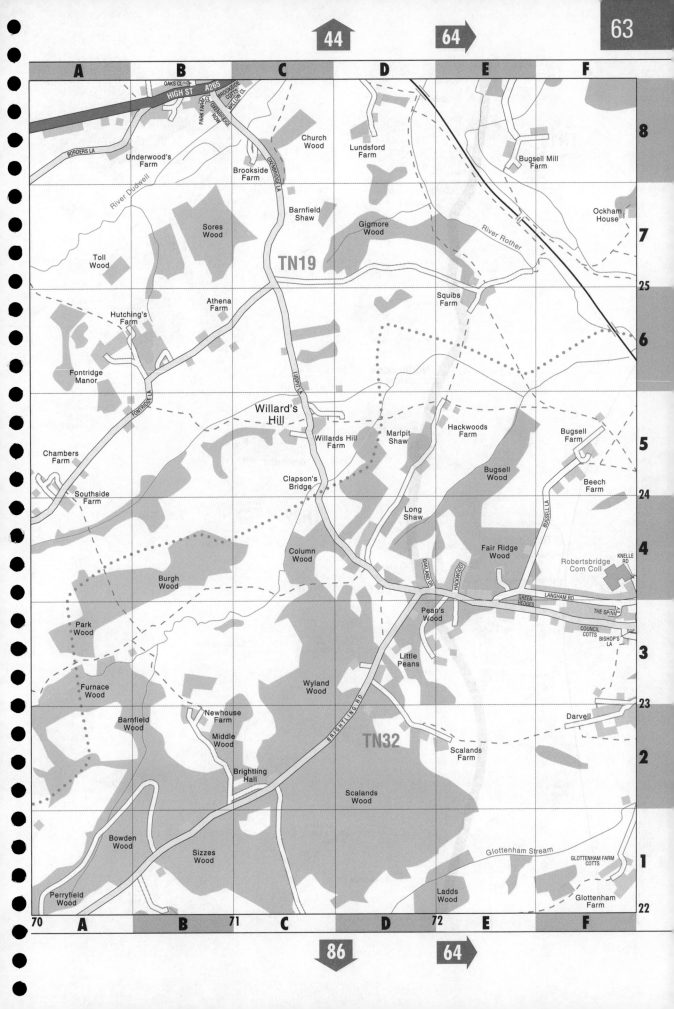

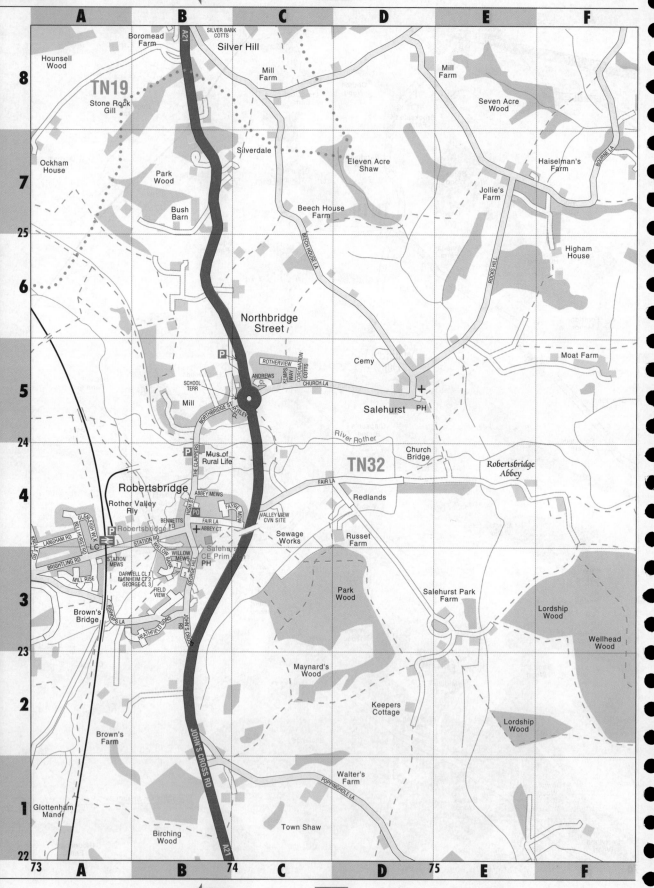

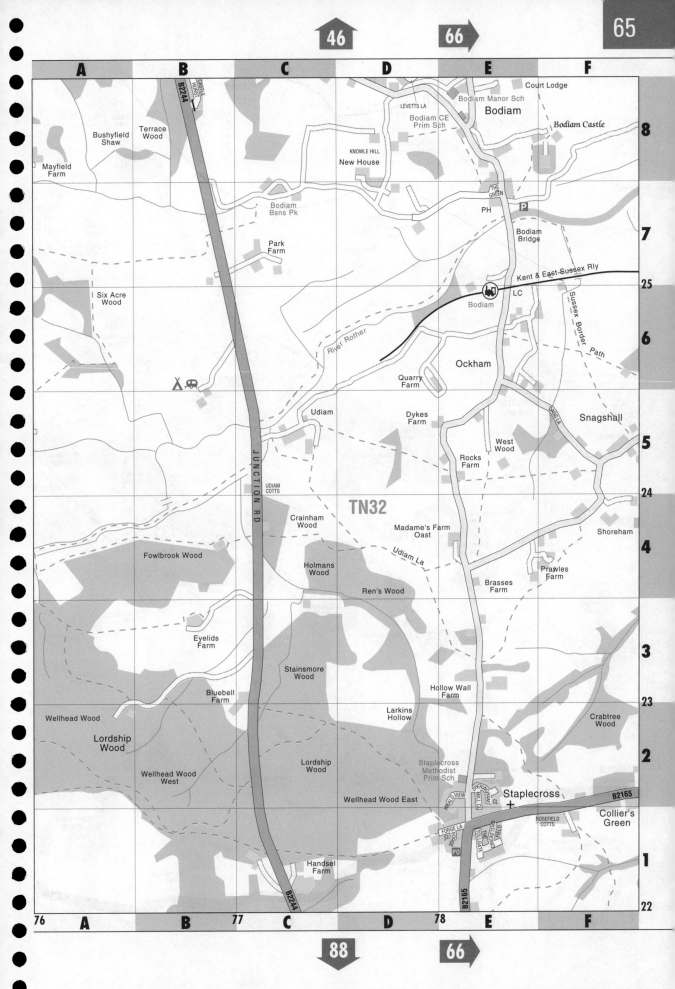

A **B** **C** **D** **E** **F**

B2244
CASTLE HURST

Bushyfield Shaw
Terrace Wood
8
Mayfield Farm

KNOWLE HILL
New House

Bodiam Bsns Pk

Park Farm

Six Acre Wood

LEVETTS LA
Bodiam CE Prim Sch
Bodiam Manor Sch
Court Lodge
Bodiam
Bodiam Castle

THE GREEN
PH
P
Bodiam Bridge
7

Kent & East-Sussex Rly
LC
25
Bodiam

River Rother
Sussex Border Path
6

Quarry Farm
Ockham

JUNCTION RD

Udiam
Dykes Farm
West Wood
Snagshall
ORGG LA
5

Rocks Farm

UDIAM COTTS
24
Crainham Wood
TN32
Madame's Farm Oast
Shoreham
4
Udiam La
Fowlbrook Wood
Holmans Wood
Prawles Farm
Ren's Wood
Brasses Farm

Eyelids Farm
3
Stainsmore Wood
Hollow Wall Farm
23
Bluebell Farm
Larkins Hollow
Crabtree Wood
Wellhead Wood
Lordship Wood
Lordship Wood
Staplecross Methodist Prim Sch
2
Wellhead Wood West
SHERINGHAM
MILL CL
CL
Staplecross
B2165
Wellhead Wood East
WEALD VIEW
Collier's Green
ROSEFIELD COTTS
FORGE LA
THE TOLLGATE
SUSSEXFIELD
PO
Handsel Farm
B2244
1
B2165
22

A   B   C   D   E   F

8

TN18   Kent Ditch

River Rother

Kent & East Sussex Rly

Dixter Halt

Dixter Wood

7

Cantise Shaw

Padgham

Little Dixter

Great Dixter Nurseries

25

Great Dixter House & Gardens

Horselands Shaw

6

Sussex Border Path

Four Acre Shaw

PH

THE GREEN

Ewhurst Green

Spital Wood

5

Snagshall

Longwood

Reach Wood

Furnace Wood

Old Steading

Sempstead Wood

24

Sogg's House

Long Wood

TN31

Coneyburrow Wood

Stumblott's Farm

TN32

Sempstead

Park Wood

Tufton Place

4

LORDINE LA

Stumblott's Wood

SEMPSTEAD LA

Birchin Wood

Wattshill Wood

Yewtree Hill

Ockford Farm

3

Flettice Wood

Martinshaw Farm

Watts Hill Farm

Lordine Wood

23

Water Twr

Spanyard's Farm

ADAMS LA

Dadland Wood

2

Collier's Green

Holmtree Wood

Lordine Court

Chantry Wood

Forstal Wood

B2165

Boyces

Sewage Works

Gate Farm

Commons Wood

1

ELLENWHORNE LA

Sparks

New House Farm

Benedict Farm

B2165

22

79   A   B   80   C   D   81   E   F

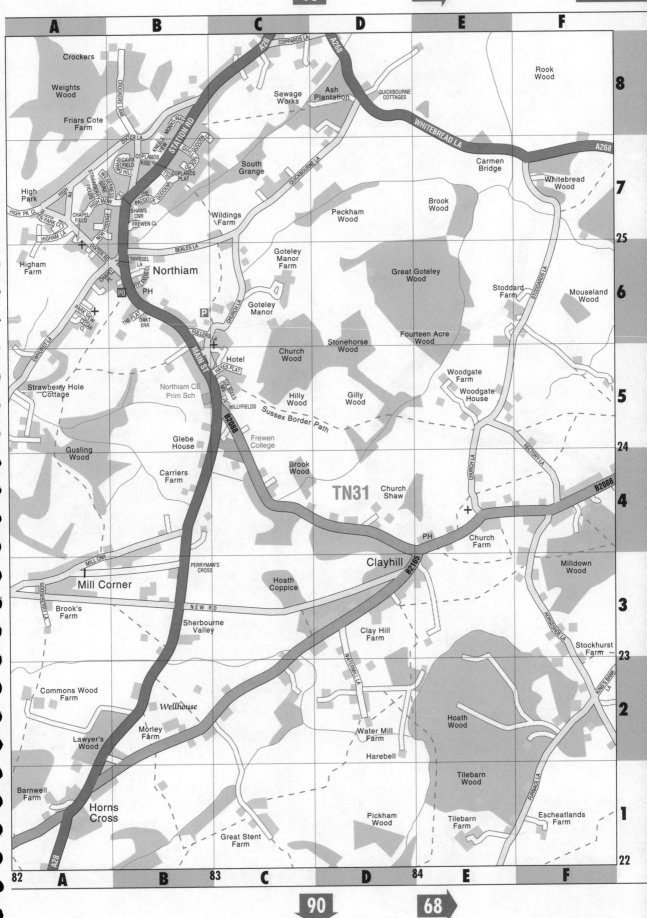

A   B   C   D   E   F

8

Great
Bellhurst
Farm

Little
Bellhurst

Little Heron
Farm

Knelle
Wood

Hope
Farm

Oxenbridge
Farm

A268

7

Little
Knelle
Farm

Decoypond Ditch

Roger's
Wood

Carpen
Wood

25

WHITEBREAD LA

Swallowtail
Hill

Sussex Border Path

High Weald Landscape Trail

Sussex Border Path

Evening
Wood

6

Dean
Wood

Hobbs'
Farm

Barber's
Wood

B2084

Turner's
Wood

Sewage
Works

Shepherds
Farm

TURNERS
COTTS

Maidland
Wood

HOBBS CL   COOMBS CL

Spring
Wood

Shepherds

Streamland
Wood

5

ROBERTS
ROW

COOMBS
COTTS

Combe
Shaw

Kitchenour

KITCHENOUR LA

B2088

24

Four
Oaks

Hop
Barn

High Weald Landscape Trail

B2088

OAKHILL
COTTS

TN31

Oaken
Wood

Mill
Wood

MACKREL HILL

Beckley

Burnt
Wood

4

Beckley CE
Prim Sch

Wish
Wood

Bartlett
Shaw

Two Hovens
Farm

King's
Bank
Farm

KING'S BANK LA

Great
Dennis
Wood

A268

Flackley
Ash

3

King's
Bank

Bixley
Wood

Little
Dennis
Wood

MILL LA

23

Weaver's
Farm

BIXLEY LA

Flatroper's Wood
(Nature Reserve)

Houseroper's
Wood

The
Firs

TANHOUSE LA

2

Little
Harmers
Farm

Fifty Acre
Wood

Watcombe

Birds
Farm

Woodlands
Farm

HORSESHOE LA

Nursery

Gate
Farm

Rockfield
Plantation

1

Great Shelley
Wood

Eggshole Brook

26

85   A   B   86   C   D   87   E   F

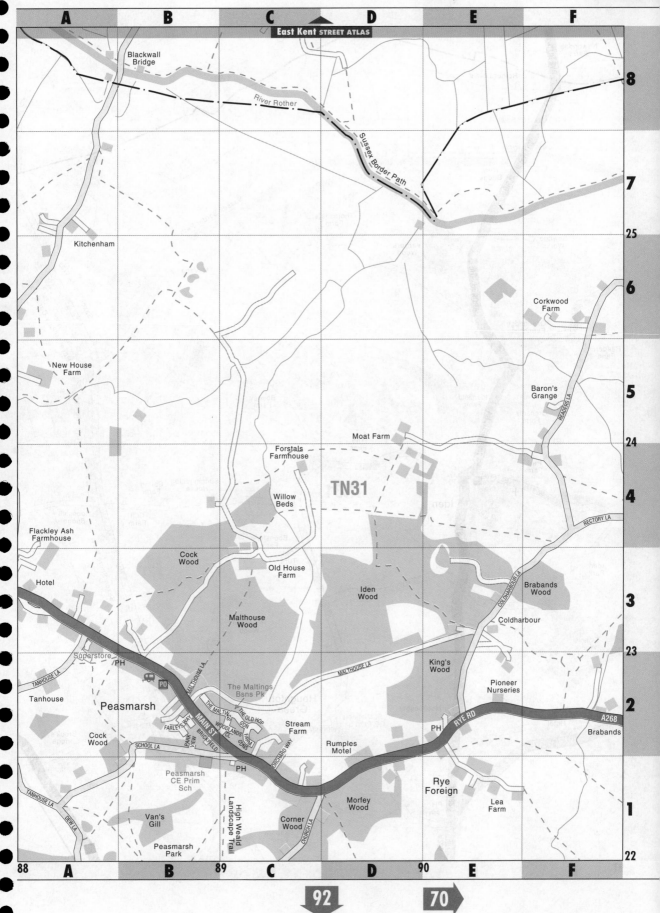

East Kent STREET ATLAS

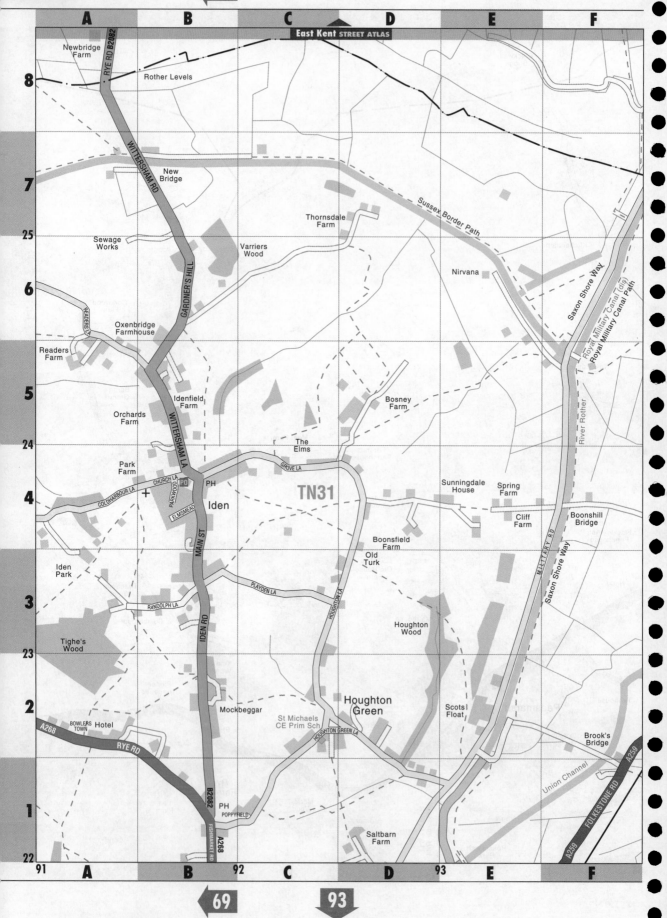

East Kent STREET ATLAS

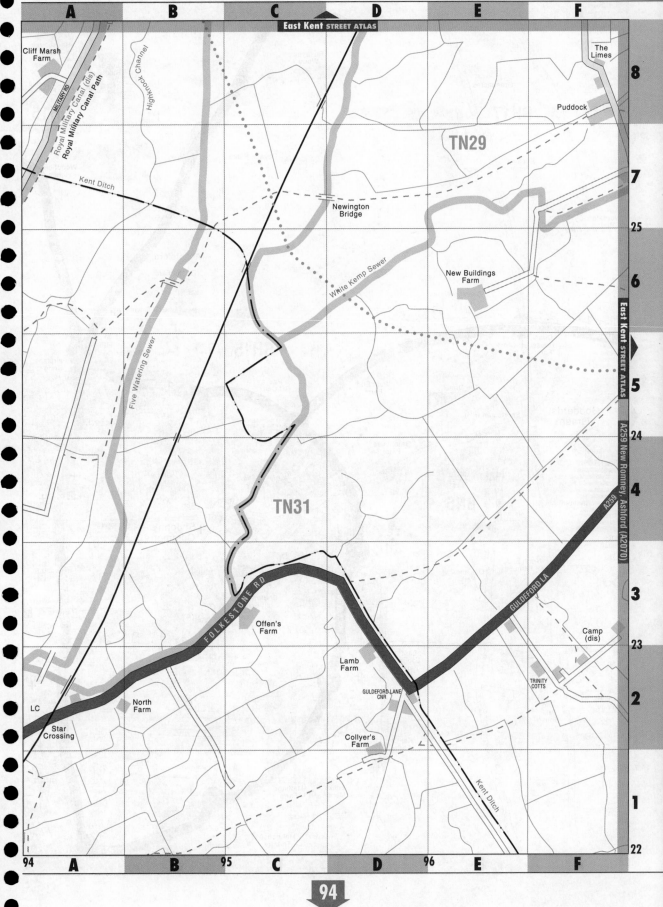

East Kent STREET ATLAS

Cliff Marsh Farm

MILITARY RD

Royal Military Canal (dis)
Royal Military Canal Path

Highknock Channel

Kent Ditch

TN29

The Limes

Puddock

8

7

25

Newington Bridge

White Kemp Sewer

New Buildings Farm

6

Five Watering Sewer

East Kent STREET ATLAS

5

A259 New Romney, Ashford (A2070)

24

TN31

4

A259

GULDEFORD LA

Camp (dis)

3

FOLKESTONE RD

Offen's Farm

Lamb Farm

TRINITY COTTS

23

North Farm

GULDEFORD LANE CNR

2

LC

Star Crossing

Collyer's Farm

Kent Ditch

1

22

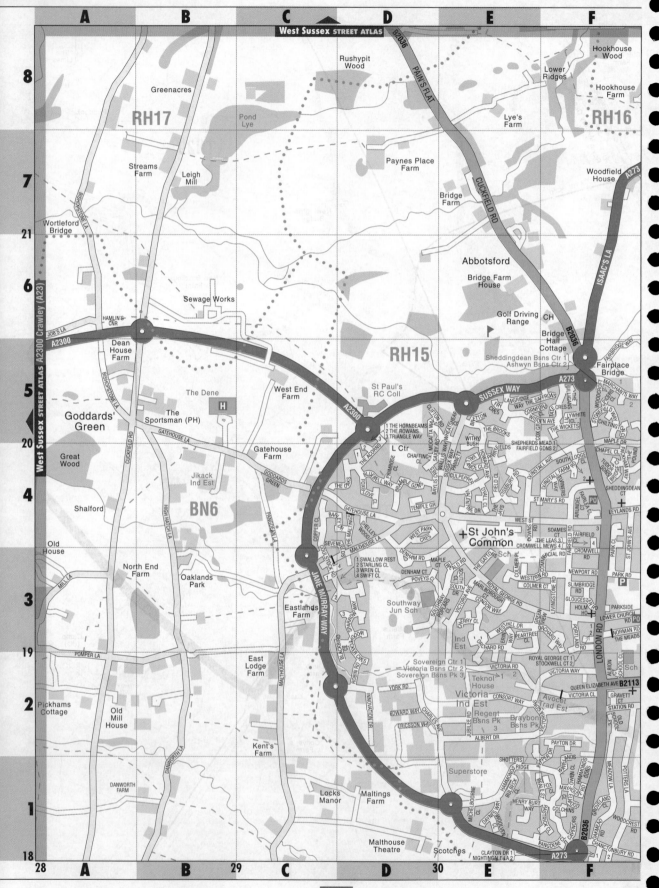

West Sussex STREET ATLAS

RH17

RH16

Greenacres

Pond Lye

Rushypit Wood

Lower Ridges

Hookhouse Wood

Hookhouse Farm

Streams Farm

Leigh Mill

Paynes Place Farm

Bridge Farm

Lye's Farm

Woodfield House

Wortleford Bridge

Abbotsford

Bridge Farm House

Sewage Works

Golf Driving Range

CH

Bridge Hall Cottage

Dean House Farm

RH15

Sheddingdean Bsns Ctr 1
Ashwyn Bsns Ctr 2

Fairplace Bridge

Goddards' Green

The Dene

West End Farm

St Paul's RC Coll

SUSSEX WAY

A273

The Sportsman (PH)

Gatehouse Farm

1 THE HORNBEAMS
2 THE ROWANS
3 TRIANGLE WAY

L Ctr

Great Wood

Goddards Green

BN6

Jikack Ind Est

St John's Common

Shalford

Old House

North End Farm

Oaklands Park

Eastlands Farm

1 SWALLOW REST
2 STARLING CL
3 WREN CL
4 SWIFT CL

Southway Jun Sch

JANE MURRAY WAY

Ind Est

Pickhams Cottage

Old Mill House

East Lodge Farm

Sovereign Ctr 1
Victoria Bsns Ctr 2
Sovereign Bsns Pk 3

Victoria Ind Est

POMPER LA

Teknol House

York Rd

Regent Bsns Pk

Brayon Bsns Pk

Kent's Farm

Queen Elizabeth Ave

B2113

Danworth Farm

Superstore

Locks Manor

Maltings Farm

SHOTTERS

Malthouse Theatre

Scotches

CLAYTON DR 1
NIGHTINGALE LA 2

A273

B2036

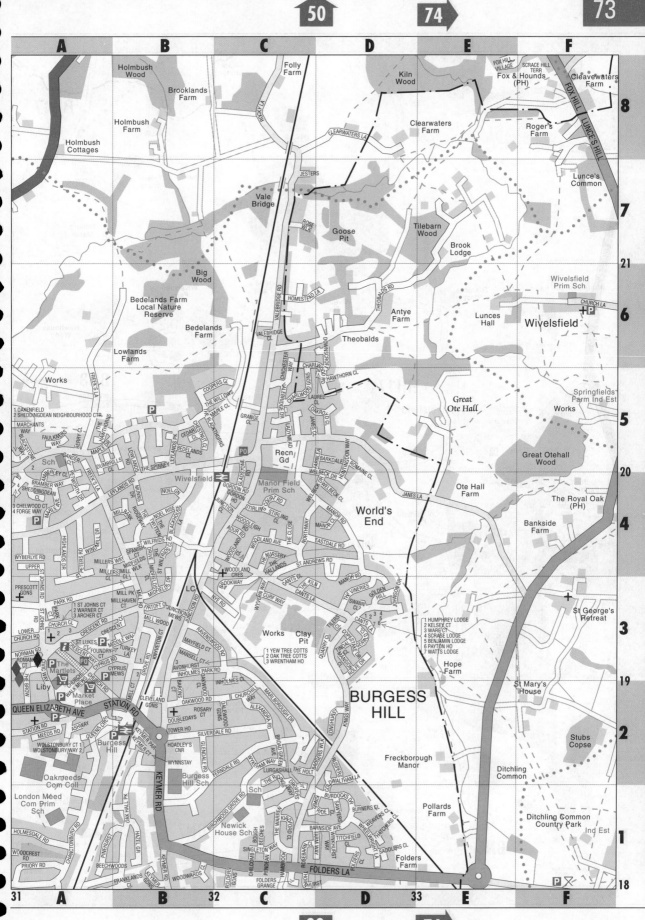

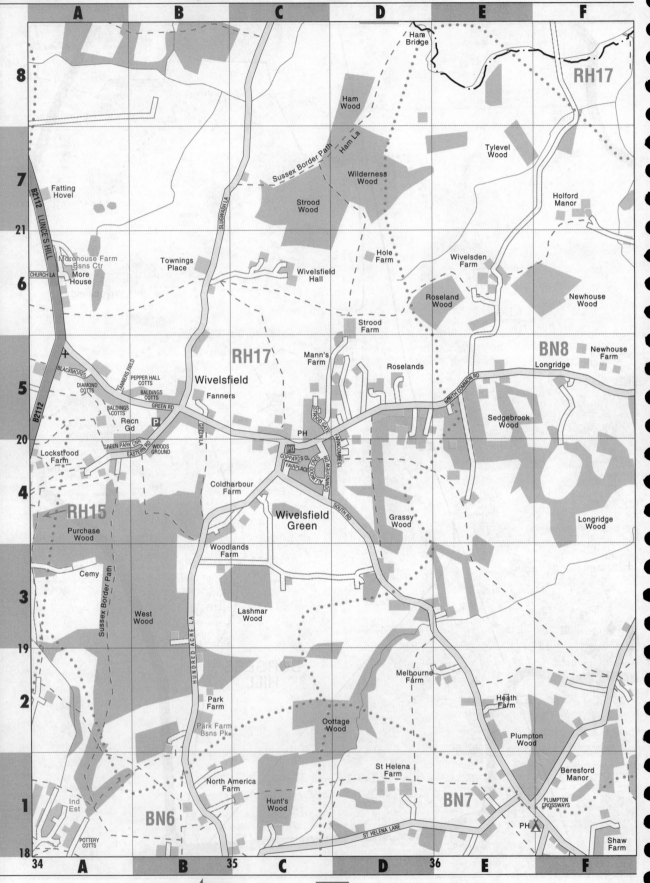

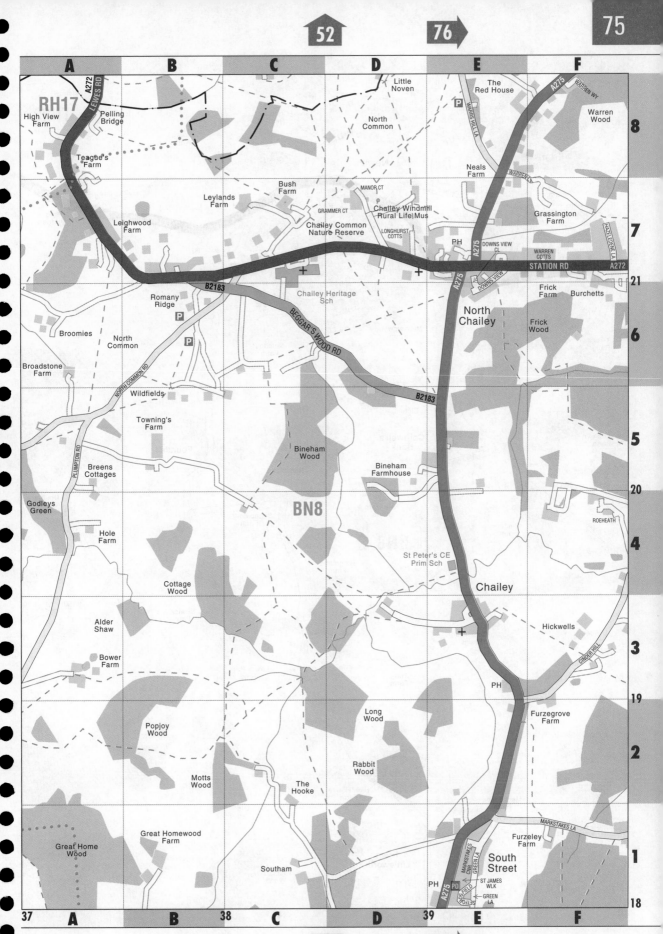

A **B** **C** **D** **E** **F**

8

Goldstrow

TN22

The Warren

Fletching Common

Cobb's Nest

Sewage Works

River Ouse

NEWICK HILL

Newick

ACERLANDS

CRICKETFIELD

ALEXANDER RD

Goldbridge Farm

Gold Bridge

Cox's Farm

7

HARMERS HILL

JACKIES LA

WESTERN RD

WOODBINE LA

NEWICK DR

GODDEN RD

PAYNTERS WAY

VERN INNS RD

NORTH LODGE

NEWLANDS PARK WAY

THE PAGETS

LEVELLER END

HIGH ST

MACKLES RD

OLDAKER RD

THE GREEN

PH

GOLDBRIDGE RD

A272

COLDHARBOUR LA

A272

STATION RD

Reedens

THE RIDINGS

WESTPOINT

NEWICK DR

THE ROUGH

GROVE RD

POWELL

BANNISTERS FIELD

PO

21

ALLINGTON CRES

MILLFIELD

ALLINGTON

SOUTH ROUGH

BADENS CL

BROOKS GDNS

HIGH HURST CL

ALLINGTON PL

BLIND LA

OXBOTTOM CL

LANGRIDGES CL

Newick CE Prim Sch

6

Great Rough

LOWER STATION RD

Mitchelswood Farm

Ketches Farm

CHURCH RD

Founthill Wood

Oxbottom

Tilehouse Farm

5

Vixengrove Farm

Cronk's Wood

CHAILEY LA

Cornwell's Bank

Beechland

Founthill

Double Barns Farm

20

Cinder Hill

Cinder Farm

New Barn Farm

Schoolhouse Farm

4

BN8

Ridgeland Farm

Cockfield La

Newick Park

MACKEREL'S ROCKS

Ades

Cockfield Bridge

3

Tutts Farm

Lower Park Pond

19

Lodge Pond

Longford Stream

Wilding Wood

2

MARKSTAKES LA

High House Farm

Old Park

1

Markstakes Farm

Shelley's Farm

Town Littleworth

Oldpark Wood

The Butletts

18

40 **A** 41 **B** **C** 42 **D** **E** **F**

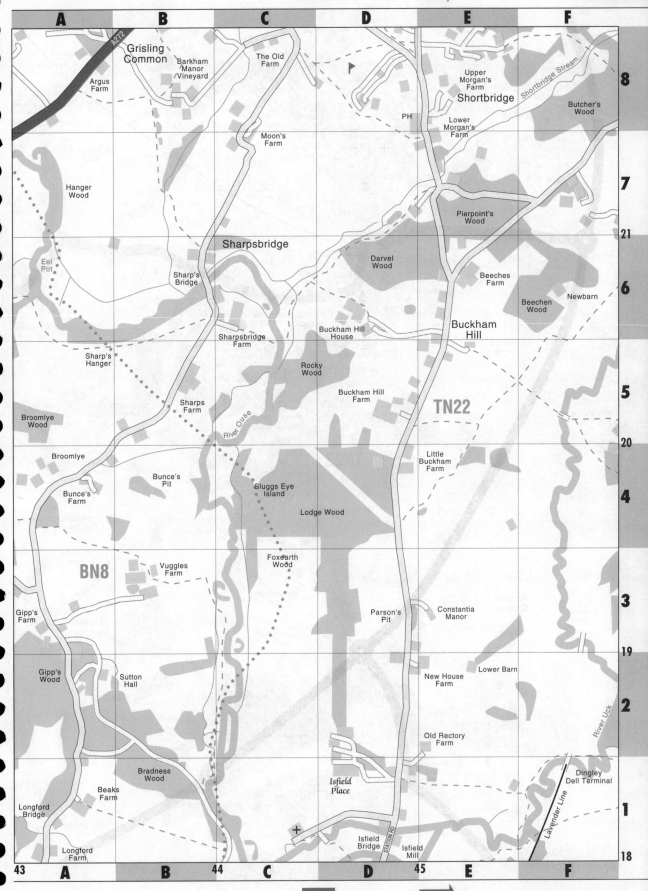

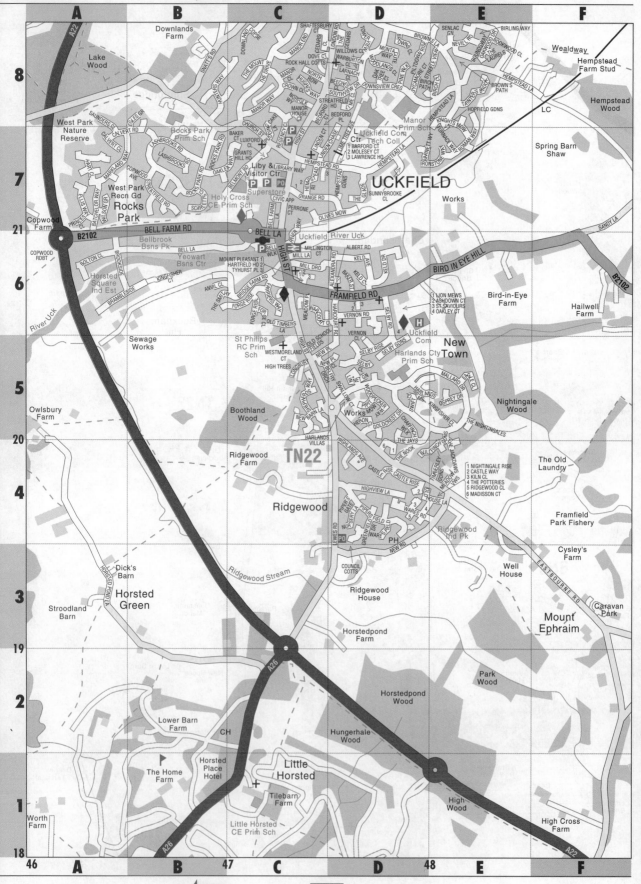

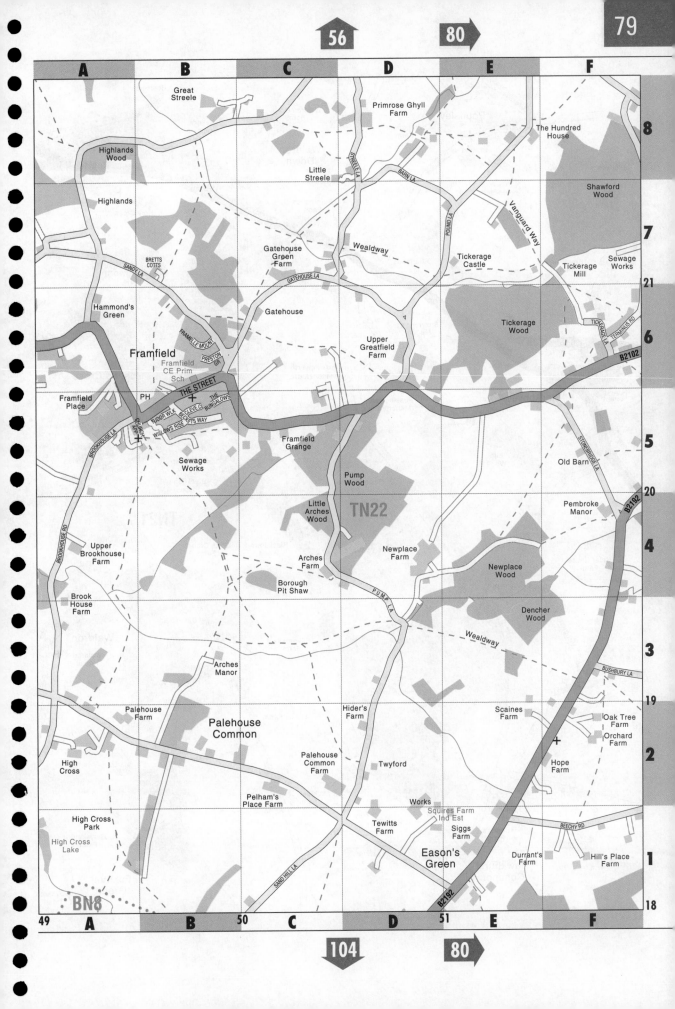

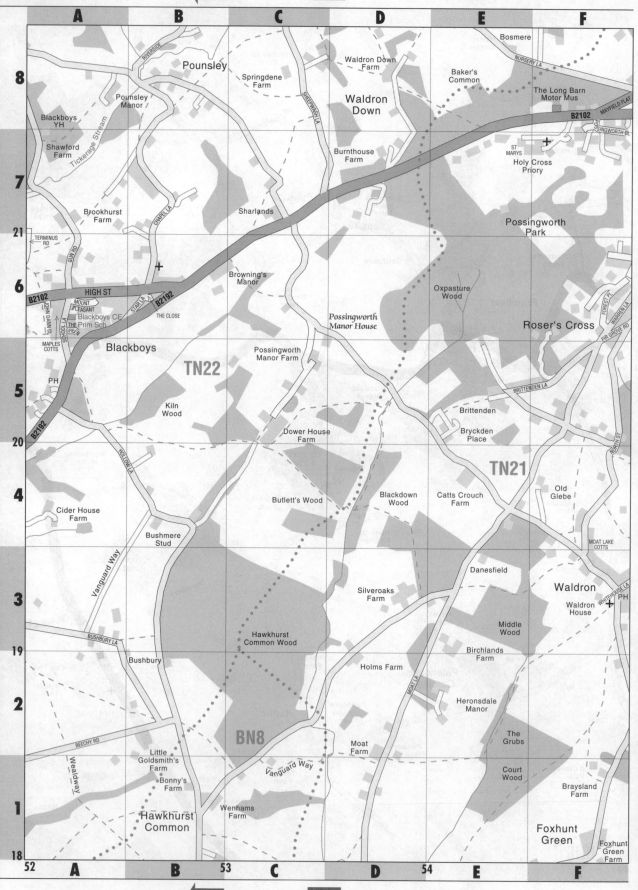

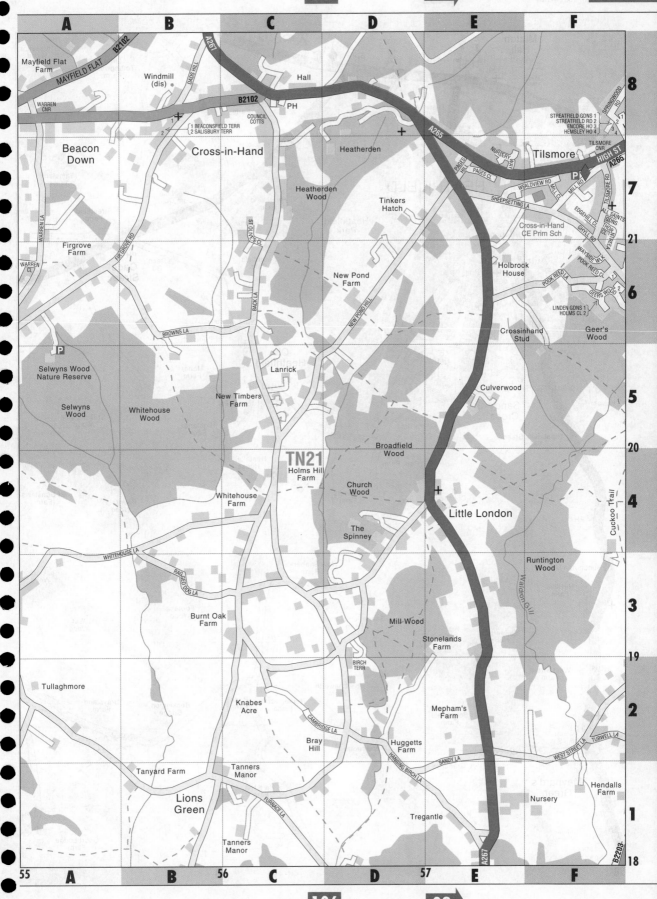

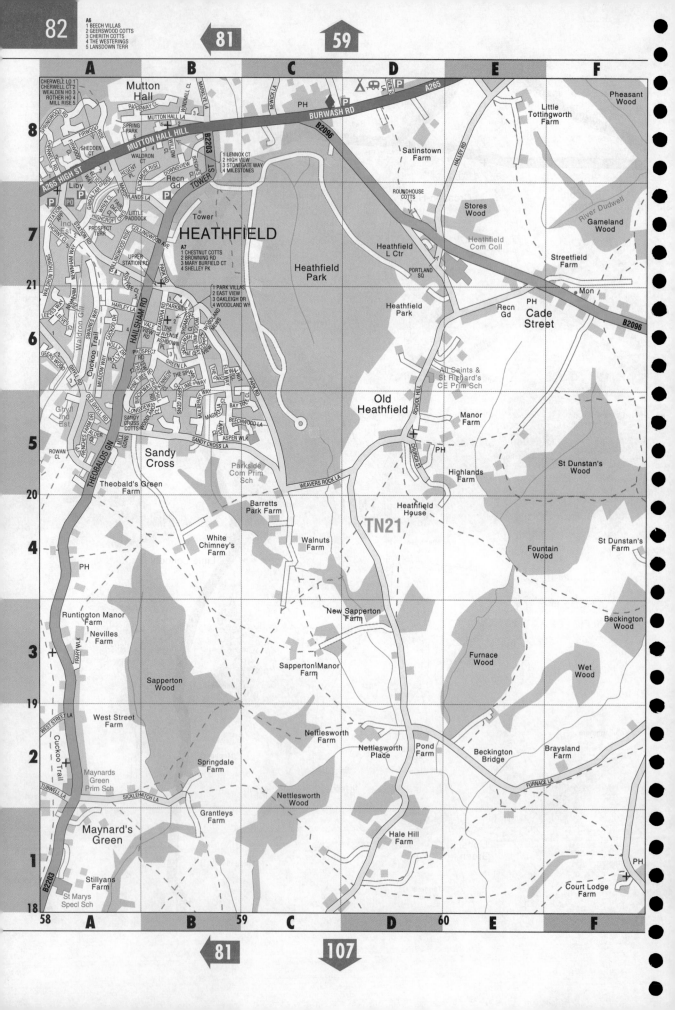

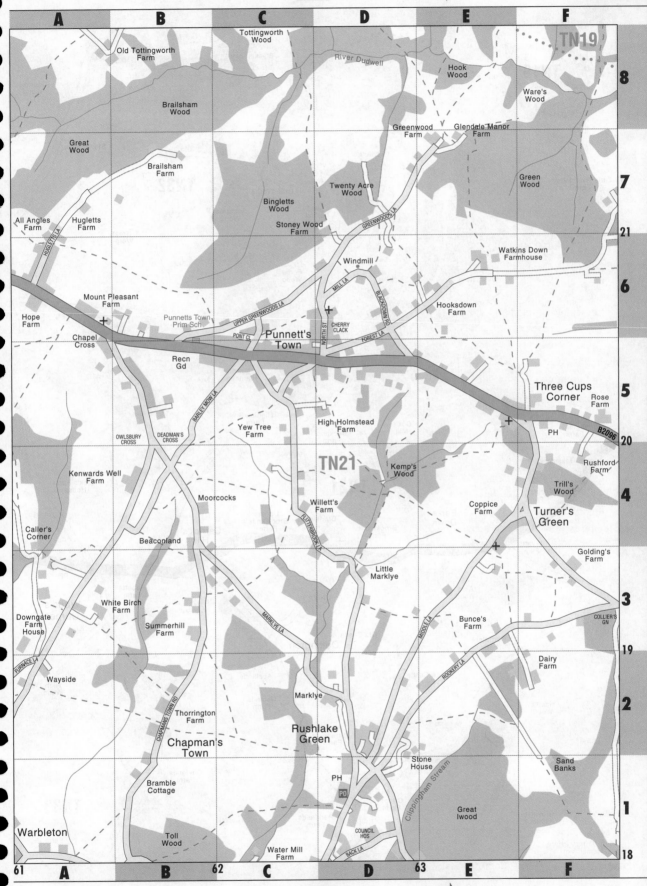

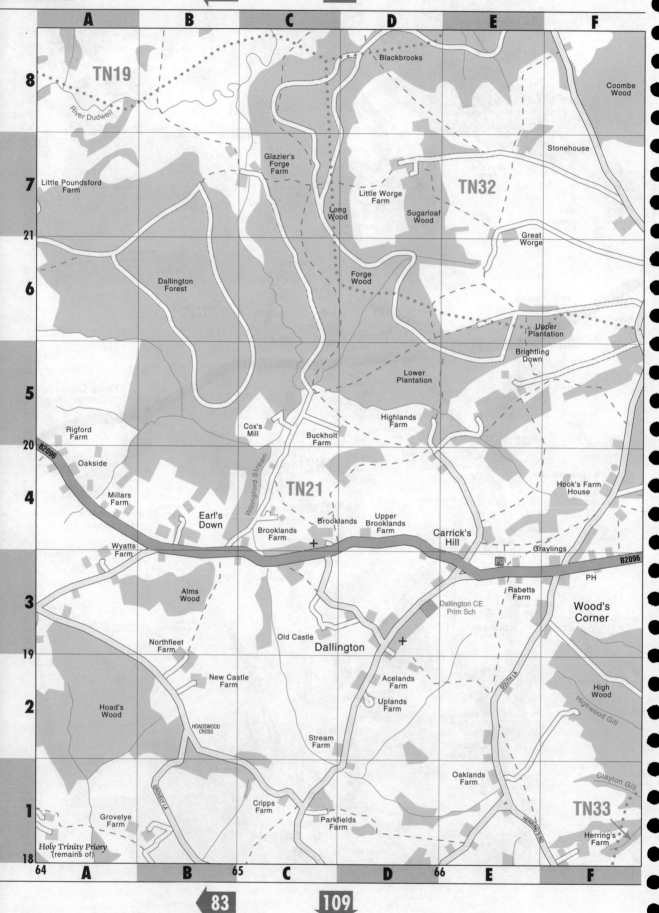

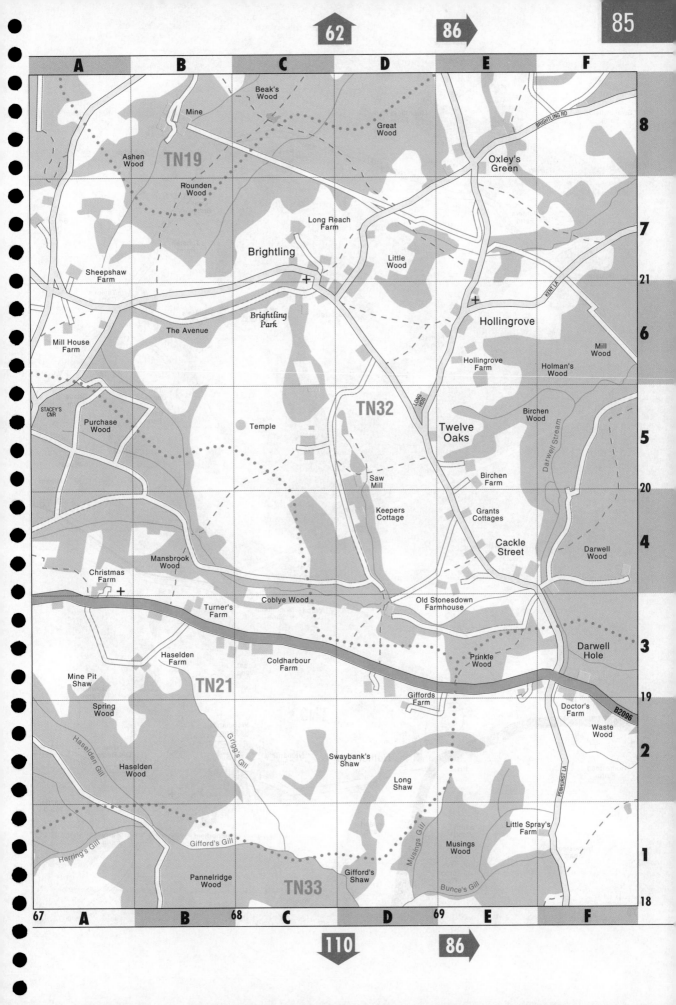

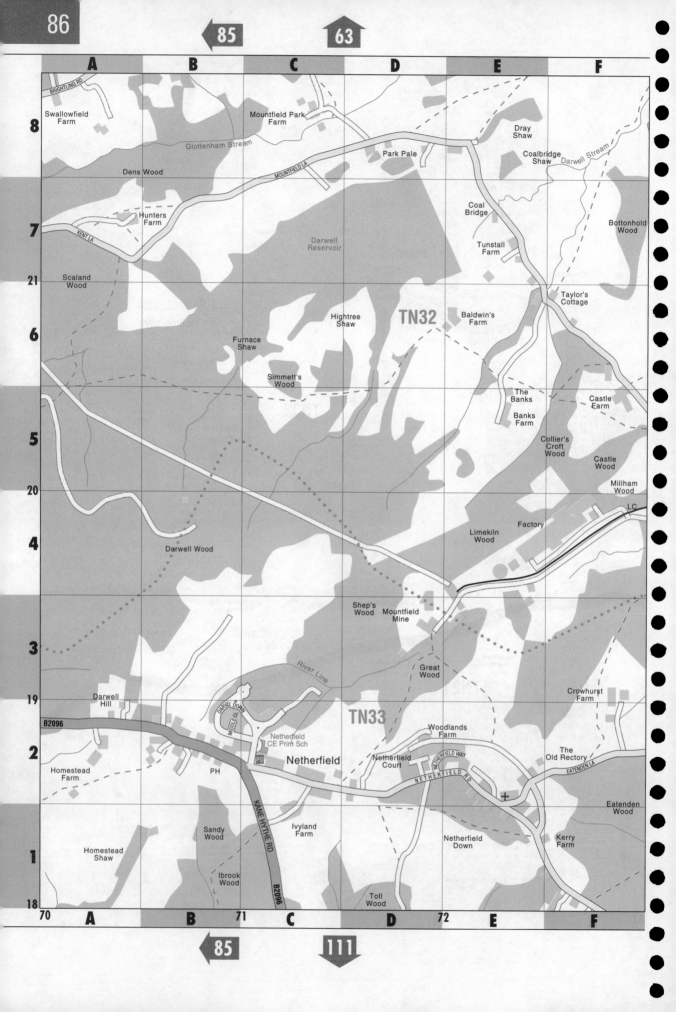

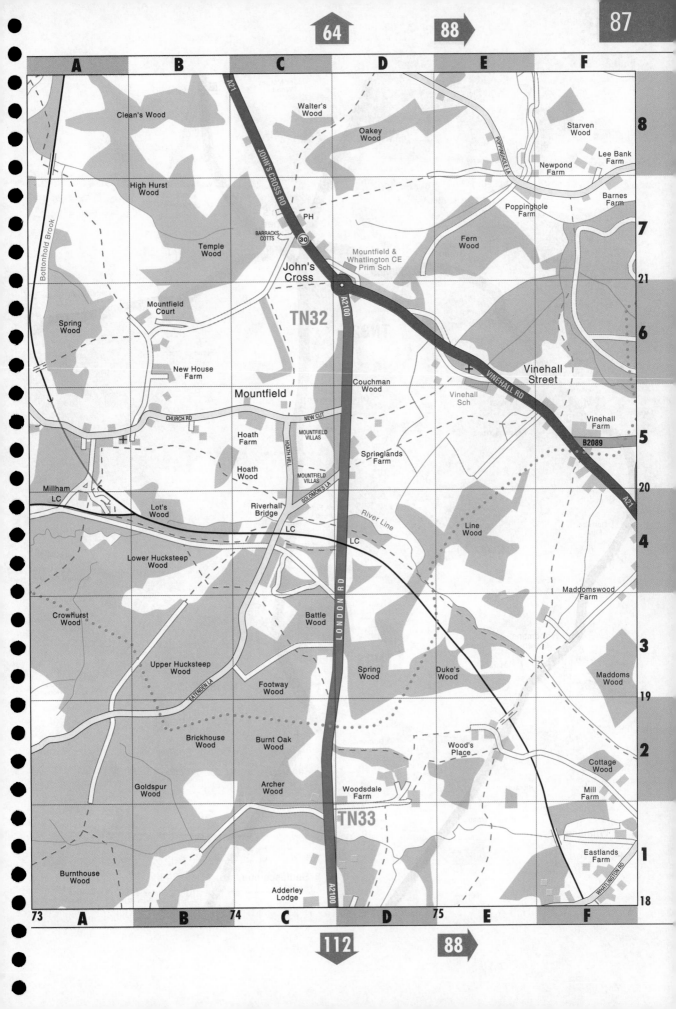

87 65

A B C D E F

8

Andrew's Gill

B2244

Upper Morgay Wood

Wattlehill

PO

B2165

Badland Wood

Strawberry Hill Farm

Badland Shaw

Wr Twr

The Beacon

BEACON LA

Miles Farm

POPPINGHOLE LA

7

Cripp's Corner
PH

B2165

Swaile's Green

B2089

21

Wimbletott's Wood

Orchard Farm

COMPASS LA

TN32

Catts Green Farm

B2089

ELLENWHORNE LA

6

Barne's Wood

Hooks Beech

Greenden Wood

Streetfield Wood

Vinehall Forest

Sedlescombe Organic Vineyard

Thorp's Wood

5

B2089

Forest Wlk

Footland Wood

Footland Farm

Mill

JUNCTION RD

B2090 PARK LA

20

Dorrells Farm

Beech Farm House

A21

4

Austford Wood

Coombe Wood

GREAT SANDERS HO

BEECH FARM RD

Hurst Wood

3

Woodmans Green

Hancox Farm

TN33

Killingan Wood

HURST LA

Hurst House

WOODMANS OAK

PH

CHURCHLAND LA

19

RICCARDS LA

WHATLINGTON RD

STREAM LA

2

Riccards Farm

Spilsted Farm

Durhamford Manor

Highfield

BALCOMBE GN

CONQUEROR TERR

Leeford Cotts

Plovers Mead

ORCHARD WAY

GORSELANDS

BREDE LA

BLACKLANDS

EAST VIEW

TERR

1

Whatlington

THE STREET

EAYOT WLK

MEADOW LA

LUKINS LA

PARK SHAW

GAMMONS WAY

STREETLANDS

Leeford Farm

River Line

A21

Sedlescombe

MEADOWSIDE 1
MANOR COTTS 2

ROSELANDS

B2244

P

Sedlescombe CE Prim Sch

Sewage Works

18

76 A 77 B C 78 D E F

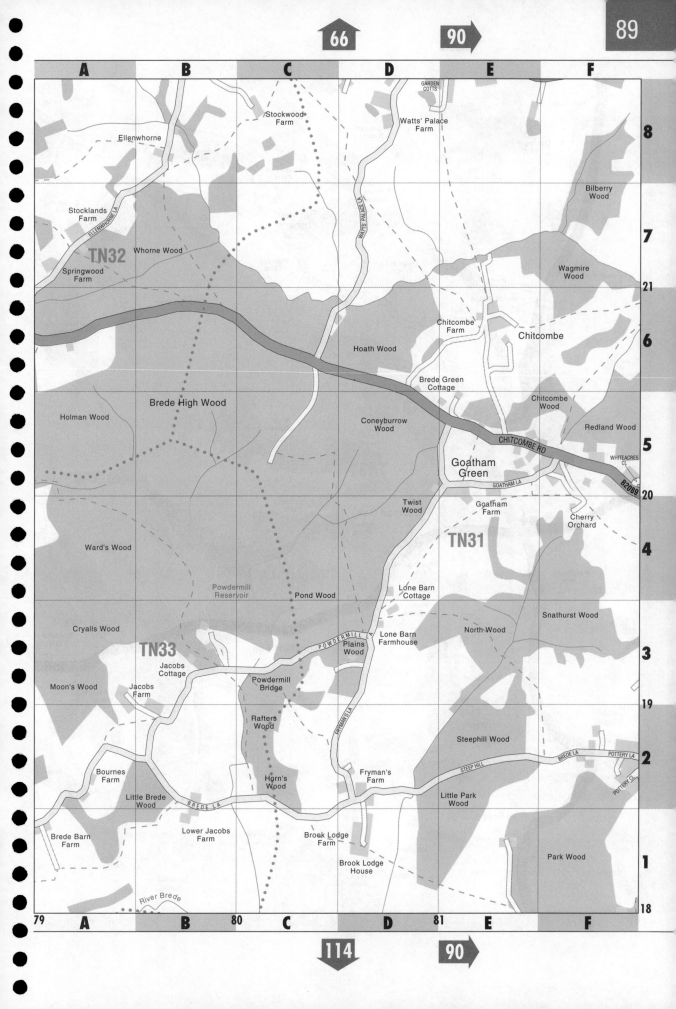

← 89
67

A B C D E F

8

Tanhouse Farm

Wharnham Wood

Garland Wood

+ Doucegrove Farm

Moore's Wood

Little Doucegrove

Glass Eye Farm

Furnace Wood

Beckley Furnace

Osier Gill

Greentiles Farm

Sheepwash Wood

7

River Tillingham

Furnace Farm

FURNACE LA

Maplestone Farm

21

Wagmary Wood

Great Conster Farm

Arnold Bridge

NORTHAM RD

Conster Manor

Burnthouse Wood

6

Austen's Wood

West Wood

Kicker Wood

Birch Wood

HOW'S CL

5

Twist Wood

TN31

Hundredhouse Bridge

WHITEACRES CL

Granary Farm

CHESTNUT CL

THE MARTLETS

FIELDWAY

THE ORCHARD

Pattendens Farm

20

B2089

CHITCOMBE RD

THE TILLINGHAM VIEW

OAKHILL DR

THE HAWTHORNES

NORTHAM RD

MOORSIDE

POND CL

REEDSWOOD RD

Broad Oak

Maidlands Farm

PO

Spring Wood

PH

THE CROSSWAYS

+ Brede Prim Sch

Reysons Farm

Gilly Wood

4

KING WOOD HILL

Moorsholm Farm

HUNDREDHOUSE LA

Reysons Oasts

UDIMORE RD

Sowdens Farm

3

Well Wood

Broadland Row

Broadlands Wood

B2089

19

Cackle Street

South Sowdens Wood

Mill Wood

2

ST MARY'S

POTTERY LA

CACKLE ST

SPRINGFIELD COTTS

STUBB LA

Groaning Bridge

Alder Wood

POTTERY CL

Brede

1

Brede Place

Pickdick Farm

+ PH

BREDE HILL

Hillyfield

B2089

Hare Cottages

Hare Farm

Stonelink Farm

18

82 A B 83 C D 84 E F

A28

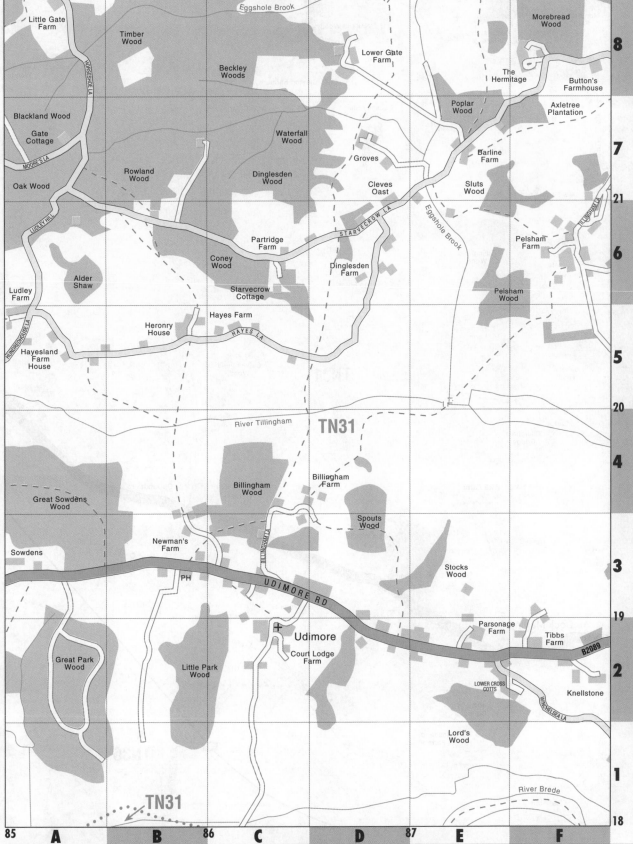

A B C D E F

Little Gate Farm

Timber Wood

Beckley Woods

Eggshole Brook

Lower Gate Farm

Morebread Wood

The Hermitage

Button's Farmhouse

HORSESHOE LA

Blackland Wood

Gate Cottage

Waterfall Wood

Groves

Poplar Wood

Axletree Plantation

MOORE'S LA

Rowland Wood

Dinglesden Wood

Cleves Oast

Barline Farm

Sluts Wood

Oak Wood

LUDLEY HILL

Partridge Farm

STARVECROW LA

Dinglesden Farm

Eggshole Brook

Pelsham Farm

TILLINGHAM LA

Coney Wood

Ludley Farm

Alder Shaw

Starvecrow Cottage

Pelsham Wood

HUNDREDHOUSE LA

Heronry House

Hayes Farm

HAYES LA

Hayesland Farm House

River Tillingham

TN31

Great Sowdens Wood

Billingham Wood

Billingham Farm

Spouts Wood

Sowdens

Newman's Farm

PH

BILLINGHAM LA

UDIMORE RD

Stocks Wood

Parsonage Farm

Tibbs Farm

B2089

Great Park Wood

Little Park Wood

Udimore

Court Lodge Farm

Lower Cross Cotts

Knellstone

WINCHELSEA LA

Lord's Wood

TN31

River Brede

A **B** **C** **D** **E** **F**

8

Morebread Farm

Peasmarsh Place
CHURCH LA

Norland Wood

STARVECROW LA
DEW LA

Wr Twr

Clayton Farm

TILLINGHAM LA
DEW LANE

Cockney Hill Wood

7

21

Dew Farm

6

Ennets Wood

Tillingham Wood

River Tillingham

High Weald Landscape Trail

Cottage Shaw

TILLINGHAM LA

Tillingham Farm

Leasam Wood

Leasam House

Secret Wood

5

Hooker's Wood

TN31

Calves Field Wood

B2089
CADBOROUGH CLIFT
OAST HOUSE DR

20

Tillingham Bridge

Gillshaw Farm

Oaklands

Cadborough Farm

4

Wick Farm

Turnpike Wood

Watlands

Cadborough Cliff

3

Hotel

Wick Wood

UDIMORE RD

Knellstone Wood

Farthing Wood

DUMB WOMAN'S LA

19

Cock Marling

B2089

1066 Country Wlk

2

Nicholls Cottages

Roadend Farm

WINCHELSEA LA

Newhouse Sewer

Winchelsea

LC

Padiam Sewer

TN36

STATION RD

1

Float Farm

STATION COTTS

18

A **B** **C** **D** **E** **F**
88   89   90

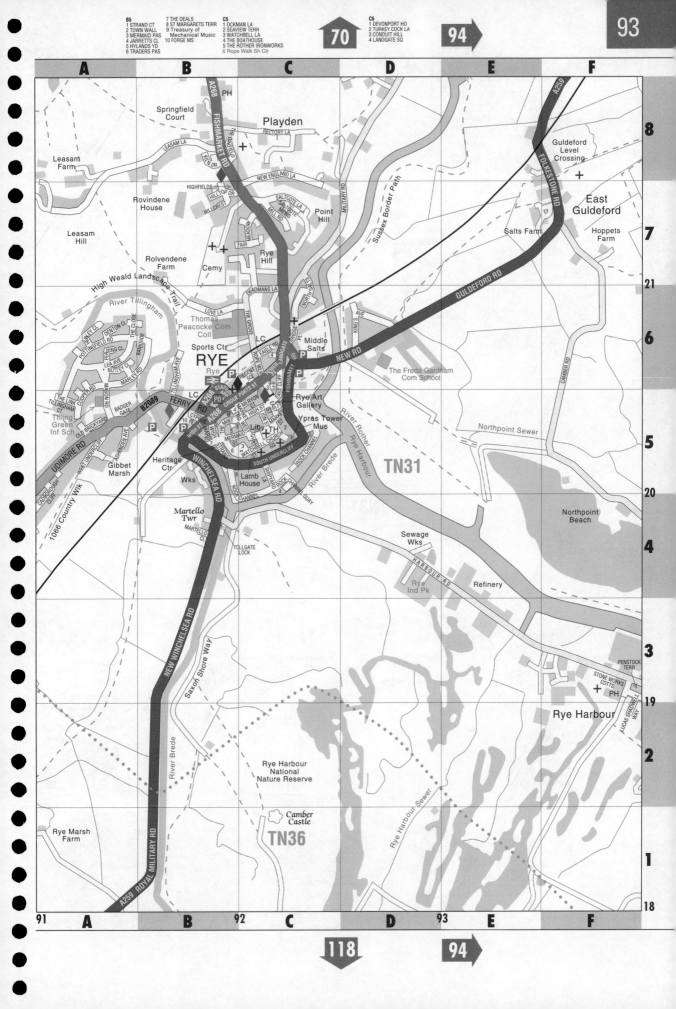

A B C D E F

8

7

East Guldeford
Level

Moneypenny

21

Black House
Farm

Guldeford Sewer

6

Tressland

Barn
Farm

Kent Ditch

5

Wainway Wall

20

TN31

Northpoint
Beach

4

Guldeford Sewer

Point
Farm

3

1 INKERMAN TERR
2 PAINES COTTS
3 MARY STANFORD GN

CH

Pound Field
Farm

FARM LA

LAPWING
CL

LIMNET
LA

WHITESAND DR

BAKER
WY

Holiday
Centre

COASTGUARD
SSJ
PH
3

HARBOUR RD

IRB
Sta

DRAFFIN LA

Motel

NEW LYDD RD

DENHAM WAY

Camber

19

1 OYSTER
CREEK
TRAM RD

P

COASTGUARD
COTTS

OLD WORLD
COTTS

P

LINKS WAY

LYDD RD

1 COACH HOUSE COTTS
2 FLEETWAY CT

Cvn
Pk

Martello
Twr

River Rother

OLD LYDD RD

PH

PETER JAMES
CL

MARCHANTS
DR

DUNE CL

DR

FIRST AVE

LYDD RD

PO

THE
SUTTONS

2

Lime Kiln
Cottage

MARINE
COTTS

P

SECOND AVE

Camber Sands

1

Rye Harbour
National Nature
Reserve

East
Pier

Rye Bay

18

A   B C D   E F

96

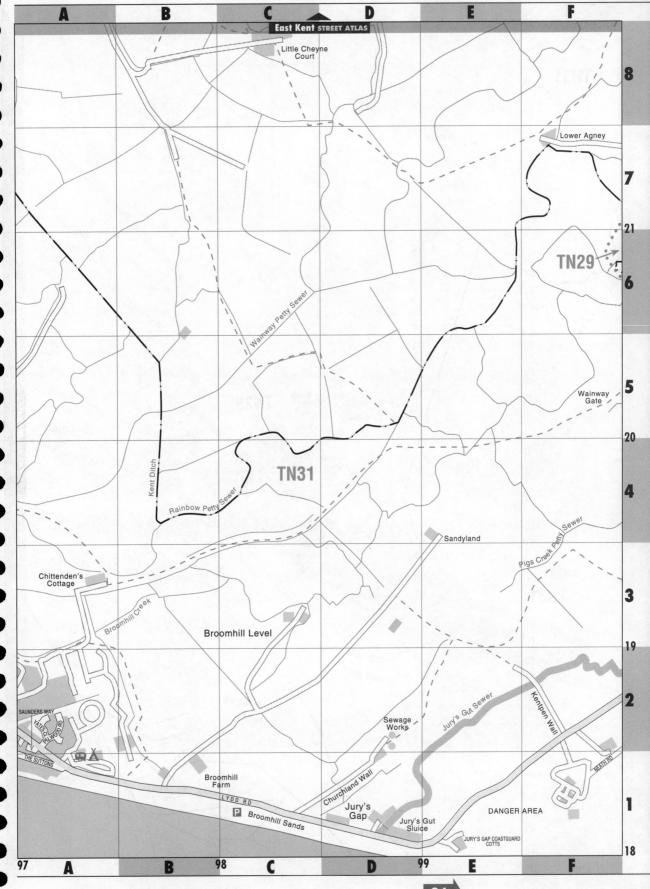

East Kent STREET ATLAS

Little Cheyne
Court

Lower Agney

21

TN29

Wainway
Gate

5

20

Wainway Petty Sewer

TN31

Kent Ditch

Rainbow Petty Sewer

Sandyland

Pigs Creek Petty Sewer

Chittenden's
Cottage

Broomhill Creek

Broomhill Level

19

Jury's Gut Sewer

Kempen Wall

Sewage
Works

SAUNDERS WAY

YATES CL

PILWOD RD

THE SUTTONS

Broomhill
Farm

DANGER AREA

HEATH RD

LYDD RD

P Broomhill Sands

Churchland Wall

Jury's
Gap

Jury's Gut
Sluice

Jury's Gap Coastguard
Cotts

A 97 B 98 C D 99 E F

95

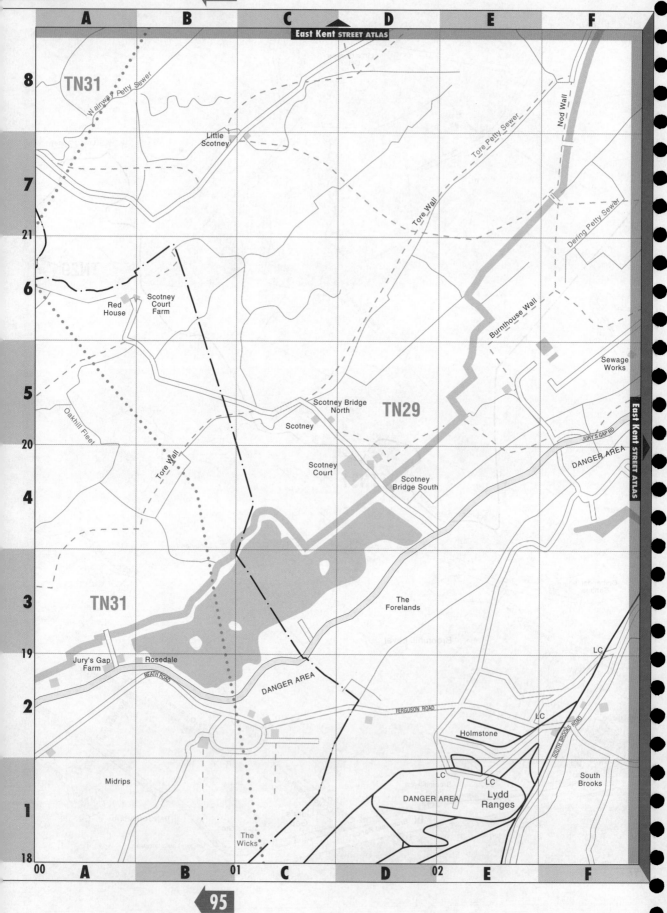

East Kent STREET ATLAS

TN31

Wainway Petty Sewer

Little
Scotney

Tore Petty Sewer

Nod Wall

Tore Wall

Dering Petty Sewer

Red
House

Scotney Court
Farm

Burnthouse Wall

Oakhill Fleet

Sewage
Works

Scotney Bridge
North

TN29

Scotney

JURY'S GAP RD

Tore Wall

DANGER AREA

Scotney
Court

Scotney
Bridge South

The
Forelands

LC

TN31

Jury's Gap
Farm

Rosedale

NEATH ROAD

DANGER AREA

FERGUSON ROAD

LC

SOUTH BROOKS ROAD

Holmstone

LC

Midrips

LC

LC

South
Brooks

DANGER AREA

Lydd
Ranges

The Wicks

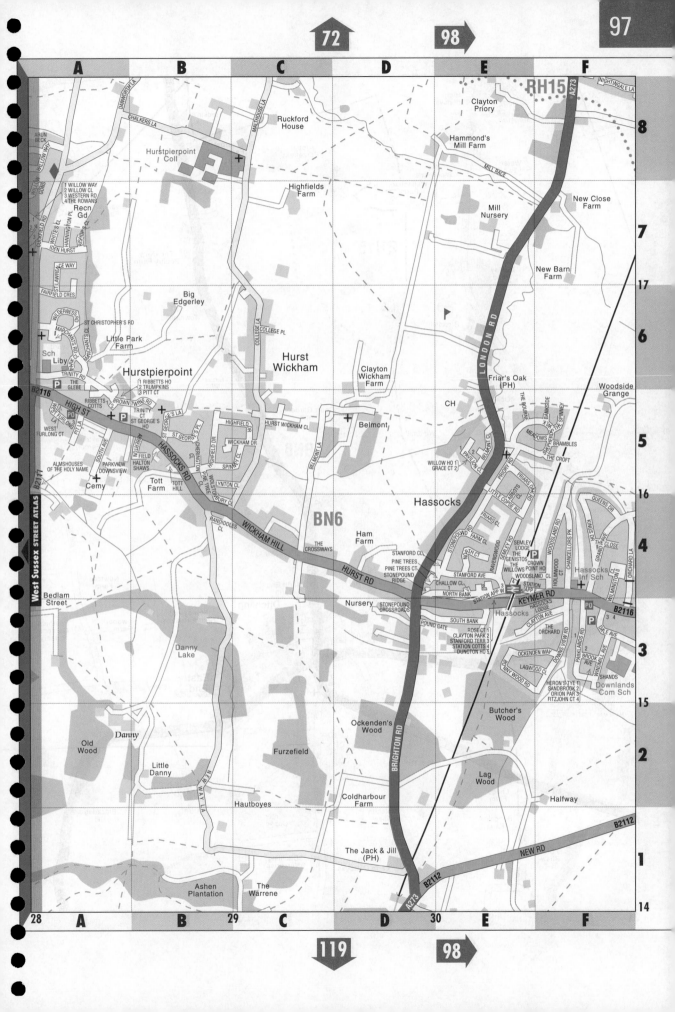

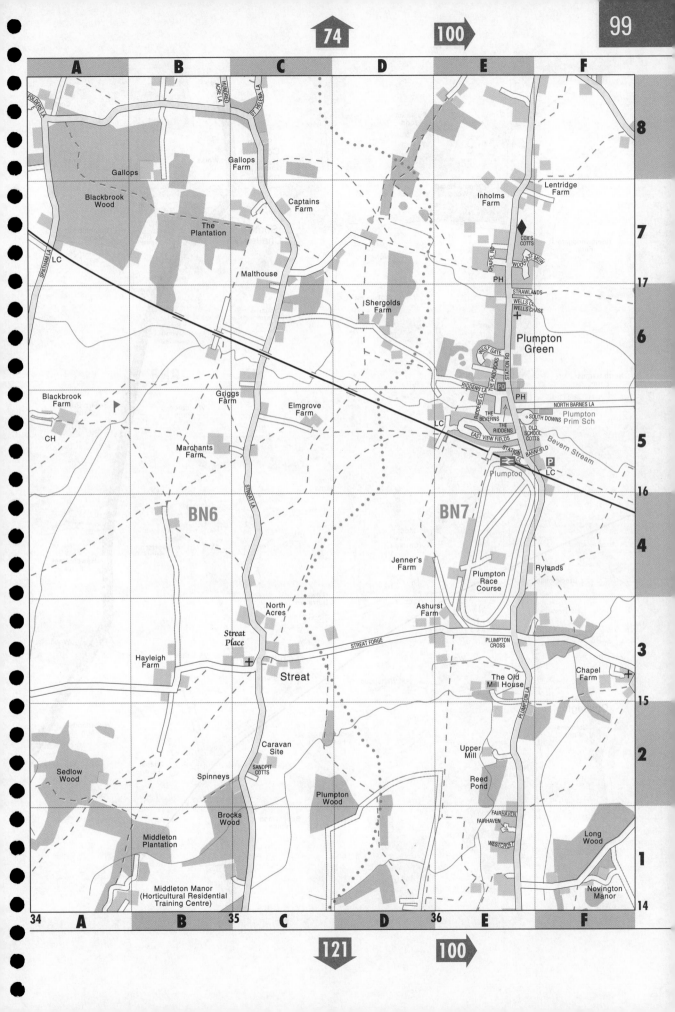

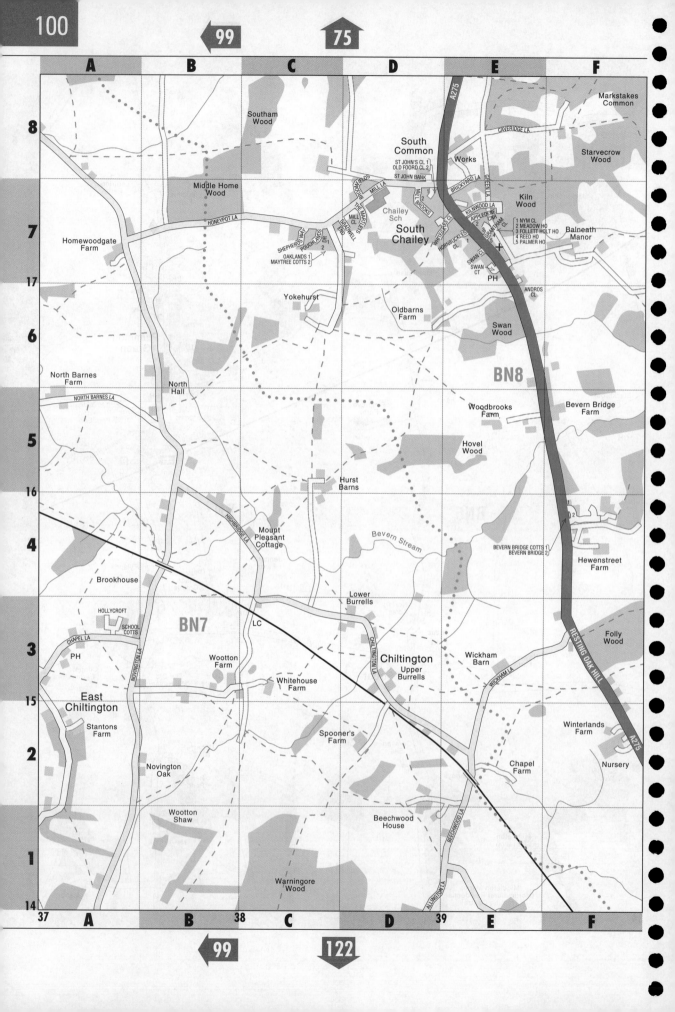

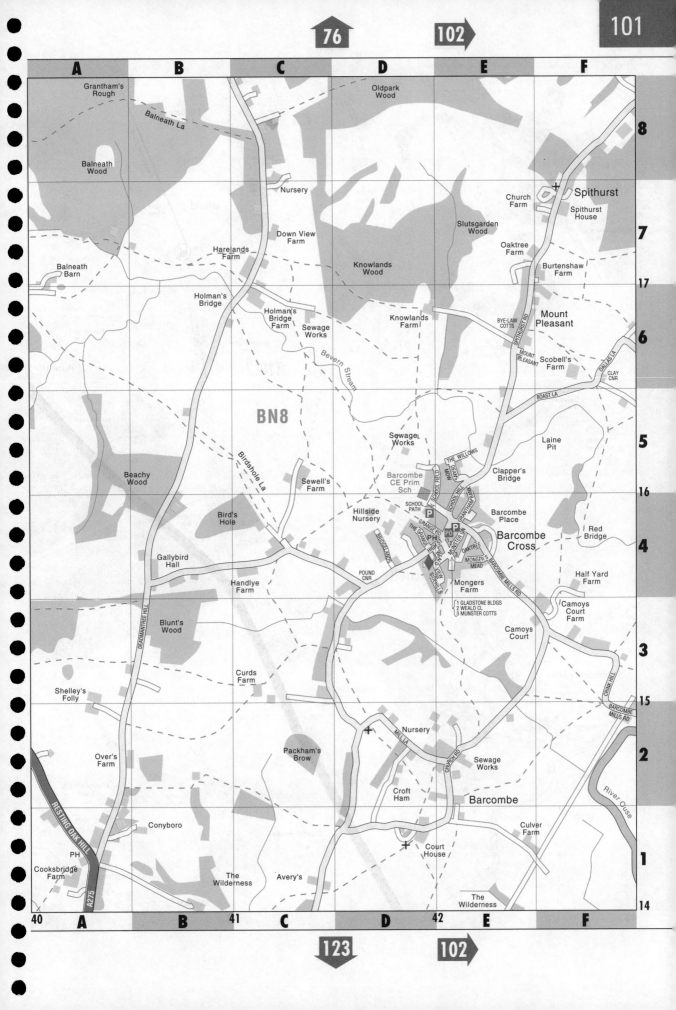

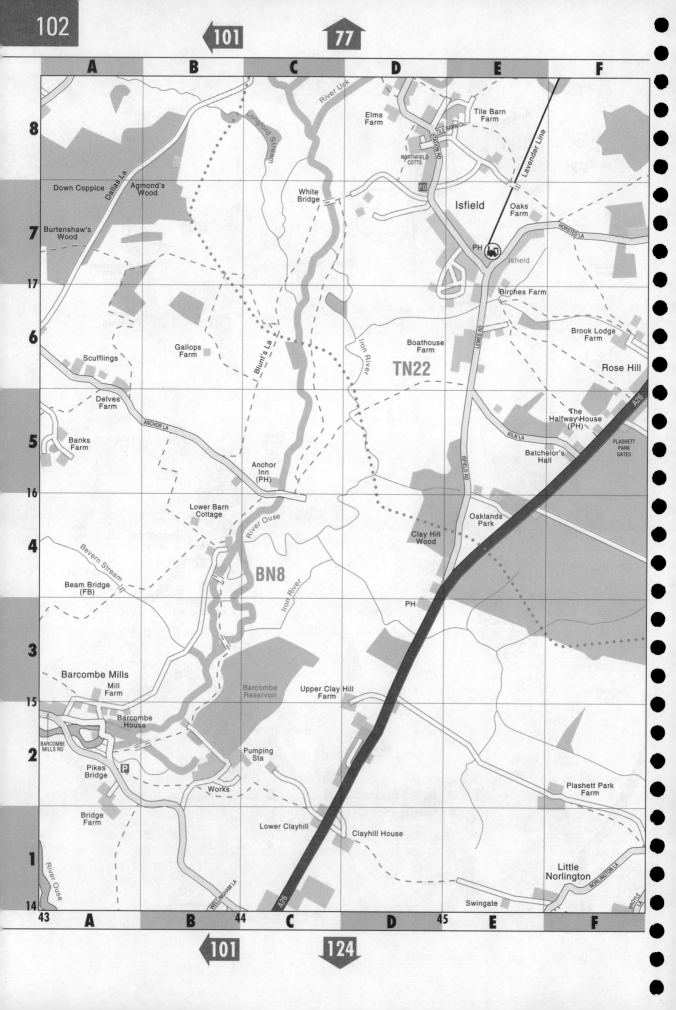

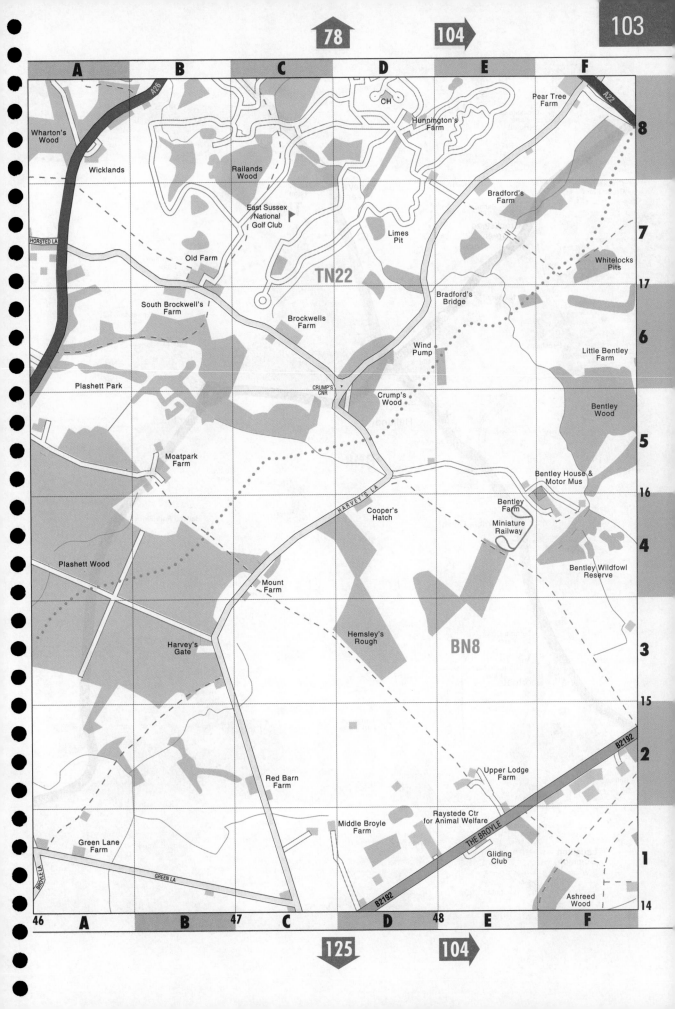

A **B** **C** **D** **E** **F**

Crockstead
Farm
(Hotel)

Slay's Wood

8

A22

SANDHILLS LA

Lower Sandhill
House

B2192

Annan
Court

Pilgrim
Hall

Crockstead
Green Farm

Sandhill

Honey's
Green

Branden
Farm

TN22

Sweetwillow
Shaw

Wealdway

7

Crockstead
Green

17

Nursery

Annandale
Farm

40 EASTBOURNE RD

Old Whyly

6

KNOWLE LA

Peckhams

IVY COTTS

OLD HEATH CL

Black
Lion Inn
(PH)

Bentley Wood

WENHAM
GDNS

5

VINE FARM
COTTS

Halland

East Hoathly
CE Prim
Sch

Hartfield
Farm

BN8

Godfrey
Cottage

Moat Wood

P

THORNS
MARKS LA

16

Vine Farm

Halland Park Farm

SOUTH ST

Terrible Down

4

White Lion
Farm

Bog Shaw

SOUTH ST

Paine's
Farm

Terrible Down
Farm

Rowland Wood

3

Shortgate Manor
Farm

PH

Shortgate

15

B2192 THE BROYLE

SHORTGATE LA

Laughton
Park Farm

PARK LA

PARK CNR

2

Bell
Farm

Walls Farm

A22

Mast

Ty
Lion

Little Common
Wood

Walls's
Hawth

Sandpit Wood

1

Laughton
Common

Upper Vert
Wood

COMMON LA

Laughton
House

14

49 **A** **B** 50 **C** **D** 51 **E** **F**

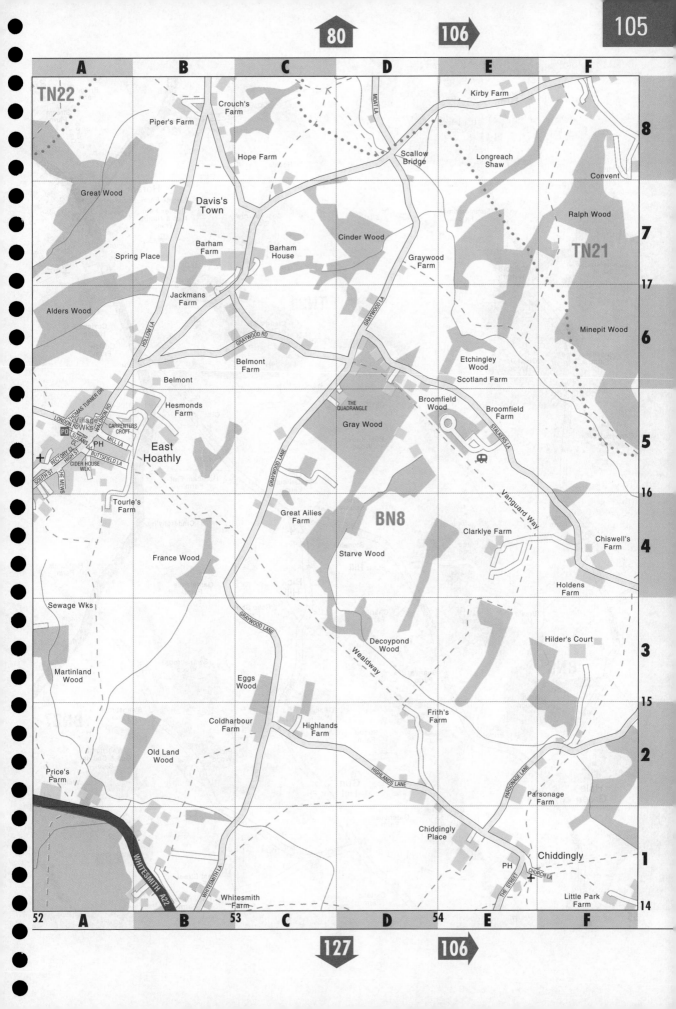

105
81

A　B　C　D　E　F

8

Dernlea Farm

Roughland Wood

FURNACE LA

SHARP'S CNR

LITTLE LONDON RD

A267

B2203

Bridge Farm

Stream Farm

Cuckoo Trail

HIGH ST

Visitation Convent

Hook's Farm

Horam

Home Farm
Sussex Farm Mus & Nature Trails

MEADOW RISE 1
HIGHFIELD RD 2
THE RISE 3

MANOR RD
THE AVENUE
MANOR CL
CHERRY CROFT
BEACON CL
DOWNLAND CL

B2203

P

PO

7

Summersbrook Farm

Coneyburrow Wood

Factory
OLD VICARAGE
CL

BEAUFORD RD
OLD LONDON RD

HOREBECH LA

HORAM PARK CL

17

Summersbrook Wood

Copford Farm

DERN LA

TN21

Clearhedge Wood

GRANGE CL

Coxlow House

Coxlow Farm

PH

6

Longshaw Farm

Great Dern Wood

JOYCE VILLAS

Oakhurst Farm

5

Coneyburrow Wood

East Knowle Wood

CH

KINGSTON VILLAS

Little Easterfields Farm

Horeham Flat Farm

Burlow

16

Stream Farm

East Knowle

Cinderghyll

4

Forge Wood

Stonehill Farm

Stone Hill

Gamelands Farm

Highlands Farm

STONEHILL

Pick Hill

Rose Bank Farm

COGGER'S LA

COGGER'S CROSS

3

BN8

Stream Mill

Mill Wood

Charity Farm

Swansbrook Wood

NORTH ST

A267

SMITHLANES LA

Beard's Farm

GUN HILL

15

Smithlands Wood

Bull Bridge

Gunhill Wood

Swansbrook Farm

BN27

2

HALE GRN

Strood Farm

D

Pickly Wood

Wellshurst Golf & Country Club

Wellshurst

CH

Hale Green

Hale Farm

Gun Hill

PH

North Street Wood

1

SCRAPER'S HILL

Gatehouse Wood

Gatehouse Farm

West Street Farm

Wealdway

Rock Harbour Farm

14

Carter's Farm

105
128

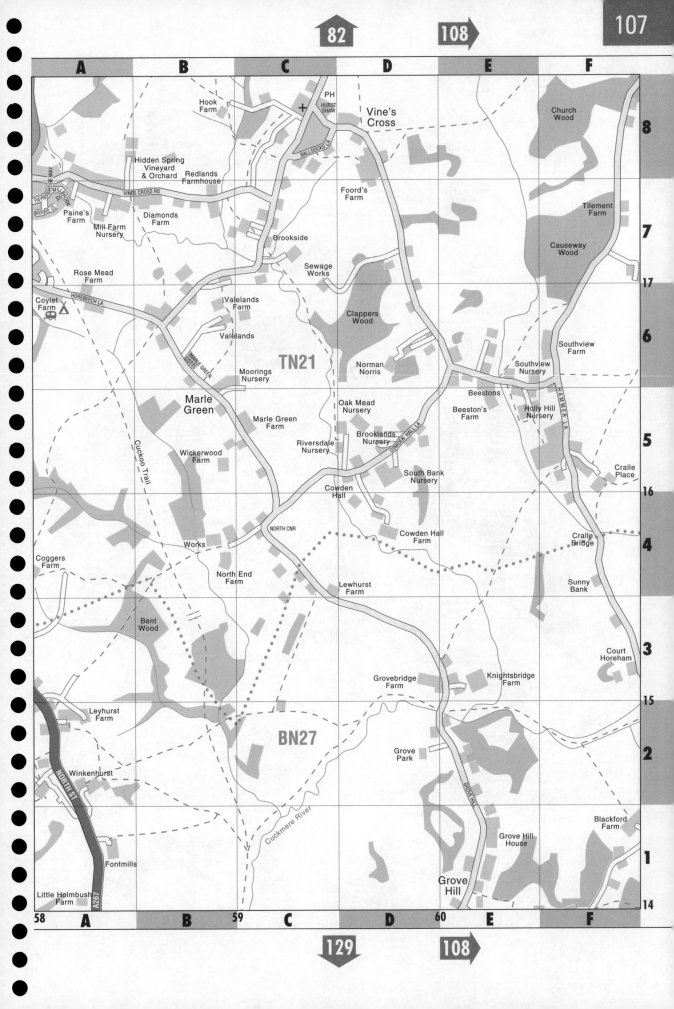

8

Hook
Farm

PH
HURST
SHAW

Vine's
Cross

Church
Wood

Hidden Spring
Vineyard
& Orchard

Redlands
Farmhouse

BALLSOCKS LA

Foord's
Farm

Tilement
Farm

7

PAYNSBRIDGE WAY
MILL BROOK
BRIDGE CL
VINES CROSS RD

Paine's
Farm

Diamonds
Farm

Brookside

Causeway
Wood

Mill Farm
Nursery

Sewage
Works

17

Rose Mead
Farm

HOREBEECH LA

Valelands
Farm

Clappers
Wood

Southview
Farm

6

Coylet
Farm

Valelands

TN21

Norman
Norris

Southview
Nursery

MARLE GREEN COTTS

Moorings
Nursery

Beestons

Marle
Green

Oak Mead
Nursery

Beeston's
Farm

Holly Hill
Nursery

HAMMER LA

5

Marle Green
Farm

Riversdale
Nursery

Brooklands
Nursery

COWDEN HALL LA

Wickerwood
Farm

Cuckoo Trail

South Bank
Nursery

Cralle
Place

Cowden
Hall

16

NORTH CNR

Cowden Hall
Farm

Cralle
Bridge

4

Works

Coggers
Farm

North End
Farm

Lewhurst
Farm

Sunny
Bank

Bent
Wood

Court
Horeham

3

Grovebridge
Farm

Knightsbridge
Farm

15

Leyhurst
Farm

BN27

Grove
Park

2

NORTH ST

Winkenhurst

GROVE HILL

Grove Hill
House

Blackford
Farm

Cuckmere River

1

A267

Fontmills

Little Holmbush
Farm

Grove
Hill

14

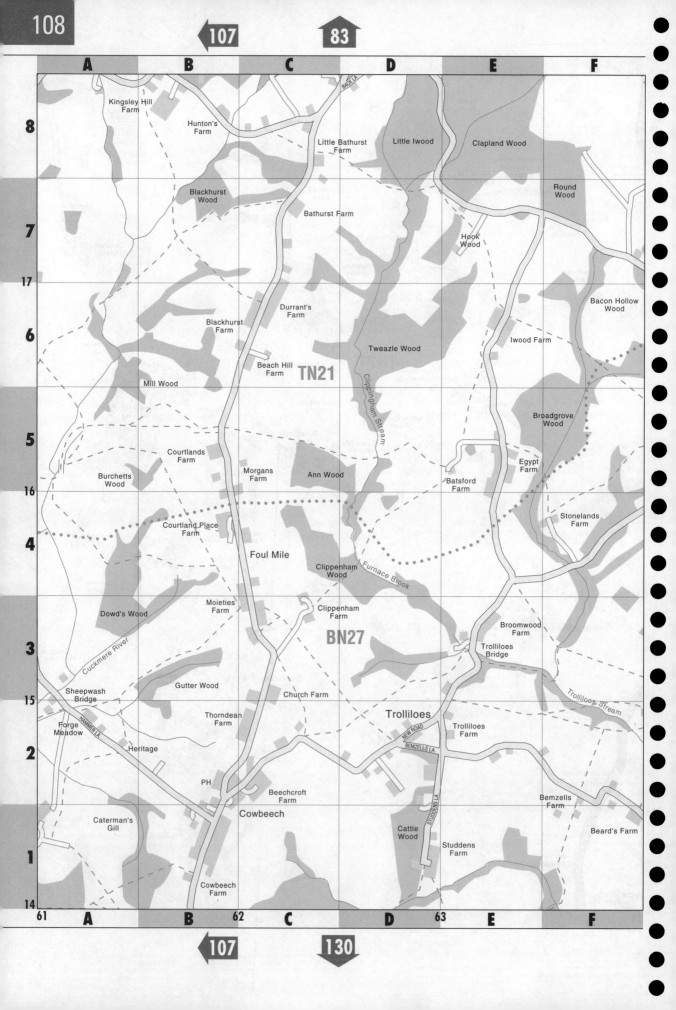

A   B   C   D   E   F

8

Kingsley Hill Farm

Hunton's Farm

Little Bathurst Farm

Little Iwood

Clapland Wood

Round Wood

Blackhurst Wood

Bathurst Farm

7

Hook Wood

17

Durrant's Farm

Bacon Hollow Wood

6

Blackhurst Farm

Tweazle Wood

Iwood Farm

Beach Hill Farm

TN21

Clippingham Stream

Broadgrove Wood

Mill Wood

Egypt Farm

5

Courtlands Farm

Batsford Farm

Burchetts Wood

Morgans Farm

Ann Wood

16

Stonelands Farm

Courtland Place Farm

4

Foul Mile

Clippenham Wood

Furnace Brook

Dowd's Wood

Moieties Farm

Clippenham Farm

Broomwood Farm

BN27

Trolliloes Bridge

3

Cuckmere River

Trolliloes Stream

Sheepwash Bridge

Gutter Wood

Church Farm

15

Trolliloes

Forge Meadow

HAMMER LA

Thorndean Farm

Trolliloes Farm

NEW ROAD

2

Heritage

BEMZELLS LA

Bemzells Farm

PH

Beechcroft Farm

Cowbeech

STUDDENS LA

Beard's Farm

Caterman's Gill

Cattle Wood

Studdens Farm

1

Cowbeech Farm

14

61   A   B   62   C   D   63   E   F

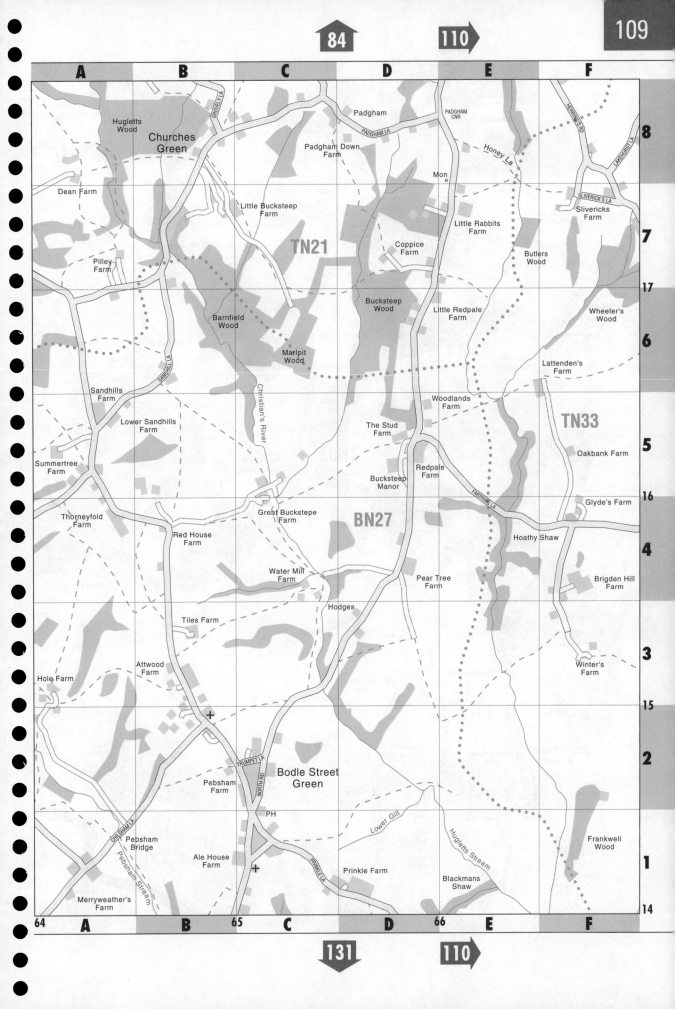

A B C D E F

8

Pleasure House
Lakehurst
LAKEHURST LA
Buckwell Wood
Buckwell Gill
Pannelridge Wood
Bunce's Farm
Link Wood
Great Spray's Farm

7

Buckwell Farm
Spring Gill
Anderson's Wood
Rocks Farm
Foxearth Wood

17

Thorndale Farm
Furnace Cottage

6

Thornden Farm
Hogstye Wood
Allfrees Wood
Penhurst
Pollyspark Wood
Church Farm
Manor House

Thornden Cottages

5

Court Lodge
Malthouse Wood
TN33
1066 Country Walk
Izlebridge Wood

16

Pontsgreen Wood
Forge Cottages

4

Ponts Green
Peens Wood
Reedlands Farm

AKEHURST FIELD
Reed Wood

3

Mon
Ash Bourne
The Bungalow
New Buildings Farm
Tent Hill

15

PH
Pigknoll Farm
Reservoir Pond
The Grove

2

Brownbread Street
Brownbread Stud
Ashburnham Place
Front Water
THE STABLES

The Pound
Linghams
Walk Wood
A271

1

1066 Country Walk
Lingham's Farm
Burrage Wood
Broad Water
Baker's Wood
Forty Acre Gill
Bray's Hill
A271

14

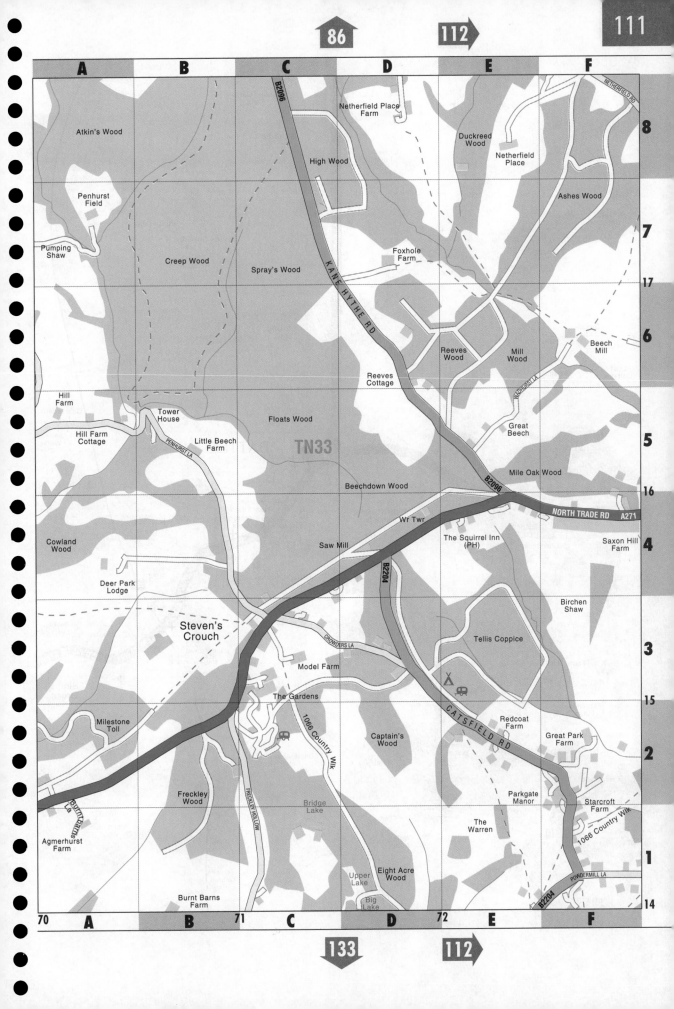

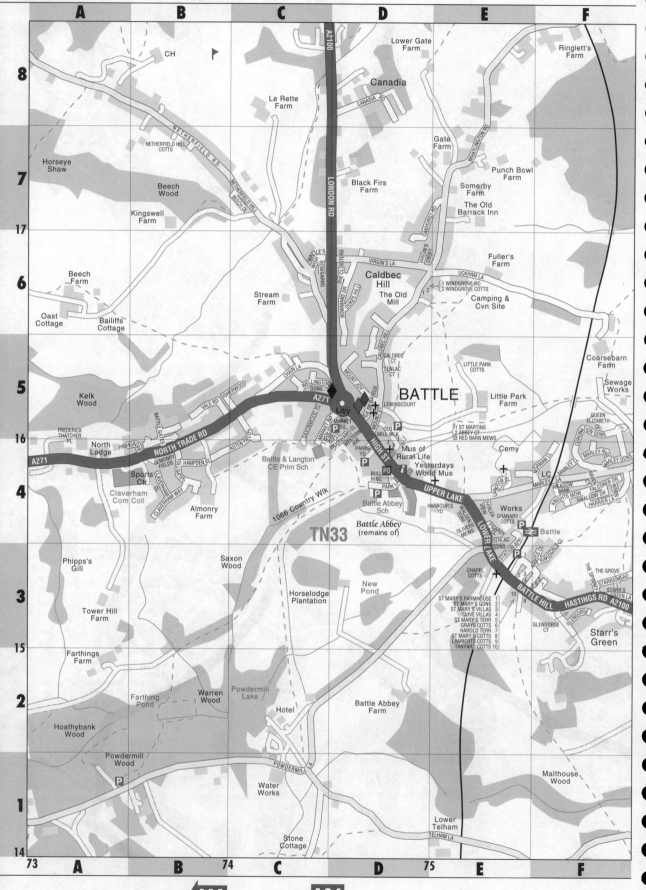

BATTLE

TN33

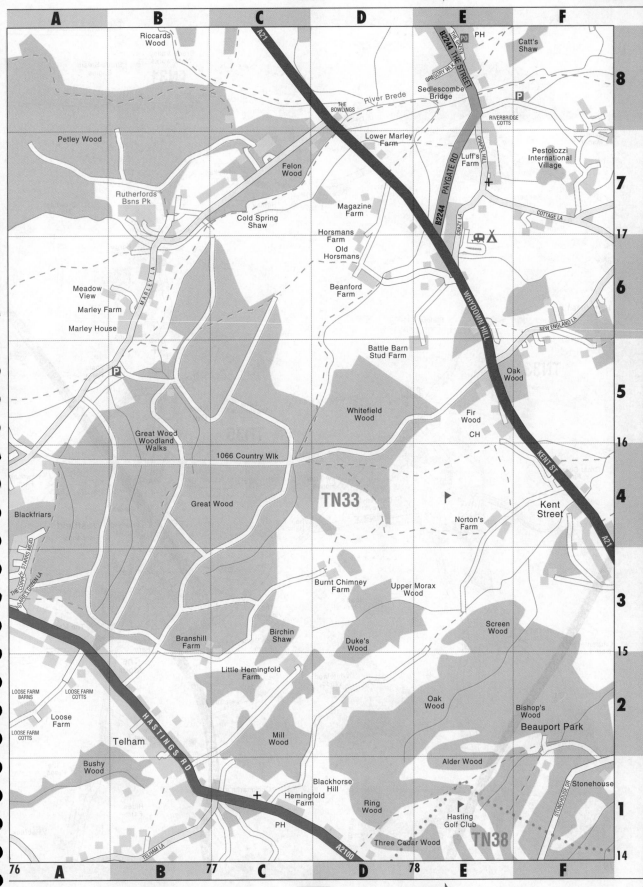

113
89

A B C D E F

8

Brassets Wood

Dean's Wood

River Brede

Brede Valley Waterworks

Brede Steam Engine

TN31

7

Oaklands Manor

Nutkin's Wood

Westfield Place

Cottage La

Rocks Farm

Redlay Farm

Keepers Cottage

Crowham Manor

17

Randall's Farm

New England La

Forge Stream

Rock's Hill

Miller's Hill

Forge Wood

6

Harts Green Farm

Platnix Farm

Benskins

A28

Dolehim La

TN33

Spray's Wood

Spray's Bridge

1066 Country Walk

Little Westbrook Farm

Westbrook La

New Cut

Cottage La

Mill La

Thala Farm

5

Great Buckhurst Farm

Spray's La

Wheel Park Farm

Yew Tree House

Nightingale Cotts

Mill Cl

Park View Rd

Fern Cl

Meadow View

Stablefield

Downoak Farm

16

Bluemans La

Bluemans

Carr Taylor Vineyard

Parsonage La

Wheel Farm Bsns Pk

Chapel La

Main Rd

Moor Rd

Westfield Prim Sch

Westfield

Fishponds Farm

4

Moat La

Wheel La

Church Field

Church La

Heathlands

Geary Pl

Moor La

Workhouse La

South Terr

Fishponds La

New Moorside

The Moor

PH

3

Hoad's Farm

Vicarage La

The Vicarage

Greenacres

Moor Farm

PH

Ireland's Farm

Church Place Farm

The Moor

15

Carpenter's Barn Farm

Kent St

Stonehouse Drive

Whiteland Wood

Whitegates Pk

Westfield La

Little Buckhurst Farm

Stonestile La

Lankhurst Farm

2

Babylon Wood

Cockmartin's Farm

A28

Little Hides

Red River

Dine's Wood

Baldslow Down

Hides Farm

Valebrook

1

TN38

Ebden's Hill

A21

Claremont Sch

TN37

79 A 80 B C 81 D E F

14

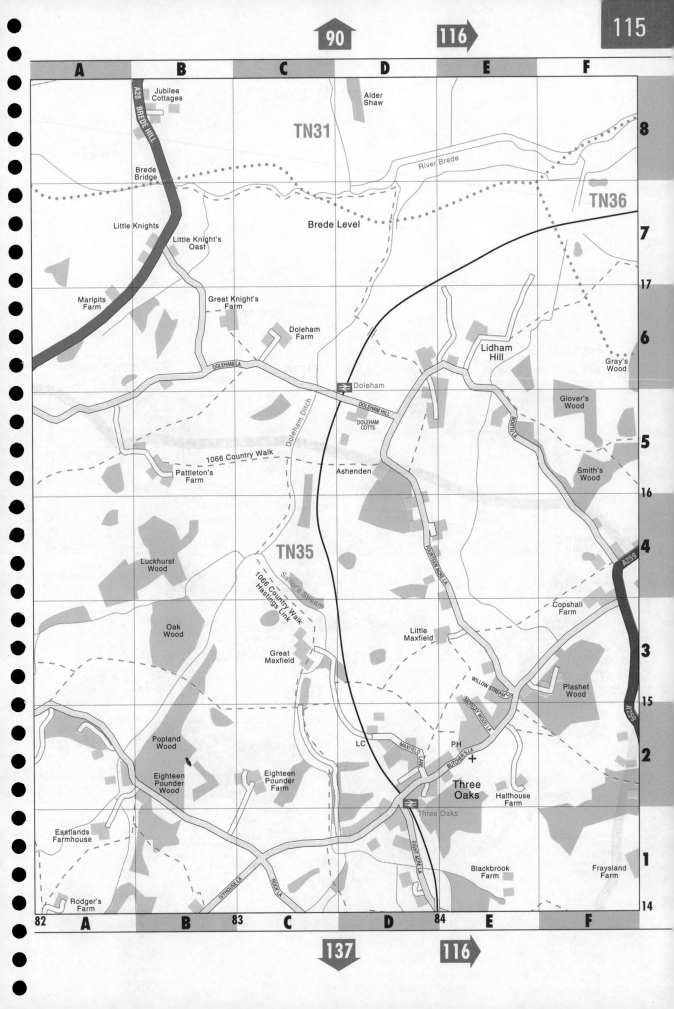

115
91

A B C D E F

8

TN31

Brede Level

River Brede

LC

Lower
Snailham

7

Snailham
Wood

17

Brook
Farm

Snaylham
Farm

1066 Country Wlk

6

Pond
Wood

Broad
Street

TN36

Icklesham
CE Prim
Sch

Five Villages
Ho

PH

PARSONAGE LA

OAST HOUSE FIELD

A259

Icklesham

Toke
Farm

Broad
Street
Wood

HIGH FORDS CL

HIGH FORDS

HAWTH CL

PETER JAMES LA

BLITHE CL

GORSTHURST FIELD

OAST
HOUSE
RD

WORKHOUSE LA

Three
Corner
Wood

Brede Valley
View

5

Stocks
Farm

MAIN RD

Little Sherwood
Ind Pk

PH

1 2

1 Seaview Cotts
2 Seaview Terr

WELLPLACE
COTTS

LAUREL LA

16

THORN
COTTS

Croft
Wood

Roughters

4

A259

Guestling
Thorn

Bench
Wood

Place
Farm

Knockbridge

Knockbridge
Farm

Little Pannel
Farm

Scrag
Oak

WATERMILL LA

3

Buckswood
Sch

Kitchen
Wood

Pickham
Mill

Pannel Sewer

TN35

15

P

Pannel
Wood

Factory
Wood

2

A259

WINCHELSEA RD

Church
Farm

1066 Country Wlk
Hastings link

Pickham
Farm

Burnt
Wood

PANNEL LA

Guestling
Wood

Pett
Wood

1

CHURCH LA

Saunders
Farmhouse

Nature
Reserve

French Court
Farm

RECTORY
PK

THE
GLEBE

Pett

ELMS LA

PETT
RD

THE OAK FIELD

Fairlight
Wood

14

85 A B 86 C D 87 E F

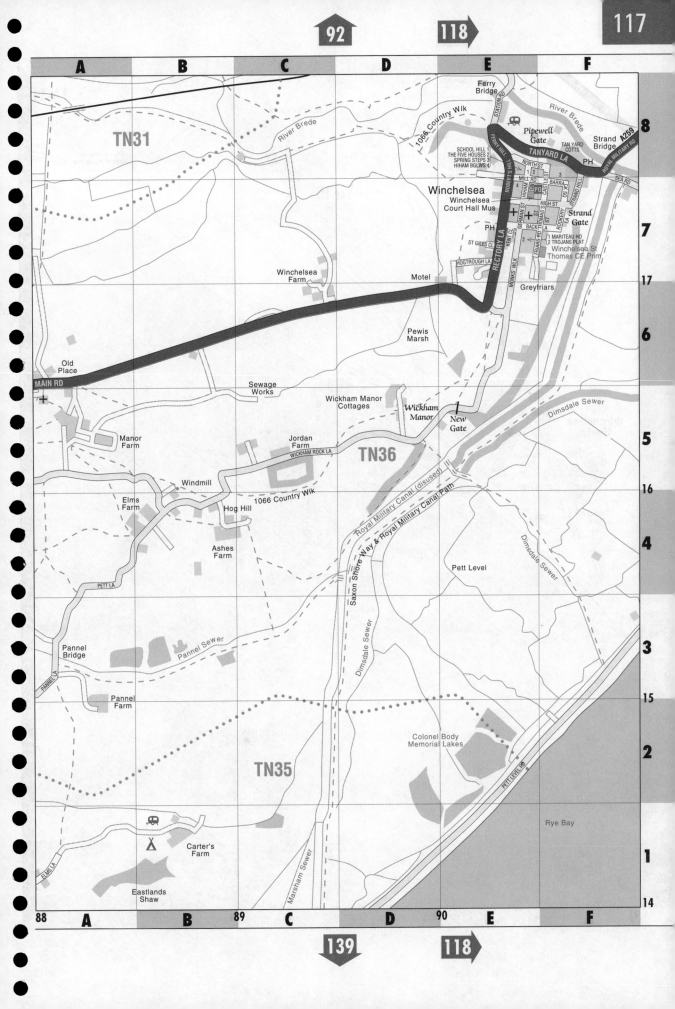

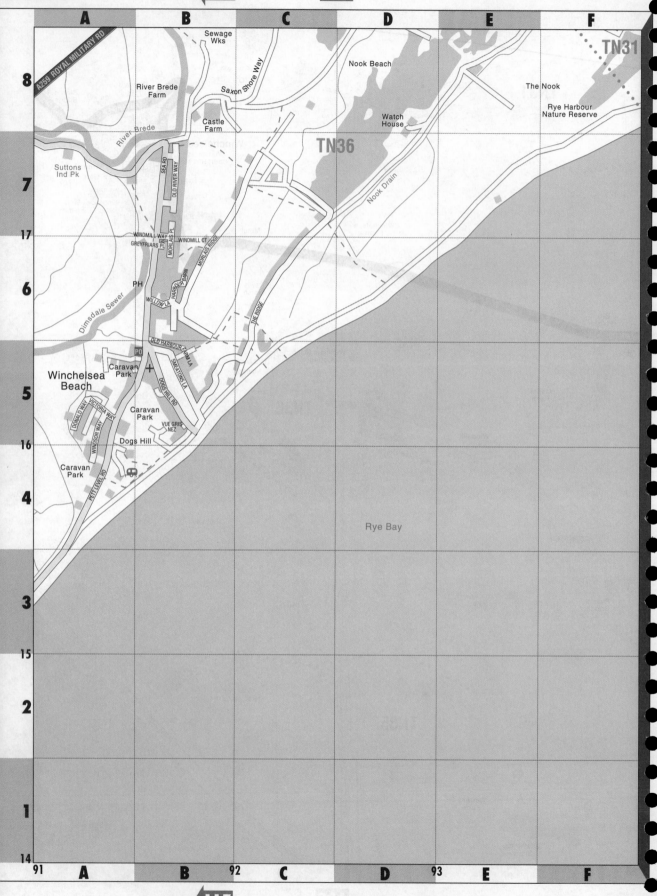

TN31

A259 ROYAL MILITARY RD

Sewage Wks

Saxon Shore Way

Nook Beach

The Nook

River Brede Farm

River Brede

Castle Farm

TN36

Watch House

Rye Harbour Nature Reserve

Suttons Ind Pk

SEA RD

OLD RIVER WAY

Nook Drain

MORLAIS PL

WINDMILL WAY

WINDMILL CT

GREYFRIARS PL

WINDMILL RIDGE

MORLAIS RIDGE

PH

HARBOUR BARN

WILLOW LA

Dimsdale Sewer

THE RIDGE

OLD HARBOUR FARM LA

PO

Caravan Park

SMEATONS LA

Winchelsea Beach

DOGS HILL RD

Caravan Park

DONALD WAY

VICTORIA WAY

VUE GRIS NEZ

WINDSOR WAY

Dogs Hill

Caravan Park

PETT LEVEL RD

Rye Bay

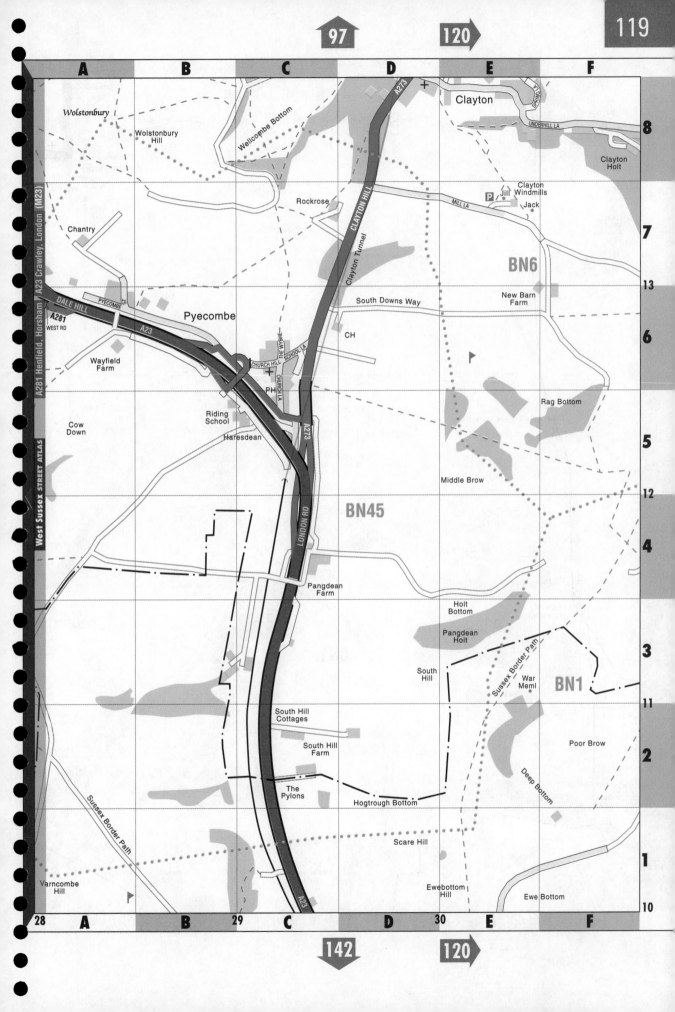

119
98

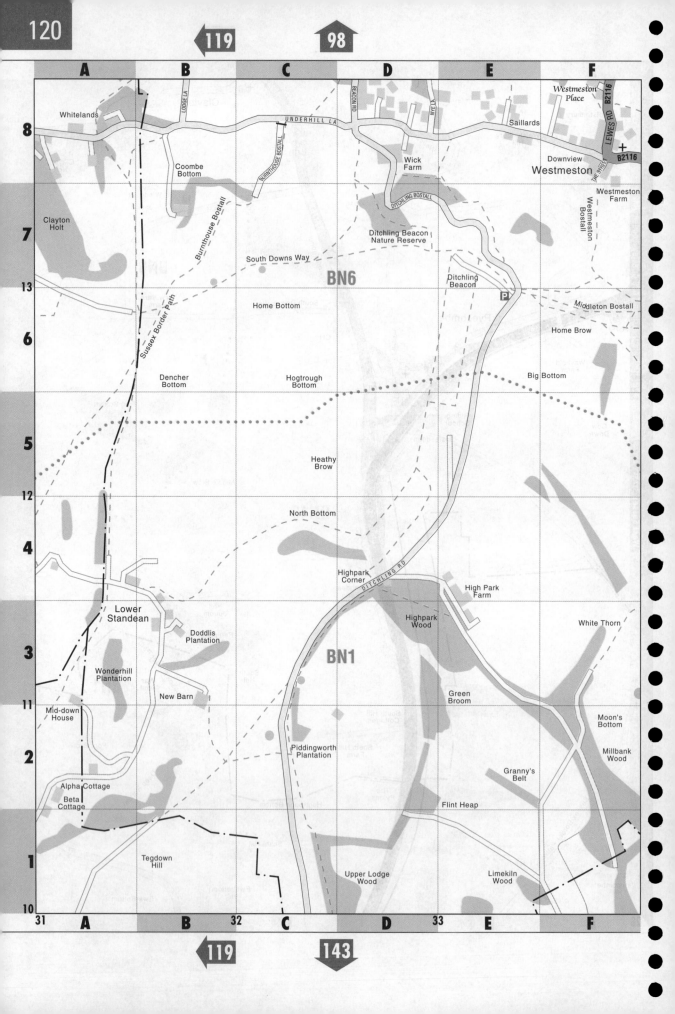

119 143

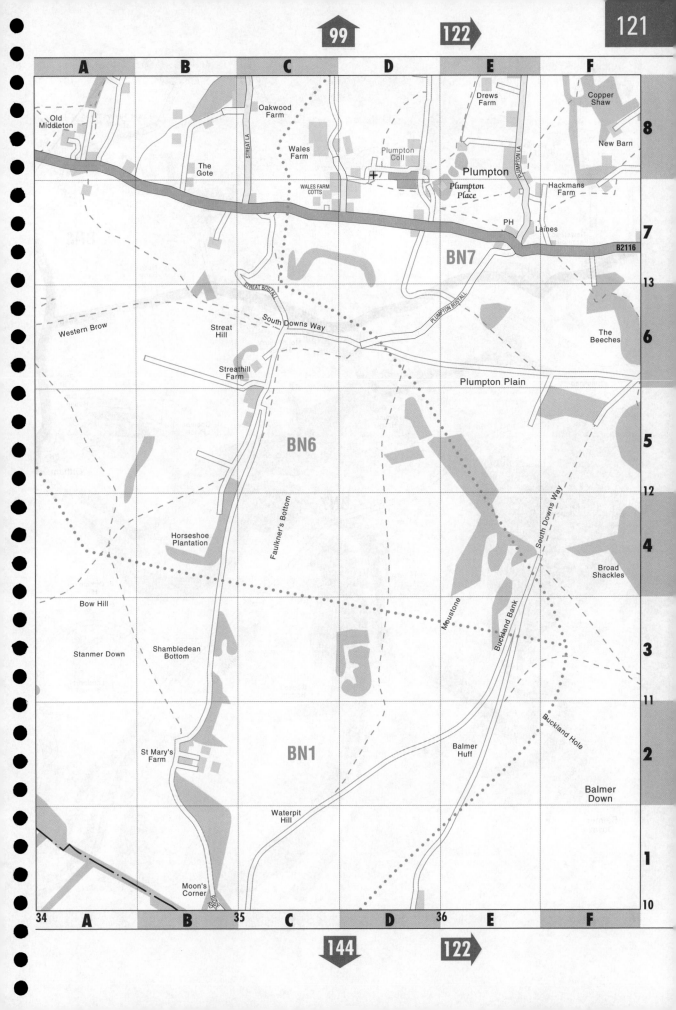

121
100

A B C D E F

8

Warningore House

Warningore Farm

NOVINGTON LA

Lower Tulleys Wells Farm

BEECHWOOD LA

Russet Shaw

Allington Farm

ALLINGTON LA

7

Newstead Farmhouse

Watershoot Shaw

Tulleys Wells Farm

BN8

A275

B2116

13

New Barn

B2116

Warningore Bostall

6

Blackcap

Courthouse Farm

Mount Harry House

Offham Farm

Offham House

Coombe Place

Mount Harry

Coombe Plantation

Offham

PH

5

12

Ashcombe Bottom

BN7

Offham Hill

4

Training Gallop

Landport Bottom

3

Cuckoo Bottom

Training Gallop

HIGHDOWN RD

FIRLE CRES

11

Training Gallop

2

South Downs Way

EAST WAY

Balmer Down

1

10

37 A B 38 C D 39 E F

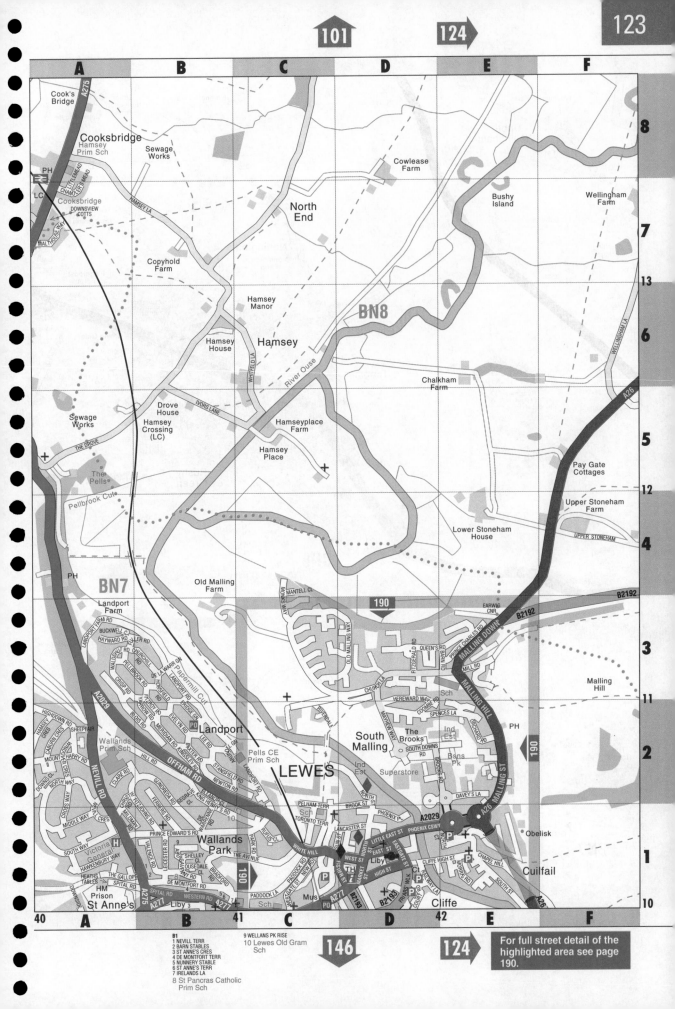

101
124
146
124

B1
1 NEVILL TERR
2 BARN STABLES
3 ST ANNE'S CRES
4 DE MONTFORT TERR
5 NUNNERY STABLE
6 ST ANNE'S TERR
7 IRELANDS LA
8 St Pancras Catholic
  Prim Sch

9 WELLANS PK RISE
10 Lewes Old Gram
   Sch

For full street detail of the highlighted area see page 190.

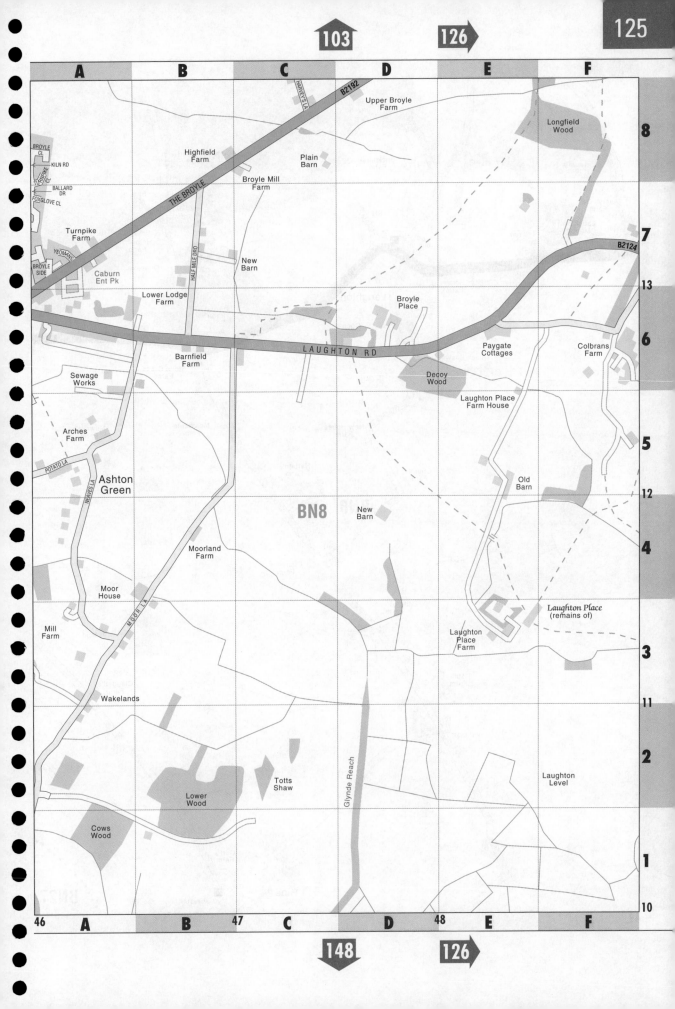

125
104

A B C D E F

8

COMMON LA

Brickhurst
Wood

Laughton Common Wood

LAUGHTON
LODGE

BRICKHURST LA

SHORTGATE LA

Brickhurst
Farm

Lower Vert
Wood

7

Averys Oak
Farm

Laughton
Manor

DUKE
HO

ELM
COTTS

ELM CL

PH

PO

POUND LA

Saw
Mill

PARK LA

Helouan
Farm

B2124 LAUGHTON RD

LEWES RD

Queeake

13

Home
Farm

Laughton

Bowen
Wood

6

Laughton
Primary
School

Coopers
Farm

Bowen
Farm

B2124

Black Shaw

Stone Cross
Farm

5

CHURCH LA

New House
Farm

Marchants
Farm

Milward's
Farm

12

Church
Farm

Harben's
Farm

BN8

4

Cleaver's
Farm

3

Little Stream
Farm

Muslins
Pit

Airfield

11

Mill
Farm

Cleggett's
Farm

2

MARK CROSS

RIPE LA

1

Curl's
Farm

10

Ripe

PO

CHANNERS LA

BN27

49 A B 50 C D 51 E F

105
128
150
128

A B C D E F

8 7 13 6 5 12 4 3 11 2 1 10

52 53 54

Vert Lane
Burchetts Farm
Whitesmith
Vert House
Randall's Farm
Shelf Wood
BN8
Hoad's Wood
Willetts Farm
Muddles Green
Bolt Wood
Chiddingly Prim Sch
Farley Farm
WILLETTS FIELD
MUDDLES GN
Vert Edge
Vanguard Way
Kiln Wood
Burghill Farm
Burgh Hill
Nash Street
Broomham
Broadoak Wood
Holmes Hill
Holme's Hill
Hazelhurst Farm
Twenty Acre Wood
Eight Acre Wood
LEWES RD
B2124
PO
Golden Cross
Works
Buffcoats Farm
Broad Oak Barn
PH
GOLDEN CROSS
A22
Broomham Farm
Brickfield's Farm
Mullany Bsns Pk
Vanguard Way
Ivy Farm
Deanland Wood
Deanland Nursery
Newhouse Farm
Mill Farm
The Old Farmhouse
BN27
Veals Wood
Deanland Rd
Tall Timbers
Herons Way
Deer Haven
Badgers Wlk
Bluebell Glade
Downsview
Foxhollow
Chestnut Rd
Sunset Av
Moondise Wa
Forest Way
The Mdws
Deanland Wood Park
Sewage Works
Bridle Gate Farm
Nickols Farm
Penny Plain Farm
Chalvington Stud Farm
Camberlot Wood
CHESTNUT AVE 1
ROSE GR 2
THE SPINNEY 3
HONEYSUCKLE LA 4
PRIMROSE WAY 5
PRIMROSE ACRE 6
CATHEDRAL WLK 7
SMALL ACRE 8
WOODPECKER WAY 9
10 SQUIRREL WLK
11 ROBINS REACH
12 SQUIRRELS DREY
13 BEECH AVE
14 OAK AVE
15 ELM AVE
Limekiln Farm
Marnhull Farm House
Martins Cottage
Green Farm
Newhouse Farm
Mount Pleasant Farm
Pollard's Wood

127
106

A B C D E F

8 Park Bridge

BN8

Scrapper's Hill Farm

Thunder's Hill

Rosemount

GWN HILL

Hamly Bridge

SCRAPPER'S HILL

THUNDERS HILL

7

Hawthbush Farm

TN21

World's End Farm

Popp's Farm

Wealdway

Westenden Wood

13 Pekes House

Pekes Farm

Leabridge Farm

A267

6 Nash Street Farm

Nash Street

Perryland Farm

Boggy Wood

The Granary Rural Bsns Ctr

NORTH ST

Broad Farm

5 Marigolds Farm

Hackhurst Farm

HACKHURST LA

B2104

Hellingly Primary School

12 Hackhurst Lane Ind Est

Cemy

A22

4 Blackbarn Farm

Northfields Bsns Pk

THE CROFT

HACKHURST LA

BN27

Caldicott's Wood

Caldicotts Farm

CALDICOTT LA

White House

B2104

LPO

Nursery

GOLDEN CROSS

BROOKLANDS TERR

3 Camberlot Farm

Camberlot Wood

The Mount

MANSERS LA

ORCHARD GRANGE

Lower Dicker

Knight's Farm

A267

A271

P

PH

Lower Horsebridge

A271

CUCKMERE CL

11 Coldharbour Farm

POTTERIES COTTS

Boship Farm Hotel

CAMBERLOT RD

COLDHARBOUR RD

Hatches Farm

2 Clover Farm

Field House

The Nurseries

Cuckmere River

Wealdway

Welbury Farm

STRUMA GDNS

1 Starnash

Plenties Farm

Hempstead Farm

HEMPSTEAD

Woodside Farm

LAVENDER CL

10 Malvern House

Bourne Farm

Chicheley Farm

A22

127
151

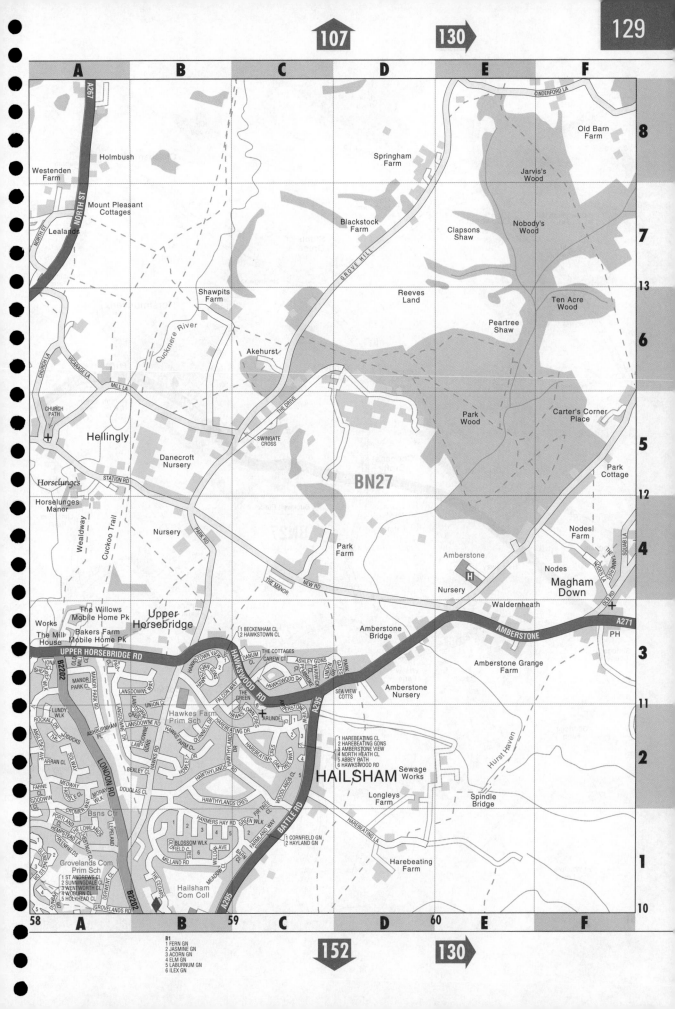

129 108

A B C D E F

8

Cinderford La

Scrip Wood

Studdens La

Kiln Wood

Chilsham

Chilsham Stream

Chilsham Farm

Scripp Farm

Greenway Fruit Farm

Cowbeech Hill Farm

Cowbeech Hill

7

Old Court

Stunts Green

Nunningham Farm

13

Oaklands

Hollingwood

New Barn Farm

Herstmonceux

West Terr
James Lane
Monceux Rd
Fairfield
Blanchard
West End
Chestnut Cl
The Ridgeway
Fairlawns
Dr
Pennies Rd
Dacre Rd
PH PO
Gardner St
Buckwell Rise
Queens Rd
P
Park New
Herstmonceux CE Prim Sch
Lime Cross

6

Twelveacres

Starvecrow Wood

Council Hos

Ginger's Green Farm

Ginger's Green

Squab La

5

Deudney's Farm

Squirrel La

Cooper's Croft

Buckwell Farm

Lime Park

Chapel Row

12

Old Rd

Upper House Farm

Cricketing La

Buckwell Place

BN27

Lime End Farm

4

Magham Down Farm

Harkaway

Butler's Farm

Butlers La

Flowers Green

Place Farm

A271

Puckridge

Under Rd

Willow Farm

Chantler's Farm

Golden Cross

Lower Rd

3

Gilridge Lodge

Sackville Farm

Ironcroft Cottage

11

Gildridge Farm

Puckridge Stream

Bowley Sewer

Iron Stream

Cherry Croft Farm

2

Magham Sewer

Mill Stream

Hurst Haven

Whelpley Level

1066 Country Wlk

1

10

61 A B 62 C D 63 E F

129 153

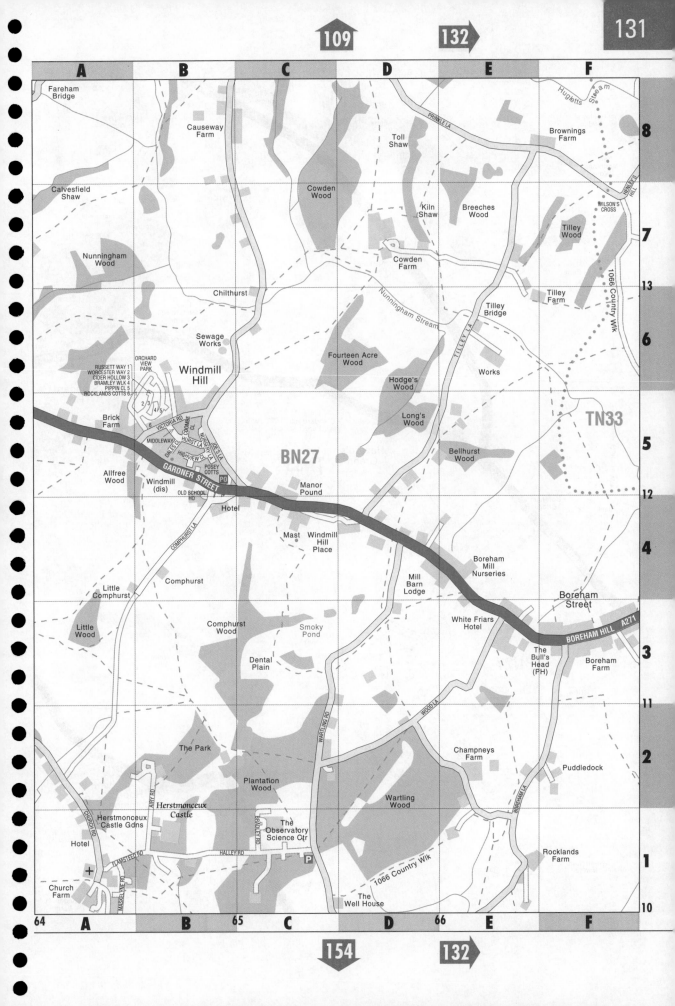

131 110

A **B** **C** **D** **E** **F**

8

The Old Kennels
A271
Compass Wood

Henley's Bridge
1066 Country Wlk
HENLEY'S HILL
Hammer Wood
Luxford's Wood

Northland Wood

7
Ash Bourne
Spring Shaw
Wilding Wood
Combe Hill Farm
Combe Hill

Wilson's Farm
Kitchenham Farm
Combe Wood

13

Ninfield Stream
Lower Standard Hill Farm
STANDARD HILL CL 1
COOKSTOWN CL 2
COMBE LA
Wr Twr

6
STANDARD HILL HIGH ST
A269
Standard Hill

Gardners Farm
1066 Country Wlk
A269
Little Standard Hill Farm
Works
Standard Hill

5
Hazard's Green
TN33
Moor Hall Farm
IVE GRANGE

12
Boreham Bridge

Blackstock Bridge

4
BOREHAM HILL
Wet Wood
Rough Wood

A271

3
Moorhall Stream
White's Wood

BN27
Hooe Level

New Barn

11
B2095
Tanyard Farm
HOOE RD

2
Waller's Haven
Waterliot Stream
Sandhall Farm
MILL LA
Hooe Common

Red Lion PH
Mobile Home Park

School Farm

1
Hogtrough Bridge
Bunts Barn
B2095
Sadlers Farm
Longdown Farm

10
67 **A** **B** 68 **C** **D** 69 **E** **F**

131 155

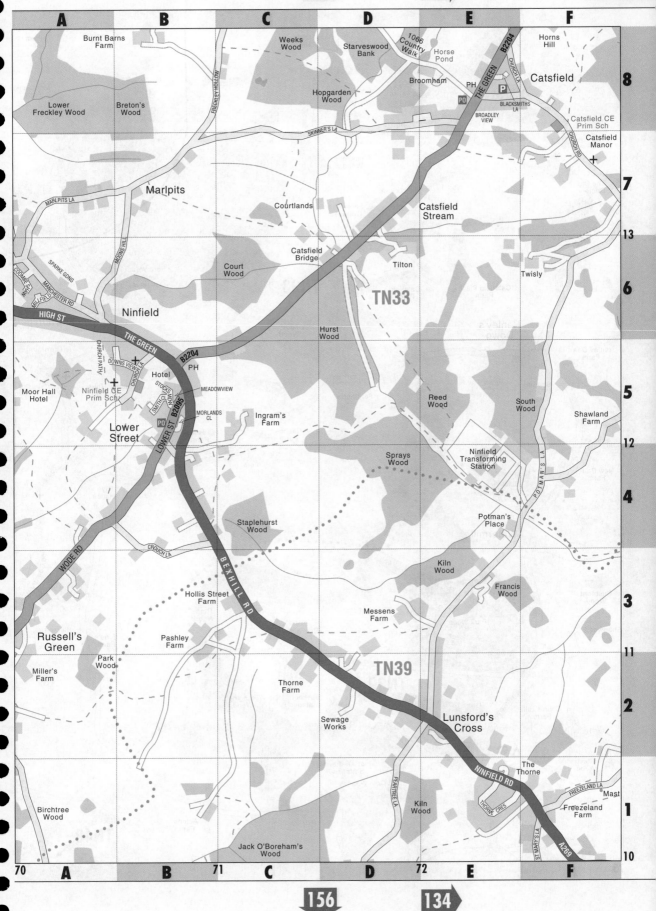

A B C D E F

8

7

13

6

TN33

5

12

4

3

11

2

1

10

70 A B 71 C D 72 E F

Burnt Barns Farm
Lower Freckley Wood
Breton's Wood
Weeks Wood
Starveswood Bank
Hopgarden Wood
1066 Country Walk
Horse Pond
Broomham
PH
PO
Horns Hill
Catsfield
B2204
CHURCH LA
THE GREEN
P
BLACKSMITHS LA
BROADLEY VIEW
Catsfield CE Prim Sch
Catsfield Manor
FRECKLEY HOLLOW
SKINNER'S LA
Marlpits
Courtlands
Catsfield Stream
MARLPITS LA
MOORS HILL
SPARKE GDNS
Catsfield Bridge
Tilton
Twisly
CHURCH RD
COOMBE
MANCHESTER RD
MILLFIELD RD
HIGH ST
Ninfield
THE GREEN
B2204
PH
Court Wood
TN33
Hurst Wood
South Wood
Shawland Farm
CHURCH PATH
DOWNS VIEW
CHURCH LA
Hotel
MEADOWVIEW
Reed Wood
Moor Hall Hotel
Ninfield CE Prim Sch
STOCKS
SMITH CL
LOWER ST
B2095
PO
MORLANDS CL
Ingram's Farm
Ninfield Transforming Station
POTMAN'S LA
Lower Street
Sprays Wood
Potman's Place
Kiln Wood
Francis Wood
WODE RD
CROUCH LA
Staplehurst Wood
BEXHILL RD
Messens Farm
Hollis Street Farm
Russell's Green
Park Wood
Pashley Farm
TN39
Miller's Farm
Thorne Farm
Lunsford's Cross
The Thorne
NINFIELD RD
FREEZELAND LA
Mast
Birchtree Wood
Sewage Works
PEARTREE LA
Kiln Wood
THORNE CRES
ST MARY'S LA
A269
Freezeland Farm
Jack O'Boreham's Wood

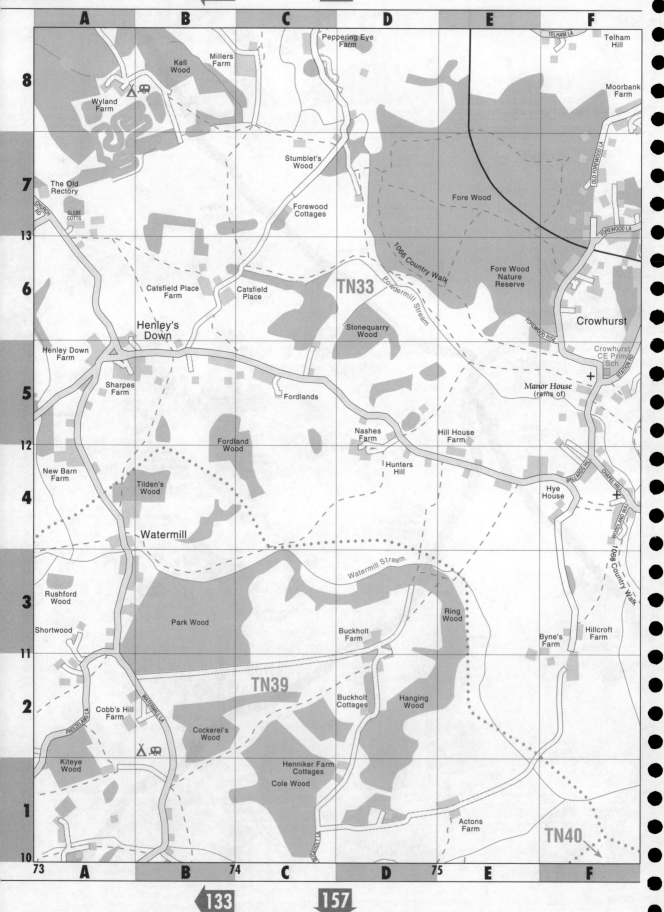

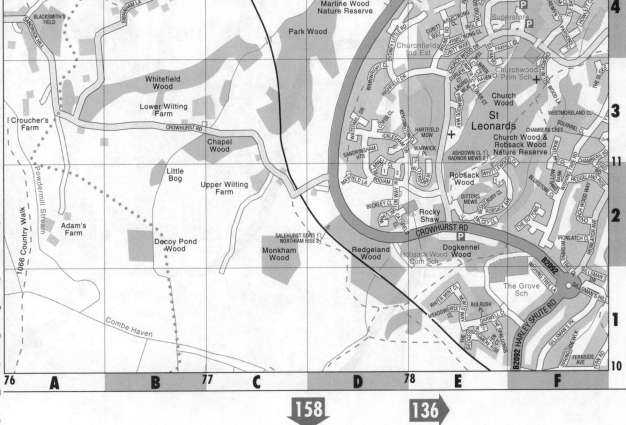

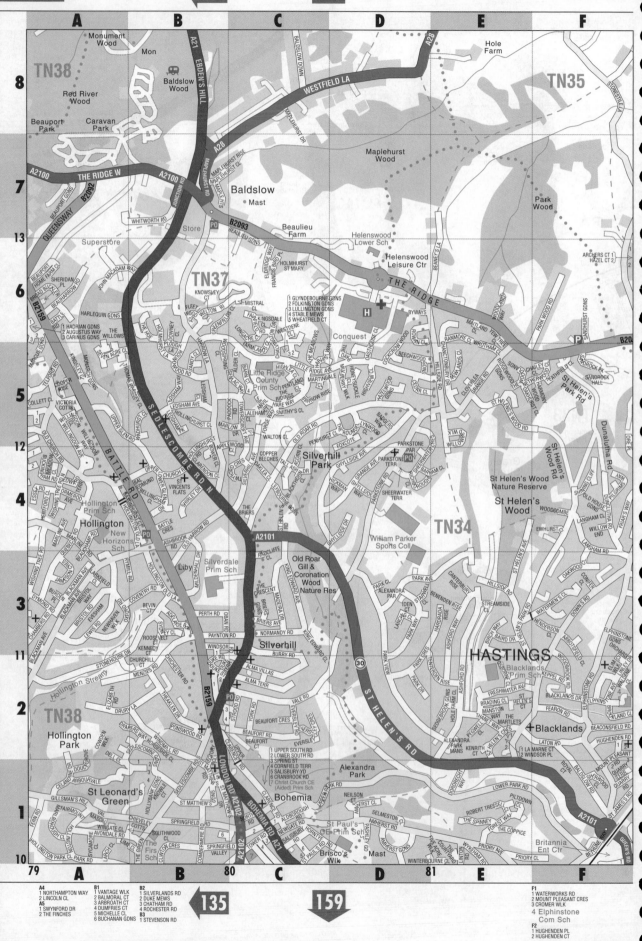

135
114

135
159

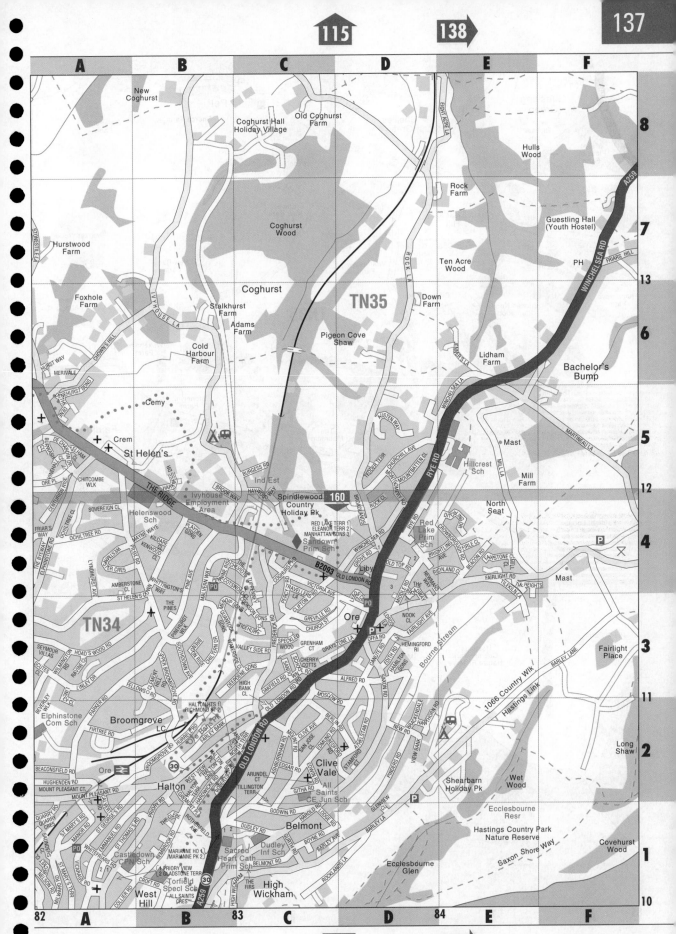

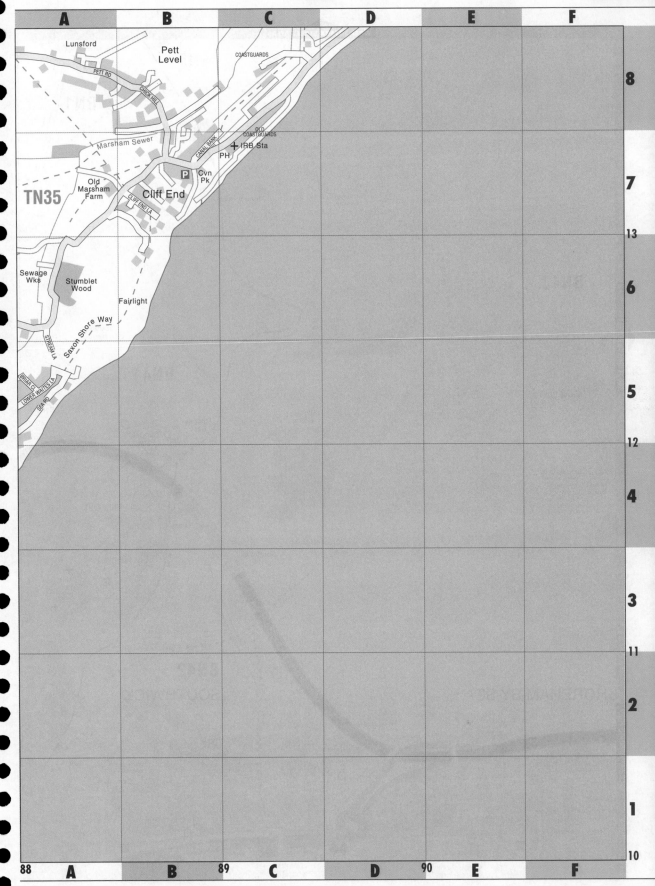

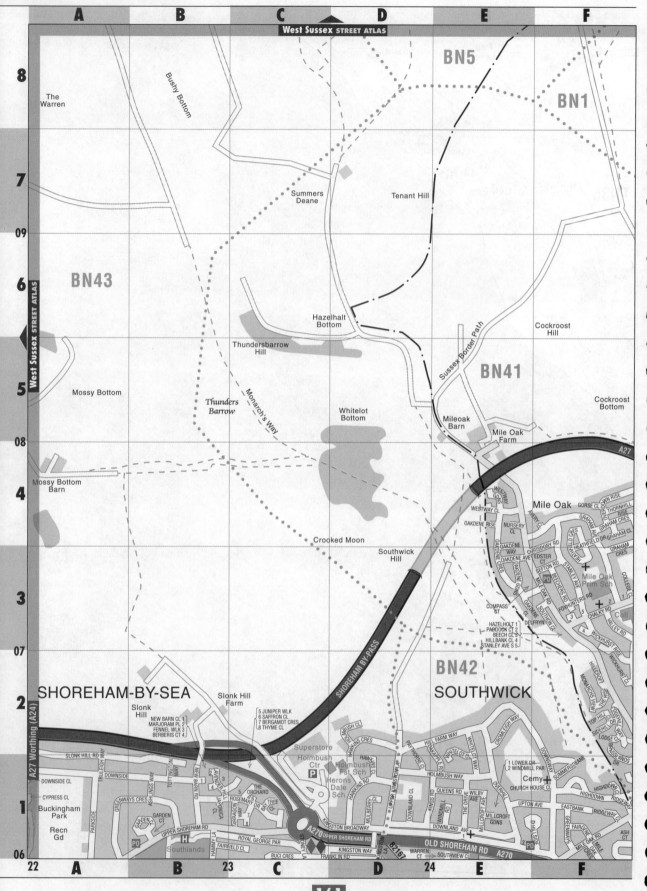

BN5

BN1

The Warren

Bushy Bottom

Summers Deane

Tenant Hill

BN43

Hazelhalt Bottom

Cockroost Hill

Mossy Bottom

Thundersbarrow Hill

Sussex Border Path

BN41

Thunders Barrow

Monarch's Way

Whitelot Bottom

Cockroost Bottom

Mossy Bottom Barn

Mileoak Barn

Mile Oak Farm

A27

Crooked Moon

Southwick Hill

Mile Oak

WESTWAY CL
WESTWAY GDNS
AVERY CL
OAKDENE RISE
NURSERY CL
OAKDENE WAY
OAKDENE AVE
OAKDENE GDNS
CHRISDORY RD
EDSTER CT
SEFTON RD
PO
STANLEY AVE
Mile Oak Prim Sch
College
GORSE CL
CROWN RISE
THORNHILL RISE
GRAHAM AVE
GRAHAM RD
HEATHFIELD DR
GRAHAM CL
GRAHAM CRES
HEATHFIELD CRES
BEECHERS RD
MILE OAK RD
FOXHUNTERS RD
VALLEY RD
CHALKY RD
WICKHURST RISE

COMPASS CT
HAZELHOLT 1
PADDOCK CT 2
BEECH CL 3
HILLBANK CL 4
STANLEY AVE S 5
DELFRYN
SUTTON CL

HILLCROFT
WICKHURST RD
MONKROSS VIEW
HILLCROFT
TOP HILL
OVERHILL WAY
SIDEHILL

BN42
SOUTHWICK

Shoreham Bypass

SHOREHAM-BY-SEA

Slonk Hill Farm

Slonk Hill

5 JUNIPER WLK
6 SAFFRON CL
7 BERGAMOT CRES
8 THYME CL

NEW BARN CL 1
MARJORAM PL 2
FENNEL WLK 3
BERBERIS CT 4

A27 Worthing (A24)

Slonk Hill Rd

DOWNSIDE

TOTTINGTON WAY

NEW BARN RD
LAVENDER HILL
JAPONICA CL
ROSEMARY DR
BAY TREE CL
THE ORCHARD

Superstore
Holmbush Ctr
P

Herons Dale Sch

Holmbush Fst Sch

CRABASH CL
HAWKINS CRES
HAWKINS RD
HAWK CL

PAYTHORNE CL
HILL FARM WAY

HILL FARM WAY
HOLMBUSH WAY

WHITELOT CL
WHITELOT WAY

CRIMSHAW WAY

SUMMERSDEANE

1 LOWER DR
2 WINDMILL PAR

Cemy
Church House Rd

HIGHDOWN
HIGHDOWN
RIDGEWAY

Buckingham Park

DOWNSIDE CL
CYPRESS CL

Recn Gd

GREENWAYS CRES
ASHLINGS WAY
PARKSIDE

GARDEN CT
GARDEN CL

PO

TRULEIGH WAY

KINGSTON BROADWAY

Upper Shoreham Rd

FAIRFIELD CL
BUCI CRES
ROYAL GEORGE PAR
FRANKLIN RD

Southlands
H

KINGSTON LA

KINGSTON WAY

MULBERRY CL
DOWNLAND CL
WINDMILL RD
QUEENS RD
WILBY AVE
THE DRIVE
MILLCROFT GDNS
DOWNLAND AVE

B2167
OLD SHOREHAM RD
A270
WARREN CT
SOUTHVIEW CL

UPTON AVE
EASTBANK
GREENWAYS
MILE OAK RD
FAIROAK
DHILSIDE

RIDGEWAY CT
ASH CT

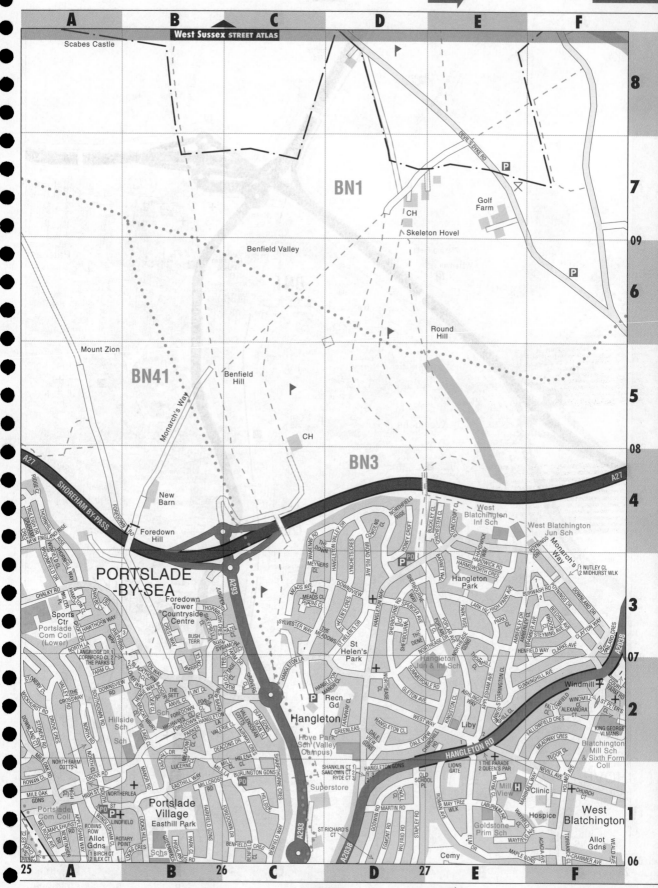

West Sussex STREET ATLAS

141
119

A B C D E F

8
7
09
6
5
08
4
3
07
2
1
06

Sweet Hill
Sports Gd
Kennels
Sussex Border Path
LONDON RD
A23
A27
Recn Gd
Recn Gd
Patcham Place (YH)
BN1
THE VILLAGE BARN
VALE AVE
Patcham
BRAESIDE AVE
HESTON AVE
SANDHILLS AVE
SOLWAY AVE
CRAIGMAIR AVE
BARRHILL AVE
MACKIE AVE
WARMDENE AVE
Liby Jun Sch
STONELEIGH CL
HIGHVIEW AVE N
HIGHVIEW AVE S
Inf Sch
High Sch
WARMDENE WAY
Old Patcham Mews 1
Greatham Ct 2
Ladies Mile Ct 3
Mile End Cotts 4
BRANGWYN WAY
PATCHAM BY-PASS
CAROL CL
WINFIELD AVE
OVERHILL WAY
UPPER WINFIELD AVE
WILMINGTON PAR
WARMDENE CL
WILMINGTON WAY
CHURCH HILL
MAYFIELD CRES
DALE CRES
DALE DR
Playing Field
Waterhall
Coney Hill
Patcham Mill (dis)
WATERHALL RD
MILL RD
WINDMILL DR
FERNWOOD RISE
DENESIDE
WAYSIDE
BRAMBLE RISE
HIGHBANK
BANKSIDE
COPSE HILL
DOWNSIDE
Loyal Par 1
Bankside Ct 2
WESTDENE DR
MILL RISE
Liby
Westdene Prim Sch
BARN RISE
ELDRED AVE
AUDREY CL
ASHBURNHAM DR
GRANGEWAYS
BRANGWYN DR
BRANGWYN AVE
RIDGESIDE AVE
GRANGE
OVERHILL DR
PATCHAM GRANGE
OLD LONDON RD
OLD FARM RD
GREENFIELD CRES
Red Hill
CH
DEVIL'S DYKE RD
GREEN RIDGE
GLEN RISE
GLEN RISE CL
Red Hill
Arundel Ct 3
Beeding Ct 4
Chailey Ct 5
Westdene
HILLCREST CT
HILLCREST
DENE VALE
FAIRWAY RISE
Durrington Ct
DENECROFT
THE DENEWAY
LIONS DENE
PRIORY
BOURNE CT
HOMELEIGH
WOODBOURNE AVE
BEECHWOOD AVE
WOODLAND WAY
SURRENDEN RD
OLD COURT CL
THE HEIGHTS
THE PARADE
WOODLAND CT
HAWTHORN CL
VALLEY DR
REDHILL DR
REDHILL
VALLEY RD
FALLSIDE WAY
HILLBROW RD
COLBOURN RD
MANDALAY CT
THE EXCELSIOR
1 Elwyn Jones Ct
2 Charles Kingston Gdns
Withdean Park
SURRENDEN RD
1 Windsor Ct
2 The Park Appartments
3 Coolwater Pk
4 Lilac Ct
Withdean
Varndean Coll
YORKLANDS
DYKE CL
TONGDEAN LA
TONGDEAN RISE
SHEPHERDS CROFT
WAYLAND HTS
WAYLAND AVE
Sports Arena
Withdean Stad (Brighton & Hove Albion FC)
Manhattan Ct 1
Park Manor 2
P&R
LONDON RD
PEACOCK LA
SURRENDEN CRES
VARNDEAN GDNS
HIGHDOWN
SURRENDEN CRES
SURRENDEN HOLT
DRAXMONT WAY
Varndean
STRINGER WAY
Dorothy Stringer Sch
KING GEORGE VI AVE
A2038
1 Goldstone Ct
2 Balmoral Ct
SANDRINGHAM DR
Queen Mary Ave
CROWNSIDE
HILL DR
THE SPINNEY
DYKE ROAD AVE
TONGDEAN RD
THE BEECHES
THE CEDARS
CEDARS GDNS
LANE CL
OAK CL
VARNDEAN RD
VARNDEAN DR
MONTEREY
FAIR EDGES
MULBURY CT
Prim Sch
Balfour Jun Sch
Queen Victoria
DEANWAY
WOODLAND
MEADOW CL
CHALK CL
TONGDEAN AVE
HAZELDENE MEADS
HAZELHOLT
LEAHURST CT RD
CURWEN PL
ELMS LEA
GROSVENOR CT
CLIVEDEN CT
CORNWALL GDNS
HARRINGTON RD
STRINGER WAY
WHITTINGEHAME GDNS
WHITTINGEHAME GDNS
Edward CL
COBTON DR
MILL DR
BARROWFIELD CL
TONGDEAN AVE
WOODLANDS
LIONS GDNS
Barrowfield Lodge
BARROWFIELD DR
WITHDEAN AVE
Pinewood Cl 7
Robinia Lodge 8
Sceptre 9
THE MEWS
SERGEANT
CLERMONT RD
CLERMONT VILLAS
TOWER PL
TIVOLI
RISSOM CT
LODER RD
BATES RD
Preston Park
SHIRLEY AVE
SHIRLEY DR
WOODRUFF AVE
MALLORY RD
MALLOW RD
TIVOLI CRES
TIVOLI CRES N
CLERMONT RD
CUMBERLAND RD
HARRINGTON RD
BAVANT RD
GORDON RD
HERBERT RD
OSBORNE RD
BALFOUR RD
King George VI Mans
HOWARD CT
COURT FARM RD
PO
NEVILL RD
WATERHOUSE WAY
GOLDSTONE CL
GOLDSTONE CRES
BENETT DR
BENETT AVE
CHARTFIELD WAY
TRESCROFT RD
STANFORD CL
HOVE PARK WAY
BISHOPS RD
THE DROVEWAY
SCARBOROUGH RD
MALDON RD
ROBERTSON RD
CUMBERLAND RD
LAURISTON RD
NORTH RD
MIDDLE RD
SOUTH RD
PRESTON DRO
SURRENDEN LODGE 1
FLORENCE CT 2
ACACIA CT 3
PRESTON RD
THE MEWS
Preston Manor Mus
Preston Park
HOVE
Blatchington Mill Sch & Sixth Form Ctr
Aldrington CE Prim Sch
Superstore
Brighton & Hove Stad
BN3
Monarch's Way
NEVILL RD
Mus
Miniature Rly
Hovel Park
1 March Ho
2 Orchard Ho
THE DROVEWAY
Mowden Sch
Preston Village Mews
1 South Rd Mews
2 Rowan Ct
3 Copper Beeches
4 Silver Birches
5 Downsview
6 Beechwood
7 Highcroft Lodge
8 Preston Grange
9 Nestor Ct
Preston
BELLEVUE CT
Hove Park Sch (Nevil Campus)
A2023
NEVILL CT
ORCHARD RD
ORCHARD AVE
PARK VIEW RD
HOVE PARK RD
GANNET HO
RIGDEN RD
LLOYD RD
PULMAR LA
WINSTON CRES
COMPTON CRES
INWOOD CRES
REIGATE RD
ROOKERY CL
WITHDEAN RD
HIGHCROFT VILLAS
GRANGE CL
A23
28 29 30

E2
1 LYNDEN CT
2 STAMFORD LODGE
3 CUMBERLAND LODGE
4 CENTENARY HO
5 SHAWCROSS HO
6 CARLTON HO

E3
1 LEAHURST CT
2 CHERRYWOOD
3 CEDARWOOD
4 MAPLEWOOD
5 PINEWOOD
6 BEECHWOOD
7 WITHDEAN CT
8 WELLINGTONIA CT

9 WITHDEAN HALL
10 THE APPROACH

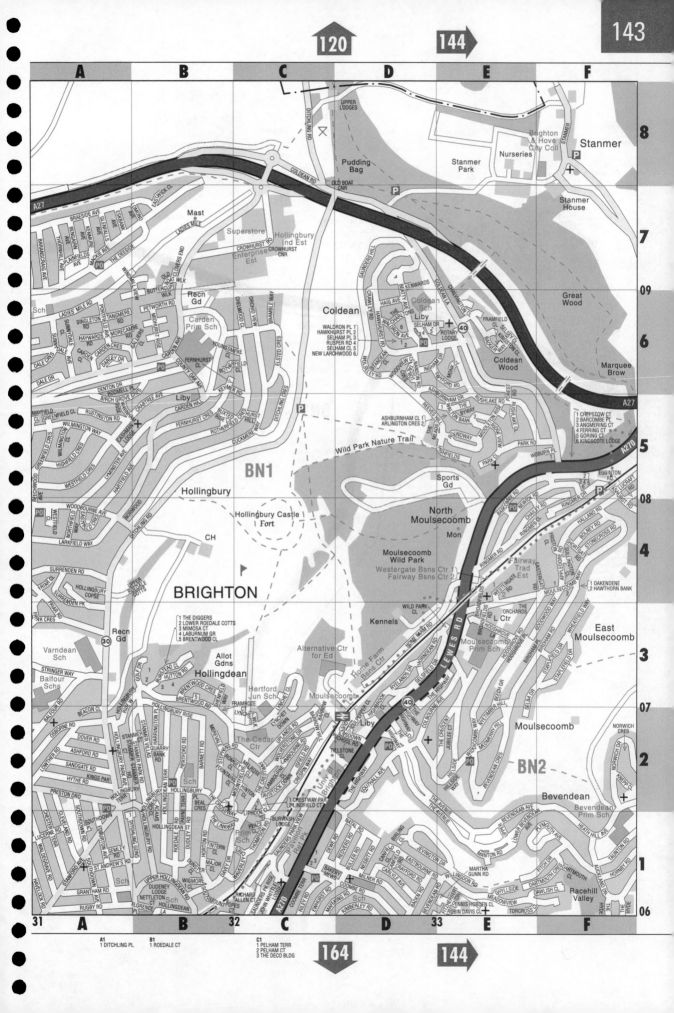

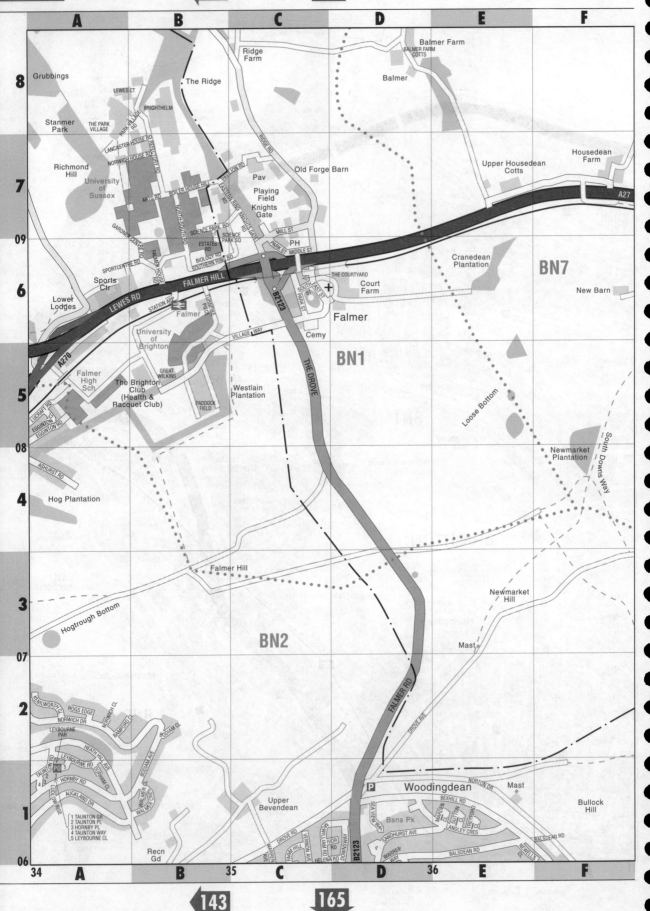

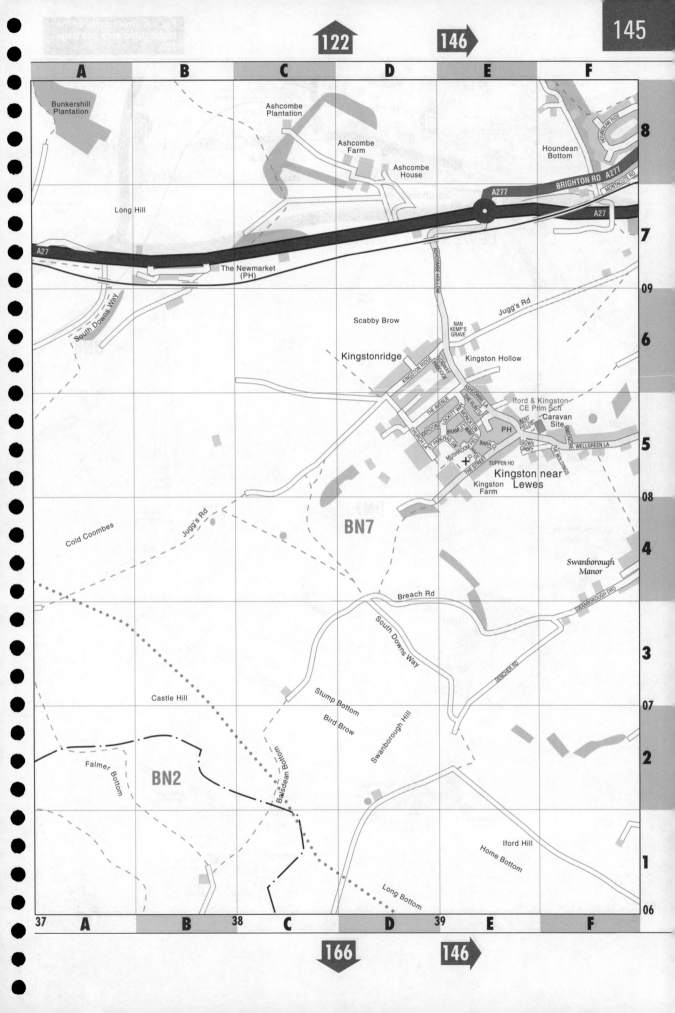

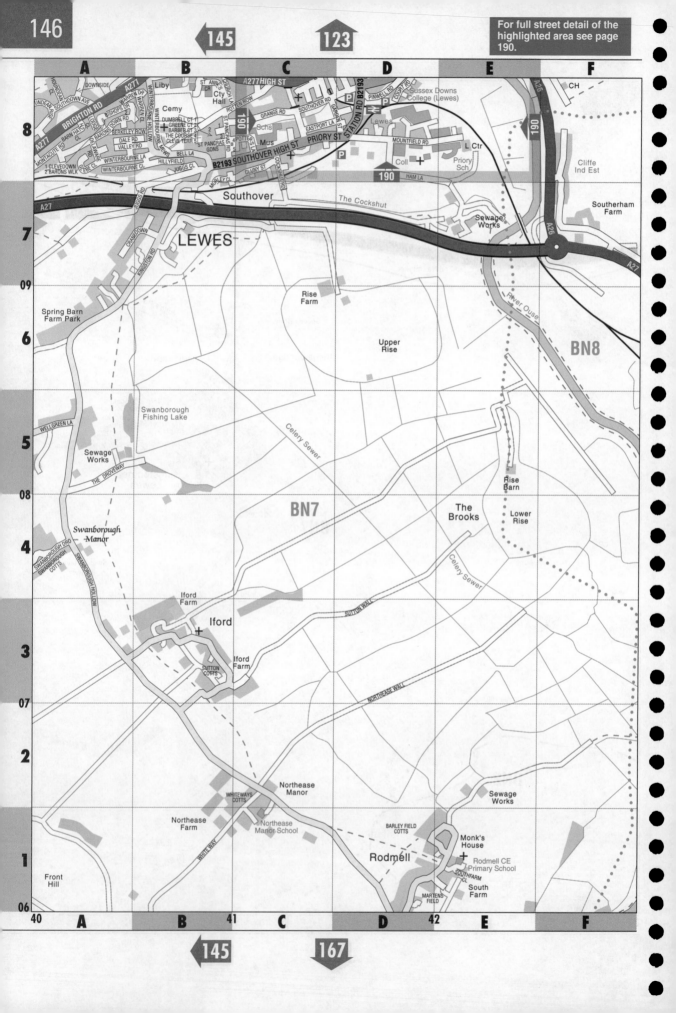

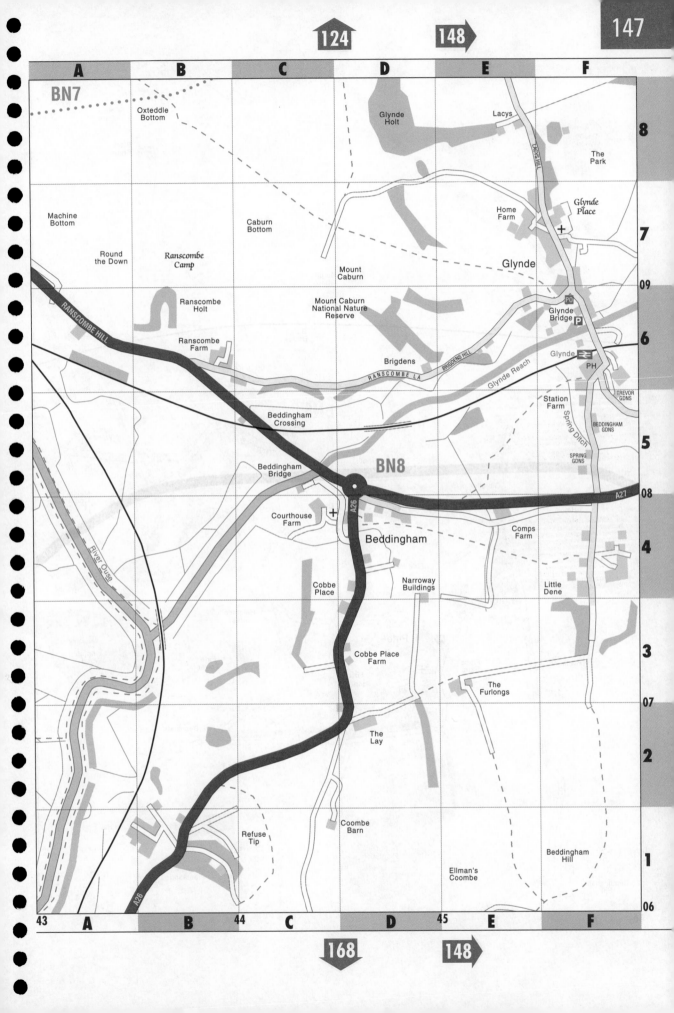

124
148
168
148

BN7

A   B   C   D   E   F

Oxteddle
Bottom

Glynde
Holt

Lacys

The
Park

LACYS HILL

Machine
Bottom

Caburn
Bottom

Home
Farm

Glynde
Place

8

Round
the Down

Ranscombe
Camp

Mount
Caburn

Glynde

7

09

Ranscombe
Holt

Mount Caburn
National Nature
Reserve

PO

Glynde
Bridge

RANSCOMBE HILL

Ranscombe
Farm

Brigdens

BRIGDENS HILL

RANSCOMBE LA.

Glynde Reach

Glynde

PH

6

TREVOR
GDNS

Station
Farm

BEDDINGHAM
GDNS

Beddingham
Crossing

Spring Ditch

SPRING
GDNS

5

River Ouse

Beddingham
Bridge

BN8

A27

08

Courthouse
Farm

A26

Beddingham

Comps
Farm

4

Cobbe
Place

Narroway
Buildings

Little
Dene

Cobbe Place
Farm

The
Furlongs

3

07

The Lay

2

Refuse
Tip

Coombe
Barn

Beddingham
Hill

1

A26

Ellman's
Coombe

06

43   A   B   44   C   D   45   E   F

| | A | B | C | D | E | F |

8

Decoy
Wood

New
Barn

Black
Shaw

7

Willow
Shaw

Glynde Reach

Barber's
Wish

09

Burgh
Shaw

Middle
Barn

LC

Bushy
Lodge

6

Burgh
Bridge

Loover
Shaw

Loover
Barn

Bushy Lodge
Farm

BN8

Newhouse
Farm

Adder
Wells

5

Garage

Wick Street

BURGH LA

STAMFORD
BLDGS

A27

Gibraltar

Middle Farm
Countryside
Ctr

08

Preston
House

CROSSWAYS

Dairy
Farm

Decoy
Pond

A27

4

Firle Park

Petland
Barn

Firle CE
Prim Sch

BOSTAL RD

CABURN VIEW
COTTS

THE STREET

P

PH

Heighton
Street

Compton
Wood

3

Newelm

CABURN VIEW
BGLWS

PO

THE ROCK

Firle

Firle
Tower

Place
Farm

+

Firle
Place

07

Beanstalk

FIRLE BOSTAL

2

Round Hill

1

Beddingham
Hill

Firle
Plantation

Roundhill
Plantation

06

| 46 | A | B | 47 | C | D | 48 | E | F |

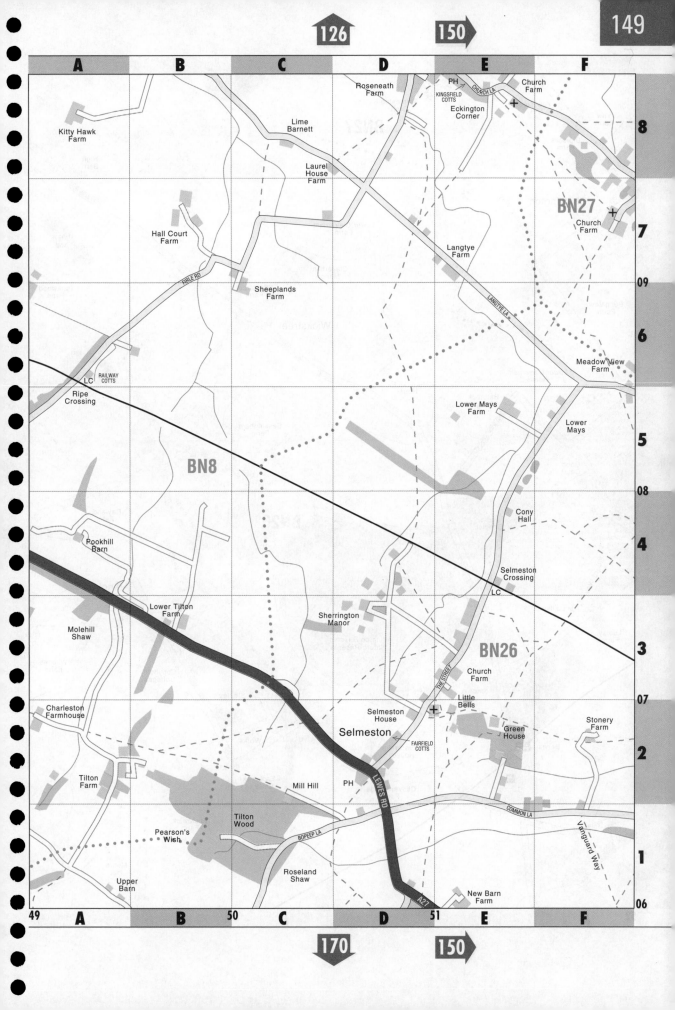

A | B | C | D | E | F

8

Yew Farm

Yew Tree (PH)

Diplocks Farm

Selmeston Croft

BN27

Clifton Farm

High Barn

HIGH BARN ROAD

Chalvington

Vanguard Way

7

Lower Claverham Farm

Park Wood

09

Claverham Manor

Wickstreet Farm

Parkwood Farm

Bungalow Farm

6

Wickstreet

WICK STREET

SESSINGHAM LANE

Lower Claverham House

Batbrooks Farm House

LOWER WICK STREET

Batbrook Cottages

Sessingham Farm

Cuckmere River

5

TYE HILL RD

08

Cobb Court

Ludlay Coppice

BN26

Raylands Farm

4

Vanguard Way

Wealdway

Arlington

Ludlay

Ludlay Farm

P

Arlington Reservoir

PH

Arlington Reservoir Nature Reserve

Copyhold Cottages

Wilbees Farm

3

PRINCES FIELD

DOWNSWAY

Polhill's Farm

Stapley's

07

Berwick

LC

Chilverbridge House

Works

2

PH

STATION RD

PO

Chilver Bridge Farm

Endlewick Cottages

1

COMMON LA

Endlewick Farm

Moors Hill

06

52 | A | B | 53 | C | D | 54 | E | F

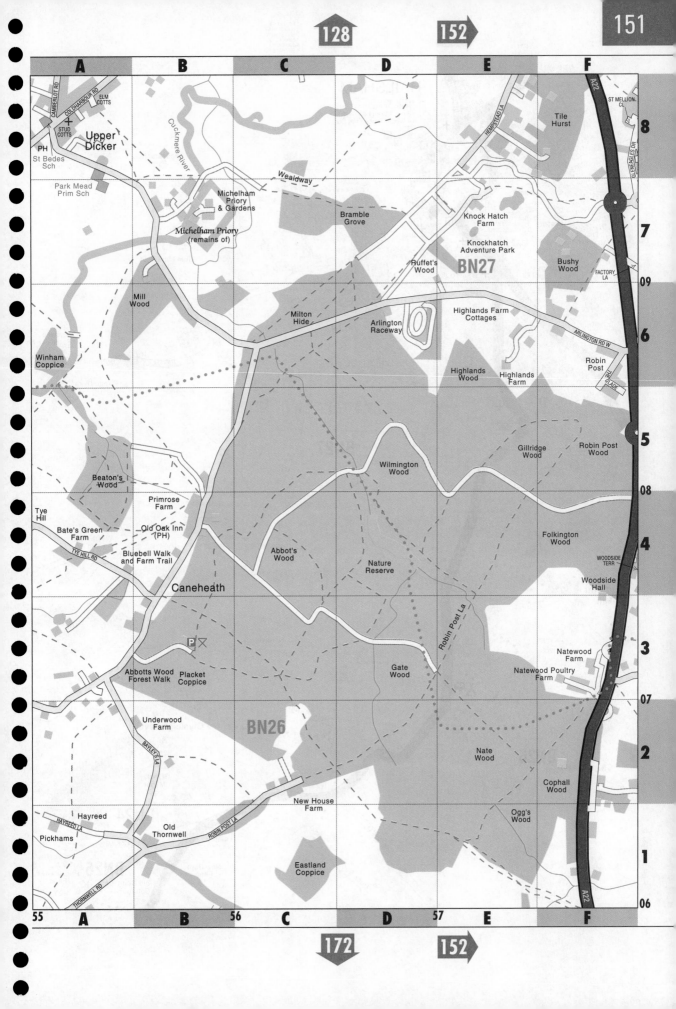

151
129

C7
1 MARKET SQ
2 ELIZABETH CT
3 SOUTHDOWN CT
4 ASHFORD CL
5 COBDEN PL
6 TERMINUS PL
7 DEER PADDOCK LA

HAILSHAM

1 ST WILFRIID'S CT
2 WELLINGTON LODGE
3 Adult Com Learning
4 White House Prim Sch

1 KINGFISHER CT
2 FIELDFARE CT
3 KESTREL CT
4 BITTERN CT
5 TEAL CT
6 REDSHANK CT
7 PLOVER CT
8 CURLEW CT
9 QUAIL CT

Marshfoot La

Old Marshfoot Farm

Marshlands Prim Sch

Little Marshfoot Farm

Lion House

White Dyke Farm

White Dyke

Mill Road

Swan Bsns Ctr

Old Swan La

New Barn Farm

Sewage Works

BN27

Nursery

Westdown Cottages

Downash Farm

Slyes Farm

Downash Manor Farm

Gassons Farm

Westfield Farm

Freshfield Farm

Seymours Farm

Little Downash Farm

Summer Hill

Coldthorn Wood

Honeycrock

The Lewens

Coppards

Mulbrooks Farm

Peel House

Glynleigh Level

BN26

Nightingale Farm

Glyndley Manor Cottage Est

Glyndley Manor

Decoy Wood

BN24

West Lodge

New Barn Farm

Glynleigh Rd

BN26

Priesthawes Farm

Duck Puddle

Old Court Cottages

Sayerland House

Bolney's Wood

Oaklands

Cemy

Cuckoo Trail

1 CHALFONT
2 COMPTON TERR
3 MOUNT VIEW TERR
4 THE LAWNS

Station Road Ind Est

North Crescent Ind Est

151
173

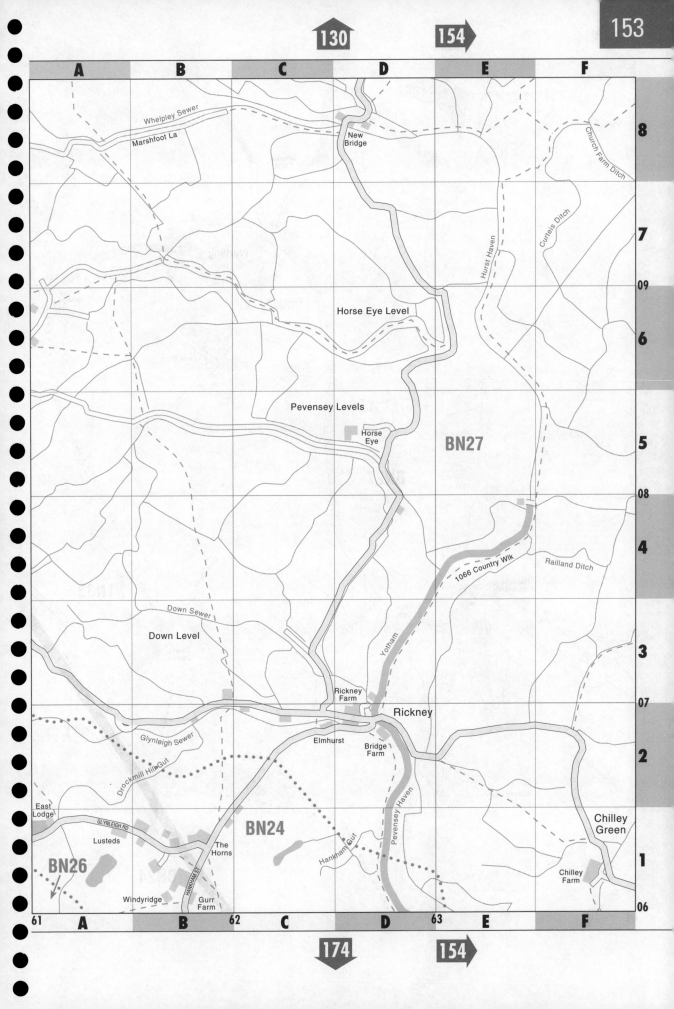

A **B** **C** **D** **E** **F**

1066 Country Wlk

MASKELYNE RD

Royal Greenwich Obsy

Hoads Hill Farm

The Reids

8

WATLING RD

Cooper's Farm

Brooks Farm

BOREHAM LA

PH

+ Wartling

HORSEWALK

7

09

Horse Bridge

Court Lodge Farm

Kentland Fleet

6

Lower Barn

Sew Ditch

Marsh Foot Farm

5

BN27

08

Dowle Stream

4

Mark Dyke

Waller's Haven

TN33

Russells in the Marsh

Church Acre Bridge

Pylons Cottages

Buck's Bridge

Lampham Dro

A259

3

07

Dowle Corner

Middle Bridge

2

Chilley Stream

Old Haven

Manxey Level

A259

1

BN24

06

64 **A** **B** **65** **C** **D** **66** **E** **F**

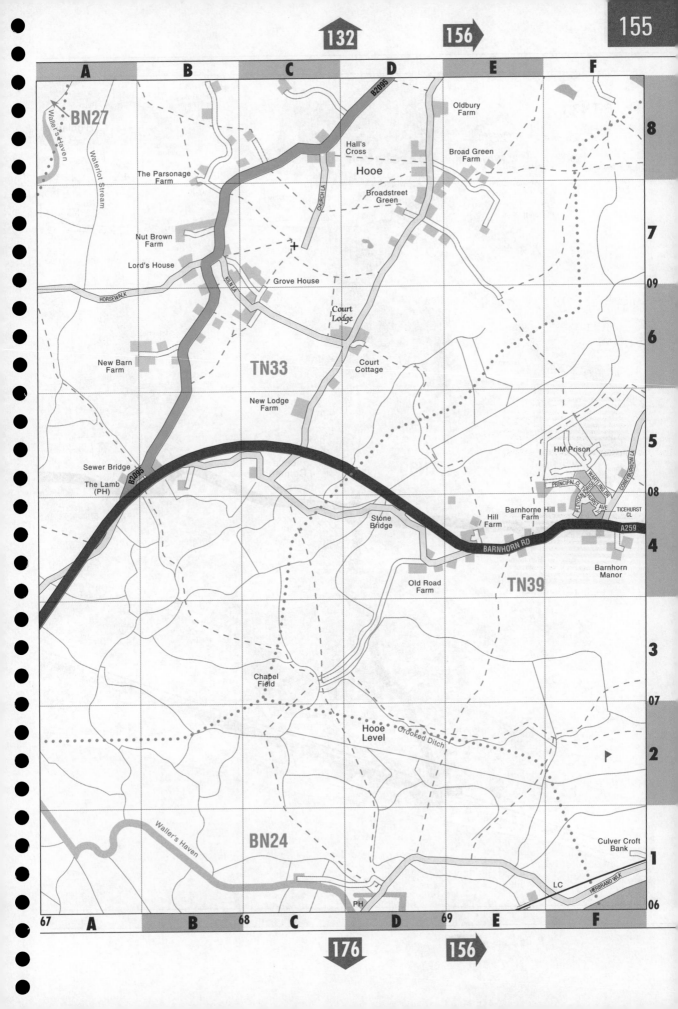

155 133 155

TN33

Holmes Farm Cotts
St Margarets Cres
Whydown Bridge
Whydown
Highwoods Farm
Holmes Farm
Highcroft
Whydown Farm
Gotham Wood
Gotham
Picknill Green
Sandhurst La
Conetsborrow La
Kite's Nest Wood
Beeches Farm

High Woods
Whydown Place
Whydown Rd
High Peartree Wood
Wet Wood
Woodstock Rd
Cowdray Park Rd
Wealden Way

Little High Wood
Clay Pit
Forest Barn
Highwoods Golf Club
Broad Oak Park

Turkey Farm
St Mary's Cotts
Ninfield Rd
A269
Recn Gd
The Highlands
Scallets Wood
Cemy
Works
Turkey Rd
CH
Bexhill High Sch
Highlands Cl
Uplands
Glenleigh Ave
Kingswood Ave
Glenleigh Ave
The Fairway
Broad View
Moleynes Mead
Fryatts Way
Primrose Hill
Roselands
Summer Hill Rd
Broadoak La
Squirrel Cl
Foxhill
Deerswood La
Broadoak
Byfields Croft
Bushy Croft
Hever Cres
Courthope Dr
Knebworth Rd
Warwick Rd
Dalmeny Rd
Redford
Colley Cnr
A259

TN39
Little Common
Recn Gd
St Marks Cl
The Twitten
Church Hill
White Hill
Little Common Rd
The Grove
White Hill Cl
Pinewoods
High Branches
Fairfield Chase
Belmaine Ct
Collington Park
Salvington Rd
Cranston Ave
Brampton Ave
Jasmine Way
Terminus Ave
Collington Wood
Normans
Normandale Ho
Saxons
Insley Ct

Barnhorn Rd
A259
The Broadwalk
Greyhorses
Kites Nest Wlk
Howards Cres
Sycamore
Oakleigh Rd
Village
Mulberry Cl
Prowting Mead
Barnhorne Manor
Barnhorne Farm
Cvn Pk
Cooden Wood

B2182
Cooden Sea Rd
Church Hill
Shepherd's La
Mayfield
Eastw
Little Common Prim Sch
Grenada Cl
Collington Gr
Birk Dale
Copse Rd
The Mead
Lake Ho
Collington Rise
Winston Dr
Bicton Gdns
Tanglewood Coppice

Cooden
Withyham Rd
Claremont Wlk
The Covert
Brackerne
Cosbench Cl
Ravens
Elsted Rd
Minsted Sq
Jevington
The Forges
The Chelgates
Westbourne Ct
Gatehouse Cl
Beaulieu Lodge
Beaulieu Rd
Hartfield Rd

Cooden Beach
Herbrand Wlk
Cole Stream
Cooden Dr
South Cliff
B2182
Mast
St Augustine's
Richmond Ave
Southcourt Ave
Pages Ave
South Cliff Ave

70 71 72

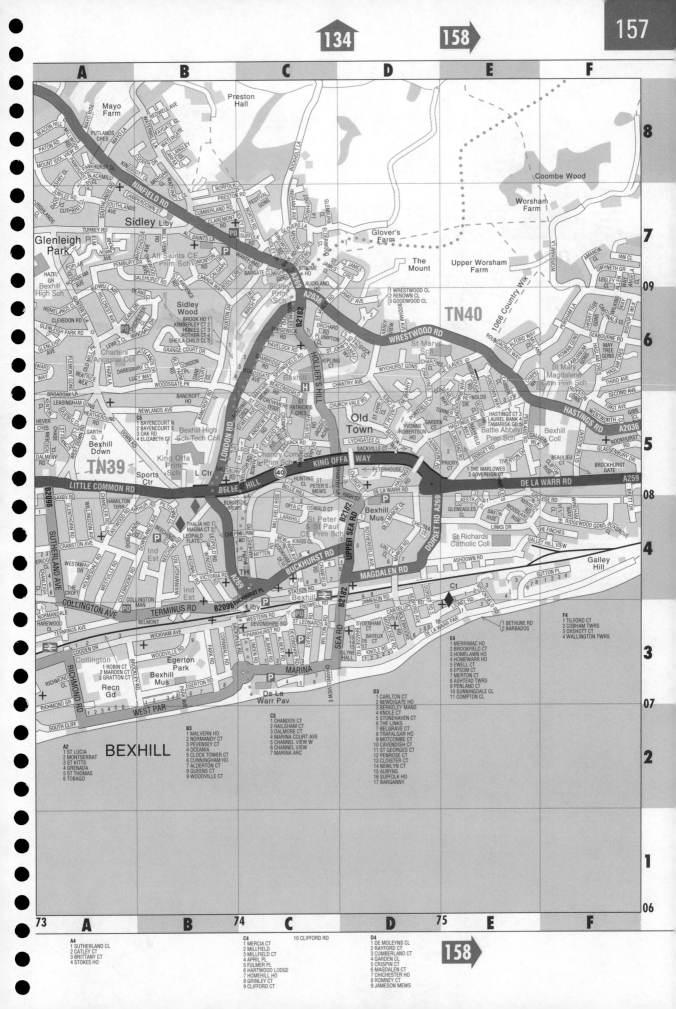

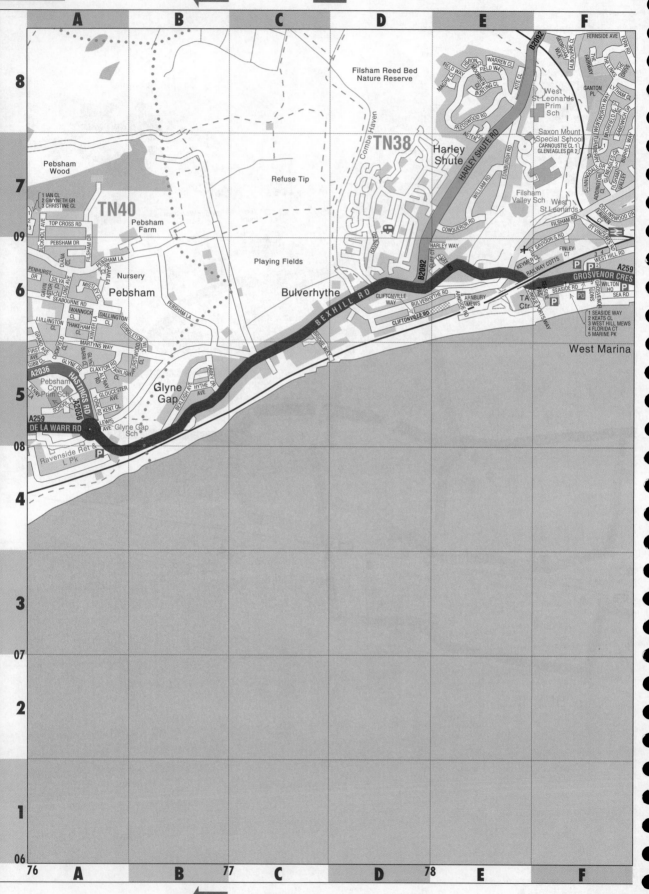

A B C D E F

8

7

09

6

5

08

4

3

07

2

1

06

Pebsham Wood

TN40

Pebsham Farm

Pebsham

Nursery

Glyne Gap

1 IAN CL
2 GWYNETH GR
3 CHRISTINE CL

TOP CROSS RD

PEBSHAM DR

PEBSHAM LA

DALLINGTON CL

MARTYNS WAY

HASTINGS RD

A2036

A2036

A259

DE LA WARR RD

Ravenside Ret & L Pk

Glyne Gap Sch

Pebsham Com Prim Sch

Filsham Reed Bed Nature Reserve

Refuse Tip

Playing Fields

Combe Haven

TN38

Harley Shute

Bulverhythe

BEXHILL RD

CLIFTONVILLE RD

CLIFTONVILLE WAY

BRIDGE WAY

BULVERHYTHE RD

West St Leonards Prim Sch

Saxon Mount Special School

CARNOUSTIE CL 1
GLENEAGLES DR 2

Filsham Valley Sch

West St Leonards

HARLEY SHUTE RD

WILLIAM RD

EDINBURGH RD

CONQUEROR RD

HARLEY WAY

B2092

B2092

HAVEN RD

CLIFF END

ST SAVIOUR'S RD

KEYMER CL

RAILWAY COTTS

FINLEY CT

TA Ctr

GROSVENOR CRES

WEST HILL RD

A259

SEASIDE RD

SEA RD

West Marina

FERNSIDE AVE

THE FAIRWAY

THE LINKS

THE DRIVE

GANTON PL

FIELD WAY

WARREN CL

KITE CL

1 SEASIDE WAY
2 KEATS CL
3 WEST HILL MEWS
4 FLORIDA CT
5 MARINE PK

76 A B 77 C D 78 E F

C7
1 STAINSBY ST
2 NORFOLK HO
3 ST RICHARDS HO
4 ROYAL TERR
5 EVERSFIELD MEWS N
6 ALAN CT

7 ASHLEY CT
8 ST MARY'S CT
9 CAVENDISH HO
10 DECIMUS BURTON WAY
11 UNION ST
12 MARLBOROUGH HO
13 BEAUFORT HO

14 ST GEORGES MOUNT
15 STOCKLEIGH CT
16 EVERSFIELD MEWS S
17 CHELSEA MEWS
18 ST MARYS COTTS
19 LOSER LA

F8
1 WATERWORKS COTTS
2 STONEFIELD PL
3 ELFORD ST
4 WALDEGRAVE ST
5 CORNWALLIS ST
6 ST ANDREW'S SQ

7 Robert Tressell Wkshps
8 QUEENS PAR
9 MIDDLE ST
10 KINGS WLK
11 PORTLAND COTTS
12 STONE ST
13 PORTLAND PL

14 WELLINGTON TERR
15 PORTLAND TERR
16 PORTLAND VILLAS
17 WELLINGTON HO
18 STATION RD
19 Priory Meadow
    S Ctr

D8
1 BAYEUX CT
2 DE CHAM AVE
3 ST CATHERINE'S CL
4 HELENSDENE WLK
5 ST PAUL'S CT

1 PRINCE'S RD
2 WARRIOR CT
3 EVERSFIELD CT
4 THE ALEXANDRA

C6
1 STANHOPE PL
2 HAROLD MEWS
3 SHEPHERD ST
4 MARINE CT
5 ST CLEMENTS PL
6 MOUNT PLEASANT
7 UNDERCLIFF TERR
8 MARKET TERR
9 MARKET PAS
10 GRAND CT

B6
1 CRABTREE HO
2 HIGHLANDS MEWS
3 ARCHERY CT
4 WEST HILL CT
5 COURTLANDS
6 SADDLER'S CT
7 ARCHIE CT
8 GREEBA CT
9 CONWAY CT

E7
1 HOLMEBURY HO
2 TRINITY VILLAS
3 TRINITY MEWS
4 WAVERLEY CT
5 SCHWERTE WAY
6 NORMAN CT
7 WHITE ROCK GDNS
8 ST MICHAEL'S PL
9 CLAREMONT
10 TRINITY ST
11 PALACE CT

E6
1 THE HERMITAGE
2 CLIFTON CT
3 HOLMESDALE TER

F7
1 ROBERTSON TERR
2 ALBANY CT
3 QUEEN'S AVE
4 YORK GDNS
5 YORK BLDGS
6 WELLINGTON PL
7 HOMEDANE HO
8 CASTLE ST
9 CASTLE GDNS

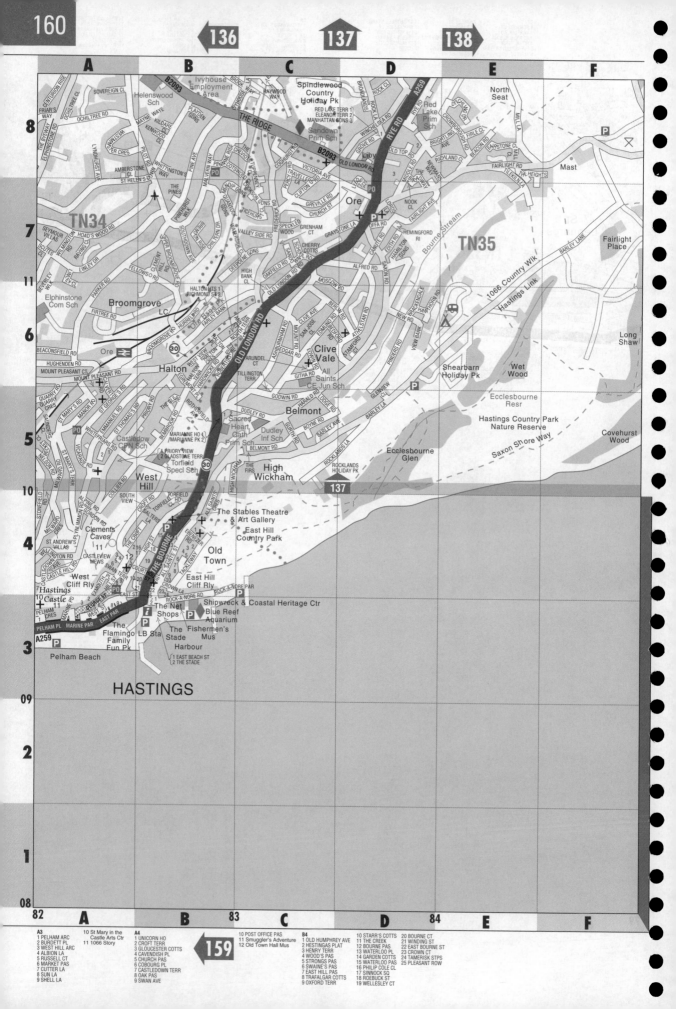

140

162

162

C8
1 LONEY CT
2 FRASER CT
3 MILWARD CT
4 PENSTONE CT
5 JULIAN CT
6 WILMOT CT

7 OSBORNE CT
8 HOLMBUSH CL
9 DOWNES CL
10 ADUR CT
11 BROADWAY CL
12 WISTON CT
13 ARUN CT

C8
14 ARUNDEL CT
15 RECTORY CT
16 CAIUS CT
17 KINGSTON CT

E7
1 SCHOOL CL
2 TWITTEN CL
3 GREEN CL
4 GREEN CT
5 WATLING CL
6 SPRING GDNS

7 STATION RD
8 WATLING CT
9 GRANGE CT
10 LOCKS CT
11 COATES CT
12 ROCK CL
13 CHANNEL VIEW

14 SEA HO

A6
1 NORTH POINT
2 ST NICHOLAS PL
3 ST MARYS PL
4 SUSSEX CT
5 THE QUAY
6 EAST POINT
7 KING JOHN CT
8 WEST POINT
9 SOUTH POINT
10 KING CHARLES PL
11 MAYFLOWER CT
12 BEACH CT
13 WATERS EDGE

B6
1 BLUEBIRD CL
2 BONAVENTURE
3 HOPEWELL CL
4 NEWPORT
5 BLESSING LODGE
6 SORLINGS REACH
7 DUNWICH
8 SEAFORD AVE
9 HASTINGS CT
10 HARRIET PL
11 GOSPORT CT

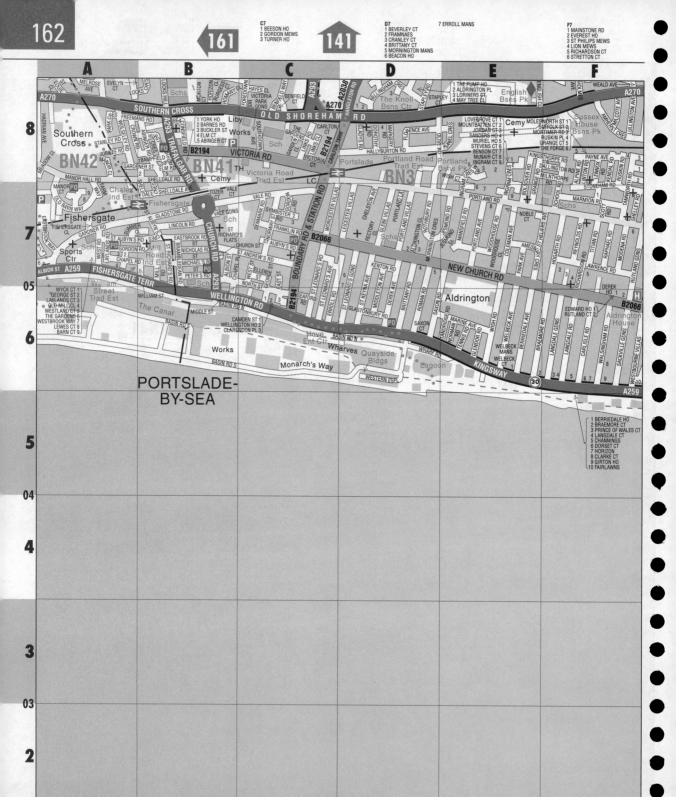

C7
1 BEESON HO
2 GORDON MEWS
3 TURNER HO

D7
1 BEVERLEY CT
2 FRAMNAES
3 CRANLEY CT
4 BRITTANY CT
5 MORNINGTON MANS
6 BEACON HO

7 ERROLL MANS

F7
1 MAINSTONE RD
2 EVEREST HO
3 ST PHILIPS MEWS
4 LION MEWS
5 RICHARDSON CT
6 STRETTON CT

PORTSLADE-BY-SEA

142

164

B7
1 CONWAY CT
2 CLARENDON HO
3 ELLEN HO
4 GOLDSTONE HO
5 LIVINGSTONE HO
6 CLIFTONVILLE CT
7 STEYNING CT
8 BRAMBER CT
9 EATON CT
10 GRANVILLE CT
11 HADDINGTON ST
12 MALVERN ST

C7
1 DEVONSHIRE CT
2 CORNWALL CT
3 SOMERSET CT
4 JANESTON CT
5 STIRLING CT
6 BRECON CT
7 ELIZABETH CT
8 PHILIP CT
9 BALTIMORE CT
10 DRIVE LODGE
11 EATON MANOR
12 VERIC
13 VALVERDE HO
14 VALENTINE CT
15 HEREFORD CT
16 GAINSBOROUGH HO
17 EATON GATE
18 CHARIS CT
19 EATON HALL
20 EATON GDNS MANS

C7
21 VANBRUGH CT

D7
1 COWDRAY CT
2 GOODWOOD CT
3 CROMWELL CT
4 WILLOW CT

D7
5 KINSALE CT
6 PALMEIRA HO
7 BELLMEAD
8 AMBER CT
9 CONISTON CT
10 SOMERHILL CT
11 CHIDDINGLY HO
12 BERESFORD CT
13 PARHAM HO
14 PETWORTH HO
15 BODIHAM HO
16 THE GALLERIES
17 VISAGE

A8
1 Hove Tech Ctr
2 St Josephs Bsns Pk
3 St Josephs Trad Est
4 WOODS HO
5 SHERIDAN MANS

A7
1 BYRON TERR
2 MONTGOMERY TERR
3 TENNYSON CT

A6
1 BLENHEIM CT
2 PEMBROKE CT
3 WENDOVER GRANGE
4 AYMER HO
5 DOLPHIN CT
6 PRINCES CT
7 VALLANCE CT
8 HOVE MANOR
9 FAIRLAWNS
10 VICEROY LODGE
11 BLUEBIRD CT
12 LANCASTER CT
13 ST AUBYN'S GDNS
14 MATTHEW HO

B5
1 ST CATHERINE'S TERR
2 THE PRIORY
3 ALBANY TWRS
4 HAMILTON MANS
5 OLIVER HO
6 VICTORIA TERR
7 VERNER HO
8 ALBEMARLE MANS
9 VICTORIA COTTS
10 BENHAM CT
11 SPA CT
12 COURTENAY TERR

B6
1 GROSVENOR MANS
2 COPTHORNE CT
3 NORMANDY HO
4 GRAND AVENUE MANS
5 COOMBE LEA
6 VICTORIA GR
7 VICTORIA GR
8 HAREWOOD CT
9 WILBURY GRANGE
10 THE AMBASSADORS
11 BOWEN CT
12 GROVE CT
13 WILBURY LODGE
14 ASHDOWN
15 SUSSEX CT
16 THE ATHENAEUM
17 SANDRINGHAM LODGE
18 HATFIELD CT
19 SALISBURY CT
20 AMBER CT
21 AVENUE CT
22 PALMEIRA MANS
23 ST JOHN'S PL
24 LANSDOWNE CT
25 PALMEIRA AVENUE MANS

B6
1 LORRAINE CT
2 PARNELL CT
4 DURHAM CT
5 WINDSOR LODGE

C6
1 MARLBOROUGH CT

D5
1 LANSDOWNE SQ
2 ALICE CL
3 BRUNSWICK MEWS
4 DONKEY MEWS
5 UPPER MARKET ST
6 LOWER MARKET ST
7 KERRISON MEWS
8 CHAPEL MEWS
9 WATERLOO HO
10 EMBASSY CT
11 GOLDEN LA
12 CAVENDISH MEWS
13 IVY MEWS
14 CROSS ST
15 FARMAN ST
16 DUDLEY MEWS
17 OLD MARKET COTTS

D6
1 CROWN CL
2 PALM CT
3 GWYDYR MANS
4 ROCHESTER CL
5 ROCHESTER CT
6 ST ANNES WELL HO
7 LANSDOWNE MEWS
8 THE COURTYARD
9 PALMEIRA GRANDE
10 GOLDSMID MEWS
11 LANSDOWNE MANS

E5
1 LITTLE WESTERN ST
2 DORCHESTER CT
3 NORFOLK PL
4 NORFOLK CT
5 NORFOLK BLDGS
6 NORFOLK MEWS
7 KINGSLEY CT
8 CAVENDISH HO
9 BEDFORD TWRS
10 ASTRA HO
11 ABBOTTS
12 METROPOLE CT
13 SUSSEX HTS
14 RUSSELL MEWS
15 REGENCY MEWS
16 FRED EMERY CT
17 SILWOOD PL
18 OSPREY HO
19 SILWOOD CT
20 SILLWOOD HALL
21 WESTERN TERR
22 SILLWOOD TERR
23 MITRE HO
24 HAMPTON ST
25 MONTPELLIER APARTMENTS
26 BURLEIGH CT
27 CASTLE MEWS

E6
1 WORCESTER CT
2 KENYA CT
3 VERNON CT
4 VERNON GDNS
5 BELVEDERE TERR
6 VICTORIA PL
7 HAMPTON TERR
8 HEATHER CT
9 MONTPELLIER LODGE
10 BOUNDARY PAS
11 BRAEMAR HO
12 YORK MANSIONS W
13 YORK MANSIONS E
14 TEMPLE HEIGHTS
15 WINDLESHAM HO
16 WINDLESHAM HALL

E7
1 WESTCOMBE
2 PRESTONVILLE CT
3 CADOGAN CT
4 BELMONT CT
5 ST ANNS MANS
6 BERKELEY CT
7 DERBY CT
8 WARWICK CT
9 RICHMOND CT
10 MARSTON CT
11 LORRAINE CT
12 CHESTER CT
13 YORK CT
14 WINDLESHAM CT
15 PAVILION CT
16 WESTMORLAND CT
17 WINDLESHAM MANS

F8
1 STANFORD CT
2 WELLEND VILLAS
3 PRESTON MANS
4 PARK GATE
5 PASTON HO

HOVE

BRIGHTON

BN3

BN1

West Pier
(dis)

King Alfred
(Swimming Pool
& Sports Ctr)

Sussex Cty
Cricket Gd

The
Brighton
Ctr

164

For full street detail of the
highlighted area see
page 189.

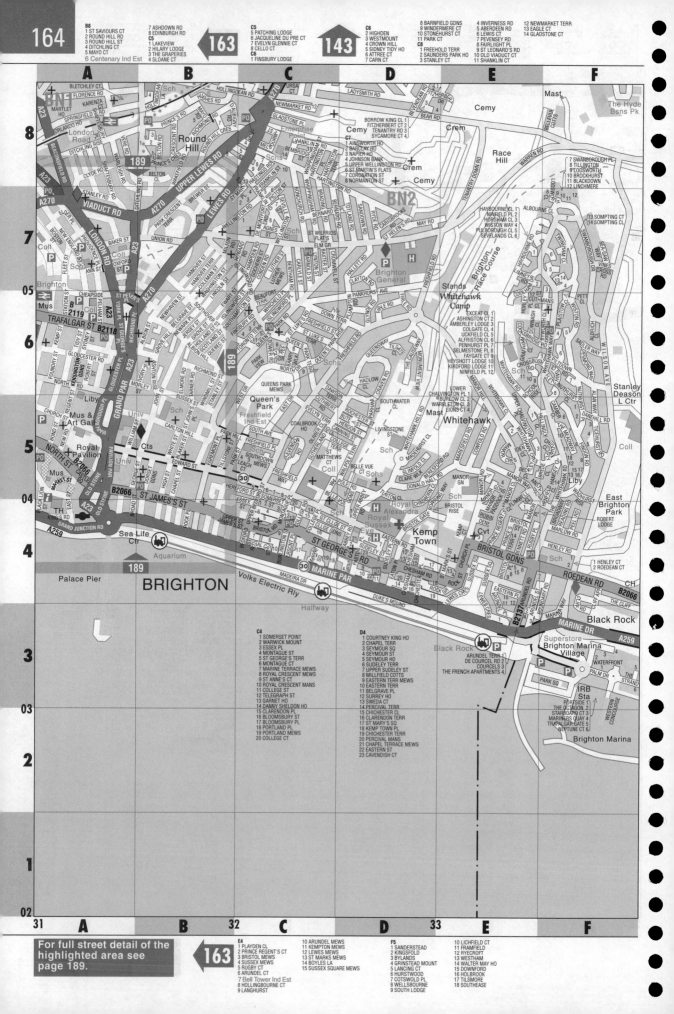

163

143

BRIGHTON

BN2

BN1

For full street detail of the highlighted area see page 189.

163

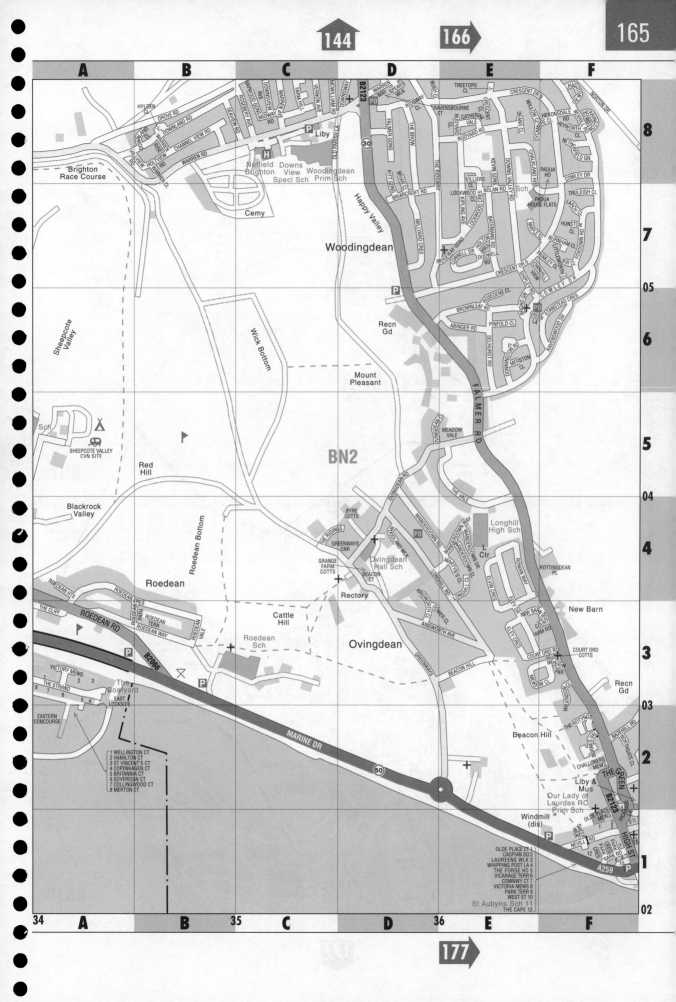

A B C D E F

8

Standean
Bottom

Whiteway
Bottom

Pickers Hill

Heathy
Brow

7

The Bostle

Monument

05

6

Highdole Hill

BN7

5

Balsdean
Farm

Balsdean
Cottages

High Hill

04

177

Pickers Hill
Farm

Telscombe
Tye

4

BN2

Coombe Bottom

Nursery

Coombe
Farm

Looes
Barn

WALDEGRAVE
CT

Westfield
Ave

COOMBE
MDW

3

WIVELSFIELD RD

TUMULUS RD

PERRY HILL

RIDGEWOOD AVE

VALE RD

STAMMER

HAILSHAM
AVE

WESTFIELD AVE N

WESTFIELD RISE

COOMBE
RISE

COOMBE VALE N

03

BAZEHILL
MANOR

BAZEHILL RD

WELLSMERE RD

GORHAM AVE

LUSTRELLS RD

DEAN COURT RD

PALMER AVE

BISHOPSTONE DR

WINTON AVE

SAXON

HILGROVE RD

HEMPSTEAD RD

ARLINGTON GDNS

HEATHFIELD AVE

GREENBANK AVE

Tenant Hill

1 CHALLONERS CL
2 TUDOR CL
3 DEAN CL

Pedlersburgh

2

NORTHFIELD
RISE

Whiteway La

Rottingdean

St Margarets
CE Sch

WESTMESTON AVE

CHORLEY AVE

LUSTRELLS CL

LUSTRELLS VALE

REMO LA

HAWTHORN

BLUNDESDANE

PALMER AVE

STRELLS CRES

CHILTINGTON WAY

CHILTINGTON

SALTDEAN VALE

MOUNT DR

GLYNDE AVE

SHEPHAM AVE

Saltdean
Prim Sch

Saltdean

HOMEBUSH AVE

ROOMEY AVE

RYE CL

IFIELD CL

1 SCHOOL LA
2 MAYFIELD CT
3 WESTBROOK
4 SOUTHDOWNS CT

1 MARINE CT
2 KIPLING CT
3 HIGHCLIFF CT
4 ST MARGARETS
5 OCEAN REACH

STEYNING RD

KNOLL AND CRES

GRAND

CHALEY AVE

NEWLANDS RD

FOUNTHILL RD

LENHAM RD

ASHDOWN AVE

FOUNTHILL DR W

SALTDEAN DR

CHICHESTER DR W

ARUNDEL DR E

CHICHESTER DR E

LINCHMERE AVE

CORSIDGE AVE

BEVENDEAN AVE

HARTFIELD RD

BANNINGS VALE

DALLEY CL

NORTHWOOD AVE

ASSBURY CRES

FINDON AVE

Telscombe Tye

The
Twitten

ST
AUBYN'S

MEAD

CHALEY AVE

TYE PARK

CRANLEIGH AVE

TYE CRES

Saltdean
Park

CHICHESTER
CL

WITHYHAM AVE

NUTLEY AVE

OAKLANDS AVE

CROWBOROUGH RD

HAMSEY
RD

ASHURST AVE

LEWES CL

BN10

1

HIGH ST

A259

ROMNEY RD

LENHAM RD W

EILEEN AVE

FREDERIC
HO

MARINE CL

ABBOTSBURY
CL

SALTDEAN PARK

Liby

WICKLANDS AVE

HOMERIDGE HO

BRAMBLETYNE AVE

02

MARINE DR

A259

GREENWAY CT

37

A B 38 C D 39 E F

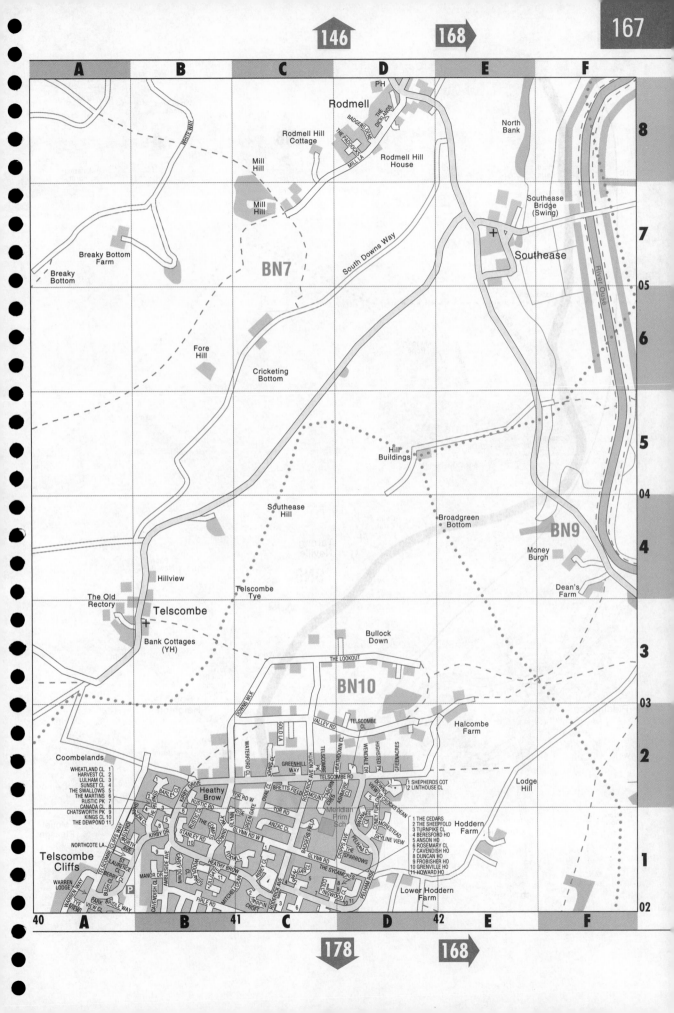

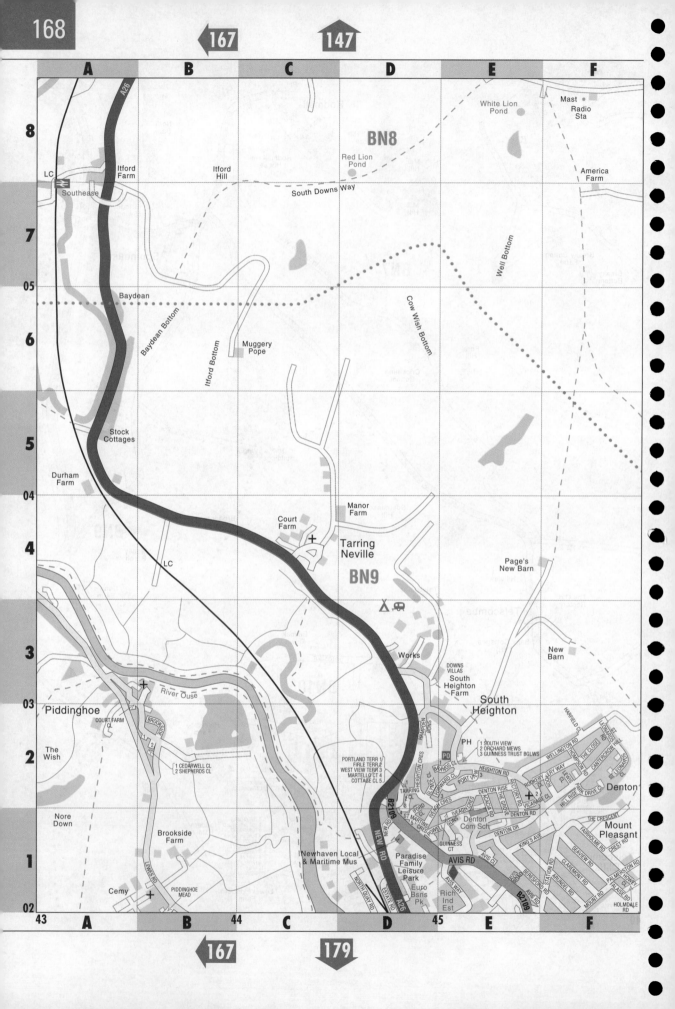

A   **B**   **C**   **D**   **E**   **F**

8

BN8

White Lion
Pond

Mast
Radio
Sta

LC
Itford Farm
Itford Hill
Red Lion
Pond

America
Farm

Southease

South Downs Way

7

Well Bottom

05

Baydean

6

Baydean Bottom

Itford Bottom

Muggery
Pope

Cow Wish Bottom

5

Stock
Cottages

04

Durham
Farm

Manor
Farm

Court
Farm

Tarring
Neville

Page's
New Barn

4

LC

BN9

New
Barn

3

Works

DOWNS
VILLAS
South
Heighton
Farm

03

Piddinghoe

South
Heighton

Court Farm
CL

Harfield

The
Wish

River Ouse

1 CEDARWELL CL
2 SHEPHERDS CL

PH

1 SOUTH VIEW
2 ORCHARD MEWS
3 GUINNESS TRUST BGLWS

Denton

2

Nore
Down

PORTLAND TERR 1
FIRLE TERR 2
WEST VIEW TERR 3
MARTELLO CT 4
COTTAGE CL 5

PO

Mount
Pleasant

THE CRESCENT

Brookside
Farm

Newhaven Local
& Maritime Mus

Denton
Com Sch

1

B2109

NEW RD

Paradise
Family
Leisure
Park

GUINNESS
CT

AVIS RD

Cemy

Piddinghoe
Mead

NORTH QUAY RD

ESTATE RD

A26

Euro
Bsns
Pk

Rich
Ind Est

AVIS WAY

B2109

HOLMDALE
RD

02

A   43   **B**   44   **C**   **D**   45   **E**   **F**

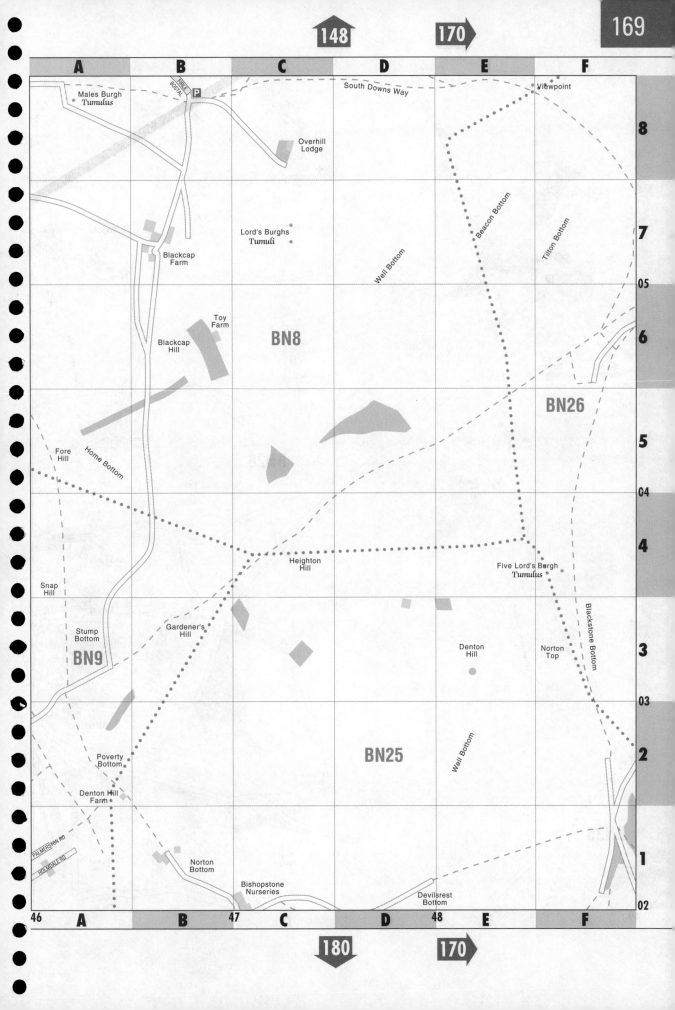

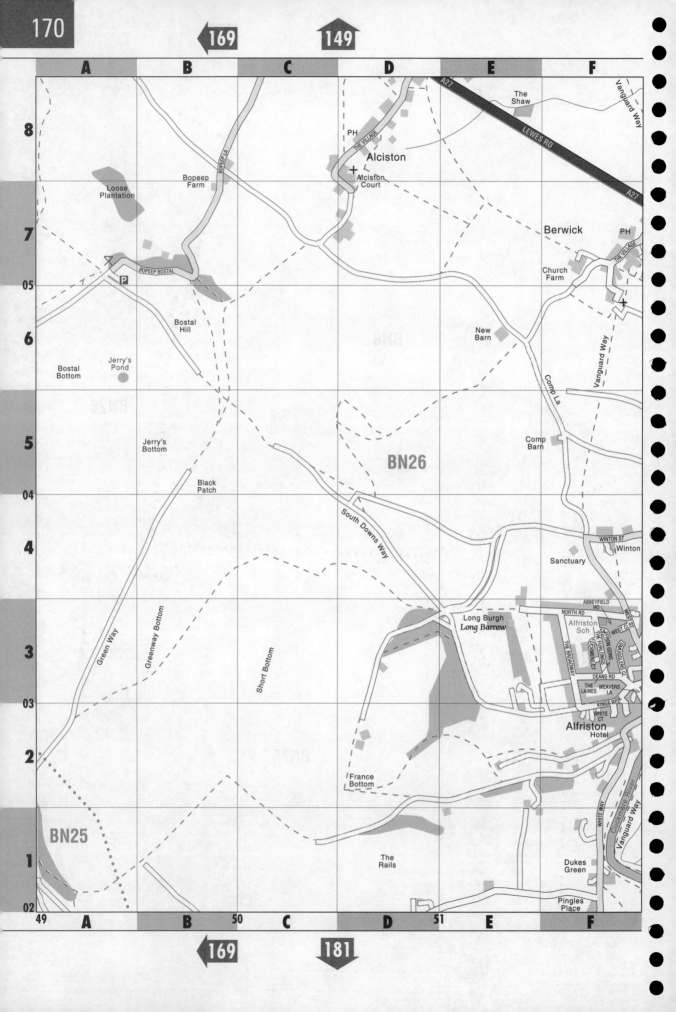

A B C D E F

8

Loose
Plantation

Bopeep
Farm

BOPEEP LA

PH

THE VILLAGE

Alciston

Alciston
Court

The
Shaw

Vanguard Way

A27

LEWES RD

A27

7   Berwick   PH

THE VILLAGE

Church
Farm

05   Bopeep Bostal

P

Bostal
Hill

New
Barn

Vanguard Way

6   Bostal
Bottom

Jerry's
Pond

BN26

Comp La

Comp
Barn

5   Jerry's
Bottom

BN26

South Downs Way

04   Black
Patch

WINTON ST

Winton

4   Sanctuary

Long Burgh
Long Barrow

ABBEYFIELD
HO

NORTH RD   WEST ST
WEST CL

Alfriston
Sch

THE FURLONGS
SAFFRON GDNS
MAGGLERS CL
COOMBE CT

Green Way

Greenway Bottom

Short Bottom

THE BROADWAY

DEANS RD

THE
LAINES
WEAVERS
LA

KINGS RIDE

3

03   WHITE
CT

Alfriston
Hotel

2   France
Bottom

WHITE WAY

Cuckmere River

Vanguard Way

BN25

1   The
Rails

Dukes
Green

Pingles
Place

02

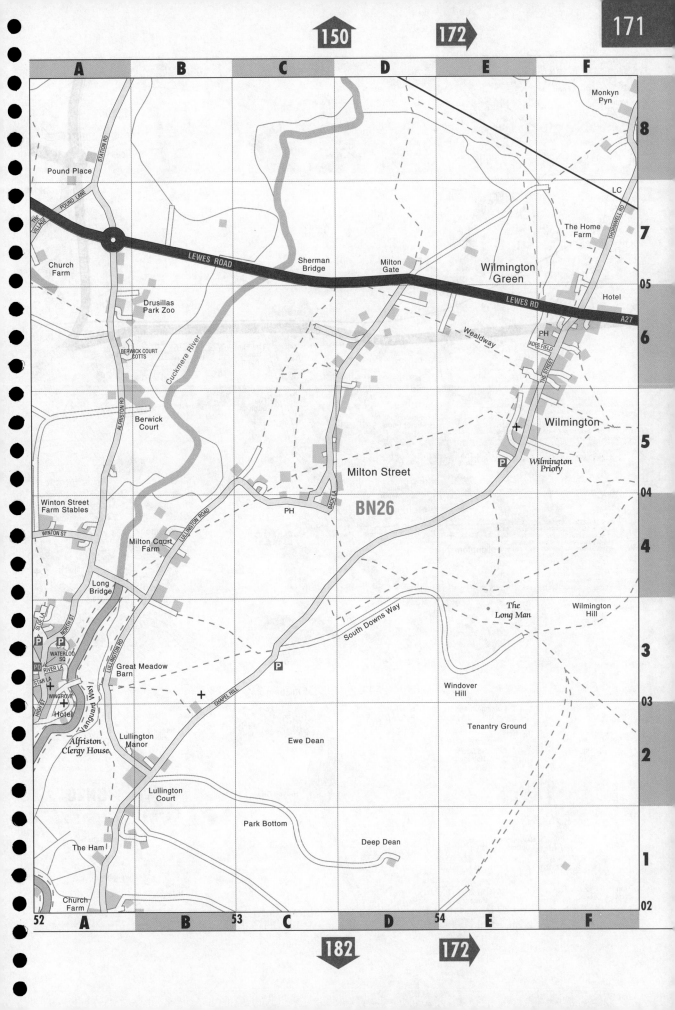

A B C D E F

8

7

05

6

THORNWELL RD
Monkyn Pyn
Warren Farm

Hide Farm

Cophall Farm

A22

BAY TREE LA

Cop Hall

A22

A27

B2247

POLEGATE BY-PASS

HAILSHAM RD

Wootton Manor

St Leonards Terr

SAYERLAND RD

GUARDIAN CT

BROOKSIDE AVE

VICTORIA AVE

UPLOCK CT

PLAZA

MANOR RD

BROOK ST

GOSFORD WAY

GRAND PAR 1
THE BERNHARD BARON COTTAGE HOMES 2

Newbarn Farm

A27

LEWES RD

A27

A2270

OLD DR

SOUTHDOWN CT

The Flint House Farm

HYPERION AVE

SUNSTAR LA

GAINSBOROUGH LA

GOLDEN MILLER LA

BRAHAM RD 1

BROWN JACK AVE

REYNOLDSTOWN LA

2

SHAD

The Stud Farm

Puddingham Wood

Folkington Manor Farm

The Rough

BERNHARD RD

BARONS WAY

NORTHFIELD

WANNOCK DR

Recn Gd

5

The Links

Wannock Coppice

WANNOCK RD

SOUTHFIELD

GROSVENOR CL

THE MILLARDS

MAYFAIR GDNS

FARMLANDS WAY

04

The Holt

Folkington Manor

MILLSTREAM GDNS

PADDOCK GDNS

FARMLANDS AVE

Wannock

LANCING WAY

MORTIMER GDNS

GLEN CL

BN26

Willingdon Com Sch

CORN HILL GDNS

MILL LA

BROAD RD

BROOK CL

4

Folkington

+

MILL CL

WANNOCK CL

WANNOCK AVE

Folkington Bottom

Middle Brow

MILL WAY

BROADWATER MEWS

HONEYWAY CL

GLEN COTS

FILCHING CL

WANNOCK LA

WANNOCK CL

THE PARAGON

THE GROVE

3

Cranedown Bottom

Crane Down

WAYFARING DOWN

Filching

03

Folkington Hill

WEALDWAY

Ash Farm

JEVINGTON RD

Dean Wood

Filching Manor Mofor Mus

Hanging Hill

Willingdon Links

2

Hill Barn

Teddard's Bottom

Helling Down

BN20

1066 Country Walk

1

SOUTH DOWNS WAY

Hayward's Bottom

The Combe

Wealdway

Holt Brow

JEVINGTON HOLT

Holt Bottom

GREEN LA

Combe Hill

02

55 A B 56 C D 57 E F

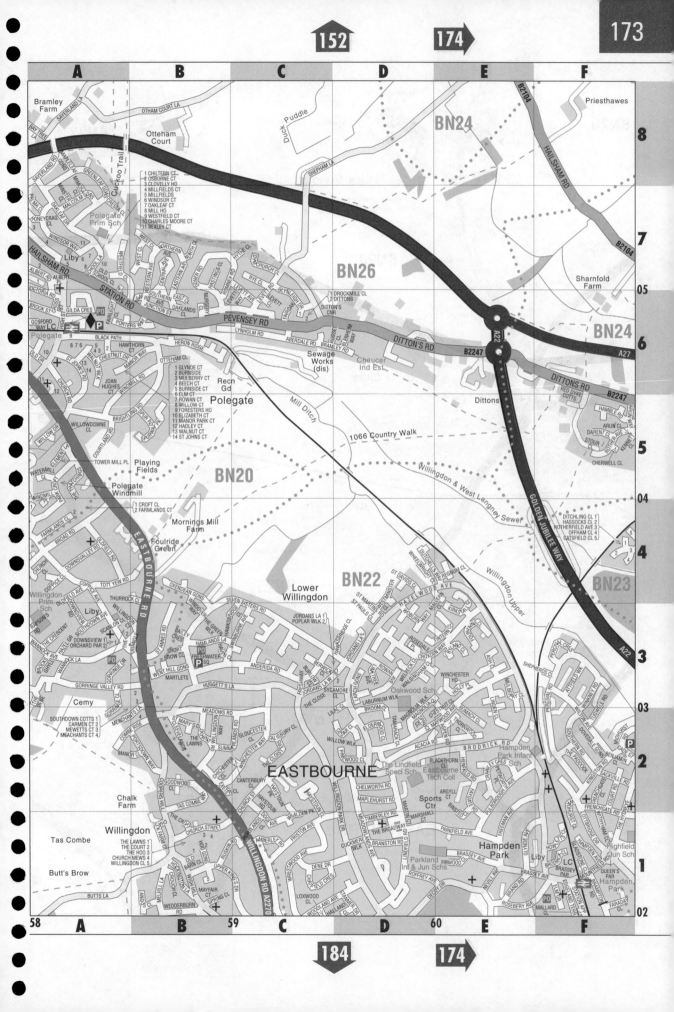

← 173
153

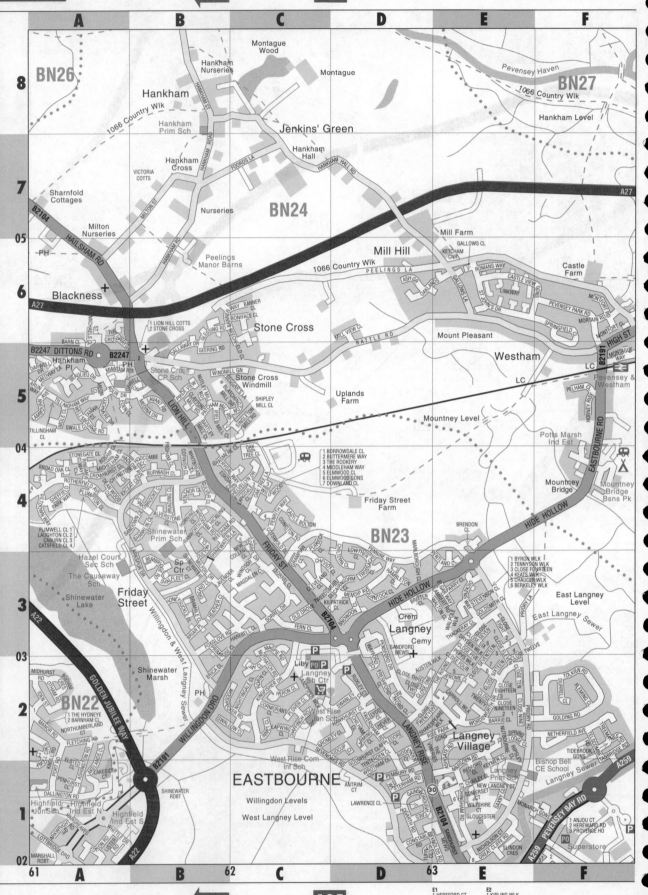

← 173
185

E1
1 HEREFORD CT
2 STAFFORD CT
3 RUTLAND CT
4 WARWICK CT
5 WORCESTER CT
6 HAMPSHIRE CT
7 WILLIAMS CT
8 PRIORY ORCH

E2
1 KIPLING WLK
2 BOSWELL WLK
3 SHELLEY WLK
4 CLOSE TWENTYFOUR
5 BROWNING WLK
6 CLOSE FIFTEEN
7 COLERIDGE WLK

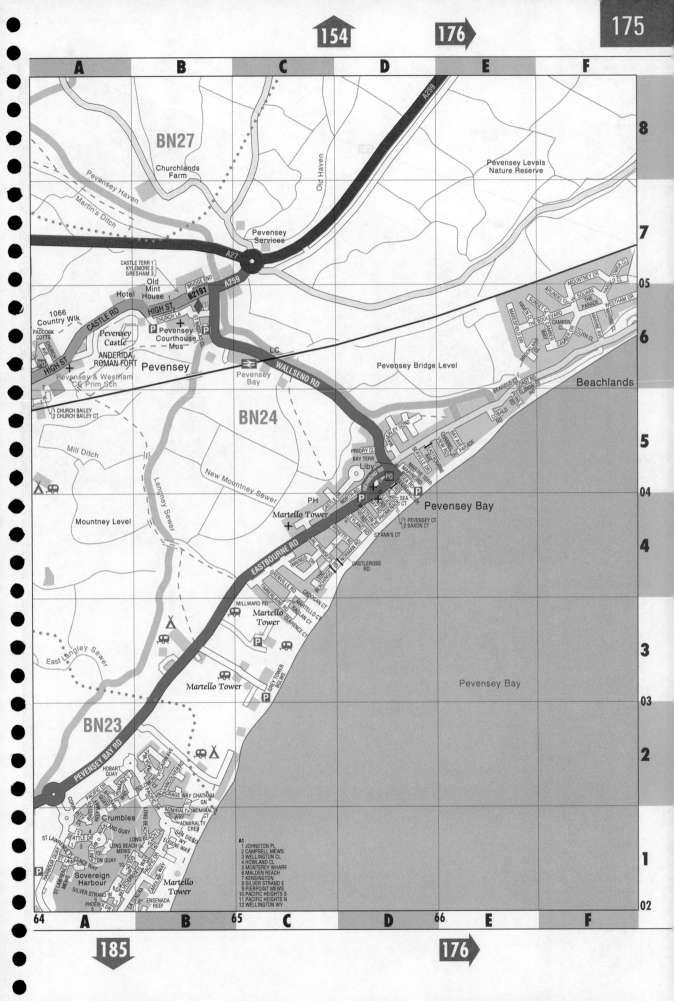

154
176
185
176

BN27

Churchlands Farm

Pevensey Haven

Martin's Ditch

A27

Pevensey Services

Old Haven

A259

Pevensey Levels Nature Reserve

CASTLE TERR 1
KYLEMORE 2
GRESHAM 3

Old Mint House 1

Hotel

BRIDGE END

A259

B2191

1066 Country Wlk

PADDOCK COTTS

CASTLE RD

HIGH ST

CHURCH LA

ST THOMAS CL

Pevensey Castle

ANDERIDA ROMAN FORT

Pevensey Courthouse Mus

Pevensey

HIGH ST

Pevensey & Westham CE Prim Sch

1 CHURCH BAILEY
2 CHURCH BAILEY CT

LC

Pevensey Bay

WALLSEND RD

Pevensey Bridge Level

Beachlands

ARUNDEL CL
MOUNTNEY DR
HARBOUR TOWER CL
THE SQUARE
THE PARADE
WESTHAM DR
MARINE CL
MARINE AVE
HAVEN CL
SUNSET CL
THE BOULEVARD
CAMBER CL
MARESFIELD RD
BROOKLAND
CAMBER WAY
CAMBER DR
SOUTH CL

BEXFIELD CL
COAST RD
OLD MERE HO
COBALD RD

BN24

Mill Ditch

New Mountney Sewer

Langney Sewer

PRIORY CL
BAY TERR
Liby

WAVERLEY GDNS

SEAVILLE DRI
EASTBOURNE
VIEW RD
BAY AVE
THE PARADE
EASTBOURNE
MARINE RD

SEA RD
PO
MARINE TERR

PH

Martello Tower

CASTLE DR
NORTH RD
RICHMOND RD

P
WESTERN
BAY TERR
THE PROMENADE
SEA CT

Pevensey Bay

EASTBOURNE RD

CASTLE OR
EYLAND RD
ROSETTI RD
NORMAN RD
VAL PRINSEP RD
INNINGS DR
THE BEACHINGS

ST ANN'S CT

1 PEVENSEY CT
2 SAXON CT

CASTLEROSS RD

Mountney Level

GRENVILLE RD
TIMBERLAINE RD
MARTELLO RD
RAGLAN CT
CADOGAN CT
CLARENCE CT

MILLWARD RD

Martello Tower

P

East Langley Sewer

Martello Tower

P

GREY TOWER BGLWS

Pevensey Bay

03

BN23

PEVENSEY BAY RD

HOBART QUAY
PACIFIC DR
PITCAIRN AVE
SOLOMON
VANCOUVER RD
ANCHORAGE WAY
CHATHAM
ADMIRALTY CT
ADMIRALTY WAY
ADMIRALTY CRES
SAN DIEGO
GN

Crumbles

CORAL REEF WY
SEATTLE DR
BRITTANY
LONG BEACH CL
EUGENE WAY
SAN DIEGO WY

ST LAWRENCE CT
HARBOUR QUAY
ST LAWRENCE WAY
ST LAWRENCE MEWS
LONG BEACH MEWS
BELVEDERE DR
CAROLINE WAY

Sovereign Harbour

SILVER STRAND W
LA SPEZIA
PHOENIX DR

Martello Tower

ENSENADA REEF

P

A1
1 JOHNSTON PL
2 CAMPBELL MEWS
3 WELLINGTON CL
4 HOWLAND CL
5 MONTEREY WHARF
6 MALDEN REACH
7 KENSINGTON
8 SILVER STRAND E
9 PIERPOINT MEWS
10 PACIFIC HEIGHTS S
11 PACIFIC HEIGHTS N
12 WELLINGTON WY

64   65   66

185   176

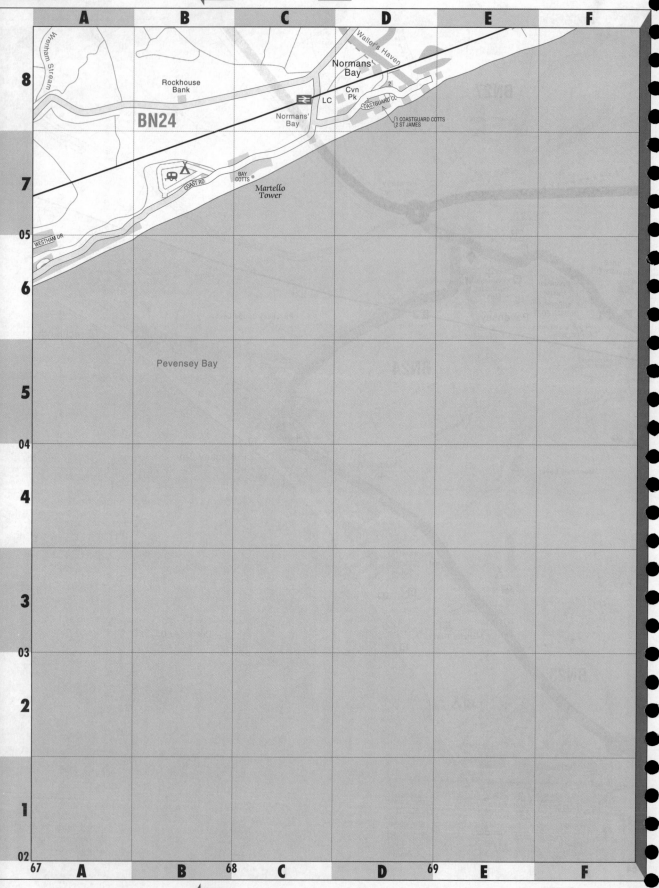

| | A | B | C | D | E | F |

BN10

Telscombe Cliffs Prim Sch

Telscombe Cliffs

Grassmere CT

WARREN WAY
PARK VIEW
PARK AVE N
TELSCOMBE CLIFFS WAY
CLIFTON WAY
CHATSWORTH AVE
ST PETER'S AVE
AMBLESIDE AVE
CENTRAL AVE
LEA RD
ROWE AVE N
SUTTON AVE N
CAVELL AVE N
RODERICK AVE
EDITH AVE N
ROSEMARY CL
FIRLE RD
CINQUE FOIL
BRAMBER BEE RD
VIEW RD
CINQUE FOIL
THE PKWY

BALCOMBE RD
ST DAVID'S CT
Hoddern County Jun Sch
Peacehaven Com Sch
BRAMBER CL
SOUTHVIEW RD
WORSHAM AVE N
DOROTHY AVE
BRAMBER AVE N

C Ctr

Third RD
Second RD
A259

HOWARD CT
Liby
L Ctr
Peacehaven Inf Sch

1 BALCOMBE CT
2 Meridian Ctr
3 RODERICK CT
The Meridian Ind Est

Peacehaven

GOLBY CT
THE ESPLANADE
PROMENADE

1 GREENACRES
2 DANA LODGE
3 CHANNEL GRANGE
4 AMBLESIDE CT
5 MARSDEN CT
6 FINCH CT

CAVELL AVE

MARGARET CT 1
FAIRFIELD 2
HOMECOAST HO 3
PARK CT 4
JUBILEE CT 5
CAVELL CT 6
FITZALAN CT 7

CRESTA CT 1
DORITA CT 2
LURELAND CT 3

ARUNDEL ROAD CENTRAL
GREENWICH WAY
JASON CL
NEWTON RD
HOYLE RD
RAZOR CT
DAMON CL
Curzy Units

ARUNDEL RD
PIDDINGHOE CL
Friar's Bay

SOUTH COAST RD

A259

30

Peacehaven Heights

Chene Gap

Friars' Bay

Motel
THE HIGHWAY
Cvn Site

LINCOLN AVE S
CARO AVE
MALINES AVE S
PHYLLIS AVE
ROWE AVE
PROMENADE
RODERICK AVE
EDITH AVE
HORSHAM AVE
DOROTHY AVE
BRAMBER AVE
STEYNING AVE
VICTORIA AVE
BOLNEY AVE
CAPEL AVE
KEYMER AVE
SLINDON AVE
MAYFIELD AVE
PIDDINGHOE AVE
GLADYS AVE
SUNVIEW AVE
SEAVIEW AVE
SOUTHDOWN AVE
VERNON AVE
FRIARS AVE
CORNWALL AVE
SEARLE AVE
ROUNDHAY AVE
ASHINGTON GDNS
DOWNLAND AVE
COSSBURY AVE
CLIFF PARK
CHICHESTER CL
CLIFF AVE
TUDOR AVE
ROSE PK
MOAT CL
CHENE RD
THE LEAS
OUTLOOK AVE

AQUARIUS CL
SLINDON CL
NEVILLE RD
BAYVIEW RD
YORK RD
JAY RD
WELLINGTON RD
PARK RD
PROM

40 41 42

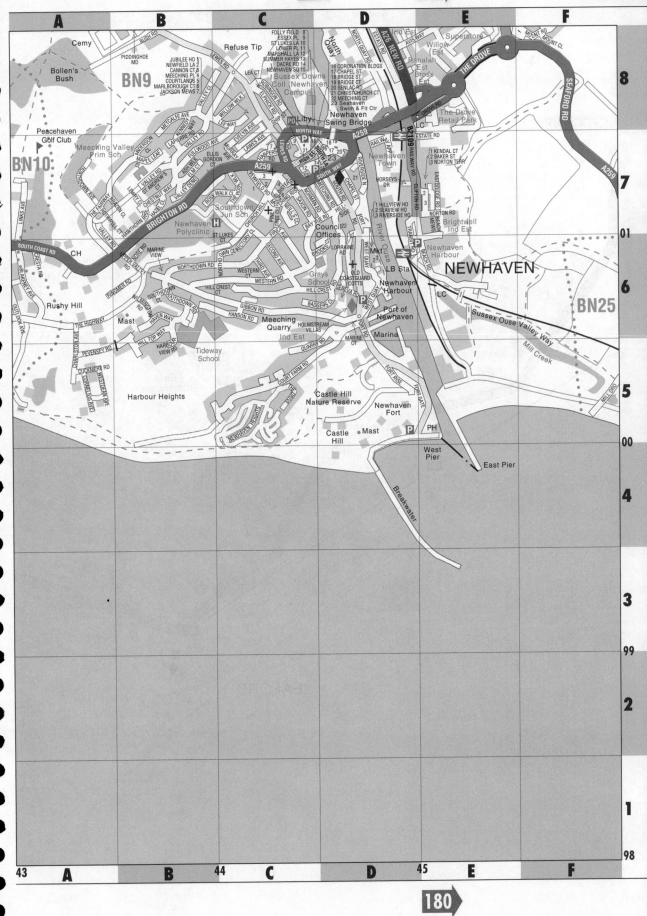

A   B   C   D   E   F

Norton

Norton Farm

Beacon Hill

Blackstone Barn

Foxhole Farm

BN9

Stud Farm

New Barn

Bullocks Barn

A259

SEAFORD RD

Bishopstone Manor Farm

Bishopstone Hill

Rookery Hill

Rosemount Rise
St Margaret's Rise
Holmes Cl
Seagrave Cl
Beneagles Cl
Troon Cl
Elizabeth Cl
Hurdis Rd
Edward Rd
Ireland Cl
Windsor Cl
Viking Cl
Harbour View Cl
St Andrews Dr
Roman Cl
Norman Cl
Antony Cl
Hanover Cl
Rochford Way
Rookery Way
Marine Dr

Bishopstone

BN25

Grand Ave

Whiteway Cl
Flint Cl
Crown Hill
The Lords
Duchess Dr
Royal Dr
Bowden Rise
Lexden Rd
Gorse Dr
Seaford Way
Chalvington Cl
CH

Newhaven Rd

MILL DRO
LC
Tide Mills

Hill Rise

Motel

Bishopstone

Hawth Valley
Hawth Rise
Station Rd
Hawth Cl
Hawth Park Rd
Hawth Cres
Hawth Way
Hawth Gr
Hawth Pl

BUCKLE BY-PASS

Clementine Ave
Churchill Rd
Caroline Cl
Dikes Cl
Charles Cl
Beacon Cl
Isabel
Pearce Way
Katherine Way
Alexandra Cl
Adelaide Cl
Princess Dr
Victor Cl
Beacon Dr
Regents Cl
Firle Cl
Carlton Cl
Kings Ride
Buckingham Cl
Kings Mead
Princes Cl
Kingsmead
Kim
Carlton Cl Way
Hamilton Ho
Belgrave Rd
Clinton La
St Peter's Rd
The Barn Ho
North Camp La
Upper Belgrave Rd
St Elizabeth's Cl
Pinewood
Morningside Cl
Homefield Cl
Rose Wlk
Mason Rd
Old Ben Home
Northcliffe

East Blatchington

St Johns Sch & Coll
Firle Grange
The Holt
The Holters
Northfield Rd
The Ridings
Offham Cl
Lexden Rd
Belgrave Cl
Lower Dr
North Way
Lucinda Way

1 Blatchington Hill Flats
2 Pine Cl

West Down Rd
Kingsway
Surrey Rd
Buckthorn Way
Bishops Cl
Buckle Dr
Kimberley Rd
Beach Cotts
Queens Park
Claremont Rd
High Beach Ho
Albany Rd
Marine Ct
Edinburgh Rd
Beach Rd
Belgrave Rd
Carlton Rd
Wellington Rd
Beacon Rd
Grosvenor Rd
Chichester Rd
Kingswood Cl
Wickinson Way
Blatchington Hill
Chapel
St Mary's Cl
Foster Cl
Sherwood Rd
Vale Rd
The Byeways

Seaford Prim Sch

Bowden House Sch

CLAREMONT RD

STATION APP

Salisbury Rd
Chichester Cl
Stafford Rd
Avondale Rd
Grove Rd
Glebe Dr
Pondsyde Ct
The Risings
East Albany Rd
Parkside Rd
Mildway Rd
Southdown Rd

SUTTON RD   A259

MILL DR

Recn Gd

Richmond
Richmond Mews

P Liby

SEAFORD

Chatham Pl

Seaford Bay

Crypt Art Gallery

Vanguard Way

Seaford Mus of Local History

Dane Rd
Dane Cl
Green La
West St
Church St
South St
John's Rd
The Steyne
Marine Par
Steyne Rd
Saxon La
Bramber La
Bramber Rd
Heathfield Rd
Cricketfield Rd
Corsica Rd
Cliff Gdns
Cliff Cl
Cliff Rd
Gerald Rd
Fitzgerald Ave
Lions Pl
Maurice Rd
The Close

Seaford Head Com Coll

Groyne

C4
1 HAWTH VALLEY CT
2 SELMESTON CT
3 OFFHAM CT
4 LITLINGTON CT
5 RODMELL CT
6 NEW COASTGUARD COTTS

1 HOMETYE HO
2 ST CRISPIANS CT
3 CLAREMONT CT

E2
1 SEAFORD CT
2 CHICHESTER CT
3 DANE HTS
4 PELHAM CT
5 TALLAND PAR
6 THE CROUCH
7 PELHAM YD
8 COURT LEET
9 FRENCH'S CT
10 CUNNINGHAM CT
11 GRANVILLE CT
12 MALLETT CL
13 THE CAUSEWAY
14 KINGS WELL CT
15 RAYFORD CT
16 STRATHNDEN CT
17 WEST VIEW CT
18 STEYNE CT
19 ESPLANADE MEWS
20 THE BOUNDARY
21 MARTELLO MEWS

E3
1 AVONDALE CT
2 RICHMOND TERR
3 OLD MARKET COTTS
4 CLINTON LA
5 CUCKMERE CT
6 SUTTON CROFT LA
7 CROFT CT
8 FITZGERALD HO
9 WELBECK CT

F2
1 KINGSFOLD CT
2 CROUCHFIELD CL
3 BRAMBER CL
4 STEYNE CL
5 SEA COTTS
6 CRICKETFIELD CT
7 WAVERLY CT

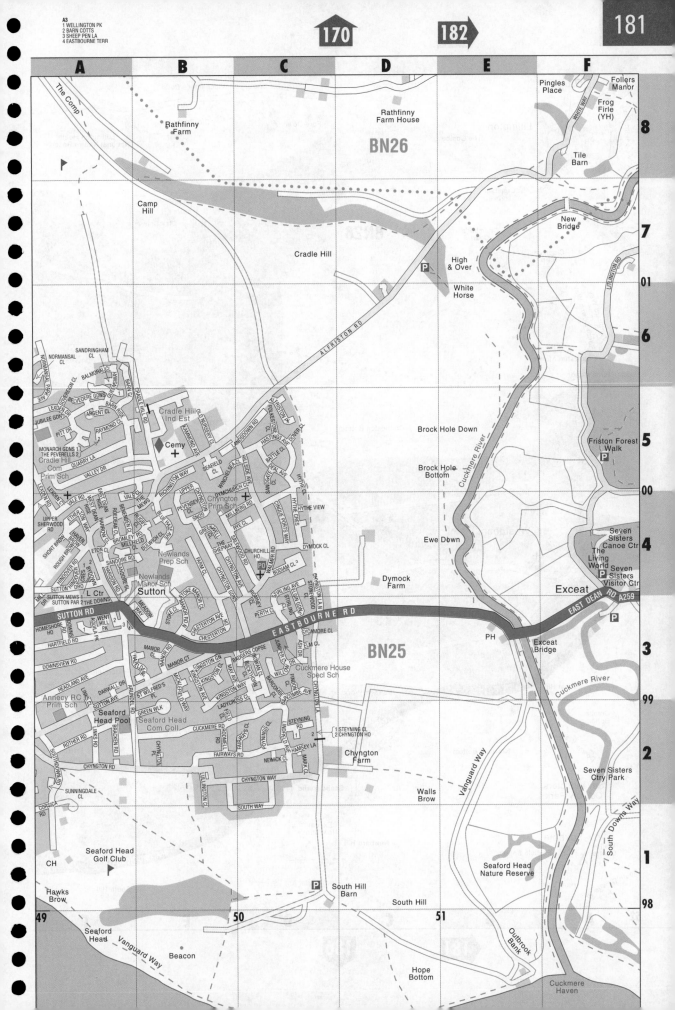

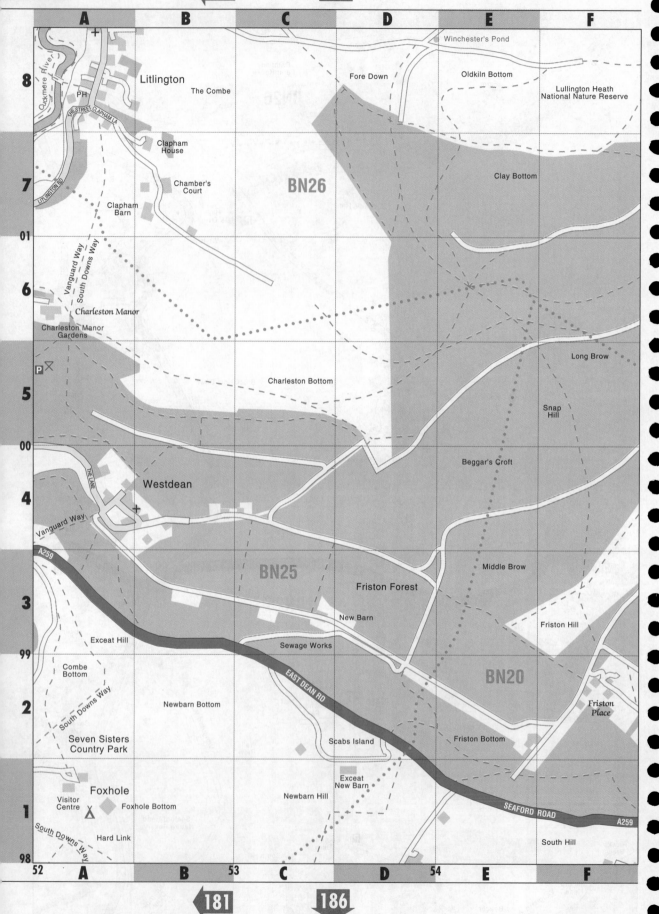

Litlington
The Combe
Oakmere River
PH
THE STREET
CLAPHAM LA
Clapham House
Clapham Court
Chamber's Court
BN26
Clapham Barn
LITLINGTON RD
Vanguard Way
South Downs Way
Charleston Manor
Charleston Manor Gardens
Charleston Bottom
Fore Down
Winchester's Pond
Oldkiln Bottom
Lullington Heath National Nature Reserve
Clay Bottom
Long Brow
Snap Hill
Beggar's Croft
P
Westdean
THE LANE
Vanguard Way
A259
BN25
Middle Brow
Friston Forest
New Barn
Friston Hill
BN20
Exceat Hill
Sewage Works
Combe Bottom
EAST DEAN RD
Newbarn Bottom
South Downs Way
Friston Place
Seven Sisters Country Park
Scabs Island
Friston Bottom
Foxhole
Visitor Centre
Foxhole Bottom
Newbarn Hill
Exceat New Barn
SEAFORD ROAD
A259
South Downs Way
Hard Link
South Hill

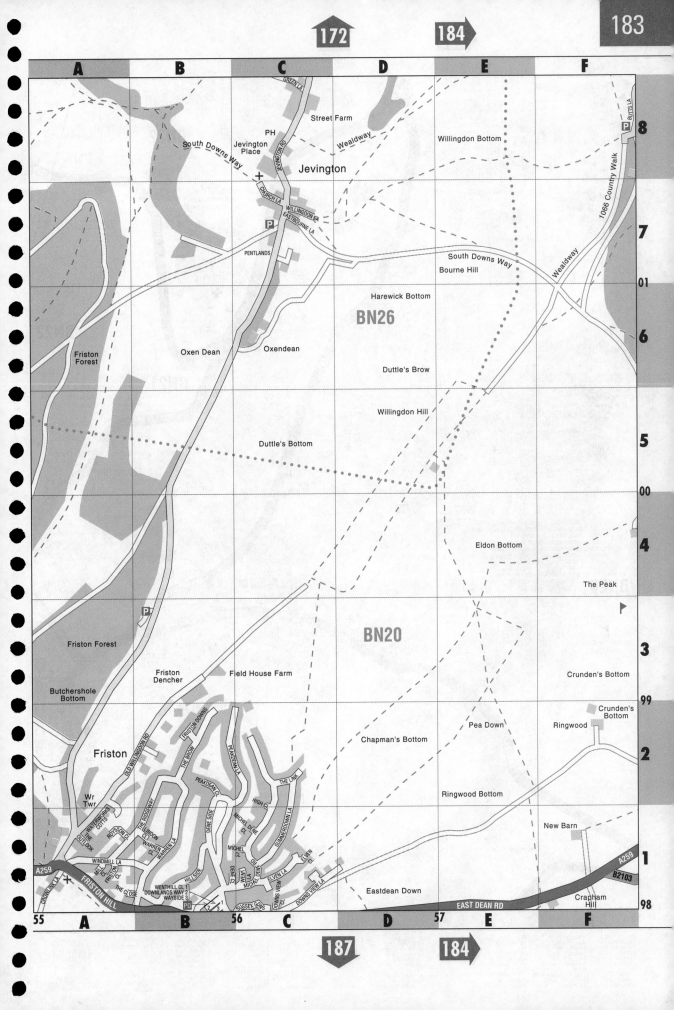

A B C D E F

South Downs Way

Jevington Place
PH
Street Farm
Wealdway
Jevington
Willingdon Bottom

8

1066 Country Walk

BUTTS LA

P

CHURCH LA
WILLINGDON LA
EASTBOURNE LA
P

7

South Downs Way
Bourne Hill
Wealdway

01

PENTLANDS

Friston
Forest

Oxen Dean
Oxendean

Harewick Bottom

BN26

6

Duttle's Brow

Willingdon Hill

5

Duttle's Bottom

00

Eldon Bottom

4

The Peak

P

Friston Forest

BN20

3

Butchershole
Bottom

Friston
Dencher
Field House Farm

Crunden's Bottom

99

Friston

OLD WILLINGDON RD
FRISTON DOWNS
THE BROW
PEAKDEAN CL
PEAKDEAN LA
THE LINK
HIGH CL

Chapman's Bottom

Pea Down

Crunden's
Bottom
Ringwood

2

Wr
Twr

THE RIDGEWAY
THE LINDON CL
WARREN LA
WARREN CL
DENE SIDE
MICHEL DENE
CL
SUMMERDOWN LA

Ringwood Bottom

New Barn

WATERWORKS
COTTS
ROYSTON CL

MICHEL
CL
LAVEN LA
ELVEN LA
ELVEN CL

A259

1

B2103

THE
OUTLOOK
WINDMILL LA
MILL
FRISTON CL
THE CLOSE
WENTHILL CL 1
DOWNLANDS WAY 2
WAYSIDE 3
HILLSIDE
MICHEL DENE
DOWNS VIEW CL
DOWNS VIEW LA
SUSSEX GDNS

Eastdean Down

EAST DEAN RD

Crapham
Hill

98

A259
CRONDIX LA
FRISTON HILL

55 56 57

A B C D E F

Map labels:

BN22 · BN23 · BN21 · BN20

Eastbourne Miniature Steam Rly Adventure Pk
Redward Bsns Pk
Allot Gdns
Southbourne Level
Stafford Junior School
St Anthony's Hill
Tollgate Junior School
Langney Village
Langney Bridge
Langney Point
Sovereign Park
Sovereign Ctr
Monarch Ho
Princes Park
St Andrews CE Inf Sch
Britland Est
Roselands Inf Sch
Roselands
Recn Gd
Courtlands Road Ind Est
Allot Gdns
Works
Spray Water Sports Centre
IRB Sta
Treasure Island Adventure Park
The Redoubt Fortress & Military Mus of Sussex
The Pavilion
Arndale Ctr
Bourne Ctn Prim Sch
Musgrave Collection Mus
Pier
EASTBOURNE
Devonshire Pk
RNLI Lifeboat Mus
Wish Tower

175 (inset — Sovereign Harbour)
BN23
Crumbles
LB Sta
Sovereign Harbour
Martello Tower
Langney Point
Wastewater Treatment Works
Panama Reach

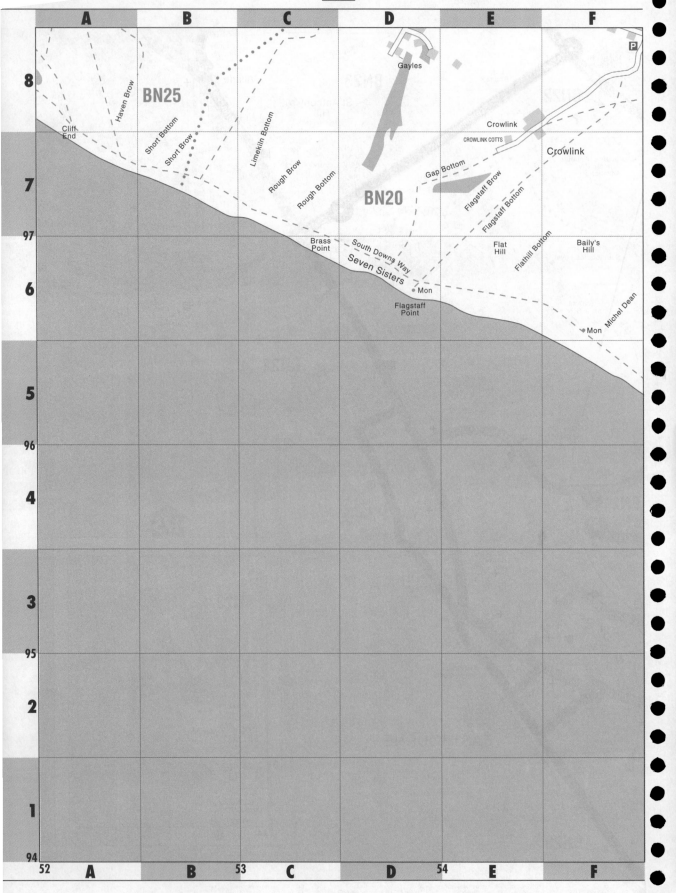

A   B   C   D   E   F

Gayles

BN25

Haven Brow

Cliff
End

Short Bottom

Short Brow

Limekiln Bottom

Rough Brow

Rough Bottom

Crowlink

CROWLINK COTTS

Crowlink

Gap Bottom

BN20

Flagstaff Brow

Flagstaff Bottom

Flathill Bottom

Flat
Hill

Baily's
Hill

Brass
Point

South Downs Way

Seven Sisters

Mon

Flagstaff
Point

Michel Dean

Mon

52   53   54

A   B   C   D   E   F

8 7 97 6 5 96 4 3 95 2 1 94

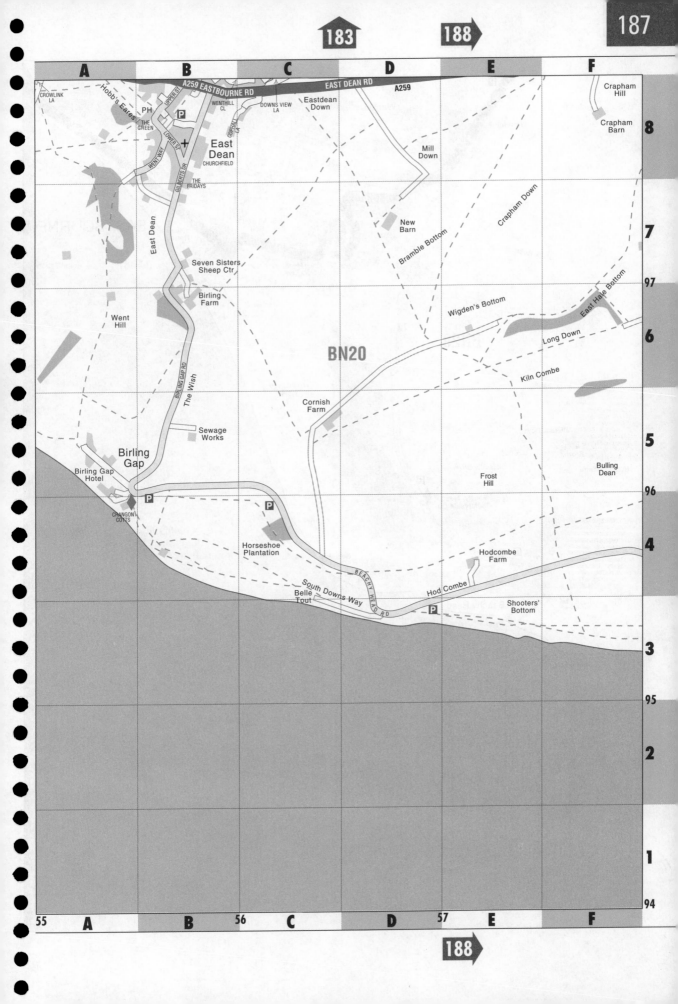

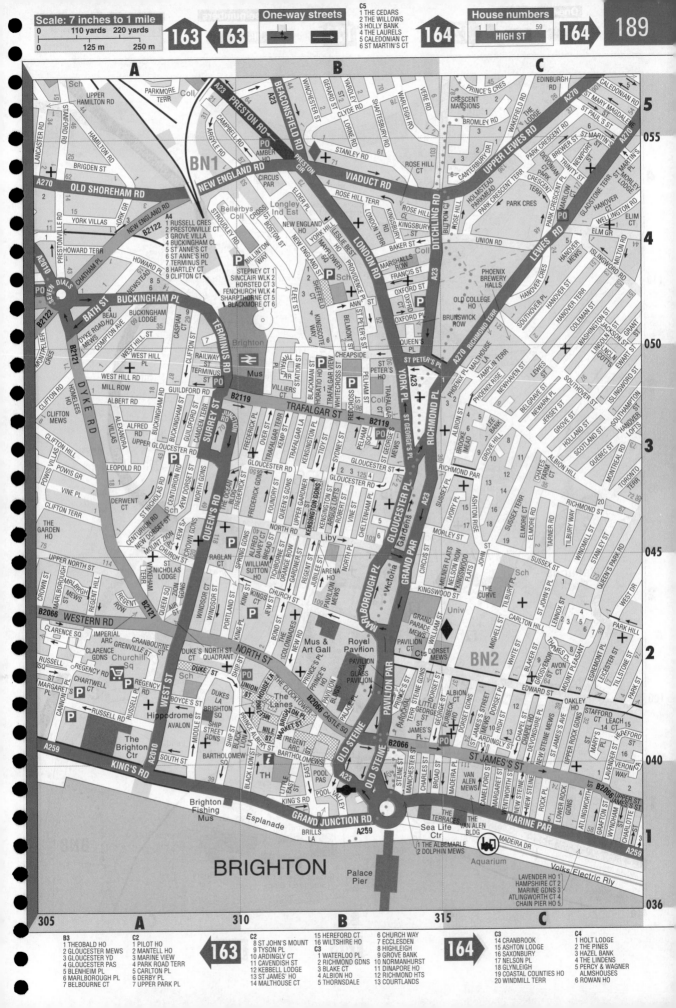

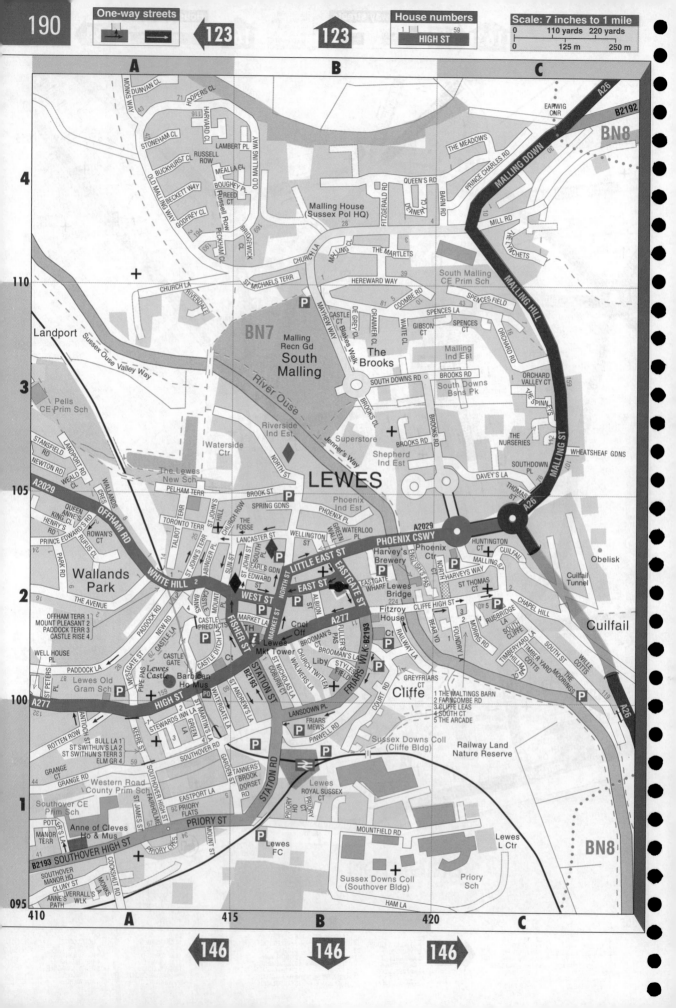

Index

Place name May be abbreviated on the map	
Location number Present when a number indicates the place's position in a crowded area of mapping	→ **Church Rd 6** Beckenham BR2.........**53** C6
Locality, town or village Shown when more than one place has the same name	
Postcode district District for the indexed place	
Page and grid square Page number and grid reference for the standard mapping	

Cities, towns and villages are listed in CAPITAL LETTERS

Public and commercial buildings are highlighted in magenta   **Places of interest** are highlighted in blue with a star★

Abbreviations used in the index

Acad	**Academy**	Comm	**Common**	Gd	**Ground**	L	**Leisure**	Prom	**Promenade**
App	**Approach**	Cott	**Cottage**	Gdn	**Garden**	La	**Lane**	Rd	**Road**
Arc	**Arcade**	Cres	**Crescent**	Gn	**Green**	Liby	**Library**	Recn	**Recreation**
Ave	**Avenue**	Cswy	**Causeway**	Gr	**Grove**	Mdw	**Meadow**	Ret	**Retail**
Bglw	**Bungalow**	Ct	**Court**	H	**Hall**	Meml	**Memorial**	Sh	**Shopping**
Bldg	**Building**	Ctr	**Centre**	Ho	**House**	Mkt	**Market**	Sq	**Square**
Bsns, Bus	**Business**	Ctry	**Country**	Hospl	**Hospital**	Mus	**Museum**	St	**Street**
Bvd	**Boulevard**	Cty	**County**	HQ	**Headquarters**	Orch	**Orchard**	Sta	**Station**
Cath	**Cathedral**	Dr	**Drive**	Hts	**Heights**	Pal	**Palace**	Terr	**Terrace**
Cir	**Circus**	Dro	**Drove**	Ind	**Industrial**	Par	**Parade**	TH	**Town Hall**
Cl	**Close**	Ed	**Education**	Inst	**Institute**	Pas	**Passage**	Univ	**University**
Cnr	**Corner**	Emb	**Embankment**	Int	**International**	Pk	**Park**	Wk, Wlk	**Walk**
Coll	**College**	Est	**Estate**	Intc	**Interchange**	Pl	**Place**	Wr	**Water**
Com	**Community**	Ex	**Exhibition**	Junc	**Junction**	Prec	**Precinct**	Yd	**Yard**

Index of towns, villages, streets, hospitals, industrial estates, railway stations, schools, shopping centres, universities and places of interest

A

Abberton Field BN6...... **97** B5
Abbey Cl BN10.......... **167** C1
Abbey Ct
　Battle TN33 ....**112** D4
　Robertsbridge TN32... **64** B4
Abbey Dr TN38......... **158** B5
Abbeyfield Ho BN26... **170** F3
Abbey Mews TN32 ..... **164** C8
Abbey Path BN27 .... **129** C2
Abbey Rd
　Brighton BN2........**164** D4
　Eastbourne BN20......**184** B5
Abbey View TN40 ..... **157** D6
Abbey Way TN33 .....**112** D5
Abbotsbury Cl BN2... **166** B1
Abbots Cl
　Battle TN33 ....**112** F3
　Hassocks BN6 .... **97** E4
ABBOTSFORD........ **72** E6
Abbot's Lodge 9 BN21.. **184** F4
Abbotts 11 BN1..... **163** E5
Abbotts CI BN22 ..... **185** A4
Abbotts Wood Forest Wlk★
　BN26..............**151** B3
Aberdale Rd BN26 .. **173** C6
Aberdeen Rd 5 BN4.. **164** C8
Abergavenny Rd BN7.. **123** B1
Abigail Ho 10 RH16.....**50** E4
Abinger Ct BN41 ..... **162** B8
Abinger Pl BN7 .... **190** A2
Abinger Rd
　Portslade-by-S BN41... **162** B8
　Woodingdean BN2..... **165** E6
Acacia Ave BN3....... **141** F1
Acacia Ct BN1 .... **142** F2
Acacia Rd
　Eastbourne BN22.......**173** D2
　Newhaven BN9 ...... **168** E2
Acer Ave TN2 .... **17** C8
Acerlands BN8...... **76** C8
Acorn Cl
　East Grinstead RH19...... **10** E8
　St Leonards TN37 ....**136** C4
Acorn Gn 3 BN27...... **129** B1
Acorns The
　Burgess Hill RH15 ....**72** D4
　Hailsham BN27 ..... **152** D7
　Stonegate TN5....... **42** F6
Acorn Way TN19 ...... **45** A3

Acre Cl RH16 .... **50** D2
Acres Rise TN5 .... **31** E1
Adam Cl
　Crowborough TN6 ...... **38** A6
　St Leonards TN38 .... **135** F4
Adams Cl BN1 ...... **143** B2
Adams La TN31 ...... **66** D2
Adastra Ave BN6...... **98** A4
Addingham Rd BN22 .. **185** C4
Addington Cl TN38 .. **158** F7
Addison Rd BN3 ...... **163** E7
Adelaide Cl BN25 .... **180** E5
Adelaide Cres BN3 ... **163** C5
Adelaide Rd TN38 .... **136** B3
Adelaide Sq BN43.... **161** B7
Ades Field BN26 .... **171** F6
Admiral's Bridge La RH19 **10** C2
Admiralty Cres BN23 .. **175** B1
Admiralty Ct BN23 ... **175** B1
Admiralty Way BN23 .. **175** B1
Adult Com Learning
　BN27............**152** B8
Adur Ct 10 BN43 ..... **161** C8
Adur Dr
　Shoreham-by-S BN43...**161** A7
　Stone Cross BN24 .... **174** A5
Adur Rd RH15.......... **73** C4
Agincourt Cl TN37 ... **135** F7
Agnes St BN2....... **164** C7
Ainsworth Ave BN2 ... **165** D3
Ainsworth Cl BN2..... **165** D3
Ainsworth Ho 1 BN2.. **164** C7
Airlie Ho BN3 .... **163** C6
Air St BN1........... **189** A2
Airy Rd BN27 .... **131** B2
Akehurst Field TN33 .. **110** B3
Alamein Ct TN6 .... **38** A8
Alan Ct 6 TN37....... **159** C7
Alan Way BN2 .... **164** F5
Albany Ct
　Eastbourne BN21......**184** F5
　2 Hastings TN34 ..... **159** F7
Albany Hill TN2 .... **8** C5
Albany Mans TN38 ... **159** B8
Albany Mews BN3.... **163** B6
Albany Rd
　Bexhill TN40......**157** C3
　Seaford BN25 ..... **180** C3
　St Leonards TN37 ... **159** B7
Albany Twrs 3 BN3.. **163** B5
Albany Villas
　Cuckfield RH17 .... **50** A6
　Hove BN3............ **163** B6

Albemarle Mans 8 BN3. **163** B5
Albemarle The BN2 ... **189** B1
Albert Cl RH16........ **51** A4
Albert Cotts TN1 ....**8** B4
Albert Dr RH15 ...... **72** E2
Albert Mews BN3 .... **163** C6
Albert Par BN21 .... **184** C4
Albert Pl BN26 ...... **173** A7
Albert Rd
　Bexhill TN40.......**157** C3
　Brighton BN3 ..... **189** A3
　Hastings TN34 ..... **159** F7
　Polegate BN26...... **173** A7
　Southwick BN42...... **161** D7
　Uckfield TN22.......... **78** D6
Albert St TN1..........**8** B4
Albert Terr BN21.... **184** C5
Albion Ct
　Brighton BN2........**189** C2
　Burgess Hill RH15 .... **72** F2
Albion Hill BN2 ...... **189** C3
Albion Ho
　4 Brighton BN2 .... **189** C3
　Southwick BN42...... **161** F7
Albion La 4 TN34..... **160** A3
Albion Mews TN1 ..... **8** C5
Albion Rd
　Eastbourne BN22.......**185** B4
　Royal Tunbridge Wells TN1.. **8** C5
Albion St
　Brighton BN2........**189** C3
　Lewes BN7........ **190** B2
　Portslade-by-S BN41.. **162** B7
　Southwick BN42...... **161** E7
Albourne Cl
　Brighton BN2........**164** F7
　St Leonards TN38 ... **158** F8
Alces Pl BN25....... **180** E5
ALCISTON........... **170** D8
Aldborough Rd TN37.. **136** C1
Aldenham Ct 1 BN21 .. **184** F2
ALDERBROOK.......... **38** A7
Alderbrook Cl TN6 ... **38** A6
Alderbrook Cotts TN6.. **38** A7
Alderbrook Path TN6.. **38** A6
Alderbrook Way TN6... **38** A6
Alder Cl
　Eastbourne BN23......**185** C8
　Heathfield TN21...... **82** A5
　St Leonards TN37 ... **136** C5
Alder Lodge TN4......**7** E4
Alders Ave RH19 ....**1** E3
Alders View Dr RH19 ...**1** E3

Alderton Ct 7 TN39... **157** B3
Aldervale Cotts TN6... **38** A7
Aldrich Cl BN2....... **164** F6
ALDRINGTON........ **162** E6
Aldrington Ave BN3 .. **163** A8
Aldrington CE Prim Sch
　BN3...............**142** A2
Aldrington Cl BN3 .... **162** D7
Aldrington House Hospl
　BN3................ **162** F6
Aldrington Pl BN3 .... **162** D8
Aldrington Sta BN3... **163** A8
Alexander Dr TN39 ... **156** E4
Alexander Mead BN8.. **76** D8
Alexandra Cl BN25 ... **180** E5
Alexandra Ct BN3.... **141** F2
Alexandra Par TN34.. **136** D3
Alexandra Park Mans
　TN34............... **136** E2
Alexandra Rd
　Burgess Hill RH15 ... **73** C2
　Eastbourne BN22......**185** D6
　Heathfield TN21...... **82** B6
　Mayfield TN20 ...... **40** C3
　St Leonards TN37 ... **159** C8
　Uckfield TN22.......... **78** D6
Alexandra Terr TN20 .. **40** C3
Alexandra The TN37.. **159** D7
Alexandra Villas BN1.. **189** A3
Alford Way TN40..... **157** E6
Alfray Rd TN40....... **158** A5
Alfred Davey Ct BN1.. **189** B3
Alfred Rd
　Brighton BN1....... **189** A3
　2 Eastbourne BN23... **185** F8
　Hastings TN35 ..... **160** D7
Alfred St TN38....... **159** C7
Alfriston Cl
　Bexhill TN39....... **156** C6
　Brighton BN2....... **164** F6
　Eastbourne BN20..... **184** C2
Alfriston Clergy Ho★
　BN26............ **171** A2
Alfriston Pk BN25.... **181** C5
Alfriston Rd
　Alfriston BN26....... **171** A5
　Seaford BN25, BN26... **181** D6
Alfriston Sch BN26.... **170** F3
Alice Bright La TN6 ... **37** F7
Alice Cl 2 BN26..... **163** D5
Alice Hudson Gdns
　BN23.............. **185** D7

Alice St BN3 .... **163** D5
Allan Cl TN4 ....**7** C4
Allandale Rd TN2 ......**8** D7
Allards TN35.......... **138** C8
Allegria Ct TN38 .... **159** B7
Allen Gardinier Ho TN2... **8** C3
Allen Rd RH16 .... **51** A4
Allen's Cl RH19 ...... **11** D6
Allen Way TN40 ..... **157** F7
Allfrey Rd BN22...... **185** D6
Allfreys La TN6 ...... **37** D6
Allington Cres BN8... **76** C7
Allington La BN7...... **122** D7
Allington Pl BN8 ..... **76** D6
Allington Rd BN8 .... **76** C6
All Saints CE Jun Sch
　TN35.............. **160** E6
All Saints CE Prim Sch
　TN39............... **157** B7
All Saints' Cres TN35... **160** B4
All Saints Gdns TN21... **81** F7
All Saints La TN39.... **157** B7
All Saints Rd TN4 ....**8** B6
All Saints Rise TN4.... **8** A6
All Saints' & St Richard's CE
　Prim Sch TN21....... **82** D6
All Saints' St TN34 ... **160** B4
Allwood Cres RH17... **74** C4
Alma Rd RH16 .... **51** B8
Alma Terr TN37..... **136** C2
Alma Villas TN37.... **136** C2
Almonry Fields TN33.. **112** B4
Almshouses of the Holy
　Name TN33 ...... **97** A5
Alpine Rd
　Hastings TN34 ......**160** A4
　Hove BN3........... **162** F8
Alternative Ctr for Ed
　BN1.............. **143** C3
Alverstone Cl BN23.. **174** B4
Amanda Ct TN40 .... **157** F7
Ambassadors The 10
　BN3............. **163** C6
Amber Ct
　20 Hove BN3 ...... **163** C6
　8 Hove BN3 ...... **163** D7
Amber Ho
　Brighton BN1....... **189** B4
　Hove BN3............ **163** C6
Amberleaze Dr TN2 ...**9** D6

Amberley Cl
Burgess Hill RH15 73 A4
Haywards Heath RH16 50 D4
Hove BN3 141 E3
Amberley Ct TN4 8 C8
Amberley Dr BN3 141 E3
Amberley Lodge BN2 164 F6
Amberley Rd BN22 173 C1
Amberstone BN27 129 E3
Amberstone Cl TN34 160 A8
Amberstone Hospl BN27 129 E4
Amberstone View BN27 129 C2
Ambleside Ave BN10 178 A8
Ambleside Ct BN10 178 A7
America La RH16 51 A5
Amesbury Cres BN3 162 E7
Amherst Cl TN34 136 D1
Amherst Cres BN3 162 F8
Amherst Gdns TN34 136 D1
Amherst Rd
Bexhill TN40 157 C4
Hastings TN34 136 D1
Royal Tunbridge Wells TN4 8 A5
Amhurst Rd BN10 177 F3
Anchorage Way BN23 175 B2
Anchor Cl BN43 161 A6
Anchor Field BN8 124 D5
Anchor Hill RH17 51 F3
Anchorhold The RH16 50 D5
Anchor La BN8 102 B5
Anderida Ct TN39 156 C4
Anderida Rd BN22 173 C3
Anderson Cl BN9 179 B7
Andrew Rd TN4 8 C8
Andrews Cl
Northbridge Street TN32 64 C5
Royal Tunbridge Wells TN2 8 D5
Andros Cl BN8 100 E6
Andwell Ct BN21 185 B2
Angela Cl TN40 157 F7
Angel Ct 1 BN21 185 A4
Angel Row TN18 47 B5
Angel Terr TN18 47 B6
Anglesea Mans TN38 159 B8
Anglesea Terr TN37, TN38 159 C8
Anglesey Ave BN27 129 A2
Angmering Ct BN1 143 F5
Angrove Ho TN6 25 D2
Angus Cl BN20 173 B1
Anjou Ct BN23 174 F1
Ann Cl BN6 98 A5
Annecy RC Prim Sch BN25 181 A2
Anne of Cleves House & Mus★ BN7 190 A1
Anne's Path BN7 190 A1
Annington Rd BN22 185 B5
Ann St
Brighton BN1 189 B4
Hastings TN34 160 C6
Anscombe 5 RH16 50 D6
Anson Cl BN23 185 E7
Anson Ho BN10 167 C1
Ansty Cl BN2 164 E5
Antares Path BN27 152 E7
Antigua Cl 14 BN23 185 F8
Antioch St BN7 190 A1
Antony Cl BN25 180 B6
Antrim Ct BN23 174 D1
Antrona Cl TN39 156 C3
Anvil Cl
Portslade-by-S BN41 141 B2
Uckfield TN22 78 B6
Anvil Ct TN37 136 C5
Anzac Cl BN10 167 C1
Apex Pk BN27 152 A7
Appledene Cnr BN8 100 E7
Appledore Cl BN23 174 D2
Appledore Ct RH16 51 A7
Appledore Gdns RH16 51 A6
Appledore Rd BN2 143 F4
Applesham Ave BN3 141 E2
Applesham Way BN41 141 A1
Apple Tree La TN2 8 D8
Applewood Cl TN37 136 B5
Approach The
10 Brighton BN1 142 E3
Dormansland RH19 1 F6
April Pl 4 TN40 157 C4
Apsley St TN4 7 D4
Aqua Ho BN10 177 F3
Aquarium Sta★ BN2 189 C1
Aquarius Cl BN10 178 C6
Aquila Pk BN25 181 A3
Araquipe Reef BN23 185 G8
Arbor Ct RH16 50 E5
Arbourvale TN38 136 A1
Arbroath Ct 3 TN38 136 B1
Arcade The BN7 190 C2
Archer Ct RH15 73 A3
Archers Ct TN35 136 F6
Archery Ct
Eastbourne BN22 185 C6
3 St Leonards TN38 159 B6
Archery Rd TN38 159 B7
Archery Wlk BN27 152 C6
Archie Ct 7 TN38 159 B6
Ardingly Ct 10 BN2 189 C2
Ardingly Rd BN2 177 D4
Ardingly St BN2 189 C2
Arena Ho BN1 189 B2
Argent Cl BN25 181 A5
ARGOS HILL 39 E5
Argos Hill Rd TN20, TN6 39 D4
Argus Lofts BN1 189 B3
Argyle Rd BN1 189 A5
Argyll Ct
3 Bexhill TN39 157 A4
Eastbourne BN22 173 E2
Arkendale RH19 1 A4
Arkwright Rd BN23 174 A1
ARLINGTON 150 F4
Arlington Cres BN1 143 E5
Arlington Ct RH16 50 E5
Arlington Gdns BN2 166 D2
Arlington Ho 7 BN21 184 D4
Arlington Raceway★ BN27 151 D6
Arlington Rd BN21 184 F3
Arlington Resr Nature Reserve★ BN26 150 C3
Arlington Road E BN27 152 A6
Arlington Road W BN27 151 F6
Armstrong Cl TN38 135 E4
Arnbury Mews TN38 158 E6
Arndale Ctr BN21 185 A3
Arnold St BN2 164 C7
Arnside Rd TN38 158 E6
Arnworth Ct BN21 184 F2
Arran Cl BN27 129 A2
Arthur Bliss Ho RH16 51 A8
Arthur Rd TN39 157 B4
Arthur St BN3 163 A8
Artisans Dwellings 8 BN21 184 F2
Arts Rd BN1 144 B7
Arun Beck BN6 97 A8
Arun Cl BN24 173 F5
Arun Ct 13 BN43 161 C8
Arundel Cl
Beachlands BN24 175 F6
Hailsham BN27 129 C2
Shoreham-by-S BN43 161 C8
Arundel Ct
6 Brighton, Black Rock BN2 164 E4
Brighton, Westdene BN1 142 C5
Burgess Hill RH15 72 F4
Hastings TN35 160 C6
14 Shoreham-by-S BN43 161 C8
Arundel Drive E BN2 166 C1
Arundel Drive W BN2 166 C1
Arundel Gn BN7 123 B2
Arundel Ho 15 BN21 184 E4
Arundel Keep 11 BN21 184 F4
Arundel Mews
10 Brighton BN2 164 E4
Haywards Heath RH16 50 F2
Arundel Pl BN2 164 E3
Arundel Rd
Brighton BN2 164 E4
Eastbourne BN21 184 F4
Newhaven BN9 168 F1
Peacehaven BN10 178 D7
Royal Tunbridge Wells TN1 8 B2
Seaford BN25 181 A3
Arundel Road Central BN10 178 B7
Arundel Road W BN10 178 B7
Arundel St BN2 164 E3
Arundel Terr BN2 164 E3
Arun Lodge BN21 184 E3
Arun Path TN22 55 E1
Arun Way BN24 173 F5
Ascham Pl BN20 184 E1
Ascot Cl BN20 188 F8
Ascot Mews TN38 159 A8
Ashampstead Pl 4 BN21 184 F3
Ashbourne Ct
13 Eastbourne BN21 185 A2
Rusthall TN4 7 D4
Ashbrook Rd TN37 136 B4
Ashburnham Cl BN1 143 E5
Ashburnham Dr BN1 143 E5
Ashburnham Gdns BN21 184 E5
Ashburnham Ho BN1 142 E5
Ashburnham Pl BN27 129 A2
Ashburnham Rd
Eastbourne BN21 184 E5
Hastings TN35 160 C6
Ashby Cl TN39 157 A8
Ash Cl
Eastbourne BN22 173 E3
Hove BN3 142 C3
Royal Tunbridge Wells TN2 17 D7
Ashcombe Dr TN39 156 D3
Ashcombe Hollow BN7 145 D7
Ashcombe La BN7 145 E5
Ashcroft 1 BN43 161 D7
Ashcroft Cl
Ringmer BN8 124 D5
Shoreham-by-S BN43 161 D8
Ash Ct
East Grinstead RH19 1 E3
Hailsham BN27 152 A7
Southwick BN42 140 F1
Ashdown 14 BN3 163 C6
Ashdown Ave BN2 166 B1
Ashdown Chase TN22 35 C5
Ashdown Cl
Forest Row RH18 12 A2
Haywards Heath RH16 51 B4
Royal Tunbridge Wells TN4 7 F4
St Leonards TN38 135 E2
Ashdown Ct
Crowborough TN6 25 E2
Uckfield TN22 78 D6
Ashdown Forest Llama Pk★ RH18 22 E4
Ashdown Forest Visitors Ctr★ RH18 23 A5
Ashdown Gate RH19 1 D2
Ashdown House Sch RH18 12 D4
Ashdown Nuffield Hospl RH16 50 D6
Ashdown Pl
Forest Row RH18 22 E8
Heathfield TN21 82 B6
Ashdown Rd
Bexhill TN40 157 E4
7 Brighton BN2 164 B8
Forest Row RH18 11 F2
Ashdown View
East Grinstead RH19 10 E7
Marlpits TN22 35 D6
Ash Dr BN25 181 C3
Ashenden Ave TN31 93 A5
Ashenden Wlk TN2 8 E8
Ashenground Cl 6 RH16 50 E3
Ashenground Rd RH16 50 E3
Asher Reeds TN3 7 A4
Ashford Cl 4 BN27 152 C7
Ashford Rd
Brighton BN1 143 A2
Eastbourne BN21 185 A3
Hastings TN34 136 E2
Ashford Sq BN21 185 A3
Ashford Way TN34 136 E3
Ashgate Rd BN23 174 E2
Ash Gr
Haywards Heath RH16 50 D2
Westham BN24 174 D6
Ashgrove Cotts RH17 33 D5
Ashington Ct BN2 164 F6
Ashington Gdns BN10 178 F6
Ashington Rd BN22 174 A1
Ashlands TN6 26 B1
Ashleigh Gdns TN6 25 E4
Ashleigh Glegg Ho BN25 180 D4
Ashley Cl BN1 142 E7
Ashley Ct
Hove BN3 163 C5
7 St Leonards TN37 159 C7
Ashley Gdns
Hailsham BN27 129 C3
Mayfield TN20 40 A2
Rusthall TN4 7 C5
Ashley Park Cl TN4 7 C5
Ashley Pk TN4 7 C5
Ashley Rd TN6 27 D1
Ashlings Way
Hove BN3 141 E2
Shoreham-by-S BN43 140 B1
Ashmore Cl BN10 167 D2
Ashtead Twrs 8 TN40 157 E4
Ashton Lodge 15 BN2 189 C3
Ashton Rise BN2 189 C3
Ashtonville Cl BN8 124 E5
Ash Tree Cl TN21 82 A7
ASHURST 5 D2
Ashurst Ave BN2 166 E1
Ashurst Hill TN3 5 D2
Ashurst Pl RH16 50 E5
Ashurst Rd
Brighton BN2 143 F5
Seaford BN25 180 F2
Stone Cross TN3 6 B2
Ashurst Sta TN3 5 D2
Ashurstwood Abbey RH19 11 F6
Ashurst Wood Prim Sch RH19 11 E6
Ashway RH15 73 A2
Ash Wlk BN9 179 B7
Ashwood Ct RH18 11 F1
Ashwyn Bsns Ctr RH15 72 F5
Aspen Cl RH16 51 B4
Aspen Ct RH19 11 A8
Aspen Rd BN22 173 E2
Aspen Way TN39 156 C4
Aspen Wlk
Haywards Heath RH16 51 B4
Heathfield TN21 82 B5
Assissi Ct RH16 50 F2
Assissi Hts RH16 50 F2
Astaire Ave BN22 185 B6
Asten Cl TN38 158 E7
Asten Fields TN33 112 C4
Astra Ho 10 BN1 163 E5
Athelstan Cl 1 BN23 185 F8
Athelstan Rd TN35 160 D6
Athenaeum The 16 BN3 163 C6
Atlantic Dr BN23 185 F7
Atlingworth Ct BN2 189 C1
Atlingworth St BN2 189 C1
Attfield Wlk BN22 173 F3
Attree Ct 6 BN2 164 C6
Attree Dr BN2 164 C6
Aubyns 15 TN40 157 D3
Auckland Dr BN2 143 F1
Auckland Ho TN40 157 C7
Auckland Quay BN23 175 A1
Auckland Rd TN1 8 C5
Audrey Cl
Brighton BN1 142 E5
Seaford BN25 180 D5
Audrey Sturley Ct TN4 7 D4
Augustines Way RH16 50 F4
Augustus Way TN37 135 F6
Aultmore Ct TN2 8 D3
Austen Cl RH19 1 B1
Austen Way TN35 137 D5
Austen Wlk BN23 174 D2
Avalon BN1 189 A2
Avard Cres BN20 184 B6
Avards Cl TN18 45 E8
Avenue Ct 21 BN3 163 C6
Avenue La BN21 184 F3
Avenue The
Brighton BN2 143 E1
Avenue The *continued*
Eastbourne BN21 184 F3
Fairlight Cove TN35 138 F4
Hailsham BN27 152 B6
Heathfield TN21 82 B6
Horam TN21 106 F8
Kingston near Lewes BN7 145 D5
Lewes BN7 190 A2
Mayfield TN20 40 B2
Avery Cl BN41 140 F4
Aviemore Rd TN6 25 D2
Avis Cl BN9 168 E1
Avis Par BN9 168 E1
Avis Rd BN9 168 E1
Avis Way BN9 168 E1
Avis Way Ind Est BN9 179 D8
Avocet BN27 152 A7
Avocet Trad Est RH15 72 F2
Avon Ct BN2 189 C2
Avondale Ct 1 BN25 180 E3
Avondale Rd
Eastbourne BN22 185 B4
Hove BN3 163 D7
Seaford BN25 180 F3
St Leonards TN38 136 A1
Avonhurst RH15 73 B3
Avonmore BN20 188 E8
Avon St TN1 8 C5
Awbrook Cl RH17 51 F3
Aylesbury BN3 163 E6
Aylesbury Ave BN23 185 E8
Aymer Ho 4 BN3 163 A6
Aymer Rd BN3 163 A6
Aynsley Ct BN3 163 C8
Ayscue Cl BN23 185 F7

B

Babylon Way BN20 184 B8
Back La
Alfriston BN26 171 C4
Cross-in-H TN21 81 C6
Fairwarp TN22 36 B2
Rushlake Green TN21 83 D1
Winchelsea TN36 117 E7
Back Rd TN18 47 B5
Backwoods Cl RH16 51 B6
Backwoods La RH16 51 B6
Baden Rd BN2 143 D1
Badens Cl BN8 76 C6
Badger Cl BN41 141 B2
Badger Dr RH16 50 C5
Badger Gate TN31 93 A5
Badgers Brow BN20 184 B8
Badgers Cl
Crowborough TN6 25 E3
Newhaven BN9 179 D6
Badgers Copse BN25 181 C3
Badgers Ct BN20 188 F8
Badgers Dene BN7 167 D8
Badgers Field BN10 167 C1
Badgers Holt TN2 8 E5
Badgers Mount TN39 156 E5
Badgers Way
East Grinstead RH19 1 F2
Hastings TN34 136 D5
Badgers Wlk
Burgess Hill RH15 73 D2
Golden Cross BN27 127 C3
Badger Way BN1 143 E6
Badlesmere Rd BN22 185 B6
Bagham La BN27 130 F6
Bahram Rd BN26 172 F6
Bailey Cres BN22 173 B3
Baillie Ave BN22 185 C5
Bainbridge Cl BN25 180 F3
Bainden Cl TN6 27 D1
Baird Dr TN34 136 E3
Baird Ho TN37 159 C8
Baker Ct TN22 78 C7
Bakers Farm Mobile Home Pk BN27 129 A3
Baker's Rd BN21 184 D3
Baker St
Brighton BN1 189 B4
Newhaven BN9 179 E7
Uckfield TN22 78 D6
Baker Way TN31 94 E3
Bakery Mews BN1 143 C1
Bakewell Rd BN21 184 D4
Balaclava La TN5 30 A6
Balcombe Ct BN10 178 C8
Balcombe Gn TN33 88 E1
Balcombe La RH17, RH19 21 E2
Balcombe Rd
Haywards Heath RH16 50 D7
Peacehaven BN10 178 B8
Baldings Cotts RH17 74 B5
Baldock Rd TN5 29 E4
BALDSLOW 136 C7
Baldslow Down TN37 136 C8
Baldslow Rd TN34 136 F1
Baldwin Ave BN21 184 C5
Baldwins Field RH19 1 C4
BALDWINS HILL 1 D4
Baldwins Hill Prim Sch RH19 1 D3
Bale Cl TN39 156 E5
Bal Edmund TN37 136 B4
Balfour Gdns RH18 11 E1
Balfour Inf Sch BN1 143 A3
Balfour Jun Sch BN1 143 A3
Balfour Rd BN1 143 A2
Ballard Dr BN8 125 A7
Ballards Hill TN33 134 F4
Ball's Gn TN7 14 B5
BALLS GREEN 14 C5
Ballsocks La TN21 107 C8
Balmer Farm Cotts BN7 144 D8
Balmoral
Brighton BN1 163 E8
East Grinstead RH19 11 A8
Balmoral Cl BN25 181 A6
Balmoral Ct
Hove BN3 142 A3
2 St Leonards TN38 136 B1
Balsdean Rd BN2 144 F1
Baltic Ho TN1 8 B5
Baltimore Ct 9 BN3 163 C7
Bamford Cl BN2 144 A2
Bampfield St BN41 162 B8
Bancroft Ho TN39 157 B5
Bancroft Rd TN39 157 B5
Bank Rd TN39 157 C7
Bankside
Brighton BN1 142 C5
Durgates TN5 29 E5
Hassocks BN6 97 F5
Rye TN31 93 B6
Bankside Ct BN1 142 C5
Banks Rd BN8 52 F1
Banner Cl BN24 174 C6
BANNER FARM 8 C2
Banner Farm Rd TN2 8 B2
Banner Way BN24 174 C6
Bannings Vale BN2 166 E1
Bannisters Field BN8 76 D7
Bannister Way RH16 50 D6
Baranscraig Ave BN1 143 A7
Barbados TN40 157 E3
Barber Ct BN7 146 B8
Barbican House Mus★ BN7 190 A2
Barbuda Quay BN23 185 G7
Barchester Pl 17 BN21 185 A2
Barclay Ho 2 BN2 164 C7
BARCOMBE 101 E2
Barcombe Ave BN25 181 C3
Barcombe CE Prim Sch BN8 101 D5
Barcombe Cl
Eastbourne BN20 184 C3
Seaford BN25 181 C3
BARCOMBE CROSS 101 E4
BARCOMBE MILLS 102 A3
Barcombe Mills Rd BN8 101 E4
Barcombe Pl
Brighton BN1 143 F5
12 Crowborough TN6 25 F3
Barcombe Rd BN1 143 E4
Barcombe Wlk BN20 184 C3
Barden Rd
Eastbourne BN22 185 C4
Speldhurst TN3 7 A8
BARDOWN 42 E7
Bardown Rd TN5 42 E7
Barford Ct TN22 78 C7
Barganny 17 TN40 157 D3
Bargate Cl TN39 157 C7
Barham Cl TN34 136 D4
Barkdale RH15 73 D5
Barley Ave TN35 160 C5
Barley Cl BN10 167 B2
Barley Dr RH15 72 D4
Barley Field Cotts BN7 146 D1
Barley La TN35 160 D5
Barley Mow La TN21 83 B5
Barming Cl BN23 174 D2
Barnard Gate RH16 50 E7
Barn Cl
Hailsham BN27 129 C1
Kingston near Lewes BN7 145 E5
Seaford BN25 181 A6
Stone Cross BN24 174 A6
Barn Cottage La RH16 51 A5
Barn Cotts 2 BN25 181 A3
Barn Ct
Southwick BN42 162 A7
St Leonards TN37 136 C5
Barnes Rd BN41 162 B8
Barnett Rd BN1 143 B2
Barnetts Way TN4 8 C8
Barnett Way TN22 78 D7
Barnet Way BN3 141 E3
Barnfield
Crowborough TN6 26 A3
Plumpton Green BN7 99 E5
Royal Tunbridge Wells TN2 16 F7
Barnfield Cl TN34 159 D8
Barnfield Gdns
8 Brighton BN2 164 C6
Ditchling BN6 98 E3
Barn Field Pl RH19 2 A3
Barnham Cl BN22 174 A2
Barnhams The TN39 156 E3
Barn Hatch Cl BN7 146 A8
Barnhorn Cl TN39 156 C4
Barnhorn Rd TN39 156 B4
Barn Ho The BN25 180 E5
Barn La TN22 79 D8
Barnmead RH16 50 D7
Barn Rd BN7 190 C4
Barn Rise
Brighton BN1 142 D5
Seaford BN25 181 A5
Barnsgate Manor Vineyard★ TN22 36 E5
Barnside Ave RH15 73 D1
Barn Stables 2 BN7 123 B1
Barons Cl BN25 180 C5
Barons Ct
Burgess Hill RH15 73 B2
Royal Tunbridge Wells TN4 8 A5
Barons Down Rd BN7 146 A8
Barons Way BN26 172 F5

Barons Wlk BN7 .... 146 A8
Barrack Rd TN40 .... 157 C5
Barracks Cotts TN32 .... 87 C7
Barrack Sq TN36 .... 117 F7
Barrhill Ave BN1 .... 142 F7
Barrie Cl BN23 .... 174 E2
Barrier Reef Way BN23 .... 175 A1
Barrington Cl RH16 .... 50 F8
Barrington Rd RH16 .... 51 A8
Barrington Wood RH16... 50 F8
Barrow Cl BN1 .... 143 C2
Barrowfield Cl BN3 .... 142 C3
Barrowfield Dr BN3 .... 142 D2
Barrowfield Lodge BN3 . 142 C2
Barrow Hill BN1 .... 143 C2
Barrow La TN3 .... 6 F2
Barrow Rise TN37 .... 136 C5
Barry Wlk BN3 .... 164 C6
Bartholomews BN1 .... 189 B2
Bartholomew Sq BN1 .... 189 B2
Bartley Mill Cl BN24 ..... 174 B5
Bartley Mill La TN3.... 18 E4
Bartley Mill Rd TN3 ..... 18 F3
Barton Cres RH19 .... 11 A8
Basin Road N BN41....... 162 B6
Basin Road S BN3, BN41 . 162 B6
Baslow Ct BN20 .... 188 D7
Baslow Rd BN20 .... 188 D7
Bassett's Forge TN5.... 29 E5
Bassetts La
  Argos Hill TN20 .... 39 F5
  Mark Cross TN6 .... 28 E2
  White Post TN8, TN11 ..... 5 C7
Batchelor Cres TN6 ..... 25 F3
Batchelors TN2 .... 9 E8
Batchelor Way TN22 ..... 78 A7
Bateman's★ TN19 .... 62 A4
Bateman's La TN19.... 62 A4
Batemans Rd BN2 .... 165 E7
Bates Rd BN1 .... 142 F2
Bath Ct BN3 .... 163 A5
Bathford Cl BN23 .... 174 D2
Bath Rd 4 BN21 .... 184 E7
Bath St BN1 .... 189 A4
Battenhurst Rd TN5 ..... 43 B4
Battery Hill TN35 .... 138 D5
BATTLE 112 D5
Battle Abbey★ TN33..... 112 D4
Battle Abbey Prep Sch
  TN40 .... 157 E5
Battle Abbey Sch TN33 . 112 C4
Battle Ct BN25 .... 181 C5
Battle Cres
  Hailsham BN27 .... 152 B8
  St Leonards TN37 .... 136 B4
Battle Gates TN33...... 112 B5
Battle Hill TN33 .... 112 E3
Battle & Langton CE Prim
  Sch TN33 .... 112 C4
Battle Rd
  Hailsham BN27 .... 129 C1
  St Leonards TN37 .... 136 A4
Battle Sta TN33 .... 112 E4
Batts Bridge Rd TN22 .. 55 A4
Bavant Rd BN1 .... 142 E2
Baxter Rd BN7 .... 123 B2
Baxters La RH17 .... 34 C6
Baxter St BN2 .... 164 C7
Bay Ave BN24 .... 175 E5
Bay Cotts BN24 .... 176 C7
Bayencourt N 1 TN40 .. 157 C5
Bayencourt S 2 TN40 .. 157 C5
Bayeux Ct
  Bexhill TN40 .... 157 D3
  St Leonards TN37 .... 159 D8
Bayhall Rd TN2 .... 8 C3
Bayham Ct TN5 .... 29 E6
Bayham Old Abbey★ TN3 . 19 B5
Bayham Rd
  Bells Yew Green TN3 ..... 18 B4
  Eastbourne BN22....... 185 C4
  Hailsham BN27 .... 152 D7
  Royal Tunbridge Wells TN2,
  TN3 .... 17 C7
Bayley's La BN26...... 151 B2
Baylis Cres RH15 .... 72 D4
Bay Pond Rd BN21 .... 184 D4
Bay Rd BN24 .... 175 D4
Bay Terr BN24 .... 175 D5
Bay Tree Cl
  Heathfield TN21 .... 82 C5
  Shoreham-by-S BN43... 140 C1
Bay Tree La BN26 .... 172 F8
Bayview Rd BN10 .... 178 E5
Bay Vue Rd BN9 .... 179 D7
Baywood Gdns BN2 .... 165 C8
Bazehill Manor BN2.... 166 A3
Bazehill Rd BN2 .... 165 F2
Beach Cl BN25 .... 180 D3
Beach Cotts BN25 .... 180 C4
Beach Ct 12 BN43 .... 161 A6
Beachings The BN24 .... 175 C4
BEACHLANDS 175 F6
Beach Mews
  7 Eastbourne BN22.... 185 C5
  Newhaven BN9 .... 179 E7
Beach Rd
  Eastbourne BN22....... 185 C5
  Newhaven BN9 .... 179 E6
Beachy Head Countryside
  Ctr★ BN20 .... 188 B4
Beachy Head Rd BN20... 188 C4
Beachy Head View TN37. 135 F7
Beacon Bsns Pk TN6 .... 38 C8
Beacon Cl
  Brighton BN1 .... 143 A4
  Crowborough TN6 .... 25 E2
  Seaford BN25 .... 180 D5

Beacon Com Coll TN6 .... 26 A2
Beacon Ct BN2 .... 165 D4
BEACON DOWN 81 A7
Beacon Dr BN25 .... 180 E5
Beaconfield Ho TN6.... 25 E2
Beacon Gdns TN6 .... 25 E3
Beacon Hill
  Bexhill TN39 .... 157 A8
  Dormansland RH7 .... 2 B8
  Ovingdean BN2 .... 165 E3
Beacon Hill Nature Reserve★
  BN2 .... 165 E2
Beacon Ho 6 BN3 .... 162 D7
Beacon Hurst BN6 .... 98 B3
Beacon La TN32 .... 88 E7
Beacon Rd
  Crowborough TN6 .... 25 E2
  Ditchling BN6 .... 98 C2
  Hastings TN35 .... 160 E8
  Seaford BN25 .... 180 D4
Beacon Road W TN6 .... 25 D2
Beaconsfield Cotts RH17. 51 F3
Beaconsfield Rd
  Bexhill TN40 .... 157 C6
  Brighton BN1 .... 164 A8
  Chelwood Gate RH17.... 34 D8
  Hastings TN34 .... 136 F2
  Portslade-by-S BN41 .... 162 B8
Beaconsfield Terr TN21 . 81 B8
Beaconsfield Villas BN1 . 142 F1
Beaconsville Ct BN1 .... 142 F1
Beagles Wood Rd TN2... 9 E7
Beal Cres BN1 .... 143 B2
Beales La TN31 .... 67 B6
Beale St RH15 .... 72 F1
Beame Ct BN25 .... 180 D3
Beamsley Rd BN22 .... 185 C4
Beaney's La TN34, TN35.. 136 E6
Bear Rd BN2 .... 164 D8
Bear Yd BN7 .... 190 B2
Beatrice La 2 BN21 .... 184 F3
Beatrice Wlk TN39 .... 157 A6
Beatty Ave BN20 .... 184 B5
Beatty Rd BN23 .... 185 E7
Beauchamp Rd TN38 .... 136 A4
Beauford Rd TN21 .... 106 F7
Beaufort Cres TN37 .... 136 C2
Beaufort Ct TN37 .... 136 C2
Beaufort Ho 13 TN37 ... 159 C7
Beaufort Rd TN37 .... 136 C2
Beaufort Terr BN2 .... 164 C6
Beauharrow Rd TN37.... 136 A6
Beau Ho BN1 .... 189 A4
Beaulieu Ct TN40 .... 157 F5
Beaulieu Dr BN24 .... 174 A5
Beaulieu Gdns TN37.... 136 C6
Beaulieu Lodge TN39 ... 156 C2
Beaulieu Rd TN39 .... 156 D2
Beauport Gdns TN37 .... 136 A7
Beauport Home Farm Cl
  TN37 .... 136 A6
Beaver Cl TN6 .... 26 A1
Beckenham Cl BN27.... 129 B3
Becket Cl TN34 .... 160 A5
Beckets Way TN22 .... 79 B5
Beckett Way
  11 East Grinstead RH19 ... 10 F8
  Lewes BN7 .... 190 A4
BECKLEY 68 A4
Beckley CE Prim Sch
  TN31 .... 68 A4
Beckley Cl
  Brighton BN2 .... 164 E5
  St Leonards TN38 .... 135 D2
BECKLEY FURNACE 90 D7
Beckworth Cl RH16 .... 51 A6
Beckworth La RH16 .... 51 A6
Bedales RH17 .... 51 D4
Bedales Cnr RH17 .... 51 D4
Bedales Hill RH16, RH17.. 51 D4
BEDDINGHAM 147 D4
Beddingham Gdns BN8.. 147 F5
Bedelands Cl RH15 .... 73 B5
Bedford Ave TN40 .... 157 D3
Bedford Ct TN22 .... 78 C8
Bedford Gr BN21 .... 184 F4
Bedford Pl
  Brighton BN1 .... 163 E6
  Uckfield TN22 .... 78 C8
Bedford Rd TN35 .... 160 C6
Bedford Sq BN1 .... 163 E6
Bedford St BN2 .... 164 C4
Bedford Terr 13 TN1 .... 8 A2
Bedfordwell Ct 3 BN22 . 185 A4
Bedfordwell Rd BN22 ... 185 A4
Bedgebury Cl TN38..... 135 E2
Bedgebury National
  Pinetum★ TN17...... 32 E8
Beecham Pl TN38 .... 135 F4
Beech Ave BN27 .... 127 C3
Beech Cl
  Battle TN33 .... 112 C7
  Bexhill TN39 .... 156 C6
  2 East Grinstead RH19 ... 1 D2
  Hawkenbury TN2 .... 8 C1
  Portslade-by-S BN41.... 140 F3
Beech Ct
  East Grinstead RH19 .... 1 D2
  Polegate BN26 .... 173 A6
  Royal Tunbridge Wells TN2.. 8 D4
Beechers Rd BN41 .... 140 F3
Beeches Cl
  Heathfield TN21 .... 82 B8
  Uckfield TN22 .... 78 D8
Beeches Farm Rd TN6.... 26 A1
Beeches La RH19 .... 11 D6
Beeches Mead RH19 .... 2 F5

Beeches Rd TN6 .... 26 B2
Beeches The
  Brighton BN1 .... 142 D3
  Crowborough TN6 .... 26 B1
  Royal Tunbridge Wells TN2.. 8 D5
  St Leonards TN37 .... 135 F6
  The Moor TN18 .... 45 E7
Beech Farm Rd TN33.... 88 D3
Beechfield Cl BN24 ..... 174 B6
Beechfields RH19 .... 1 F3
Beech Gr BN2 .... 143 E3
Beech Green La TN7 .... 14 B7
Beech Hill RH16 .... 51 B4
Beech House La TN19,
  TN32 .... 64 C6
Beech Hurst TN2 .... 9 D7
Beech Hurst Cl RH16 .... 50 C4
Beech Hurst Cotts RH16.. 50 C4
Beeching Cl TN39 .... 157 B4
Beeching Park Ind Est
  TN39 .... 157 B4
Beeching Rd TN39 .... 157 B4
Beeching Way RH19...... 1 E1
Beechlands Cotts TN5... 28 F3
Beech Manor TN2 .... 8 D3
Beech Rd TN18 .... 48 C3
Beech St TN1 .... 8 B4
Beech Villas 1 TN21.... 82 A6
Beechwood 6 BN1 .... 142 E3
Beechwood Ave BN1 .... 142 F4
Beechwood Cl
  Brighton BN1 .... 142 F4
  Burwash RH19 .... 62 B7
  Hailsham BN27 .... 152 C5
Beechwood Cres BN20... 184 B5
Beechwood Gdns TN37.. 136 D5
Beechwood La
  Cooksbridge BN7, BN8... 122 F8
  Heathfield TN21 .... 82 B5
Beechwood Mews TN2... 8 E4
Beechwoods RH15 .... 73 A1
Beechwood Sacred Heart
  Sch TN2 .... 8 E4
Beechy Ave BN20 .... 184 B5
Beechy Gdns BN20 .... 184 B5
Beechy Rd TN22 .... 80 A2
Beeding Ave BN3 .... 141 F4
Beeding Ct
  Brighton BN1 .... 142 C5
  4 Shoreham-by-S BN43.. 161 B8
Bee Rd BN10 .... 178 C8
Beeson Ho 1 BN41 .... 162 C7
Beggar's La TN38 .... 136 A4
Beggar's Wood Rd BN8.. 75 C6
Belbourne Ct 7 BN1.... 189 B3
Belfast St BN3 .... 163 B7
Belfield Rd TN2 .... 9 D6
Belfry Orch TN22 .... 78 D5
Belfry The BN27 .... 152 A8
Belgrave Ct 7 TN40 .... 157 D3
Belgrave Pl 11 BN2.... 164 D4
Belgrave Rd
  Royal Tunbridge Wells TN1.. 8 B4
  Seaford BN25 .... 180 E4
Belgrave St BN2 .... 189 C3
Bellagio Pl RH19 .... 1 D3
Bell Alley Rd TN19 .... 62 B5
Bell Banks Rd BN27 .... 152 C7
Bellbrookbus Pk TN22... 78 B6
Belle Hill TN35 .... 157 B5
Bellerbys Coll BN1 .... 189 B4
Bellevue Cotts BN2 .... 164 F8
Bellevue Ct
  Brighton BN1 .... 142 F1
  3 Eastbourne BN22..... 185 C5
Belle Vue Ct BN2 .... 164 D5
Belle Vue Gdns BN2 .... 164 D4
Belle Vue Rd 5 BN22... 185 C5
Bell Farm La TN2 .... 78 C7
Bell Farm Rd TN22 .... 78 B6
Bell Hammer RH19 .... 10 E8
Bellhurst Rd TN32 .... 64 A4
Bellingham Cl TN37 .... 136 B4
Bellingham Cres BN3 ... 162 D8
Bell La
  Lewes BN7 .... 146 B8
  Nutley TN22 .... 35 A4
  Uckfield TN22 .... 78 B6
Bellmead 8 BN2 .... 163 D7
BELLS YEW GREEN 17 F5
Bell Tower Ind Est 7
  BN2 .... 164 E4
Bell Wlk TN22 .... 78 C6
Belmaine Ct TN39 .... 156 F4
BELMONT 137 C1
Belmont
  Bexhill TN39 .... 157 B3
  Brighton BN1, BN3 ...... 163 E7
Belmont Cl BN6 .... 97 E5
Belmont Ct
  4 Brighton BN1 .... 163 E7
  Hailsham BN27 .... 152 B7
Belmont La BN6 .... 97 C5
Belmont Rd
  Hastings TN35 .... 160 C5
  Uckfield TN22 .... 78 C7
Belmont St BN1 .... 189 B3
Belmore Rd BN22 .... 185 B4
Belton Cl BN2 .... 164 B8
Belton Rd BN2 .... 164 B8
Beltring Rd
  Eastbourne BN22....... 185 B4
  Royal Tunbridge Wells TN4.. 8 A6
Beltring Terr BN22 .... 185 B4
Belvedere
  Brighton BN1 .... 163 E8

Belvedere continued
  Eastbourne BN23....... 175 A1
Belvedere Ct 13 BN21 ... 184 F4
Belvedere Gdns
  Crowborough TN6 .... 26 A1
  Seaford BN25 .... 181 A5
Belvedere Pk TN38 .... 159 A8
Belvedere Terr 5 BN1 .. 163 E6
Belvedere Wlk BN3 .... 50 C3
Bembridge Rd BN23..... 174 B3
Bembridge St BN2 .... 164 C8
Bembrook Rd TN34 .... 160 B5
Benbow Ave BN23 .... 185 E6
Benbow Ho TN39 .... 156 E4
Benchfield Cl RH19 ..... 2 B1
Bending Cres TN40...... 157 C5
Benenden Cl BN25 .... 181 A4
Benenden Rise TN34 .... 136 E3
Benett Ave BN3 .... 142 B2
Benett Dr BN3 .... 142 B2
Benfield Cl BN41 .... 141 C1
Benfield Cres BN41 ..... 141 C1
Benfield Jun Sch BN41.. 162 C8
Benfield Valley Rd BN41.. 141 C1
Bengairn Ave BN1 .... 143 A7
Benhall Mill Rd TN2, TN3.. 17 D8
Benham 10 BN3 .... 163 B5
Benjamin Cl BN22 .... 173 F2
Benjamin Lodge RH15... 73 D3
Bennett Meml Diocesan Sch
  TN4 .... 7 E6
Bennett Rd BN2 .... 164 E4
Bennetts Yd TN32 .... 64 B4
Benson Ct BN3 .... 162 E7
Bentham Hill TN3 .... 7 D8
Bentham Rd BN2 .... 164 C7
Bentley House & Motor
  Mus★ BN8 .... 103 F5
Bentley Wildfowl Reserve★
  BN8 .... 103 F4
Bentswood Cres RH16... 51 A5
Bentswood Rd RH16 .... 50 F5
Berberis Ct BN43 .... 140 B1
Beresford Cl TN17 .... 20 F2
Beresford 12 BN3 .... 163 D7
Beresford Ho BN10...... 167 C1
Beresford Rd
  Brighton BN2 .... 164 D5
  Newhaven BN9 .... 168 E1
Bergamot Cres BN43 .... 140 C1
Beristede Cl BN20 .... 184 E1
Berkeley Cl TN2 .... 9 E7
Berkeley Ct
  4 Eastbourne BN21..... 185 A1
  6 Hove BN3 .... 163 E7
Berkeley Mans 3 TN40.. 157 D3
Berkeley Rd 7 TN1 .... 8 A2
Berkeley Row BN7 .... 146 A8
Berkeley Wlk BN3 .... 174 E3
Berkley Rd TN20 .... 39 E1
Berkshire Ct 7 BN22.... 185 B4
Berlin Rd TN35 .... 160 C6
Bermuda Pl BN23 .... 185 G8
Bernard La BN1 .... 184 F3
Bernard Pl BN2 .... 164 C7
Bernard Rd BN2 .... 164 C7
Bernhard Baron Cottage
  Homes The BN26 .... 172 F5
Bernhard Gdns BN26.... 172 F5
Berriedale Ave BN3 ..... 162 E6
Berriedale Ho BN3 .... 162 E6
Berry Cl
  Burgess Hill RH15 .... 73 A5
  Telscombe Cliffs BN10... 167 A1
BERWICK 170 F7
Berwick Cl
  Bexhill TN39 .... 156 C6
  Eastbourne BN22....... 173 C3
  Seaford BN25 .... 180 D4
Berwick Ct 1 BN21 .... 185 B3
Berwick Ct Cotts BN26.. 171 A6
Berwick Rd BN2 .... 166 D3
Berwick Sta BN26...... 150 B2
BEST BEECH HILL 29 B3
Betchley Cl RH19 .... 1 E3
Betherinden Cotts TN18.. 47 A4
Bethune Rd TN40 .... 157 C3
Bethune Way TN34 .... 136 F1
Beulah Rd TN1 .... 8 C4
Beuzeville Ave BN27 .... 152 B8
BEVENDEAN 143 F2
Bevendean Ave BN2..... 166 D1
Bevendean Cres BN2 ... 143 E2
Bevendean Prim Sch
  BN2 .... 143 F1
Bevendean Rd BN2 .... 143 D1
Beverington Cl BN21 ... 184 D6
Beverington Rd BN21 ... 184 D6
Beverley Cl 1 BN3 .... 162 D7
Beverley Wlk TN34 .... 160 A6
Bevern Bridge BN8...... 100 F4
Bevern Bridge Cotts
  BN8 .... 100 F4
Beverns The BN7 .... 99 E5
Bevin Ct TN38 .... 136 B3
Bewl Bridge Cl TN5 .... 32 B3
Bewlbridge La
  Lamberhurst TN3, TN5... 20 B1
  Lower Cousley Wood TN5.. 30 F4
Bewl Water Outdoor Ctr
  TN3 .... 31 A8
Bewl Water Visitors Ctr★
  TN3 .... 31 B3
Bewl Wr★ TN5 .... 31 C6
Bexfield Ct
  Beachlands BN24 .... 175 E6

Bexfield Ct continued
  6 Eastbourne BN20...... 184 F1
BEXHILL 157 A2
Bexhill Cl BN25 .... 157 F5
Bexhill High Sch TN39... 157 A7
Bexhill High Sch Tech Coll
  TN39 .... 157 B5
Bexhill Hospl TN40 .... 157 C5
Bexhill Mus★ TN39 ..... 157 B3
Bexhill Mus of Costume &
  Social History★ TN40 . 157 D4
Bexhill Rd
  Eastbourne BN22....... 185 C5
  Lower Street TN33, TN39.. 133 C3
  St Leonards TN38, TN40.. 158 D6
  Woodingdean BN2 ...... 144 A1
Bexhill Sta TN40 .... 157 C4
Bexleigh Ave TN38 ..... 158 D5
Bexley Cl BN27 .... 129 B2
Bexley Ct BN26 .... 173 A7
Bicton Gdns TN39 .... 156 E4
Biddenden Cl BN23 ..... 174 D2
Bidwell Ave TN39 .... 157 A7
Bigwood Ave BN3 .... 163 D6
Bilbury Mews BN1 .... 184 F5
Billingham La TN31 ..... 91 C3
Billington Ct RH19 .... 1 E2
Billinton Way BN1 .... 189 B4
Binsted Cl BN22 .... 173 E1
Biology Rd BN1 .... 144 B6
Birch Ave RH17 .... 51 A3
Birch Cl
  Eastbourne BN23....... 185 D7
  Haywards Heath RH17... 51 B3
  Royal Tunbridge Wells TN2.. 8 D1
  Uckfield TN22 .... 78 E8
Birch Ct BN42 .... 141 A1
BIRCHDEN 15 D5
Birchden Cotts TN3 ..... 15 C6
Birchen La RH16 .... 50 F8
Birches Cl TN6 .... 25 F4
Birches Ind Est RH19 .... 1 A4
Birch Est The BN23...... 185 C7
Birchetts Ave TN3 .... 6 E3
BIRCHETT'S GREEN 30 F3
Birchetts Green La TN5.. 31 A2
Birch Grove Cres BN1... 143 A5
Birchgrove La RH17 .... 22 A1
Birchgrove Rd RH17 .... 33 C7
Birchington Cl TN39..... 156 D4
Birch Kiln Cotts TN5 .... 30 A6
Bircholme TN2 .... 8 D7
Birch Path TN22 .... 78 D8
Birch Rd BN23 .... 185 C7
Birch Rdbt BN23 .... 185 C7
Birch Terr TN21 .... 81 D7
Birch Tree Gdns RH19 ... 1 B3
Birch View TN39 .... 157 C6
Birch Way
  Hailsham BN27 .... 152 B6
  Hastings TN34 .... 136 E3
  Haywards Heath RH17... 51 A2
  Heathfield TN21 .... 82 A5
  Royal Tunbridge Wells TN2.. 8 D7
Birchwood Grove Com Prim
  Sch RH15 .... 73 C1
Birchwood Gr Rd RH15.. 73 C1
Birdham Pl BN23 .... 143 E3
Birdham Rd BN2 .... 143 F3
Bird in Eye Hill TN22 .... 78 E6
Bird in Hand St TN3 .... 15 B8
Bird La TN5 .... 29 B5
Birkdale TN1 .... 8 B6
Birk Dale TN39 .... 156 D4
Birken Rd TN2 .... 8 D6
Birling Cl
  Brighton BN2 .... 143 D3
  Seaford BN25 .... 180 D4
BIRLING GAP 187 A5
Birling Gap Rd BN20 .... 187 B6
Birling Park Ave TN2.... 17 B8
Birling Rd TN2 .... 17 B8
Birling St BN21 .... 184 D4
Birling Way TN22 .... 78 E8
Biscay Ave BN23 .... 185 F6
Bishop Bell CE Sch
  BN23 .... 174 E1
Bishops Cl BN25 .... 180 C4
Bishop's Cl
  Hurstpierpoint BN6 ...... 97 A7
  Ringmer BN8 .... 124 E6
Bishops Ct TN4 .... 7 E5
Bishop's Down TN4 ...... 7 E5
Bishop's Down Park Rd
  TN4 .... 7 F4
Bishop's Down Prim Sch
  TN4 .... 7 E5
Bishop's Down Rd TN4 .. 7 F3
Bishops Dr BN7 .... 146 A8
Bishop's La
  Ringmer BN8 .... 124 D6
  Robertsbridge TN32..... 64 A3
Bishops Rd BN3 .... 142 C1
BISHOPSTONE 180 C6
Bishopstone Dr BN2 .... 166 B2
Bishopstone La BN6, RH17.. 72 A7
Bishopstone Rd BN25... 180 C6
Bishopstone Sta BN25... 180 B4
Bishop's Wlk TN40 .... 157 F6
Bittern Ct BN27 .... 152 D7
Bixley La TN31 .... 68 B2
Blackberry La★ RH19 .... 1 E8
Blackberry Rd RH19, RH7.. 1 D8
Blackbird Cl RH15 .... 72 D3

BLACKBOYS 80 A5
Blackboys CE Prim Sch
  TN22 . . . . 80 A6
Blackboys YH★ TN22 . . . . 80 A8
Blackbrook La BN8, RH17 . 52 E2
Blackdon Hill TN3 . . . . 27 B6
Blackdown BN2 . . . . 164 F7
Blackdown Rd TN21 . . . . . . 83 D6
Blackdown Rdbt TN22 . . . . 55 B3
Blackfields Ave TN39 . . . . 156 F5
BLACKHAM 5 A4
Black Hill RH16 . . . . 51 A7
Blackhorse Mews TN4 . . . . . 9 C6
Blackhouse La RH15 . . . . . 73 B4
BLACKHURST 8 F5
Blackhurst La TN2 . . . . 8 F6
BLACKLANDS 136 F2
Blacklands TN33 . . . . 88 F1
Blacklands Cres RH18 . . . . 11 F2
Blacklands Dr★ TN32 . . . . 136 F2
Blacklands Prim Sch
  TN34 . . . . 136 E2
Black Lion La BN1 . . . . . . 189 A2
Black Lion St BN1 . . . . . . 189 B1
Blackman Ave TN38 . . . . . 136 A3
Blackman St BN1 . . . . 189 B3
Blackmill Cl TN39 . . . . 157 A8
Blackmore Ct BN1 . . . . . . 189 B4
Blackmores RH17 . . . . 74 A5
BLACKNESS
  Crowborough 26 A1
  Eastbourne 174 A6
Blackness Rd TN6 . . . . 38 A8
Blackness Villas TN6 . . . . . 38 A8
Black Path BN26 . . . . 173 A6
BLACK ROCK 164 F3
Black Rock (for Marina)
  Sta★ BN2 . . . . 164 E3
Blacksmiths Copse
  BN27 . . . . 152 A6
Blacksmiths Field TN32 . . 46 C1
Blacksmith's Field TN33 . 135 A4
Blacksmiths La TN33 . . . . 133 E8
Blacksmith's La TN5 . . . . . 30 A5
Blackstone Way RH15 . . . . 73 A5
Blackthorn Cl
  Brighton BN1 . . . . 142 D3
  Eastbourne 173 E2
  Portslade-by-S BN41 . . . . 141 B2
  St Leonards TN37 . . . . . . 136 C4
Blackthorns RH16 . . . . 51 A7
Blackthorns Cl RH16 . . . . . 51 A6
Blackthorns Com Prim Sch
  RH16 . . . . 51 A6
Blackthorns The RH15 . . . 73 B5
Blackthorn Way TN35 . . . 138 F4
Blackwater Rd BN20,
  BN21 . . . . 184 F1
BLACKWELL 1 E3
Blackwell Farm Rd RH19 . . 1 F3
Blackwell Hollow RH19 . . . . 1 F2
Blackwell Prim Sch RH19 . 1 E3
Blackwell Rd RH19 . . . . 1 F2
Blake Ct ③ BN2 . . . . 189 C3
Blakeney Ave BN10, BN9 . 179 A6
Blaker St BN2 . . . . 189 C2
Blakes Way BN23 . . . . 185 F6
Blake Way TN2 . . . . 8 D7
Blanshard Cl BN2 . . . . . . 130 E6
Blatchington Cl BN25 . . . . 180 E4
Blatchington Hill BN25 . . 180 E4
Blatchington Hill Flats
  BN25 . . . . 180 F5
Blatchington Mill Dr
  BN24 . . . . 174 C5
Blatchington Mill Sch & Sixth
  Form Coll BN3 . . . . 142 A2
Blatchington Rd
  Hove BN3 . . . . 163 B7
  Royal Tunbridge Wells TN1 . . 8 B1
  Seaford BN25 . . . . 180 E3
Blenheim Cl RH19 . . . . 2 A3
Blenheim Ct
  ① Hove BN3 . . . . 163 A6
  Robertsbridge TN32 . . . . . 64 B3
Blenheim Fields RH18 . . . 11 E3
Blenheim Mews RH16 . . . 50 F2
Blenheim Pl ⑤ BN1 . . . . 189 B3
Blenheim Way
  Flimwell TN5 . . . . 32 C3
  Polegate BN26 . . . . 173 D6
Blessing Lodge ⑤ BN43 . 161 B6
Bletchinglye La TN6 . . . . . . 27 E1
Bletchley Ct BN1 . . . . 164 A8
Blind La BN8 . . . . 76 E6
Blois Rd BN7 . . . . 123 B2
Blomfield Rd TN37 . . . . . 159 D8
Bloomsbury Pl ⑰ BN2 . . 164 C4
Bloomsbury St ⑯ BN2 . . 164 C4
Blossom Wlk BN27 . . . . . 129 B1
Blount Ave RH19 . . . . 1 C1
Blowers Hill
  Cowden TN8 . . . . 4 D8
  Speldhurst TN3 . . . . 7 B8
Bluebell Bsns Est TN22 . . 53 A4
Bluebell Cl
  East Grinstead RH19 . . . . 1 B1
  Haywards Heath RH16 . . . 50 F4
Bluebell Glade BN27 . . . 127 B4
Bluebell Rly Mus★ TN22 . 53 A4
Bluebell Rly The★ TN22 . 53 A5
Bluebell Way RH15 . . . . . . 72 D4
Bluebell Wlk & Farm Trail★
  BN26 . . . . 151 B4
Bluebird Cl ① BN43 . . . . 161 B6

Bluebird Ct ⑪ BN3 . . . . 163 A6
Blue Haze Ave BN25 . . . . 181 B4
Bluemans La TN33 . . . . . 114 A4
Blue Reef Aquarium★
  TN34 . . . . 160 B3
Bluestone Cl TN38 . . . . . 135 F2
Blunts Wood Cres RH16 . 50 B6
Blunts Wood Rd RH16 . . . 50 C6
Blytons The RH19 . . . . 1 B1
Boarders La TN5 . . . . 31 C3
BOARSHEAD 26 C6
Boast La BN8 . . . . 101 F5
Boathouse The ④ TN31 . . 93 C5
Boatyard The BN2 . . . . . . 165 A3
Bocking Cl TN5 . . . . 29 E4
Bocks Hill TN32 . . . . 64 E6
Boddingtons La BN6 . . . . . 98 D3
BODIAM 65 E8
Bodiam Ave
  Bexhill TN40 . . . . 157 D6
  Brighton BN2 . . . . 144 B1
Bodiam Bsns Pk TN32 . . . 65 C7
Bodiam Castle★ TN32 . . . 65 F8
Bodiam CE Prim Sch
  TN32 . . . . 65 E8
Bodiam Cl
  Brighton BN2 . . . . 144 B2
  Seaford BN25 . . . . 181 C4
Bodiam Cres BN22 . . . . . 174 A2
Bodiam Ct RH16 . . . . 50 E5
Bodiam Dr TN38 . . . . 135 D2
Bodiam Manor Sch TN32 . 65 F3
Bodiam Rd TN18, TN32 . . 46 F3
Bodiam Ho ⑮ BN3 . . . . . 163 D7
Bodle Cres TN39 . . . . 157 B7
BODLE STREET GREEN . . 109 C2
Bodmin Dr BN20 . . . . 184 C3
BOHEMIA 136 C1
Bohemia Rd TN34, TN37 . 159 D8
Boiler House Hill BN1 . . . 144 B7
Bolding Way RH16 . . . . . . 50 E2
Bolebrooke Rd TN40 . . . . 157 D3
Bolney Ave BN10 . . . . 178 C6
Bolney Rd BN2 . . . . 143 F4
Bolnore RH16 . . . . 50 B4
Bolnore Rd RH16 . . . . 50 C4
BOLNORE VILLAGE 50 C2
Bolsover Ct BN20 . . . . . . 188 F8
Bolsover Rd
  Eastbourne BN20 . . . . . . 188 F8
  Hove BN3 . . . . 162 F8
Bolton Cl TN22 . . . . 78 A6
Bolton Rd BN21 . . . . 185 A2
Boltro Rd RH16 . . . . 50 D5
Bonaventure ② BN43 . . . 161 B6
Bonchurch Rd BN2 . . . . . 164 C7
Bond St BN1 . . . . 189 B2
Bonfire La RH17 . . . . 33 D5
Boniface CE Prim Sch
  TN22 . . . . 55 B4
Bonny Wood Rd BN6 . . . . 97 E3
Booker Cl TN6 . . . . 26 A1
Booth Mus of Natural
  History★ BN1 . . . . 163 E8
Bopeep Bostal BN26 . . . . 170 B7
Bopeep La BN26 . . . . 170 B8
Border Ct RH19 . . . . 1 F4
Borders La TN5 . . . . 62 F7
Boreham Hill BN27, TN33 . 132 A4
Boreham La BN27 . . . . . . 131 C2
BOREHAM STREET 131 F4
Borodales TN39 . . . . 156 E4
Borough La BN20 . . . . . . 184 D3
Borough St BN1 . . . . 163 E6
Borrowdale Cl BN23 . . . . 174 C4
Borrow King Cl BN2 . . . . 164 D8
Boscawen Cl BN23 . . . . . 185 F7
Boscobel Cl TN38 . . . . . . 159 A6
Boscobel Lodge TN38 . . . 159 B7
Boscobel Rd TN38 . . . . . 159 A7
Boscobel Road N TN38 . . 159 A7
Boship Cl BN23 . . . . 174 A4
Bostal Rd BN8 . . . . 148 B4
Boston Cl BN23 . . . . 185 F7
Boston Ct RH16 . . . . 51 A5
Boston Rd RH16 . . . . 51 A5
Boston St BN1 . . . . 189 B4
Boswell Wlk ② BN23 . . . 174 E2
Bough Beeches RH15 . . . 73 C1
Boughey Pl BN7 . . . . 190 A4
Boulevard The BN24 . . . . 175 F6
Boundary Pas ⑩ BN3 . . . 163 E6
Boundary Rd
  Brighton BN2 . . . . 164 F4
  Portslade-by-S BN3, BN41 162 C7
  Royal Tunbridge Wells TN2 . . 8 D1
Boundary The
  Langton Green TN3 . . . . . 7 B3
  ⑳ Seaford BN25 . . . . . . 180 E2
Boundsway TN22 . . . . 78 E8
Bourg-de-Peage Ave RH19 2 A1
Bourne Ct
  Brighton BN1 . . . . 142 D4
  ⑳ Hastings TN34 . . . . . . 160 B4
Bourne Cty Prim Sch
  BN22 . . . . 185 B3
Bourne La
  Northbridge Street TN32 . 64 F7
  Sandhurst Cross TN18 . . . 46 E4
Bourne Pas ⑫ TN34 . . . . 160 B4
Bourneside Ct ⑫ BN22 . . 185 B3
Bourne St BN21 . . . . 185 B3
Bourne The
  Hassocks BN6 . . . . 97 E5
  Hastings TN34 . . . . 160 B4

Bowden House Sch
  BN25 . . . . 180 E4
Bowden Rise BN25 . . . . . 180 E6
Bowen Ct ⑪ BN3 . . . . . . 163 C6
Bowen Rd TN4 . . . . 7 B4
Bower Cl TN37 . . . . 136 B4
Bowerhill Cotts RH19 . . . . 21 F6
Bower The RH16 . . . . 50 D5
Bowlers Town TN31 . . . . . 70 A2
Bowles Outdoor Ctr TN6 . . 26 E6
Bowley Rd BN27 . . . . 152 C7
Bowlings The TN33 . . . . . 113 D8
Bowmans Dr TN33 . . . . . 112 D6
Bowood Ave BN22 . . . . . . 185 B6
Bowrey Pl TN40 . . . . 157 C5
Bowring Way BN2 . . . . . . 164 D4
Bowsprit Mews TN38 . . . 135 E7
Boxes La RH17 . . . . 33 C5
Boxgate TN6 . . . . 25 D4
Boxgrove Cl TN40 . . . . . . 157 F4
Box La RH17 . . . . 11 E6
Box's La RH17 . . . . 34 C6
Boyce's La BN1 . . . . 189 A2
Boyles La ⑭ BN2 . . . . . . 164 E4
Boyne Pk TN4 . . . . 7 F4
Boyne Rd TN35 . . . . 160 C5
Brackenbury Cl BN41 . . . 141 B2
Bracken Cl
  Crowborough TN6 . . . . . . 26 C1
  Royal Tunbridge Wells TN2 . . 8 E5
Brackendale TN35 . . . . . . 160 D6
Brackenhill TN7 . . . . 13 A1
Bracken Rd
  Eastbourne BN20 . . . . . . 184 B5
  Royal Tunbridge Wells TN2 . . 8 E5
  Seaford BN25 . . . . 181 A4
Bracken Way TN21 . . . . . . 59 E1
Brackerne Cl TN39 . . . . . 156 C2
Bradford Ct ⑨ BN22 . . . 185 B4
Bradford Rd BN7 . . . . 123 B1
Bradford St BN21 . . . . . . 184 B1
Brading Cl
  Eastbourne BN23 . . . . . . 174 B4
  Hastings TN34 . . . . 136 B4
Brading Rd BN2 . . . . 164 C7
Bradley Rd
  Wartling BN27 . . . . 131 C1
  White Post TN3 . . . . 5 D5
Braemar Ct ② TN39 . . . . 157 A4
Braemar Ho ⑪ BN1 . . . . 163 E6
Braemore Ct BN3 . . . . . . 162 E6
Braemore Rd BN3 . . . . . . 162 E6
Braeside Ave BN1 . . . . . . 143 A7
Bramber Ave
  Hove BN3 . . . . 141 F3
  Peacehaven BN10 . . . . . . 178 C7
Bramber Avenue N
  BN10 . . . . 178 C8
Bramber Cl
  Haywards Heath RH16 . . . 50 D4
  Peacehaven BN10 . . . . . . 178 C8
  ③ Seaford BN25 . . . . . . 180 F2
Bramber Ct
  ⑧ Hove BN3 . . . . 163 B7
  ② Shoreham-by-S BN43 . 161 B8
Bramber Ho ⑰ BN1 . . . . 184 E4
Bramber La BN25 . . . . . . 180 F2
Bramber Rd BN25 . . . . . . 180 F2
Bramber Way RH15 . . . . . 73 A4
Bramble Cl BN23 . . . . 174 B3
Bramble Croft TN6 . . . . . . 26 A2
Brambledean Rd BN41 . . 162 B7
Bramble Dr BN27 . . . . 152 A7
Bramble Gdns RH15 . . . . 72 D4
Bramble Rise BN1 . . . . . . 142 C5
Brambles BN6 . . . . 97 F5
Brambleside TN22 . . . . . . 78 A6
Brambles The RH17 . . . . . 50 A6
Bramble Twitten RH19 . . . 2 A1
Brambletye La RH18 . . . . 11 D4
Brambletye Prep Sch
  RH19 . . . . 11 C5
Brambletye Ave BN2 . . . . 166 D1
Bramble Way
  Brighton BN1 . . . . 143 C6
  Fairlight Cove TN35 . . . . . 138 F4
Bramble Wlk TN2 . . . . 8 D7
Bramlea Cl TN40 . . . . 158 A6
Bramley Rd BN26 . . . . . . 173 D6
Bramleys BN7 . . . . 145 E5
Bramley Wlk BN27 . . . . . 131 B5
Brampton Ave TN39 . . . . 156 F4
Brampton Ct TN39 . . . . . 156 F4
Brampton Rd BN22 . . . . . 184 F8
Brampton Road Trad Est
  BN22 . . . . 185 A8
Brand Rd BN22 . . . . 173 E1
Brands Cl BN2 . . . . 168 E2
Brangwyn Ave BN1 . . . . . 142 E5
Brangwyn Cres BN1 . . . . 142 E6
Brangwyn Ct BN1 . . . . . . 142 E5
Brangwyn Dr BN1 . . . . . . 142 E5
Brangwyn's Acre BN6 . . . 98 D3
Brangwyn Way BN1 . . . . . 142 E5
Branksome Rd TN38 . . . . 159 A8
Branston Rd BN22 . . . . . . 173 D1
Brassey Ave BN22 . . . . . . 173 E1
Brassey Par BN22 . . . . . . 173 F1
Brassey Rd TN40 . . . . 157 D3
Brasslands Dr BN41 . . . . 140 F1
Braybon Ave BN1 . . . . . . 142 F4
Braybon Bsns Pk RH15 . . 72 E2
Braybrooke Cl TN34 . . . . 159 E8
Braybrooke Rd TN34 . . . . 159 E8
Braybrooke Terr TN34 . . 159 E8
Braypool La BN1 . . . . 142 D7
Brazen Cl BN9 . . . . 179 B7
Breadsell La TN38 . . . . . 135 D6

Bread St BN1 . . . . 189 B3
Brecon Cotts TN6 . . . . 39 A8
Brecon Ct ⑥ BN3 . . . . . . 163 C7
Brecon Terr TN6 . . . . 39 A8
BREDE 90 B1
Brede Cl
  Brighton BN2 . . . . 164 F5
  Eastbourne BN22 . . . . . . 185 D6
Brede Hill TN31 . . . . 115 B8
Brede La TN31, TN33 . . . . 89 B2
Brede Prim Sch TN31 . . . 90 B4
Brede Valley View TN36 . 116 E5
Breeds TN34 . . . . 159 F7
Brendon Cl
  Eastbourne BN23 . . . . . . 174 E4
  Royal Tunbridge Wells TN2 . . 8 D5
Brendon Rise TN34 . . . . . 160 B7
Brentor Ct TN2 . . . . 8 D6
Brentwood Cl BN1 . . . . . 143 B3
Brentwood Cres BN1 . . . 143 B3
Brentwood Rd BN1 . . . . . 143 B3
Bretland Ct TN4 . . . . 7 D4
Bretland Rd TN4 . . . . 7 D4
Brett Dr TN40 . . . . 157 F4
Bretton RH15 . . . . 72 E5
Bretts Cotts TN22 . . . . . . 79 B7
Bretts Field TN10 . . . . . . 167 C2
Brewers Gr TN20 . . . . 40 B2
Brewer St
  Brighton BN2 . . . . 189 C4
  Lamberhurst TN3 . . . . 20 A5
Brian Cres TN4 . . . . 8 B8
Briar Cl
  Fairlight Cove TN35 . . . . . 139 A5
  Woodingdean BN2 . . . . . . 165 D7
Briarcroft Rd BN2 . . . . . . 165 D7
Briar Pl BN23 . . . . 174 B3
Briary The TN40 . . . . 157 D5
Brickfield TN31 . . . . 69 B2
Brickfields TN2 . . . . 9 E8
Brickhurst La BN8 . . . . . . 126 F6
Brick Kiln La TN20, TN22 . 57 E6
Brickyard Cotts TN6 . . . . 28 A4
Brickyard La
  Mark Cross TN6 . . . . 27 C5
  South Chailey BN8 . . . . . 100 E7
Bricky The BN10 . . . . 178 D8
Bridge Cl
  Burgess Hill RH15 . . . . . . 72 F4
  Horam TN21 . . . . 107 A2
Bridge Ct BN9 . . . . 179 D7
Bridge End BN24 . . . . 175 B7
Bridge Farm Rd TN22 . . . 78 C6
Bridge Ho TN4 . . . . 8 B5
Bridgelands BN8 . . . . 101 D4
Bridge Pl TN31 . . . . 93 C6
Bridge Rd RH16 . . . . 50 F6
Bridge Rd Bsns Pk RH16 . 50 F7
Bridges Ho RH16 . . . . 50 E6
Bridgersmill RH16 . . . . . . 50 D6
Bridger Way TN6 . . . . 26 A1
Bridge St BN9 . . . . 179 D7
Bridge Way TN38 . . . . . . 158 C6
Bridgewick Cl BN7 . . . . . 190 B4
Bridle Way BN10 . . . . 167 A1
Briers Ave TN34 . . . . 136 C3
Briers Gdns TN34 . . . . . . 136 C3
Briers The TN34 . . . . 136 C4
Brigdens Hill BN8 . . . . . . 147 E6
Brigden St BN1 . . . . 189 A4
Brighthelm BN1 . . . . 144 B8
Brighton & Hove High Sch
  Jun Dept BN3 . . . . 163 D8
BRIGHTLING 85 C7
Brightling Ave TN35 . . . . 160 C8
Brightling Rd
  Polegate BN26 . . . . 173 B5
  Robertsbridge TN32 . . . . 63 D2
BRIGHTON 189 B3
Brighton Coll BN2 . . . . . . 164 C5
Brighton Coll Prep Sch
  BN2 . . . . 164 C4
Brighton Fishing Mus★
  BN1 . . . . 189 A1
Brighton General Hospl
  BN2 . . . . 164 D7
Brighton & Hove City Coll
  BN1 . . . . 143 F8
Brighton & Hove High Sch
  BN1 . . . . 163 E6
Brighton & Hove Stad
  BN3 . . . . 142 B1
Brighton, Hove & Sussex
  Sixth Form Coll BN3 . . . . 163 E8
Brighton Marina BN2 . . . . 164 F2
Brighton Marina Village
  BN2 . . . . 164 F3
Brighton Mus & Art Gall★
  BN1 . . . . 189 B2
Brighton Pl BN1 . . . . 189 B2
Brighton Race Course
  BN2 . . . . 165 A8
Brighton Rd
  Hassocks BN6 . . . . 97 D2
  Kingston near Lewes BN7 . 145 F8
  Lewes BN7 . . . . 146 A8
  Newhaven BN9 . . . . 179 B7
  Shoreham-by-S BN43 . . . . 161 B7
Brighton Sea Life Ctr★
  BN1 . . . . 189 B1
Brighton Sq BN1 . . . . 189 B2
Brighton Sta BN1 . . . . . . 189 B3
Brighton Steiner Sch Ltd
  BN2 . . . . 164 F4

Brighton Toy & Model Mus
  The★ BN1 . . . . 189 B3
Bright Ridge TN4 . . . . 7 E8
Brightwell Ind Est BN9 . . 179 E7
Brills La BN1 . . . . 189 B1
Brincliffe TN6 . . . . 25 E3
Brinkers La TN5 . . . . 30 A2
Brisbane Quay BN23 . . . . 175 A2
Bristol Gate BN2 . . . . 164 D4
Bristol Gdns BN2 . . . . . . 164 E4
Bristol Mews ③ BN2 . . . 164 E4
Bristol Pl BN2 . . . . 164 E4
Bristol Rd
  Brighton BN2 . . . . 164 C4
  St Leonards TN38 . . . . . . 136 A3
Bristol Rise BN2 . . . . 164 D4
Bristol St BN2 . . . . 164 E4
Bristol Way TN38 . . . . . . 136 A3
Britannia Ave BN43 . . . . 161 B6
Britannia Ct BN2 . . . . 165 A3
Britannia Ent Ctr TN34 . . 136 F1
British Engineerium Mus★
  BN3 . . . . 142 B2
Britland Est BN22 . . . . . . 185 C6
Brittany Ct
  ⑤ Bexhill TN39 . . . . 157 A4
  ④ Hove BN3 . . . . 162 D7
Brittany Ho TN6 . . . . 37 D8
Brittany Mews TN38 . . . . 159 B7
Brittany Rd
  Hove BN3 . . . . 162 D6
  St Leonards TN37, TN38 . 159 B8
Britten Cl BN23 . . . . 174 D3
Brittenden La TN21 . . . . . 80 E5
Britts Farm Rd TN22 . . . . 56 C3
Britts Orch TN22 . . . . 56 C3
Broad Buckler TN37 . . . . 136 A6
Broadcroft TN2 . . . . 16 F8
Broadfields BN2 . . . . 143 E3
Broadfields Rd BN2 . . . . 143 E3
Broad Gn BN2 . . . . 165 E6
Broad Gr TN2 . . . . 8 A1
Broad Green Ave RH15 . . 73 C2
Broadhill Cl TN21 . . . . . . 59 E1
Broad La TN3 . . . . 6 A4
BROADLAND ROW 90 D3
Broadlands
  Burgess Hill RH15 . . . . . . 98 B8
  Hastings TN35 . . . . 160 D8
Broadley View TN33 . . . . 133 E8
Broadmead TN2 . . . . 16 F8
Broadmead Ave TN2 . . . . 16 F8
Broad Oak
  Buxted TN22 . . . . 56 C3
  Groombridge TN3 . . . . . . 15 C6
BROAD OAK
  Hastings 90 C4
  Heathfield 59 F1
Broad Oak Cl
  Broad Oak TN31 . . . . 90 B5
  Eastbourne BN23 . . . . . . 174 A4
  Royal Tunbridge Wells TN2 . . 7 F1
Broadoak La TN39 . . . . . . 156 E5
Broad Oak Prim Sch TN21 59 F2
Broad Rd BN20 . . . . 173 A4
Broad Rig Ave BN3 . . . . . 141 D3
Broads Cotts TN19 . . . . . 62 B6
Broad St
  Brighton BN2 . . . . 189 B1
  Cuckfield RH17 . . . . 50 A6
  Icklesham TN36 . . . . 116 C6
  Seaford BN25 . . . . 180 E3
Broadstone RH18 . . . . . . 12 A2
BROAD STREET 116 C6
Broad View
  Bexhill TN39 . . . . 156 F6
  Broad Oak TN21 . . . . 59 E1
Broadview Cl BN20 . . . . . 172 F4
Broadwalk The TN39 . . . 156 B4
Broadwater Ct TN2 . . . . . 16 E8
BROADWATER DOWN . . . 16 E7
Broadwater Down TN2 . . 16 F8
Broadwater Down Prim Sch
  ① TN2 . . . . 7 F1
Broadwater Forest La
  TN3 . . . . 16 B7
Broadwater La TN2, TN4 . . 7 F1
Broadwater Mews BN26 . 172 E3
Broadwater Rise TN2 . . . . 7 F1
Broadwater Way BN22 . . 184 F8
Broadway
  Fairlight Cove TN35 . . . . . 138 F5
  Southwick BN42 . . . . 161 F8
Broadway Ct ⑪ BN43 . . 161 C8
Broadway The
  Alfriston BN26 . . . . 170 F3
  Brighton BN2 . . . . 164 F4
  Crowborough TN6 . . . . . . 25 F3
  Eastbourne BN22 . . . . . . 173 D1
  Hastings TN35 . . . . 160 D8
  Haywards Heath RH16 . . . 50 E5
  Lamberhurst TN3 . . . . 20 B5
Brockhurst BN2 . . . . 164 C7
Brockhurst Gate TN40 . . 157 F5
Brockley Rd TN39 . . . . . . 157 A3
Brocks Ghyll BN20 . . . . . 173 A3
Brodie Rd BN21 . . . . 184 D4
Brodrick Cl BN22 . . . . . . 173 F1
Brodrick Rd BN22 . . . . . . 173 E2
Brokes Way TN4 . . . . 8 B7
Bromley Cl
  Eastbourne BN23 . . . . . . 174 C2
  Keymer BN6 . . . . 98 A4
Bromley Rd
  Brighton BN2 . . . . 189 C5
  Seaford BN25 . . . . 181 A4
Brompton Cl BN1 . . . . . . 142 E6
Brontes The RH19 . . . . 1 D1

Brook Ave BN6 ... 97 F3
Brook Cl
Crowborough TN6 ... 26 D1
East Grinstead RH19 ... 2 B1
Brooke Mead BN2 ... 189 C3
Brooker Pl BN3 ... 163 A7
Brooker St BN3 ... 163 A7
Brookfield TN18 ... 47 B5
Brookfield Ct 2 TN40 ... 157 E4
Brookfield Rd TN40 ... 157 E4
Brook Ho TN39 ... 157 C6
Brookhouse Bottom TN22 34 D4
Brookhouse La TN22 ... 79 A5
Brookhouse Rd TN22 ... 79 A4
Brook La
Beddingham BN8 ... 147 A6
Haywards Heath RH16 ... 50 F8
Brookland Cl
Beachlands BN24 ... 175 E6
Hastings TN34 ... 136 F2
Brookland Ho 5 RH19 ... 1 E1
Brooklands
Haywards Heath RH16 ... 50 C1
Royal Tunbridge Wells TN2... 8 D7
Brooklands Ave TN6 ... 37 F7
Brooklands Farm Cl TN3 .. 6 A6
Brooklands Terr BN27 ... 128 E3
Brooklands Way RH19 ... 10 D8
Brooklyn Rd BN25 ... 180 E3
Brook Manor RH19 ... 10 D7
Brookmead Cl BN22 ... 185 B5
Brook Rd TN2 ... 8 D7
Brooks Cl
Lewes BN7 ... 190 B3
Newhaven BN9 ... 179 D6
Brooks Gdns BN8 ... 76 D6
Brookside
Piddinghoe BN9 ... 168 B2
Uckfield TN22 ... 78 A6
Brookside Ave BN26 ... 172 F7
Brookside Cotts TN19 ... 63 B8
Brooks Rd BN7 ... 190 B3
Brook St
Hastings TN34 ... 159 F8
Lewes BN7 ... 190 B2
Polegate BN26 ... 172 F6
BROOKS THE ... 190 B3
Brooks The RH15 ... 72 E5
Brook Terr TN6 ... 25 D4
Brook View TN6 ... 25 D4
Brookway
Burgess Hill RH15 ... 73 C3
Lindfield RH16 ... 51 A8
Brook Way TN35 ... 160 B8
Brooman's Ct BN7 ... 190 B2
Broomans La BN7 ... 190 B2
Broom Cl BN22 ... 173 D2
Broomfield Ave BN10 ... 177 F4
Broomfield Dr BN41 ... 141 A3
Broomfields BN8 ... 100 D7
Broomfield St BN20,
BN21 ... 184 C4
Broomgrove Rd TN34 ... 160 B6
Broomham La BN8 ... 127 B7
Broomhill Bank Sch TN3 .. 7 C5
Broom Hill Cotts TN5 ... 32 B3
Broomhill Pk Rd TN4 ... 7 F8
Broomhill Rd TN3 ... 7 D7
Broom La TN3 ... 6 E2
Broom Pk TN3 ... 6 E3
BROOMSGROVE ... 137 A2
Bross Est BN9 ... 179 D8
BROWNBREAD STREET ... 110 A2
Browning Rd 2 TN21 ... 82 A7
Brownings The 1 RH19 ... 1 C1
Browning Wlk 5 BN23 ... 174 E2
Brown Jack Ave BN26 ... 172 F6
Brownleaf Rd BN2 ... 165 E6
Browns Cl TN22 ... 78 D8
Browns La TN21 ... 81 B6
Brown's La TN22 ... 78 D8
Brown's Path TN22 ... 78 E8
Browns Wood RH19 ... 1 E4
Brown Twins Rd BN6 ... 97 B5
Brow The
Burgess Hill RH15 ... 73 A2
Friston BN20 ... 183 B2
Woodingdean BN2 ... 165 D8
Broyle Cl BN8 ... 125 A8
Broyle La BN8 ... 124 F8
Broyle Paddock BN8 ... 124 F7
Broyleside BN8 ... 125 A7
BROYLE SIDE ... 124 F8
Broyle The BN8 ... 125 B7
Bruce Cl RH16 ... 50 E3
Brunel Rd TN38 ... 135 E4
Brunswick Mews 3
BN3 ... 163 D5
Brunswick Pl BN3 ... 163 D6
Brunswick Rd BN3 ... 163 D6
Brunswick Row BN1 ... 189 B4
Brunswick Sq BN3 ... 163 D5
Brunswick Street E BN3 163 D5
Brunswick Street W
BN3 ... 163 D5
Brunswick Terr
Hove BN1, BN3 ... 163 D5
Royal Tunbridge Wells TN1... 8 A2
Brushes La RH16 ... 51 B8
Bryants Field TN6 ... 25 E3
Brydges Cl BN22 ... 185 C6
Buchanan Gdns TN38 ... 136 B1
Buci Cres BN43 ... 140 C1
BUCKHAM HILL ... 77 E6
Buckholt Ave TN40 ... 158 A7
Buckholt La TN39 ... 157 C8
Buckhurst Cl
Eastbourne BN20 ... 184 B8
Buckhurst Cl *continued*
East Grinstead RH19 ... 1 C3
Lewes BN7 ... 190 A4
Buckhurst La TN5 ... 29 A6
Buckhurst Mead RH19 ... 1 C4
Buckhurst Pl TN39 ... 157 C4
Buckhurst Rd
Bexhill TN40 ... 157 C4
Telscombe Cliffs BN10 ... 177 F3
Buckhurst Way RH19 ... 1 C3
Buckingham Cl
4 Brighton BN1 ... 189 A4
Seaford BN25 ... 180 E4
Shoreham-by-S BN43 ... 161 A8
Buckingham Ct BN20 ... 184 B6
Buckingham Dr RH19 ... 11 A8
Buckingham Hts 2
BN22 ... 185 A4
Buckingham Lodge BN1 . 189 A4
Buckingham Pl BN1 ... 189 A4
Buckingham Rd
Brighton BN1 ... 189 A3
Royal Tunbridge Wells TN1... 8 B2
St Leonards TN38 ... 136 A4
Buckingham St BN1 ... 189 A3
Buckland Rd BN25 ... 180 F5
Buckle By-pass BN25 ... 180 C4
Buckle Cl BN25 ... 180 C4
Buckle Dr BN25 ... 180 C4
Buckle Rise BN25 ... 180 C4
Bucklers Cl TN2 ... 8 C3
Buckler St BN41 ... 162 B8
Buckley Cl BN3 ... 141 E4
Buckswood Sch TN35 ... 116 A3
Buckthorn Cl BN25 ... 181 C3
Buckwell Ct BN7 ... 123 A3
Buckwell Rise BN27 ... 130 E5
Buddens Gn TN31 ... 68 B5
BUDLETT'S COMMON ... 55 C3
Budletts Rdbt TN22 ... 55 C4
Bugsell La TN32 ... 63 F4
Bulbeck Cl RH15 ... 72 E1
Buller Cl TN6 ... 26 A1
Buller Rd BN2 ... 143 D1
Bullfinch Gdns TN22 ... 78 E4
BULLINGSTONE ... 6 E7
Bullingstone Cotts TN3 ... 6 E7
Bullingstone La TN3 ... 6 F7
Bull La BN7 ... 190 A1
Bull La Cotts TN3 ... 19 C4
Bull Ring TN33 ... 112 D4
Bulls Pl TN2 ... 9 D6
Bulrushes Bsns Pk RH19 . 10 D6
Bulrush Pl TN38 ... 135 E1
BULVERHYTHE ... 158 C6
Bulverhythe Rd TN38 ... 158 D6
Bungalows The TN22 ... 79 B5
Bunny La TN3 ... 16 E5
Bunting Cl TN38 ... 158 E8
Burchetts Cl RH16 ... 50 E2
Burden Pl TN38 ... 136 A3
Burdett Pl 2 TN34 ... 160 A3
Burdett Rd
Crowborough TN6 ... 26 C1
Rusthall TN4 ... 7 B4
Burdocks Dr RH15 ... 73 D1
Burfield Park Ind Est
BN27 ... 152 B6
Burfield Rd BN22 ... 185 B3
Burgess Ct BN41 ... 162 B8
Burgess Hill Sch RH15 ... 73 B2
Burgess Hill Sta RH15 ... 73 B2
Burgess Rd TN35 ... 137 C5
BURGH HILL ... 44 E3
Burgh Hill TN19 ... 44 E2
Burgh Hill Rd BN8 ... 127 E6
Burgh La BN8 ... 148 E5
Burgundy Ho 3 BN23 ... 185 F8
Burhill Way TN38 ... 158 F7
Burleigh Ct 26 BN1 ... 163 E5
Burleigh Pl BN22 ... 185 C6
Burlington Ct 18 BN21 ... 185 A2
Burlington Gdns BN41 ... 141 C1
Burlington Mans 23
BN21 ... 185 A2
Burlington Pl BN21 ... 185 A2
Burlington Rd BN21 ... 185 B2
Burlington St BN2 ... 164 C4
Burlington Villas 22
BN21 ... 185 B3
BURLOW ... 106 F5
Burlow Cl
Brighton BN2 ... 164 E5
Eastbourne BN22 ... 173 C3
Burma Cl RH16 ... 51 C4
Burners Cl RH15 ... 73 D1
Burnes Vale BN2 ... 165 F2
Burnham Cl BN2 ... 165 F7
Burnside BN26 ... 173 A6
Burnside Ct BN26 ... 173 A6
Burnside Mews TN39 ... 157 B4
Burns Way RH19 ... 1 C1
Burnthouse Bostall BN6 . 120 C8
Burnt House Cl TN18 ... 47 C5
Burnt House La TN3 ... 7 A5
Burnt Lodge La TN5 ... 31 B2
BURNT OAK ... 37 F3
Burnt Oak Rd TN22, TN6... 37 C2
Burrell Rd RH16 ... 50 D6
Burrells La TN22 ... 55 A7
Burrells The BN43 ... 161 B6
Burrow Down BN20 ... 184 B5
Burrow Down Cl BN20 ... 184 A5
Burrswood Villas TN3 ... 15 B7
Burry Rd TN37 ... 136 C3
Burslem Rd TN2 ... 8 E7
Burstead Cl BN1 ... 143 B3
Burston Gdns RH19 ... 1 D4
Burton Rd BN21 ... 184 E5
Burton Villas BN3 ... 163 D8
Burton Way TN38 ... 159 B6
Burton Wlk BN27 ... 152 B7
BURWASH ... 62 B6
Burwash CE Prim Sch
TN19 ... 62 B6
Burwash Cl
Eastbourne BN23 ... 174 B4
Hastings TN34 ... 137 A5
BURWASH COMMON ... 61 A4
Burwash Lodge BN1 ... 143 C1
Burwash Rd
Broad Oak TN21 ... 82 C8
Hove BN3 ... 141 F3
BURWASH WEALD ... 61 C3
Burwood Ho TN2 ... 8 E5
Busby Ct 21 BN21 ... 185 B3
Bushbury La TN22 ... 80 A3
Bush Cl
Telscombe Cliffs BN10 ... 167 A1
Woodingdean BN2 ... 165 D8
Bush Cottage Cl BN41 ... 141 C2
Busheyfields BN27 ... 152 A8
Bush Farm Dr BN41 ... 141 C3
Bush Rd BN9 ... 179 B8
Bush Terr BN41 ... 141 B3
Bushy Croft TN39 ... 156 F5
Bushy Gill TN3 ... 7 A3
Butcherfield La TN7 ... 13 B6
BUTCHER'S CROSS ... 58 B8
Butcher's Cross TN7 ... 13 B7
Butcher's La TN35 ... 115 E2
Bute St BN2 ... 164 D5
Butler Cl TN6 ... 25 E1
Butler's Green Ho RH16 .. 50 B5
Butler's Green Rd RH16 .. 50 C4
Butler's La BN27 ... 130 E3
Butlers Way BN8 ... 124 C5
Butterbox La RH17 ... 52 D4
Buttercup Wlk BN1 ... 143 B7
Butterfield RH19 ... 1 B3
Buttermere Way BN23 ... 174 C4
Button Ct BN2 ... 189 C4
Butts Field BN27 ... 152 C6
Buttsfield La BN8 ... 105 A5
Butts La
Cousley Wood TN5 ... 30 C7
Eastbourne BN20 ... 173 A1
Butts Rd BN42 ... 161 E7
BUXTED ... 56 B4
Buxted CE Prim Sch TN22 55 F3
Buxted Ct TN22 ... 56 C3
Buxted Rise BN1 ... 143 B5
Buxted Sta TN22 ... 56 B3
Buxted Wood La TN22 ... 56 E5
Buxton Dr TN39 ... 157 B6
Buxton Rd
Brighton BN1 ... 163 E7
Eastbourne BN20 ... 188 E8
Bydown BN25 ... 181 A4
Bye-law Cotts BN8 ... 101 E6
Byeways The BN25 ... 180 F4
Byeway The
Bexhill TN39 ... 156 D5
Hastings TN34 ... 160 A8
Byfields Croft TN39 ... 156 F5
Byland Cl BN22 ... 173 E3
Bylands 3 BN2 ... 164 F5
Byng Rd TN4 ... 7 F5
Byre Cotts BN2 ... 165 D4
Byron Ct 1 RH16 ... 50 D5
Byron Gr 2 RH19 ... 1 C1
Byron St BN3 ... 163 A7
Byron Terr 1 BN3 ... 163 A7
Byron Wlk BN23 ... 174 E3
By Sunte RH16 ... 50 F8
Byways TN34 ... 136 D6
Byway The BN1 ... 143 E5
Byworth Cl
Bexhill TN39 ... 156 C6
Brighton BN2 ... 164 F6

C

Cabbages & Kings Gdn★
TN22 ... 57 C3
Cabbage Stalk La TN4 ... 7 E2
Cabot Cl BN23 ... 185 G7
Caburn Cl BN23 ... 174 A4
Caburn Cres BN7 ... 123 A2
Caburn Ent Pk BN8 ... 125 A7
Caburn Rd BN3 ... 163 E7
Caburn View Bglws BN8. 148 B3
Caburn View Cotts BN8 . 148 B3
Caburn Way BN27 ... 152 B6
Cacklebury Cl BN27 ... 152 A6
Cackle St
Cackle Street TN31 ... 90 A2
Dodd's Hill TN22 ... 35 E2
CACKLE STREET
Battle ... 85 E4
Hastings ... 90 A2
Uckfield ... 35 E2
Cadborough Cliff TN31 ... 93 A4
Cade St BN22 ... 173 F2
CADE STREET ... 82 E6
Cadogan Ct
3 Brighton BN1 ... 163 E7
Pevensey Bay BN24 ... 175 C4
Cadogan Gdns 6 TN1 ... 8 B4
Cairngorm Cl BN23 ... 174 D3
Cairo Ave BN10 ... 178 A8
Cairo Ave S BN10 ... 178 A7
Caister's Cl BN3 ... 163 C8
Caius Ct 16 BN43 ... 161 C8
Calbourne RH16 ... 50 D5
Caldbec Ct TN33 ... 112 D5
CALDBEC HILL ... 112 D6
Caldbec Hill TN33 ... 112 D5
Caldicotts La BN27 ... 128 C4
Caledonian Ct 5 BN2 ... 189 C5
Caledonian Rd BN2 ... 189 C5
Caley Rd TN2 ... 8 D7
Calgary Rd TN39 ... 157 B7
Callao Quay BN23 ... 185 G8
Callums Wlk TN40 ... 157 E5
Calverley Ct TN1 ... 8 C3
Calverley Park Cres 1 TN1 8 B3
Calverley Park Gdns TN1 .. 8 C4
Calverley Pk TN1 ... 8 B3
Calverley Rd
6 Eastbourne BN21 ... 184 F2
Royal Tunbridge Wells TN1... 8 B3
Calverley St TN1 ... 8 B4
Calverley Wlk 7 BN21 .. 184 F2
Calvert Cl TN22 ... 78 A7
Calvert Rd
Hastings TN34 ... 160 A6
Uckfield TN22 ... 78 A7
CAMBER ... 94 F2
Camber Castle★ TN36 ... 93 C1
Camber Cl
Beachlands BN24 ... 175 F6
Bexhill TN40 ... 157 E6
Brighton BN2 ... 164 F5
Camber Dr BN24 ... 175 F6
Camberlot Rd BN27 ... 128 A2
Camber Rd TN31 ... 94 B3
Camber Way BN24 ... 175 F6
Cambrian Rd TN4 ... 8 C7
Cambridge Gardens Coll
TN34 ... 159 E7
Cambridge Gdns
Hastings TN34 ... 159 E7
Royal Tunbridge Wells TN2... 8 B2
Cambridge Gr BN3 ... 163 C7
Cambridge La TN21 ... 81 C2
Cambridge Mews BN3 ... 163 C7
Cambridge Rd
Bexhill TN40 ... 157 C6
Eastbourne BN22 ... 185 C4
Hastings TN34 ... 159 E7
Hove BN3 ... 163 D6
Cambridge St TN2 ... 8 C3
Cambridge Way TN22 ... 55 C1
Camden Ave TN2 ... 9 C6
Camden Ct
Pembury TN2 ... 9 D6
2 Royal Tunbridge Wells
TN1 ... 8 B4
Camden Ctr TN1 ... 8 B4
Camden Hill TN2 ... 8 B3
CAMDEN PARK ... 8 C2
Camden Pk TN2 ... 8 C2
Camden Rd
5 Eastbourne BN21 ... 184 F2
Royal Tunbridge Wells TN1... 8 B4
Camden St BN41 ... 162 C6
Camden Terr BN1 ... 189 A3
Camelford St BN2 ... 189 C1
Cameron Cl BN27 ... 152 A8
Campbell Cl TN22 ... 55 C1
Campbell Cres RH19 ... 1 B1
Campbell Ct TN38 ... 159 A8
Campbell Mews 2 BN23 175 A1
Campbell Rd
Brighton BN1 ... 189 A5
Royal Tunbridge Wells TN4... 8 A6
Camperdown St TN39 ... 157 B7
Canada Cl BN10 ... 167 B1
Canada Way TN39 ... 157 B7
CANADIA ... 112 D8
Canadia Rd TN33 ... 112 D8
Canal Bank TN35 ... 139 B7
Canary Quay 15 BN23 ... 185 F8
CANEHEATH ... 151 B4
Canfield Cl BN2 ... 143 D1
Canfield Rd BN2 ... 143 D1
Canning St BN2 ... 164 D5
Cannon Pl BN1 ... 189 A2
Cansiron La
Ashurst Wood RH19 ... 11 F6
Holtye TN7, TN8 ... 3 E2
Cantelupe Ho 1 RH19 ... 1 F1
Cantelupe Mews 7 RH19 ... 1 E1
Cantelupe Rd
Bexhill TN40 ... 157 D3
East Grinstead RH19 ... 1 F1
Canterbury Cl BN22 ... 173 C2
Canterbury Dr 5 BN2 ... 189 C4
Canterbury Rd TN2 ... 9 E6
Canterbury Rise TN34 ... 136 E3
Cantercrow Hill BN9 ... 168 F2
Canton 3 RH16 ... 50 D6
Cants Cl RH15 ... 73 C3
Cants La RH15 ... 73 C3
Canute Cl BN23 ... 185 F8
Canute Rd TN35 ... 160 D7
Capel Ave BN10 ... 178 D7
Capella Path BN27 ... 152 D7
Capenors RH15 ... 72 F1
Cape The BN2 ... 165 F1
Caple Ct TN38 ... 159 B8
Caple Gdns TN38 ... 159 B7
Carden Ave BN1 ... 142 F5
Carden Cl BN1 ... 143 A6
Carden Cres BN1 ... 143 A6
Carden Hill BN1 ... 143 B5
Carden Prim Sch BN1 ... 143 B6
Card Hill RH18 ... 11 F1
Cardiff Rd TN38 ... 159 C7
Cardinal Newman RC Sch
BN3 ... 163 D8
Cardinals Cl TN40 ... 157 F6
Carew Ct
7 Eastbourne BN21 ... 185 A4
Hailsham BN27 ... 129 C3
Carew Lodge 1 BN21 ... 184 F4
Carew Rd BN21 ... 184 F4
Carew Views 2 BN21 ... 184 F4
Carey Down BN10 ... 167 B1
Carfax Cl TN39 ... 157 B8
Carinus Gdns TN37 ... 136 A6
Carisbrooke Cl BN23 ... 174 B4
Carisbrooke Rd
Brighton BN2 ... 164 D7
St Leonards TN38 ... 159 C7
Carlisle Bldngs 2 BN21 . 185 A1
Carlisle Par TN34 ... 159 F7
Carlisle Rd
Eastbourne BN20, BN21 .. 184 F1
Hove BN3 ... 162 F6
Carlton Cl BN25 ... 180 E4
Carlton Cres TN1 ... 8 C4
Carlton Ct
1 Bexhill TN40 ... 157 D3
Portslade-by-S BN41 ... 162 C8
Carlton Hill BN2 ... 189 C2
Carlton Hill Prim Sch
BN2 ... 189 C2
Carlton Ho 6 BN1 ... 142 E2
Carlton Pl 5 BN2 ... 189 C2
Carlton Rd
Eastbourne BN22 ... 185 C4
Royal Tunbridge Wells TN1... 8 C4
Seaford BN25 ... 180 D4
Carlton Terr
3 Crowborough TN6 ... 37 F8
Portslade-by-S BN3, BN41 162 C8
Carlyle Ave BN2 ... 143 D1
Carlyle St BN2 ... 164 C7
Carmel Cl TN39 ... 156 D3
Carmel Ho BN3 ... 163 A7
Carmelstead Cl RH16 ... 51 A3
Carmen Ct BN20 ... 173 B3
Carn Ct 7 BN2 ... 164 C6
Carnoustie Cl TN38 ... 158 F7
Carnoustie Ct 18 RH16 ... 50 E4
Carol Cl BN1 ... 142 F6
Caroline Cl BN25 ... 180 D5
Caroline Way BN23 ... 175 B1
Carpenter Dr TN38 ... 135 F4
Carpenters Croft BN8 ... 105 A5
Carpenters Way BN27 ... 152 A6
Carrier's Path BN27 ... 152 B8
Carriers Pl TN3 ... 5 B4
Carroll Wlk BN23 ... 174 E2
Carr Taylor Vineyard★
TN35 ... 114 C4
Carvel Ct TN37 ... 135 E7
Cashman Lodge BN1 ... 143 A5
Caspian Ct BN1 ... 189 A4
Caspian Sq BN2 ... 165 F1
Castle Banks BN7 ... 190 A2
Castle Bolton BN23 ... 174 C4
Castle Ct BN7 ... 190 B3
Castle Ditch La BN7 ... 190 A2
Castledown Ave TN34 ... 160 A4
Castledown CPN Sch
TN34 ... 160 A5
Castledown Terr 7
TN34 ... 160 A4
Castle Dr BN24 ... 175 C4
Castle Farm Cotts TN7 ... 13 E4
Castlefields TN7 ... 13 E4
Castle Gate BN7 ... 190 A2
Castle Gdns 9 TN34 ... 159 F7
Castleham Ind Est TN38 . 135 F5
Castleham Rd TN38 ... 135 F5
CASTLE HILL ... 39 A4
Castle Hill TN6 ... 39 A5
Castle Hill Nature Reserve★
BN9 ... 179 D5
Castle Hill Pas TN34 ... 159 F8
Castle Hill Rd TN34 ... 159 F7
Castle Hurst TN32 ... 65 B8
Castle La BN7 ... 190 A2
Castle Mews 27 BN1 ... 163 E5
Castle Mount BN20 ... 184 D1
Castle Prec BN7 ... 190 A2
Castle Rd
Pevensey BN24 ... 175 A6
Royal Tunbridge Wells TN4... 8 A3
Castle Rise
Lewes BN7 ... 190 A2
Uckfield TN22 ... 78 D4
Castleross Rd BN24 ... 175 C4
Castle Sq BN1 ... 189 B2
Castle St
Brighton BN1 ... 163 E5
8 Hastings TN34 ... 159 F7
2 Royal Tunbridge Wells
TN1 ... 8 A2
Winchelsea TN36 ... 117 F7
Castle Terr BN24 ... 175 B6
Castle View Gdns BN24 . 174 E6
Castleview Mews TN34 .. 160 A4
Castle Way TN22 ... 78 D4
Castle Wlk TN5 ... 29 E4
Cathedral Wlk BN27 ... 127 B3
Catherine Pl 7 TN1 ... 8 B4
Catherine Vale BN2 ... 165 E8
Catkin Way RH16 ... 51 B4
Catley Ct 4 TN39 ... 157 A4
CATSFIELD ... 133 F8
Catsfield CE Prim Sch
TN33 ... 133 F8
Catsfield Cl
Eastbourne BN23 ... 173 F4

Catsfield Cl continued
St Leonards TN38......135 D2
Catsfield Rd TN33......111 E2
CATSFIELD STREAM......133 E7
Cat St TN7......12 F1
Catt's Corner Cotts TN6..27 D1
Catt's Hill TN6......27 E1
Cattswood La RH16......50 C2
Causeway Sch BN23....174 A3
Causeway The
Brighton BN2......164 D6
13 Seaford BN25......180 E4
Cavalier Way RH19......10 F7
Cavalry Cres BN20......184 B7
Cavell Ave BN10......178 B7
Cavell Avenue N BN10....178 A8
Cavell Ct BN10......178 B7
Cavendish Ave
Eastbourne BN22......185 B4
St Leonards TN38......159 A7
Cavendish Cl BN10......167 B1
Cavendish Ct
10 Bexhill TN40......157 D3
23 Brighton BN2......164 D4
Cavendish Dr TN2......8 B1
Cavendish Ho
8 Brighton BN1......163 E5
Haywards Heath RH16....50 F2
Peacehaven BN10......167 C1
9 St Leonards TN37......159 C7
Cavendish Mews **12** BN1 163 D5
Cavendish Pl
Brighton BN1......163 E5
Eastbourne BN21......185 B3
4 Hastings TN34......160 A4
Cavendish Sch The
BN21......184 C5
Cavendish St **11** BN2....189 C2
Caveridge La BN8......100 E8
Caves Rd TN38......159 A6
Cavix Field TN31......67 B7
Caxton Way **15** RH16....50 E4
Cecil Ct **2** BN21......184 F2
Cedar Cl
Burgess Hill RH15......73 B5
Eastbourne BN22......173 D2
Northiam TN31......67 A6
St Leonards TN37......136 D5
Cedar Ct TN4......8 A5
Cedar Ctr The BN1......143 C2
Cedar Ho TN4......7 E4
Cedar Lodge TN4......7 F3
Cedar Ridge TN2......8 D5
Cedars Cl TN22......78 C8
Cedars Gdns BN1......142 E3
Cedars The
1 Brighton BN2......189 C5
Brighton, Withdean BN1..142 E3
Hailsham BN27......129 B1
Haywards Heath RH16....50 D7
Peacehaven BN10......167 C1
Uckfield TN22......78 D8
Cedar Way RH16......51 B4
Cedarwell Cl BN9......168 B2
Cedarwood **3** BN1......142 E3
Celandine Dr TN38......136 A1
Cello Ct **8** BN2......164 C5
Centenary Ho **4** BN1....142 E2
Centenary Ind Est **6**
BN2......164 B8
Central Ave
Eastbourne BN20......184 B5
Polegate BN26......173 B7
Telscombe Cliffs BN10....178 A8
Central Par TN5......29 F4
Central Sussex Coll
(Haywards Heath Campus)
RH16......50 D6
Centurion Rd BN1......189 A3
Centurion Rise TN34....160 A8
Ceylon Pl BN21, BN22....185 B3
Ceylon Wlk TN39......156 E3
Chadborn Cl BN2......164 D5
Chaffinch Cl RH15......72 D4
Chaffinch Rd BN23......174 C2
Chaffinch Wlk TN22......78 D5
Chafford Cotts TN3......5 F5
Chafford La TN3......5 F5
CHAILEY......75 E4
Chailey Ave BN2......166 A1
Chailey Cl
Eastbourne BN23......174 C1
Hastings TN34......136 F5
Chailey Comm Nature
Reserve★ BN8......75 D7
Chailey Cres BN2......166 E1
Chailey Ct
Brighton BN1......142 C5
2 Haywards Heath RH16..50 F3
Chailey Heritage Sch BN8 75 C7
Chailey La BN8......76 B5
Chailey Rd BN1......143 E4
Chailey Sch BN8......100 D7
Chailey Windmill Rural Life
Mus★......75 D7
Chain La TN33......112 C5
Chain Pier Ho BN2......189 C1
Chalden Pl TN39......156 C6
Chalex Ind Est BN42....162 A7
Chalfont BN27......152 C6
Chalfont Dr BN3......142 C3
Chalkers La BN6......97 B8
Chalket La TN2......9 C5
Chalk Farm Cl BN20....173 B1
Chalkland Rise BN2....165 E8

Chalky Rd BN41......141 A3
Challoners RH17......33 C4
Challoners Cl BN2......166 A2
Challoners Mews BN2..165 F2
Challow Cl BN6......97 E4
Chaloner Cl RH16......51 B7
Chaloner Rd RH16......51 B7
CHALVINGTON......150 A7
Chalvington Cl
Brighton BN1......143 E6
Seaford BN25......180 F6
Chalvington Dr TN37....136 C6
Chalvington Ho **10** BN21 184 D4
Chalvington Rd BN21....184 C7
Chamberlaines La BN8..124 F6
Chamberlain Rd BN21..184 C4
Chambers Cres TN38....135 F3
Chambers Rd TN38......135 F3
Champions Row BN3....163 C8
Chancellor Ho TN4......7 F3
Chancellors Pk BN6......97 F4
Chanctonbury Dr TN34 136 C5
Chanctonbury Rd
Burgess Hill RH15......73 A1
Hove BN3......163 E2
Chandler Rd TN39......157 A4
Chandler's Mead BN8..123 A7
Chandos Cl **1** TN40....157 C3
Chandos Rd TN40......8 C5
Channel Grange BN10..178 A7
Channel View
6 Bexhill TN40......157 C3
13 Southwick BN42......161 E7
Channel View E TN40....157 C3
Channel View Rd
Eastbourne BN22......185 D5
Pevensey Bay BN24......175 E5
Woodingdean BN2......165 B8
Channel View W **5**
TN40......157 C3
Channel Way TN35......138 E3
Channers La BN8......126 E1
Chant La TN6......27 C1
Chantlers Cl RH19......1 C2
Chantlers Mead TN8......4 A5
Chantry Ave TN40......157 D6
Chantry Com Prim Sch
TN40......157 C5
Chantry La TN40......157 C5
Chantry The **12** BN21..184 E4
Chapel Barn Cl BN27....152 C7
Chapel Cl
Burgess Hill RH15......72 F4
Seaford BN25......180 E4
Chapel Cotts TN33......112 E3
Chapel Field TN31......67 A7
Chapel Gn TN6......25 F2
Chapel Hill
Alfriston BN26......171 B3
Crowhurst TN33......134 F4
Lewes BN7......190 C2
Sedlescombe TN33......113 E7
Chapel Ho BN2......189 C2
Chapel La
Ashurst Wood RH19......11 D6
Blackboys TN22......80 B7
East Chiltington BN7....100 A3
Forest Row RH18......11 F2
Guestling Green TN35....138 A8
Horsted Keynes RH17....33 C5
Westfield TN35......114 E4
Chapel Mews **8** BN3....163 D5
Chapel Park Rd TN37....159 C8
Chapel Pl
Northiam TN31......67 B6
Portslade-by-S BN41......162 B7
14 Royal Tunbridge Wells
TN1......8 A2
Ticehurst TN5......31 E1
Chapel Rd
Plumpton Green BN7......99 E2
Portslade-by-S BN41......162 A7
CHAPEL ROW......130 F5
Chapel St
Brighton BN2......189 C2
Newhaven BN9......179 D7
Chapel Terr **2** BN2....164 D4
Chapel Terr Mews **21**
BN2......164 D4
Chapel Wlk TN40......157 E6
Chapman's La RH19......1 D1
Chapman's Town Rd TN21 83 B2
Chapman Way TN2......8 C8
Charis Ct **18** BN3......163 C7
Charity Farm Way TN6..26 A3
Charles Ave RH15......72 D2
Charles Bennett Ct RH16..51 A4
Charles Cl
Hove BN3......142 A3
Seaford BN25......180 D5
Charles Ct TN2......8 C3
Charles Kingston Gdns
BN1......142 E4
Charles Moore Ct BN26..173 A7
Charles Rd TN38......159 C8
Charles Road W TN38..159 B8
Charles St
Brighton BN1......189 B1
Royal Tunbridge Wells TN4..8 A8
Charleston Farmhouse★
BN8......149 A2
Charleston Manor Gdns★
BN25......182 A6
Charleston Rd BN21....184 D4
Charlesworth Pk RH16..51 C4
Charlotte St BN2......189 C1
Charlston Ave BN9......179 A5

Charlton Gdns BN6......98 D3
Charltons The BN1......143 D6
Charlton's Way TN4......7 E1
Charlwood Gdns RH15..73 C5
Charlwood Rd RH15......73 D6
Charlwoods Bsns Ctr RH19 1 D2
Charlwoods Pl RH19......1 E3
Charlwoods Rd RH19......1 E3
Charter Gate RH14......50 D5
Charters Ancaster Coll
TN39......157 A6
Chartfield BN3......142 A2
Chartfield Way BN3......142 B2
Chartres TN40......157 D6
Chartres Cl TN40......157 D6
Chartwell Cl BN25......180 E6
Chartwell Ct BN1......189 A2
Chates Farm Ct BN2....189 C3
Chatfield Cl TN38......135 F4
Chatfield Cres BN22....173 C1
Chatfield Rd RH17......50 A6
Chatham Gn BN23......175 B2
Chatham Pl
Brighton BN1......189 A4
Seaford BN25......180 E2
Chatham Rd **3** TN38....136 B2
Chatsworth Ave BN10..167 A1
Chatsworth Cl BN10....178 A8
Chatsworth Ct BN1......163 E8
Chatsworth Gdns BN20 188 F8
Chatsworth Pk BN10....167 B1
Chatsworth Rd BN1......163 E8
Chatsworth Sq BN3......163 D7
Chaucer Ave **3** RH19....1 C1
Chaucer Ct **2** RH16......50 D5
Chaucer Ind Est BN26..173 A6
Chaucer Wlk BN23......174 C3
Chawbrook Mews BN22 185 B4
Chawbrook Rd BN22....185 B4
Cheapside BN1......189 B3
Cheeleys RH17......33 C5
Chelgates BN20......156 C2
Chelmsford Ct **4** BN20..184 F1
Chelsea Cl TN40......157 D4
Chelsea Mews **17** TN38 159 C7
Chelston Ave BN3......162 D7
Cheltenham Pl BN1......189 B3
Chelwood Cl BN1......143 C6
Chelwood Ct **5** BN1......73 A4
Chelwood Gate Rd RH17,
TN22......34 F7
Chelworth Rd BN22......173 D2
Chene Rd BN10......178 F6
Chenies Cl TN2......17 A8
Chepbourne Rd TN40....157 C4
Chepstow Ct BN1......143 F5
Chequer Grange RH18....11 E1
Chequer Rd RH19......1 F1
Chequers Cl TN6......26 A2
Chequers Way TN6......26 A2
Cherington Cl BN6......97 B5
Cherith Cotts **3** TN21....82 A6
Cheriton Ct BN20......184 C4
Cherry Cl RH15......72 E3
Cherry Clack TN21......83 D6
Cherry Cotts
Fletching TN22......54 A4
Hastings TN35......160 C7
Cherry Garden Rd BN20 184 B3
Cherry Gdns
Heathfield TN21......82 B5
High Hurstwood TN22....56 B8
Cherry Pl **10** RH16......50 C2
Cherry Side BN27......152 A7
Cherry Tree Ct TN37....159 D8
Cherry Tree Ct TN21....106 F7
Cherry Tree Gdns TN40..157 F6
Cherry Tree Rd TN2......7 E1
Cherrywood **2** BN1......142 E3
Cherwell Cl BN24......173 F5
Cherwell Ct TN21......82 A8
Cherwell Lo TN21......82 A8
Cherwell Rd TN21......82 A8
Chesham Pl BN2......164 D4
Chesham Rd BN2......164 D4
Chesham St BN2......164 D4
Cheshire Ct **6** BN22....185 B4
Chester Ave TN2......8 D2
Chester Ct **12** BN3......163 E7
Chesterfield Gdns BN20 188 E8
Chesterfield Rd BN20....188 E8
Chester Terr BN1......143 A1
Chesterton Ave BN25....181 B3
Chesterton Cl RH19......10 F7
Chesterton Dr BN25....181 B3
Chestnut Ave
Golden Cross BN27......127 B4
Royal Tunbridge Wells TN4..8 B8
Chestnut Cl
Broad Oak TN31......90 B5
Burgess Hill RH15......73 B5
Eastbourne BN22......173 E2
East Grinstead RH19......2 A1
Hailsham BN27......129 A1
Herstmonceux BN27......130 E6
Royal Tunbridge Wells TN4..8 B8
Chestnut Cotts
Fletching TN22......53 F3
1 Heathfield TN21......82 A7
Chestnut Ct TN2......17 A8
Chestnut Dr BN26......173 A6
Chestnut Pl TN8......4 A6
Chestnuts Cl RH16......51 A7
Chestnuts The
Haywards Heath RH16....50 F7
The Moor TN18......45 F8
Chestnut Way BN9......179 B7

Chestnut Wlk
Bexhill TN39......156 C5
Felcourt RH19......1 C8
Cheviot Cl BN23......174 C3
Cheviots The TN34......160 C8
Cheyne BN43......161 C7
Chichester Cl
Bexhill TN39......157 B6
15 Brighton BN2......164 D4
Eastbourne BN22......173 B2
Hove BN3......141 E4
Peacehaven BN10......178 F7
Saltdean BN2......166 C1
Seaford BN25......180 E3
Chichester Ct
Bexhill TN39......156 C5
2 Seaford BN25......180 E2
Chichester Drive E BN2..166 C1
Chichester Drive W BN2 166 B1
Chichester Ho **7** TN40..157 D4
Chichester Lodge BN25 180 E3
Chichester Pl BN2......164 D4
Chichester Rd
Seaford BN25......180 E3
St Leonards TN38......136 B2
Chichester Terr **19** BN2..164 D4
Chichester Way RH15....73 C5
Chick Hill TN35......139 B8
Chicks La TN17......20 F2
CHIDDINGLY......105 E1
Chiddingly Cl BN2......164 F5
Chiddingly Ho **11** BN3..163 D7
Chiddingly Prim Sch
BN8......127 E7
Chieveley Cotts TN38....136 B1
Chieveley Dr TN2......8 D1
Chilcomb RH15......73 C1
Chilham Cl BN23......174 D2
Chillies La TN22, TN6....37 B3
Chilling St RH19......21 D3
Chillis Wood Rd RH16....50 C5
Chilsham La BN27......130 E7
Chilston Cl TN4......8 A5
Chilston Rd TN4......8 A5
Chiltern Cl
Eastbourne BN23......174 D3
Shoreham-by-S BN43....161 C8
Chiltern Ct BN26......173 A7
Chiltern Dr TN34......160 B7
Chiltern Wlk TN2......8 D4
CHILTINGTON......100 D3
Chiltington Cl
Burgess Hill RH15......72 F5
Saltdean BN2......166 C2
Chiltington La BN7......100 D3
Chiltington Way BN2....166 C2
Chiswick Pl BN21......185 A2
CHITCOMBE......89 E6
Chitcombe Rd TN31......89 E5
Chitcombe Wlk TN34....137 A5
Chorley Ave BN2......166 B2
Chownes Mead La RH16..50 B4
Chown's Hill TN35......137 A6
Chrisdory Rd BN41......140 F3
Christ Church Ave **1** BN2 8 A2
Christ Church CE (Aided)
Prim Sch TN37......136 C1
Christchurch Ct BN9....179 D7
Christie Ave BN8......124 D6
Christie Rd BN7......123 A2
Christies RH19......10 D8
Christine Cl TN40......158 A7
Christopher Rd RH19......1 E1
CHUCK HATCH......24 D7
Chuck Hatch Rd TN7....24 C6
Church App TN22......79 B5
Church Ave
Haywards Heath RH16....50 E6
Westham BN24......175 A6
Church Bailey BN24......175 A5
Church Bailey Ct BN24..175 A5
Church Cl
Brighton BN1......142 F5
Burgess Hill RH15......73 A3
Eastbourne BN20......173 A4
Church Ct
3 Haywards Heath RH16..50 E4
Hove BN3......141 F1
Churchdale Ave BN22....185 C6
Churchdale Pl BN22......185 B6
Churchdale Rd BN22....185 C6
CHURCHES GREEN......109 B8
Church Farm Cl TN19....44 C1
Churchfield
East Dean BN20......187 B8
Westfield TN35......114 D3
Churchfields TN22......35 C4
Churchfields Ind Est
TN38......135 E4
Churchfield Sq **16** BN21 184 F4
Church Gn BN43......161 C7
Church Hill
Bexhill TN39......156 D4
Brighton BN1......142 E7
Etchingham TN19......44 B2
Newhaven BN9......179 C7
Pyecombe BN45......119 C6
Ringmer BN8......124 D6
Church Hill Ave TN39....156 D4
Church House Cl BN42..141 F2
Churchill Ave TN35......137 D5
Churchill Cl BN20......184 D3
Churchill Ct TN38......136 B2
Churchill Ho
Hove BN3......141 E2
Seaford BN25......181 C4
Churchill Rd
Heathfield TN21......82 B6

Churchill Rd continued
Lewes BN7......123 D3
Seaford BN25......180 D5
Churchill Sq BN1......189 A2
Churchill Way RH15......73 C2
Church in the Wood La
TN38......135 F3
Church La
Burgess Hill RH17......73 F6
Buxted TN22......56 C5
Catsfield TN33......133 E8
Chiddingly BN8......105 E1
Clayhill TN31......67 E4
Danehill RH17......34 A3
Ditchling BN6......98 D3
1 Eastbourne BN21......184 D3
East Grinstead RH19......1 F1
Etchingham TN19......44 C1
Frant TN3......17 B4
Guestling Green TN35....116 B1
Hellingly BN27......129 A6
Hooe TN33......155 C7
Horsted Keynes RH17....33 C5
Iden TN31......70 B4
Jevington BN26......183 C7
Kingston near Lewes BN7 145 D5
Laughton BN8......126 C5
Lewes, St Anne's BN7....146 B8
Lewes, South Malling BN7 190 B4
Ninfield TN33......133 B5
Northbridge Street TN32....64 C5
Northiam TN31......67 C6
Pevensey BN24......175 B6
Pyecombe BN45......119 C6
Ripe BN27, BN8......149 E8
Rye Foreign TN31......92 B8
Seaford BN25......180 E2
Southwick BN42......161 D7
Westfield TN35......114 E3
Churchland La TN33......88 E3
Church Marks La BN8....104 F5
Church Mead BN6......98 B3
Church Mews BN20......173 B1
Church Pas **5** TN34......160 A4
Church Path
Hellingly BN27......129 A5
Ninfield TN33......133 A5
Church Pl BN2......164 E4
Church Rd
Barcombe BN8......101 E2
Burgess Hill RH15......73 A3
Buxted TN22......56 B4
Catsfield TN33......133 F7
Crowborough TN6......25 F2
Flowers Green BN27......131 A1
Haywards Heath RH16....50 E4
Hove BN3......163 B6
Kilndown TN17......20 F3
Lamberhurst TN3......20 C6
Mountfield TN32......87 B5
Newick BN8......76 E6
Pembury TN2......9 D8
Polegate BN26......173 A6
Portslade-by-S BN41......162 B7
Rotherfield TN6......39 A8
Royal Tunbridge Wells TN1...8 A3
Sandhurst Cross TN18....46 F4
Scaynes Hill RH17......51 F3
St Leonards TN37......159 D7
Church Row BN7......190 A2
Churchsettle La TN5......42 B7
Church Sq TN31......93 C3
Church St
Bexhill TN40......157 D5
Brighton BN1......189 B2
Cowden TN8......4 B5
Eastbourne BN20, BN22..173 C2
Eastbourne, Old Town BN20,
BN21......184 D3
Hartfield TN7......13 D4
Hastings TN35......160 C7
Old Heathfield TN21......82 D5
Portslade-by-S BN41......162 B7
Seaford BN25......180 E2
Ticehurst TN5......31 D1
Uckfield TN22......78 C7
Wadhurst TN5......30 A4
Church Twitten BN7......190 B2
Church Vale Rd TN40....157 D5
Church Walk Mews RH15 73 A3
Church Way **6** BN2......189 C3
Church Wlk RH15......73 A3
Church Wood Dr TN38..135 E4
Churchwood Prim Sch
TN38......135 F3
Church Wood & Robsack
Wood Nature Reserve★
TN38......135 F3
Church Wood Way TN38 135 F2
Churchyard Cotts TN3....7 A8
Chyngton Ave BN25......181 B4
Chyngton Cl BN23......174 A4
Chyngton Gdns BN25....181 B4
Chyngton Ho BN25......181 C2
Chyngton La BN25......181 C3
Chyngton Lane N BN25..181 C3
Chyngton Pl BN25......181 B2
Chyngton Prim Sch
BN25......181 B4
Chyngton Rd BN25......181 A2
Chyngton Way BN25....181 C2
Cider Hollow BN27......131 B5
Cider House Rd TN31....131 B5
Cider House Wlk BN8....105 A5
Cinderford La BN27......129 F8
Cinder Hill
Chailey BN8......75 F3
Cinder Hill RH19......21 B1
Cinquefoil BN10......178 C8

Cinque Ports St TN31 .... 93 B5
Cinque Ports Way
  Seaford BN25 .... 181 C4
  St Leonards TN38 ...... 158 E6
Circus Par BN1 .... 189 B4
Circus St BN2 .... 189 B2
Circus The BN23 .... 185 D8
Cissbury Ave BN10 ...... 178 E7
Cissbury Cres BN2 ...... 166 E1
Cissbury Rd
  Burgess Hill RH15 ...... 72 E4
  Hove BN3 .... 163 E7
City Coll Brighton & Hove
  Brighton BN1 .... 189 A5
  Brighton BN1 .... 189 B5
  Brighton, Whitehawk BN2 . 164 F5
  Hove BN3 .... 163 A6
Civic App TN22 .... 78 C7
Civic Way
  Burgess Hill RH15 ...... 73 D2
  Royal Tunbridge Wells TN1 .. 8 A3
CJ Gallards Almshouses
  TN4 .... 8 A8
Clackhams La TN6 .... 38 D7
Clair Ct RH16 .... 50 E5
Clair Rd RH16 .... 50 E5
Clanricarde Gdns **1** TN1 .. 8 A3
Clanricarde Rd **2** TN1 ... 8 A3
Clapham La BN26 .... 182 A8
Claphatch La TN5 .... 31 A5
Clappers The TN32 ...... 64 B4
Claremont **9** TN34 ..... 159 E7
Claremont Ct
  4 Royal Tunbridge Wells
  TN2 .... 8 C7
  Seaford BN25 .... 180 D3
Claremont Gdns TN2 ..... 8 B2
Claremont Pl TN22 ...... 55 C1
Claremont Prim Sch TN2 .. 8 B2
Claremont Rd
  Bexhill TN39 .... 157 B7
  Newhaven BN9 .... 168 F1
  Royal Tunbridge Wells TN1 .. 8 B2
  Seaford BN25 .... 180 D3
Claremont Rise TN22 .... 55 C1
Claremont Sch TN37 .... 114 B1
Clarence Ct BN24 ...... 175 C3
Clarence Dr **2** RH19 .... 10 F7
Clarence Gdns BN1 ..... 189 A2
Clarence Rd
  Eastbourne BN22 ...... 185 B4
  Royal Tunbridge Wells TN1 .. 8 A3
  St Leonards TN37 ..... 136 C1
Clarence Row TN1 .... 8 A3
Clarence Sq BN1 .... 189 A2
Clarendon Cl TN37 ..... 136 B4
Clarendon Gdns TN2 .... 8 A1
Clarendon Ho **2** BN3 .. 163 B7
Clarendon Pl
  15 Brighton BN2 ..... 164 C4
  Portslade-by-S BN41 ... 162 C6
Clarendon Rd
  Hove BN3 .... 163 B7
  Shoreham-by-S BN42,
  BN43 .... 161 D8
Clarendon Terr **16** BN2 . 164 D4
Clarendon Villas BN3 .. 163 B7
Clarendon Way TN2 ..... 8 A1
Clare Rd BN7 .... 123 A2
Clare Wlk BN3 .... 164 D5
Claridge TN1 .... 8 B6
Clarke Ave BN3 .... 141 F3
Clarke Ct BN3 .... 162 F6
Clarks Ind Est BN3 .... 163 B8
Clark's Yd TN5 .... 32 A3
Claverham Cl TN33 .... 112 B4
Claverham Com Coll
  TN33 .... 112 A4
Claverham Way TN33 .. 112 B4
Clavering Wlk TN39 ... 156 B2
Claxton Cl BN21 ...... 184 D5
Claxton Rd TN40 ..... 158 A5
Clay Cnr BN8 .... 101 F6
Clayfields BN10 ...... 178 B7
CLAYHILL 67 D3
Clay Hill Rd TN3 ...... 19 D6
Clays Cl RH19 .... 10 E8
Clayton Ave BN6 ...... 97 F3
Clayton Dr RH15 ..... 72 F1
Clayton Hill BN6, BN45 .. 119 D7
Clayton Mill Rd TN4 .. 174 B5
Clayton Pk BN6 ...... 97 E4
Clayton Rd
  Brighton BN2 .... 164 D7
  Ditchling BN6 .... 98 C3
Clayton's La TN3 ..... 5 E2
Clayton Way BN3 ..... 141 F3
Clayton Windmills★
  BN6 .... 119 E7
Clearwater RH17 ..... 52 A3
Clearwaters La RH16 .. 73 D8
Cleeve Ave TN2 ...... 8 D2
Cleevelands BN22 .... 173 B2
Clement Hill Rd TN34 . 160 B7
Clementine Ave BN25 . 180 D5
Clement La BN26 ..... 173 A5
Clerks Acre BN6 ..... 98 A4
Clermont Cl BN1 ..... 142 E2
Clermont Rd BN1 ..... 142 E2
Clermont Terr BN1 ... 142 E2
Cleve Cl TN22 .... 79 B5
Clevedon Rd TN39 ... 157 A6
Clevedown BN7 ...... 146 A8
Cleveland TN8 .... 3 D4
Cleveland Cl BN23 ... 174 C3
Cleveland Gdns RH15 . 73 B2
Cleveland Rd BN1 ... 143 A1
Clevelands RH16 .... 50 E6

Cleve Terr BN7 .... 146 B8
Cliff App TN4 .... 164 F4
Cliff Ave BN10 .... 178 A8
Cliff Cl BN25 .... 180 F1
Cliff Ct TN38 .... 158 D6
CLIFFE 190 B6
Cliffe High St BN7 ... 190 B2
Cliffe Ind Est BN8 ... 146 F8
Cliffe Leas BN7 ..... 190 C2
CLIFF END 139 B7
Cliff End La TN35 .... 139 B7
Cliff Gdns
  Seaford BN25 .... 180 F1
  Telscombe Cliffs BN10 . 177 F4
Cliff Park Cl BN10 ... 178 F7
Cliff Rd
  Brighton BN2 .... 164 F4
  Eastbourne BN20 .... 188 E7
  Seaford BN25 .... 180 F1
Cliff The BN2 .... 164 F4
Cliff Way TN35 ...... 138 F5
Clifton Cl BN22 ..... 184 D8
Clifton Cotts TN2 .... 8 D8
Clifton Ct
  9 Brighton BN1 ... 189 A4
  Hastings TN34 ...... 159 E7
Cliftonville Ct **6** BN1 . 163 B7
Cliftonville Rd TN38 . 158 D6
Cliftonville Way TN38 . 158 D6
Clifton Way BN10 ... 178 A8
Climping Cl RH16 ... 50 D3
Clinch Green Ave TN39 . 156 F7
Clinton Cres TN38 ... 136 B1
Clinton Hill RH7 ..... 2 A8
Clinton La **4** BN25 . 180 E3
Clinton Pl BN25 .... 180 E3
Clinton Way TN35 ... 138 F5
Clive Ave TN35 ..... 160 C6
Clive Ct RH16 ...... 50 E6
Cliveden Ct BN1 .... 142 E3
Clive Villas TN33 ... 112 E3
CLIVE VALE 137 C2
Clockhouse TN1 ..... 8 F6
Clock House La TN22 . 35 C4
Clock Tower Ct **5** TN39 . 157 B3
Clocktower The BN1 . 189 B2
Cloister Ct **13** TN40 . 157 D3
Cloisters BN9 ...... 179 C7
Cloisters The
  Battle TN33 .... 112 C6
  Eastbourne BN22 ... 173 C2
  St Leonards TN37 ... 159 D7
Close Eight BN23 ... 174 E3
Close Eighteen BN23 . 174 E2
Close Eleven BN23 .. 174 E3
Close Fifteen **6** BN23 . 174 E3
Close Five BN23 .... 174 E3
Close Four BN23 .... 174 E3
Close Fourteen BN23 . 174 E3
Close Nine BN23 .... 174 E3
Close Nineteen BN23 . 174 E2
Close One BN23 .... 174 E3
Close Seven BN23 .. 174 E3
Close Seventeen BN23 . 174 E2
Close Six BN23 ..... 174 E3
Close Sixteen BN23 . 174 E2
Close Ten BN23 .... 174 E3
Close The
  Blackboys TN22 .... 80 B6
  Brighton BN1 ...... 142 E5
  Burgess Hill RH15 .. 73 C4
  Crowborough TN6 ... 25 E3
  Eastbourne BN22 ... 173 C3
  East Grinstead RH19 . 10 D8
  Fairlight TN35 ..... 138 C4
  Friston BN20 ...... 183 A1
  Groombridge TN3 ... 15 C6
  Hassocks BN6 ..... 97 F4
  Newhaven BN9 ..... 168 B2
  Royal Tunbridge Wells TN2 .. 8 D8
  Rye TN31 .... 93 A6
  Seaford BN25 ..... 180 F2
Close Three BN23 .. 174 D2
Close Twelve BN23 . 174 E2
Close Twenty BN23 . 174 E2
Close Twentyfive BN23 . 174 D2
Close Twentyfour **4**
  BN23 .... 174 E2
Close Two BN23 ... 174 D2
Cloudesley Rd TN37 . 159 C8
Clovelly Ho BN26 ... 173 A7
Clover Ct **2** RH16 . 50 E4
Cloverlea TN34 .... 136 E3
Clovers End BN1 ... 143 B7
Clover Way BN41 .. 141 B4
Cluny St BN7 ...... 190 A1
Clyde Pk BN27 .... 152 E2

Clyde Rd
  Brighton BN2 .... 189 B5
  St Leonards TN37, TN38 . 159 C7
Coach & Horses La RH17 . 34 C6
Coach & Horses Pas **18**
  TN2 .... 8 A2
Coach House Cotts TN31 . 94 F2
Coach La RH17 ...... 34 C6
Coach Rd TN4 ...... 7 C3
Coalbrook Ho BN2 ... 164 C5
Coastal Counties Ho **19**
  BN2 .... 189 C3
Coastguard Cl BN24 . 176 D8
Coastguard Cotts
  Camber TN31 ...... 94 D2
  Normans' Bay BN24 . 176 D8
Coastguard La TN35 . 138 C4
Coastguards TN35 .. 139 C8
Coastguard Sq
  3 Eastbourne BN22 . 185 C4
  Rye Harbour TN31 .. 94 A3
Coast Rd BN24 ..... 176 B7
Coates Ct **11** BN42 . 161 E7
Cobald Rd BN24 ... 175 E5
COBBARN 15 A3
Cobbetts Mead RH16 . 51 B3
Cobbett's Ride TN2 . 7 F1
Cobblers Field TN19 . 61 E4
Cobbold Ave BN21 .. 184 C5
Cobden Pl **5** BN27 . 152 C7
Cobden Rd BN2 .... 164 C7
Cobdown La TN22 .. 55 C5
Cobhams TN3 ..... 7 A8
Coburg Pl **6** TN34 . 160 A4
Cobton Dr BN3 .... 142 A3
Coburn Ct BN7 .... 190 B2
Cochrane Cl BN23 . 185 E7
Cockcrow Wood TN37 . 136 D5
Cockhaise Cotts RH16 . 52 A8
COCK MARLING 92 A2
Cockmount La TN5 . 29 F5
Cockshut Rd BN7 .. 190 A1
Cogger's Cross TN21 . 106 F3
Cogger's La TN21 .. 106 F4
COGGINS MILL 40 D4
Coggins Mill La TN20 . 40 D4
Coghurst Hall Holiday Village
  TN35 .... 137 C8
Coghurst Rd TN35 . 160 C8
Colbourne Ave BN2 . 143 D2
Colbourne Rd BN3 . 163 E7
Colchester Vale RH18 . 11 E2
Colchins RH15 .... 72 F1
COLDEAN 143 D6
Coldean La BN1 ... 143 E6
Coldean Prim Sch BN1 . 143 D6
Coldean Rd BN1 .. 143 C8
Coldharbour Cl TN6 . 26 A1
Coldharbour La
  Iden TN31 .... 70 A4
  Newick BN8 ...... 76 A7
  Peasmarsh TN31 .. 69 E3
Coldharbour Rd
  Lower Dicker BN27 . 128 B2
  White Post TN8, TN11 . 5 E8
Coldthorn La BN26, BN27. 152 A4
Coldwaltham La RH15 . 73 D2
Colebrooke Rd TN39 . 157 A4
Colebrook Rd
  Brighton BN1 ...... 142 D4
  Royal Tunbridge Wells TN4 . 8 C8
  Southwick BN42 ... 161 F7
Coleman Ave BN3 .. 162 E7
COLEMAN'S HATCH . 23 C7
Colemans Hatch Rd
  Coleman's Hatch RH18,
  TN7 .... 23 C6
  Forest Row RH18 .. 22 E5
Coleman St BN2 ... 189 C4
Coleridge St BN3 .. 163 A8
Coleridge Wlk **7** BN23 . 174 E2
Coles Ct TN2 ..... 8 C3
Colgate Ct BN2 ... 164 F6
College Cl
  East Grinstead RH19 . 1 F1
  Portslade-by-S BN41 . 140 F3
College Ct
  Brighton BN2 ..... 164 C4
  22 Eastbourne BN21 . 185 A2
College Dr TN2 ... 8 D4
College Gdns BN2 . 164 C4
College Gn BN21 .. 184 E4
College La
  East Grinstead RH19 . 1 F1
  Hurst Wickham BN6 . 97 C6
College Pl
  Brighton BN2 ..... 164 C4
  Hurst Wickham BN6 . 97 C6
College Rd
  Bexhill TN40 ..... 157 F5
  Brighton BN2 ..... 164 C4
  Eastbourne BN21 .. 184 F2
  Haywards Heath RH16 . 50 E7
  Seaford BN25 .... 180 F2
College St **11** BN2 . 164 C4
College Terr BN2 . 164 D5
Coller Mews TN6 . 38 D8
Collett Cl TN38 .. 135 F5
Colley Cnr TN39 . 156 F4
Collier Cl BN22 .. 185 B7
Collier Rd
  Hastings TN34 ... 160 A5
  Pevensey Bay BN24 . 175 D4
Collier's Gn TN21 . 83 C3
COLLIER'S GREEN . 66 A2
Collingford La RH17 . 34 B4
Collington Ave TN39 . 156 F2

Collington Cl BN20 ... 184 E1
Collington Gr TN39 .. 156 E4
Collington Lane E TN39 . 156 F4
Collington Lane W TN39 . 156 D3
Collington Man TN39 . 157 B3
Collington Park Cres
  TN39 .... 156 F4
Collington Rise TN39 . 156 E4
Collington Sta TN39 . 157 A3
Collingwood Ave TN21 . 82 F7
Collingwood Cl
  Eastbourne BN23 .. 185 E6
  4 East Grinstead RH19 . 10 F7
  Peacehaven BN10 .. 167 D1
Collingwood Ct BN2 . 165 A3
Collingwood Rise **4** BN2 . 82 A7
Collinstone Rd TN38 . 159 A7
Collinswood Dr TN38 . 159 A7
Coll of St Barnabas RH7 . 1 F8
Colmer Ct RH15 ... 72 E3
Colmer Rd RH15 .. 72 E3
Colonnade Gdns **13**
  BN21 .... 185 B3
Colonnade Rd **14** BN21 . 185 B3
Colonnades The BN1 . 189 B2
Coltstocks Rd BN20 . 188 D8
Columbus Dr BN23 . 185 G7
Colville Ct **2** BN21 . 184 E4
Colwell Cl RH16 .. 50 F3
Colwell Gdns RH16 . 50 F3
Colwell La
  Haywards Heath, Fox Hill
  RH17 .... 50 F1
  Haywards Heath, Franklands
  Village RH16 ..... 51 B3
Colwell Rd RH16 .. 50 F2
Colwood Cres BN20 . 184 B6
Combe End TN6 .. 37 E8
Combe La
  Eastbourne BN20 .. 188 D7
  Standard Hill TN33 . 132 F6
Combe Rise BN20 . 173 A2
Combe The BN20 .. 184 E2
Commanders Wlk TN35 . 138 E4
Command Rd BN20 . 184 B5
Commercial Mews N **8**
  BN21 .... 185 A4
Commercial Rd
  Burgess Hill RH15 .. 72 F3
  Eastbourne BN21 .. 185 A4
  Royal Tunbridge Wells TN1 . 8 B5
Commercial Sq RH16 . 50 E6
Common La
  Ditchling BN6 .... 98 D6
  Laughton BN8 ... 126 A8
  Selmeston BN26 .. 149 E1
Common View TN4 . 7 C2
Common Wood Rise TN6 . 25 F4
Compass Ct BN41 . 140 E3
Compasses La TN32 . 88 C6
Comphurst La BN27 . 131 B4
Compton Ave BN1 . 189 A4
Compton Cl **11** TN40 . 157 E4
Compton Dr BN20 . 184 C2
Compton Grange BN20 . 184 E1
Compton Lodge BN21 . 184 E2
Compton Place Rd BN20,
  BN21 .... 184 E2
Compton Rd
  Brighton BN1 ..... 142 D1
  Lindfield RH16 ... 51 B8
Compton St BN21 . 185 A1
Compts The BN10 . 167 B1
Conan Doyle Ct TN6 . 25 E2
Concord Ct TN2 .. 8 C4
Concorde Cl TN39 . 156 F6
Condor Way TN15 . 72 E3
Conduit Hill **3** TN31 . 93 C6
Coneyburrow Gdns TN38 . 135 E4
Coneyburrow La TN39 . 155 F5
Coneyburrow Rd **8** TN2 . 8 E5
Coney Furlong BN10 . 167 D1
Conghurst La TN18 . 46 B6
Congress Theatre★ **15**
  BN21 .... 185 A1
Conifer Cl TN34 .. 136 F3
Conifers The **8** BN21 . 184 F4
Coniston Ave TN4 . 7 E5
Coniston Ct **9** BN3 . 163 D7
Coniston Rd BN23 . 174 C4
Connaught Rd
  1 Eastbourne BN21 . 185 A2
  Hove BN3 .... 163 A6
  Seaford BN25 .... 180 C3
Connaught Terr BN3 . 163 B7
Connaught Way TN4 . 7 F5
Connell Dr BN2 .. 165 E7
Conqueror Ind Est TN38 . 135 F6
Conqueror Rd TN38 . 158 E7
Conqueror Terr TN33 . 88 F1
Conquest Hospl TN37 . 136 D6
Consort Way RH15 . 72 E2
Constable Rd BN23 . 174 D1
Constable Way TN40 . 157 E5
Conway Ct
  1 Hove BN3 ..... 163 B7
  9 St Leonards TN38 . 159 B6
Conway Pl BN3 .. 163 A8
Conway St BN3 .. 163 B8
COODEN 156 D2
Cooden Beach Sta TN39 . 156 B2
Cooden Cl TN35 .. 156 C3
Cooden Dr TN39 . 156 E2
Cooden Ledge TN38 . 135 F7
Cooden Sea Rd TN39 . 156 C3
Cook Ave BN23 .. 185 E6

Cookham Dene TN40 ... 157 C4
COOKSBRIDGE 123 A8
Cooksbridge Rd BN8 ... 164 E6
Cooksbridge Sta BN8 .. 123 A7
Cookson Gdns TN35 ... 160 C3
Cookstown Cl TN33 ... 132 F6
Coolham Dr BN2 ...... 164 E2
Coolwater Pk BN1 .... 142 D4
Coombe Cl BN27 ..... 131 B5
Coombe Hall Pk RH19 . 10 D6
Coombe Hill Rd RH19 . 10 D6
Coombe La TN5 ..... 41 C7
Coombe Lea **5** BN2 . 163 C6
Coombe Lodge BN25 . 180 C3
Coombe Mdw BN2 ... 166 E3
Coombe Rd
  Brighton BN2 ...... 143 D1
  Eastbourne BN20 ... 184 C4
  Lewes BN7 .... 190 B3
Coombe Rd Prim Sch
  BN2 .... 143 D1
Coombe Rise BN2 . 166 D3
Coombers La RH16 . 51 B5
Coombe Shaw TN33 . 133 A6
Coombe Terr BN2 . 143 C1
Coombe Vale BN2 . 166 D3
Coombs Cl TN31 .. 68 C5
Coombs Cotts TN31 . 68 C5
Cooper Dr TN39 .. 157 B8
Cooper Rd TN31 .. 93 A5
Cooper Rise TN37 . 136 A5
Coopers Cl RH15 . 73 B5
COOPER'S GREEN .. 55 D4
Coopers Hill BN20 . 173 B2
Coopers La
  Crowborough TN6 . 25 D4
  Poundsbridge TN11, TN3 . 6 C7
Coopers Row TN22 . 55 D4
Coopers Way BN27 . 152 A6
Coopers Wood TN6 . 25 D4
Copenhagen Ct BN2 . 165 A3
Copestake Dr RH15 . 73 D3
Cophall La RH16 .. 187 B8
Cophall Rd BN20 . 184 E1
Coppards Ct RH17 . 74 C4
Coppards La TN31 . 67 C8
Copper Beeches
  Brighton BN1 ..... 142 E1
  St Leonards TN37 . 136 C4
Copper Cl RH15 .. 72 C4
Copperfields La TN4 . 8 A8
Coppers Ct TN4 .. 8 A8
Copper's Hill TN19 . 61 E4
Coppice Ave BN20 . 173 A4
Coppice BN20 ... 173 A4
Coppice The
  Battle TN33 ...... 113 A3
  Hastings TN34 ... 136 E1
  Pembury TN2 .... 9 D7
  Scaynes Hill RH17 . 51 F3
Coppice View TN21 . 82 B6
Coppice Way RH16 . 50 D3
Copse Cl
  East Grinstead RH19 . 2 A3
  St Leonards TN38 . 135 D3
Copse Hill BN1 .. 142 D5
Copse Rd TN39 .. 156 E4
Copse The RH16 . 51 B5
Copt Hall TN18 .. 48 D3
Copthorne Ct **2** BN3 . 163 C6
Copthorne Ho **19** BN21 . 184 E4
Copwood Ave TN22 . 78 B7
Copwood Rdbt TN22 . 78 A6
Copyhold La RH17 . 50 A4
Copyhold Rd RH19 . 10 D8
Copythorne Ho **1** RH16 . 50 E6
Coral Reef Cl BN23 . 175 A1
Corbyn Cres BN43 . 161 A7
Cordons BN43 ... 145 D5
Cormorant Cl BN23 . 174 C2
Cornelius Ave BN9 . 179 A5
Cornelius Ho BN3 . 163 A6
Corner Gn BN8 .. 124 D5
Cornfield Cl BN25 . 180 F3
Cornfield Gn BN27 . 129 C1
Cornfield La BN21 . 185 A2
Cornfield Rd
  Eastbourne BN21 . 185 A2
  Seaford BN25 .... 180 F3
Cornfield Terr
  11 Eastbourne BN21 . 185 A2
  St Leonards TN37 . 136 C1
Cornford La
  Burgess Hill RH15 . 72 E5
  Crowborough TN6 . 26 A1
  Pembury TN2 .... 9 B6
  Portslade-by-S BN41 . 141 B4
Cornford La TN2 . 9 B5
Cornford Pk TN2 . 9 C6
Cornish Cl BN23 . 174 B4
Cornish Mews BN1. 163 E8
Cornmill Gdns BN26 . 172 E4
Cornwall Ave BN10 . 178 E6
Cornwall Ct
  Eastbourne BN20 . 184 C4
  2 Hove BN3 .... 163 C7
Cornwall Gdns
  Brighton BN1 .... 142 E2
  6 East Grinstead RH19 . 10 F8
Cornwall Ho BN1 . 142 E2
Cornwallis Cl BN23 . 185 E7
Cornwallis Gdns TN34 . 159 E8
Cornwallis St **5** TN34 . 159 F8
Cornwallis Terr TN34 . 159 E8

Cornwall Rd TN39 . . . . . . 157 B3
CORNWELL'S BANK 76 C5
Coronation Bldgs BN9 . . . 179 D7
Coronation Cotts
 Burwash TN19 . . . . 62 A6
 Northbridge Street TN32 . . 64 C5
 Ticehurst TN5 . . . . 31 F2
Coronation Gdns
 Battle TN33 . . . . 112 F5
 Hurst Green TN19 . . . . . . 44 F3
Coronation Rd RH19 . . . . . 10 E7
Coronation St 7 BN2 . . . 164 C7
Corseley Rd TN5 . . . . 15 B5
Corsica Cl BN25 . . . . 180 F2
Corsica Rd BN25 . . . . 180 F1
Costells Edge RH17 . . . . . 51 F3
Cotchford Cl
 Eastbourne BN23 . . . . . . 174 C4
 Hastings TN34 . . . . 160 B8
Cotswold Pl 7 BN2 . . . . . 164 F5
Cotswolds The BN42 . . . . 161 E8
Cottage Cl BN9 . . . . 168 D2
Cottage Homes BN6 . . . . . 98 E6
Cottage La
 Hailsham BN27 . . . . 152 E1
 Westfield TN33, TN35 . . . 114 C7
Cottages The BN27 . . . . . 129 C3
COTTENDEN 43 B5
Cottenden Rd TN5 . . . . . . 43 A6
Cottesmore St Mary's RC
 Prim Sch BN3 . . . . 163 D8
Coulstock Rd RH15 . . . . . 72 C3
Council Cotts
 Cross-in-H TN21 . . . . . . 81 C8
 Crowborough TN6 . . . . . . 38 A8
 Robertsbridge TN32 . . . . 63 F3
 Uckfield TN22 . . . . 78 D3
Council Hos
 Ginger's Green BN27 . . . . 130 C6
 Rushlake Green TN21 . . . . 83 D1
Countess of Thanet's
 Almshouses TN8 . . . . 3 F3
County Oak Ave BN1 . . . . 143 B6
Courcels BN2 . . . . 164 E3
Course The BN7 . . . . 146 B8
Court Cl
 Brighton BN1 . . . . 142 E7
 East Grinstead RH19 . . . . . 1 F1
Court Cres RH19 . . . . 1 F1
Courtenay Gate BN3 . . . . 163 B5
Courtenay Terr 2 BN3 . . . 163 B5
Courtenwell TN3 . . . . 6 F4
Court Farm Cl BN9 . . . . . 168 A2
Court Farm Rd
 Hove BN3 . . . . 142 A2
 Newhaven BN9 . . . . 179 C5
 Rottingdean BN2 . . . . . . 165 F3
Courthope Ave TN5 . . . . . . 29 F4
Courthope Dr TN39 . . . . . 156 F5
Courthouse St TN34 . . . . 160 B4
Court La TN22 . . . . 55 D4
Courtland Rd BN26 . . . . . 173 A5
Courtlands
 13 Brighton BN2 . . . . . . 189 C3
 Dodd's Hill TN22 . . . . . . 35 D2
 Haywards Heath RH16 . . . 50 E3
 Newhaven BN9 . . . . 179 C7
 5 St Leonards TN38 . . . . 159 B6
Courtlands Pl TN6 . . . . . . 25 E1
Courtlands Rd BN22 . . . . 185 A5
Courtlands Road Ind Est
 BN22 . . . . 185 A5
Court Leet 8 BN25 . . . . . 180 E2
Court Mdw TN6 . . . . 39 B8
Court Meadow Cl TN6 . . . . 39 B7
Court Meadow Sch RH17 . . 50 A8
Courtney King Ho 1
 BN2 . . . . 164 D4
Court Ord Cotts BN2 . . . . 165 F3
Court Ord Rd BN2 . . . . . . 165 F3
Court Rd
 Eastbourne BN22 . . . . . . 173 F2
 Lewes BN7 . . . . 190 B2
 Royal Tunbridge Wells TN4 . . 7 F4
Court Royal TN2 . . . . 16 E8
Court The BN20 . . . . 173 B1
Courtyard The
 12 Eastbourne BN21 . . . . 184 F3
 East Grinstead RH19 . . . . . 2 B1
 Falmer BN1 . . . . 144 C6
 Hastings TN34 . . . . 136 E1
 Haywards Heath RH16 . . . 50 F4
 Hove BN3 . . . . 163 B8
 8 Hove BN3 . . . . 163 D6
 Sheffield Green TN22 . . . . 53 C5
COUSLEY WOOD 30 C7
Cousley Wood Rd TN5 . . . . 30 C7
Coventry Ct BN22 . . . . . . 185 D6
Coventry Rd TN38 . . . . . . 136 B3
Coventry St BN1 . . . . . . 163 E8
Coverdale Ave TN39 . . . . 156 C3
Coverdale Ct RH19 . . . . . . 1 C3
Covers The BN25 . . . . . . 180 F2
Covert The TN39 . . . . 156 C2
COWBEECH 108 C1
COWBEECH HILL 130 B7
COWDEN 4 A6
Cowden Cl TN18 . . . . 45 E8
Cowden Cross TN8 . . . . . . 4 C7
Cowden Hall La TN21 . . . 107 D5
Cowden La TN18 . . . . 45 E7
Cowden Mews TN8 . . . . . . 4 A5
Cowden Rd BN2 . . . . 177 D4

Cowdens Cl BN3 . . . . 141 D4
Cowden Sta TN8 . . . . 4 D8
Cowden Wlk TN38 . . . . . . 136 A2
Cowdray Cl TN39 . . . . . . 156 D6
Cowdray Ct 1 BN3 . . . . . 163 D7
Cowdray Park Rd TN39 . . . 156 C6
Cowfold Rd BN2 . . . . 164 E5
Cowley Dr BN2 . . . . 165 F7
Cownwy Ct BN2 . . . . 165 F1
Cowper St BN3 . . . . 163 A7
Cox Gr RH15 . . . . 72 E5
Coxheath Cl TN38 . . . . . . 135 E7
Cox's Cotts BN7 . . . . 99 E7
Crabtree Ave BN1 . . . . . . 143 B5
Crabtree Ho 1 TN38 . . . . 159 B8
Crackendale Field BN8 . . . 124 E6
Cradle Hill Com Prim Sch
 BN25 . . . . 181 A5
Cradle Hill Ind Est BN25 . . 181 B5
Cradle Hill Rd BN25 . . . . 181 B5
Craig Cl TN33 . . . . 135 A6
Craig Mdws BN8 . . . . 124 C5
Craigmore Hall TN6 . . . . . 26 A1
Craignair Ave BN1 . . . . . 142 F7
Cranborne Ave BN20 . . . . 188 C8
Cranbourne St BN1 . . . . . 189 A2
Cranbrook 14 BN2 . . . . . 189 C3
Cranbrook Rd TN37 . . . . . 136 C1
Cranedown BN7 . . . . 146 B7
Cranfield Rd TN40 . . . . . . 157 C4
Crangon Cotts BN20 . . . . 187 A4
Cranleigh Ave BN2 . . . . . 166 B1
Cranleigh Cl 3 BN3 . . . . 162 D7
Cranmer Ave TN39 . . . . . 157 A4
Cranmer Cl BN7 . . . . 190 B3
Cranston Ave TN39 . . . . . 157 A4
Cranston Cl TN39 . . . . . . 156 F4
Cranston Rd RH19 . . . . 1 F2
Cranston Rise TN39 . . . . . 156 F4
Cranwell Rd TN4 . . . . 7 C4
Crates Yd TN4 . . . . 8 A5
Craven Rd BN2 . . . . 164 D6
Crawford Way RH19 . . . . . . 1 F3
Crawley Cres BN22 . . . . . 173 E2
Crawley Rd BN1 . . . . 143 D6
Crayford Rd BN2 . . . . . . 143 D1
Crazy La TN33 . . . . 113 E7
Crecy Cl TN37 . . . . 135 F7
Creek The 11 TN34 . . . . . 160 B4
Crendon Pk TN4 . . . . 8 A8
Crescent Cl
 Burgess Hill RH15 . . . . . 73 B3
 Woodingdean BN2 . . . . . 165 E8
Crescent Drive N BN2 . . . . 165 E8
Crescent Drive S BN2 . . . . 165 E7
Crescent Mans BN2 . . . . . 189 C5
Crescent Pl BN2 . . . . 164 C4
Crescent Rd
 Brighton BN2 . . . . 164 B8
 Burgess Hill RH15 . . . . . 73 A3
 East Grinstead RH19 . . . . . 1 D1
 Royal Tunbridge Wells TN1 . . 8 B3
Crescent The
 Brighton BN2 . . . . 143 E2
 Eastbourne BN20 . . . . . . 173 A5
 Eastbourne, Downside
  BN20 . . . . 184 B5
 Felcourt RH19 . . . . 1 C8
 Groombridge TN3 . . . . . . 15 C7
 Hastings TN34 . . . . 136 C3
 Keymer BN6 . . . . 98 B3
 Newhaven BN9 . . . . 168 F1
 Southwick BN42 . . . . . . 161 F8
Crescent Way RH15 . . . . . 73 A3
Crespin Way BN1 . . . . . . 143 C2
Cresta Cl BN26 . . . . 173 A7
Cresta Ct BN10 . . . . 178 C6
Cresta Rd BN9 . . . . 179 A6
Crest Rd BN9 . . . . 168 F1
Crest Way BN41 . . . . 141 B3
Crestway Par BN1 . . . . . . 143 C2
Crestway The BN1 . . . . . . 143 C2
Cricket Ct RH19 . . . . 1 E3
Cricketers Cl TN3 . . . . . . 18 A5
Cricketers Field TN32 . . . . 65 E1
Cricketfield BN8 . . . . 76 D8
Cricketfield Ct 6 BN25 . . . 180 F2
Cricketfield Rd BN25 . . . . 180 F2
Cricketing La BN27 . . . . . 130 C4
Criers La TN20, TN22 . . . . 57 F7
Crink Hill BN8 . . . . 101 F3
Cripland Ct RH16 . . . . 51 B6
Cripps Ave BN10 . . . . . . 167 D1
CRIPP'S CORNER 88 D7
Crittle's Ct TN5 . . . . 29 F4
Crockers Hatch Cnr TN3 . . . 6 D2
Crockers La TN31 . . . . . . 67 B8
Crocks Dean BN10 . . . . . 167 D2
Croft Ave BN42 . . . . 161 F7
Croft Cl BN26 . . . . 173 A4
Croft Ct
 2 Eastbourne BN21 . . . . 185 B3
 7 Seaford BN25 . . . . . . 180 E3
Croft Dr BN41 . . . . 141 A3
Croft La BN25 . . . . 180 E3
Crofton Park Ave TN39 . . . 156 F3
Croft Rd
 Brighton BN1 . . . . 142 D4
 Crowborough TN6 . . . . . . 25 F2
 Hastings TN34 . . . . 160 B4
Croft Terr 2 TN34 . . . . . 160 A4
Croft The
 Bexhill TN39 . . . . 157 A4
 14 Eastbourne BN21 . . . . 184 F4

Croft The continued
 Eastbourne, Willingdon
  BN20 . . . . 173 B1
 Hassocks BN6 . . . . 97 F5
 Hastings TN34 . . . . 160 A4
 Lower Dicker BN27 . . . . . 128 B4
 Southwick BN42 . . . . . . 161 E8
Croft Works BN27 . . . . . . 152 B7
Croham Rd 11 TN6 . . . . . . 25 F3
Cromarty Wlk 17 BN23 . . . 185 F8
Cromer Way BN27 . . . . . . 129 A1
Cromer Wlk 3 TN34 . . . . 136 F1
Cromleigh Way BN42 . . . . 140 E2
Cromwell Ct 3 BN3 . . . . . 163 D7
Cromwell Mews RH15 . . . . 72 F4
Cromwell Pl 1 RH19 . . . . . 10 F7
Cromwell Rd
 Burgess Hill RH15 . . . . . 72 F3
 Hove BN3 . . . . 163 C7
 Royal Tunbridge Wells TN2 . . 8 C3
Cromwell St BN2 . . . . . . 164 C7
Crooked La BN25 . . . . . . 180 F2
Crossbush Rd BN2 . . . . . 164 E6
CROSS-IN-HAND 81 B7
Cross-in-Hand CE Prim Sch
 TN21 . . . . 81 F7
Cross La TN5 . . . . 31 D1
Cross La Gdns TN5 . . . . . 31 D1
Cross Levels Way BN21,
 BN22 . . . . 184 C7
Cross Rd BN42 . . . . 161 D8
Cross Road Cl BN42 . . . . 161 D8
Cross St
 Brighton BN1 . . . . 189 B4
 14 Hove BN1, BN3 . . . . . 163 D5
 Polegate BN26 . . . . 173 A6
 St Leonards TN37 . . . . . 159 C7
Cross Way BN7 . . . . 123 A2
Crossways BN8 . . . . 148 B4
Crossways Ave RH19 . . . . . 1 C1
Crossways The
 Broad Oak TN31 . . . . . . 90 B4
 Hassocks BN6 . . . . 97 C4
 Stone Cross BN24 . . . . . 174 A6
Crossway The
 Brighton BN1 . . . . 143 B2
 Portslade-by-S BN41 . . . . 141 A2
 Royal Tunbridge Wells TN4 . . 7 D2
Crouch Dr BN20 . . . . 173 B1
Crouchfield Cl 2 BN25 . . . 180 F2
Crouch La
 Linkhill TN18 . . . . 47 D6
 Lower Street TN33 . . . . . 133 B3
 Seaford BN25 . . . . 180 E2
Crouch The 6 BN25 . . . . 180 E2
CROWBOROUGH 26 C1
Crowborough Ct 4 TN6 . . . 25 F3
Crowborough Hill TN6 . . . . 26 B1
Crowborough Mews TN6 . . 25 E2
Crowborough Rd
 Hastings TN35 . . . . 160 E8
 Marlpits TN22 . . . . 35 E6
 Saltdean BN2 . . . . 177 D4
Crowborough Sta TN6 . . . . 38 C8
CROWBOROUGH
 WARREN 25 C1
Crowders La TN33 . . . . . . 111 D3
CROWHURST 134 F6
Crowhurst CE Prim Sch
 TN33 . . . . 134 F5
Crowhurst Cl BN23 . . . . . 174 A4
Crowhurst Cnr BN1 . . . . . 143 C7
Crowhurst La TN39 . . . . . 157 C7
Crowhurst Rd
 Brighton BN1 . . . . 143 C7
 St Leonards TN38 . . . . . 135 E2
Crowhurst Sta TN33 . . . . 135 A6
CROWLINK 186 F7
Crowlink Cotts BN20 . . . . 186 E7
Crowlink La BN20 . . . . . . 183 A1
Cromere Ave BN2 . . . . . . 157 C5
Crowmere Terr TN40 . . . . 157 C5
Crown Cl
 Hailsham BN27 . . . . 152 A7
 1 Hove BN3 . . . . 163 C6
 Uckfield TN22 . . . . 78 C8
Crown Ct 23 TN34 . . . . . 160 B4
Crowne Ho 8 BN21 . . . . . 184 E4
Crown Gdns BN1 . . . . . . 189 A2
Crown Hill
 4 Brighton BN2 . . . . . . 164 C6
 Seaford BN25 . . . . 180 E2
Crown Ho TN3 . . . . 20 B5
Crown La TN34 . . . . 160 B4
Crown Point Ho BN6 . . . . . 97 F4
Crown Rd
 Portslade-by-S BN41 . . . . 162 A8
 Shoreham-by-S BN43 . . . 161 B8
Crown St
 Brighton BN1 . . . . 189 A2
 13 Eastbourne BN21 . . . . 184 D4
Croxden Way BN22 . . . . . 173 D3
Croxton La RH16 . . . . 51 B6
Croydon Cotts 8 TN6 . . . . 25 F3
Crump's Cnr TN22 . . . . . 103 D6
Crunden Rd BN20 . . . . . . 184 C4
Crypt Art Gall ✦ BN25 . . . 180 E2
Cubitt Way TN38 . . . . . . 135 E4
Cuckfield Cl TN40 . . . . . . 158 A5
Cuckfield Rd
 Burgess Hill RH15 . . . . . 72 E7
 Goddards' Green BN6, RH17 72 A4
 Hurstpierpoint BN6 . . . . . 97 A7
Cuckmere Cl BN27 . . . . . 128 F3
Cuckmere Ct
 Alfriston BN26 . . . . 170 F3
 5 Seaford BN25 . . . . . . 180 E3
Cuckmere Dr BN24 . . . . . 174 A5

Cuckmere Ho BN24 . . . . . 175 E5
Cuckmere House Specl Sch
 BN25 . . . . 181 C2
Cuckmere Path TN22 . . . . 55 E1
Cuckmere Rd
 Newhaven BN9 . . . . 179 A5
 Seaford BN25 . . . . 181 B2
Cuckmere Rise TN21 . . . . 82 B8
Cuckmere Way BN1 . . . . . 143 C5
Cuckmere Wlk BN25 . . . . 173 D1
Cuckoo Dr TN21 . . . . 82 A6
CUILFAIL 190 C2
Cuilfail BN7 . . . . 190 C2
Culpepper Ave RH15 . . . . 72 E4
Culpepper Cl BN2 . . . . . . 143 D2
Culross Ave RH16 . . . . . . 50 D5
Cultural Ctr ✦ 16 BN21 . . 185 A1
Culver Cl BN23 . . . . 174 B4
Culverden Ave TN4 . . . . . . 8 A6
Culverden Down TN4 . . . . . 7 F5
Culverden Park Rd TN4 . . . . 7 F5
Culverden Pk TN4 . . . . 7 F5
Culverden Sq TN4 . . . . 8 A5
Culverden St TN1 . . . . 8 A4
Cumballa Ct BN20 . . . . . 188 F8
Cumberland Ct
 3 Bexhill TN40 . . . . . . 157 D4
 Eastbourne BN20 . . . . . . 184 B6
Cumberland Dr BN1 . . . . . 142 E2
Cumberland Gdns
 10 Royal Tunbridge Wells
  TN1 . . . . 8 A2
 St Leonards TN38 . . . . . 159 B8
Cumberland Lodge 3
 BN1 . . . . 142 E2
Cumberland Mews 12 TN1 . 8 A2
Cumberland Rd
 Bexhill TN39 . . . . 157 B7
 Brighton BN1 . . . . 142 E2
Cumberland Wlk TN1 . . . . . 8 A2
Cumberland Yd 11 TN1 . . . 8 A2
Cumnor House Sch RH17 . . 34 B5
Cunningham Cl
 Hailsham BN27 . . . . 152 D7
 St Leonards TN38 . . . . . 135 E3
Cunningham Ct 10 BN25 . . 180 E2
Cunningham Dr BN23 . . . . 185 E7
Cunningham Ho 6 TN39 . . 157 B3
Cunningham Rd TN4 . . . . . 8 B7
Curf Way RH15 . . . . 73 C3
Curlew Ct
 Hailsham BN27 . . . . 152 D7
 St Leonards TN38 . . . . . 135 E3
Curlews The BN43 . . . . . . 161 A8
Currie Rd TN4 . . . . 8 A5
Curve The BN2 . . . . 189 C2
Curwen Pl BN1 . . . . 142 E3
Curzon Ho BN2 . . . . 177 C4
Cuthbert Cl TN39 . . . . . . 157 A7
Cuthbert Rd BN2 . . . . . . 164 C5
Cutter La 7 TN34 . . . . . . 160 A3
Cypress Cl TN38 . . . . . . 159 A7
Cypress Gr TN2 . . . . 17 C8
Cyprus Mews RH15 . . . . . 73 B3
Cyprus Pl TN31 . . . . 93 B5
Cyprus Rd RH15 . . . . 73 A3
Cyril Richings Bsns Ctr
 BN43 . . . . 161 B7

D

Dacre Pk BN27 . . . . 152 D7
Dacre Rd
 Eastbourne BN20, BN21 . . 184 C4
 Herstmonceux BN27 . . . . 130 E6
 Newhaven BN9 . . . . 179 D7
Dads Hill TN21 . . . . 81 B8
Dagg La TN32 . . . . 65 F5
Dairy Gn TN6 . . . . 38 D8
Dakins The RH19 . . . . 10 E8
Dale Ave
 Brighton BN1 . . . . 142 F5
 Keymer BN6 . . . . 98 A3
Dale Cres BN1 . . . . 142 F6
Daledene RH19 . . . . 10 F8
Dale Dr BN1 . . . . 143 A6
Dale Hill BN45 . . . . 119 A6
Dalehurst TN6 . . . . 38 C7
Dalehurst Rd TN39 . . . . . 157 B7
Dale Rd
 Forest Row RH18 . . . . . . 11 F1
 Lewes BN7 . . . . 146 A8
Dales Cl BN27 . . . . 131 B5
Dale St TN1 . . . . 8 B4
Dale View BN3 . . . . 141 D2
Dale View Gdns BN3 . . . . 141 D2
Dalewood Gdns RH15 . . . . 73 C2
Dallas La BN8 . . . . 101 F6
Dallaway Dr BN24 . . . . . . 174 B5
Dallaway Gdns RH19 . . . . . 1 E1
DALLINGTON 84 D3
Dallington CE Prim Sch
 TN21 . . . . 84 D3
Dallington Cl TN40 . . . . . 158 A6
Dallington Rd
 Eastbourne BN22 . . . . . . 174 A1
 Hove BN3 . . . . 162 F8
Dalmeny Rd TN39 . . . . . . 157 A5
Dalmore Ct 3 TN40 . . . . . 157 C3
Dalton Rd BN20 . . . . 188 E8
Damian Way BN6 . . . . 98 B4
Damon Cl BN10 . . . . 178 C6
Dana Lodge BN10 . . . . . . 178 A7
Dane Cl BN25 . . . . 180 D2
Dane Ct TN31 . . . . 157 B6
Danehill CE Prim Sch
 RH17 . . . . 34 B4
Danehill La RH17 . . . . . . 33 E5
Danehill Rd BN2 . . . . 164 F5

Dane Hts 3 BN25 . . . . . . 180 E2
Dane Rd
 Seaford BN25 . . . . 180 E3
 St Leonards TN38 . . . . . 159 B8
Daniel Way TN31 . . . . 94 F2
Dannfields Ho BN25 . . . . . 180 E3
Danny Sheldon Ho 14
 . . . . 164 C4
Danum Cl BN27 . . . . 129 C3
Danworth Farm BN6 . . . . . 72 A1
Danworth La BN6 . . . . 72 B2
Darby's La TN5 . . . . 30 B2
Darcey Dr BN1 . . . . 143 A6
Darent Cl BN24 . . . . 173 F5
Daresbury Cl TN39 . . . . . 157 B6
Darley Rd BN20 . . . . 188 D7
Darrick Ct 6 BN21 . . . . . 185 A1
Dart Ct RH19 . . . . 2 A3
Dartmouth Cl BN2 . . . . . 143 F1
Dartmouth Cres BN2 . . . . 143 F1
Darvel Down TN33 . . . . . . 86 B2
Darwall Dr BN25 . . . . . . 181 A3
Darwell Cl
 Robertsbridge TN32 . . . . 64 B3
 St Leonards TN38 . . . . . 135 E1
Darwell Dr BN24 . . . . . . 174 A5
DARWELL HOLE 85 F3
D'Aubigny Rd BN2 . . . . . . 164 B8
Davey Dr BN1 . . . . 143 B1
Davey's La BN7 . . . . 190 C3
David Lloyd Club The
 BN22 . . . . 184 F8
Davids Hts BN21 . . . . . . 184 E5
Davigdor Inf Sch BN3 . . . . 163 D6
Davigdor Rd BN3 . . . . . . 163 E7
Davis Dr TN39 . . . . 157 A7
Dawber Bldgs BN27 . . . . . 152 B7
Dawes Ho TN19 . . . . 62 A6
Dawlish Cl BN2 . . . . 143 F1
Dawson Terr BN2 . . . . . . 164 C6
Daynes Way RH15 . . . . . . 72 E1
Daytona Quay 19 BN23 . . 185 F8
Deacons Dr BN41 . . . . . . 141 C2
Deadman's Cross TN21 . . . 83 B5
Deadmans La TN31 . . . . . 93 C6
Deadmantree Hill BN8 . . . 101 B3
Deal Ave BN25 . . . . 181 C5
Deals The 7 TN31 . . . . . . 93 B5
Dean Cl
 Portslade-by-S BN41 . . . . 141 C2
 Rottingdean BN2 . . . . . . 166 A2
Dean Ct Rd BN2 . . . . 166 A2
Deanery Cl BN7 . . . . 190 B4
Dean Gdns BN41 . . . . . . 141 C2
Deanland Rd BN27 . . . . . 127 B4
DEANLAND VILLAGE 127 B4
Deanland Wood Pk
 BN27 . . . . 127 B3
Dean Rd BN25 . . . . 180 F2
Deans Cl
 Bexhill TN39 . . . . 157 B6
 Woodingdean BN2 . . . . . 165 E8
Deans Dr TN39 . . . . 157 A6
Deans Mdw BN8 . . . . 101 E5
Deans Rd BN26 . . . . 170 F3
Dean St BN1 . . . . 163 E5
Deanway BN3 . . . . 142 B3
Dean Wood Cl BN23 . . . . 174 A4
De Cham Ave TN37 . . . . . 159 D8
De Cham Rd TN37 . . . . . . 159 C8
De Chardin Dr TN34 . . . . 137 A5
Decimus Burton Way 10
 TN37 . . . . 159 C7
Decimus Pl TN1 . . . . 8 B4
Deco Bldg The 3 BN2 . . . 143 C1
De Courcel Rd BN2 . . . . . 164 E3
Decoy Dr BN22 . . . . 173 D1
Deepdene TN5 . . . . 30 A6
Deepdene Gdns TN35 . . . . 160 C7
Deepdene Sch BN3 . . . . . 162 D7
Deer Haven BN27 . . . . . . 127 C4
Deerhurst Pk RH18 . . . . . 12 A2
Deer Paddock La 7
 BN27 . . . . 152 C7
Deers Leap RH16 . . . . . . 50 C1
Deerswood La TN39 . . . . . 156 E5
Deeside The BN1 . . . . . . 143 A7
De Grey Cl BN7 . . . . 190 B3
Deilsfoot Cotts TN21 . . . . 28 A3
Delamere Ct 3 BN21 . . . . 184 F2
Delavall Wlk BN23 . . . . . 185 F6
Delaware Dr TN37 . . . . . 135 F6
Delaware Rd BN7 . . . . . . 146 A8
De La Warr Gn BN7 . . . . . 123 B3
De La Warr Par TN40 . . . . 157 E3
De La Warr Pav TN40 . . . . 157 C3
De La Warr Rd
 Bexhill TN39 . . . . 157 C5
 East Grinstead RH19 . . . . . 1 F1
Delfryn BN41 . . . . 140 F3
Dell Cl TN38 . . . . 136 A1
Dell Dr TN2 . . . . 8 D4
Dellney Ave RH16 . . . . . . 50 F3
Dell The
 East Grinstead RH19 . . . . . 2 B1
 Haywards Heath RH16 . . . 50 C5
Delmonden Rd TN18 . . . . . 45 C8
Delves Ave TN2 . . . . 8 C1
Delves Cl BN8 . . . . 124 D6
Delves Ho BN8 . . . . 124 D6
Delves Way BN8 . . . . 124 D6
De Moleyns Cl 1 TN40 . . . 157 D4
De Montfort Rd
 Brighton BN2 . . . . 164 C7
 Lewes BN7 . . . . 123 B1
De Montfort Terr 4
 BN7 . . . . 123 B1
Denbigh Cl TN39 . . . . . . 156 E4

Denbigh Ct TN39...... 156 E5
Denbigh Rd TN4...... 8 C7
Dencher Rd BN7...... 145 B3
Dene Cl BN20...... 183 B1
Denecroft BN1...... 142 D5
Dene Dr BN22...... 173 C1
Dene Hospl The BN6... 72 B5
Denehurst Gdns TN35.. 137 A5
Dene Path TN22...... 55 D1
Deneside BN20...... 183 B1
Dene The
　Eastbourne BN20..... 173 A3
　Hastings TN35...... 137 A5
　Hove BN3...... 141 D3
　Uckfield TN22...... 55 D1
Dene Vale BN1...... 142 D5
Dene Way TN3...... 7 A7
Deneway The BN1...... 142 D4
Denham Cl TN38...... 135 F4
Denham Ct RH15...... 72 D3
Denham Rd RH15...... 72 D3
Denham Way TN31...... 94 E2
Den Hill BN20...... 184 A4
Denman's Cl RH16...... 51 A8
Denman's La RH16...... 51 A7
Denmark Mews BN3...... 163 B7
Denmark Pl TN34...... 159 F7
Denmark Rd BN41...... 162 C7
Denmark Terr BN1...... 163 E6
Denmark Villas BN3...... 163 B7
Dennis Hobden Cl BN2.. 143 E1
DENNY BOTTOM...... 7 E4
DENTON...... 168 F2
Denton Cl TN31...... 93 A6
Denton Com Sch BN9... 168 E1
Denton Dr
　Brighton BN1...... 143 A6
　Newhaven BN9...... 168 E1
Denton Rd
　Eastbourne BN20..... 188 D8
　Newhaven BN9...... 168 E1
Denton Rise BN9...... 168 E2
Dentons The BN20...... 188 D8
Derby Ct [7] BN3...... 163 E7
Derby Pl [6] BN2...... 189 C2
Derek Ave BN3...... 162 D6
Derek Ho BN3...... 162 F6
Dern La TN21...... 106 B7
De Roos Ct BN21...... 184 E5
De Roos Rd BN21...... 184 E4
Dervia Ho BN3...... 163 C7
Derwent Cl BN27...... 129 A1
Derwent Ct BN1...... 189 A3
Derwent Dr TN4...... 7 E5
Derwent Rd BN20...... 188 E8
Desmond Rd BN22...... 185 D5
Desmond Way BN2...... 164 F6
Devil's Dyke Rd BN1... 141 E7
Devonian Ct BN2...... 189 C4
Devonport Ho [1] TN31... 93 C6
Devonshire Cl TN2...... 16 F8
Devonshire Ct [1] BN3.. 163 C7
Devonshire Lodge [1]
　BN22...... 185 C5
Devonshire Park Theatre★
　[14] BN21...... 185 A1
Devonshire Pl
　Brighton BN2...... 189 C2
　Eastbourne BN21..... 185 A2
Devonshire Rd
　Bexhill TN40...... 157 C3
　Hastings TN34...... 159 F8
Devonshire Sq TN40..... 157 C3
Devon Villas RH16...... 50 F4
De Walden Mews BN20.. 188 E8
De Warrenne Rd BN7... 123 B1
Dewe Rd BN2...... 143 C1
Dewhurst Cotts TN5..... 29 A7
Dewhurst La TN5...... 29 B8
Dew La TN31...... 92 A8
Dewlands Hill TN20..... 38 F2
Dewpond The BN10..... 167 B1
Dexter Dr RH19...... 10 E8
Dharma Sch The BN1... 143 A6
Diamond Cotts RH17.... 74 A5
Diana Cl TN40...... 158 A6
Dickens Cl RH19...... 1 C1
Dickens Way RH23...... 174 E3
Dicklands The BN7...... 167 D8
Diggers The BN1...... 143 B3
Dillingburgh Rd BN20... 184 C4
Dillon Way TN2...... 8 D7
Dinapore Ho [11] BN2... 189 C3
Diplock Cl BN26...... 172 F6
Diplocks Bldgs BN27.... 152 A7
Diplocks The BN27...... 152 A8
Diplocks Way BN27..... 152 A8
Diplocks Wlk BN27...... 152 A8
Dirty La RH19...... 11 E7
Ditchling Beacon Nature
　Reserve★ BN6...... 120 D7
Ditchling Bostall BN6... 120 D7
Ditchling Cl BN23...... 173 F4
Ditchling Comm Ctry Pk★
　BN6...... 73 B6
Ditchling Cres BN1...... 143 C5
Ditchling Ct [4] BN1.... 164 B8
Ditchling Dr TN35...... 160 E8
Ditchling Gdns BN1..... 143 B1
Ditchling Mus★ BN6.... 98 C3
Ditchling Pl [1] BN1.... 143 A1
Ditchling Rd
　Brighton BN1, BN2.... 143 D4
　Westmeston BN1, BN6.. 120 D4
Ditchling Rise BN1...... 164 A8
Ditchling St Margaret's CE
　Prim Sch BN6...... 98 D3

Ditchling Way BN27..... 152 B6
Dittons BN26...... 173 C6
Ditton's Cnr BN27...... 173 C6
Ditton Mews TN38...... 135 E2
Dittons Rd BN21...... 184 E3
Ditton's Rd BN26...... 173 D6
Dixter La TN31...... 67 B8
Dixter Rd TN31...... 67 A6
Dock The BN8...... 148 C3
Dodd'S HILL...... 35 D2
Dodshill TN6...... 26 A1
Dog Cotts RH19...... 3 B1
Dog Kennel La TN22.... 57 F6
Dogs Hill Rd TN36...... 118 B5
Doleham Cotts TN35.... 115 D5
Doleham La TN35...... 115 B6
Doleham Sta TN35...... 115 D5
Dolphin Ct
　Eastbourne BN20..... 188 E7
　[5] Hove BN3...... 163 A6
Dolphin Ind Est BN43... 161 B7
Dolphin Mews
　Brighton BN1...... 189 B1
　Shoreham-by-S BN43... 161 A7
Dolphin Rd
　Haywards Heath RH16... 50 D4
　Shoreham-by-S BN43... 161 B7
Dolphin Way BN43...... 161 B7
Dominica Ct BN23...... 185 G7
Donald Hall Rd BN2..... 164 D5
Donald Way TN36...... 118 A5
Donkey Mews [4] BN3.. 163 D5
Donnington Rd BN2..... 165 E6
Dorchester TN1...... 8 B6
Dorchester Ct
　[2] Brighton BN1...... 163 E5
　[3] Eastbourne BN21... 184 E4
Dordrecht Way TN34.... 136 E1
Dorin Ct TN2...... 8 C3
Dorita Ct BN10...... 178 C6
Dorking Rd TN1...... 8 C6
Dorman's Cl RH7...... 2 A8
Dormans Gdns RH19.... 1 E6
Dormans High St RH7... 2 A8
Dormans Park Rd
　Dormans Park RH19.... 1 E6
　East Grinstead RH19... 1 D3
Dormans Sta RH7...... 1 F8
Dormans Sta Rd RH7.... 1 F7
Dornden Dr TN3...... 7 A4
Dorothy Ave BN10...... 178 C7
Dorothy Avenue N BN10. 178 C8
Dorothy Rd BN3...... 162 D8
Dorset Ave RH19...... 1 C3
Dorset Cotts TN7...... 14 B4
Dorset Ct
　[6] Eastbourne BN22... 185 B3
　Hove BN3...... 162 F6
Dorset Gdns
　Brighton BN2...... 189 C2
　East Grinstead RH19... 1 C3
Dorset Mews
　Brighton BN2...... 189 B2
　East Grinstead RH19... 1 C3
Dorset Pl
　Brighton BN2...... 189 C2
　Hastings TN34...... 159 E7
Dorset Rd
　Bexhill TN40...... 157 E5
　Lewes BN7...... 190 B1
　Royal Tunbridge Wells TN1.. 8 D2
Dorset Road S TN40.... 157 D4
Dorset St BN2...... 189 B2
Doubledays RH15...... 73 B2
Doucegrove TN38...... 136 A1
Douglas Cl BN27...... 129 B2
Douglas Rd TN6...... 27 D1
Douro Stables TN4...... 8 A4
Dove Ct TN22...... 78 D6
Dovedale Gdns BN22.... 173 F2
Dover Cl BN25...... 181 C5
Dover Rd
　Brighton BN1...... 143 A2
　Polegate BN26...... 173 B7
Dowding Way TN2...... 8 D8
Dower Cl BN2...... 165 D3
Downash Cl BN2...... 164 E6
Downash Ct TN5...... 32 A3
Downash Ho TN5...... 32 A3
Down Ave TN3...... 20 A4
Downes Ct [9] BN43.... 161 C8
Downey Ct TN37...... 136 B6
Downford [15] BN2..... 164 F5
Downhill View BN2...... 165 E7
Down La TN3...... 28 C8
Downland Ave
　Peacehaven BN10..... 178 E6
　Southwick BN42...... 140 F1
Downland Cl
　Eastbourne BN23..... 174 C4
　Southwick BN42...... 140 D1
　Woodingdean BN2..... 165 B8
Downland Copse TN22.. 78 C8
Downland Cres BN3..... 141 B8
Downland Cl BN41...... 141 A2
Downland Dr BN3...... 141 B3
Downland Rd BN2...... 165 B8
Downlands Ave TN38.... 157 B4
Downlands Cl TN39..... 157 A4
Downlands Com Sch BN6 97 F3
Downlands Way BN20... 183 B1
Downline TN21...... 106 F7
Down Rd TN39...... 157 A5

DOWNSIDE...... 184 C4
Downside
　Brighton BN1...... 142 D5
　Hove BN3...... 142 B3
　Shoreham-by-S BN43... 140 A1
Downside Cl BN20...... 184 C3
Downs Inf Sch BN1..... 164 B8
Downs Jun Sch BN1.... 143 A1
Downs Rd
　Burgess Hill RH15..... 72 E4
　Eastbourne BN22..... 173 B2
　Seaford BN25...... 181 A3
Down's Rd TN34...... 136 F3
Downs The BN25...... 181 A3
DOWN STREET...... 54 C5
Downsvalley Rd BN20... 173 A4
Downs Valley Rd BN2... 165 E8
Downsview
　Brighton BN1...... 142 E1
　Eastbourne BN20..... 173 A3
　Heathfield TN21...... 82 B8
　Hove BN3...... 141 D3
　Hurstpierpoint BN6.... 97 A5
Downs View
　Ninfield TN33...... 133 B5
　North Chailey BN8..... 75 E7
　Peacehaven BN10..... 167 D2
Downsview Ave BN2..... 165 C8
Downs View Cl
　East Dean BN20...... 183 C1
　North Chailey BN8..... 75 E7
Downsview Cotts BN8... 123 A7
Downsview Cres BN27... 78 B8
Downsview Dr RH17..... 74 C4
Downs View La BN20.... 183 C1
Downsview Rd
　Eastbourne BN20..... 173 A3
　Golden Cross BN27.... 127 B3
　Portslade-by-S BN41... 141 A2
　Seaford BN25...... 181 A3
Downs View Rd BN6.... 97 F3
Downs View Specl Sch
　BN2...... 165 C8
Downsview Way BN27... 152 B7
Downs Villas BN9...... 168 E3
Downsway
　Arlington BN26...... 150 B3
　Southwick BN42...... 140 F1
　Woodingdean BN2..... 144 D1
Downs Wlk BN10...... 167 C2
Down Terr BN2...... 164 C6
DOWN THE...... 20 A3
Down The BN3...... 141 B4
Downton Cotts TN18.... 46 F4
Draffin La TN31...... 94 D3
Drake Ave BN23...... 185 E7
Drake Cl BN25...... 180 E2
Drake Ho TN39...... 156 E4
Drapers Way TN38...... 136 B2
Draxmont Way BN1..... 142 F3
Drayton Rise TN39...... 156 D4
Drive Lodge [10] BN3... 163 C7
Drive Prep Sch The BN3 163 C8
Drive Pl
　Burgess Hill RH15..... 73 B4
　Crowborough TN6..... 25 D2
　Fordcombe TN3...... 6 A5
　Hailsham BN27...... 152 B6
　Hellingly BN27...... 129 C5
　Hove BN3...... 163 C7
　Maresfield Park TN22.. 55 A7
　Maresfield TN22...... 55 A5
　Newhaven BN9...... 179 C5
　Royal Tunbridge Wells TN2. 8 B1
　Southwick BN42...... 158 F8
　St Leonards TN38..... 158 F8
　Uckfield TN22...... 78 C8
　Walter's Green TN3.... 5 F5
Drockmill Cl BN26...... 173 C6
Drove Ave BN2...... 144 D2
Drove Cres BN41...... 141 B4
Drove Rd
　Newhaven BN9...... 179 D8
　Portslade-by-S BN41... 141 A1
　Woodingdean BN2..... 165 B8
Drove Ret Pk The BN9... 179 E8
Drovers Cl BN41...... 141 C2
Drovers Way RH15...... 73 C1
Drove The
　Brighton BN1...... 142 D1
　Falmer BN1...... 144 C3
　Newhaven BN9...... 179 E8
　Offham BN7, BN8..... 123 C3
Droveway The
　Haywards Heath RH16.. 50 F4
　Hove BN3...... 142 B1
　Lewes BN7...... 146 A5
Drummond Ct RH16..... 50 D4
Drummond Cl RH16..... 50 D4
Drury La TN38...... 136 A2
Drury Lo [6] RH19..... 1 F2
Drusillas Park Zoo★
　BN26...... 171 B6
Dryden Wlk BN23...... 174 E3
Duchess Dr BN25...... 180 E6
DUDDLESWELL...... 36 B4
Dudeney Lodge BN1.... 143 B1
Dudley Inf Sch TN35.... 160 C5
Dudley Lodge TN2...... 8 C4
Dudley Mews [16] BN3.. 163 D5
Dudley Rd
　Brighton BN1...... 143 B1
　Eastbourne BN22..... 185 B4
　Hastings TN35...... 160 C5

Dudley Rd continued
　Royal Tunbridge Wells TN1.. 8 A4
Dudwell Rd BN2...... 165 E7
Duke Bernard Ct [8]
　BN22...... 185 C5
Duke Ho BN8...... 126 B7
Duke Mews [2] TN37.... 136 B2
Duke Rd TN37...... 136 B2
Dukes Barn Ct RH16.... 51 B7
Dukesbury Ho BN21..... 184 E3
Dukes Cl BN25...... 180 D5
Duke's Ct BN2...... 189 A2
Duke's Dr BN20...... 188 E7
Dukes Hill TN33...... 112 C6
Dukes La BN1...... 189 A2
Duke's Mound BN2..... 164 D4
Duke St
　Bexhill TN39...... 156 F5
　Brighton BN1...... 189 A2
　St Leonards TN37..... 136 B2
Duke Terr TN37...... 136 B2
Dulwich Cl BN25...... 181 B4
Dumbrell Ct BN7...... 146 B8
Dumbrells Ct BN6...... 98 D4
Dumbrells Ct Rd BN6... 98 D4
Dumbrills Cl RH15...... 73 A5
Dumb Woman's La TN31. 92 D3
Dumfries Ct [4] TN38... 136 B1
Dunbar Dr BN27...... 129 A1
Duncan Ho BN10...... 167 D1
Dunclutha Rd TN34..... 136 F4
Duncton Cl RH16...... 50 D4
Duncton Ho BN6...... 97 E4
Dundale Rd TN3...... 9 C1
Dunes Ave TN31...... 94 F2
Dunning's Rd RH19..... 10 E7
Dunorlan Farm Cotts TN2. 8 E4
Dunstall Ave RH15...... 72 E4
Dunstall Farm Rd RH15.. 72 F4
Dunstan Gr TN4...... 8 B6
Dunstan Rd TN4...... 8 B6
Dunstans Croft TN20.... 40 C3
Dunster Cl BN21...... 143 B1
Dunvan Cl BN7...... 190 A4
Dunwich [7] BN43...... 161 B6
DURGATES...... 29 E5
Durham Cl BN2...... 144 A1
Durham Ct
　Eastbourne BN20..... 184 B6
　[4] Hove BN3...... 163 B6
Durkins Rd RH19...... 1 D3
Durrell Cl BN23...... 174 F2
Durrington Ct BN1...... 142 D5
Dursley Rd BN22...... 185 A4
Dutchells Way BN22.... 173 E4
Dyall Cl RH15...... 72 E4
Dyke Cl BN3...... 142 B4
Dyke Rd BN1, BN3...... 163 E7
Dyke Road Ave BN1, BN3. 142 C3
Dyke Road Dr BN1..... 163 F8
Dyke Road Mews BN1... 189 A4
Dyke Road Pl BN1...... 142 C3
Dymchurch Cl
　Polegate BN26...... 173 C7
　Seaford BN25...... 181 C5
Dymock Cl BN25...... 181 C4
Dymock's The BN5...... 98 D3
Dymond Rd TN38...... 136 A3
Dynevor Rd TN4...... 8 C7

E

Eagle Cl TN22...... 78 E5
Eagle Ct [13] BN2...... 164 C8
Eagle Rd TN31...... 93 C6
Earle Ho [2] RH19...... 1 F2
Earls Cl BN25...... 180 C5
Earl's Down...... 84 B4
Earls Gdn BN7...... 190 B2
Earl's Rd TN4...... 7 F4
Earl St TN34...... 159 F8
Earwig Cnr BN8...... 190 C4
East Albany Rd BN25... 180 F3
East Ascent TN38...... 159 C6
East Beach St TN34..... 160 B3
East Beeches Rd TN6... 26 B2
EAST BLATCHINGTON... 180 E5
EASTBOURNE...... 185 B2
Eastbourne Ave BN24... 175 D5
Eastbourne Coll
　Eastbourne BN20..... 184 F1
　Eastbourne BN21..... 184 F4
Eastbourne District General
　Hospl BN21...... 184 E7
Eastbourne Her Ctr★ [18]
　BN22...... 185 A1
Eastbourne La BN21.... 183 C7
Eastbourne Miniature Steam
　Rly Adventure Pk★
　BN23...... 185 A2
Eastbourne Rd
　Brighton BN2...... 143 D1
　Eastbourne BN20..... 173 B4
　East Dean BN20...... 187 B8
　Halland BN8...... 104 C6
　Pevensey Bay BN24.... 175 C4
　Seaford BN25...... 181 C3
　Uckfield TN22...... 78 F3
　Westham BN3, BN24.... 174 F4
Eastbourne Sports Pk
　BN21...... 174 E5
East Bourne St [22] TN34. 160 B4
Eastbourne Sta BN21... 184 F3

Eastbourne Tech Coll
　BN22...... 173 E2
Eastbourne Terr [4]
　BN25...... 181 A3
Eastbridge Rd BN9..... 179 E7
Eastbrook Rd BN41..... 162 B7
Eastbrook Way BN42.... 162 A2
EAST CHILTINGTON... 100 A3
East Cl BN26...... 173 B6
East Cliff TN31...... 93 C6
East Cliff Rd TN4...... 8 A6
Eastcourt Villas [3] RH19.. 1 F2
Eastdale Rd RH15...... 73 D4
EAST DEAN...... 187 B8
East Dean Rd BN20..... 184 B2
East Dean Rise BN25... 181 A4
East Dr BN2...... 164 C5
EAST END...... 98 E3
East End La BN6...... 98 D3
Eastergate TN39...... 156 D6
Eastgate Rd BN2...... 143 F4
Eastern Ave
　Polegate BN26...... 173 B5
　Shoreham-by-S BN43... 161 A7
Eastern Cl BN43...... 161 A7
Eastern Concourse BN2. 165 A3
Eastern Cotts RH16..... 51 B7
Eastern Pl BN2...... 164 E4
Eastern Rd
　Brighton BN2...... 164 D4
　Haywards Heath RH16.. 50 F3
　Lindfield RH16...... 51 C7
　Wivelsfield RH17..... 74 B4
Eastern Ring Rd BN1... 144 C2
Eastern Rd BN25...... 164 D4
Eastern Terr [10] BN2... 164 D4
Eastern Terr Mews [9]
　BN2...... 164 D4
Eastfield Cres BN1...... 143 A4
Eastgate St BN7...... 190 B2
Eastgate Wharf BN7.... 190 B2
East Gdns BN6...... 98 D3
East Grinstead Sta RH19. 1 C1
East Grinstead Town Mus★
　RH19...... 1 F1
EAST GULDEFORD... 93 C7
East Hill RH19...... 1 E6
East Hill Cliff Rly★ TN34. 160 B4
East Hill Ctry Pk★ TN35. 160 C4
Easthill Dr BN41...... 141 B2
East Hill Pas [7] TN34... 160 B4
Easthill Way BN41...... 141 B1
EAST HOATHLY...... 105 B5
East Hoathly CE Prim Sch
　BN8...... 104 F5
Eastlands Cl TN4...... 16 E8
Eastlands Rd TN4...... 7 E1
East Lockside BN2...... 165 A3
East Mascalls La RH16.. 51 E6
East Meadway BN43.... 161 A6
EAST MOULSECOOMB.. 143 F3
East Par TN34...... 160 A3
East Point [6] BN43..... 161 A6
Eastport La BN7...... 190 A1
East St
　Brighton BN1...... 189 B1
　Coggins Mill TN20..... 40 D3
　Falmer BN1...... 144 C6
　Hastings TN34...... 160 A4
　Lewes BN7...... 190 B2
　Portslade-by-S BN41... 162 C7
　Rye TN31...... 93 C5
　Seaford BN25...... 180 E3
East View TN21...... 82 B6
Eastview Cotts BN8..... 124 E5
East View Fields BN7... 99 E5
East View Terr TN33.... 88 F1
Eastway TN39...... 156 D4
East Way BN7...... 122 F2
Eastwell Pl BN27...... 152 B8
East Wick RH16...... 51 C7
Eastwick Cl BN1...... 143 B7
Eastwood Rd TN39..... 157 A4
Eatenden La TN32, TN33.. 87 B3
Eaton Ct [3] BN3...... 163 B7
Eaton Gate [17] BN3.... 163 C6
Eaton Gdns BN3...... 163 C7
Eaton Gdns Mans [20]
　BN3...... 163 C7
Eaton Gr BN3...... 163 C7
Eaton Hall [19] BN3.... 163 C7
Eaton Manor [11] BN3... 163 C7
Eaton Pl BN2...... 164 D4
Eaton Rd BN3...... 163 C7
Eaton Villas BN3...... 163 B7
Eaton Wlk TN33...... 88 D1
Ebbisham Ct RH19...... 1 A4
Ebden's Hill TN37...... 136 B8
Ebenezer Rd TN34..... 160 B4
Ecclesden [7] BN2...... 189 C3
Ecmod Rd BN22...... 185 C6
Edburton Ave BN1...... 143 A1
Edenbridge Rd TN7..... 13 E7
Eden Cl BN24...... 174 A5
Eden Ct TN5...... 43 D8
Eden Dr TN39...... 156 F4
Eden Rd TN1...... 8 A2
Edensor Rd BN20...... 188 D7
Eden Vale
　Dormans Park RH19.... 1 F5
　East Grinstead RH19... 1 D4
Eden Wlk [9] TN1...... 8 A2
Edgar Rd TN35...... 160 C6
Edgehill Cl TN21...... 81 F7
Edgehill Way BN41..... 140 F2

Edgeland Terr BN22.....173 F1
Edinburgh Ct
  Eastbourne BN20.....184 C5
  Seaford BN25.....180 D3
Edinburgh Rd
  Bexhill TN40.....157 C5
  8 Brighton BN2.....164 C8
  Seaford BN25.....180 D3
  St Leonards TN38.....158 E7
Edinburgh Way RH19.....10 F7
Edison Rd BN23.....174 A1
Edith Ave BN10.....178 B7
Edith Avenue N BN10.....178 C8
Edith Rd TN35.....160 D7
Edmond Cl BN23.....185 E8
Edmonton Rd TN39.....157 B7
Edmund Rd TN35.....160 C6
Edster Ct BN41.....140 F3
Edward Ave
  Hove BN3.....142 A3
  Saltdean BN2.....166 D3
Edward Cl
  Hove BN3.....142 A3
  Seaford BN25.....180 A6
Edward Ho BN3.....162 F6
Edward Rd
  Haywards Heath RH16.....50 E2
  St Leonards TN37.....159 D7
Edward St
  Brighton BN2.....189 C2
  Lewes BN7.....190 B2
  Royal Tunbridge Wells TN4.....7 B7
  Rusthall TN4.....7 C4
Edward Terr TN35.....136 A4
Edward Way RH15.....72 D2
Edwin Rd TN35.....160 C6
Effingham Cl BN2.....166 C2
Effingham Dr TN39.....156 D3
Egbert Cl BN23.....185 E8
Egerton Ho BN20.....188 E8
Egerton Rd TN39.....157 B3
Egginton Cl BN1.....144 A5
Egginton Rd BN2.....143 F5
Egles Gr TN22.....78 B8
Egmont Rd BN3.....141 D1
Egremont Pl
  Brighton BN2.....189 C2
  Hastings TN34.....160 B6
Eight Acre La TN35.....115 D1
Eight Bells Cl TN22.....56 C4
Eileen Ave BN2.....166 B1
Eisenhower Dr TN37.....135 F6
Elder Cl BN41.....141 B2
Elder Pl BN1.....189 B4
Elderwood Cl
  Bexhill TN39.....157 C7
  Eastbourne BN22.....173 D2
Eldon Rd BN21.....184 C5
Eldred Ave BN1.....142 D5
Eldridge Way TN37.....136 C6
Eleanor Cl
  Lewes BN7.....123 B2
  Seaford BN25.....180 D5
Eleanor Terr TN35.....160 D8
Eley Cres BN2.....165 E3
Eley Dr BN2.....165 E3
Elford St 3 TN34.....159 F8
Elgar Way BN23.....174 E3
Elgin Gdns BN25.....181 C3
Elim Ct BN2.....189 C4
Elim Ct Gdns TN6.....25 E4
Elim Wlk TN34.....136 F2
Eliot Ho 5 RH16.....50 E3
Elizabethan Cl TN33.....132 F2
Elizabeth Ave BN3.....142 A3
Elizabeth Cl
  Hove BN3.....142 A3
  Seaford BN25.....180 A6
Elizabeth Cres RH19.....1 F3
Elizabeth Ct
  4 Bexhill TN40.....157 C5
  Eastbourne BN20.....184 C5
  2 Hailsham BN27.....152 C7
  7 Hove BN3.....163 C7
  Polegate BN26.....173 A6
Elizabeth Garlick Ct 1
  TN1.....8 B4
Elizabeth Rd
  Shoreham-by-S BN43.....161 C8
  St Leonards TN38.....136 A2
Ellen Ho 3 BN3.....163 B7
Ellenslea Rd TN37.....159 C7
Ellen St
  Hove BN3.....163 B7
  Portslade-by-S BN41.....162 C7
Ellenwhorne La TN32.....89 A7
Ellerslie La TN39.....156 F6
Elliots Way TN21.....82 A8
Ellis Cl TN34.....159 E7
Ellis Gordon Ct BN9.....179 B7
Ellison Cl TN6.....25 E4
Ellis Way TN22.....78 A7
Elm Ave BN27.....127 C3
Elm Cl
  Bexhill TN39.....157 A7
  Hove BN3.....142 C2
  Laughton BN8.....126 C7
  Seaford BN25.....181 C3
Elm Cotts
  Laughton BN8.....126 C7
  Upper Dicker BN27.....151 A8
Elm Ct
  Brighton BN1.....163 E8
  3 East Grinstead RH19.....1 D2

Elm Ct *continued*
  East Grinstead, Sunnyside
  RH19.....10 E8
  Newhaven BN9.....179 B7
  Polegate BN26.....173 A6
  Portslade-by-S BN41.....162 B8
Elm Dr
  East Grinstead RH19.....2 A1
  Hove BN3.....141 A1
Elm Gn 4 BN27.....129 B1
Elm Gr
  Brighton BN2.....164 C7
  Eastbourne BN22.....173 F1
  Lewes BN7.....190 A1
Elm Green Prim Sch
  BN2.....164 C7
Elmhurst Ave TN2.....9 D8
Elmore Cl BN2.....189 C3
Elmore Rd BN2.....189 C3
Elm Rd BN41.....162 B8
Elms Ave BN21.....185 B2
Elmsdown Pl BN27.....152 C7
Elms La TN35.....116 F1
Elms Lea Ave BN1.....142 E3
Elmsmead TN31.....70 B4
Elms Rd BN2.....185 B2
Elmstead RH19.....10 E8
Elmstead Rd TN40.....157 E5
Elms The BN8.....124 C5
Elm Way TN21.....82 B6
Elmwood 12 BN21.....184 F4
Elmwood Cl BN23.....174 C4
Elmwood Gdns BN23.....174 C4
Elphick Pl TN6.....25 F3
Elphick Rd
  Broyle Side BN8.....124 F7
  Newhaven BN9.....179 C8
Elphick's Pl TN1.....17 B8
Elphinstone Ave TN34.....136 F2
Elphinstone Com Sch
  TN34.....160 A6
Elphinstone Gdns TN34.....136 F3
Elphinstone Rd TN34.....136 F2
Elrington Rd BN3.....142 C1
Elsted Cl BN22.....174 A1
Elsted Cres BN1.....143 C6
Elsted Rd TN39.....156 C2
Elven Cl BN20.....183 C1
Elven La BN20.....183 C1
Elvin Cres BN2.....165 E4
Elwood Cl RH15.....72 F1
Elwyn Jones Ct BN1.....142 E4
Ely Cl TN5.....8 B4
Embassy Ct
  10 Brighton BN1.....163 D5
  4 Haywards Heath RH16.....50 E6
Emerald Quay BN43.....161 A6
Emerson Coll RH18.....12 B3
Emmanuel Rd TN34.....160 A4
Encore Ho TN21.....81 F8
Endcliffe Ct BN20.....188 E8
Endwell Rd TN40.....157 C3
Engalee RH19.....1 C2
English Bsns Pk BN3.....162 E8
English Cl BN3.....162 E8
English's Pas BN7.....190 B2
Enholms La RH17.....34 A4
Ensenada Reef BN23.....175 B1
Enterprise Ctr The BN21.....184 F3
Enterprise Pl BN21.....143 C7
Enterprise Point BN2.....164 C8
Enys Rd BN21.....184 F4
Epsom Cl TN38.....159 A8
Epsom Ct 6 TN40.....157 E4
Erica Ct BN2.....174 B2
Ericsson Way RH15.....72 C2
Eridge Ct TN39.....157 A4
Eridge Ct TN2.....7 F1
Eridge Dr TN6.....26 A3
Eridge Gdns TN6.....26 A3
Eridge Gn BN7.....123 B2
ERIDGE GREEN.....16 B3
Eridge La TN3, TN6.....27 B2
Eridge Rd
  Crowborough TN6.....26 C1
  Eastbourne BN21.....184 D7
  Groombridge TN3.....15 D5
  Hove BN3.....142 A2
  Royal Tunbridge Wells TN2,
  TN4.....7 E1
Eridge Sta TN3.....15 E2
Erin Way RH15.....72 E3
Erroll Mans 7 BN3.....162 D7
Erroll Rd BN3.....162 C6
Ersham Rd BN27.....152 B5
Ersham Way BN27.....152 B5
Erskine Park Rd TN4.....7 C4
Esher Cl BN25.....180 F4
Eshton Rd BN22.....185 C5
Eskbank Ave BN1.....143 A7
Eskdale Cl BN23.....174 C4
Esplanade BN25.....180 E2
Esplanade Mews 19
  BN25.....180 E2
Esplanade The BN10.....177 F3
Essenden Rd TN38.....159 A7
Essex Cl TN2.....16 F8
Essex Ct BN20.....184 B6
Essex Pl
  3 Brighton BN2.....164 C4
  Newhaven BN9.....179 C7
Essex St BN2.....164 C4
Estate Rd BN1.....144 B7
Estates Rd BN1.....144 B7
Estcots Dr RH19.....2 A1
Estcots Prim Sch RH19.....2 A1
ETCHINGHAM.....44 B1

Etchingham CE Prim Sch
  TN19.....44 D2
Etchingham Rd BN23.....174 E1
Etchingham Sta TN19.....44 C1
ETCHINGWOOD.....56 D1
Ethelred Cl BN23.....185 E8
Ethel St BN3.....163 B7
Etherington Hill TN3.....7 C8
Etherton Way BN25.....181 A4
Ethnam La TN18.....47 A4
Eton Cl BN25.....181 A4
Eton Mews 3 BN21.....185 A3
Eugene Way BN23.....175 B1
Euro Bsns Pk BN9.....168 D1
Eurythmy Sch RH19.....10 E6
Evelyn Ave BN9.....179 C7
Evelyn Clark Ho RH18.....11 F2
Evelyn Cl BN41.....162 A8
Evelyn Glennie Ct 7
  BN2.....164 C5
Evelyn Rd BN7.....123 B2
Evelyn Terr BN2.....164 C5
Everest Ho 2 BN2.....162 F7
Eversfield Ct TN37.....159 D7
Eversfield Hospl TN38.....159 A6
Eversfield Mews N 5
  TN37.....159 C7
Eversfield Mews S 16
  TN37.....159 C7
Eversfield Pl TN37.....159 D7
Eversfield Rd BN21.....184 F4
Evershed Way BN43.....161 B7
Eversley Cl TN37.....136 C2
Eversley Cres TN37.....136 C2
Eversley Rd BN21.....184 F4
Eversley Rd
  Bexhill TN40.....157 C3
  St Leonards TN37.....136 C2
Everton Cotts TN19.....62 B6
Evesham TN38.....136 A3
Ewart St BN2.....189 C3
Ewehurst La TN3.....6 F6
Ewell Ct 5 TN40.....157 E4
Ewhurst Cl TN34.....136 F4
EWHURST GREEN.....66 B5
Ewhurst La TN31.....66 F4
Ewhurst Rd BN2.....143 C1
EXCEAT.....181 F4
Exceat Cl
  Brighton BN2.....164 E6
  Eastbourne BN23.....174 B4
Excelsior The BN1.....142 D4
Exchange Mews 4 TN4.....8 A5
Exeter Cl BN22.....173 B2
Exeter St BN1.....163 E8
Exmouth Pl TN34.....160 A4

F

Factory La BN27.....152 A6
Fairbanks RH16.....50 E4
Fairbridge Way RH15.....72 F5
Faircrouch La TN5.....29 B5
Fairdene BN42.....140 F1
Fairfax Ave TN37.....135 F7
Fairfield
  Herstmonceux BN27.....130 E6
  Peacehaven BN10.....178 B7
Fairfield Ave TN2.....8 C5
Fairfield Chase TN39.....156 F4
Fairfield Cl
  Burgess Hill RH15.....72 F4
  Shoreham-by-S BN43.....140 C1
Fairfield Cotts BN26.....149 D2
Fairfield Cres BN6.....97 A6
Fairfield Gdns
  Burgess Hill RH15.....72 F4
  Portslade-by-S BN41.....141 B1
Fairfield Lodge BN20.....188 E8
Fairfield Rd
  Burgess Hill RH15.....72 F4
  Eastbourne BN20.....184 E1
  East Grinstead RH19.....10 F8
  St Leonards TN37.....136 C6
Fairfield Way RH16.....50 D8
Fairford Cl RH16.....50 E5
Fairglen Cotts TN5.....29 B3
Fairglen Rd TN5.....29 B4
Fairhaven BN7.....99 E1
Fairholme BN7.....190 A1
Fairholme Ct TN6.....25 F1
Fairholme Rd BN9.....168 F1
Fairhurst BN10.....177 F3
Fairisle Cl BN27.....129 A2
Fair Isle Cl BN23.....185 E8
Fair La TN32.....64 B4
Fairlawn 1 RH16.....50 E4
Fairlawn Cres RH19.....1 B2
Fairlawn Dr RH19.....1 B2
Fairlawns
  9 Hove BN3.....163 A6
  Shoreham-by-S BN43.....161 A6
Fairlawns Dr BN27.....130 E6
Fairlea Cl RH15.....72 F4
Fairlie Gdns BN1.....142 E3
FAIRLIGHT.....138 C4
Fairlight TN22.....55 E1
Fairlight Ave
  Hastings TN35.....160 D7
  Telscombe Cliffs BN10.....177 F3
Fairlight Cl
  Bexhill TN40.....158 A5
  Polegate BN26.....173 A6
FAIRLIGHT COVE.....138 F5
Fairlight Field BN8.....124 D5
Fairlight Gdns TN35.....138 F4

Fairlight Pl 8 BN2.....164 C8
Fairlight Prim Sch BN2.....164 C8
Fairlight Rd
  Eastbourne BN22.....185 C5
  Fairlight TN35.....138 A4
  Hastings TN35.....160 E8
Fairmile Rd TN2.....8 E5
Fairmount Rd TN40.....136 A1
Fairmount Rd TN40.....157 C5
Fairoak BN26.....173 C6
Fair Oak Cl TN21.....82 A7
Fairplace RH17.....74 C4
Fairview Cotts TN6.....25 E4
Fair View Cotts TN5.....30 A6
Fairview Ct 13 RH19.....10 F8
Fairview La TN6.....25 E4
Fairview Rise BN1.....142 D5
FAIRWARP.....36 B2
Fairway Bsns Ctr BN2.....143 E4
Fairway Cl BN20.....184 C2
Fairway Cres BN41.....141 C2
Fairways BN1.....163 E8
Fairways Cl BN25.....181 C2
Fairways Rd BN25.....181 B2
Fairways The TN4.....8 A7
Fairway The
  Bexhill TN39.....156 F6
  Newhaven BN9.....179 A4
  St Leonards TN38.....158 F8
Fairway Trad Est BN2.....143 E4
Falaise Fitness Ctr TN34.....159 D7
Falaise Rd
  Hastings TN34.....159 D7
  Newhaven BN9.....168 F1
Falconbury Dr TN39.....156 D3
Falcon Cl BN43.....161 C6
Falconer Dr TN33.....112 F4
Falcon Way BN27.....129 B3
Fallowfield Cl BN3.....141 F2
Fallowfield Cres BN3.....141 F2
Falmer Ave BN2.....166 B2
Falmer Gdns BN2.....165 D8
Falmer High Sch BN1.....144 A5
Falmer Hill BN1.....144 B6
Falmer House Rd BN1.....144 B6
Falmer Rd BN2.....165 C5
Falmer Sta BN1.....144 B6
Falmouth Cl BN23.....185 F8
Famet Ct RH19.....1 C3
Faraday Ave RH19.....10 F6
Faraday Cl BN22.....173 F1
Faraday Lodge TN2.....8 E5
Farlaine Rd BN21.....184 C6
Farley Bank TN35.....160 B6
Farleys Way TN31.....69 B2
Farley Way TN35.....138 E5
Farlington Ave RH16.....50 F5
Farlington Cl RH16.....50 F5
Farman St 15 BN3.....163 D5
Farm Cl
  East Grinstead RH19.....11 B8
  Hassocks BN6.....97 A4
  Portslade-by-S BN41.....141 A2
  Seaford BN25.....181 B4
Farmcombe Cl TN2.....8 B2
Farmcombe La TN2.....8 B2
Farmcombe Rd TN2.....8 C2
Farm Cotts RH16.....50 C3
Farm Gdns TN31.....69 C2
Farm Hill BN2.....165 C8
Farm La
  Camber TN31.....94 D3
  Ditchling BN6.....98 E3
Farmlands Ave BN26.....172 F4
Farmlands Cl
  Polegate BN26.....173 A4
  St Leonards TN37.....136 C5
Farmlands Ct BN26.....173 A4
Farmlands Way BN26.....172 F5
Farmland Way BN27.....129 C1
Farm Mews BN3.....163 D6
Farm Rd BN3.....163 D6
Farm Way
  Burgess Hill RH15.....73 D1
  Southwick BN42.....162 A7
Farmway BN3.....141 D2
**Farm World, Great Knelle
  Farm (Childrens Farm)**★
  TN31.....68 A8
Farncombe Cl RH17.....74 D4
Farncombe Rd BN7.....190 D2
Farne Cl BN27.....129 A2
Farnham Ave BN6.....98 A5
Farnham Cl TN3.....7 A3
Farnham Ct TN3.....7 A3
Farnham La TN3.....7 A4
Farnham Pl TN3.....7 A3
Farningham Rd TN6.....38 C8
Farnlea RH15.....73 D5
Farnol Ho 6 BN21.....184 D4
Farrance Cl TN1.....8 B4
Farriers Pl BN8.....124 D5
Farriers Way TN22.....78 C6
Farthing Hill TN5.....31 E1
Farthing La BN27, TN33.....109 E4
Farthings The TN6.....26 A3
Fastnet Cl BN23.....185 E8
Faulkners Way RH15.....73 A5
Faversham Rd BN23.....174 D2
Faygate Cl TN39.....157 B8
Faygate Ct BN2.....164 E6
Faygate Rd BN22.....173 E2
Fayre Mdw TN32.....64 C4
Fazan Ct TN5.....29 F4
Fearon Rd TN34.....136 F2

Felbridge Cl RH19.....1 C3
Felbridge Rd RH19.....1 A4
Felbridge Ctr The RH19.....1 A3
Felcourt Cotts RH19.....1 C8
Felcourt La RH19.....1 C8
Felcourt Rd RH19, RH7.....1 C7
Feld The RH19.....1 A4
Fellows Rd TN34.....160 B7
Felride RH16.....50 E3
Felwater Ct RH19.....1 A3
Fenchurch Wlk BN1.....189 B4
Fen Ct TN38.....135 E1
Fennell's Cl BN21.....184 E5
Fennel Wlk BN43.....140 B1
Ferbies TN3.....7 A7
Ferbies Ct TN3.....7 A7
Ferdinand Terr TN3.....15 C7
Ferguson Rd TN29.....96 D2
Fermor Rd TN6.....38 A7
Fermor Row 2 TN6.....37 F8
Fermor Way TN6.....38 A8
Fernbank Sh Ctr TN6.....25 F3
Fern Cl BN23.....174 C3
FERNDALE.....8 C5
Ferndale TN2.....8 D5
Ferndale Cl TN2.....8 C4
Ferndale Point TN2.....8 C4
Ferndale Rd
  Burgess Hill RH15.....73 C2
  Hove BN3.....163 D7
Fern Gn 1 BN27.....129 B1
Fernhurst Cl BN1.....143 B6
Fernhurst Cres BN1.....143 B5
Fernlea TN35.....114 E4
Fern Rd TN38.....158 F8
Fernside RH19.....1 D2
Fernside Ave TN38.....135 F1
Ferns The TN1.....8 C4
Fernwood Rise BN1.....142 D5
Ferrers Rd BN7.....123 B1
Ferring Cl TN31.....93 A6
Ferring Ct BN1.....143 F5
Ferringham TN4.....7 A4
Ferry Hill TN36.....117 E8
Ferry Rd TN31.....93 B5
Festival Gdns TN39.....157 C7
Feversham Cl BN43.....161 B6
Field Cl
  Burgess Hill RH15.....72 E4
  Seaford BN25.....181 B2
Field End TN22.....55 A4
Fielden La TN6.....25 D1
Fielden Rd TN6.....25 D2
Fieldfare BN27.....152 D7
Fields End Cl RH16.....50 F4
Field View TN32.....64 B3
Fieldway
  Broad Oak TN31.....90 C5
  Ditchling BN6.....98 D3
  Haywards Heath RH16.....50 F8
Field Way TN38.....158 E8
Fiennes Cl BN21.....184 C4
Fiennes Rd BN27.....130 E6
Figg La TN6.....37 D3
FILCHING.....172 D3
Filching Cl BN26.....172 E3
Filching Ct BN20.....184 B5
Filching Manor Motor Mus★
  BN26.....172 D2
Filching Rd BN20.....184 B5
Filder Cl BN22.....185 A6
Filsham Dr TN40.....158 A6
Filsham Hurst TN39.....159 A7
Filsham Rd TN38.....159 A8
**Filsham Reed Beds Nature
  Reserve**★ TN38.....158 D8
Filsham Valley TN38.....158 F7
Filsham Valley Sch TN38.....158 F7
Finch Cl BN10.....178 A7
Finches Gdns RH16.....51 A8
Finches La RH16.....51 A8
Finches Park Rd RH16.....51 A8
Finches The
  Bexhill TN40.....157 F4
  Shoreham-by-S BN43.....161 A8
  2 St Leonards TN38.....136 A5
Findon Ave BN2.....166 E2
Findon Cl
  Bexhill TN39.....156 F3
  Hove BN3.....141 F3
  Seaford BN25.....181 C3
Findon Rd BN2.....164 F5
Finistere Ave BN23.....185 E8
Finley Ct TN38.....158 F6
Finmere Cl BN22.....185 C6
Finmere Ct BN22.....185 C6
Finmere Rd BN22.....185 C6
Finsbury Lodge 1 BN2.....164 C6
Finsbury Rd BN2.....164 C6
Firbank Way RH19.....1 D1
Fir Cl BN2.....142 E3
Fircroft Cl BN1.....142 E3
Firehills Cotts TN35.....138 C3
Fir Green Rd TN21.....81 B6
Firlands RH16.....50 F4
Firle Bostal BN8.....148 A2
Firle CE Prim Sch BN8.....148 B4
Firle Cl
  Hastings TN35.....160 E8
  Seaford BN25.....180 E5
Firle Cres BN7.....122 F2
Firle Dr BN25.....180 E5
Firle Gn TN22.....55 E1
Firle Grange BN25.....180 E5
Firle Pl★ BN8.....148 C3
Firle Rd
  Bexhill TN39.....156 D4
  Brighton BN2.....164 D6

Firle Rd *continued*
Eastbourne BN22 . . . . **185** A4
Peacehaven BN10 . . . . . . **178** C8
Ripe BN8 . . . . **149** B7
Seaford BN25 . . . . **180** E6
Firle Terr BN9 . . . . **168** D2
Firs Ct TN4 . . . .**7** F6
Firs Sch The TN38 . . . . **136** B1
First Ave
Bexhill TN40 . . . . **157** F5
Camber TN31 . . . . **94** F2
Hove BN3 . . . . **163** C6
Newhaven BN9 . . . . **179** C7
Firs The TN35 . . . . **160** C5
Firstone Ho TN20 . . . . . . **39** F2
First St TN3 . . . .**6** F3
Firtoft Cl RH15 . . . . **73** B3
Fir Toll Cl TN20 . . . . **39** F2
Fir Toll Rd TN20 . . . . **39** E2
Fir Tree Cl
Bexhill TN39 . . . . **156** C3
Hailsham BN27 . . . . **129** C2
Firtree Rd TN34 . . . . **160** A6
Fir Tree Rd TN4 . . . .**7** F3
Fir Tree Way BN6 . . . . . . **98** A4
Firwood Cl
Eastbourne BN22 . . . . . . **173** E1
Heathfield BN27 . . . . **82** A8
Firwood Rise TN21 . . . . . **82** A8
Fisher Cl BN23 . . . . **185** F7
Fishermen's Mus★ TN34. **160** B3
FISHERSGATE **162** A7
Fishersgate Cl BN41. . . . **162** A7
Fisher's Gate Cotts TN7 . . **14** A1
Fishersgate Fst Sch
BN41 . . . . **162** A7
Fishersgate Sta BN41 . . **162** B7
Fishersgate Terr BN41 . **162** A7
Fisher St BN7 . . . . **190** B2
Fishmarket Rd TN31 . . . . . **93** C6
Fishponds La TN35 . . . . . **114** E3
Fitch Dr BN2 . . . . **143** F1
Fitzalan Ct BN10 . . . . . . **178** B7
Fitzalan Ho 10 BN1 . . . . **184** F4
Fitzgerald Ave BN25. . . . **180** E3
Fitzgerald Cl BN20 . . . . . **184** F1
Fitzgerald Ho 8 BN25. . . **180** E3
Fitzgerald Pk BN25 . . . . **180** E3
Fitzgerald Rd TN39 . . . . . **190** B4
Fitzherbert Ct BN2 . . . . . **164** D8
Fitzherbert Dr BN2 . . . . . **164** D8
Fitzjohn Ct BN6 . . . . **97** F3
Fitzjohns Rd BN7 . . . . . . **123** B1
Fitzmaurice Ave BN22 . . **185** B5
Fitzroy Cl BN7 . . . . **123** B2
Five Acre Wlk TN34 . . . . **136** E1
FIVE ASH DOWN **55** D5
FIVE ASHES **58** B7
Five Ashes CE Prim Sch
TN20 . . . . **58** B6
Five Ashes Rd TN20 . . . . . **39** A5
Five Chimneys La TN22 . . **57** A6
Five Hos The TN36 . . . . . **117** E8
Five Villages Ho TN36 . . **116** F6
Five Ways TN1 . . . .**8** A4
FLACKLEY ASH **68** F3
Flag Ct BN3 . . . . **163** B5
Flamingo Family Fun Pk
The★ TN34 . . . . **160** A3
Flamsteed Rd BN27 . . . . **131** A1
Fleet St BN1 . . . . **189** B4
Fleetway Ct TN31 . . . . **94** F2
Fleet Wood Cl TN37 . . . . **136** B6
Fleming Cl BN23 . . . . **174** F2
Fleming Wlk TN37 . . . . . . **10** F6
Fletcher Ave TN37 . . . . . **135** F7
Fletcher Cl BN23 . . . . **152** C7
Fletcher Way 4 RH16 . . . **50** C2
FLETCHING **53** F4
Fletching CE Prim Sch
TN22 . . . . **53** F3
Fletching Cl RH16 . . . . . **164** F6
FLETCHING COMMON . . . **53** C1
Fletching Rd BN22 . . . . . **174** A2
Fletching St TN20 . . . . . . **40** B3
FLIMWELL **32** C3
Flimwell Cl
Brighton BN2 . . . . **164** E5
Eastbourne BN23 . . . . . . **174** A4
Flimwell TN5 . . . . **32** D4
St Leonards TN38 . . . . . . **135** D3
Flint Cl
Portslade-by-S BN41 . . . . **141** B2
Seaford BN25 . . . . **180** E6
Flint Halls 5 BN21 . . . . **184** D3
Flints The BN7 . . . . **145** E5
Flitterbrook La TN21 . . . . . **83** C4
Florance La TN3 . . . . **15** B6
Florence Ave BN3 . . . . . . **162** D8
Florence Cl BN1 . . . . **142** F2
Florence Pl BN1 . . . . **143** B1
Florence Rd BN1 . . . . **164** A8
Florida Ct TN38 . . . . **158** F6
FLOWERS GREEN **130** F3
Floyd Cl TN4 . . . .**8** A7
Folders Cl RH15 . . . . **73** D1
Folders Gdns RH15 . . . . . **73** C1
Folders Grange RH15 . . . . **73** C1
Folders La RH15 . . . . **73** D1
Folders Lane E
Ditchling BN6 . . . . **98** F8
Plumpton Green BN7 . . . . . **99** A8
Fold Sch The BN3 . . . . . **162** D7
Foley Cl BN23 . . . . **185** E7
Folkestone Cl BN25 . . . . **181** C4
Folkestone Rd TN31 . . . . . **93** F8
FOLKINGTON **172** B4
Folkington Gdns TN37 . . **136** C5

Folkington Rd BN26 . . . . **172** D5
Follett Holt Ho BN8 . . . . **100** E7
Folly Field BN9 . . . . **179** C7
Fonthill Rd BN3 . . . . **163** B8
Fonthill Lodge Sch RH19 . **10** C6
Fontridge La TN19 . . . . . . **62** E3
Fontwell Ave TN39 . . . . . **156** C5
Foords La BN24 . . . . **174** C7
Foots La TN19 . . . . **61** B3
Fordbrook Hill TN6 . . . . . . **37** F2
FORDCOMBE **6** B5
Fordcombe CE Prim Sch
TN3 . . . .**6** B5
Fordcombe Rd TN3 . . . .**6** C4
Ford Rd TN38 . . . . **135** F2
FORD'S GREEN **35** C3
Foredown Cl
Eastbourne BN20 . . . . . . **184** C2
Portslade-by-S BN41 . . . . **141** B2
Foredown Dr BN41 . . . . . . **141** C1
Foredown Rd
Portslade-by-S BN41 . . . . **141** B5
Portslade-by-S BN41 . . . . **141** B4
Foredown Tower
Countryside Ctr★
BN41 . . . . **141** B3
Forest Dene
Crowborough TN6 . . . . **26** D1
Royal Tunbridge Wells TN2 . .**8** C1
Foresters Ho TN33 . . . . . **173** A6
Forest Fold Cotts TN6 . . . **25** D5
Forest La TN21 . . . . **83** D6
Forest Lodge
Crowborough TN6 . . . . **37** D8
2 East Grinstead RH19 . . **10** F8
Forest Pk
Crowborough TN6 . . . . **25** D2
Maresfield TN22 . . . . **54** C5
Forest Pl TN21 . . . . **80** F6
Forest Rd
Brighton BN1 . . . . **143** E6
Forest Row RH18 . . . . **12** B2
Royal Tunbridge Wells TN2 . .**8** C1
Forest Ridge RH19 . . . . . **21** A6
Forest Rise TN6 . . . . **26** D1
Forest Row Bsns Pk RH18 **11** F3
Forest Row CE Prim Sch
RH18 . . . . **11** F2
Forest View
Hailsham BN27 . . . . **152** A8
Nutley TN22 . . . . **35** C3
Forest View Rd RH19 . . . . **10** E6
Forest Way
Golden Cross BN27 . . . . . **127** C3
Hastings TN34 . . . . **136** E1
Pembury TN2 . . . . **9** D8
Royal Tunbridge Wells TN2 . .**8** D1
Forewood La TN33 . . . . . **135** A7
Forewood Rise TN33 . . . **134** F6
Forge Cl
Portslade-by-S BN41 . . . . **141** B2
Staplecross TN32 . . . . **65** E1
Uckfield TN22 . . . . **78** C6
Forge Field TN5 . . . . **42** F6
Forgefield Cotts TN18 . . . **47** A4
Forge Ho The BN2 . . . . . **165** F1
Forge La TN32 . . . . **65** E1
Forge Lane Cotts TN32 . . . **55** A8
Forge Mews 10 TN31 . . . . **93** B5
Forge Rd TN3 . . . . **15** C2
Forge Rise TN22 . . . . **78** C5
Forge The
Hove BN3 . . . . **162** F8
Ringmer BN8 . . . . **124** C5
Forge Way
Burgess Hill RH15 . . . . . . **73** A4
St Leonards TN37 . . . . . . **136** C5
Forstall TN3 . . . .**7** A4
Forstal The
Cobbarn TN3 . . . . **15** F3
Pembury TN2 . . . .**9** E8
Fort Gate BN9 . . . . **179** E5
Forthaven BN43 . . . . **161** C6
Fort La BN22 . . . . **185** D6
Fort Rd
Eastbourne BN22 . . . . . . **185** D6
Newhaven BN9 . . . . **179** D6
Fort Rise BN9 . . . . **179** D5
Forward Cl BN9 . . . . **168** E2
Fosse The BN7 . . . . **190** B4
Foster Cl BN25 . . . . **180** E4
Foster Ct BN3 . . . . **163** E6
Foundry Ct RH15 . . . . **73** B3
Foundry La BN7 . . . . **190** C2
Foundry St BN1 . . . . **189** B4
Fountains Cl
Brighton BN1 . . . . **143** B2
Eastbourne BN22 . . . . . . **173** E3
Founthill Ave BN2 . . . . . . **166** B1
Founthill Rd BN2 . . . . **166** B1
FOUR OAKS **68** C5
Fourteen Acre La TN35 . . **115** D4
Fourth Ave BN3 . . . . **163** B6
FOUR THROWS **46** D8
Fowey Cl BN43 . . . . **161** B6
Fowlers Cl TN39 . . . . **156** E5
Fowly La TN22 . . . . **56** C7
Fox Cl RH15 . . . . **72** F1
Foxcote TN37 . . . . **136** D5
Foxdown Rd BN2 . . . . **165** F7
Foxglove Cl
Broyle Side BN8 . . . . **125** A4
Burgess Hill RH15 . . . . . . **72** D4
Foxglove Rd BN23 . . . . . . **174** B3
Foxhill
Bexhill TN39 . . . . **156** E5
Peacehaven BN10 . . . . . . **167** B1
FOX HILL **50** E1

Fox Hill RH16 . . . . **50** E1
Fox Hill Cl RH16 . . . . **50** F1
Foxhill Ct 3 RH16 . . . . . . **50** F1
Fox Hill Village RH16 . . . . **50** F1
FOXHOLE **182** A1
Foxhole La
Four Throws TN18 . . . . . . **46** D8
Wadhurst TN5 . . . . **30** B4
Foxhunters Rd BN41 . . . . **140** F3
Fox in the Wood TN5 . . . . **29** C6
Foxwarren RH16 . . . . **50** C5
Fox Way BN41 . . . . **141** B2
Framele Mount TN22 . . . . **79** B6
FRAMFIELD **79** B6
Framfield 11 BN2 . . . . . . **164** F5
Framfield CE Prim Sch
TN22 . . . . **79** B6
Framfield Cl BN1 . . . . **143** E6
Framfield Rd
Buxted TN22 . . . . **56** B3
Uckfield TN22 . . . . **78** D6
Framfield Way BN21 . . . . **184** D6
Framnaes 2 BN3 . . . . . . **162** D7
Framroze Ct BN1 . . . . **143** B2
Francis Bird Pl TN37 . . . . **136** C6
Francis Rd RH16 . . . . **51** B8
Francis St BN1 . . . . **189** B4
Frankfield Rise TN2 . . . . . . **8** A1
Franklands Cl RH15 . . . . . **73** B1
Franklands Gdns RH15 . . **98** A8
FRANKLANDS VILLAGE . . **51** A4
Franklands Way RH15 . . . **98** A8
Franklin Rd
Brighton BN2 . . . . **164** C7
Portslade-by-S BN41 . . . . **141** D2
Shoreham-by-S BN43 . . . . **140** D1
Franklin St BN2 . . . . **164** C8
Franklynn Ct RH16 . . . . . . **50** F3
Franklynn Rd RH16 . . . . . . **50** F3
Frankton Ave RH16 . . . . . . **51** A3
FRANT **17** C3
Frant Ave TN39 . . . . **156** C5
Frant CE Prim Sch TN3 . . **17** B4
Frant Cl TN39 . . . . **156** C5
Frant Green Rd TN3 . . . . . **17** B3
Frant Rd
Hove BN3 . . . . **142** A2
Royal Tunbridge Wells TN2,
TN3 . . . . **17** A7
Frant Sta TN3 . . . . **17** F5
Frary Wlk TN31 . . . . **82** A3
Fraser Ave BN23 . . . . **185** E7
Fraser Ct 2 BN43 . . . . . . **161** C8
Freckley Hollow TN33 . . . **111** C1
Freda Gardham Com Sch The
TN31 . . . . **93** D6
Fred Emery Ct 16 BN1 . . **163** E5
Frederic Ho BN1 . . . . **166** B1
Frederick Cotts RH16 . . . . **51** B7
Frederick Gdns BN1 . . . . **189** B3
Frederick Pl BN1 . . . . **189** B3
Frederick Rd TN35 . . . . . . **160** C7
Frederick St BN1 . . . . **189** B3
Frederick Thatcher Pl
TN33 . . . . **112** A5
Freedom Leisure Ctr
TN34 . . . . **159** D8
Free Heath Rd TN3, TN5 . . **19** C3
Freehold Terr 1 BN2 . . . . **164** C8
Freeland Cl BN25 . . . . **180** A6
Freeland Ho 6 BN20 . . . . **184** F1
Freeman Ave BN22 . . . . . **173** E1
Freemans Rd BN41 . . . . . **162** A8
Freezeland La TN39 . . . . . **134** A2
Fremlin Cl TN4 . . . .**7** B4
French Apartments The
BN2 . . . . **164** E3
Frenches Farm Dr TN21 . . **82** A5
Frenchgate Cl BN22 . . . . **173** F2
Frenchgate Rd BN22 . . . . **173** F2
French Gdns RH16 . . . . . . **51** A6
French's Ct 9 BN25 . . . . **180** E2
Freshfield Bank RH18 . . . **11** E2
Freshfield Cl BN27 . . . . . **152** B6
Freshfield Crossway
RH17 . . . . **52** C8
Freshfield Ind Est BN2 . . **164** C5
Freshfield La RH17 . . . . . . **33** C2
Freshfield Pl BN2 . . . . **164** C5
Freshfield Rd BN2 . . . . . . **164** D6
Freshfield St BN2 . . . . **164** C6
Freshfield Way BN2 . . . . . **164** C6
Freshford Cl BN23 . . . . . . **174** D2
Freshwater Ave TN34 . . . **136** E2
Freshwater Sq BN22 . . . . **173** B3
Freshway TN2 . . . . **173** C3
Frewen Cl TN31 . . . . **67** B7
Frewen Coll TN31 . . . . **67** C5
Frewyn Ct TN38 . . . . **135** F4
Friar Cl BN1 . . . . **143** B3
Friar Cres BN1 . . . . **143** A3
Friar Rd BN1 . . . . **143** A3
Friars' Ave BN10 . . . . **178** E6
Friars Bank TN35 . . . . **138** B7
Friars Cl BN6 . . . . **97** E4
Friar's Cres TN35 . . . . **138** B7
FRIAR'S GATE **25** B7
Friars Hill TN35 . . . . **137** F7
FRIAR'S HILL **138** B7
Friar's Hill Terr TN35 . . . . **138** A7
Friars Mews BN7 . . . . **190** B1
Friars Oak Rd BN6 . . . . **97** E5
Friars Rd TN36 . . . . **117** F7
Friars Vale TN6 . . . . **25** C5

Friars Way TN2 . . . .**8** D6
Friar's Way TN34 . . . . **136** F4
Friars' Wlk BN7 . . . . **190** B2
Friar Wlk BN1 . . . . **142** F4
Friday St BN23 . . . . **174** C3
Fridays The BN20 . . . . **187** B2
FRIDAY STREET **174** A3
Friezland Rd TN4 . . . .**7** D1
Frimley Cl BN2 . . . . **165** F7
FRISTON **183** A4
Friston Ave BN22 . . . . **173** C1
Friston Cl
Brighton BN2 . . . . **143** F4
Friston BN20 . . . . **183** A1
Seaford BN25 . . . . **180** C4
Friston Downs BN20 . . . . **183** B2
Friston Hill BN20 . . . . **183** A1
Frith Pk RH19 . . . .**1** E3
Frith Rd BN3 . . . . **163** A8
Frobisher Cl BN23 . . . . . . **185** E1
Frobisher Ho RH16 . . . . . **167** D1
Frog Hole La TN20, TN21 . . **58** C5
Frog La TN1 . . . .**8** A2
Front Cotts TN5 . . . . **31** E1
Fruitfields TN5 . . . . **32** C3
Fryatts Way TN39 . . . . **156** F6
Fry Cres RH15 . . . . **72** F5
Fryman's La TN31 . . . . **89** D2
Fulbourne Ho BN20 . . . . . **184** E1
Fulford St TN38 . . . . **159** A8
Fuller Cl TN5 . . . . **29** E5
Fuller Rd BN7 . . . . **123** A3
Fullers La TN31 . . . . **67** B6
Fuller's Pas BN7 . . . . **190** B2
Fullwood Ave BN9 . . . . . . **179** B7
Fulmar Cl BN3 . . . . **142** D1
Fulmar Dr RH19 . . . .**2** B3
Fulmer Pl 5 TN40 . . . . . . **157** C4
Furlongs The BN26 . . . . . **170** F3
Furnace Ave TN3 . . . . **20** A3
Furnace La
Beckley Furnace TN31 . . . . **90** D7
Hook Green TN3 . . . . **19** E4
Horam TN21 . . . . **106** D8
Warbleton TN21 . . . . **82** E2
Furnace Way TN22 . . . . . . **78** E7
Furness Rd BN20, BN21 . . **184** F2
Furnival Ct TN2 . . . . **16** F8
Furze Croft
Hove BN3 . . . . **163** D6
St Leonards TN38 . . . . . . **159** A8
Furzedene BN3 . . . . **163** D6
Furzefield Ave TN3 . . . .**7** A8
Furzefield Chase RH19 . . . .**1** E6
Furzefield Rd RH19 . . . .**1** D4
Furze Hill BN3 . . . . **163** D6
Furze Hill Ct BN3 . . . . **163** D6
Furze Hill Ho BN3 . . . . **163** D6
Furze La RH19 . . . .**1** B4
Fyning Pl TN39 . . . . **156** C5
Fyrsway TN35 . . . . **138** E4
Fysie La TN19 . . . . **44** D3

G

Gables Ct 2 BN21 . . . . . **185** A3
Gableson Ave BN1 . . . . . **142** B4
Gables The TN34 . . . . **136** E3
Gage Ridge RH18 . . . . **11** E2
Gages The BN27 . . . . **152** D7
Gainsborough Cres
BN23 . . . . **174** D1
Gainsborough Ho 16
BN3 . . . . **163** C7
Gainsborough La BN26 . . **172** E6
Gainsborough Rd TN40 . . **157** E6
Galleries The 16 BN3 . . . **163** D7
Galley Hill View TN40 . . . **157** E4
Galliers Cl BN1 . . . . **143** B6
Gallipot Hill TN7 . . . . **13** B2
Gallops The BN7 . . . . **123** A1
Gallows Cl BN24 . . . . **174** E1
Gallows La BN24 . . . . **174** E6
GALLYPOT STREET **13** B3
Galveston Cl BN23 . . . . . **185** F7
Gammons Way TN33 . . . . . **88** E1
Gander Cl RH15 . . . . **73** A5
Gander Gn TN6 . . . . **50** F7
Gander Hill RH16 . . . . **50** F7
Gannet Ho
5 Eastbourne BN21 . . . . **185** A2
Hove BN3 . . . . **142** B1
Ganton Pl TN38 . . . . **158** F8
Garden Cl
4 Bexhill TN40 . . . . **157** D4
East Grinstead RH19 . . . . . **10** F7
Portslade-by-S BN41 . . . . **162** C8
Shoreham-by-S BN43 . . . . **140** B1
Garden Cotts
Goatham Green TN31 . . . . . **89** D8
14 Hastings TN34 . . . . . **160** A6
Garden Ct
Bexhill TN40 . . . . **157** D5
19 Eastbourne BN21 . . . . **185** A2
Shoreham-by-S BN43 . . . . **140** B1
Gardener St BN41 . . . . . . **162** B8
Garden Ho The BN1 . . . . . **189** A3
Garden House La RH19 . . . **10** F7
Garden Mews BN20 . . . . . **188** D8
Garden Rd TN1 . . . .**8** B4
Garden St
Lewes BN7 . . . . **190** B1
Royal Tunbridge Wells TN1 . .**8** B4
Gardens The BN42 . . . . . . **161** B4
Garden Wood Rd RH19 . . . **10** C8
Gardner Ctr Rd BN23 . . . . **185** E7
Gardner Ctr Rd BN1 . . . . . **144** B6

Gardner Rd BN41 . . . . **162** A7
Gardner's Hill TN31 . . . . . . **70** B6
Gardner St
Brighton BN1 . . . . **189** B2
Herstmonceux BN27 . . . . **130** F6
Gardner Way BN3 . . . . **159** B6
Garfield Rd BN27 . . . . **152** C7
Garland Rd RH19 . . . .**1** D2
Garnet Dr BN20 . . . . **184** C7
Garnet Ho 13 BN2 . . . . . **164** C4
Garston Pk TN19 . . . . **62** B6
Garth Cl TN39 . . . . **157** A5
Gatehouse Cl TN39 . . . . . **156** C2
Gatehouse La
Framfield TN22 . . . . **79** C7
Goddards' Green BN6, RH15 **72** C4
Gatelands Dr TN39 . . . . . . **157** B6
Gatesmead RH15 . . . . **72** E3
Gattons Inf Sch The RH15 **72** E3
Gattons The RH15 . . . . **72** E3
Gatwick Farm Cotts RH19 . .**3** A4
Gaudick Cl BN20 . . . . **184** E1
Gaudick Pl BN20 . . . . **188** E8
Gaudick Rd BN20 . . . . **184** E1
Gavin Astor Cl TN40 . . . . **158** A6
Geary Pl TN35 . . . . **114** E3
Geering Pk BN27 . . . . **152** D7
Geering Rd BN24 . . . . **174** D5
Geers Wood TN21 . . . . **81** F6
Geerswood Cotts 2 TN21 **82** A6
Gemini Bsns Ctr BN3 . . . . **163** B8
Gemma 2 BN21 . . . . **152** E7
Geneva Rd BN9 . . . . **179** D6
Genistos The BN6 . . . . **97** E4
Gensing Rd TN38 . . . . **159** C7
George Cl TN32 . . . . **64** B3
George Hill TN32 . . . . **64** B3
George St
Brighton BN2 . . . . **189** B2
Hailsham BN27 . . . . **152** C7
Hastings TN34 . . . . **160** A3
Hove BN3 . . . . **163** B6
Portslade-by-S, Aldrington
BN41 . . . . **162** C7
Portslade-by-S, Fishersgate
BN41 . . . . **162** A7
Royal Tunbridge Wells TN2 . .**8** C3
Sparrow's Green TN5 . . . . **29** F5
Georgian Cl TN40 . . . . **157** E5
Georgian Wlk TN38 . . . . . **158** F8
Georgia Pl TN2 . . . .**8** C4
Gerald Cl RH15 . . . . **73** C3
Gerald Rd BN25 . . . . **180** F1
Gerard St BN1 . . . . **189** B5
German St TN36 . . . . **117** E7
Ghyll Ind Est TN21 . . . . . . **82** A5
Ghyll Rd
Crowborough TN6 . . . . **25** E4
Heathfield TN21 . . . . **82** A6
Ghyllside BN2 . . . . **143** E1
Ghyllside Ave TN34 . . . . . **136** D4
Ghyllside Dr TN34 . . . . . . **136** D4
Ghyll Side Rd TN31 . . . . . . **67** B7
Ghyllside Way TN34 . . . . . **136** D4
Gibb Cl TN40 . . . . **158** A5
Gibbetts TN3 . . . .**6** F3
Gibbon Rd BN9 . . . . **179** C6
Gibraltar Rise TN21 . . . . . . **82** A7
Gibson Ct BN7 . . . . **190** B3
Giffards Cl RH19 . . . .**1** F1
Gilbert Rd
Eastbourne BN22 . . . . . . **185** B4
St Leonards TN37, TN38 . . **159** B8
Gilberts Dr BN20 . . . . **187** B8
Gilbert Way BN27 . . . . **152** B5
Gilda Cres BN26 . . . . **173** A6
Gildredge Rd
Eastbourne BN21 . . . . . . **184** F2
Seaford BN25 . . . . **180** F3
Gilham La RH18 . . . . **11** E2
Gilham Wood Ave TN39 . . **156** D3
Gilham Wood Rd TN39 . . . **156** D3
Gilligans The RH15 . . . . . . **72** F5
Gill Ridge Gn TN6 . . . . **25** F4
Gillridge La TN6 . . . . **25** E5
Gillsman's Dr TN38 . . . . . **135** F1
Gillsman's Hill TN38 . . . . **136** A1
Gillsman's Pk TN38 . . . . . **135** F1
Gill The TN2 . . . .**9** E8
Gimble Way TN2 . . . .**9** D8
Gingerbread La TN18 . . . . **32** F2
GINGER'S GREEN **130** C6
Gipps Cross La TN3 . . . .**6** F3
Girton Ho BN3 . . . . **162** F6
Githa Rd TN35 . . . . **160** C6
Gladepoint RH16 . . . . **50** E5
Glades The
Bexhill TN40 . . . . **157** E6
East Grinstead RH19 . . . . . .**2** B1
Glade The
Hailsham BN27 . . . . **151** F6
Mayfield TN20 . . . . **40** A3
Uckfield TN22 . . . . **78** D7
Gladstone Bldgs BN8 . . . **101** E4
Gladstone Cl BN22 . . . . . . **173** F1
Gladstone Ct 14 BN2 . . . . **164** C8
Gladstone Pl BN2 . . . . **164** C8
Gladstone Rd
Burgess Hill RH15 . . . . . . **73** C4
Crowborough TN6 . . . . **25** F1
Portslade-by-S BN41 . . . . **162** B2
Rusthall TN4 . . . .**7** B4
Gladstone Terr
Brighton BN2 . . . . **189** C4
Hastings TN34 . . . . **160** A5

Gladys Ave BN10........178 D6
Gladys Rd BN3..........162 D8
Glanfield Ct TN1..........8 C5
Glassenbury Dr TN40....157 F5
Glass Pavilion BN1......189 B2
Glastonbury Rd BN3....162 D6
Gleave Cl RH19..........2 A2
Glebe Cl
   Bexhill TN39..........156 D3
   Eastbourne BN20......184 D3
   Lewes BN7............146 A8
   Southwick BN42.......161 F7
Glebe Com Mid Sch
   BN42..................161 D8
Glebe Cotts TN33.......134 A7
Glebe Dr BN25..........180 E3
Glebelands Cl BN43.....161 B8
Glebelands The TN6......25 F2
Glebe The
   Felbridge RH19.........1 A4
   Hastings TN34.........160 B5
   Hurstpierpoint BN6.....97 A6
   Lindfield RH16.........51 A8
   Pembury TN2............9 D8
   Pett TN35.............116 F1
   Southwick BN42.......161 E8
Glebe Villas BN3........162 D7
Glenburn Cl TN39.......157 C7
Glen Cl BN26............172 F4
Glencoe TN6..............25 F2
Glen Cotts BN26........172 F3
Glendale Ave BN21......184 C5
Glendale Ct TN2..........8 D6
Glendale Rd
   Burgess Hill RH15......73 B2
   Hove BN3.............163 D7
Glendor Rd BN3.........162 E6
Glendyne Cl RH19........11 A8
Glendyne Way RH19.....11 A8
Gleneagles Cl
   Bexhill TN40..........157 E5
   Seaford BN25..........180 A6
Gleneagles Ct 13 RH16...50 E4
Gleneagles Dr
   Hailsham BN27........152 A8
   St Leonards TN38......158 F7
Glenfalls Ave BN1.......143 A7
Glenfergus 3 RH16.......50 E6
Glenfalls Ave RH16......50 E6
Glengorse TN33.........112 F3
Glengorse Ct TN33......112 F3
Glenham Pl RH19.........21 A5
Glenleigh Ave TN39.....156 F6
GLENLEIGH PARK.........157 A7
Glenleigh Park Rd TN39..157 A6
Glenleigh Wlk TN32......64 A4
Glenmore Mews 4
   BN21..................185 A3
Glenmore Pk TN2........16 F8
Glenmore Rd TN6........25 C3
Glenmore Road E TN6....25 D3
Glen Rise BN1...........142 B5
Glen Rise Cl BN1........142 B5
Glenside 1 RH19..........1 E1
Glen The TN22...........55 D1
Glenthorne Ho 17 BN21..184 F4
Glenthorn Rd TN39......157 C4
Glenview Cl TN35........160 D5
Glen Vue RH19............1 E1
Glessing Rd BN24.......174 B6
Gleton Ave BN3.........141 D2
Glottenham Farm Cotts
   TN32..................63 F1
Gloucester Ave TN40....158 A5
Gloucester Cl
   Eastbourne BN23......173 C2
   East Grinstead RH19...11 A8
Gloucester Cotts 3
   TN34..................160 A4
Gloucester Ct BN23.....174 E1
Gloucester Mews 2
   BN1..................189 B3
Gloucester Pas 4 BN1...189 B3
Gloucester Pl BN1.......189 B3
Gloucester Rd
   Brighton BN1.........189 B3
   Burgess Hill RH15......72 F3
   Turner's Green TN5.....29 F6
Gloucester St BN1......189 B3
Gloucester Yd 3 BN1....189 B3
Glovers La TN39........157 C7
Glovers Yd BN1.........142 F1
GLYNDE.................147 E7
Glynde Ave
   Eastbourne BN22......173 E1
   Saltdean BN2.........166 D2
Glyndebourne Ave BN2..166 C2
Glyndebourne Gdns
   TN37..................136 C6
Glyndebourne Opera Ho★
   BN8..................124 E2
Glynde Cl BN9..........168 D2
Glynde Ct
   Bexhill TN39..........156 C3
   Polegate BN26........173 A6
Glynde Ho BN3..........163 D6
Glynde Pl★ BN8.........147 F7
Glynde Rd BN2..........164 D6
Glynde Sta BN8.........147 E5
Glyndley Manor Cottage Est
   BN24..................152 F2
Glyne Ascent TN40......157 F5
Glyne Barn Cl TN40.....158 A5
Glyne Dr TN40..........158 A5
GLYNE GAP.............158 B5

Glyne Gap Sch TN40.....158 A5
Glyne Hall TN40........157 D3
Glynleigh 18 BN2.......189 C3
Glynleigh Dr BN26......173 C6
Glynleigh Rd BN24......153 A1
Glynn Rd BN10..........167 C1
Glynn Rise BN10........167 B1
Glynn Road W BN10......167 C1
GOATHAM GREEN...........89 E5
Goatham La TN31.........89 E5
Gochers Ct BN2.........164 C7
Goddards Gn BN6.........72 C4
Godden Cl TN31..........67 B7
Godden Rd BN8...........76 C7
Goddens Gill TN31.......67 B7
Goddens The RH19.......10 E7
Godfrey Cl BN7.........190 A4
Godwin Rd
   Hastings TN35.........160 C5
   Hove BN3.............141 D1
Goffs The BN21.........184 E3
Golby Ct BN10..........178 A7
Goldbridge Rd BN8, TN22..76 E7
Goldcrest Dr TN22.......78 D5
GOLDEN CROSS BN27.....127 E5
GOLDEN CROSS
   Hailsham.............127 D6
   Herstmonceux.........130 E3
Golden Gate Way BN23..175 B1
Golden Hill TN3.........73 D3
Golden Jubilee Way BN23,
   BN24.................173 F4
Golden La 11 BN1.......163 D5
Golden Miller La BN26..172 F6
Goldhurst Gn TN36......116 E5
Golding Rd BN23........174 F2
Gold La BN10...........167 C2
Goldsmid Mews 10 BN3..163 D6
Goldsmid Rd BN3........163 E7
Goldsmith Cl BN23......174 E3
Goldsmiths Ave TN6......25 D3
Goldsmiths Leisure Ctr
   TN6...................25 D4
Goldstone Cres BN3.....142 A2
Goldstone Cl BN3.......142 B3
Goldstone Ct BN3.......142 A3
Goldstone Ho 4 BN3....163 B7
Goldstone Prim Sch BN3 141 E1
Goldstone Ret Pk BN3...163 B8
Goldstone St BN3.......163 B7
Goldstone Villas BN3...163 B7
Goldstone Way BN3.....142 A2
Golf Dr BN1............143 B3
Goodensfield TN5........29 E5
Goods Sta Rd BN1........8 B4
Goodtrees La TN8.........4 B2
Goodwin Cl BN27........129 A2
Goodwins Cl RH19........1 D3
Goodwins The TN2........7 F1
Goodwood Cl
   Bexhill TN40..........157 D6
   Eastbourne BN20......173 B6
Goodwood Ct 2 BN3.....163 D7
Goodwood Way BN2......143 F3
Gooseberry La TN31......67 A3
Gordon Ave BN43........161 A7
Gordon Cl RH16..........50 E6
Gordon Ho RH15..........73 C4
Gordon Mews 2 BN41....162 C7
Gordon Pl TN39.........157 B6
Gordon Rd
   Brighton BN1.........142 F2
   Burgess Hill RH15......73 C4
   Buxted TN22...........56 C3
   Crowborough TN6......25 F2
   Hailsham BN27........152 B7
   Hastings TN34........160 A4
   Haywards Heath RH16...50 E6
   Portslade-by-S, Aldrington
   BN41.................162 C7
   Portslade-by-S, Fishersgate
   BN41.................162 A7
   Royal Tunbridge Wells TN4...8 C7
   Shoreham-by-S BN43...161 A7
Gore Park Ave BN21.....184 D4
Gore Park Rd BN21......184 D4
Gorham Ave BN2........166 A2
Gorham Cl BN2..........166 A2
Gorham Ct TN31.........177 E4
Gorham Way BN10.......177 E4
Goring Ct BN1..........143 F5
Gorringe Cl
   Eastbourne BN20......173 A3
   Shoreham-by-S BN43...161 D7
Gorringe Dr BN20.......173 A3
Gorringe Rd BN22.......185 A4
Gorringe Valley Rd
   BN20.................173 A3
Gorse Cl
   Eastbourne BN20......184 B5
   Portslade-by-S BN41...140 A7
Gorse Dr BN25..........180 F6
Gorse Hill TN21.........59 F1
Gorselands TN33.........88 C1
Gorse Rd TN2............8 E5
Gorses The TN39........156 C2
Gorsethorn Way TN35...138 E4
Gorseway The TN39......156 C5
Gosford Way BN26......172 F6
Gosport Ct 11 BN43....161 B6
Gote La BN8............124 D4
Goudhurst Cl BN23......174 D1
Gower Rd RH16..........50 E3
Gows Croft BN7.........145 E5
Grace Cl BN6............97 E3
Gradwell End BN8.......100 D7

Graffham Cl BN2........164 E6
Grafton St BN2.........189 C1
Graham Ave
   Brighton BN1.........142 F5
   Portslade-by-S BN41...140 F4
Graham Cl BN41.........140 F4
Graham Cres BN41......140 F4
Grammer Ct BN8.........75 D7
Grampian Cl
   Eastbourne BN23......174 C3
   Royal Tunbridge Wells TN2...8 D5
Granary Cotts TN33.....112 F3
Granary Rural Bsns Ctr The
   BN27.................128 F6
Grand Ave
   Bexhill TN40..........158 A5
   Hassocks BN6..........97 A3
   Hove BN3.............163 C6
   Seaford BN25.........180 D6
Grand Ave Mans 4 BN3..163 C6
Grand Cres BN2.........166 A1
Grand Ct
   3 Eastbourne BN21....185 A1
   10 St Leonards TN37...159 C8
Grand Hotel Bldgs 8
   BN21.................185 A1
Grand Junc Rd BN1......189 B1
Grand Mans 10 BN20....185 A1
Grand Par
   Brighton BN2.........189 B2
   Eastbourne BN21......185 B2
   Polegate BN26........172 F6
   St Leonards TN37, TN38 159 C6
Grand Parade Mews
   BN2..................189 B2
Grange Ave TN34........136 D4
Grange Cl
   Brighton BN1.........142 E1
   Burgess Hill RH15......73 C5
   Crowborough TN6......25 D1
   Horam TN21...........106 C3
Grange Court Dr TN39...157 B6
Grange Ct
   Eastbourne BN21......184 F2
   Hove BN3.............162 F8
   Lewes BN7............190 A1
   9 Southwick BN42.....161 E7
Grange End BN20........184 F1
Grange Farm Cotts BN2.165 D4
Grange Gdns TN4.........7 D4
Grange Ind Est The
   BN42.................161 D7
Grange Mus & Art Gall★
   BN2..................165 F2
Grange Rd
   Barcombe Cross BN8...101 D4
   Eastbourne BN21......184 F1
   Hastings TN34........136 E5
   Hove BN3.............162 E8
   Lewes BN7............190 A1
   Rusthall TN4...........7 D4
   Southwick BN42.......161 E7
   Uckfield TN22..........78 C7
Grange The
   Barcombe Cross BN8...101 D4
   21 Eastbourne BN21...185 A2
   Felcourt RH19..........1 D7
   Langton Green TN3......6 F3
   Saltdean BN2.........177 D6
Grangeways BN1.........142 E5
Grantham Bank BN8.....101 E4
Grantham Cl BN8........100 E7
Grantham Rd BN1.......143 A1
Grants Hill Ho TN22.....78 C7
Grant St BN2...........189 C4
Granville Ct
   2 Eastbourne BN20....184 F1
   10 Hove BN3..........163 B6
   11 Seaford BN25......180 E2
Granville Rd
   Eastbourne BN20......184 F1
   Hove BN3.............163 E7
   Royal Tunbridge Wells TN1...8 C5
Graperies The 3 BN2....164 C5
Grasmere BN23..........174 B4
Grassington Rd BN20...184 F1
Grassmere Ave BN10....177 F4
Grassmere Ct BN10.....178 A8
Gratton Ct TN39........157 A3
Gravelye Cl RH16........51 B5
Gravelye La
   Haywards Heath RH16...51 A4
   Walstead RH16.........51 B6
Gravett Ct RH15.........72 F2
Graycoats Dr TN6........25 F2
Grays Cotts TN33.......112 F3
Grays Sch BN9..........179 D6
Graystone La TN35......160 D7
Graywood La BN8.......105 D6
Graywood Rd BN8.......105 C6
Grazebrook Cl TN39.....156 C3
Great Brooms Rd TN4.....8 C8
Great Cliffe Rd BN23....174 E1
Great Coll St BN2.......164 C4
Great Courtlands TN3....7 A3
Great Dixter House & Gdns★
   TN31..................66 F7
Great Dixter Nurseries★
   TN31..................66 F7
Greater Paddock BN8...124 E6
Great Field Pl RH19......2 B3
Great Footway TN3.......6 F3
Great Hall Arc 3 TN1.....8 B3
Greatham Ct BN1.......142 E6
Great Heathmead RH16..50 D4
Great House Ct 4 RH19..10 F8
Great Oak TN19..........45 A3
Great Rough BN8........76 A6

Great Sanders Ho TN33...88 D4
Great Walstead Sch RH16..51 F6
Great Wilkins BN1......144 B5
Great Wood Woodland
   Walks★ BN6...........113 B5
Grecian Rd TN1..........8 B2
Greeba Ct 8 TN38......159 B6
Greenacres
   Brighton BN1.........142 F1
   Peacehaven BN10......167 D2
   Westfield TN35........114 E3
Greenacres Dr
   Hailsham BN27........152 C7
   Ringmer BN8..........124 D4
Greenacres Way BN2...152 C8
Greenbank Ave BN2.....166 D2
Green Cl
   Ringmer BN8..........124 E6
   4 Southwick BN42.....161 E7
Green Ct 3 BN42........161 E7
Greene Ct BN7..........146 B8
Greenfield Cl
   Brighton BN1.........143 A5
   Rusthall TN4...........7 C5
Green Field Cl BN42....161 E8
Greenfield Cres BN1....142 F5
Greenfield Dr TN22......78 D4
Greenfield Rd
   Burwash RH19.........62 C7
   Eastbourne BN21......184 D4
Greenfields BN27.......129 A1
Greenfields Cl TN37....136 B6
Greenfields Sch RH18...11 C1
Green Gate BN10.......167 C1
Green Gr BN2...........152 B8
Green Hedges TN32......63 E4
Green Hedges Ave RH19..1 D2
Green Hedges Cl RH19...1 D2
Greenhill Pk RH17.......51 A2
Greenhill Way
   Haywards Heath RH17...51 A2
   Peacehaven BN10......167 C2
Green La
   Bexhill TN40..........156 D5
   Broyle Side BN8.......103 D1
   Crowborough TN6......26 B2
   Heathfield TN21........82 B6
   Jevington BN26........172 C1
   Lewes BN7............190 A1
   Seaford BN25.........180 E2
   South Chailey BN8....100 E7
   South Street BN8......75 E1
   Wivelsfield RH17.......74 B5
   Woodingdean BN2.....165 E6
Greenlands Cl RH15......98 B8
Greenlands Dr RH15.....98 B8
Greenleaf Gdns BN26...173 A8
Greenleas
   Hove BN3.............141 D2
   Pembury TN2...........9 C6
Green Mdws RH16........51 B8
Green Park Cnr RH17....74 B4
Green Rd RH17..........74 B5
Green Ridge BN1.......142 B5
Green Sq TN5............29 F5
Green St BN21..........184 C4
Greenstede Ave RH19....1 F2
GREEN STREET..........135 B4
Green The
   Blackboys TN22........80 A6
   Bodiam TN32...........65 E7
   Catsfield TN33.........133 E8
   East Dean BN20.......187 B8
   Ewhurst Green TN32....66 B5
   Frant TN3.............17 C3
   Hailsham BN27........129 C2
   Horsted Keynes RH17...33 C5
   Hove BN3.............142 C5
   Langton Green TN3......6 E3
   Newick BN8............76 D7
   Ninfield TN33.........133 B5
   Ringmer BN8..........124 D5
   Rottingdean BN2......165 F2
   Sedlescombe TN33.....113 E8
   Southwick BN42.......161 E7
   St Leonards TN38......159 B8
Green View RH15.........72 E3
Green Wall BN7.........190 B2
Greenway TN2............8 E8
Greenway Ct BN2.......166 A1
Greenways
   Bexhill TN39..........156 F7
   Haywards Heath RH16...50 F6
   Ovingdean BN2........165 D3
   Portslade-by-S BN41...141 B1
   Southwick BN42.......140 C1
Greenways Cnr BN2.....165 D4
Greenways Cres BN43...140 A1
Greenwoods La TN21....83 D7
Greenwich Rd BN27.....152 D7
Greenwich Way BN10...178 C7
Green Wlk
   Hailsham BN27........129 C1
   Seaford BN25.........181 B2
Green Wlk The BN22....173 B3
Greenwoods La TN21....83 D7
Greggs Wood Rd TN2.....8 E7
Gregory Ct 2 RH19......1 E1
Gregory La BN24........174 F5
Gregory Wlk TN33......113 E8
Grenada 4 TN39........157 A6
Grenada Cl
   Bexhill TN36..........156 D4
   Eastbourne BN23......185 G7
Grenham Ct TN35.......160 C7
Grenville Ho RH16......167 D1
Grenville Rd BN24......175 C4

Grenville St BN1.......189 A2
Gresham............175 B6
Gresham Cl BN21.......184 C6
Gresham Way TN38.....159 A8
Gresley Rd TN38........135 F5
Greville Rd TN35.......160 C7
Grey Alders RH16.......51 B6
Greyfriars BN3.........163 D8
Greyfriars Ct BN7......190 B2
Greyfriars Pl TN36.....118 B6
Greyhorses TN39.......156 B4
Greys Rd BN20.........184 D3
Greystones Ct TN6......25 D4
Grey Tower Bglws BN24..157 C3
Grinley Ct 8 TN40......157 C4
Grinstead La
   East Grinstead RH19...10 B1
   Sharpthorne RH19.....21 C7
Grinstead Mount 4 BN2 164 F5
GRISLING COMMON........77 B8
Gromenfield TN3.........15 C7
GROOMBRIDGE............15 C7
Groombridge Hill TN3....6 D1
Groombridge Pl★ TN3...15 C8
Groombridge Pl Gdns★
   TN3...................15 C8
Groombridge St Thomas CE
   Prim Sch TN3.........15 C6
Groombridge Sta TN3....15 C7
Grosvenor Bridge TN1....8 B5
Grosvenor Cl BN26......172 F5
Grosvenor Cres TN38...159 A6
Grosvenor Ct
   Brighton BN1.........142 E3
   Seaford BN25.........180 D3
Grosvenor Gdns TN38...158 F6
Grosvenor Ho RH19.......1 E3
Grosvenor Mans 1 BN3..163 B6
Grosvenor Pk TN1........8 A4
Grosvenor Rd
   East Grinstead RH19...1 D1
   Royal Tunbridge Wells TN1...8 A4
   Seaford BN25.........180 E4
Grosvenor St BN2.......189 C2
Grosvenor Wlk TN1.......8 A4
Grove Ave TN1...........8 A2
Grove Bank 9 BN2.....189 C3
Grovebury BN27.........152 C7
Grove Ct 12 BN3.......163 C6
GROVE HILL............107 E4
Grove Hill
   Brighton BN2.........189 C3
   Grove Hill RH19.......129 D7
Grove Hill Gdns TN1......8 B2
Grove Hill Rd TN1.......8 B3
Grove La TN31..........70 C4
Grovelands Cl RH15......72 F1
Grovelands Com Prim Sch
   BN27.................129 A1
Grovelands Rd BN27....129 A1
Grovely La TN21.........84 B1
Grove Park Specl Sch
   TN6...................25 E1
Grove Rd
   Burgess Hill RH15......73 B3
   Eastbourne BN21......184 F2
   Hastings TN35........160 D8
   Seaford BN25.........180 F3
Grover Ct 3 TN1.........8 A4
Grove Sch TN38.........135 F1
Grove St BN2...........189 C3
Grove The
   Battle TN33...........112 F3
   Bexhill TN39..........156 E5
   Crowborough TN6......25 E1
   Eastbourne BN20......184 B7
   Eastbourne, Wannock
   BN20.................172 F3
   Hailsham BN27........152 B6
   Haywards Heath RH16...51 B3
   Mayfield TN20.........40 A2
   Newhaven BN9........168 E2
   Pembury TN2...........9 D8
   Rye TN31..............93 C6
Grove Villa 3 BN1......189 A4
Growers End BN8........76 D7
Guardian Ct BN26......172 F7
Guestling Bradshaw CE Prim
   Sch TN35.............138 A8
GUESTLING GREEN.......138 A8
Guestling Rd BN22.....185 D5
Guildford Rd
   Brighton BN1.........189 A3
   7 Royal Tunbridge Wells
   TN1...................8 B3
Guildford St BN1.......189 A3
Guinness Ct BN9........168 E1
Guinness Trust Bglws
   BN9..................168 E2
Guldeford La TN29, TN31..71 F3
Guldeford Lane Cnr TN31..71 D2
Guldeford Rd TN31......93 E7
Gundreda Rd BN7.......123 B2
GUN HILL..............106 C2
Gun Hill
   Gun Hill TN21.........106 D3
   Lower Dicker BN27, TN21 128 B8
Gun Rd TN22............80 A6
Gunter's La TN39.......157 A6
Gurth Rd TN35..........160 C5
Gwent Ct 7 BN22.......185 C4
Gwydyr Mans 3 BN3....163 D6
Gwyneth Gr TN40.......157 F7
Gwynne Gdns RH19.......1 C2

H

Hackenden Cl RH19 1 E3
Hackenden La RH19 1 E3
Hackhurst La BN27 128 B4
Hackhurst Lane Ind Est
BN27 128 B4
Hackwood TN32 63 E4
Haddington Cl BN3 163 B6
Haddington St 11 BN3 163 B7
Hadley Ct
Polegate BN26 173 A6
Royal Tunbridge Wells TN4 7 F6
Hadley Ho 7 BN21 184 F3
Hadlow Ave BN23 174 B4
Hadlow Cl BN2 164 D6
HADLOW DOWN 57 C5
Hadlow Down Rd TN6 38 B4
Hadrian Ave BN42 162 A8
Hadrian Gdns TN37 136 A6
Haig Ave BN1 143 D6
HAILSHAM 152 C8
Hailsham Ave BN2 166 D3
Hailsham Com Coll
BN27 152 B8
Hailsham Ct 2 TN40 157 C3
Hailsham Rd
Heathfield TN21 82 A6
Herstmonceux BN27 130 E5
Polegate BN26 172 F7
Stone Cross BN24, BN26 173 F8
Hairpin Croft BN10 167 C1
Hale Gn BN8 106 A2
HALE GREEN 106 A2
Half Mile Dro BN8 125 B7
Halfway Sta★ BN2 164 C4
HALLAND 104 C5
Halland Cl BN22 173 D1
Halland Rd BN2 143 F4
Hallands The RH15 73 C4
Hallett Rd BN2 164 D7
Halley Pk BN27 152 D7
Halley Rd
Cade Street TN21 82 E8
Wartling BN27 131 B1
Hall La TN22 57 C5
Halls Cotts TN5 29 F5
Hall's Hole Rd TN2 8 E4
Hallyburton Rd BN3 162 D8
Halsford Croft RH19 1 B3
Halsford Gn RH19 1 B3
Halsford La RH19 1 C3
Halsford Park Prim Sch
RH19 1 C2
Halsford Park Rd RH19 1 C2
HALTON 137 B2
Halton Cres TN34 160 B6
Halton Hts TN34 160 B6
Halton Pl TN34 160 B6
Halton Rd BN22 185 C4
Halton Shaws BN6 97 B5
Halton Terr TN34 160 B6
Hamble Rd BN24 173 F5
Hambleton Cl BN23 174 D3
Hambrook RH15 73 C1
Ham Bsns Ctr BN43 161 A7
Hamelsham Ct BN27 152 A8
Hamilton Cl BN41 141 A3
Hamilton Ct
Brighton BN2 165 A3
Royal Tunbridge Wells TN4 8 A5
Hamilton Gdns TN35 160 D7
Hamilton Ho
13 Eastbourne BN21 184 E4
1 Royal Tunbridge Wells
TN4 8 A5
Seaford BN25 180 E4
Hamilton Lodge Sch
BN2 164 D5
Hamilton Mans 4 BN3 163 B5
Hamilton Rd BN1 189 A4
Hamilton Terr TN39 157 A4
Ham La
Burwash TN19 62 B6
Lewes BN7 190 B1
Ringmer BN8 124 C6
Scaynes Hill RH17 51 E3
Hamlands La BN22 173 B3
Hamlin's Cnr BN6 72 A6
Hammer La BN27, TN21 107 F5
HAMMERWOOD 3 B3
Hammerwood Pk★ RH19 3 C2
Hammerwood Rd RH19 11 E6
Hammonds Dr BN23 185 C7
Hammonds Gdns RH15 72 F1
Hammonds Ridge RH15 72 E1
Hammy Cl BN43 161 C8
Hammy La BN43 161 B8
Hammy Way BN43 161 B8
Hampden Ave BN22 173 F1
Hampden Cl TN33 112 B4
Hampden Gdns BN9 168 D2
HAMPDEN PARK 173 E1
Hampden Park Dr BN22 184 E8
Hampden Park Inf Sch
BN22 173 E2
Hampden Park Sta BN22 173 F1
Hampden Rd BN2 164 C7
Hampden Terr 8 BN22 185 C4
Hampshire Ct
Brighton BN2 189 C1
6 Eastbourne BN23 174 E1
Hampstead Rd BN1 142 D1
Hampton Pl BN1 163 E5
Hampton St 24 BN1 163 E5
Hampton Terr 7 BN1 163 E6
Hampton Way RH19 10 F7
HAMSEY 123 C6
Hamsey Cl
Brighton BN2 164 F5
Eastbourne BN20 184 B6
Hamsey Cres BN7 123 A2
Hamsey La
Cooksbridge BN8 123 B7
Seaford BN25 181 C2
Hamsey Prim Sch BN8 123 A8
Hamsey Rd
Saltdean BN2 166 D1
Sharpthorne RH19 21 A6
Hamshaw Ct BN22 184 F8
Hamsland RH17 33 C4
Hanbury La RH16 51 A5
Hancock Way BN43 161 B6
Hangdown Mead Bsns Pk
RH19 21 B5
Hanging Birch La TN21 81 D1
Hangleton Cl BN3 141 D2
Hangleton Gdns BN3 141 D1
Hangleton Jun & Inf Sch
BN3 141 E2
Hangleton La BN41 141 B2
Hangleton Manor Cl
BN3 141 D2
Hangleton Rd BN3 141 E2
Hangleton Valley Dr
BN3 141 D4
Hangleton Way BN3 141 D3
HANKHAM 174 B8
Hankham Hall Rd BN24 174 D7
Hankham Prim Sch
BN24 174 B8
Hankham Rd BN24 174 B6
Hankham St BN24 174 B8
Hanlye La RH17 50 B8
Hannington Pl BN6 97 A7
Hanover Cl
Bexhill TN40 157 C5
Seaford BN25 180 B6
Hanover Cres BN2 189 C4
Hanover Ct
Brighton BN2 189 C4
Eastbourne BN21 184 D5
Haywards Heath RH16 50 D4
Hanover Lofts BN2 189 C3
Hanover Mews BN2 189 C4
Hanover Rd
Eastbourne BN22 185 C4
Royal Tunbridge Wells TN1 8 A4
Hanover St BN2 189 C4
Hanover Terr BN2 189 C4
Hanson Rd BN9 179 C6
Harbour Barn TN36 118 B6
Harbour Ct BN42 161 F7
Harbour Ho BN43 161 B6
Harbour Quay BN23 175 A1
Harbour Rd TN31 93 D4
Harbour's Yd TN33 112 E4
Harbour View Cl BN25 180 B6
Harbour View Rd BN9 179 B5
Harbour Way
Shoreham-by-S BN43 161 B6
St Leonards TN38 135 E7
Harcourt Cl TN22 78 C6
Harcourt Rd TN22 78 D6
Harding Ave BN22 185 B6
Hardrada Rise TN34 136 E3
Hardwicke Rd TN34 160 B6
Hardwick Rd
Eastbourne BN21 185 A2
Hove BN3 141 E3
Hardwick Way BN3 141 E3
Hardy Dr BN23 185 F6
Harebeating Cl BN27 129 C2
Harebeating Cres BN27 129 C2
Harebeating Dr BN27 129 C2
Harebeating Gdns BN27 129 C2
Harebeating La BN27 129 D1
Harebell Cl BN23 174 C3
Harebell Dr BN41 141 A3
Harecombe Rd TN6 37 F8
Harecombe Rise TN6 37 F8
Haremere Hill TN19 44 D2
Harescroft TN2 16 F7
Hare Way TN37 136 C5
Harewood Cl TN39 157 A3
Harewood Ct 8 BN3 163 C6
Harfield Cl BN9 168 F2
Hargate Cl TN2 16 F8
Hargreaves Rd BN23 174 A1
Harison Rd BN25 181 A4
Harkness Dr TN34 137 B5
Harlands Cl RH16 50 C6
Harlands Cty Prim Sch
TN22 78 D5
Harlands Ho RH16 50 D6
Harlands Mews TN22 78 D5
Harlands Prim Sch RH16 50 D7
Harlands Rd RH16 50 D6
Harlands Villas TN22 78 D5
Harlequin Gdns TN37 136 A6
Harlequin La TN6 37 E8
Harlequin Pl TN6 37 E8
Harley La TN21 82 A6
HARLEY SHUTE 158 E7
Harley Shute Rd TN38 158 E7
Harley Way TN38 158 E6
Harlow Sports Ctr BN21 184 E7
Harmans Dr RH19 2 B1
Harmans Mead RH19 2 B1
Harmers Hay Rd BN27 129 B1
Harmers Hill BN8 76 C7
Harmony St TN4 7 D4
Harmony Wood TN34 136 F5
Harmsworth Cres BN3 141 E3
Harold Cl BN24 175 F7
Harold Dr BN23 185 F8
Harold Ho 2 TN2 8 C7
Harold Mews 2 TN38 159 C6
Harold Pl TN34 159 F7
Harold Rd TN35 160 C5
Harold Terr TN33 112 F3
Harpers Rd BN9 179 C7
Harrier La TN33 112 F4
Harriers Ct BN27 152 D7
Harries Rd TN2 8 E7
Harriet Pl 10 BN43 161 B6
Harrington Ct BN1 142 E2
Harrington Mans BN1 142 E2
Harrington Pl BN1 143 B2
Harrington Rd BN1 142 E2
Harrington Villas BN1 142 F2
Harris Ct BN21 185 A3
Harrisons La BN8 124 E5
Harrow Cl BN25 181 A4
Harrow La TN37 136 B5
Hart Cl TN22 78 A7
HARTFIELD 13 D4
Hartfield Ave BN1 143 A5
Hartfield Ho TN22 78 C6
Hartfield La BN21 184 F4
Hartfield Mdw TN38 135 D3
Hartfield Rd
Bexhill TN39 156 E2
Cowden TN8 4 C6
Eastbourne BN21 184 F3
Forest Row RH18 11 F2
Saltdean BN2 166 D1
Seaford BN25 181 A3
Harting Combe TN38 159 B8
Hartington Mans 7
BN21 185 A2
Hartington Pl
Brighton BN2 164 C8
Eastbourne BN21 185 A2
Hartington Rd BN2 164 C8
Hartington Terr BN2 164 C8
Hartington Villas BN3 163 B8
Hartley Ct 8 BN1 189 A4
Hartwood Lodge 6
TN40 157 C4
Harvard Cl BN7 190 A4
Harvard Rd BN8 124 D5
Harvest Cl
Lindfield RH16 51 B7
Telscombe Cliffs BN10 167 B2
Harvesters RH16 50 D2
Harvest Hill RH19 10 E8
Harvest Way TN37 136 C5
Harvey Cl TN38 135 F4
Harvey's La BN8, TN22 103 D4
Harveys Way BN7 190 C2
Harvington Bsns Pk
BN22 184 F8
Harwood Cl BN23 185 E7
Harwoods Cl 3 RH19 10 F7
Harwoods La RH19 10 F7
Haslam Cres TN40 157 F6
Hasletts Cl TN1 8 B6
Hassocks Cl BN23 173 F4
Hassocks Inf Sch BN6 97 F4
Hassocks Lodge BN6 97 F3
Hassocks Rd BN6 97 B5
Hassocks Sta BN6 97 E4
HASTINGS 159 F7
Hastings Ave BN25 181 C5
Hastings Castle & 1066
Story★ 11 TN34 160 A4
Hastings Cl BN26 173 B7
Hastings Coll of Art & Tech
TN38 159 B6
Hastings Com It TN34 159 E7
Hastings Ct
Bexhill TN40 157 E5
9 Shoreham-by-S BN43 161 B6
Hastings Ctry Park Nature
Reserve★ TN35 160 E5
Hastings Ctry Park Visitor
Ctr★ TN35 138 C4
Hastings Mus & Art Gall★
TN34 159 E7
Hastings Rd
Battle TN33 113 B2
Bexhill TN40 157 E5
Brighton BN2 164 C8
Newenden TN17, TN18 48 C6
Pembury TN2 9 F5
The Moor TN18 45 F6
Hastings Sta TN34 159 E8
Hatch End RH18 11 F2
Hatchgate Cl RH17 50 A6
Hatchgate La RH17 50 A6
Hatfield Ct 18 BN3 163 C6
Hatherley Rd TN37 159 C7
Havana Ct 12 BN23 185 F8
Havelock Rd
Bexhill TN40 157 C6
Brighton BN1 142 F1
Eastbourne BN22 185 B4
Hastings TN34 159 F7
Haven Brow BN25 181 A4
Haven Cl
Beachlands BN24 175 E6
Eastbourne BN22 173 B3
Haven Rd TN38 158 D6
Haven The BN27 152 C6
Haven VA CE Prim Sch The
BN23 185 F7
Haven Way BN9 179 B6
Havering Cl TN2 8 F6
HAWKENBURY 8 D2
Hawkenbury Cl TN2 8 D2
Hawkenbury Mead TN2 8 D1
Hawkenbury Rd TN2, TN3 8 E1
Hawkenbury Way BN7 123 A1
Hawkes Farm Prim Sch
BN27 129 B3
Hawkhurst Cl BN23 174 D2
Hawkhurst Pl BN1 143 D6
Hawkhurst Rd
Brighton BN1 143 D6
Flimwell TN5, TN18 32 E2
Hawkhurst Way TN39 156 E3
Hawkins Cl BN43 140 D1
Hawkins Cres BN43 140 D2
Hawkins Rd BN43 140 D1
Hawkins Way BN27 152 B8
Hawksbridge Cl BN22 173 C3
Hawks Farm Cl BN27 129 B2
Hawks Rd BN27 129 B2
Hawkstown Cl BN27 129 B3
Hawks Town Cres BN27 129 C2
Hawkstown Gdns BN27 129 B3
Hawkstown View BN27 129 B3
Hawkswood Dr BN27 129 C3
Hawkswood Rd BN27 129 C3
Hawth Cl BN25 180 C4
Hawth Cres BN25 180 C4
Hawth Gr BN25 180 C4
Hawth Hill BN25 180 C5
Hawthorn Ave TN39 156 D3
Hawthorn Bank BN2 143 F4
Hawthorn Cl
Burgess Hill RH15 73 D5
Saltdean BN2 166 C2
Hawthorn Ct BN26 173 B6
Hawthorne Cl TN21 82 B6
Hawthornes The TN31 90 B4
Hawthorn Pl 13 RH16 50 C2
Hawthorn Rd
Eastbourne BN23 185 C7
Hastings TN35 160 D6
Hawthorn Rise BN9 179 B7
Hawthorns The
Burgess Hill RH15 73 A5
Hailsham BN27 152 A7
The Moor TN18 45 F8
Hawthorn Way BN41 141 A3
Hawthorn Wlk TN2 8 E8
Hawth Park Rd BN25 180 C4
Hawth Pl BN25 180 C4
Hawth Rise BN25 180 C5
Hawth Valley Ct 1 BN25 180 C4
Hawth Way BN25 180 D4
Hawthylands Cres BN27 129 B2
Hawthylands Dr BN27 129 B2
Hawthylands Rd BN27 129 B2
Haybourne Cl BN2 164 E7
Haybourne Rd BN2 164 E7
Hayes Cl
Portslade-by-S BN41 162 C8
Ringmer BN8 124 D5
Hayes La TN31 91 C5
Hayes Plat TN31 67 C5
Hayland Gn BN27 129 C1
Hayland Ind Units TN38 135 F5
Haylind Rd RH16 51 B5
Hayreed La BN26 151 A1
Haystoun Cl BN22 173 C2
Haystoun Ho BN22 173 C2
Haystoun Pk BN22 173 C2
Hayward Rd BN7 123 A3
Haywards Heath Sta RH16 50 E6
Haywards Rd
Brighton BN1 143 A6
Haywards Heath RH16 50 E3
Haywards Villas RH16 50 F3
Haywood Way TN35 160 C8
HAZARD'S GREEN 132 C5
Hazelbank TN3 6 F3
Hazel Bank 3 BN2 189 C4
Hazel Cl
Hove BN41 141 C3
Newhaven BN9 179 B7
Hazel Ct TN35 136 F6
Hazel Ct Sch BN21 184 E7
Hazel Ct Sec Sch BN23 174 A3
Hazeldene BN25 181 B3
Hazeldene Meads BN1 142 D3
Hazeledene La BN8 75 F7
Hazel Gr
Bexhill TN39 157 A7
Burgess Hill RH15 73 B1
Eastbourne BN20 173 A3
Hazelgrove Gdns 8 RH16 50 E4
Hazelgrove Rd RH16 50 E4
Hazelholt BN41 140 F3
Hazelwood BN1 142 D3
Hazelwood Ave BN22 173 D4
Hazelwood Cl
Bexhill TN39 156 C3
Royal Tunbridge Wells TN2 8 D8
Hazelwood Cotts TN5 31 D1
Hazelwood Gdns TN37 136 D5
Hazleden Cross RH19 10 B6
Headland Ave BN25 181 A3
Headland Cl BN10 178 E7
Headway Ct TN4 7 B4
Heansill La TN18 45 E8
Heasewood RH16 50 C3
Heath Cl 9 RH16 50 E4
Heathcote Dr RH19 1 C2
Heath Ct RH16 50 E5
Heathdown Cl BN10 167 D2
Heather Bank RH16 50 C5
Heather Cl BN23 174 B3
Heather Ct 8 BN1 163 E6
Heatherdune Rd TN39 157 A5
Heather Way TN35 138 F4
Heather Wlk TN6 26 D1
HEATHFIELD 82 B7
Heathfield Ave BN2 166 D2
Heathfield Cl TN34 136 F5
Heathfield Com Coll TN21 82 E7
Heathfield Cres BN41 140 F3
Heathfield Dr BN41 140 F4
Heathfield Gdns TN32 64 B3
Heathfield L Ctr TN21 82 D7
Heathfield Rd BN25 180 F3
Heathfields TN2 8 D4
Heath Hill Ave BN2 143 F1
Heathlands TN35 114 E3
Heath Rd RH16 50 E5
Heath Sq RH16 50 D5
Heath Stables BN7 123 A1
Heathy Brow BN10 167 B1
Heavegate Rd TN6 37 C8
Heaven Farm★ RH17 34 B1
Hebrides Wlk BN23 185 E7
Hectors La RH19 11 C7
Heighton Cl TN39 156 D3
Heighton Cres BN9 168 D2
Heighton Rd BN9 168 E2
Heights The
Brighton BN1 142 B5
Hastings TN35 160 E8
6 Haywards Heath RH16 50 E4
Helena Cl BN41 141 C2
Helena Ct TN38 159 B7
Helena Rd BN2 144 C1
Helensdene Wlk TN37 159 D8
Helenswood Leisure Ctr
TN37 136 D6
Helenswood Lower Sch
TN37 136 D6
Helenswood Sch
Hastings TN34 160 B8
St Leonards TN37 136 D6
HELLINGLY 129 A5
Hellingly Cl BN2 164 F5
Hellingly Prim Sch BN27 128 F5
Helmsman Rise TN38 135 F7
Helvellyn Dr BN23 174 C4
Hemingford Rise TN35 160 D7
Hempstead Gdns TN22 78 D7
Hempstead La
Hailsham BN27 128 F1
Uckfield TN22 78 E8
Hempstead Rd
Saltdean BN2 166 D3
Uckfield TN22 78 C7
Hempstead Rise TN22 78 C7
Hemsley Ho TN21 81 F8
Henderson Cl TN34 136 F3
Hendon St BN2 164 D5
Henfield Cl BN2 164 F5
Henfield Rd BN22 173 E2
Henfield Way BN3 141 F3
Henge Way BN41 141 B2
Hengist Cl BN23 185 F8
Henleaze BN21 184 E3
Henley Cl
Royal Tunbridge Wells TN2 8 C4
Rye TN31 93 A6
Henley Ct BN2 164 F4
Henley Rd BN2 164 F4
HENLEY'S DOWN 134 B6
Henley's Hill BN27 131 F7
Henry Burt Way RH15 72 E1
Henry Terr 3 TN34 160 B4
HENWOOD GREEN 9 E6
Henwood Green Rd TN2 9 E6
Henwoods Cres TN2 9 D6
Henwoods Mount TN2 9 E6
Herbert Rd BN1 142 F2
Herbrand Wlk TN39 156 A1
Hereford Ct
15 Brighton BN2 189 C2
1 Eastbourne BN23 174 E1
15 Hove BN3 163 C7
Hereford St BN2 164 C5
Hereward Rd BN23 185 F8
Hereward Way BN7 190 B4
Hermitage La RH19 10 F8
Hermitage Rd RH19 1 D3
Hermitage The TN34 159 E8
Herne Down TN6 38 A7
Herne Jun Sch TN6 37 F8
Herne Rd TN6 37 F8
Heron Cl
Eastbourne BN23 174 C2
St Leonards TN38 158 E8
Uckfield TN22 78 D5
Heron Cotts TN18 48 D3
Heron Ct BN27 152 D7
Heron Pl RH19 10 F8
Heron Ridge BN26 173 B6
Heronsdale Rd BN2 165 F8
Herons Dale Sch BN43 140 C1
HERON'S GHYLL 36 E3
Herons The BN43 161 A8
Heron's Tye BN6 97 F3
Herons Way
Golden Cross BN27 127 C4
Pembury TN2 9 E8
Herontye Dr RH19 11 A8
Herontye Ho RH19 10 F7
Herring's Rd TN21, TN33 109 F8
HERSTMONCEUX 130 E6
Herstmonceux Castle Gdns★
BN27 131 A1
Herstmonceux CE Prim Sch
BN27 130 E6
Hertford Cl TN38 136 A4
Hertford Inf Sch BN1 143 B2
Hertford Jun Sch BN1 143 C2
Hertford Rd BN1 143 B2

Heskett Pk TN2 .... 9 E6
Hestingas Plat **2** TN34 .. 160 B4
Heston Ave BN1 .... 142 F7
Hever Cl BN23 .... 174 D2
Hever Cres TN39 .... 156 F5
Heyworth Cl BN2 .... 165 F8
Heyworth Prim Sch RH16 . 50 F4
Heyworth Ride RH16 ...... 50 C3
Hickling Cl BN23 .... 174 B4
Hickman's Cl RH16 .... 51 B8
Hickmans Ct RH16 .... 51 A7
Hickman's La RH16 ...... 51 A8
Hickman Way TN34 ..... 136 D4
Hidden Spring Vineyard &
 Orch★ TN21 .... 107 B8
Hide Hollow BN23 ...... 174 D3
Higglers Cl TN22 .... 56 C3
Higham Gdns TN35 ..... 138 A8
Higham La TN31 .... 67 A7
Highbank
 Brighton BN1 .... 142 C5
 Haywards Heath RH16 ... 50 C1
High Bank TN35 .... 160 C7
High Bank Cl TN35 ..... 160 C6
High Barn Rd BN26 .... 150 F7
High Beach Ho BN25 ... 180 C3
High Beech Cl TN37 .... 135 F6
High Beech Ctry Club (Chalet
 Pk) The TN37 .... 135 F6
High Beeches TN 8 D6
High Branches TN39 .... 156 E4
Highbridge La BN7 ..... 100 B4
Highbrook Cl BN2 ...... 143 D3
High Broom La TN6 ..... 37 E7
High Broom Rd TN6 .... 37 F7
HIGH BROOMS 8 C8
High Brooms Ind Pk TN2 . 8 C8
High Brooms Rd TN4 .... 8 C7
High Brooms Sta TN4 ... 8 C7
High Cl
 East Dean BN20 .... 183 C2
 Portslade-by-S BN41 ... 141 A1
Highcliff Ct BN2 .... 166 A1
Highcombe BN20 .... 188 D7
Highcroft Cres TN21 ..... 82 A7
Highcroft Lodge BN1 ... 163 E8
Highcroft Mews BN1 ... 142 D1
Highcroft Rd RH19 ...... 21 A6
Highcroft Villas BN1 ... 163 E8
HIGH CROSS 39 C6
High Cross Fields TN6 ... 25 F3
Highden **2** BN2 .... 164 C6
Highdown BN42 .... 140 F1
Highdown BN42 .... 140 F1
Highdown Cotts TN17 ... 20 F3
Highdown Ct BN1 .... 142 E3
Highdown Rd
 Hove BN1, BN3 .... 163 E7
 Lewes BN7 .... 123 A2
Highfield Cl TN2 .... 9 D6
Highfield Cres BN1 ..... 143 A5
Highfield Ct **7** RH16 .... 50 E4
Highfield Dr
 Hurstpierpoint BN6 ..... 97 C5
 St Leonards TN38 ..... 135 D2
Highfield Gdns TN39 ... 157 C7
Highfield Ind Est N
 BN23 .... 174 A1
Highfield Ind Est S BN23 174 A1
Highfield Jun Sch BN22 . 174 A1
Highfield Rd
 East Grinstead RH19 ..... 1 D3
 Horam TN21 .... 106 F7
 Royal Tunbridge Wells TN4 . 8 C7
Highfields
 Brighton BN1 .... 143 E5
 Burwash TN19 .... 62 A6
 Forest Row RH18 .... 11 F2
 Horsted Keynes RH17 ... 33 C4
 Rye TN31 .... 93 B7
High Fords TN36 .... 116 E5
High Fords Cl TN36 .... 116 E5
HIGHGATE 11 F1
Highgate Flats TN6 ..... 27 B1
Highgate Rd RH18 .... 11 F1
Highgrove
 Battle TN33 .... 112 B4
 Royal Tunbridge Wells TN2 . 17 A8
High Hatch La BN6 ...... 72 B4
High Hurst Cl BN8 ...... 76 D7
HIGH HURSTWOOD 37 A1
High Hurstwood CE Prim Sch
 TN22 .... 37 A1
Highland Ct RH16 .... 50 E4
Highland Grange TN4 ... 25 E3
Highland Lodge BN21 .. 184 F4
Highland Rd RH16 .... 50 F3
Highlands TN2 .... 8 D7
Highlands Ave TN22 ..... 78 D4
Highlands Cl
 Bexhill TN39 .... 156 F7
 Crowborough TN6 ...... 25 E3
 Keymer BN6 .... 98 A3
Highlands Ct TN6 .... 25 E3
Highlands Dr
 Burgess Hill RH15 ...... 73 A4
 St Leonards TN38 ..... 159 B7
Highlands Gdns TN38 .. 159 B7
Highlands La BN8 ...... 105 D2
Highlands Mews **2**
 TN38 .... 159 B6
Highlands Rd
 Portslade-by-S BN41 .. 141 B1
 Seaford BN25 .... 180 F3
HIGHLANDS THE 156 F8

Highlands The TN39 .... 156 F7
Highlea Cl TN37 .... 136 C5
Highleigh **8** BN2 ..... 189 C3
High Mdw TN31 .... 67 B7
High Park Ave BN3 .... 141 E3
High Park Cl TN31 ...... 67 A7
High Pk TN31 .... 67 A7
High Point RH16 .... 51 A3
High Rd TN22 .... 24 B2
High Rocks★ TN3 .... 7 B1
High Rocks La TN3, TN4 .. 7 C1
High Rocks Sta★ TN3 .... 7 B1
High St (School Hill)
 TN22 .... 55 B4
High St
 Alfriston TN26 .... 171 A2
 Barcombe Cross BN8 ... 101 E4
 Battle TN33 .... 112 D4
 Bexhill TN40 .... 157 D5
 Blackboys TN22 .... 80 A6
 Brighton BN2 .... 189 C2
 Burwash TN19 .... 62 A6
 Buxted TN22 .... 56 C3
 Cowden TN8 .... 4 B5
 Crowborough TN6 ...... 25 F3
 Ditchling BN6 .... 98 D3
 Eastbourne BN21 ..... 184 E3
 East Grinstead RH19 ... 10 F8
 East Hoathly BN8 ..... 105 A5
 Etchingham TN19 ...... 44 C1
 Flimwell TN5 .... 32 C3
 Frant TN3 .... 17 C4
 Hailsham BN27 .... 152 C8
 Hartfield TN7 .... 13 D1
 Hastings TN34 .... 160 B4
 Heathfield TN21 .... 82 A8
 Horam TN21 .... 106 F8
 Hurstpierpoint BN6 .... 97 A5
 Lamberhurst TN3 ...... 20 B5
 Lewes BN7 .... 190 A2
 Lindfield RH16 .... 51 B8
 Maresfield TN22 .... 55 B4
 Mayfield TN20 .... 40 B2
 Newhaven BN9 .... 179 C7
 Newick BN8 .... 76 D7
 Ninfield TN33 .... 133 A6
 Nutley TN22 .... 35 C3
 Pembury TN2 .... 9 C6
 Pevensey BN24 .... 175 B6
 Polegate BN26 .... 173 A6
 Portslade-by-S BN41 .. 141 A1
 Robertsbridge TN32 .... 64 B4
 Rotherfield TN6 .... 39 B8
 Rottingdean BN2 ..... 165 F1
 Royal Tunbridge Wells TN1 . 8 A2
 Rye TN31 .... 93 C5
 Seaford BN25 .... 180 E2
 Ticehurst TN5 .... 31 C1
 Uckfield TN22 .... 78 C6
 Wadhurst TN5 .... 29 F4
 Westham BN24 .... 175 A6
 Winchelsea TN36 ..... 117 F7
Highsted Pk BN10 ..... 167 D2
High Trees
 4 Eastbourne BN21 .. 184 F4
 Haywards Heath RH16 .. 50 F5
 Uckfield TN22 .... 78 C5
High View
 Eastbourne BN21 ..... 184 E5
 Heathfield TN21 .... 82 B8
Highview Avenue N BN1 . 142 E6
Highview Avenue S BN1 . 142 E6
Highview Cl
 St Leonards TN37 .... 136 D5
 Windmill Hill BN27 ... 131 B5
Highview Ct BN20 ..... 184 E5
Highview La TN22 ...... 78 D4
Highview Rd
 Brighton BN1 .... 142 E6
 Broad Oak TN21 .... 59 E1
 Telscombe Cliffs BN10 . 177 F4
Highview Way BN1 .... 142 E6
Highwater View TN37 .. 135 F7
Highway Cl BN2 .... 143 D2
Highways BN41 .... 141 B2
Highway The
 Brighton BN2 .... 143 D3
 Newhaven BN10, BN9 .. 179 A6
HIGH WICKHAM 137 C1
High Wickham TN35 ... 160 B5
Highwoods Ave TN39 .. 156 C6
Highwoods Ct TN39 ... 156 E5
High Woods La TN35 ..... 9 B3
Hiham Bglws TN36 .... 117 E7
Hiham Gn TN36 .... 117 E7
Hilary Cl BN26 .... 172 F5
Hilary Lodge **2** BN2 . 164 C5
Hilbert Cl TN2 .... 8 C5
Hilbert Rd TN2 .... 8 C5
Hilders Farm Cl TN6 .... 26 B1
Hilgrove Rd BN2 ...... 166 C5
Hillary Rd RH19 .... 2 A3
Hillbank Cl BN41 ...... 140 F3
Hill Brow BN3 .... 142 B3
Hillbrow (Brighton Univ)
 BN20 .... 184 E1
Hillbrow Rd BN1 ...... 142 D4
Hillbury Gdns TN5 ...... 31 D1
Hill Cl TN16 .... 25 E1
Hillcrest
 Brighton BN1 .... 142 C5
 Horsted Keynes RH17 .. 33 C5
 Rye TN31 .... 93 B7
Hill Crest
 Dormans Park RH19 .... 1 E6
 Royal Tunbridge Wells TN4 . 8 B8
Hillcrest Ave TN39 .... 157 A6

Hillcrest Cl RH17 .... 51 F3
Hillcrest Cl BN9 .... 142 C5
Hill Crest Ct BN9 ..... 179 C6
Hillcrest Dr TN2 .... 8 D7
Hillcrest La RH17 .... 51 F3
Hill Crest Rd BN9 ..... 179 D6
Hillcrest Sch TN35 .... 137 E5
Hillcroft BN41 .... 140 F7
Hill Dr BN3 .... 142 B3
Hill Farm Way BN42 .. 140 E2
Hillgarth TN4 .... 8 A8
Hillman Cl BN7 .... 190 C2
Hill Mead TN22 .... 35 C4
Hill Rd
 Eastbourne BN20 ..... 184 B5
 Fairlight TN35 .... 138 C4
 Lewes BN7 .... 123 B4
 Newhaven BN9 .... 168 F2
 Saltdean BN2 .... 166 B1
Hill Rise
 Newhaven BN9 .... 168 F2
 Seaford BN25 .... 180 C5
Hillside
 Brighton BN2 .... 143 E2
 6 Crowborough TN6 .. 37 F8
 Forest Row RH18 ...... 11 F3
 Friston BN20 .... 183 B1
 Mayfield TN20 .... 40 B2
 Newhaven BN9 .... 179 D7
 Portslade-by-S BN41 .. 141 C5
 Southwick BN42 ...... 140 F1
Hillside Ave BN3 ...... 181 C5
Hillside Cl RH19 .... 1 E3
Hillside Cotts TN35 ..... 30 B8
Hillside Dr TN21 ...... 106 F7
Hillside Rd
 Bexhill TN40 .... 157 C5
 Hastings TN34 .... 136 E5
 Hollington BN41 ..... 141 B2
Hillside Way
 Brighton BN2 .... 143 E2
 Brighton, Westdene BN1 . 142 C4
Hillside Wlk RH16 ...... 50 C6
Hills Rd RH19 .... 1 A3
Hill St
 Hastings TN34 .... 160 A4
 Royal Tunbridge Wells TN1 . 8 B5
Hill Top BN1 .... 142 B5
Hilltop Dr TN31 .... 93 B7
Hill Top Way BN1 .... 142 B4
Hillview Ho BN9 ...... 179 D6
Hill View Rd TN4 .... 7 C4
Hillyfield BN7 .... 146 B8
Hillyfields TN31 .... 67 C5
Hillyglen Cl TN34 .... 159 E8
Hilton Ct **11** TN34 .... 159 E7
Hindleap La RH17, RH18 . 22 C4
Hindleap Warren Outdoor Ed
 Ctr RH18 .... 22 D5
Hindover Cres BN25 ... 181 A4
Hindover Rd BN25 .... 181 A4
Hinton Cl BN1 .... 143 C2
Hither Chantlers TN3 ..... 7 A2
Hoadley's Cnr RH15 .... 73 B2
Hoadleys La TN6 .... 25 D5
Hoad Rd BN2 .... 185 B4
Hoadswood Cross TN21 . 84 B2
Hoad's Wood Rd TN34 . 160 A4
Hoathdown Ave BN9 .. 179 A7
Hoath Hill TN32 .... 87 C5
Hobart Quay BN23 ... 175 A2
Hobbs Cl TN31 .... 68 C5
Hobbs La TN31 .... 68 D6
Hoblands RH16 .... 51 B4
Hobney Rise BN24 ... 174 F5
Hockington La BN20 .. 173 B1
Hodcombe Cl BN24 ... 174 B4
Hoddern Ave BN10 ... 178 B8
Hoddern Cty Jun Sch
 BN10 .... 178 B8
Hodshrove La BN2 ... 143 E3
Hodshrove Pl BN2 ... 143 E3
Hodshrove Rd BN2 ... 143 E3
Hoe The TN37 .... 136 B6
Hogarth Ho TN38 .... 159 A8
Hogarth Rd
 Eastbourne BN23 .... 174 D1
 Hove BN3 .... 162 F7
Hog Hole La TN3 .... 19 F2
Hogs Edge BN2 .... 144 A2
Hogtrough La TN36 ... 117 E7
Holbrook **16** BN2 ... 164 F5
Holbrook Cl BN20 .... 188 E8
Holden Pk Rd TN4 ...... 8 A8
Holdings The
 Kingston near Lewes
 BN7 .... 145 F5
 Upper Wellingham BN8 . 124 B7
Hole Farm Cl TN34 ... 136 E2
Hollamby Pk BN27 ... 152 D7
Holland Ave TN39 .... 156 C4
Holland Mews BN3 ... 163 D5
Holland Rd BN3 ...... 163 D6
Hollands Ct RH19 .... 2 A4
Holland St BN2 .... 189 C3
Hollands Way RH19 ..... 2 A4
Hollier's Hill TN40 ... 157 C6
Hollies The TN20 .... 40 A2
Hollin Cl TN4 .... 7 F4
Hollingbourne Ct **8**
 BN2 .... 164 E4
HOLLINGBURY 143 B5
Hollingbury Copse BN1 . 143 A4
Hollingbury Cres BN1 . 143 B2
Hollingbury Ind Est BN1 143 C7

Hollingbury Park Ave
 BN1 .... 143 A2
Hollingbury Pl BN1 ... 143 B2
Hollingbury Rd BN1 .. 143 B1
Hollingbury Rise BN1 . 143 B1
Hollingbury Rise W BN1 143 A3
Hollingbury Terr BN1 . 143 A2
HOLLINGDEAN 143 B3
Hollingdean La BN1 .. 164 B8
Hollingdean Rd BN2 . 164 B8
Hollingdean St BN1 .. 143 B1
Hollingdean Terr BN1 143 A2
HOLLINGROVE 85 E6
HOLLINGTON 136 A4
Hollington Ct TN38 ... 159 A8
Hollington Old La TN38 136 A4
Hollington Park La TN38 136 A1
Hollington Park Rd
 TN38 .... 136 A4
Hollington Prim Sch
 TN38 .... 136 A4
Hollow La
 Blackboys TN22 .... 80 B4
 Dormansland RH19, RH7 .. 2 D6
 East Hoathly BN8 ..... 105 B6
Hollow The RH16 .... 51 B5
Holly Bank **3** BN2 ... 189 C5
Holly Bank Cl TN6 ..... 26 B2
Hollybank Gdns TN38 . 136 B1
Holly Bech La TN20 .... 58 B8
Holly Cl
 Bexhill TN39 .... 156 C6
 Brighton BN1 .... 142 E3
 Hailsham BN27 .... 152 B6
 Heathfield TN21 .... 82 A6
Hollycroft BN7 .... 100 A3
Holly Ct TN6 .... 25 E2
Hollydene Rd TN5 ...... 29 F6
Holly Dr TN21 .... 82 A6
Holly Pl BN2 .... 173 E3
Holly Rd RH16 .... 51 A3
Hollyshaw TN2 .... 8 C2
Hollyshaw Cl TN2 .... 8 C2
Hollywood Ct RH16 .... 50 E5
Holmbush Cl
 Haywards Heath RH16 .. 50 E2
 Shoreham-by-S BN43 .. 140 D2
Holmbush Ct **8** BN43 161 C8
Holmbush Ctr BN43 .. 140 D1
Holmbush Fst Sch BN43 140 D1
Holmbush Way BN42 . 140 E1
Holmdale Rd BN9 .... 168 F1
Holmebury Ho **1** TN34 159 E7
Holmes Ave BN3 ..... 141 F1
Holmes Cl BN25 ...... 180 A6
Holmesdale Cl TN5 .... 29 E5
Holmesdale Ct TN34 . 159 E8
Holmesdale Gdns TN34 159 E7
Holmesdale Rd
 Bexhill TN39 .... 157 A4
 Burgess Hill RH15 ..... 73 A1
Holmes Farm Cotts
 TN39 .... 156 A8
Holmes Hill BN8 ...... 127 C6
Holmewood House Sch
 TN3 .... 7 A2
Holmewood Rd TN4 ..... 8 C7
Holmewood Ridge TN3 .. 6 F3
Holm Ho RH15 .... 72 F3
Holmhurst Cl TN4 .... 7 F4
Holmhurst La TN37 ... 136 B5
Holmhurst St Mary TN37 136 C6
Holm Oak Cl TN39 ... 156 E3
Holmstead BN2 ...... 189 C4
Holmwood Cl BN6 ..... 97 F4
Holters Way BN25 ... 180 F5
Holt Lodge **1** BN2 .. 189 C4
HOLTON HILL 61 E7
Holton Hill BN2 ...... 165 E7
Holt The
 Burgess Hill RH15 ..... 73 C2
 Hailsham BN27 .... 152 A6
 Seaford BN25 .... 180 F5
Holtview Rd BN2 ..... 165 B8
HOLTYE 3 F3
Holtye Ave RH19 .... 2 A3
Holtye Pl RH19 .... 2 B3
Holtye Rd RH19 .... 2 B3
Holy Cross CE Prim Sch
 TN22 .... 78 C7
Holyhead Cl BN27 ... 129 A1
Holyrood RH19 .... 11 A8
Holywell Cl BN20 .... 188 E7
Holywell Rd BN20 ... 188 E7
Holywell Wlk BN27 .. 152 B7
Homebush Ave
 Saltdean BN2 .... 166 D1
 Saltdean BN7 .... 166 F3
Homecoast Ho BN10 . 178 B7
Homedane Ho **7** TN4 159 F7
Homedrive Ho BN3 ... 163 C8
Home Farm Bsns Ctr
 BN1 .... 143 D3
Home Farm Ct
 Frant TN3 .... 17 C4
 Horsted Keynes RH17 .. 33 C5
Home Farm La TN2 ..... 8 E8
Home Farm Rd BN1, BN2 143 D3
Homefield Cl BN25 ... 180 F4
Homefield Rd BN25 .. 180 F4
Homegate Ho **3** BN21 184 F3
Homeglade Ho BN20 . 188 B8
Homehill Ho **7** TN40 157 C4
Homelands BN1 ...... 157 A6
Homelatch Ho **1** BN21 185 A3

Homelawn Ho **3** TN40 157 E4
Homelees Ho BN1 .... 189 A3
Homeleigh BN1 .... 189 A3
Homeopathic Hospl TN1 .. 8 A3
Home Platt RH19 ...... 21 A6
Home Rd BN1 .... 142 E1
Homeridge Ho BN2 .. 166 D1
Homeshore Ho BN25 . 181 A3
Homestall Rd RH19 .... 11 E8
Homestead La RH15 ... 73 C6
Homestead The TN3 ... 15 C7
Hometye Ho BN25 ... 180 D3
Homewarr Ho **4** TN40 157 E4
Homewood Cl BN22 .. 185 B6
Homewood Rd TN3 ..... 6 F3
Honeycrag Cl BN26 .. 173 A7
Honey Croft BN3 ..... 141 C4
Honey La BN8 .... 149 D7
Honeypot La BN7, BN8 . 100 B7
Honeysuckle Cl
 Eastbourne BN23 .... 174 B3
 Hailsham BN27 .... 152 B5
 St Leonards TN37 .... 136 D5
Honeysuckle La BN27 . 127 B3
Honeyway Cl BN26 ... 172 F3
Honies Ct TN39 .... 157 C6
Hood Cl BN23 .... 185 E7
HOOE 155 D8
HOOE COMMON 132 F2
Hoo Gdns BN20 ...... 173 B1
HOOK GREEN 19 C4
Hook Hill TN5 .... 31 A6
Hookswood Cl TN6 .... 26 A3
Hoopers Cl BN7 ...... 190 A4
Hoo The BN20 .... 173 B1
Hoover Cl TN37 ...... 135 F7
Hope Cotts BN42 .... 161 E8
Hopehouse La TN17, TN18. 47 E7
Hopewell Cl **3** BN43 161 B6
Hopfield Gdns TN22 .. 78 E8
Hopgarden Cl
 Hastings TN34 .... 159 E8
 Lamberhurst TN3 ..... 20 A5
Hop Gdn TN22 .... 36 C2
Hoppers Croft La TN19 . 62 B6
Hopwood Gdns TN4 ..... 8 A6
HORAM 106 E7
Horam Pk Cl TN21 ... 106 F7
Horatio Ho BN1 ...... 189 B3
Horebeech La TN21 .. 107 A6
Horizon BN3 .... 162 F6
Horizon Cl
 Portslade-by-S BN41 .. 162 B8
 Royal Tunbridge Wells TN4 . 8 B8
Horleigh Green Rd TN20. 39 C1
Horley Pl BN2 .... 164 E6
Hornbeam TN19 .... 62 B7
Hornbeam Ave TN39 . 157 A4
Hornbeams The RH15 . 72 D4
Hornblower Cotts TN19 . 44 C1
Hornbuckles Cl BN8 .. 100 E7
Hornby Pl BN2 .... 144 A1
Hornby Rd BN2 ...... 144 A1
HORNEY COMMON 54 E8
Horning Cl BN23 ..... 174 B4
HORNS CROSS 67 A1
Horns Rd TN18 .... 45 D8
Horntye Park Sports & Con
 Ctr TN34 .... 159 D8
Horntye Pk TN37, TN38 .. 159 D8
Horntye Rd TN37 ..... 136 C1
Horsa Cl BN23 .... 185 E8
Horsegrove Ave TN5 ... 31 F1
Horsegrove La TN6 ..... 39 B8
Horseshoe Cl TN38 .. 136 B2
Horseshoe La TN31 .... 68 A1
Horsewalk BN27, TN33 . 154 E7
Horseys Dr BN9 ...... 179 D7
Horsfield Rd BN7 .... 123 B3
Horsgate Ho RH17 ..... 50 A8
Horsgate La RH17 ..... 50 A6
Horsham Ave BN10 .. 178 C7
Horsham Avenue N
 BN10 .... 178 C8
Horsham Cl BN2 ..... 164 F6
Horsted Ct BN1 ...... 189 B4
HORSTED GREEN 78 A3
Horsted Ho **1** RH16 . 50 F3
Horsted Keynes Ind Pk
 RH17 .... 33 B7
Horsted Keynes Sta RH17 33 A7
Horsted La
 Danehill RH17 .... 34 A4
 Isfield TN22 .... 102 F7
 Sharpthorne RH19 ..... 21 B3
Horsted Pond La TN22 . 78 A3
Horsted Square Ind Est
 TN22 .... 78 A6
Horsye Rd BN22 ..... 185 B7
Horton Rd BN1 ...... 143 B1
Hoskins Pl RH19 .... 2 A4
Hosmers Field TN6 .... 39 D8
HOUGHTON GREEN 70 D2
Houghton Green La TN31. 70 C2
Houghton La TN31 ..... 70 C3
Houndean Cl BN7 .... 146 A8
Houndean Rise BN7 .. 145 F8
Hova Villas BN3 ...... 163 B6
Hove Bsns Ctr BN3 .. 163 B8
Hovedene BN3 .... 163 C7
Hove Ent Ctr BN41 .. 162 C6
Hove Manor **8** BN3 .. 163 A6
Hove Mus & Art Gall★
 BN3 .... 163 A6
Hove Park Gdns BN3 . 142 B1
Hove Park Rd BN3 ... 142 C1
Hove Park Sch (Nevill
 Campus) BN3 .... 142 A1

Hove Park Sch (Valley Campus) BN3. . . . . 141 D2
Hove Park Villas BN3. . . . 163 B8
Hove Park Way BN3. . . . . 142 C1
Hove Pl BN3. . . . . 163 B5
Hove St BN3. . . . . 163 A6
Hove Sta BN3. . . . . 163 B8
Hove Tech Ctr 1 BN3 . . . 163 A8
Howard Ave RH15. . . . . . . 72 E4
Howard Cl BN27 . . . . 152 D6
Howard Ct
Hove BN3. . . . . 142 A2
Peacehaven BN10 . . . . . . 178 B7
Howard Gdns TN2. . . . . 8 A1
Howard Ho
Bexhill TN39. . . . . 156 E4
1 Eastbourne BN21. . . . . . 185 A1
Peacehaven BN10 . . . . . . 167 D1
Howard Pl BN1 . . . . 189 A4
Howard Rd BN2. . . . . 164 C7
Howards Cres TN39 . . . . 156 C4
Howard Sq BN21. . . . . . . 185 A2
Howard Terr BN1 . . . . . . 189 A4
Howbourne La TN22 . . . . . 56 E5
Howes Cotts TN18 . . . . . . 45 F8
Howey Cl BN9 . . . . 168 F1
Howland Cl 4 BN23. . . . . 175 A1
Howlett Cl TN38 . . . . 135 F4
Howlett Dr BN27. . . . . . . 129 B2
Howletts Cl BN22 . . . . . . 173 F1
How's Cl TN31. . . . . 90 B5
How We Lived Then Mus of Shops & Social History★ 24 BN21. . . . . 185 A2
Hoyle Rd BN10. . . . . 178 C7
Hubbards Hill TN6 . . . . 25 B6
Hudson Cl BN23 . . . . 185 G7
Hudson Ct BN22 . . . . 185 C6
Huggett's La BN22 . . . . . . 173 B3
Hughenden Ct 2 TN34 . . 136 F2
Hughenden Pl 1 TN34 . . 136 F2
Hughenden Rd TN34 . . . . 160 A6
Hughes Rd BN2. . . . . 164 B8
Hughes Way TN22. . . . . 78 C8
Hugletts La TN21. . . . . 83 A7
Humboldt Ct TN2 . . . . 8 D5
Humphrey Lodge RH15 . . . 73 D3
Humphrey's Gap BN43 . . . 161 A7
Hundred Acre La BN6, RH17 . . . . 74 B2
Hundredhouse La TN31 . . 90 F4
HUNGERSHALL PARK 7 E2
Hungershall Park Cl TN4 . . . 7 E1
Hungershall Pk TN4. . . . . . . 7 E2
Hunloke Ave BN22 . . . . . . 185 B6
Hunston Cl BN2. . . . . 165 F7
Hunters Way
Royal Tunbridge Wells TN2. . . 7 F1
Uckfield TN22. . . . . 78 B8
Hunting Cl TN40 . . . . 157 C5
Huntingdon Rd TN6. . . . . . 25 F1
Huntingdon Way RH15 . . . 73 D5
Huntington Ct BN7. . . . . 190 C2
Huntley Mill Rd TN5. . . . . . 31 E3
Huntleys Pk TN4 . . . . 7 F5
Hunt's Gate RH17 . . . . 52 E3
Hurdis Rd BN25. . . . . 180 A6
Hurrell Rd TN34. . . . . 160 B6
Hurst Cres BN41 . . . . 162 B8
Hurst Ct BN1 . . . . 142 D1
Hurst Farm Rd RH19 . . . . . 10 D7
Hurstfield Cl RH17 . . . . . . 51 A2
HURST GREEN 45 B3
Hurst Green CE Sch TN19. . 45 A2
Hurst Hill BN1 . . . . 143 C5
Hurst La
Eastbourne BN21. . . . . . . 184 D4
Sedlescombe TN33 . . . . . . 88 F3
Windmill Hill BN27. . . . . . 131 B5
Hurstpierpoint Coll BN6. . 97 B8
Hurst Rd
Eastbourne BN21. . . . . . . 184 D5
Hassocks BN6 . . . . 97 D4
Hurst Shaw TN21 . . . . 107 C8
Hurst The TN2. . . . . 8 E7
Hurst Way TN35. . . . . 137 A6
Hurst Wickham Cl BN6. . . . 97 C5
Hurstwood 6 BN2 . . . . . . 164 F5
Hurstwood Cl TN40 . . . . . 158 B5
Hurstwood La
Haywards Heath RH17 . . . . 51 A2
Royal Tunbridge Wells TN4. . . . 7 F3
Sharpthorne RH17, RH19 . . 21 D1
Hurstwood Park Hospl RH17. . . . . 51 A2
Hurstwood Pk TN4. . . . . 7 F3
Hurstwood Rd TN22. . . . . . 56 A6
Hurtis Hill TN6. . . . . 37 E7
Hutton Rd BN1. . . . . 143 B3
Hyde Bsns Pk The BN2 . . 164 F8
Hyde Cl BN7 . . . . 145 E5
Hyde Gdns BN21. . . . . 185 A2
Hydehurst Cl TN6. . . . . 25 F1
Hyde Rd BN21 . . . . 184 F2
Hyde Tynings Cl BN20 . . . 188 D8
Hydneye The BN22 . . . . . . 173 F1
Hydney St BN22. . . . . 185 C5
Hylands Cl TN31 . . . . 67 B6
Hylands Yd 5 TN31 . . . . . . 93 B5
Hylden Cl BN2 . . . . 165 B8
Hyperion Ave BN26 . . . . . 172 E6
Hythe Ave TN38. . . . . 158 B5
Hythe Cl
Polegate BN26. . . . . 173 C7
Seaford BN25 . . . . 181 C5
Hythe Cres BN25. . . . . 181 C4
Hythe Rd BN1. . . . . 143 A2
Hythe View BN25 . . . . 181 C4

I

Ian Cl TN40. . . . . 157 F7
ICKLESHAM. 116 E6
Icklesham CE Prim Sch TN36. . . . . 116 E6
Icklesham Dr TN38. . . . . . 135 D3
IDEN. 70 B4
Iden Cl BN2. . . . . 164 E5
Iden Ct TN34. . . . . 136 D3
Iden Hurst BN6 . . . . 97 A7
Iden Rd TN31 . . . . 70 B3
Iden's La TN21. . . . . 82 D8
Iden St BN22. . . . . 174 A2
Ifield Cl BN2. . . . . 166 E2
Ifield Mill Cl BN24. . . . . . . 174 B5
IFORD 146 B3
Iford Cl BN9 . . . . 168 D1
Iford & Kingston CE Prim Sch BN7. . . . . 145 F5
Ilex Ct BN42 . . . . 141 A1
Ilex Gn 6 BN27 . . . . 129 B1
Image Cross RH19 . . . . 21 A5
Imberhorne Bsns Ctr RH19 . 1 B3
Imberhorne La RH19 . . . . 1 B2
Imberhorne Lower Sch RH19. . . . . 1 D3
Imberhorne Sch RH19. . . . . . 1 B3
Imberhorne Way RH19 . . . . . 1 B3
Impala Gdns TN4 . . . . 8 B6
Imperial Arc BN1 . . . . 189 A2
Independent Bsns Pk The RH19. . . . . 1 A3
Ingham Dr BN1 . . . . 143 D6
Ingleside TN38. . . . . 135 E4
Ingleside Dr TN6. . . . . 25 E2
Inglewood Gdns TN38 . . . 135 E4
Ingram Crescent E BN3. . 162 E8
Ingram Crescent W BN3. 162 E8
Ingram Ct BN3. . . . . 162 E7
Ingrams Ave TN39. . . . . . . 157 C7
Ingrams Ho 4 RH16. . . . . . . 50 E3
Ingrams Way BN27. . . . . . . 152 A6
Inholmes Cl RH15 . . . . 73 C3
Inholmes Park Rd RH15 . . 73 B3
Inkerman Terr TN31. . . . . . . 94 A3
Inkpen La RH18. . . . . 11 F1
Innham's Wood TN6 . . . . . . 25 E4
Innings Dr BN24 . . . . 175 C4
Innovation Dr RH15 . . . . . . 72 D2
Insley Ct TN39. . . . . 156 F3
Institute Wlk 6 RH19 . . . . . . 1 E1
International Coll of Oriental Medicine The RH19 . . . . . . 1 D2
Inverness Rd 4 BN2 . . . . . 164 C8
Inwood Cres BN1 . . . . 142 E1
Iona Cl BN27. . . . . 129 A3
Iona Way 12 RH16. . . . . 50 E4
Irelands La 7 BN7 . . . . 123 B1
Ironlatch Ave TN38. . . . . . 135 F2
Ironlatch Cl TN38 . . . . 135 F2
Ironstones TN3 . . . . 7 B3
Ironstone Way TN22. . . . . . 78 E7
Irving Ho TN1. . . . . 8 B5
Isaac's La RH16, RH15. . . . . 50 A2
Isabel Cl BN25 . . . . 180 E5
Isabel Cres BN3. . . . . 162 E8
Isenhurst Cresent TN21 . . 58 C3
ISFIELD 102 E7
Isfield Rd
Brighton BN1. . . . . 143 C2
Isfield BN8, TN22. . . . . 102 E5
Isfield Sta★ TN22 . . . . 102 E7
Isherwood TN33 . . . . 112 B5
Islingword Pl BN2. . . . . . . 164 C6
Islingword Rd BN2. . . . . . . 164 C7
Islingword St BN2. . . . . . . 189 C3
Ismay Lodge TN39 . . . . . . 156 D3
Iveagh Cres BN9 . . . . 168 D2
Ive Grange TN33 . . . . 132 F5
Ivor Rd BN2 . . . . 144 C1
Ivors La BN8. . . . . 123 B5
Ivory Pl BN2. . . . . 189 C3
Ivy Cotts BN8 . . . . 104 C6
Ivydene Ind Est RH19. . . . . 11 D7
Ivy Dene La RH19 . . . . 11 D6
Ivyhouse Employment Area TN35. . . . . 160 B8
Ivyhouse La TN35 . . . . 137 B6
Ivy La TN3. . . . . 18 A5
Ivy Mews 13 BN3. . . . . 163 D5
Ivy Pl BN1, BN3 . . . . 163 D5
Ivy Terr BN21. . . . . 184 F3

J

Jackdaws The TN22. . . . . . 78 E4
Jackies La BN8 . . . . 76 B7
Jack O'Dandy Cl BN21. . . 184 C7
Jacks Hill TN7 . . . . 13 D2
Jackson Mews BN9 . . . . . 179 C7
Jackson St BN2. . . . . 189 C4
Jacobs Acre TN40. . . . . . . 157 C5
Jacqueline Du Pre Ct 6 BN2 . . . . 164 C5
Jamaica Way BN23. . . . . . 185 F8
James Ave BN27 . . . . 130 E6
James Bradford Almhouses RH16 . . . . 50 C4
Jameson Cres TN38. . . . . 136 A3
Jameson Mews 9 TN40 157 D4
Jameson Rd TN40. . . . . . . 157 D4
Jane Murray Way BN6, RH15 . . . . 72 C3
Janes Cl RH15 . . . . 73 C5
Janes La RH15. . . . . 73 D4
Janeston Ct 4 BN3 . . . . . 163 C7
Japonica Cl BN43 . . . . 140 B1
Jardine Ct TN6 . . . . 25 F2
Jarretts Cl 4 TN31. . . . . . . 93 B5
JARVIS BROOK. 38 D8
Jarvisbrook Cl TN39. . . . . 156 D3
Jarvis Brook Ctry Pk TN6. 38 B8
Jarvis Brook Prim Sch TN6. . . . . 38 C7
Jasmine Cotts TN3. . . . . . . 15 C7
Jasmine Ct
Brighton BN1. . . . . 142 F5
Hove BN3. . . . . 163 D7
Jasmine Gn 2 BN27 . . . . 129 B1
Jasmine Way TN39. . . . . . 156 F3
Jason Cl BN10 . . . . 178 C7
Jay Cl BN23. . . . . 174 C2
Jay Rd BN10. . . . . 178 E6
Jays The
Burgess Hill RH15 . . . . 72 E4
Uckfield TN22. . . . . 78 D4
Jefferies RH17. . . . . 33 C4
Jefferies Way TN6 . . . . 25 F4
Jefferson Way TN37. . . . . 135 F6
Jeffreys Way TN22. . . . . . . 55 D1
Jellicoe Cl BN23 . . . . 185 F7
JENKINS' GREEN 174 C8
Jenner's La TN35 . . . . 137 E6
Jenner's Way BN7 . . . . . . 190 B3
Jephson Cl BN20. . . . . 188 F8
Jerome Cl BN23 . . . . 174 E2
Jersey St BN2 . . . . 189 C3
Jervis Ave BN23 . . . . 185 E6
Jesmond Cl BN3 . . . . 162 E7
Jesmond Rd BN3 . . . . 162 E7
Jesters RH16 . . . . 73 C7
JEVINGTON. 183 C8
Jevington Cl TN39 . . . . . . 156 D2
Jevington Ct BN43 . . . . . . 161 D6
Jevington Dr
Brighton BN2. . . . . 143 D1
Seaford BN25 . . . . 180 D4
Jevington Gdns BN21 . . . 185 A1
Jevington Ho 9 BN21. . . . 184 D4
Jevington Rd BN26. . . . . . 172 D2
Jew St BN1. . . . . 189 B2
Jikack Ind Est BN6. . . . . . . 72 B4
Jireh Ct RH16. . . . . 50 E5
Joan Hughes Ct BN26 . . . 173 A6
Joan Nightingale Ho RH16 . . . . 50 C4
Joe's La BN27 . . . . 131 B5
John Dann Cl TN22. . . . . . . 80 A6
John MacAdam Way TN37 . . . . 136 A6
Johns Cl BN10 . . . . 167 C2
JOHN'S CROSS 87 C7
John's Cross Rd TN32 . . . . 87 C8
Johnson Bank 4 BN2 . . . 164 C7
Johnson Cl TN37. . . . . 135 F6
Johnson Dr RH15 . . . . 73 D3
John Spare Ct TN4. . . . . 8 A6
John St
Brighton BN2. . . . . 189 C3
Royal Tunbridge Wells TN4. . . 8 A5
Johnston Pl 1 BN23 . . . . . 175 A1
John Whittle Lodge BN2 143 C1
Jonas Dr TN5. . . . . 29 E5
Jonas La TN5. . . . . 29 E5
Jordan Ct BN3. . . . . 162 E8
Jordans La BN22. . . . . 173 D3
Jordans Lane E BN22. . . . 173 D3
Jordans Lane W BN22. . . 173 C3
Jordans The RH19 . . . . 10 E8
Joyce Villas TN21. . . . . . . 106 E5
Jubilee Cl RH16. . . . . 51 A4
Jubilee Cotts 4 TN6. . . . . . 37 F8
Jubilee Ct
Brighton BN2. . . . . 143 E2
Peacehaven BN10 . . . . 178 B7
Jubilee Gdns BN25. . . . . . 181 A5
Jubilee Ho
Eastbourne BN22. . . . . 185 B4
Newhaven BN9 . . . . 179 C7
Jubilee Rd
Bexhill TN39. . . . . 157 A7
Burgess Hill RH15 . . . . 72 E2
Portslade-by-S BN41 . . . . . 162 A8
Jubilee St BN1. . . . . 189 B2
Judges Cl RH19. . . . . 10 E8
Judge's Terr RH19 . . . . 10 E8
Juggs Cl BN7 . . . . 146 B8
Juggs Rd BN7 . . . . 146 A7
Jugg's Rd BN7. . . . . 146 B7
Julian Ct 5 BN43 . . . . 161 C8
Julian Rd BN3 . . . . 163 E7
Junction Cl RH15 . . . . 73 C4
Junction Mews RH15. . . . . . 73 B3
Junction Rd
Bodiam TN18, TN32 . . . . . . 46 A3
Brighton BN1. . . . . 189 A3
Burgess Hill RH15 . . . . 73 B3
Cripp's Corner TN32, TN33 . 88 D5
Eastbourne BN21. . . . . 185 A3
Staplecross TN32. . . . . 65 C5
St Leonards TN37 . . . . 136 B7
Junction St BN26 . . . . 173 B6
Juniper Cl
Portslade-by-S BN41 . . . . . 141 B3
Seaford BN25 . . . . 181 C3
St Leonards TN38 . . . . 135 E3
Juniper Ct 11 RH16. . . . . . . 50 C2
Juniper Wlk BN43. . . . . . . 140 C1
JURY'S GAP 95 D1
Jury's Gap Coastguard Cotts TN31 . . . . 95 E1
Jury's Gap Rd TN29 . . . . . 96 F5

K

Kammond Ave BN25 . . . . 181 B5
Kane Hythe Rd TN33 . . . . 111 D6
Karenza Ct BN1. . . . . 164 A8
Katherine Way BN25 . . . . 180 D5
Keaton Ho 2 RH16. . . . . . . 50 E6
Keats Cl TN38. . . . . 158 F6
Keats Pl RH19 . . . . 1 D1
Keats Wlk BN23. . . . . 174 E3
Kebbell Lodge 12 BN2. . . 189 C2
Kedale Rd BN25. . . . . 180 E4
Keel Gdns TN4. . . . . 7 E8
Keere St BN7 . . . . 190 A1
Keith Wlk BN23. . . . . 185 F6
Keld Ave TN22 . . . . 78 D6
Keld Cl TN22. . . . . 78 D6
Keld Dr TN22 . . . . 78 D6
Kelly Rd BN3 . . . . 142 D1
Kelsey Cotts BN8 . . . . 124 E6
Kelsey Ct RH15 . . . . 73 D3
Kemble Cl TN2. . . . . 8 E7
Kemp Ct BN2 . . . . 164 E4
Kemps Farm Rd TN6 . . . . . 26 B1
Kemp St BN1 . . . . 189 B3
Kemps Way TN32 . . . . 64 C5
KEMP TOWN. 164 D4
Kemptown Mews 11 BN2 . . . . 164 E4
Kemp Town Pl 18 BN2. . . 164 D4
Kendal Ct BN9 . . . . 179 E7
Kendall Ct RH16 . . . . 50 F2
Kendal Pk TN4. . . . . 7 E5
Kendal Rd BN3 . . . . 162 F8
Kenilworth Cl BN2 . . . . . . 144 A2
Kenilworth Rd TN38. . . . . 159 B7
Kenmure Ave BN1 . . . . . . 143 A7
Kennard Ct RH18. . . . . 11 E3
Kennedy Ave RH19. . . . . 1 D3
Kennedy Cl TN21. . . . . 82 B6
Kennedy Ct TN38 . . . . 136 B3
Kennedy Rd TN40 . . . . 157 E4
Kennedy Way BN9 . . . . . . 179 B8
Kennel Cnr BN8. . . . . 124 F6
Kennel La TN39. . . . . 156 C4
Kennett Cl BN24 . . . . 173 F5
Kenrith Ct TN34. . . . . 136 E2
Kensington 7 BN23. . . . . . 175 A1
Kensington Cl TN38 . . . . . 135 D3
Kensington Gdns BN1. . . . 189 B3
Kensington Pl BN1. . . . . . 189 B3
Kensington St BN1. . . . . . 189 B3
Kent Cl
Bexhill TN40. . . . . 158 A5
Shoreham-by-S BN43. . . . . 161 C7
Winchelsea TN36. . . . . 117 E7
Kent Ct BN20 . . . . 184 B6
Kent & E Sussex Steam Rly★ TN17. . . . . 49 C5
Kent Fields BN7 . . . . 145 E5
Kent Ho TN1. . . . . 8 C6
Kentish Gdns TN2. . . . . 16 E8
Kentish Mans 15 TN1. . . . . . 8 A2
Kent La TN32 . . . . 85 F6
Kenton Cl TN39 . . . . 157 A5
Kenton Ct 7 BN21 . . . . 185 A1
Kenton Rd BN3 . . . . 162 D7
Kent Rd
Royal Tunbridge Wells TN4. . . 8 A6
St Leonards TN38 . . . . 135 F4
Kent's La BN6. . . . . 99 C7
Kents Rd RH16. . . . . 50 F3
Kent St TN33 . . . . 114 A3
Kent & Sussex Hospl TN4. . 8 A4
Kenwards BN1. . . . . 143 D7
Kenwood Cl TN34 . . . . 160 B8
Kenya Ct 2 BN1 . . . . 163 E6
Keppel Rd TN34. . . . . 136 F2
Kepplestone BN20. . . . . . . 188 E8
Kerrara Terr BN22 . . . . . . 185 B5
Kerrison Mews 7 BN3 . . 163 D5
Kestrel Cl
Bexhill TN40. . . . . 157 E4
Hove BN3. . . . . 163 D8
Kestrel Ct BN27. . . . . 152 D7
Kestrels The
Shoreham-by-S BN43. . . . . 161 A8
St Leonards TN38 . . . . 135 F5
Ketcham Cnr BN24. . . . . . . 174 E6
Ketche's La RH17, TN22 . . . 52 E7
Kevin Gdns BN2. . . . . 165 E8
Kewhurst Ave TN39 . . . . . 156 D3
Kewhurst Ho TN39 . . . . . . 156 E4
Kew St BN1. . . . . 189 A3
Keymer Ave BN10 . . . . 178 D7
Keymer Cl
Eastbourne BN23. . . . . 174 E1
St Leonards TN38 . . . . 158 E6
Keymer Ct RH15 . . . . 73 B2
Keymer End RH16. . . . . 50 D3
Keymer Gdns RH15. . . . . . . 73 B1
Keymer Ho 18 BN21 . . . . . 184 E4
Keymer Par RH15 . . . . 73 B2
Keymer Pk BN6. . . . . 98 B3
Keymer Rd
Brighton BN1. . . . . 143 B6
Burgess Hill RH15. . . . . 98 B8
Hassocks BN6 . . . . 97 F3
Key W BN23 . . . . 185 G8
Kibbles La TN4 . . . . 7 E8
Kidbrook RH16 . . . . 51 B6
Kidbrooke Rise RH18. . . . . . 11 E2
Kidd's Hill TN7. . . . . 24 A4
Kilburn Terr 6 BN21. . . . . 185 A3
Kildare Cl TN34 . . . . 160 B8
Kildare Ct BN20. . . . . 184 C3
Kilda St 1 BN22 . . . . 185 B4
Kilnbank TN2 . . . . 8 C7
Kilnbarn Ct RH16 . . . . 50 D2
Kilnbarn Way RH16 . . . . . . 50 D2
Kiln Cl TN22 . . . . 78 D4
KILNDOWN 20 F3
Kiln Dr TN31. . . . . 93 B8
Kiln La
Haywards Heath RH16 . . . . 51 B5
Hooe TN33. . . . . 155 B7
Isfield TN22. . . . . 102 E5
Kiln Rd BN8 . . . . 125 A8
Kiln The RH15 . . . . 73 C3
Kilnwood La BN8 . . . . 100 E7
Kilpatrick Cl BN23 . . . . . . 174 D3
Kimberley Ct TN39 . . . . . . 157 C6
Kimberley Rd
Brighton BN2. . . . . 143 D1
Seaford BN25 . . . . 180 C4
Kindersley Cl RH19. . . . . 2 B3
Kinfauns Ave BN22. . . . . . 185 B6
King Charles Pl 10 BN43. 161 A6
King Edward Ave TN34 . . 136 C3
King Edward Cl TN34. . . . 136 C3
King Edward's Par BN20. 188 F8
Kingfisher Cl TN22. . . . . . . 78 E5
Kingfisher Ct
Hailsham BN27 . . . . 152 D7
Uckfield TN22. . . . . 78 B6
Kingfisher Dr
Eastbourne BN23. . . . . 174 C2
Haywards Heath RH16 . . . . 50 C1
Kingfisher Rise RH19. . . . . 10 F8
King George Ave RH19 . . . . 1 C3
King George Rd BN43 . . . 161 D8
King George V Hill TN1. . . . 8 C5
King George VI Ave BN3. 142 A3
King George VI Dr BN3. . 142 A4
King George VI Mans BN3 . . . . 141 F2
King Henry's Rd BN7 . . . . 123 B2
King John Ct 7 BN43 . . . . 161 A6
King Offa Prim Sch TN39. . . . . 157 B5
King Offa Way TN40. . . . . 157 C5
King Pl BN1 . . . . 189 A2
King's Ave
Eastbourne BN21. . . . . 184 E5
Newhaven BN9 . . . . 168 E1
Rye TN31. . . . . 93 D6
KINGS BANK 68 A3
King's Bank La TN31 . . . . . 68 A3
Kingsbury Rd BN1 . . . . . . 189 B4
Kingsbury St BN1 . . . . 189 B4
Kings Chase TN6. . . . . 25 D3
Kings Cl
Bexhill TN40. . . . . 157 C4
Eastbourne BN21. . . . . 184 F5
Peacehaven BN10 . . . . 167 B1
King's Cl BN21. . . . . 184 E5
Kings Copse 9 RH19. . . . . . 10 F8
Kingscote Lodge BN1 . . . . 143 F5
Kingscote Way BN1 . . . . . 189 B4
Kingscott Cl TN39 . . . . 157 B8
Kings Court E 4 BN23 . . . 185 F8
Kings Court S 6 BN23 . . . 185 F8
Kings Court W 5 BN23. . . 185 F8
Kings Ct
Brighton BN1. . . . . 189 B2
Crowborough TN6 . . . . 25 E2
Kingsdale Cl
Battle TN33 . . . . 112 F3
St Leonards TN37 . . . . 136 C6
Kings Dr
Eastbourne BN21. . . . . 184 E6
Hassocks BN6 . . . . 97 F4
King's Dr BN21 . . . . 184 D7
King's Espl BN3. . . . . 163 A5
Kingsfield Cl BN42 . . . . . . 161 E8
Kingsfield Cotts BN8. . . . 149 E8
Kingsfold 2 BN2 . . . . 164 F5
Kingsfold Ct 1 BN25. . . . . 180 F2
Kingsford BN23. . . . . 185 D7
Kings Gate
Haywards Heath RH16 . . . . 50 E6
Hove BN3. . . . . 163 C8
King's Gdns BN3. . . . . 163 B5
King's Hill Rd TN19 . . . . . . 62 B3
Kingsland 3 BN20. . . . . . . 184 F1
Kingsland Cl BN43 . . . . . . 161 C7
Kingsley Cl TN37. . . . . 136 A5
Kingsley Ct
7 Brighton BN1 . . . . 163 E5
Wadhurst TN5 . . . . 30 A4
Kingsley Rd
Brighton BN1. . . . . 142 D1
Lewes BN7. . . . . 123 B2
King's Manor Com Coll BN43. . . . . 161 D8
Kingsmarsh Cotts TN20 . . 58 B6
Kingsmead BN25. . . . . 180 E5
Kingsmead Cl BN25 . . . . . 180 E4
Kings Mead Ct BN20 . . . . 188 D7
King's Mead La BN25. . . . 180 D4
Kingsmead Way BN25 . . . 180 E4
Kingsmead Wlk BN25 . . . 180 E4
Kingsmere BN1. . . . . 142 E2
Kingsmere Ct 4 BN21. . . . 184 D4
Kingsmere Way BN23 . . . 185 F8
Kings Mews BN3. . . . . 163 B6
Kings Par BN1 . . . . 143 A2
Kings Pk TN2 . . . . 8 D3
Kings Rd BN42 . . . . 140 E1
King's Rd
Brighton BN1, BN3 . . . . . . 163 E5
Haywards Heath RH16 . . . . 50 F3

King's Rd *continued*
St Leonards TN37 .... 159 C7
Kings Ride
Alfriston BN26 .... 170 F3
Burgess Hill RH15 .... 73 D1
Seaford BN25 .... 180 D4
King St
Brighton BN1 .... 189 B2
East Grinstead RH19 .... 1 E1
Kingsthorpe Rd BN3 .... 162 F8
Kings Toll Rd TN2 .... 9 F6
Kingston Ave BN25 .... 181 B3
Kingston Bay Rd BN43 .... 161 C6
Kingston Broadway
BN43 .... 140 D1
Kingston Buci Fst Sch
BN43 .... 161 B8
KINGSTON BY SEA 161 C7
Kingston Cl
Brighton BN1 .... 143 E6
Hove BN3 .... 141 E2
Seaford BN25 .... 181 B3
Shoreham-by-S BN43 .... 161 C8
Kingston Ct 17 BN43 .... 161 C8
Kingston Gn BN25 .... 181 B3
Kingston Ho 15 BN21 .... 184 F4
Kingston La BN42, BN43 .... 161 D7
Kingston Quay 13 BN23 .... 185 F8
Kingston Rd
Eastbourne BN22 .... 173 F2
Lewes BN7 .... 146 B7
KINGSTONRIDGE 145 D6
Kingston Ridge BN7 .... 145 D6
Kingston Villas TN21 .... 106 E5
Kingston Way
Seaford BN25 .... 181 B3
Shoreham-by-S BN43 .... 140 D1
Kingsway
Hove BN3 .... 163 B5
Seaford BN25 .... 180 D4
Kings Way RH15 .... 73 D2
Kingsway Ct
Hove BN3 .... 163 C5
Seaford BN25 .... 180 D4
Kings Well Ct 14 BN25 .... 180 E2
Kings Wlk 10 TN34 .... 159 F8
Kingswood Ave TN39 .... 156 F6
Kingswood Cl TN2 .... 8 C3
Kingswood Flats BN2 .... 189 C2
Kingswood Rd TN2 .... 8 C3
Kingswood St BN2 .... 189 B2
King Wood Hill TN31 .... 90 A3
Kinross Ct 5 BN21 .... 185 A4
Kinsale Ct 5 BN3 .... 163 D7
Kinver La TN40 .... 158 A6
Kipling Ave BN2 .... 165 E7
Kipling Ct
Bexhill TN40 .... 157 C6
3 Haywards Heath RH16 .... 50 D5
Rottingdean BN2 .... 166 A1
Kipling Way RH19 .... 1 C1
Kipling Wlk 1 BN23 .... 174 E2
Kirby Dr BN10 .... 167 B1
Kirdford Cl RH15 .... 73 C1
Kirkdale Rd TN1 .... 8 B4
Kirkstall Cl BN22 .... 173 E3
Kirk Way BN20 .... 184 B5
Kitchenour La TN31 .... 68 E5
Kite Cl TN38 .... 158 E8
Kites Nest Wlk TN39 .... 156 B4
Kitilear Ct BN3 .... 163 D6
Knebworth Rd TN39 .... 156 F5
Knelle Rd TN32 .... 64 A4
Knelle View TN31 .... 67 B7
Knepp Cl BN2 .... 143 F2
Knightsbridge Cl TN4 .... 7 F5
Knightsbridge Ct TN1 .... 8 B6
Knights Cl TN2 .... 9 D7
Knights Gate Rd BN1 .... 144 C7
Knights Gdn BN27 .... 152 B6
Knights Mdw
Battle TN33 .... 112 F4
Uckfield TN22 .... 78 E8
Knights Pk TN2 .... 8 F8
Knight's Ridge TN2 .... 9 D7
Knights Way TN2 .... 8 F8
Knockhatch Adventure Pk★
BN27 .... 151 E7
Knole Ct 4 TN40 .... 157 D3
Knole Gr RH19 .... 1 C3
Knole Rd
Bexhill TN40 .... 157 D3
Rottingdean BN2 .... 166 A1
Knoll Bsns Ctr The BN3 .... 162 D8
Knoll Cl BN3 .... 141 D1
Knoll Cres BN22 .... 174 A1
Knoll Pl RH16 .... 51 B5
Knoll Rd BN22 .... 174 A2
Knoll Rise TN38 .... 159 A7
Knowle Cl
Crowborough TN6 .... 38 C8
Langton Green TN3 .... 6 F3
Knowle Cotts TN3 .... 17 E1
Knowle Ct TN38 .... 136 B1
Knowle Hill
Bodiam TN32 .... 65 D8
Mayfield TN20 .... 40 A1
Knowle La BN8 .... 104 A6
Knowle Pk
Crowborough TN6 .... 25 D2
Mayfield TN20 .... 40 A1
Knowle Rd TN35 .... 138 E5
Knowsley Ct TN37 .... 136 B6
Knoyle Rd BN1 .... 142 E2
Knyveton Ct RH15 .... 73 B3
Kylemore BN24 .... 175 B6
Kymer Gdns BN6 .... 98 A3

L

Laburnum Ave BN3 .... 141 E1
Laburnum Ct TN2 .... 8 C7
Laburnum Gdns TN40 .... 157 F6
Laburnum Gn 5 BN27 .... 129 B1
Laburnum Gr BN1 .... 143 B3
Laburnum Way RH16 .... 51 B4
Laburnum Wlk BN22 .... 173 D3
Labyrinth The 20 BN21 .... 185 A2
Lacys Hill BN8 .... 147 F8
Ladies Mile
Brighton BN1 .... 143 B7
Withyham TN6, TN7 .... 14 D4
Ladies Mile Cl BN1 .... 142 F6
Ladies' Mile Ct BN1 .... 142 E6
Ladies' Mile Rd BN1 .... 142 F6
Lady Bee Marina Ind Est
BN42 .... 161 E6
Ladycross Cl BN25 .... 181 C3
Ladyfern Ct TN2 .... 8 C4
Ladymead RH15 .... 73 C5
Lady Oak La TN5, TN17 .... 32 C7
Lady's Gift Rd TN4 .... 7 F8
Ladysmith Rd BN2 .... 164 D8
Lagwood Cl BN6 .... 97 F3
Laine Cl BN1 .... 142 E3
Laines The BN26 .... 170 F3
Lake Dr BN10 .... 178 B8
Lake Ho TN39 .... 156 D3
Lake House Cl TN39 .... 156 D4
Lakehurst La TN33 .... 110 B8
Lakelands Cl BN22 .... 174 A1
Lakelands Dr TN39 .... 156 D4
Lakeman Way TN4 .... 8 B7
Lake Rd TN4 .... 7 E4
Lakeside TN2 .... 8 E6
Lakeside Ct BN22 .... 174 A1
Lake St TN20, TN6 .... 40 D7
Lakeview 1 BN2 .... 164 C5
Lake View Rd RH19 .... 1 F5
Laleham Cl
Eastbourne BN21 .... 184 E4
St Leonards TN37 .... 136 C5
La Marne Ct TN34 .... 136 E2
LAMBERHURST 20 B5
Lamberhurst Rd TN3,
TN12 .... 20 C8
Lamberhurst St Mary's CE Prim Sch TN3 .... 20 B4
Lamberhurst Vineyard★
TN3 .... 20 A4
Lambert Pl BN7 .... 190 B4
Lambert Rd BN23 .... 174 E3
Lamberts Cotts TN33 .... 112 E3
Lamberts Rd TN2 .... 8 D8
Lamb House★ TN31 .... 93 C5
Lambourn Ave BN24 .... 174 A5
Lambourn Cl RH19 .... 1 E3
Lambourne Cl BN1 .... 143 C2
Lambourne Rd BN1 .... 143 C2
Lambourn Way TN2 .... 8 D1
Lampington Row TN3 .... 6 E3
Lampool Cnr TN22 .... 55 A7
Lampool Rdbt TN22 .... 55 A7
Lanark Ct BN20 .... 184 B6
Lancaster Ct
16 Eastbourne BN22 .... 185 B3
12 Hove BN3 .... 163 A6
Lancaster Dr RH19 .... 2 A3
Lancaster House Rd BN1 .... 144 B7
Lancaster Rd
Brighton BN1 .... 189 A4
St Leonards TN38 .... 135 F5
Lancaster St BN7 .... 190 B2
Lancing Cl TN34 .... 136 D3
Lancing Ct 5 BN2 .... 164 F5
Lancing Way BN26 .... 172 F4
Landgate TN31 .... 93 C6
Landgate Sq 4 TN31 .... 93 C6
LANDPORT 123 B2
Landport Farm Rd BN7 .... 123 A3
Landport Rd BN7 .... 190 A3
Landsdowne Way TN40 .... 157 E5
Landsdown Rd BN25 .... 181 C5
Landseer Rd BN3 .... 163 A8
Lanes The★ BN1 .... 189 B2
Lane The
Fordcombe TN3 .... 6 C5
Foxhole BN25 .... 182 A4
Langdale Cl BN23 .... 174 C4
Langdale Ct BN3 .... 162 F6
Langdale Gdns BN3 .... 162 F6
Langdale Rd BN3 .... 162 F6
Langham Cl
Hastings TN34 .... 136 F4
Ringmer BN8 .... 124 D5
Langham Rd
Hastings TN34 .... 136 F4
Robertsbridge TN32 .... 63 F4
Langholm Rd TN3 .... 6 F3
Langhurst 9 BN2 .... 164 E4
Langley Cl TN39 .... 157 B8
Langley Cres BN2 .... 144 E1
LANGNEY 174 D3
Langney Gn BN23 .... 185 E8
Langney Prim Sch BN23 .... 174 E1
Langney Rd BN21, BN22 .... 185 B3
Langney Rise BN23 .... 174 D2
Langney Sh Ctr BN23 .... 174 C2
LANGNEY VILLAGE 174 E2
Langridge Cl TN6 .... 37 D8
Langridge Dr
East Grinstead RH19 .... 10 E8
Langridge Dr *continued*
Portslade-by-S BN41 .... 141 B3
Langridge La RH16 .... 51 A5
Langridges Cl BN8 .... 76 C7
Langridge Way RH15 .... 72 E5
Langton Cl TN33 .... 112 E4
LANGTON GREEN 6 E3
Langton Green Prim Sch
TN3 .... 6 E4
Langton Rd
Rusthall TN3, TN4 .... 7 C3
Speldhurst TN3 .... 7 A7
Langton Ridge TN3 .... 7 B3
Langtye La BN26, BN8 .... 149 E6
Lansdowne Cres BN27 .... 129 B2
Lansdowne Ct
5 Eastbourne BN21 .... 185 A1
24 Hove BN3 .... 163 C6
Lansdowne Dr BN27 .... 129 A2
Lansdowne Gdns BN27 .... 129 B2
Lansdowne Mans 11
BN3 .... 163 D6
Lansdowne Mews 7
BN3 .... 163 D6
Lansdowne Pl BN3 .... 163 D6
Lansdowne Rd
Hailsham BN27 .... 129 B2
Hove BN1, BN3 .... 163 D6
Royal Tunbridge Wells TN1 .... 8 B4
Lansdowne Sq
1 Hove BN3 .... 163 D5
8 Royal Tunbridge Wells
TN1 .... 8 B4
Lansdowne St BN3 .... 163 D6
Lansdowne Way BN27 .... 129 B3
Lansdown Pl BN7 .... 190 B1
Lansdown Terr 5 TN21 .... 82 A6
Lanthorne Mews
Royal Tunbridge Wells,
Calverley Park TN1 .... 8 B3
Royal Tunbridge Wells TN1 .... 8 B5
Lapierre Rd BN9 .... 179 B7
Lapwing Cl
Camber TN31 .... 94 E3
Eastbourne BN23 .... 174 C2
Lapwing Ct BN27 .... 152 D7
Larch Cl
Heathfield TN21 .... 82 B5
St Leonards TN38 .... 136 A1
Woodingdean BN2 .... 165 F7
Larches Ho RH19 .... 2 B4
Larch Gdns BN22 .... 173 D3
Larch Way RH16 .... 51 B4
Larke Cl BN43 .... 161 C7
Larkfield Cl TN38 .... 136 A3
Larkfield Way BN1 .... 143 A4
Larkhill TN40 .... 157 C4
Lark Hill BN3 .... 141 E3
Lark Rise Cl RH16 .... 51 B5
Larkspur Dr BN23 .... 174 B3
Larnach Cl TN22 .... 78 D8
Lascelles Terr BN21 .... 185 A1
La Senera Pl BN23 .... 175 B1
Laser La 19 TN37 .... 159 C7
Lashbrooks Rd TN22 .... 78 B7
Latimer Rd BN22 .... 185 C4
Laton Rd TN34 .... 136 F2
LAUGHTON 126 C6
Laughton Cl BN23 .... 174 A4
Laughton Lodge BN8 .... 126 A8
Laughton Prim Sch BN8 .... 126 C6
Laughton Rd
Ringmer BN8 .... 125 D6
Woodingdean BN2 .... 165 F8
Laundry La RH17 .... 22 D1
Laureens Wlk BN2 .... 165 F1
Laurel 2 RH16 .... 50 D6
Laurel Bank
Bexhill TN40 .... 157 E5
Royal Tunbridge Wells TN4 .... 8 B8
Wadhurst TN5 .... 30 A4
Laurel Cl RH15 .... 73 D5
Laurel Dene RH19 .... 1 F1
Laurel La TN36 .... 116 F5
Laurel Rd TN2 .... 8 D7
Laurels The
4 Brighton BN2 .... 189 C5
1 Crowborough TN6 .... 25 F3
Uckfield TN22 .... 78 E8
Laurel Way TN2 .... 8 D7
Laurel Wlk TN38 .... 135 E3
Lauren Ct TN38 .... 158 F7
Lauriston Rd BN1 .... 142 E2
Lavant Cl TN39 .... 156 C6
Lavant Rd BN24 .... 174 B5
Lavender Cl
Eastbourne BN23 .... 174 B3
Hailsham BN27 .... 128 F1
Lavender Gdns TN5 .... 31 E1
Lavender Hill BN43 .... 140 B1
Lavender Ho BN2 .... 189 C1
Lavender Line★ TN22 .... 102 E8
Lavender St BN2 .... 189 C1
Lawes Ave BN9 .... 179 C7
Lawns Ave BN21 .... 184 D4
Lawns The
Eastbourne BN20 .... 173 B1
Eastbourne, Roselands
BN22 .... 185 C5
Hailsham BN27 .... 152 C6
Lawn The TN38 .... 159 C7
Lawrence Cl BN23 .... 174 D1
Lawrence Ho TN22 .... 78 C7
Lawrence Rd BN3 .... 162 F7
Lawrie La RH16 .... 51 B5
Laylands Ct BN41 .... 162 A7
Laylands Rd BN41 .... 162 A7
Lazanby Ct TN38 .... 159 B8
Lea Ave TN31 .... 93 A6
Leach Ct BN2 .... 164 C5
Leacroft RH19 .... 1 D2
Lea Ct BN9 .... 179 C8
Leaf Hall Rd 10 BN22 .... 185 B3
Leaf Hospl (Univ of Brighton)
BN21 .... 184 F4
Leaf Rd BN21 .... 185 A3
Leahurst Ct 1 BN1 .... 142 E3
Leahurst Ct Rd BN1 .... 142 E3
Lealands Cl TN3 .... 15 C6
Lealands Dr TN22 .... 55 C1
Leamland Wlk BN27 .... 152 B7
Leap Cross Small Bsns Ctr
BN27 .... 129 A1
Lea Rd BN10 .... 178 B8
Leasam La TN31 .... 93 B8
Leasingham Gdns TN39 .... 157 A5
Leas The
Burgess Hill RH15 .... 72 F4
Peacehaven BN10 .... 178 F6
St Leonards TN38 .... 159 A6
Turner's Green TN5 .... 30 A6
Le Brun Rd BN21 .... 184 F5
Ledsham Ave TN37 .... 136 B5
Ledsham Cl TN37 .... 136 B5
Ledsham Pk TN37 .... 136 B5
Ledsham Way TN37 .... 136 B5
Lee Bank BN2 .... 189 C3
Leeds Ave BN23 .... 185 D7
Leeds Cl TN35 .... 160 D8
Leeds La TN20 .... 58 D6
Leeford Cotts TN33 .... 88 A1
Lee Rd BN7 .... 123 B2
Leeves Cl TN21 .... 82 A6
Leeves Way TN21 .... 82 A6
Leeward Quay 11 BN23 .... 185 F8
Lee Way BN9 .... 179 C8
Leggs' La TN3 .... 6 E5
Legsheath La
Forest Row RH19 .... 10 D1
Sharpthorne RH18, RH19 .... 21 F8
Leicester Ct 5 BN22 .... 185 B4
Leicester Dr TN2 .... 16 F8
Leicester Rd BN7 .... 123 B1
Leicester St BN2 .... 189 C2
Leicester Villas BN3 .... 162 D7
Leighton Cl TN4 .... 8 A7
Leighton Rd
Horsted Keynes RH17 .... 33 C5
Hove BN3 .... 163 A8
Leighton Villas RH17 .... 33 C5
Leneda Dr TN2 .... 16 E8
Lenham Ave BN2 .... 166 B1
Lenham Road E BN2 .... 166 B1
Lenham Road W BN2 .... 166 A1
Lennox Cl BN20 .... 184 B5
Lennox Ct TN21 .... 82 B8
Lennox Rd
Hove BN3 .... 162 F8
Shoreham-by-S BN43 .... 161 B8
Lennox St BN2 .... 189 C2
Leopald Flats TN39 .... 157 B4
Leopold Rd
Bexhill TN39 .... 157 B4
Brighton BN1 .... 189 A3
Lepeland BN27 .... 129 A1
Lesley Cl TN40 .... 157 F7
Leslie Best Ho BN1 .... 189 B4
Leslie St BN22 .... 185 B4
Letheren Pl BN21 .... 184 D3
Leveller End BN8 .... 76 D7
Leveller Rd BN8 .... 76 D7
Levett Ave BN26 .... 173 C6
Levett Cl BN26 .... 173 C6
Levett Rd BN26 .... 173 C6
Levetts La TN32 .... 46 D1
Levett Way BN26 .... 173 C6
LEWES 190 B3
Lewes Castle★ BN7 .... 190 A2
Lewes Cl
Bexhill TN39 .... 157 A6
Saltdean BN2 .... 166 E1
Lewes Cres BN2 .... 164 E4
Lewes Ct
5 Eastbourne BN21 .... 184 F4
Falmer BN1 .... 144 A8
Southwick BN42 .... 162 A7
Lewes Ho 7 BN21 .... 184 F4
Lewes Leisure Ctr BN7 .... 190 C1
Lewes Mews 12 BN2 .... 164 E4
Lewes New Sch The
BN7 .... 190 A2
Lewes Old Gram Sch
BN7 .... 190 A2
Lewes Rd
Ashurst Wood RH19 .... 11 C6
Brighton BN1, BN2 .... 143 E3
Chelwood Gate RH17 .... 22 C1
Danehill RH17 .... 34 B3
Ditchling BN6 .... 98 E2
Eastbourne BN21 .... 184 F5
Forest Row RH18 .... 11 E2
Horsted Keynes RH17 .... 33 C5
Isfield TN22 .... 102 E6
Laughton BN8 .... 126 C7
Lindfield RH16 .... 51 B7
Newhaven BN9 .... 179 C8
Polegate BN26 .... 172 C6
Ringmer BN8 .... 124 D6
Scaynes Hill RH17 .... 51 D4
Selmeston BN26 .... 149 D2
Uckfield TN22 .... 78 D4
Lewes St BN2 .... 189 C3
Lewes Sta BN7 .... 190 B1
Lewinscourt TN33 .... 112 D5
Lewis Ave TN40 .... 158 A5
Lewis Cl BN9 .... 168 F2
Lewis Ct 6 BN2 .... 164 C8
Lewis Rd TN38 .... 136 A3
Lewry Cl BN9 .... 179 B7
Lexden Ct BN25 .... 181 A4
Lexden Dr BN25 .... 181 A5
Lexden Lodge Ind Est
TN6 .... 38 D8
Lexden Rd BN25 .... 180 F6
Leybourne Cl BN2 .... 144 A1
Leybourne Gdns TN37 .... 136 C4
Leybourne Par BN2 .... 144 A1
Leybourne Rd BN2 .... 144 A1
Leyland Rd BN24 .... 175 D4
Leylands Pk RH15 .... 73 B5
Leylands Rd RH15 .... 73 B4
Library Way TN22 .... 78 C7
Lichfield Ct 10 BN2 .... 164 F5
LIDHAM HILL 115 E6
Lilac Cl BN22 .... 173 D3
Lilac Ct BN1 .... 142 D4
Lillesden Cotts TN18 .... 45 E7
Lillywhite Cl RH15 .... 72 F5
Limden Cl TN5 .... 42 F6
Lime Cl
Frant TN3 .... 17 B3
St Leonards TN38 .... 136 B1
Uckfield TN22 .... 78 D8
Lime Cross BN27 .... 130 F5
Lime Hill Rd TN1 .... 8 A4
Limekiln Ct TN6 .... 26 C3
Limes La TN22 .... 56 D3
Limes The
Dormans Park RH19 .... 1 A5
14 Eastbourne BN21 .... 184 E4
Limetree Ave BN22 .... 173 D3
Lime Tree Ave TN22 .... 78 D7
Lime Tree Gr RH16 .... 51 C7
Lime Tree Terr TN19 .... 62 A6
Lime Way TN21 .... 82 B6
Limney Rd BN2 .... 164 E7
Limousin Ho BN23 .... 185 F8
Linchmere BN2 .... 164 F7
Linchmere Ave BN2 .... 166 C1
Lincoln Ave BN10 .... 178 A7
Lincoln Avenue S BN10 .... 178 A7
Lincoln Cl
Eastbourne BN20 .... 188 C8
2 St Leonards TN38 .... 136 A4
Lincoln Cotts BN2 .... 189 C3
Lincoln Ct
Eastbourne BN20 .... 184 B7
Hove BN3 .... 163 C8
Peacehaven BN10 .... 178 A7
Lincoln Rd BN41 .... 162 B7
Lincoln St BN2 .... 189 C4
Lincoln Way TN6 .... 38 A8
Lincoln Wood RH16 .... 50 C5
Linden Ave RH19 .... 1 C2
Linden Chase TN22 .... 78 D7
Linden Cl
Eastbourne BN22 .... 173 E2
Royal Tunbridge Wells TN4 .... 8 A2
Linden Ct TN22 .... 78 C7
Linden Fields TN2 .... 8 A1
Linden Gdns
Heathfield TN21 .... 81 F6
Royal Tunbridge Wells TN2 .... 7 F1
Linden Gr
Hailsham BN27 .... 129 C3
Lindfield RH16 .... 51 B7
Linden Park Rd TN2 .... 8 A2
Linden Rd TN40 .... 157 C3
Lindens The 4 BN2 .... 189 C4
Lindfield BN41 .... 141 A1
Lindfield Ave BN25 .... 181 C2
Lindfield Cl BN2 .... 166 B2
Lindfield Ct BN1 .... 143 C2
Lindfield Dr BN27 .... 152 B7
Lindfield Ent Pk RH16 .... 51 C6
Lindfield Prim Sch RH16 .... 51 A7
Lindfield Rd BN22 .... 173 D1
Lindfield Specl Sch The
BN22 .... 173 D2
Lindon Cl BN20 .... 183 B1
Lindsay Cl BN20 .... 184 C2
Lingfield Rd RH19 .... 1 D3
Linkden Cotts TN18 .... 47 E5
LINKHILL 47 E4
Link Ho 2 TN6 .... 25 F3
Link Rd BN20 .... 184 D1
Links Ave BN10, BN9 .... 179 A7
Links Cl
Crowborough TN6 .... 25 D2
Portslade-by-S BN41 .... 162 C8
Seaford BN25 .... 181 A2
Links Dr TN40 .... 157 E4
Links Rd
Portslade-by-S BN41 .... 162 C8
Seaford BN25 .... 181 A2
Links The
6 Bexhill TN40 .... 157 D3
St Leonards TN38 .... 158 F8
Links Way TN31 .... 94 E2
Linkswood BN21 .... 184 E2
Link The
East Dean BN20 .... 183 C2
Rye TN31 .... 93 A5
Linkway
Eastbourne BN20 .... 184 B7
Westham BN24 .... 174 E6
Link Way TN2 .... 8 E8
Linkway The BN1 .... 143 B1
Linley Cl
Bexhill TN40 .... 157 D4
Hastings TN34 .... 160 A7
Linley Dr TN34 .... 160 A7
Linnet Cl BN23 .... 174 C2
Linnet Gn TN22 .... 78 D5

Linnet La TN31 . . . . **94** E3
Linosa Ct TN22 . . . . **185** B3
Linthouse Cl BN10 . . . . **167** D2
Linton Cres TN34 . . . . . . **159** E8
Linton Ct TN34 . . . . **159** E8
Linton Rd
    Hastings TN34 . . . . **159** E8
    Hove BN3 . . . . **162** F8
Lionel Rd TN40 . . . . **157** E3
Lion Hill BN23, BN24 . . . **174** B5
Lion Hill Cotts BN24 . . . . **174** B5
Lion La BN21 . . . . **185** B3
Lion Mews
    ◢ Hove BN3 . . . . **162** F7
    Uckfield TN22 . . . . **78** D6
Lions Ct BN2 . . . . **164** E5
Lions Dene BN1 . . . . . . **142** D4
Lions Gate BN3 . . . . . . **141** E1
Lions Gdns BN1 . . . . . . **142** D2
Lions Pl BN25 . . . . **180** F2
Lion St TN31 . . . . **93** C5
Liphook Cl BN1 . . . . **143** A7
Lipscombe Rd TN2 . . . . . . **8** D6
Liptraps La TN2 . . . . **8** D7
Lismore Rd BN21 . . . . . **185** A2
Lister Ave RH19 . . . . **10** F6
Lister Rd BN23 . . . . **174** A1
LITLINGTON **182** B8
Litlington Ct ◢ BN25 . . . **180** C4
LITTLE BAYHAM **18** F4
Little Bayham Cotts TN3 . . **18** F4
Little Bentswood RH16 . . . **50** F5
Little Bentswood Cl RH16 . **50** F5
Little Black Hill RH16 . . . . **51** B7
LITTLE COMMON **156** D5
Little Comm Prim Sch
    TN39 . . . . **156** D4
Little Comm Rd TN39 . . . **156** D5
Little Copse BN6 . . . . **97** E4
Little Cres BN2 . . . . **166** B1
Little East St
    Brighton BN2 . . . . **189** B1
    Lewes BN7 . . . . **190** B2
Little Footway TN3 . . . . . . **6** F3
Little George St BN2 . . . . **189** B1
LITTLE HORSTED **78** C1
Little Horsted CE Prim Sch
    TN22 . . . . **78** C1
Little Iridge Farm Cotts
    TN19 . . . . **45** C1
Little King St RH19 . . . . **1** E1
LITTLE LONDON **81** E4
Little London Rd TN21 . . **106** F8
Little Mallett TN3 . . . . **6** F3
Littlemead
    Cooksbridge BN8 . . . . **123** A7
    Nutley TN22 . . . . **35** C3
Little Mount Sion TN1 . . . . **8** A2
LITTLE NORLINGTON . . . **102** F1
Little Paddock
    Crowborough TN6 . . . . . **25** E1
    Heathfield TN21 . . . . . . **82** A7
    Ringmer BN8 . . . . **124** E6
Little Park Cotts TN33 . . **112** E5
LITTLE PARROCK **12** D1
Little Pk TN5 . . . . **29** E5
Little Preston St BN1 . . . **163** E5
Little Ridge Ave TN37 . . . **136** C5
Little Ridge Cty Prim Sch
    TN37 . . . . **136** C5
Little Sherwood Ind Pk
    TN36 . . . . **116** D5
Little Sunnyside TN6 . . . . **25** E1
Little Trogers La TN20 . . . **40** B4
Little Twitten TN39 . . . . . **156** C6
Little Western St ◢ BN1 **163** E5
Littlewood La TN22 . . . . . **56** C4
Littleworth Cl BN2 . . . . . **165** F7
Livingstone Ho ◢ BN3 . . **163** B7
Livingstone Rd
    Burgess Hill RH15 . . . . **72** F3
    Hove BN3 . . . . **163** B7
Livingstone St BN2 . . . . **164** D5
Living World The★ BN25 . **181** F4
Lloyd Cl BN3 . . . . **163** C8
Lloyd Rd BN3 . . . . **163** C8
Lockhart Ct RH16 . . . . . . **50** F2
Lockitt Way BN7 . . . . . . **145** E5
Locks Cres BN41 . . . . . . **141** B1
Locks Ct ◢ BN42 . . . . . **161** E7
Locks Hill BN41 . . . . **141** B1
Lockwood Cl BN2 . . . . . **165** E7
Lockwood Cres BN2 . . . . **165** E7
Loder Pl BN1 . . . . **142** F2
Loder Rd BN1 . . . . **142** F2
Lodge Ave TN33 . . . . . . **173** C1
Lodge Cl
    East Grinstead RH19 . . . . **1** D1
    Lewes BN7 . . . . **146** A8
    Portslade-by-S BN41 . . **140** F2
Lodge Hill La BN6 . . . . . . **98** C4
Lodge La
    Keymer BN6 . . . . **98** A2
    Royal Tunbridge Wells TN3 . **16** A8
Lodge Rd TN35 . . . . **160** C5
Lodge The
    Brighton BN2 . . . . **189** C5
    ◢ Eastbourne BN21 . . **185** A2
Lodsworth BN2 . . . . **164** F7
Lodsworth Cl BN2 . . . . . **164** F7
Lomaria Ct TN2 . . . . **8** C4
Lomas La TN18 . . . . **47** F5
Lomond Ave BN1 . . . . . . **143** B7
London Meed Com Prim Sch
    RH15 . . . . **73** A1
London Rd
    Bexhill TN39 . . . . **157** B5
    Brighton BN1 . . . . **189** B4

London Rd *continued*
    Brighton, Withdean BN1 . . **142** D4
    Burgess Hill RH15 . . . . . **72** F3
    Crowborough TN6 . . . . . **25** E4
    Danehill RH17 . . . . **34** A4
    East Grinstead RH19 . . . . **1** C3
    East Hoathly BN8 . . . . **105** A5
    Flimwell TN5 . . . . **32** D3
    Forest Row RH18 . . . . . . **11** E4
    Hailsham BN27 . . . . . . **129** A2
    Hassocks BN6, RH15 . . . . **97** E6
    Hurst Green TN19 . . . . . **45** A3
    John's Cross TN32, TN33 . . **87** D3
    Maresfield TN22 . . . . . . **55** B4
    Pyecombe BN1, BN45 . . **119** C4
    Royal Tunbridge Wells, Mount
        Sion TN1 . . . . **8** A3
    Royal Tunbridge Wells TN4 . . **8** B2
    St Leonards TN37, TN38 . **159** C8
    Uckfield TN22 . . . . **55** D2
London Rd (Brighton) Sta
    BN1 . . . . **164** A8
London Terr BN1 . . . . . . **189** B4
Loney Ct ◢ BN43 . . . . . **161** C8
Longacre Ct TN37 . . . . . **136** C6
Long Acre Cl BN21 . . . . . **184** D5
Long Ave TN40 . . . . **158** A6
Long Barn Motor Mus The★
    TN21 . . . . **80** F8
Long Beach Cl BN23 . . . . **175** B1
Long Beach Mews BN23 . . **175** B1
Long Beach View BN23 . . **175** B1
Longbury TN22 . . . . **78** C5
Longhill Cl BN2 . . . . **165** E4
Longhill High Sch BN2 . . **165** E4
Longhill Rd BN2 . . . . . . **165** E4
Long Hos TN32 . . . . **85** D3
Longhurst RH15 . . . . **73** D2
Longhurst Cotts BN8 . . . . **75** D7
Long La TN33 . . . . **88** E1
Longland Rd BN20 . . . . . **184** C4
Longley Ind Est BN1 . . . . **189** B4
Long Man of Wilmington
    The★ BN26 . . . . **171** E3
Long Meads TN3 . . . . **7** B4
Long Park Cnr BN6 . . . . . **98** D2
Longridge Ave BN2 . . . . **166** D1
Long Slip TN3 . . . . **7** A3
Longstone Rd BN21 . . . . **185** A3
Longview TN21 . . . . **82** A5
Longview Way TN2 . . . . . . **8** D7
Longwall RH19 . . . . **1** A4
Long Wlk RH16 . . . . **51** B4
Lonsdale Gdns TN1 . . . . . . **8** A3
Looes Barn Cl BN2 . . . . . **166** D3
Lookout The BN10 . . . . . **167** B8
Loose Farm Barns TN33 . . **113** A2
Loose Farm Cotts TN33 . . **113** A2
Lordine La TN32 . . . . **66** B4
Lords La TN35 . . . . **160** D7
Lordslaine Cl BN20 . . . . . **188** D8
Lords The BN25 . . . . **180** E6
Lordswell La TN6 . . . . **37** E8
Loriners Ct BN3 . . . . **162** D8
Lorna Rd BN3 . . . . **163** D7
Lorne Rd BN1 . . . . **189** B5
Lorraine Ct
    ◢ Hove BN3 . . . . **163** B6
    ◢◢ Hove BN3 . . . . . . **163** E7
Lorraine Rd BN9 . . . . . . **179** D7
Lossenham La TN18 . . . . . **48** D3
Lottbridge Dr BN22 . . . . **173** F1
Lottbridge Dro BN23 . . . **185** B7
Lottbridge Rdbt BN23 . . **185** A8
Lovat Mead TN38 . . . . . **158** E6
Lovegrove Ct BN3 . . . . . **162** E8
Love La
    Eastbourne BN20 . . . . **184** D3
    Mayfield TN20 . . . . **39** F2
    Rye TN31 . . . . **93** B6
Lovell Ct ◢ BN21 . . . . . **184** D4
Lover's Walk Cotts BN1 . . **163** F8
Lover's Wlk BN1 . . . . . . **163** F8
Lowdells Cl RH19 . . . . **1** C4
Lowdells Dr RH19 . . . . **1** D4
Lowdells La RH19 . . . . **1** C4
Lower Bevendean Ave
    BN2 . . . . **143** E1
Lower Chalvington Pl
    BN2 . . . . **164** E5
Lower Church Rd RH15 . . . **72** F3
LOWER COUSLEY WOOD . . **30** E8
Lower Cross Cotts TN31 . . **91** E2
Lower Dene RH19 . . . . **2** A1
LOWER DICKER **128** C3
Lower Dr
    Seaford BN25 . . . . **180** F5
    Southwick BN42 . . . . . **140** E1
Lower Glen Rd TN37 . . . **136** B4
LOWER GREEN
    Pembury **9** D8
    Royal Tunbridge Wells **7** C5
Lower Green Rd
    Pembury TN2 . . . . **9** D7
    Rusthall TN3, TN4 . . . . . . **7** C6
Lower Hazelhurst TN5 . . . **31** A4
Lower High St TN5 . . . . . . **30** A4
LOWER HORSEBRIDGE . . **128** F3
Lower Lake TN33 . . . . . . **112** E4
Lower Market St ◢ BN3 **163** D5
Lower Mere RH16 . . . . . . **10** F8
Lower Park Rd TN34 . . . **136** E1
Lower Pl BN9 . . . . **179** C7
Lower Platts TN5 . . . . **31** F1
Lower Rd
    Eastbourne BN21 . . . . . **184** D4
    Forest Row RH18 . . . . . . **11** F3

Lower Rd *continued*
    Herstmonceux BN27 . . . . **130** E3
Lower Rock Gdns BN2 . . **189** C1
Lower Roedale Cotts
    BN1 . . . . **143** B8
Lower St Mary's TN5 . . . . **31** E1
Lower Saxonbury TN6 . . . **25** F2
Lower South Rd TN37 . . . **136** C1
Lower Sq RH18 . . . . **11** F3
Lower St
    East Dean BN20 . . . . . **187** B8
    Lower Street TN33 . . . . **133** B5
LOWER STANDEAN **120** A3
Lower Sta Rd BN8 . . . . . . **76** A6
LOWER STREET **133** B5
Lower Village ◢ RH16 . . . **50** C2
Lower Village ◢◢ RH16 . . **50** C1
Lower Waites La TN35 . . . **138** F4
Lower Wick St BN26 . . . . **150** B5
LOWER WILLINGDON **173** C4
Lowfield Rd RH16 . . . . . . **50** F3
Lowlands Rd RH15 . . . . . . **73** B5
Lowlands Rd TN29 . . . . . **129** A1
Lowther Cl BN23 . . . . . . **174** D3
Lowther Rd BN1 . . . . . . **143** A2
Loxdale (The Swedish Folk
    High Sch) BN41 . . . . **141** B1
Loxfield Cl TN20 . . . . **40** A2
Loxfield Gdns TN6 . . . . . . **26** B1
Loxwood Cl
    Bexhill TN39 . . . . **156** D5
    Eastbourne BN22 . . . . **173** C1
Loyal Par BN1 . . . . **142** C5
Lucas RH17 . . . . **33** D5
Lucas Cl
    East Grinstead RH19 . . . . **2** A1
    ◢ High Brooms TN2 . . . . **8** C7
Lucas Grange RH16 . . . . . **50** D5
Lucas Shadwell Way TN31 **93** F2
Lucastes Ave RH16 . . . . . **50** D6
Lucastes La RH16 . . . . . . **50** C6
Lucastes Rd RH16 . . . . . . **50** C5
Lucas Way RH16 . . . . **50** C5
Lucerne Cl BN41 . . . . . . **141** B1
Lucerne Rd BN1 . . . . . . **143** A1
Lucinda Way BN25 . . . . . **180** F6
Lucraft Rd BN2 . . . . **143** F5
Lucy Way TN39 . . . . **157** B6
Ludley Hill TN31 . . . . **91** A6
Ludlow Rise BN2 . . . . . . **144** A1
Ludpit La TN19, TN32 . . . . **63** C6
Luke Lade BN27 . . . . **152** C7
Lulham Cl BN10 . . . . **167** B2
Lullington Ave BN3 . . . . **162** F8
Lullington Cl
    Bexhill TN40 . . . . **158** A6
    Eastbourne BN21 . . . . **184** C7
    Seaford BN25 . . . . **181** B2
Lullington Gdns TN37 . . . **136** C5
Lullington Heath National
    Nature Reserve★ BN26 . **182** E8
Lullington Ho ◢ BN21 . . **184** E4
Lullington Rd BN26 . . . . . **171** A3
Lunce's Hill RH16, RH17 . . **73** F8
Lundy Wlk
    ◢ Eastbourne BN23 . . **185** F8
    Hailsham BN27 . . . . . . **129** A2
LUNSFORD'S CROSS **133** D2
Lureland Ct BN10 . . . . . **178** C6
Lurgashall RH15 . . . . **73** C1
Lushington La BN21 . . . . **185** A2
Lushington Rd BN21 . . . . **185** A2
Lustrells Cl BN2 . . . . . . **166** B2
Lustrells Cres BN2 . . . . . **166** C2
Lustrells Rd BN2 . . . . . . **166** A2
Lustrells Vale BN2 . . . . . **166** C2
Luther Mews BN2 . . . . . **164** C7
Luther St BN2 . . . . **164** C7
Luton Cl BN21 . . . . **184** C6
Luxford Cl TN22 . . . . **78** C7
Luxford Cotts TN6 . . . . . . **38** A8
Luxford Dr TN6 . . . . **38** A8
Luxford La TN6 . . . . **38** A8
Luxford Rd
    Crowborough TN6 . . . . . **38** A8
    Lindfield RH16 . . . . **51** B7
Luxford's La RH19 . . . . . . **11** B6
Lychgates Cl TN40 . . . . . **157** D5
Lydd Cl BN23 . . . . **174** D2
Lydd Rd TN31 . . . . **94** F2
LYE GREEN **14** D1
Lymden La TN5 . . . . **43** A7
Lyminster Ave BN1 . . . . . **143** A5
Lynchet Cl BN1 . . . . **143** C3
Lynchet Down BN1 . . . . . **143** C2
Lynchets Cres BN3 . . . . . **141** D3
Lynchets The BN7 . . . . . **190** C4
Lynchet Wlk BN1 . . . . . . **143** C2
Lynden Ct ◢ BN1 . . . . . **142** E2
Lyndhurst Ave TN34 . . . . **160** A8
Lyndhurst Cl BN3 . . . . . **163** D7
Lyndhurst Rd BN3 . . . . . **163** D7
Lynholm Rd BN26 . . . . . **173** C4
Lynton Cl
    East Grinstead RH19 . . . . **2** A2
    Hurstpierpoint BN6 . . . . . **97** B5
Lynton Park Ave RH19 . . . . **2** A2
Lynton St BN2 . . . . **164** C7
Lynwood TN3 . . . . **15** C6
Lynwood Cl TN37 . . . . . **136** D5
Lynwood Rd BN2 . . . . . . **177** C4
Lyon Cl BN3 . . . . **163** D7
Lyoth La RH16 . . . . **51** C4
Lyoth Villas RH16 . . . . . . **51** C4
Lytham Cl TN38 . . . . **158** F8**

M

Mabb's Hill TN5 . . . . **42** F7
Maberley Rd TN40 . . . . . **157** C6
McGechie Ho RH19 . . . . . . **1** D3
McIndoe Rd RH19 . . . . **1** D3
Mackenzie Ho RH19 . . . . . **1** A4
Mackerel Hill TN31 . . . . . . **69** E7
Mackerel's Rocks BN8 . . . **76** F3
Mackie Ave
    Brighton BN1 . . . . **143** A7
    Keymer BN6 . . . . **98** A5
McMichaels Way TN19 . . . **45** A3
Macmillan Dr BN21 . . . . **184** C5
McNair Ct BN2 . . . . **162** E7
MacQuarie Quay BN23 . . **185** G8
McWilliam Rd BN2 . . . . . **144** C1
Madehurst Cl BN2 . . . . . **164** D5
Madeira Dr
    Brighton BN2 . . . . **164** C4
    Hastings TN34 . . . . . . **136** C3
MADEIRA PARK **8** B2
Madeira Pk TN2 . . . . **8** B2
Madeira Pl BN2 . . . . **189** C1
Madeira Way BN23 . . . . **185** F8
Madisson Ct TN22 . . . . . . **78** D4
Magdalen Cl BN23 . . . . . **174** C3
Magdalen Ct ◢ TN40 . . **157** D4
Magdalen Rd
    Bexhill TN40 . . . . **157** D4
    St Leonards TN37 . . . . **159** D7
Magellan Way BN23 . . . . **185** G7
MAGHAM DOWN **129** F4
Magna Ct TN40 . . . . **157** B4
Magnolia Cl TN21 . . . . . . **82** B5
Magnolia Dr BN22 . . . . . **173** D2
Magnolia Wlk BN22 . . . . **173** D2
Magpie Cl
    Bexhill TN39 . . . . **156** C6
    St Leonards TN38 . . . . **158** E8
Magpie Rd BN23 . . . . . . **174** C3
Magreed La TN21 . . . . . . **59** E2
Maidstone Rd TN2 . . . . **9** E8
Main Rd
    Icklesham TN35, TN36 . . **116** D5
    Westfield TN35 . . . . . . **114** E4
Main St
    Iden TN31 . . . . **70** B4
    Northiam TN31 . . . . **67** B5
    Peasmarsh TN31 . . . . . . **69** B2
Mainstone Rd ◢ BN1 . . **162** F7
Maitland Cl TN34 . . . . . . **136** E6
Major Cl BN1 . . . . **143** B1
Major York's Rd TN4 . . . . . **7** F2
Malcolm Ct BN1 . . . . **143** B1
Malcolm Gdns BN26 . . . . **173** A7
Malden Reach ◢ BN23 . . **175** A1
Maldon Rd BN1 . . . . **142** D2
Malines Ave BN10 . . . . . **178** B8
Malines Ave S BN10 . . . . **178** A7
Mallard Cl
    Eastbourne BN22 . . . . **184** F8
    Hampden Park BN22 . . **173** F1
Mallard Dr TN22 . . . . **78** D4
Mallard Pl RH19 . . . . **10** F8
Mallett Cl ◢◢ BN25 . . . . **180** E2
Malling Cl BN7 . . . . **190** B4
Malling Down BN7, BN8 . . **190** C3
Malling Hill BN7 . . . . . . **190** C3
Malling Ind Est BN7 . . . . **190** C3
Malling St BN7 . . . . **190** C2
Mallory Rd BN3 . . . . **142** C2
Malthouse Cl ◢◢ BN25 . . **189** C2
Malthouse La
    Brighton BN2 . . . . **189** C3
    Burgess Hill BN6, RH15 . . **72** C2
    Peasmarsh TN31 . . . . . . **69** B2
Malt House Trad Est
    BN43 . . . . **161** B7
Malthouse Way RH16 . . . **123** A7
Maltings Barn The BN7 . . **190** C2
Maltings The
    Burgess Hill RH15 . . . . **72** D4
    Peasmarsh TN31 . . . . . . **69** B2
Malton Way TN2 . . . . **8** F7
Malvern Cl BN22 . . . . . . **173** E4
Malvern Ho TN37 . . . . . . **157** B3
Malvern St ◢◢ BN3 . . . . **163** B4
Malvern Way TN34 . . . . . **160** B8
Manaton Cl RH16 . . . . . . **50** F4
Manchester Rd TN33 . . . **133** A6
Manchester St BN2 . . . . **189** B1
Mandalay Ct BN1 . . . . . . **142** D4
Manhattan Ct BN1 . . . . . **142** D3
Manhattan Gdns TN35 . . **160** D8
Manifold Rd BN22 . . . . . **185** B4
Manning Ct RH19 . . . . **1** D2
Mann St TN1 . . . . **159** F8
Manor Ave BN6 . . . . **98** A5
Manor Cl
    Brighton BN2 . . . . **164** E5
    Broyle Side BN8 . . . . . **124** F7
    Burgess Hill RH15 . . . . **73** D4
    Eastbourne BN20 . . . . **173** D2
    Horam TN21 . . . . **106** F7
    Icklesham TN36 . . . . . **116** F5
    Royal Tunbridge Wells TN4 . . **7** E3
    Seaford BN25 . . . . **181** B3
    Southwick BN42 . . . . . **162** A8
    Uckfield TN22 . . . . **78** C8
Manor Cotts
    Lamberhurst TN3 . . . . . **20** B5
    Sedlescombe TN33 . . . . **88** E1
Manor Cres BN2 . . . . . . **164** E5

Manor Ct
    North Chailey BN8 . . . . **75** D7
    Seaford BN25 . . . . **181** B3
    Southwick BN42 . . . . . **162** A7
Manor Dr BN10 . . . . **167** B1
Manor End TN22 . . . . **78** C8
Manor Field Prim Sch
    RH15 . . . . **73** C4
Manor Gdns BN2 . . . . . . **164** E5
Manor Gn BN2 . . . . **164** E5
Manor Hall Fst Sch
    BN42 . . . . **161** F7
Manor Hall Mid Sch
    BN42 . . . . **161** F8
Manor Hall Rd BN42 . . . . **161** F8
Manor Hill BN2 . . . . **164** E6
Manor House Ct TN22 . . . **78** C8
Manor Paddock BN2 . . . . **164** E4
Manor Park BN27 . . . . . **129** A3
Manor Park Ct BN26 . . . **173** A6
Manor Park Rd BN27 . . . **129** A3
Manor Pk TN4 . . . . **7** E3
Manor Pl BN2 . . . . **164** E4
Manor Prim Sch TN22 . . . **78** D8
Manor Rd
    Bexhill TN40 . . . . **157** D4
    Brighton BN2 . . . . **164** E5
    Burgess Hill RH15 . . . . **73** D4
    Eastbourne BN22 . . . . **174** A2
    East Grinstead RH19 . . . . **1** C2
    Hastings TN34 . . . . . . **160** A5
    Horam TN21 . . . . **106** F8
    Portslade-by-S BN41 . . **141** B1
    Rusthall TN4 . . . . **7** C4
    Seaford BN25 . . . . **181** B3
Manor Road N BN25 . . . . **181** B3
Manor Terr BN7 . . . . **190** A1
Manor The
    Hailsham BN27 . . . . . . **129** C4
    Royal Tunbridge Wells TN2 . . **8** E5
Manor Way
    Brighton BN2 . . . . **164** E5
    Crowborough TN6 . . . . . **37** E8
    Eastbourne BN20 . . . . **184** B8
    Polegate BN26 . . . . . . **173** B6
    Uckfield TN22 . . . . **78** C8
Mansell Cl TN39 . . . . . . **156** C4
Mansell Ct RH15 . . . . . . **73** B3
Mansell Rd BN43 . . . . . . **161** B8
Mansers La BN27 . . . . . . **128** C3
Mansfield Rd BN3 . . . . . **162** E7
Mansion Cl RH15 . . . . . . **73** D3
Manston Way TN34 . . . . **136** E2
Mantell Cl BN7 . . . . **123** C4
Mantell Ho ◢◢ BN2 . . . . **189** C2
Manton Ct BN23 . . . . . . **185** D8
Manton Rd BN21 . . . . . . **143** C1
Manvers Rd BN20 . . . . . **184** B3
Maple Ave TN39 . . . . . . **156** C3
Maple Cl
    Bexhill TN39 . . . . **156** C3
    Burgess Hill RH15 . . . . **73** B5
    Haywards Heath RH16 . . **51** B3
    Maresfield TN22 . . . . . . **55** A4
    Royal Tunbridge Wells TN2 . . **8** A1
    Woodingdean BN2 . . . . **165** E7
Maple Ct RH15 . . . . **72** D3
Maple Ct
    Hailsham BN27 . . . . . . **152** A8
    Royal Tunbridge Wells TN4 . . **7** E4
Maple Dr
    Burgess Hill RH15 . . . . **73** A5
    East Grinstead RH19 . . . . **2** A1
Maple Gdns
    Hove BN3 . . . . **141** F1
    Madeira Park TN2 . . . . **17** B8
Maple Hts TN37 . . . . . . **136** C8
Maplehurst Cl TN37 . . . . **136** C8
Maplehurst Dr TN37 . . . . **136** C8
Maplehurst Rd
    Eastbourne BN22 . . . . **173** D2
    Portslade-by-S BN41 . . **141** A1
    St Leonards TN37 . . . . **136** B7
Maplehurst Rise TN37 . . . **136** B7
Maple Leaf Cl BN9 . . . . . **179** B7
Mapleleaf Gdns BN26 . . . **173** A8
Maple Rd
    Eastbourne BN23 . . . . **185** D7
    Peacehaven BN10 . . . . **178** F6
Maples Cotts TN22 . . . . . **80** A6
Maples The BN8 . . . . . . **124** A6
Maple Wlk TN39 . . . . . . **156** C3
Maplewood ◢ BN1 . . . . . **142** E3
Marbles Rd BN8 . . . . **76** D7
Marchants Cl BN6 . . . . . . **97** A6
Marchants Dr TN31 . . . . . **94** E2
Marchants Rd BN6 . . . . . . **97** A6
Marchants Way RH15 . . . . **72** F5
March Ho BN3 . . . . **142** B1
Marcia Cl BN20 . . . . **184** A8
Marcus Gdns TN37 . . . . **136** A5
Mardan Ct TN38 . . . . . . **159** B7
Marden Cl BN2 . . . . **144** C1
Marden Ct TN39 . . . . . . **157** A3
MARDEN'S HILL **25** B3
Marden's Hill TN6 . . . . . . **25** C5
Mare Bay Cl TN38 . . . . . **135** E7
MARESFIELD **55** A5
Maresfield Dr BN24 . . . . **175** E6
MARESFIELD PARK **55** A6
Maresfield Rd BN2 . . . . . **164** E5
Margaret Ct BN10 . . . . . **178** B7
Margaret St BN2 . . . . . . **189** C1
Margery Rd BN3 . . . . . . **162** D8
Marianne Ho TN35 . . . . . **160** B5**

Marianne Pk TN35 . . . . . 160 B5
Marina
 Bexhill TN40. . . . . .157 C3
 St Leonards TN38 . . . . . . 159 B6
Marina Arc **7** TN40. . . . 157 C3
Marina Court Ave 4
 TN40. . . . . 157 C3
Marina Way BN2 . . . . . . 164 F3
Marina Wlk BN23 . . . . . 185 E8
Marine Ave
 Beachlands BN24 . . . . . . 175 F6
 Hove BN3. . . . . 162 E6
Marine Cl
 Beachlands BN24 . . . . . . 175 F6
 Saltdean BN2. . . . . 166 B1
Marine Cotts TN31 . . . . 94 E2
Marine Cres BN25. . . . . 180 F2
Marine Ct
 Newhaven BN9 . . . . .179 D6
 Rottingdean BN2 . . . . . . 166 A1
 Seaford BN25 . . . . 180 C3
 4 St Leonards TN38 . . 159 C6
 Telscombe Cliffs BN10. . 177 F3
Marine Dr
 Rottingdean BN2 . . . . . . 165 C2
 Saltdean BN2. . . . . 177 B5
 Seaford BN25 . . . . 180 B5
Marine Gdns BN2 . . . . . 189 C1
Marine Hts TN38 . . . . . 159 A6
Marine Par
 Brighton BN2. . . . . 164 C4
 Eastbourne BN21, BN22 . 185 B3
 Hastings TN34 . . . . 160 A3
 Seaford BN25 . . . . 180 C3
Marine Parade Rd 15
 BN21 . . . . 185 B3
Marine Pk TN38 . . . . . . 158 F6
Marine Rd
 Eastbourne BN22. . . . . . 185 B3
 Pevensey Bay BN24. . . . 175 D5
Mariners Quay BN2 . . . 164 F3
Marine Sq BN2 . . . . 164 C4
Marine Terr BN24 . . . . . 175 D5
Marine Terrace Mews 7
 BN2 . . . . 164 C4
Marine View
 3 Brighton BN2. . . . . 189 C2
 Newhaven BN9 . . . . .179 B6
Mariteau Ho TN36. . . . . 117 E7
Marjoram Pl BN43 . . . . 140 B1
Mark Cl BN25 . . . . 181 C2
MARK CROSS 28 A4
Mark Cross TN6 . . . . . . 126 B2
Mark Cross CE Prim Sch
 TN6. . . . . 28 A3
Market La BN7. . . . . 190 B2
Market Pas
 6 Hastings TN34 . . . . 160 A3
 9 St Leonards TN38 . . 159 C6
Market Pl
 Hailsham BN27 . . . . 152 C7
 Haywards Heath RH16 . . 50 D6
 16 Royal Tunbridge Wells
 TN2 . . . . 8 A2
Market Place Sh Ctr
 RH15. . . . . 73 A2
Market Rd
 Battle TN33 . . . . .112 C5
 Rye TN31 . . . . 93 C5
Market Sq
 Battle TN33 . . . . .112 D5
 1 Hailsham BN27. . . . 152 C7
Market St
 Brighton BN1. . . . . 189 B2
 Hailsham BN27 . . . . 152 C7
 Lewes BN7. . . . . 190 A4
 17 Royal Tunbridge Wells
 TN2 . . . . 8 A2
 Rye TN31 . . . . 93 C5
 St Leonards TN38 . . . . . 159 C6
Market Terr **8** TN38 . . 159 C6
Mark La BN25 . . . . 185 A4
Markland Way TN22. . . . 78 A7
Marklye La
 Heathfield TN21. . . . . . . 59 B2
 Rushlake Green TN21 . . . 83 C3
Markstakes Cnr BN8 . . . 75 E1
Markstakes La BN8 . . . . 76 C2
MARK STREET 34 F3
Markwick Terr TN38 . . . 159 B8
Marlborough Cl
 Eastbourne BN23. . . . . . 174 D3
 Royal Tunbridge Wells TN4. . . 7 E4
 St Leonards TN38 . . . . . 136 A1
Marlborough Ct
 Burgess Hill RH15. . . . . 72 E3
 8 Eastbourne BN21. . . 184 F3
 1 Hove BN3. . . . . 163 C6
 Newhaven BN9 . . . . .179 C7
Marlborough Dr RH15. . 73 C2
Marlborough Ho 12
 TN37. . . . . 159 C7
Marlborough Mews BN1. 189 A2
Marlborough Pl 6 BN1,
 BN2 . . . . 189 B3
Marlborough St BN1 . . . 189 A2
Marle Ave RH15. . . . . . . 73 A4
MARLE GREEN 107 B5
Marle Green Cotts TN21. 107 B6
Marley Cl TN33 . . . . 112 F4
Marley Gdns TN33 . . . . 112 F4
Marley La TN33 . . . . 113 B6
Marley Rd TN31. . . . . . . 93 A6
Marley Rise TN33 . . . . . 112 F4
Marline Rd TN38 . . . . . . 136 A4

Marline Rd TN38 . . . . . . 136 A4
Marlinespike The BN43. . 161 A6
Marline Wood Nature
 Reserve★ TN38 . . . . . . 135 D4
Marlings The RH16 . . . . 50 C3
Marlow Ave BN22 . . . . . 185 B6
Marlow Ct
 Brighton BN2. . . . . 189 C4
 5 Crowborough TN6 . . 37 F8
Marlow Dr
 Haywards Heath RH16 . . 51 C4
 St Leonards TN37 . . . . . 136 C5
Marlowes The TN40. . . . 157 E5
Marlow Rd BN2 . . . . 164 F4
Marlpit Cl RH19. . . . . . . 1 E4
Marlpit Gdns TN5 . . . . . 31 E1
Marlpit Rd RH19 . . . . . . 21 A6
MARLPITS
 Bexhill 133 B7
 Crowborough 35 E6
Marlpits La TN33 . . . . . . 133 A7
Marlpit The TN5 . . . . . . 29 E5
Marmion Rd BN3 . . . . . . 162 F7
Marsden Ct BN10 . . . . . 178 A4
Marsden Rd BN23 . . . . . 174 E1
Marshall Ct BN22 . . . . . 173 D1
Marshall La BN9 . . . . . . 179 C7
Marshall Rd BN23 . . . . . 185 A8
Marshall Rdbt BN23 . . . 174 A1
Marshalls Row BN1 . . . . 189 B4
Marshall Way BN3 . . . . 141 F1
Marshfoot La BN27 . . . . 152 D8
Marsh Ho **3** BN42 . . . . 161 D7
Marshlands La TN21 . . . 82 A7
Marshlands Prim Sch
 BN27. . . . . 152 D8
Marsh Quarter La TN18. . 47 C3
Marston Ct **10** BN3 . . . . 163 E7
Martello Ct
 Newhaven BN9 . . . . .168 D2
 Pevensey Bay BN24. . . . 175 C3
Martello Mews **21** BN25 . 180 E2
Martello Rd
 Eastbourne BN22. . . . . . 185 D6
 Seaford BN25 . . . . 180 E2
Martens Field BN7 . . . . 146 E1
Martha Gunn Rd BN2. . . 143 E1
Martin Ct BN22 . . . . 173 D1
Martineau La TN35. . . . . 137 F5
Martingale Cl TN37 . . . . 136 C5
Martinique Way BN23 . . 185 G7
Martin Rd BN3 . . . . 141 D1
Martins The BN10 . . . . . 167 B1
Martlet Ct **5** BN2 . . . . . 164 C5
Martlet Ho
 Brighton BN1. . . . . 164 A8
 Saltdean BN2. . . . . 177 D4
Martlets
 Bexhill TN40. . . . . 157 E5
 Eastbourne BN22. . . . . . 173 B3
Martlets Ct TN6. . . . . . . 25 F1
Martlets Sh Ctr The RH15. 73 A3
Martlets The
 Broad Oak TN31. . . . . . . 90 C4
 Crowborough TN6 . . . . . 25 F1
Martlets The BN27 . . . . . 152 A7
Martletts The
 Hastings TN34 . . . . 136 E2
 Lewes BN7. . . . . 190 B4
 South Chailey BN8. . . . . 100 D7
Martlet The BN3 . . . . . . 142 D1
Martletts The
 Burwash Common TN19 . . 60 F3
 Ringmer BN8 . . . . 124 E6
Martyn's Cl BN2 . . . . . . 165 E4
Martyns Pl RH19 . . . . . . 11 A8
Martyns Way TN40 . . . . 158 A5
Marwick Ct TN38. . . . . . 159 B8
Maryan Ct BN27. . . . . . . 152 B8
Mary Burfield Ct **3** TN21. 82 A7
Maryland Rd TN2 . . . . . . 8 D1
Marylands RH16 . . . . . . 50 F5
Mary Stanford Gn TN31 . 94 A3
Maskelyne Rd BN27. . . . 131 A1
Mason Cl RH19 . . . . .1 E2
Mason Rd
 Rye TN31 . . . . 93 A5
 Seaford BN25 . . . . 180 F4
Matlock Rd
 Brighton BN1. . . . . 142 D2
 Eastbourne BN20. . . . . . 188 E8
Matthew Ho **14** BN3 . . . . 163 A6
Maudlin Ct TN38 . . . . . . 159 C8
Maunsell Ct RH16 . . . . . 50 F3
Maunsell Rd TN38. . . . . 135 F5
Maurice Rd BN25 . . . . . 180 F1
Maxfield Ct BN20 . . . . . 184 B5
Maxfield La TN35 . . . . . . 115 D2
May Ave BN25 . . . . 181 B3
Maycroft Pl TN20 . . . . . 39 F2
Mayfair Cl BN26 . . . . . . 172 F4
Mayfair Ct BN20 . . . . . . 173 B1
Mayfair Mews TN40. . . . 157 C5
MAYFIELD 40 A2
Mayfield Ave BN10. . . . . 178 D6
Mayfield CE Prim Sch
 TN20. . . . . 40 B3
Mayfield Cl
 Brighton BN1. . . . . 143 A5
 Mayfield TN20 . . . . 39 F2
Mayfield Cres BN1 . . . . 142 F5
Mayfield La
 Bexhill TN39. . . . . 156 C4
 Broad Oak TN21. . . . . . . 59 E1
 Burgess Hill RH15. . . . . 73 B3
 Saltdean BN2. . . . . 166 C2
Mayfield Flat TN21, TN22. . 81 A8

Mayfield La
 Durgates TN5. . . . . 29 D4
 St Leonards TN38 . . . . . 135 D2
Mayfield Pk TN5 . . . . . . 29 E5
Mayfield Pl BN22 . . . . . 185 A4
Mayfield Rd
 Mark Cross TN6 . . . . . . 28 A8
 Mark Cross TN6. . . . . . . 28 A8
 Rotherfield TN6 . . . . 39 A7
 Royal Tunbridge Wells TN4. . . 7 E4
Mayfield Way TN40 . . . . 157 E5
Mayflower Ct
 Haywards Heath RH16 . . 50 F4
 11 Shoreham-by-S BN43. 161 A6
Mayflower Rd RH16. . . . 50 F4
Mayflower Sq BN1 . . . . 189 B4
Mayhew Way BN7. . . . . . 190 B3
Mayhouse Rd RH15 . . . . 72 F1
MAYNARD'S GREEN . . . 82 A1
Maynards Green Prim Sch
 TN21. . . . . 82 A2
Mayne Waye TN34 . . . . . 160 B8
Mayo Ct **5** BN2 . . . . . . 164 B8
Mayo La TN39 . . . . 157 A8
Mayo Rd BN2 . . . . 164 B8
Mayo Rise BN9 . . . . 157 A8
Maypole Cotts TN22. . . . 56 B8
Maypole Rd
 Ashurst Wood RH19. . . . 11 E6
 East Grinstead RH19 . . . .1 D2
Maytham Rd TN17. . . . . . 49 C7
May Tree Cl BN3 . . . . . . 162 D8
May Tree Gdns TN40 . . . 157 F6
May Tree Wlk BN3 . . . . . 141 E1
Mayvern Ct **5** TN6. . . . . 25 F3
Mayview Cl TN31. . . . . . 59 E1
Maywood Ave BN22 . . . . 173 E2
Maze Hill TN38 . . . . 159 B7
Maze Hill Terr TN38 . . . 159 B7
Meachants Ct BN20 . . . . 173 B2
Meachants La BN20 . . . . 173 B2
Meadow Bank TN33 . . . . 112 F4
Meadow Cl
 Hailsham BN27 . . . . 129 B1
 Hove BN3. . . . . 142 B3
 Portslade-by-S BN41. . . . 141 C1
 Rottingdean BN2 . . . . . . 165 F3
 Southwick BN42. . . . . . . 162 A8
Meadow Cres TN39 . . . . 157 C7
Meadowcroft Cl RH19 . . . 1 C2
Meadow Dr RH16 . . . . . 51 B6
Meadow Hill Rd **6** TN1. . .8 B3
Meadow Ho BN8 . . . . . . 100 E7
Meadow La
 Burgess Hill RH15 . . . . . 72 F1
 Lindfield RH16 . . . . 51 B6
 Sedlescombe TN33 . . . . 88 D1
Meadowlands Ave BN22 . 173 D1
Meadow Par BN2 . . . . . . 165 F3
Meadow Pl TN22 . . . . . . 78 C6
Meadow Rd
 Groombridge TN3 . . . . . 15 C7
 Hailsham BN27 . . . . 152 A6
 Royal Tunbridge Wells TN1. . . 7 A4
 Rusthall TN4. . . . . .7 C2
Meadow Rise TN21. . . . . 106 F7
Meadow Side BN13 . . . . 88 D1
Meadowside Cotts TN5. . 31 F1
Meadows Rd BN22 . . . . 173 B2
Meadows The
 Crowborough TN6 . . . . . 25 F2
 Golden Cross BN27 . . . . 127 B3
 Hove BN3. . . . . 141 C3
 Lewes BN7. . . . . 190 C4
 St Leonards TN37 . . . . . 136 C5
Meadowsweet Cl TN38. . 135 E1
Meadow The TN20 . . . . . .9 E8
Meadow Vale BN2 . . . . . 165 E5
Meadowview
 Brighton BN2. . . . . 143 E1
 Lower Street TN33. . . . . 133 B5
Meadow View
 Rotherfield TN6 . . . . 39 B7
 Union Street TN5. . . . . . 32 A3
 Westfield TN35 . . . . 114 E4
Meadow View Cotts TN19. 45 A3
Meadow Views TN22. . . . 78 E4
Meadow Way
 Fairlight Cove TN35 . . . . 138 E4
 Heathfield TN21. . . . . . . 82 A6
 Seaford BN25 . . . . 181 B3
MEADS. 188 E8
Meads Ave
 Bexhill TN39. . . . . 156 C4
 Hove BN3. . . . . 141 C3
Meads Brow BN20 . . . . . 188 D8
Mead Sch The TN2 . . . . .8 A1
Meads Cl BN3 . . . . 141 C3
Meads Ct BN20 . . . . 184 E1
Meads Gate BN20 . . . . . 188 E8
Meads Prim Sch RH19. . 10 E7
Meads Rd
 Bexhill TN39. . . . . 156 C4
 Eastbourne BN20. . . . . . 184 E1
 Seaford BN25 . . . . 180 F3
Meads St BN20 . . . . 188 E8
Meads The
 Brighton BN1. . . . . 143 D5
 Burgess Hill RH15. . . . . 73 B4
 East Grinstead RH19 . . . 10 E7
 Royal Tunbridge Wells TN2. . 8 C2
Meadsway BN20 . . . . . . 188 E8
Mead The TN39 . . . . 156 D4

Meadway Cres BN3 . . . . 141 F2
Meadway Ct BN42. . . . . 161 D8
Meadway The
 Brighton BN2. . . . . 164 F5
 Shoreham-by-S BN43. . . 161 A6
Mealla Cl BN7 . . . . 190 A4
Medina Dr BN24 . . . . . . 174 B5
Medina Pl BN3. . . . . 163 B6
Medina Terr
 Hove BN3. . . . . 163 B5
 St Leonards TN38 . . . . . 159 A6
Medina Villas BN3 . . . . . 163 B6
Medmerry Hill BN2. . . . . 143 E2
Medway
 Crowborough TN6 . . . . . 26 C1
 Hailsham BN27 . . . . 129 A2
Medway Dr
 East Grinstead RH19 . . . 10 D6
 Forest Row RH18 . . . . . 12 A2
Medway La BN24. . . . . . 174 A5
Medway Rd TN1 . . . . .8 B5
Medway View RH18 . . . . 12 A2
Meeching Cl BN9 . . . . . . 179 D7
Meeching Pl BN9 . . . . . . 179 C7
Meeching Rd BN9 . . . . . 179 D7
Meeching Rise BN9 . . . . 179 D7
Meeching Valley Prim Sch
 BN9. . . . . 179 B7
Meeds Rd RH15 . . . . . . 73 A4
Meeting House La BN1 . 189 B2
Megrims Hill TN18 . . . . . 47 A6
Melbourne Rd BN22 . . . 185 B4
Melbourne St BN2 . . . . . 164 C8
Melfort Rd TN6 . . . . 25 D1
Melrose Ave BN41 . . . . . 141 A1
Melrose Cl
 Brighton BN1. . . . . 143 C2
 Hailsham BN27 . . . . 152 A8
Melrose Ho TN6 . . . . . . 25 E1
Melville Rd BN3. . . . . . . 163 E7
Melvill La BN20 . . . . 173 B1
Mendip Ave BN20 . . . . . 174 D3
Mendip Gdns TN34 . . . . 160 B7
Mendip Wlk TN2. . . . . . . .8 D5
Menzies Rd TN38 . . . . . 136 B2
Meon Cl BN24 . . . . 174 A5
Mercatoria TN38 . . . . . . 159 C6
Mercers TN3 . . . . .7 A3
Mercer St TN1. . . . . .8 B5
Mercia Ct **1** TN40 . . . . . 157 C4
Mercread Rd BN25 . . . . 180 F3
Meres La TN20 . . . . 58 D7
Merevale BN1 . . . . 143 B6
Merewood Ct BN21 . . . . 184 E4
Mereworth Rd TN4. . . . . .8 A6
Meridian Ctr BN10 . . . . 178 C8
Meridian Ind Est The
 BN10. . . . . 178 C7
Meridian Prim Sch BN10. 167 C1
Meridian Rd BN7 . . . . . . 123 B2
Meridian Way
 East Grinstead RH19. . . . .1 F3
 Peacehaven BN10 . . . . . 178 C7
Merivale TN35 . . . . 137 A6
Merlin Cl BN3 . . . . 163 D8
Merlin Ct BN27 . . . . 152 E2
Merlin Way RH19 . . . . . .2 A3
Merlynn **12** BN21 . . . . . . 185 A2
Mermaid Pas 3 TN31 . . . 93 B5
Mermaid St TN31 . . . . . 93 B5
Merrimac Ho 1 TN40 . . . 157 E4
Merrimede Cl TN38 . . . . 159 A7
Merriments Gdns★ TN19 . 45 D5
Merriments La TN18, TN19 45 D5
Merrion Cl TN4. . . . . .8 B7
Merrion Way TN4. . . . . . .8 B7
Merston Ct BN2 . . . . 165 E6
Merton Ct
 7 Bexhill TN40. . . . . 157 E4
 Brighton BN2. . . . . 165 A3
Meryon Ct TN31. . . . . . . 93 C5
Metcalfe Ave BN9 . . . . . 179 B8
Metropole Ct
 12 Brighton BN1. . . . . 163 E6
 11 Eastbourne BN22. . 185 B3
Mewetts Ct BN20 . . . . . 173 B3
Mews Ct RH19 . . . . 10 F6
Mews Rd TN38. . . . . 159 C6
Mews The
 Brighton BN1. . . . . 142 E2
 East Hoathly BN8. . . . . . 105 A5
 Pembury TN2 . . . . .9 C6
 5 Royal Tunbridge Wells
 TN1. . . . . 8 B3
 Seaford BN25 . . . . 181 B4
Meyners Ct BN3 . . . . . . 141 C3
Michael Fields RH18 . . . 11 E2
Michael Hall Sch RH18. . 11 D1
Michelbourne Cl RH15 . . 72 E1
Michel Cl BN20 . . . . 183 C1
Michel Dene Cl BN20. . . 183 C1
Michel Dene Rd BN20. . . 183 C1
Michele Cl **5** TN38 . . . . 136 B1
Michel Gr BN21 . . . . 184 E4
Michelham Ct BN23 . . . . 174 A4
Michelham Priory & Gdns★
 BN27. . . . . 151 B7
Michelham Rd TN22. . . . 55 C3
Michelson Cl TN38 . . . . 135 F4
Micklefield Way BN25. . . 181 B3
Middle Cl TN33 . . . . 86 B2
Middle Dr TN22 . . . . 55 A6
Middle Farm Countryside
 Ctr★ BN8 . . . . 148 F4
Middle Field TN2 . . . . . . .9 E8
Middle Furlong BN25. . . 180 F3
Middleham Cl BN8 . . . . . 124 C4
Middleham Way BN23 . . 174 C4

Middle La TN21 . . . . 83 E3
Middle Rd
 Bells Yew Green TN3 . . . 18 A5
 Brighton BN1. . . . . 142 E1
 Hastings TN35 . . . . 160 D8
 Shoreham-by-S BN43. . . 161 B7
Middle Row **1** RH19 . . . 10 F8
Middle St Prim Sch BN1 189 A2
Middlesex Ct **4** BN2 . . . 185 B4
Middlesex Rd TN40. . . . . 157 D3
Middle St
 Brighton BN1. . . . . 189 A2
 Falmer BN1 . . . . 144 C6
 9 Hastings TN34 . . . . 159 F8
 Portslade-by-S BN41. . . . 162 B6
Middleton Ave BN3 . . . . 162 D6
Middleton Dr BN23. . . . . 185 E7
Middleton Rise BN1 . . . . 143 E5
Middle Village RH16 . . . 50 C2
Middleway BN27 . . . . . . 131 B5
Middle Way
 Burgess Hill RH15 . . . . . 73 B3
 Lewes BN7. . . . . 123 A1
Middle Wlk TN2. . . . . . . .8 E8
Midfields Cl RH15 . . . . . 73 B3
Midfields Dr RH15 . . . . . 73 B3
Midfields Wlk RH15 . . . . 73 B3
Midhurst Rd BN22. . . . . . 173 F2
Midhurst Rise BN1 . . . . 143 B6
Midhurst Wlk BN3 . . . . . 141 F3
Midway Rd BN20 . . . . . . 165 C8
Midway The TN4 . . . . . . .7 D2
Mighell St BN2 . . . . 189 C2
Milchester Ho BN20. . . . 188 E8
Milcote Ave BN3 . . . . . . 162 F8
Mildenhall Dr TN37 . . . . 136 B3
Mildmay Cl BN8. . . . . . . 124 D6
Mildmay Rd BN7 . . . . . . 123 A1
Mile End Cotts BN1 . . . . 142 E6
MILE OAK 140 F4
Mile Oak Cres BN42 . . . 140 F1
Mile Oak Gdns BN41 . . . 141 A1
Mile Oak Prim Sch BN41 140 F3
Mile Oak Rd
 Portslade-by-S BN41 . . . 140 F3
 Southwick BN42. . . . . . . 140 F1
Milestones TN21 . . . . . . 82 B8
Miles Wlk BN3 . . . . 163 B6
Milfoil Dr BN23 . . . . 174 B3
Military Rd TN30, TN31. . 70 F3
Milland Cl TN40 . . . . 157 E6
Milland Rd BN27 . . . . . . 129 B1
Millbank RH15 . . . . 73 B4
Millberg Rd BN25 . . . . . 181 C4
MILLBROOK 35 C6
Millbrook Bsns Pk TN6 . . 38 D8
Millbrook Gdns BN20. . . 184 B6
Millbrook Ind Est TN6 . . 38 D8
Millbrook Rd TN6 . . . . . 26 A3
Mill Brooks BN8 . . . . . . 100 D7
Mill Cl
 Burgess Hill RH15 . . . . . 73 B4
 East Grinstead RH19 . . . 10 E7
 Friston BN20 . . . . 183 A1
 Hastings TN35 . . . . 160 E8
 Heathfield TN21. . . . . . . 81 F7
 Polegate BN26 . . . . 172 F4
 Portslade-by-S BN41. . . . 141 C1
 Ringmer BN8 . . . . 124 E5
 South Chailey BN8. . . . . 100 D7
 Staplecross TN32. . . . . . 65 E2
 Westfield TN35 . . . . 114 E5
Mill Cnr TN31. . . . . 67 A3
MILL CORNER 67 A3
Mill Cotts RH19 . . . . 10 E7
Mill Cres TN6 . . . . 25 F3
Millcroft BN1 . . . . 142 C5
Millcroft Ave BN41 . . . . 140 E1
Millcroft Gdns BN42. . . . 140 E1
Millcross Rd BN41 . . . . . 141 B1
Mill Ct RH15. . . . . 73 B2
Milldown Rd BN25 . . . . . 180 F3
Mill Dr
 Crowborough TN6 . . . . . 25 F3
 Hove BN3. . . . . 142 A3
 Seaford BN25 . . . . 181 A3
Mill Dro
 Seaford BN25 . . . . 180 A5
 Uckfield TN22. . . . . 78 C6
Miller Pl BN43 . . . . 141 A3
Millers Cl RH15 . . . . 73 A4
Miller's Hill TN35 . . . . . . 114 E6
Miller's Rd BN1 . . . . 142 E1
Millers Rise BN27 . . . . . 152 A6
Millers Way RH15 . . . . . 73 B4
Millfield
 2 Bexhill TN40. . . . . 157 C4
 Ninfield TN33. . . . . 133 A6
Millfield Cl
 Newick BN8 . . . . 76 C7
 Seaford BN25 . . . . 181 B4
Millfield Cotts **8** BN20. . 164 D4
Millfield Ct **3** TN40. . . . . 157 C4
Millfield Rise TN40. . . . . 157 C4
Millfields BN26 . . . . 173 A7
Millfields BN23 . . . . 173 A7
Mill Gap Rd BN21 . . . . . 184 F4
Mill Gdns
 Heathfield TN21. . . . . . . 82 A5
 Ringmer BN8 . . . . 124 D5
Mill Green Ind Est RH16. . 50 E6
Mill Green Rd RH16 . . . . 50 E6
Millham Ct TN36 . . . . . . 156 F5
Millhaven Ct RH15 . . . . . 73 B3
MILL HILL 174 D6
Mill Hill Cl RH16 . . . . . . 50 E7
Mill Ho BN26 . . . . 173 A7

Millington Ct TN22 . . . . . . 78 C6
Mill La
  Barcombe BN8 . . . . . . 101 D2
  Clayton BN6, BN45 . . . . 119 E7
  Crowborough TN6 . . . . . 25 E2
  Dormansland RH7 . . . . 1 F8
  East Hoathly BN8 . . . . . 105 A5
  Flackley Ash TN31 . . . . . 68 F3
  Goddards' Green BN6 . . . 72 A3
  Hastings TN35 . . . . . . 137 E5
  Hellingly BN27 . . . . . . 129 A6
  Hooe Common TN33 . . . 132 F2
  Mark Cross TN6 . . . . 28 A3
  Portslade-by-S BN41 . . . 141 B1
  Punnett's Town TN21 . . . 83 D6
  Rodmell BN7 . . . . 167 D8
  South Chailey BN8 . . . . 100 D7
  Uckfield TN22 . . . . 78 C6
  Westfield TN35 . . . . . . 114 E5
Mill Mead BN8 . . . . . . 124 E5
Mill Path BN8 . . . . 124 E5
Mill Pk RH15 . . . . 73 B3
Mill Race BN6 . . . . 97 E8
Millrace The BN26 . . . . 172 F4
Mill Rd
  Brighton BN1 . . . . 142 C6
  Burgess Hill RH15 . . . . . 73 B3
  Eastbourne BN21 . . . . . 184 E5
  Hailsham BN27 . . . . . . 152 D6
  Heathfield TN21 . . . . . . 81 F7
  Lewes BN7 . . . . 190 C4
  Portslade-by-S BN41 . . . 162 B7
  Ringmer BN8 . . . . 124 D5
  Rye TN31 . . . . 93 C7
  Winchelsea TN36 . . . . . 117 E8
Mill Rd Ind Est BN41 . . . 162 B7
Mill Rise
  Brighton BN1 . . . . 142 C5
  Heathfield TN21 . . . . . . 82 A8
  Robertsbridge TN32 . . . . 64 A3
Mill Row BN1 . . . . 189 C4
Mill St
  Falmer BN1 . . . . 144 C7
  Sandhurst TN18 . . . . . . 47 B8
Millstream Cl TN3 . . . . . . 5 D2
Millstream BN26 . . . . . 172 F4
Mill Stream Mdw RH16 . . 50 D7
Mill View BN8 . . . . 124 C4
Mill View Cl BN24 . . . . . 174 D6
Mill View Hospl BN3 . . . 141 E1
Mill View Rd TN39 . . . . 157 B7
Millward Rd BN24 . . . . . 175 C3
Mill Way
  East Grinstead RH19 . . . . 10 E7
  Polegate BN26 . . . . . . 172 E4
Mill Wood RH15 . . . . . . 73 B3
Millwood Cl TN22 . . . . . 55 D4
Millwood La TN22 . . . . . 55 C4
Millwood Rd TN39 . . . . 157 A8
Millyard Cres BN2 . . . . 165 D7
Milner Flats BN2 . . . . . 189 C2
Milner Rd BN3 . . . . 141 D1
Milnthorpe Gdns BN20 . . 188 E8
Milnthorpe Rd
  Eastbourne BN20 . . . . . 188 E8
  Hove BN3 . . . . 162 F8
Milton Cres
  Eastbourne BN21 . . . . . 184 C4
  East Grinstead RH19 . . . . 10 C8
Milton Ct RH16 . . . . . . 50 D5
Milton Dr
  Royal Tunbridge Wells TN2 . . 8 D7
  Southwick BN42 . . . . . 161 F8
Milton Rd
  Brighton BN2 . . . . 189 C4
  Eastbourne BN24 . . . . . 184 C4
  Haywards Heath RH16 . . . 50 D6
Milton St BN24 . . . . . . 174 B7
MILTON STREET 171 D5
Milward Cres TN34 . . . . 160 A4
Milward Ct 3 BN43 . . . . 161 C8
Milward Rd TN34 . . . . . 160 A5
Mimosa Cl BN26 . . . . . 173 A4
Mimosa Ct BN1 . . . . . . 143 B3
Mimram Rd BN24 . . . . . 174 A5
Mindelheim Ave RH19 . . . 2 B7
Minnels The BN6 . . . . . . 98 A3
Minsted Sq TN39 . . . . . 156 C2
Minster Ct BN26 . . . . . 173 A7
Mint The TN31 . . . . 93 B5
Mistley Cl TN40 . . . . . . 158 A6
Mistral Cl TN37 . . . . . . 136 C6
Mitchelldean BN10 . . . . 167 C1
Mitre Ho 23 BN1 . . . . . 163 E6
Mitten Rd TN40 . . . . . . 157 C4
Moat Croft Ct BN21 . . . . 184 E3
Moat Croft Rd BN21 . . . 184 E4
Moat Farm TN2 . . . . 17 A7
Moat Ho BN21 . . . . 184 E3
Moat La
  Cowden TN8 . . . . 4 E7
  Waldron TN21 . . . . 80 D2
  Westfield TN33 . . . . . . 114 B3
Moat Lake Cotts TN21 . . . 80 F4
Moat Rd RH19 . . . . 1 E2
Mocatta Way RH15 . . . . 72 D5
Modena Rd BN3 . . . . . . 162 F7
Moira House Girls Sch
  BN20 . . . . 188 D8
Moira House Jun Sch
  BN20 . . . . 184 D1
Mole Cl BN24 . . . . 174 A5
Molesey Ct TN22 . . . . . 78 C7
Molesworth St BN3 . . . . 162 F8
Molineux Pl RH16 . . . . . 50 D5
Molyneux Almshouses TN4 7 B4
Molyneux Ct TN4 . . . . . . 7 F4
Molyneux Park Gdns TN4 . . 7 F4

Molyneux Park Rd TN4 . . . 7 F4
Monarch Gdns
  Eastbourne BN23 . . . . . 174 F1
  Seaford BN25 . . . . 181 A5
  St Leonards TN37 . . . . . 136 A5
Monarch Ho BN22 . . . . . 185 E5
Monarchs View BN41 . . . 140 F2
Mona Rd BN22 . . . . 185 B5
Monastery Gdns TN6 . . . . 39 B8
Monceux Rd
  Eastbourne BN21 . . . . . 184 C4
  Herstmonceux BN27 . . . 130 E6
Monckton Way BN41 . . . 145 E5
Monger's Mead BN8 . . . 101 E4
Monk Cl BN1 . . . . 143 E6
Monk's House ★ BN7 . . . 146 E1
Monks La
  Lewes BN7 . . . . 190 A1
  Newbury's TN5 . . . . . . 30 B8
Monks Way
  Lewes BN7 . . . . 190 A4
  Northiam TN31 . . . . 67 B8
Monks' Wlk TN36 . . . . . 117 E7
Monson Rd TN1 . . . . 8 B4
Monson Way 5 TN1 . . . . . 8 B4
Montacute Gdns TN2 . . . . 7 F2
Montacute Mews TN2 . . . . 8 A1
Montacute Rd
  Kingston near Lewes
    BN7 . . . . 145 F8
  Lewes BN7 . . . . 146 A8
  Royal Tunbridge Wells TN2 . . 8 A1
Montacute Way TN22 . . . 78 D8
Montague Cl BN43 . . . . . 161 D7
Montague Ct
  6 Brighton BN2 . . . . . 164 C4
  2 Shoreham-by-S BN43 . 161 D7
Montague Pl BN2 . . . . . 164 C4
Montague St 4 BN2 . . . . 164 C4
Montague Way BN24 . . . 174 F5
Montana St TN38 . . . . . 135 E6
Montargis Way TN6 . . . . 26 A1
Monteith St TN1 . . . . 7 A3
Monterey Cl TN39 . . . . . 156 E3
Monterey Ct BN1 . . . . . 142 E3
Monterey Gdns TN39 . . . 156 E3
Monterey Wharf 5
  BN23 . . . . 175 A1
Montes Hill RH16 . . . . . 51 F8
Monteswood La RH16,
  RH17 . . . . 52 B8
Montford Cl BN43 . . . . . 161 D8
Montfort Cl BN24 . . . . . 174 F6
Montfort Rd BN24 . . . . . 174 F6
Montgomery Rd
  Hastings TN35 . . . . . . 137 D5
  Royal Tunbridge Wells TN4 . . 8 B7
Montgomery St BN3 . . . 163 A7
Montgomery Terr 2
  BN3 . . . . 163 A7
Montpelier Cres BN1 . . . 163 E6
Montpelier Lodge 9
  BN1 . . . . 163 E6
Montpelier Pl BN1 . . . . . 163 E6
Montpelier Rd BN1 . . . . 163 E5
Montpelier St BN1 . . . . . 163 E6
Montpelier Terr BN1 . . . 163 E6
Montpelier Villas BN1 . . 163 E6
Montpellier Apartments 25
  BN1 . . . . 163 E5
Montreal Rd BN2 . . . . . 189 C3
Montserrat 2 TN39 . . . . 157 A2
Monument View BN2 . . . 164 D6
Moonrise Way BN27 . . . 127 C3
Moons Hill TN33 . . . . . 133 B6
Moon's La RH7 . . . . 2 B8
Moons Yd TN6 . . . . 39 B8
Moore Pk BN27 . . . . . . 152 D7
Moore's La TN31 . . . . . . 90 E8
Moor Hall Dr TN33 . . . . 132 F6
Moorhen Cl TN38 . . . . . 158 E8
Moor Hill TN18 . . . . 45 F8
Moorhurst Rd TN38 . . . . 135 F5
Moorings The
  Eastbourne BN20 . . . . . 188 E8
  East Grinstead RH19 . . . . 1 A3
  Lewes BN7 . . . . 190 C2
  Shoreham-by-S BN43 . . . 161 C6
Moor La
  Ringmer BN8 . . . . 125 B3
  Westfield TN35 . . . . . . 114 E3
Moor Pl RH19 . . . . 1 D2
Moor Rd TN35 . . . . 114 E4
MOOR THE 45 F8
Moor The TN18 . . . . 45 F8
Moray Wlk BN27 . . . . . 129 A2
Morecambe Rd BN1 . . . . 143 A6
Morehouse Farm Bsns Ctr
  RH7 . . . . 74 A6
Morestead BN10 . . . . . 167 D1
Morgan Cl TN39 . . . . . . 157 B8
Morgay Wood La TN35 . . 115 E2
Morlais Pl TN36 . . . . . . 118 B6
Morlais Ridge TN36 . . . 118 B6
Morland Dr TN3 . . . . 20 B5
Morlands Cl TN33 . . . . . 133 B5
Morley Cl BN7 . . . . 146 B8
Morley Lodge BN2 . . . . 189 C4
Morley St BN2 . . . . 189 C3
Morningside Cl BN25 . . . 180 F4
Mornington Cres BN3 . . 162 D7
Mornington Mans 5
  BN3 . . . . 162 D7
Morris Rd BN7 . . . . 190 C2
Mortain Pk BN27 . . . . . 152 D7
Mortain Rd BN24 . . . . . 174 F6
Mortimer Gdns BN26 . . . 172 F4

Mortimer Mews BN3 . . . 163 A8
Mortimer Rd
  Eastbourne BN22 . . . . . 185 A6
  Hove BN3 . . . . 162 F8
Morton Ct BN41 . . . . . . 162 B8
Morton Rd RH19 . . . . . . 10 E7
Moscow Rd TN35 . . . . . 160 C7
Moss Ho BN21 . . . . 184 F2
Motcombe Com Inf Sch
  BN21 . . . . 184 C5
Motcombe Ct 9 TN40 . . . 157 D3
Motcombe La BN21 . . . . 184 D4
Motcombe Pool BN21 . . 184 D4
Motcombe Rd BN21 . . . . 184 D4
Motte Field TN7 . . . . 13 E4
Mottins Hill TN6 . . . . . . 38 D8
MOTT'S MILL 15 A3
MOULSECOOMB 143 E2
Moulsecoomb Prim Sch
  BN2 . . . . 143 E3
Moulsecoomb Sta BN2 . . 143 F4
Moulsecoomb Way BN2 . 143 F4
Mountain Ash Cl BN27 . . 152 A8
Mountbatten Cl TN35 . . . 137 D5
Mountbatten Ct BN3 . . . 162 E8
Mountbatten Dr BN23 . . 185 F7
Mount Caburn Cres
  BN10 . . . . 167 C2
**Mount Caburn National
  Nature Reserve** ★ BN8 . . 147 C5
Mount Cl BN9 . . . . 179 F8
Mount Dr BN2 . . . . 166 D2
Mount Edgcumbe Rd TN4 . . 8 A3
MOUNT EPHRAIM 7 F4
Mount Ephraim TN4 . . . . 8 A4
MOUNT EPHRAIM 78 F3
Mount Ephraim Ct TN4 . . . 7 F4
Mount Ephraim Rd TN1 . . 8 A4
MOUNTFIELD 87 C5
Mountfield Ct 4 TN1 . . . . 8 B3
Mountfield Hill TN33 . . . . 8 B3
Mountfield La TN32 . . . . 86 C8
Mountfield Rd
  Eastbourne BN22 . . . . . 173 F1
  Lewes BN7 . . . . 190 B1
  Royal Tunbridge Wells TN1 . . 8 B3
Mountfields BN1 . . . . . 143 C2
Mountfield Villas TN32 . . 87 C5
**Mountfield & Whatlington CE
  Prim Sch** TN32 . . . . . . 87 D7
Mount Harry Rd BN7 . . . 123 A2
Mount Idol View TN39 . . 157 A8
Mount Joy TN33 . . . . . . 112 D5
Mountney Bridge Bsns Pk
  BN24 . . . . 174 F4
Mountney Dr BN24 . . . . 175 F7
Mountney Rd BN21 . . . . 184 C4
Mount Pl BN7 . . . . 190 A2
Mount Pleasant
  Blackboys TN22 . . . . . . 80 A6
  Brighton BN2 . . . . 189 C4
  Crowborough TN6 . . . . . 38 B7
  Durgates TN5 . . . . 29 E5
  Lamberhurst TN3 . . . . . 19 E6
MOUNT PLEASANT 101 F6
Mount Pleasant BN7 . . . 190 A2
MOUNT PLEASANT 168 F1
Mount Pleasant
  Spithurst BN8 . . . . 101 E6
  6 St Leonards TN38 . . . 159 C6
  The Moor TN18 . . . . . . 45 F8
  Uckfield TN22 . . . . 78 C6
Mount Pleasant Ave 2
  TN1 . . . . 8 B3
Mount Pleasant Cres 2
  TN34 . . . . 136 F1
Mount Pleasant Ct TN34 . 160 A6
Mount Pleasant La 2 . . . 20 A6
Mount Pleasant Rd
  Hastings TN34 . . . . . . 160 A6
  Royal Tunbridge Wells TN1 . . 8 A3
Mount Rd
  Eastbourne BN20 . . . . . 188 F8
  Hastings TN35 . . . . . . 160 C7
  Newhaven BN9 . . . . . . 179 F8
Mountreed TN20 . . . . . . 58 D7
MOUNT SION 8 A2
Mount Sion TN1 . . . . 8 A2
Mount St
  Battle TN33 . . . . 112 D5
  Lewes BN7 . . . . 190 A1
Mount The
  Hailsham BN27 . . . . . . 152 C6
  St Leonards TN38 . . . . 159 B7
  Uckfield TN22 . . . . 78 C6
Mount View Terr BN27 . . 152 C6
Mount Zion Pl BN1 . . . . 189 A3
Mowden Sch BN3 . . . . . 142 D1
Moy Ave BN22 . . . . 185 B5
Moyne Cl BN3 . . . . 141 E1
Muddles Gn BN8 . . . . . 127 E7
MUDDLES GREEN 127 F8
Muirfield Ct 16 RH16 . . . 50 E4
Muirfield Rise TN38 . . . . 158 F8
Mulberry Cl
  Bexhill TN39 . . . . 156 C4
  Brighton BN1 . . . . 142 F3
  Eastbourne BN22 . . . . . 173 E3
  Shoreham-by-S BN43 . . . 140 D1
Mulberry La BN6 . . . . . . 98 D3
Mulberry Pk TN22 . . . . . 55 B5
Mulberry Way TN21 . . . . 82 B5
Mulberry Wlk TN37 . . . . 136 C5
Mullany Bsns Pk BN27 . . 127 B4
Munns Dr RH15 . . . . 73 B4
Munster Cotts BN8 . . . . 101 E4
Munster Gn BN8 . . . . . . 101 E4

Muriel Ho BN3 . . . . 162 E8
Murray Ave BN9 . . . . . . 179 C7
Museum of Local History
  TN33 . . . . 112 D4
Museum of Rural Life ★
  TN32 . . . . 64 B4
Musgrave Ave RH19 . . . . 10 E8
Musgrave Collection Mus ★
  BN22 . . . . 185 B2
Mushroom Field BN7 . . . 145 E5
Muskerry Ct TN4 . . . . 7 B4
Muster Ct RH16 . . . . . . 50 D4
Muster Green RH16 . . . . 50 D4
Muster Green S RH16 . . . 50 D4
MUTTON HALL 82 A8
Mutton Hall Hill TN21 . . . 82 B8
Mutton Hall La TN21 . . . . 82 B8
Mutton Hill TN6 . . . . 2 B7
Myrtle Cotts 3 TN6 . . . . . 25 F3
Myrtle Rd
  Crowborough TN6 . . . . . 25 F1
  Eastbourne BN22 . . . . . 185 D6

N

Namrik Mews BN3 . . . . . 163 A6
Nan Kemp's Grave BN7 . . 145 E6
Nanson Rd BN3 . . . . . . 143 D6
Nan Tucks La TN22 . . . . . 56 C2
Naomi Cl BN20 . . . . 184 E1
Napier Ho 3 BN2 . . . . . 164 C7
Napier Rd
  Royal Tunbridge Wells TN2 . . 8 D2
  St Leonards TN38 . . . . 135 E4
Nash La RH17 . . . . 52 B4
NASH STREET 128 A6
Natal Rd BN2 . . . . 143 D1
Neale Cl RH19 . . . . 1 B3
Neath Rd TN31 . . . . 96 A3
Neaves La BN8 . . . . 125 A5
Neill's Cl BN9 . . . . 179 C7
Neills Rd TN33 . . . . 19 D2
Neilson Ct TN34 . . . . . . 136 D1
Nellington Ct TN4 . . . . . . 7 B4
Nellington Rd TN3, TN4 . . . 7 B4
Nelson Dr BN23 . . . . . . 185 E6
Nelson Rd TN39 . . . . . . 156 E4
Nelson Pl 17 BN2 . . . . . 189 C3
Nelson Rd
  Hastings TN34 . . . . . . 160 A5
  Royal Tunbridge Wells TN2 . . 8 D2
Nelson Row BN2 . . . . . . 189 C2
Neptune Ct BN2 . . . . . . 164 F3
Nesbitt Rd BN2 . . . . . . 143 D1
Nestor Ct BN1 . . . . 163 E8
NETHERFIELD 86 C2
Netherfield Ave BN23 . . 174 F2
Netherfield CE Prim Sch
  TN33 . . . . 86 C2
Netherfield Gn BN2 . . . . 165 F8
Netherfield Hill TN33 . . . 112 C7
Netherfield Hill Cotts
  TN33 . . . . 112 B7
Netherfield Rd TN33 . . . 111 F8
Netherfield Way TN33 . . . 86 D2
Nether La TN22 . . . . 35 C3
Netherwood Cl TN34 . . . 136 F5
Net Shops The ★ TN35 . . 160 B3
Nettleton St BN1 . . . . . . 143 B1
Nevill Ave
  Eastbourne BN22 . . . . . 173 E1
  Hove BN3 . . . . 141 F1
Nevill Cl
  Crowborough TN6 . . . . . 37 C8
  Hove BN3 . . . . 142 A2
Nevill Cotts BN6 . . . . . . 98 D2
Nevill Cres BN7 . . . . . . 123 A1
Nevill Ct
  Crowborough TN6 . . . . . 37 C8
  Hove BN3 . . . . 142 A1
Nevill Gate TN2 . . . . 8 B1
Nevill Gdns BN3 . . . . . . 142 A2
Nevill Gn TN22 . . . . 55 D1
Nevill Lodge TN2 . . . . . . 8 C4
NEVILL PARK 7 D2
Nevill Pk TN4 . . . . 7 E3
Nevill Pl BN3 . . . . 142 A2
Nevill Rd
  Crowborough TN6 . . . . . 25 F3
  Hove BN3 . . . . 142 A2
  Lewes BN7 . . . . 123 A2
  Rottingdean BN2 . . . . . 165 F1
  Uckfield TN22 . . . . 55 D1
Nevill Ridge TN4 . . . . . . 7 D3
Nevill St TN2 . . . . 8 A2
Nevill Terr
  7 Crowborough TN6 . . . 25 F3
  1 Lewes BN7 . . . . . . 123 B1
  Royal Tunbridge Wells TN2 . . 7 F2
Nevill Way BN3 . . . . . . 142 A2
Newark Pl BN2 . . . . 189 C3
New Barn Cl
  Hailsham BN27 . . . . . . 152 C6
  Portslade-by-S BN41 . . . 141 B2
  Shoreham-by-S BN43 . . . 140 D1
New Barn La TN22 . . . . . 78 C5
New Barn Rd
  Rottingdean BN2 . . . . . 165 F3
  Shoreham-by-S BN43 . . . 140 B1
NEWBRIDGE 23 F6
Newbury Cotts TN5 . . . . 30 B8
Newbury La TN5 . . . . . . 30 B8
NEWBURY'S 30 B8
New Church Rd BN3 ★ . . 162 E7

New Coastguards Cotts 6
  BN25 . . . . 180 C4
New College Cl BN23 . . . 174 C4
Newcomen Rd TN4 . . . . . 8 A5
New Cotts
  Crowborough TN6 . . . . . 38 C8
  Eastbourne BN20 . . . . . 188 B8
  Poundford TN20 . . . . . . 58 B6
  Scaynes Hill RH17 . . . . . 51 F1
  The Moor TN18 . . . . . . 45 B7
NEW CUT 114 E5
New Cut
  Mountfield TN32 . . . . . . 87 C5
  Westfield TN35 . . . . . . 114 E4
Newdigate Ho 2 TN40 . . 157 D3
New Dorset St BN1 . . . . 189 A3
Newells Cl BN2 . . . . 144 E1
NEWENDEN 48 D3
New England Ho BN1 . . . 189 B4
New England La
  Rye TN31 . . . . 93 C8
  Sedlescombe TN33 . . . . 113 F6
New England Rd
  Brighton BN1 . . . . 189 A4
  Haywards Heath RH16 . . . 50 F4
  Royal Tunbridge Wells TN4 . . 8 A7
New England Rise BN41 . 141 A4
New England St BN1 . . . 189 B4
New Farthingdale RH7 . . . 2 B8
Newfield La BN9 . . . . . . 179 C7
Newfield Rd BN9 . . . . . . 179 C7
Newgate Rd TN37 . . . . . 136 C1
NEWHAVEN 179 E6
Newhaven Fort ★ BN9 . . 179 D5
Newhaven Harbour Sta
  BN9 . . . . 179 D6
Newhaven Hts BN9 . . . . 179 C5
**Newhaven Local & Maritime
  Mus** ★ BN9 . . . . 168 D1
Newhaven Polyclinic
  BN9 . . . . 179 C7
Newhaven Rd BN25 . . . . 180 B5
Newhaven Sq BN9 . . . . 179 D7
Newhaven St BN2 . . . . . 189 C4
Newhaven Town Sta
  BN9 . . . . 179 D8
Newhaven Wlk TN38 . . . 136 A3
New Horizons Best Ctr
  TN38 . . . . 135 F4
New Horizons Sch TN38 . 136 A4
NEWICK 76 C8
Newick CE Prim Sch BN8 . 76 C6
Newick Cl BN25 . . . . . . 181 C2
Newick Dr BN8 . . . . 76 C7
Newick Hill BN8 . . . . . . 76 C8
Newick House Sch RH15 . 73 C1
Newick La TN20, TN21 . . . 59 C5
Newick Rd
  Brighton BN1 . . . . 143 E4
  Eastbourne BN20 . . . . . 184 C6
Newington Ct TN5 . . . . . 31 E1
Newlands TN3 . . . . 7 A3
Newlands Ave TN39 . . . . 157 B5
Newlands Cl
  Hastings TN34 . . . . . . 136 E5
  Keymer BN6 . . . . 98 B3
Newlands Cres RH19 . . . . 1 D2
Newlands Manor Sch
  BN25 . . . . 181 B4
Newlands Park Way BN8 . 76 C7
Newlands Pl RH18 . . . . . 11 F3
Newlands Prep Sch
  BN25 . . . . 181 B4
Newlands Rd
  Rottingdean BN2 . . . . . 166 A1
  Royal Tunbridge Wells TN4 . . 8 B7
Newlands Rise TN4 . . . . . 8 A6
Newlands Way TN4 . . . . . 8 B7
New Langney Ct BN23 . . 174 E1
New Larchwood BN1 . . . 143 D6
New Lydd Rd TN31 . . . . . 94 E2
Newlyn Ct 14 TN40 . . . . 157 D3
Newmans Way TN35 . . . 160 D8
Newmarket Rd BN2 . . . . 164 C8
Newmarket Terr 12 BN2 . 164 C8
New Moorsite TN35 . . . . 114 E4
Newnham Rd TN21 . . . . . 82 A6
Newnham Way TN21 . . . . 82 A7
New Park Ave TN40 . . . . 157 C4
New Pl
  Eastbourne BN21 . . . . . 184 D3
  Uckfield TN22 . . . . 78 C5
New Place Cl TN22 . . . . . 78 C6
New Pond Hill TN21 . . . . 81 D6
Newport 4 BN43 . . . . . . 161 B6
Newport Rd RH15 . . . . . 72 F3
Newport St BN2 . . . . . . 189 C4
New Rd
  Brighton BN1 . . . . 189 B2
  Crowborough TN6 . . . . . 25 D3
  Eastbourne BN2 . . . . . 185 B4
  Fairlight TN35 . . . . . . 138 D4
  Hailsham BN27 . . . . . . 129 C4
  Hastings TN35 . . . . . . 160 D6
  Keymer BN6 . . . . 98 B2
  Lewes BN7 . . . . 190 A2
  Mill Corner TN31 . . . . . 67 B3
  Newhaven BN9 . . . . . . 168 D1
  Polegate BN26 . . . . . . 173 B6
  Ringmer BN8 . . . . 124 D3
  Rotherfield TN6 . . . . . . 39 C8
  Rye TN31 . . . . 93 D6
  Saint's Hill TN11 . . . . . . 6 A8
  Trolliloes BN27 . . . . . . 108 D2
  Uckfield TN22 . . . . 78 D3

Newstead BN1 189 A4
New Steine BN2 189 C1
New Steine Mews BN2 189 C2
Newtimber Dr BN41 141 A1
Newton Ave RH19 10 F6
Newton Cl RH16 51 B7
Newton Ct RH16 50 E5
Newton Pk BN27 152 D7
Newton Rd
Lewes BN7 123 B2
Lindfield RH16 51 C7
Peacehaven BN10 178 C7
Royal Tunbridge Wells TN1 8 B4
Newtons Hill TN7 13 D3
NEWTON'S HILL 13 C3
Newton's Hill TN7 13 D3
Newton Willows TN3 15 E2
NEW TOWN 78 E5
Newtown Rd BN3 163 B8
Newts Way TN38 135 E1
New Upperton Rd 7 BN21 184 E4
New Way La BN6 97 B2
New Winchelsea Rd TN31, TN36 93 B3
Nicholson Ct BN23 174 E1
Nicolson Dr BN43 161 A8
Nightingale Cl
Eastbourne BN23 174 C2
East Grinstead RH19 10 D7
Haywards Heath RH16 50 F4
Nightingale Cotts TN35 114 D4
Nightingale La RH15 97 F8
Nightingale Rise TN22 78 D4
Nightingales The
Royal Tunbridge Wells TN4 8 A5
Uckfield TN22 78 E5
Nile St BN1 189 B2
NINFIELD 133 B6
Ninfield CE Prim Sch TN33 133 B5
Ninfield Pl BN2 164 E6
Ninfield Rd TN39 157 B7
Nizells Ave BN3 163 E7
Noahs Ark La RH16 51 C7
Noble Ct BN3 162 E7
Nodes La BN27 129 F4
Noel Gn RH15 73 B4
Noel Rise RH15 73 B4
Nolan Rd BN2 165 E7
Nook Cl TN35 160 D7
Nook The TN22 78 D4
Norbury Cl TN6 25 E4
Nore Rd BN9 179 B6
Norfolk Bldgs 5 BN1 163 E5
Norfolk Cl TN39 157 B7
Norfolk Ct
4 Brighton BN1 163 E5
4 Eastbourne BN22 185 C4
Norfolk Dr TN38 135 F5
Norfolk Ho 2 TN37 159 C7
Norfolk Mews 6 BN1 163 E5
Norfolk Pl 3 BN1 163 E5
Norfolk Rd
Brighton BN1 163 E6
Royal Tunbridge Wells TN1 8 B2
Norfolk Sq BN1 163 E5
Norfolk St BN1 163 E5
Norfolk Terr BN1 163 E6
Norfolk Way TN22 78 C8
NORLINGTON 124 D7
Norlington Ct BN8 124 D6
Norlington Fields BN8 124 D6
Norlington La BN8 124 D7
Norman Cl
Battle TN33 112 F4
Seaford BN25 180 B6
Norman Ct 6 TN34 159 E7
Normandale TN39 156 F3
Normandale Ho TN39 156 F3
Normandy Cl 7 RH19 10 F8
Normandy Ct 2 TN39 157 B3
Normandy Ho 3 BN3 163 C6
Normandy Rd TN34 136 C3
Normanhurst 10 BN2 189 C3
Norman Rd
Burgess Hill RH15 73 A3
Hove BN3 162 E6
Newhaven BN9 179 C7
Pevensey Bay BN24 175 D4
Royal Tunbridge Wells TN1 8 B5
St Leonards TN37 159 C6
Normans TN39 156 F3
Normansal Cl BN25 181 A6
Normansal Park Ave BN25 181 A6
NORMANS' BAY 176 D8
Normans' Bay Sta BN24 176 C8
Normansland TN22 36 B2
Normanton St 8 BN2 164 C7
Norstead Gdns TN4 8 B8
Northampton Way 1 TN38 136 A4
North Ave BN20 184 B5
North Bank BN6 97 E4
North Barnes La BN7 100 A5
North Beeches Rd TN6 26 A2
Northbourne Rd BN22 185 C6
Northbridge St TN32 64 B5
NORTHBRIDGE STREET 64 C6
North Camp La BN25 180 F5
NORTH CHAILEY 75 E6
North Cl
Polegate BN26 173 B7
Portslade-by-S BN41 141 A2
Northcliffe Cl BN25 180 F4
North Cnr TN21 107 C4
North Common Rd BN8, RH17 74 E5
Northcote La BN10 167 A1
North Crescent Ind Est BN27 152 A7
North Ct
Hassocks BN6 97 E4
Lewes BN7 190 C2
Northdown Cl BN9 179 C6
Northdown Rd BN9 179 B6
Northdown Terr RH19 1 D3
North Dr
Brighton BN2 164 C6
Dormansland RH19 2 B6
Northease Cl BN3 141 D2
Northease Dr BN3 141 E3
Northease Gdns BN3 141 E3
Northease Manor Sch BN7 146 C1
Northease Wall BN7 146 D3
North End BN6 98 D4
Northerlea BN41 141 A1
Northern Ave BN26 173 B7
North Farm Cotts BN41 141 A2
North Farm Rd TN2 8 C8
Northfield BN26 172 F5
Northfield Cl BN25 180 F5
Northfield Cotts TN22 102 D8
Northfield Rise
Hove BN3 141 D4
Rottingdean BN2 166 A2
Northfields TN3 7 A8
Northfields Bsns Pk BN27 128 A4
Northfield Way BN1 143 A4
Northgate Cl BN2 165 F2
North Gdns BN1 189 A3
North Heath Cl BN27 129 C2
NORTHIAM 67 B6
Northiam CE Prim Sch TN31 67 B5
Northiam Rd
Broad Oak TN31 90 A6
Eastbourne BN20, BN21 184 C4
Northiam Rise TN38 135 D2
Northiam Sta★ TN31 48 C2
North La
Portslade-by-S BN41 141 A3
Three Oaks TN35 115 E5
Northlands Ave RH16 51 B4
Northlands Cotts TN32 46 C1
Northlands Wood Com Prim Sch RH16 51 B4
North Lodge BN8 76 D7
NORTH MOULSECOOMB 143 E4
North Pl BN1 189 B2
North Point 1 BN43 161 A6
North Quay Rd BN9 179 D8
North Rd
Alfriston BN26 170 F3
Bexhill TN39 157 C7
Bodle Street Green BN27 109 C2
Brighton BN1 189 B3
Brighton, Preston BN1 142 E1
Haywards Heath RH16 51 A4
Pevensey Bay BN24 175 D5
Portslade-by-S BN41 141 A2
Ringmer BN8 124 D6
St Leonards TN37 136 C1
Northridge TN31 67 A7
North Road Cotts BN8 124 D6
North Row TN22 78 C8
North St Quadrant BN1 189 A2
North Salts TN31 93 C6
North-South Rd BN1 144 B7
North St
Alfriston BN26 171 A3
Brighton BN1 189 B2
Cowden TN8 4 A6
Eastbourne BN21 185 B3
Hailsham BN27 152 B8
Hellingly BN27 129 A7
Lewes BN7 190 B3
Lower Horsebridge BN27 107 A2
Mayfield TN20 40 B3
Portslade-by-S BN41 162 C7
Punnett's Town TN21 83 D6
Roser's Cross TN21 80 F5
Rotherfield TN6 39 B8
Royal Tunbridge Wells TN2 8 C3
St Leonards TN38 159 C7
Winchelsea TN36 117 E8
North Terr TN34 160 C6
North Trade Rd TN33 112 B4
Northumberland Ct BN22 174 A2
Northway RH15 73 C4
North Way
Lewes BN7 123 A2
Newhaven BN9 179 C8
Seaford BN25 180 F5
Northwood Ave BN2 166 E1
NORTON 180 C8
Norton Cl BN3 163 B6
Norton Dr BN2 144 E1
Norton Rd
Hove BN3 163 B6
Newhaven BN9 179 E7
Norton Terr BN9 179 E7
Norton Wall BN7 146 C4
Norway Rd BN22 185 D6
Norway St BN41 162 C7
Norwich Cl BN2 144 A2
Norwich Cres BN2 143 F2
Norwich Dr BN2 143 F2
Norwich House Rd BN1 144 B7
Norwood BN1 143 A4
Nottidge Rd TN4 7 D1
Novington La BN7 100 A3
Nuffield Hospl TN2 8 C3
Nuffield Hospl Brighton BN2 165 C8
Nunnery La TN11 5 F8
Nunnery Stables 5 BN7 123 B1
Nurseries The BN7 190 C3
Nursery Cl
Hailsham BN27 152 C8
Haywards Heath RH16 50 D5
Polegate BN26 173 B6
Portslade-by-S BN41 140 E4
Shoreham-by-S BN43 161 B8
Union Street TN5 32 B3
Nursery Field TN22 56 C4
Nursery La
Maresfield Park TN22 55 B7
Nutley TN22 35 C4
Uckfield TN22 78 D4
Waldron Down TN21, TN22 80 E8
Windmill Hill BN27 131 B5
Nursery Path BN27 152 B6
Nursery Rd TN4 8 B8
Nursery The RH15 73 C4
Nursery Way TN21 81 E7
Nutbourne Cl BN23 174 E2
Nuthatch Rd BN23 174 C2
Nuthurst Cl BN2 164 F6
Nuthurst Pl BN2 164 F5
NUTLEY 35 C4
Nutley Ave BN2 166 C1
Nutley CE Prim Sch TN22 35 C5
Nutley Cl
Hove BN3 141 F3
Rye TN31 93 A6
Nutley Mill Rd BN24 174 B5
Nutley Windmill★ TN22 35 E7
Nye Cl TN6 25 F1
Nye La
Ditchling BN6 98 D1
Westmeston BN6 120 D8
Nye Rd RH15 73 C3
Nyetimber Hill BN2 143 E2
Nym Cl BN8 100 E7

O

Oakapple Rd BN42 140 E1
Oak Ave BN27 127 C3
Oak Bank RH16 50 F7
Oak Cl BN1 142 E3
Oak Croft RH19 11 A8
Oakdale Rd
Haywards Heath RH16 50 F3
Royal Tunbridge Wells TN4 7 F4
Oakdene RH16 50 D5
Oakdene Ave BN41 140 E3
Oakdene Cl BN41 140 E3
Oakdene Cres BN41 140 E3
Oakdene Gdns BN41 140 E3
Oakdene Rise BN41 140 E4
Oakdene Way BN41 140 E4
Oakdown Ct TN19 61 A4
Oakendene BN2 143 F4
Oakenfield RH15 73 A5
Oakfield Cl RH16 51 A7
Oakfield Court Rd TN2 8 C3
Oakfield Rd TN35 160 C7
Oakfield The TN31 93 B8
Oak Field The TN35 116 F1
Oakfield Way
Bexhill TN39 156 C6
East Grinstead RH19 1 F3
Oak Hall Pk RH15 73 B1
Oakhill Cotts TN31 68 C4
Oakhill Dr TN31 90 B5
Oak Ho 3 TN2 8 C7
Oakhurst RH16 50 D8
Oakhurst Cl TN34 136 E5
Oakhurst Dr TN6 26 A3
Oakhurst Gdns RH19 1 C2
Oakhurst La RH16 50 D8
Oakhurst Rd TN33 112 D7
Oakland Dr TN32 63 D4
Oaklands
Crowborough TN6 26 B1
6 Eastbourne BN21 185 A4
South Chailey BN8 100 C7
Westham BN24 174 D6
Oaklands Ave BN2 166 D1
Oaklands Cl BN26 173 B6
Oaklands Rd
Groombridge TN3 15 B6
Haywards Heath RH16 50 D5
Oaklands Way BN27 152 A6
Oakland Villas TN3 15 B7
Oaklea Cl TN37 136 C4
Oaklea Ct TN7 13 D4
Oakleaf Ct BN26 173 A7
Oakleaf Dr BN26 173 A7
Oaklea Way TN22 78 C7
Oakleigh Dr TN21 82 B6
Oakleigh Rd TN39 156 C4
Oakley Cl RH19 11 B7
Oakley Cotts RH19 11 C7
Oakley Ct TN22 78 D6
Oakley Ho BN2 189 C2
Oakley Sch TN2 9 A5
Oak Lodge TN2 8 D2
Oakmead Rd RH15 72 F1
Oakmede Way BN8 124 D5
Oakmeeds Com Coll RH15 73 A2
Oak Pas 8 TN34 160 A4
Oak Rd
3 Bexhill TN40 157 C5
Royal Tunbridge Wells TN2 8 D7
Oakroyd Cl RH15 73 D5
Oaks Cl TN19 63 B8
Oaks Forstal TN18 47 C5
Oaks The
Burgess Hill RH15 72 D4
East Grinstead RH19 11 B8
Haywards Heath RH16 51 A4
Heathfield TN21 82 B6
St Leonards TN37 136 D5
Oak Terr TN31 67 B6
Oaktree BN8 101 E4
Oak Tree Cl
Eastbourne BN23 174 C4
East Grinstead RH19 1 C3
Royal Tunbridge Wells TN2 8 A1
Oak Tree Cotts
Burgess Hill RH15 73 B3
Danehill RH17 34 A4
Oak Tree Ct TN22 78 D8
Oak Tree La BN23 174 C4
Oak Tree Way BN27 129 C2
Oakwood RH16 50 D4
Oakwood Ave TN39 157 B7
Oakwood Cl
Burgess Hill RH15 73 B2
Hastings TN34 136 F3
Oakwood Dr TN22 78 E8
Oakwood Pk
Forest Row RH18 11 F2
Nutley TN22 35 C4
Oakwood Rd
Burgess Hill RH15 73 B2
Haywards Heath RH16 50 D4
Oakwood Rise TN2 8 E7
Oakwood Sch BN22 173 D3
Oast Cl TN2 8 D7
Oasthouse Cl TN37 136 D5
Oast House Dr TN31 92 F4
Oast House Field TN36 116 F6
Oast House Rd TN36 116 F5
Oathall Ave RH16 50 F6
Oathall Com Coll RH16 50 F6
Oathall Rd RH16 50 E5
Oban Rd TN37 136 B3
Observatory Science Ctr The★ BN27 131 C1
Observatory View BN27 152 D7
Ocean Bldg The BN1 189 A3
Ocean Ct BN23 185 F7
Oceania 4 TN39 157 B3
Ocean Reach BN2 166 A1
Ochiltree Cl TN34 160 A8
Ochiltree Rd TN34 160 A8
Ocho Rios Mews 9 BN23 185 F8
Ockenden Way BN6 97 E3
Ockley Hill BN6, RH15 98 B6
Ockley La
Burgess Hill RH15 98 B7
Keymer BN6 98 B4
Ockley Way BN6 98 A5
Ockling Piece BN21 184 D5
Ocklynge Ave 3 BN21 184 D4
Ocklynge Cl TN39 156 C5
Ocklynge Ct 2 BN21 184 D4
Ocklynge Jun Sch BN20 184 C6
Ocklynge Rd BN21 184 D4
Ockman La 1 TN31 93 C5
Octagon The BN2 164 F3
Offa Ct TN40 157 C4
Offa Rd TN35 160 D7
OFFHAM 122 F5
Offham Cl
Eastbourne BN23 173 F4
Seaford BN25 180 F5
Offham Ct 3 BN25 180 C4
Offham Rd BN7 123 B2
Offham Terr BN7 190 A2
Okehurst Rd BN21 184 C3
Oldaker Rd BN8 76 D7
Old Barn Cl BN20 173 B1
Old Barn Ct RH16 50 D2
Old Barn Way BN42 162 A7
Old Ben Homes BN25 180 F4
Old Boat Cnr BN1 143 D8
Old Boat Wlk BN1 143 B7
Old Brickyard TN31 93 A5
Old Camp Rd BN20 184 C2
Old Church Rd TN38 136 A4
Old Coastguard Cotts BN9 179 D6
Old Coastguards TN35 139 C7
Old College Ho BN2 189 C4
Old Convent The RH19 1 E2
Old Court Cl BN1 142 F4
Old Dr BN26 172 F6
Old Dro BN23 174 C3
Olde Place Ct BN2 165 F1
Olde Place Mews BN2 165 F1
Old Farm Cl RH17 51 A2
Old Farm Rd
Bexhill TN39 157 B6
Brighton BN1 142 F5
Oldfield Ave BN20 173 A4
Oldfield Cres
Hailsham BN27 129 B1
Southwick BN42 161 E8
Oldfield Rd BN20 173 A4
Old Fire Sta The 5 BN22 185 A3
Old Foord Cl BN8 100 D7
Old Forest La TN6 38 E8
Old Forewood La TN33 134 F7
Old Forge La TN22 36 A1
Old Fort Rd BN43 161 B6
Old Gardens Cl TN2 17 B8
Old Ghyll Rd TN21 82 A5
Old Harbour Farm La TN36 118 B5
Old Harrow Rd TN37 136 B4
Old Heath Cl BN8 104 C6
OLD HEATHFIELD 82 D5
Old Hop Gdn The TN31 69 C2
Old House Gdns TN34 136 F4
Old House La
Langton Green TN3 6 D4
Uckfield TN22 78 E4
Old Humphrey Ave 1 TN34 160 B4
Old La
Crowborough, Poundfield TN6 26 B1
Crowborough, St John's TN6 25 D3
Mayfield TN20 40 A2
Oldlands Ave BN6 98 A4
Oldlands Hall TN22 36 D4
Oldlands Hill TN22 36 C2
Old Lodge Nature Reserve★ TN22 24 A2
Old London Rd
Brighton BN1 142 E6
Hastings TN34, TN35 160 C6
Old Lydd Rd TN31 94 E2
Old Malling Way BN7 190 A4
Old Manor Cl TN40 157 D4
Old Mansion Cl BN20 184 A8
Old Market Cotts
17 Hove BN3 163 D5
3 Seaford BN25 180 E3
Old Mill Cl
Brighton BN1 142 E5
Hailsham BN27 129 A3
Portslade-by-S BN41 162 A7
Old Mill Ct TN6 25 E2
Old Mill La BN26 172 F4
Old Mill Mews BN1 163 E8
Old Mill Pk TN39 157 A6
Old Mill Wlk TN33 112 D5
Old Mint House★ BN24 175 B6
Old Motcombe Mews 11 BN21 184 D4
Old Nursery Cl BN25 181 B5
Old Orch TN18 47 B5
Old Orchard Pl BN27 152 B7
Old Orchard Rd BN21 184 F2
Old Parish La BN2 165 C8
Old Park Cl RH17 50 A6
Old Patcham Mews BN1 142 E6
Old Rd
East Grinstead RH19 1 F1
Magham Down BN27 130 A4
Old Rectory Gdns BN42 161 D8
Old Riding Sch The TN3 15 B2
Old River Way TN36 118 B7
Old Roar Gill & Coronation Wood Nature Reserve★ TN34 136 C3
Old Roar Rd TN37 136 C5
Old School Cl
Polegate BN26 173 A7
Ringmer BN8 124 E6
Old School Cotts BN7 99 E5
Old School Ct RH16 51 B7
Old School Fields TN22 78 C5
Old School Ho BN27 131 B5
Old School Pl
Burgess Hill RH15 72 F2
Portslade-by-S BN3 141 D1
Old Shoreham Rd
Portslade-by-S BN3, BN41 162 C8
Southwick BN42 140 E1
Old Station Rd TN5 29 E6
Old Steine BN1 189 B2
Old Surgery The 4 RH19 1 F2
Old Swan La BN27 152 D6
Old Timbers La TN22 78 C6
Old Top Rd TN35 160 D8
OLD TOWN
Bexhill 157 D5
Eastbourne 184 D3
Hastings 160 B4
Old Town Hall Mus★ 12 TN34 160 A4
Old Viaduct Ct 10 BN2 164 C8
Old Vicarage Cl TN21 106 F7
Old Wardsdown TN5 32 B3
Old Wickham La RH16 50 E7
Old Willingdon Rd BN20 183 B2
Old Wish Rd BN21 184 F1
Old World Cotts TN31 94 D2
Oliver Cl
Crowborough TN6 26 A1
Hastings TN34 159 E7
Olive Rd BN3 162 D8
Oliver Ho 5 BN3 163 B5
Olivers Mews TN33 112 E4
Olives Mdw TN22 78 D7
Olivier Cl BN2 164 C5
Onslow Rd BN3 142 C2
Open Univ (South East) The RH19 1 E1
Orange Row BN1 189 B2
Orchard Ave BN3 142 A1
Orchard Bsns Ctr TN2 8 D8
Orchard Cl
Fairwarp TN22 36 B2
Hastings TN34 136 F2
Haywards Heath RH16 50 D8
Royal Tunbridge Wells TN2 8 D6
Scaynes Hill RH17 51 F3
Southwick BN42 161 F8

Orchard Cnr RH16 . . . . 51 B5
Orchard Cotts TN6 . . . . 39 B8
Orchard Gdns BN3 . . . . . . 142 B1
Orchard Gr TN1 . . . . .8 B5
Orchard Grange BN27 . . 128 C3
Orchard Ho BN3 . . . . 142 B1
Orchard La
  Ditchling BN6 . . . . 98 D4
  Hassocks BN6 . . . . 97 F4
Orchard Mews BN9 . . . . . . 168 E2
Orchard Par BN20 . . . . 173 A3
Orchard Rd
  Bexhill TN40 . . . . 157 C6
  Burgess Hill RH15 . . . . 72 E3
  Hove BN3 . . . . 142 B1
  Lewes BN7 . . . . 190 C3
Orchard Rise TN3 . . . . 15 B7
Orchards Sh Ctr RH16 . . . . 50 E4
Orchards The BN2 . . . . 143 E3
Orchard The
  Broad Oak TN31 . . . . 90 B4
  Etchingham TN19 . . . . 44 C1
  Hassocks BN6 . . . . 97 F3
  Nutley TN22 . . . . 35 C4
  Shoreham-by-S BN43 . . . . 140 C1
Orchard View Pk BN27 . . 131 B6
Orchard Way
  Burgess Hill RH15 . . . . 72 F3
  East Grinstead RH19 . . . . . . 1 E1
  Haywards Heath RH16 . . . 50 D8
  Peasmarsh TN31 . . . . 69 C1
  Sedlescombe TN33 . . . . . . 88 E1
Orchid Cl BN23 . . . . 174 B3
Orchidhurst TN2 . . . . 8 D7
Orchid Pk RH16 . . . . 51 C4
Orchid View BN1 . . . . 143 C6
ORE 137 D3
Ore Bsns Pk TN35 . . . . 160 B6
Ore Pl TN34 . . . . 137 A5
Ore Sta TN34 . . . . 160 A6
Oriental Pl BN1 . . . . 163 E5
Orion Cl BN27 . . . . 152 D7
Orion Par BN6 . . . . 97 F3
Orkney Ct BN20 . . . . 184 B6
Orlando Ho BN1 . . . . 164 A8
Ormerod Ave TN38 . . . . . . 136 A4
Ormerod Ct RH16 . . . . 50 E5
Orpen Rd BN3 . . . . 142 D1
Orwell Cl BN24 . . . . 174 B5
Osbern Cl TN39 . . . . 156 C3
Osborne Cl TN34 . . . . 136 E2
Osborne Ct
  Polegate BN26 . . . . 173 A7
  7 Shoreham-by-S BN43 . . 161 C8
Osborne Hill TN6 . . . . 38 C8
Osborne Mews RH16 . . . . . 50 D4
Osborne Rd
  Brighton BN1 . . . . 143 A2
  Crowborough TN6 . . . . . . 38 C8
  Eastbourne BN20 . . . . . . 184 B4
Osborne Villas BN3 . . . . . . 163 B6
Osmers Hill TN5 . . . . 29 F7
Osmond Gdns BN3 . . . . . . 163 E7
Osmond Rd BN3 . . . . 163 E7
Osmunda Bank RH19 . . . . . 1 E6
Osmunda Ct TN2 . . . . 8 C4
Osprey Dr TN22 . . . . 78 E5
Osprey Ho **18** BN1 . . . . . . 163 E5
Ospringe Pl TN2 . . . . .8 F6
Oswald St TN40 . . . . 157 C4
Otham Court La BN26 . . . 173 B8
Otham Pk BN27 . . . . 152 D7
Otham Rd BN22 . . . . 174 A2
Ottafield Ct RH16 . . . . 50 F6
Otteham Cl BN26 . . . . 173 B6
Otterbourne Pl RH19 . . . . . 1 B1
Oulton Cl BN24 . . . . 174 B4
Our Lady of Lourdes RC Prim
  Sch TN4 . . . . 165 F1
Ousedale Cl BN7 . . . . 123 E6
Outlook Ave BN10 . . . . . . 178 F6
Outlook The BN20 . . . . . . 183 A1
Oval CI BN10 . . . . 167 C2
Overdown Rise BN41 . . . . 140 F4
Overhill BN42 . . . . 140 E1
Overhill Dr BN1 . . . . 142 E5
Overhill Gdns BN1 . . . . . . 142 E5
Overhill Way BN1 . . . . 142 E6
Over St BN1 . . . . 189 B3
Overton Cl RH19 . . . . .1 E1
Overton Shaw RH19 . . . . . 1 E4
Ovingdean Cl BN2 . . . . . . 165 D5
Ovingdean Hall Sch BN2 165 D4
Ovingdean Rd BN2 . . . . . . 165 D5
Owen Cl RH15 . . . . 72 F1
Owlsbury Cross TN21 . . . 83 B5
Owls Gdns TN5 . . . . 42 F5
OXBOTTOM 76 B5
Oxbottom Cl BN8 . . . . 76 B6
Oxenbridge La TN19 . . . . . 63 C8
Oxenbridge Row TN19 . . . . 63 B8
Oxendean Gdns BN22 . . . 173 B4
Oxford Cl BN1 . . . . 189 B4
Oxford Mews BN3 . . . . . . 163 C7
Oxford Pl BN1 . . . . 189 B4
Oxford Rd
  8 Eastbourne BN22 . . . 185 B4
  St Leonards TN38 . . . . . . 136 A3
Oxford St BN1 . . . . 189 B4
Oxford Terr **9** TN34 . . . . 160 B4
Ox Lea TN3 . . . . .7 A3
OXLEY'S GREEN 85 E8
Oxshott Ct **3** TN40 . . . . 157 F4
Oyster Creek TN31 . . . . . . 94 A3

P

Pacific Dr BN23 . . . . 175 B2
Pacific Heights N **11**
  BN23 . . . . 175 A1
Pacific Heights S **10**
  BN23 . . . . 175 A1
Packer Cl RH19 . . . . 2 A3
Packham Way RH15 . . . . . 72 F4
Paddock Cl
  Bexhill TN40 . . . . 157 D6
  Fordcombe TN3 . . . . .6 B5
Paddock Cotts BN24 . . . . 175 A6
Paddock Ct BN41 . . . . 140 F3
Paddock Field BN1 . . . . . . 144 B5
Paddock Gdns
  East Grinstead RH19 . . . . . 10 E7
  Polegate BN26 . . . . 172 F4
Paddockhall Rd RH16 . . . . 50 D5
Paddock La BN7 . . . . 190 A2
Paddock Rd
  Lewes BN7 . . . . 190 A2
  St Leonards TN37 . . . . . . 136 C5
Paddocks The
  Cowden TN8 . . . . 4 B7
  Hailsham BN27 . . . . 129 A2
  Haywards Heath RH16 . . . 50 C3
  Plumpton Green BN7 . . . . 99 E6
  Rodmell BN7 . . . . 167 D8
Paddock Terr BN7 . . . . . . 190 A2
Paddock The
  Eastbourne BN22 . . . . . . 173 F2
  Hove BN3 . . . . 142 C1
  Maresfield TN22 . . . . 55 A4
  Northiam TN31 . . . . 67 B7
  Pembury TN2 . . . . .9 C6
  Walter's Green TN3 . . . . . . .5 F5
Padgham Cnr TN21 . . . . . 109 E8
Padgham La TN21 . . . . . . 109 D8
Padua Ho BN2 . . . . 165 F8
Padua House Flats BN2 . . 165 F8
Pages Ave TN39 . . . . 156 F2
Pages Cl TN21 . . . . 81 E7
Pages Hill TN21 . . . . 81 E7
Pages La TN39 . . . . 156 E3
Pagets The BN8 . . . . 76 D7
Pagham Cl BN23 . . . . 174 B4
Paine's Cnr TN21 . . . . 60 C4
Paines Cotts TN31 . . . . 94 A3
Pain's Flat RH15, RH17 . . . 72 D8
Palace Ct **11** TN34 . . . . . 159 E7
Palace Pier* BN2 . . . . 189 B1
Palace Pl BN1 . . . . 189 B2
Palesgate La TN6 . . . . 26 C2
Palesgate Way BN20 . . . . 184 B5
Palliser Cl BN23 . . . . 185 E6
Palma Cl BN26 . . . . 173 A7
Palm Ct **2** BN3 . . . . 163 D6
Palm Dr BN2 . . . . 164 F3
Palmeira Ave BN3 . . . . 163 C6
Palmeira Avenue Mans **25**
  BN3 . . . . 163 C6
Palmeira Ct BN3 . . . . 163 C6
Palmeira Grande **9**
  BN3 . . . . 163 D6
Palmeira Ho **6** BN3 . . . . 163 D7
Palmeira Mans **22** BN3 . 163 C6
Palmeira Pl BN3 . . . . 163 D7
Palmeira Sq BN3 . . . . 163 C6
Palmer Ho BN8 . . . . 100 E7
Palmers Row BN2 . . . . 152 B7
Palmerston Rd BN9 . . . . . 168 F1
Palmyra Rd BN23 . . . . 185 G8
Panama Reach BN23 . . . . 185 G8
Pangdean La BN6, RH15 . . 72 C4
Pangdene Cl RH15 . . . . 72 F1
Pankhurst Ave BN2 . . . . . 164 D6
Pankhurst Ct BN2 . . . . 164 D6
Pankhurst Rise TN39 . . . . 157 A8
Pannel La TN35, TN36 . . . 116 E2
Pannell Cl RH19 . . . . 1 D1
Pannett RH15 . . . . 72 E4
Pantiles The **20** TN2 . . . . .8 A2
Parade The
  Beachlands BN24 . . . . . . 175 F6
  Brighton BN1 . . . . 142 B4
  Crowborough TN6 . . . . . . 25 F3
  Hove BN3 . . . . 141 E2
  Pevensey Bay BN24 . . . . 175 E5
Paradise Cl BN20 . . . . 184 D2
Paradise Dr BN20 . . . . 184 D2
Paradise Family L Pk*
  BN9 . . . . 168 D1
Paragon The BN20 . . . . . . 172 F3
Parham Cl BN2 . . . . 164 D5
Parham Ho **13** BN3 . . . . 163 D7
Park Aparments The
  BN1 . . . . 142 D4
Park Ave
  Bexhill TN39 . . . . 157 B3
  Eastbourne BN21, BN22 . 184 D7
  Hastings TN34 . . . . 136 D3
  Hove BN3 . . . . 162 E7
  Keymer BN6 . . . . 98 A2
  Shoreham-by-S BN43 . . . 161 A8
  Telscombe Cliffs BN10 . . . 178 A8
Park Cl
  Brighton BN1 . . . . 143 E6
  Burgess Hill RH15 . . . . . . 72 F4
  Eastbourne BN20 . . . . . . 184 D3
  Hailsham BN27 . . . . 152 B6
  Hastings TN34 . . . . 136 D3
  Hove BN3 . . . . 141 E3
  Hurstpierpoint BN6 . . . . . 97 A6
  Portslade-by-S BN41 . . . . 141 B1
Park Cnr BN8 . . . . 104 F2
Park Coll BN21 . . . . 184 D7

Park Cres
  Brighton BN2 . . . . 189 C4
  Crowborough TN6 . . . . . . 25 F3
  Forest Row RH18 . . . . 12 A2
  Hastings TN34 . . . . 136 D2
  Portslade-by-S BN41 . . . . 162 A8
  Rottingdean BN2 . . . . . . 165 F1
Park Crescent Pl BN2 . . . . 189 C4
Park Crescent Rd BN2 . . . 189 C4
Park Crescent Terr BN2 . . 189 C4
Park Croft BN26 . . . . 173 A5
Park Ct
  11 Brighton BN2 . . . . . 164 C6
  Brighton, Patcham BN1 . . 142 E6
  Brighton, Preston BN1 . . . 142 F1
  Burgess Hill RH15 . . . . . . 73 A3
  4 Haywards Heath RH16 . 50 E4
  Hove BN3 . . . . 163 D6
  Peacehaven BN10 . . . . . 178 B7
Park Dr TN34 . . . . 136 D2
Park Drive Cl BN9 . . . . 168 F2
Park E RH16 . . . . 50 F2
Parker Cl BN21 . . . . 184 E5
Parker Ct BN41 . . . . 141 B2
Parker Rd TN34 . . . . 160 A7
Park Farm Bsns Pk RH17 . . 74 B2
Park Farm Cl TN19 . . . . . . 63 B8
Parkfield Ave BN22 . . . . . 173 E1
Parkfield Way RH16 . . . . . 50 C3
Park Gate
  4 Brighton BN1 . . . . . . 163 F8
  Hailsham BN27 . . . . 129 D3
  Hove BN3 . . . . 163 D6
Park Gates **16** BN21 . . . 185 A2
Park Hill BN2 . . . . 189 C2
Parkhurst Rd TN40 . . . . . . 157 C3
Park La
  Ashurst Wood RH19 . . . . . 11 D6
  Battle TN33 . . . . 112 D4
  Bexhill TN39 . . . . 157 A6
  6 Crowborough TN6 . . 25 F3
  Eastbourne BN21 . . . . . . 184 C8
  Flimwell TN17 . . . . 32 E8
  Laughton BN8 . . . . 126 E7
  Southwick BN42 . . . . 161 D7
  Whatlington TN33 . . . . 88 A5
Park Lodge
  10 Eastbourne BN21 . . 185 A2
  Hove BN3 . . . . 163 D8
Park Lodge Ct TN38 . . . . . 159 B7
Park Manor BN1 . . . . 142 D3
Parkmead BN2 . . . . 189 C4
Park Mead Prim Sch
  BN27 . . . . 151 A7
Parkmore Terr BN1 . . . . . . 189 A5
Park Par RH16 . . . . 50 E4
Park Rd
  Bexhill TN39 . . . . 157 B3
  Brighton BN1 . . . . 143 E5
  Burgess Hill RH15 . . . . . . 73 A3
  Crowborough TN6 . . . . . . 25 F3
  Dormans Park RH19 . . . . . .1 F6
  East Grinstead RH19 . . . . . 1 D1
  Forest Row RH18 . . . . 11 F2
  Hailsham BN27 . . . . 129 B4
  Haywards Heath RH16 . . . 50 E4
  Heathfield TN21 . . . . 82 C6
  Lewes BN7 . . . . 190 A2
  Peacehaven BN10 . . . . . 178 F6
  Rottingdean BN2 . . . . . . 165 F1
  Royal Tunbridge Wells TN4 . .8 B5
  Seaford BN25 . . . . 180 D3
  Shoreham-by-S BN43 . . . 161 A8
Park Rd Terr **4** BN2 . . . . 189 C4
Park Rise BN3 . . . . 141 E3
Park Royal BN1 . . . . 163 E6
Park Shaw TN33 . . . . 88 E1
Parkside
  Burgess Hill RH15 . . . . . . 72 F3
  East Grinstead RH19 . . . . . 1 C1
  Heathfield TN21 . . . . 82 B6
  Keymer BN6 . . . . 98 A4
  Shoreham-by-S BN43 . . . 140 A1
Parkside Com Prim Sch
  TN21 . . . . 82 C5
Parkside Rd BN25 . . . . 180 F4
Park Sq BN2 . . . . 164 F3
Park St
  Brighton BN2 . . . . 189 C2
  Falmer BN1 . . . . 144 C6
  Royal Tunbridge Wells TN2 . . 8 C3
Parks The BN1 . . . . 141 B3
Parkstone Par TN34 . . . . . 136 D4
Parkstone Rd TN34 . . . . . . 136 D4
Parkstone Terr TN34 . . . . . 136 D4
Parks Yd TN33 . . . . 112 D4
Park Terr BN2 . . . . 165 F1
Park The
  Crowborough TN6 . . . . . . 25 F2
  Rottingdean BN2 . . . . . . 166 A1
Parkview
  Hurstpierpoint BN6 . . . . . 97 A5
  Royal Tunbridge Wells TN2 . . 8 D4
Park View
  Brighton BN2 . . . . 164 C6
  Brighton, Preston BN1 . . . 163 E8
  Buxted TN22 . . . . 56 C4
  Hastings TN34 . . . . 136 D2
  Herstmonceux BN27 . . . 130 C5
  Northiam TN31 . . . . 67 A6

Park View continued
  Peasmarsh TN31 . . . . 69 B2
Park View Cl BN10 . . . . . . 167 A1
Parkview Rd TN22 . . . . 55 D1
Park View Rd
  Hove BN3 . . . . 142 B1
  Westfield TN35 . . . . 114 E4
Park View Rise BN10 . . . . 178 A8
Park View Terr BN1 . . . . . . 163 E8
Park Village Rd BN1 . . . . . 144 B8
Park Village The BN1 . . . . 144 A8
Park Villas TN21 . . . . 82 B6
Park W RH16 . . . . 50 F2
Parkway BN20 . . . . 184 B8
Park Way
  Hastings TN34 . . . . 136 D3
  Southwick BN42 . . . . 161 F8
Park Way Cl BN42 . . . . 161 F8
Parkwood TN2 . . . . .9 C6
Parkwood Ct TN34 . . . . 8 C6
Park Wood Rd TN34 . . . . . 136 F6
Parnell Ct **3** BN3 . . . . . . 163 B6
Parochial Terr BN2 . . . . . . 189 B2
Parrock La TN7 . . . . 12 E2
Parry Cl BN23 . . . . 174 E3
Parsonage Cl TN4 . . . . .7 B5
Parsonage La
  Chiddingly BN8 . . . . 105 D3
  Icklesham TN36 . . . . 116 F6
  Lamberhurst TN3 . . . . 20 B6
  Westfield TN35 . . . . 114 C4
Parsonage Rd
  Eastbourne BN21 . . . . . . 184 D4
  Rusthall TN4 . . . . .7 B5
Parsons Cl TN38 . . . . 135 F4
Partridges La TN5 . . . . 28 E6
Parve Ct TN40 . . . . 157 C4
Pashley Down Inf Sch
  BN20 . . . . 184 B4
Pashley Gdns TN34 . . . . . 136 D1
Pashley Manor Gdns*
  TN5 . . . . 44 B7
Pashley Rd BN20 . . . . 184 C2
Paston Ho **5** BN1 . . . . . 163 F8
Paston Pl BN2 . . . . 164 D4
Pasture Hill Rd RH16 . . . . . 50 D6
Patagonia Ho TN2 . . . . 8 C3
Patcham By-pass BN1 . . . 142 E6
Patcham Grange BN1 . . . 142 E5
Patcham High Sch BN1 . . 142 F6
Patcham House Specl Sch
  BN1 . . . . 142 E6
Patcham Inf Sch BN1 . . . . 142 E6
Patcham Jun Sch BN1 . . . 142 F6
Patcham Mill Rd BN24 . . . 174 F5
Patchdean BN1 . . . . 142 E5
Paton Rd TN39 . . . . 157 A8
Paul Cl BN27 . . . . 129 A3
Pavilion Bldgs BN1 . . . . . . 189 B2
Pavilion Cl BN6 . . . . 97 E5
Pavilion Ct
  15 Brighton BN1 . . . . . 163 E7
  Brighton BN1 . . . . 189 B2
Pavilion Mews BN1 . . . . . . 189 B2
Pavilion Par BN1 . . . . 189 B2
Pavilion Rd BN1 . . . . 144 C7
Pavilion Ret Pk BN2 . . . . . 143 C1
Pavilion St BN2 . . . . 189 B2
Pavilion Way RH19 . . . . . . 10 E8
Paxhill Cl TN38 . . . . 135 E4
Paygate Rd TN33 . . . . 113 E7
Payne Ave BN3 . . . . 162 F8
Payne Terr BN1 . . . . 143 B1
Paynsbridge Way TN21 . . 107 A7
Paynton Rd TN37 . . . . 136 B3
Paythorne Cl BN42 . . . . . . 140 D1
Payton Dr RH15 . . . . 72 F2
Payton Ho RH15 . . . . 73 D3
Peace Cl BN1 . . . . 143 C1
PEACEHAVEN 178 D7
Peacehaven Com Sch
  BN10 . . . . 178 C8
Peacehaven Inf Sch
  BN10 . . . . 178 B7
Peacock Ind Est BN3 . . . . 163 D7
Peacock La BN1 . . . . 142 E4
Peakdean Cl BN20 . . . . . . 183 B2
Peakdean La BN20 . . . . . . 183 B2
Pearl Ct **3** BN21 . . . . . . 185 A2
Pearse Pl TN3 . . . . 20 B5
Peartree Cl RH15 . . . . 72 E3
Peartree Field TN36 . . . . . 116 F6
Peartree Hill TN5 . . . . 42 E4
Peartree La TN39 . . . . 156 D6
PEASMARSH 69 B2
Peasmarsh CE Prim Sch
  TN31 . . . . 69 B1
Pebble Rd BN24 . . . . 175 E5
PEBSHAM 158 A6
Pebsham Com Prim Sch
  TN40 . . . . 158 A5
Pebsham Dr TN40 . . . . . . 158 A6
Pebsham La TN38, TN40 . . 158 A6
Peckham Cl BN7 . . . . 190 A4
Peelings La BN24 . . . . 174 D6
Peelings Manor Barns
  BN24 . . . . 174 B6
Peel Rd BN2 . . . . 164 F4
Peeps La TN6 . . . . 39 A6
Pegasus Way RH19 . . . . . . .2 B3
Pegwell Cl TN34 . . . . 136 E2
Pelham Arc **1** TN34 . . . . 160 A3
Pelham Cl
  Peacehaven BN10 . . . . . 167 D1
  Westham BN24 . . . . 174 F5
Pelham Cres
  Hailsham BN27 . . . . 152 C6

Pelham Cres continued
  Hastings TN34 . . . . 160 A3
Pelham Ct
  2 Brighton BN2 . . . . . . 143 C1
  4 Seaford BN25 . . . . . . 180 E2
Pelham Pl TN34 . . . . 160 A3
Pelham Pl Cotts RH16 . . . . 51 A7
Pelham Rd
  Lindfield RH16 . . . . 51 A6
  Seaford BN25 . . . . 180 E2
Pelham Rise BN10 . . . . . . 167 D1
Pelham Sq BN1 . . . . 189 B3
Pelham St
  Brighton BN1 . . . . 189 B3
  Hastings TN34 . . . . 159 F7
Pelham Terr
  1 Brighton BN2 . . . . . . 143 C1
  Lewes BN7 . . . . 190 A3
Pelham Yd **7** BN25 . . . . . 180 E2
Pellbrook Rd BN7 . . . . 123 B3
Pell Cl TN5 . . . . 30 A6
PELL GREEN 30 A7
Pellings Farm Cl TN6 . . . . 26 B2
Pellings Rise TN6 . . . . 26 B3
Pells CE Prim Sch BN7 . . 190 A3
Pelwood Rd TN31 . . . . 95 A2
Pembroke Ave BN3 . . . . . 163 A4
Pembroke Ct BN27 . . . . . 129 C3
Pembroke Cres BN3 . . . . . 163 A7
Pembroke Ct
  2 Hove BN3 . . . . 163 A6
  St Leonards TN37 . . . . . . 159 C8
Pembroke Gdns BN3 . . . . 163 A6
Pembroke Ho **6** BN21 . . 184 F3
PEMBURY 9 C6
Pembury Cl
  Haywards Heath RH16 . . . 51 B3
  Pembury TN2 . . . . .9 D7
Pembury Gr TN39 . . . . 157 A7
Pembury Grange TN2 . . . . .9 A6
Pembury Hospl TN2 . . . . . .9 B7
Pembury Prim Sch TN2 . . .9 D8
Pembury Rd
  Camden Park TN2 . . . . 8 C3
  Eastbourne BN23 . . . . . . 174 D1
  Royal Tunbridge Wells TN2 . . 8 E4
Pendean BN23 . . . . 174 C1
Pendragon Ct BN3 . . . . . . 163 A8
Pendrill Pl TN5 . . . . 29 F5
Penhale Rd BN22 . . . . 185 D5
PENHURST 110 E6
Penhurst Cl
  Eastbourne BN22 . . . . . . 174 A1
  St Leonards TN37 . . . . . . 136 D5
Penhurst Dr TN40 . . . . 158 A6
Penhurst La TN33 . . . . 110 E6
Penhurst Pl BN2 . . . . 164 F6
Penland Cl RH16 . . . . 50 D7
Penland Ct **9** TN40 . . . . 157 E4
Penland Rd
  Bexhill TN40 . . . . 157 E5
  Haywards Heath RH16 . . . 50 D7
Penn Cres
  Haywards Heath RH16 . . . 51 A5
  Ringmer BN8 . . . . 124 D5
Pennett Ho RH16 . . . . 50 D2
Pennine Rise TN34 . . . . . . 160 B8
Pennine Way BN23 . . . . . . 174 D3
Pennine Wlk TN2 . . . . 8 D5
Pennington Ho RH16 . . . . 51 A3
Pennsbridge La TN20 . . . . 40 D5
Penn Yd TN2 . . . . 9 C6
Penny La TN40 . . . . 158 A5
Penrith Way BN23 . . . . . . 174 C4
Penrose Ct **12** TN40 . . . 157 D3
Pensford Dr BN23 . . . . 174 D3
Penshurst Rd TN11, TN3 . . . 6 E8
Penstock Terr TN31 . . . . . . 93 F3
Penstone Ct **4** BN43 . . . 161 C8
Pentland Cl
  Eastbourne BN23 . . . . . . 174 E3
  St Leonards TN37 . . . . . . 136 C5
Pentlands BN26 . . . . 183 C7
Peppercombe Rd BN20 . . 184 B4
Pepper Dr RH15 . . . . 72 F2
Pepper Hall Cotts RH17 . . 74 B5
Pepys Wlk TN2 . . . . 174 E3
Percival Cres BN22 . . . . . 173 F3
Percival Mans **20** BN2 . . 164 D4
Percival Rd BN22 . . . . 173 F3
Percival Terr **14** BN2 . . . 164 D4
Percy Rd TN35 . . . . 160 C7
Percy Terr TN4 . . . . 8 A6
Percy & Wagner Almshouses
  5 BN2 . . . . 189 C4
Perrone Ct TN22 . . . . 78 C7
Perry Ave RH19 . . . . .1 E3
Perryfields RH15 . . . . 72 E4
Perry Hill BN2 . . . . 166 C3
Perryhill Cotts TN7 . . . . . . 13 E8
Perryhill La TN7 . . . . 13 E8
Perrymans La TN22 . . . . . . 36 F1
Perryman's La RH17 . . . . . 34 D3
Perrymans's Cross TN31 . . 67 B3
Perrymount Rd RH16 . . . . . 50 E5
Perth Cl BN25 . . . . 181 C3
Perth Ct **4** BN21 . . . . . . 185 A4
Perth Rd TN37 . . . . 136 B3
Peter Gladwin Prim Sch
  BN41 . . . . 141 B2
Peterhouse TN40 . . . . 157 D5
Peter James Cl TN31 . . . . 94 E2
Peter James La TN35 . . . . 138 C6
Petersfield TN2 . . . . .9 E7
Petlands Gdns RH16 . . . . . 50 F3

Petlands Rd RH16 . . . . 50 E3
PETT 116 F1
Pett Cl BN2 . . . . 164 F6
Pett La TN36 . . . . 117 A4
PETT LEVEL 139 B8
Pett Level Rd TN35 . . . . 139 B7
Pett Rd TN35 . . . . 138 C8
Petworth Dr RH15 . . . . 73 A4
Petworth Ho 14 BN3 . . . . 163 D7
Petworth Pl BN22 . . . . 173 E2
Petworth Rd BN1 . . . . 143 B6
PEVENSEY 175 B6
PEVENSEY BAY 175 D4
Pevensey Bay Rd BN23 . . . . 175 A2
Pevensey Bay Sta BN24 . . . 175 C6
Pevensey Castle ★ BN24 . . . 175 A6
Pevensey Cl BN25 . . . . 181 B4
Pevensey Courthouse Mus ★
 BN24 . . . . 175 B6
Pevensey Ct
 3 Bexhill TN39 . . . . 157 B3
 Pevensey Bay BN24 . . . . . . 175 D4
Pevensey Levels National
 Nature Reserve ★ BN24 . 175 B8
Pevensey Park Rd BN24 . 174 F6
Pevensey Rd
 7 Brighton BN2 . . . . 164 C8
 Eastbourne BN21, BN22 . . 185 B3
 Newhaven BN9 . . . . 179 B5
 Polegate BN26 . . . . 173 C6
 St Leonards TN38 . . . . 159 B7
Pevensey & Westham CE
 Prim Sch BN24 . . . . 175 A6
Pevensey & Westham Sta
 BN24 . . . . 174 F5
Peverells The BN25 . . . . 181 A5
Peyton Cl BN23 . . . . 185 F7
Philip Cole Cl 16 TN34 . . . . 160 B4
Philip Ct 8 BN3 . . . . 163 C7
Phoenix Brewery Halls
 BN2 . . . . 189 C4
Phoenix Cl
 Eastbourne BN23 . . . . 185 G8
 Hailsham BN27 . . . . 152 E7
Phoenix Cres BN42 . . . . 161 D8
Phoenix Ct 9 BN3 . . . . 185 B3
Phoenix Dr BN23 . . . . 175 A1
Phoenix Ho 10 TN6 . . . . 25 F3
Phoenix Ind Est BN7 . . . . . . 190 B2
Phoenix La RH19 . . . . 11 E6
Phoenix Pl
 Brighton BN2 . . . . 189 C3
 Lewes BN7 . . . . 190 B2
Phoenix Rise BN2 . . . . 189 C3
Phoenix Terr RH19 . . . . 11 E6
Phoenix Way BN42 . . . . 161 D8
Phyllis Ave BN10 . . . . 178 B8
Piazza The BN23 . . . . 185 F8
Picardy Cl TN33 . . . . 112 E4
Picardy Pl BN23 . . . . 185 E8
Piccadilly La TN20 . . . . 40 C1
Pickers Gn RH16 . . . . 51 A8
Picketts La TN22 . . . . 54 D8
Pickforde La TN5 . . . . 31 D1
PICK HILL 106 D4
Pick Hill TN21 . . . . 106 D4
Picton St BN2 . . . . 164 C7
PIDDINGHOE 168 A2
Piddinghoe Ave BN10 . . . . . 178 D6
Piddinghoe Cl BN10 . . . . . . 178 D7
Piddinghoe Mead BN9 . . . . 168 B1
Pierces La 7 RH16 . . . . 50 C2
Pierpoint Mews 9 BN23 175 A1
Pilgrims Way TN34 . . . . 136 F4
Pilmer Rd TN6 . . . . 25 F4
Pilot Ho 1 BN2 . . . . 189 C2
Pilot Rd TN34 . . . . 160 B8
PILTDOWN 54 B1
Piltdown Cl
 Bexhill TN39 . . . . 157 B4
 Hastings TN34 . . . . 136 E1
Piltdown Rd BN2 . . . . 164 F6
Piltdown Rise TN22 . . . . 78 D8
Piltdown Way BN23 . . . . 174 A4
Pinders Rd TN35 . . . . 160 D6
Pine Ave TN34 . . . . 160 B8
Pine Ct BN25 . . . . 180 F5
Pine Gr
 Crowborough TN6 . . . . 25 E2
 East Grinstead RH19 . . . . . . 1 B3
Pineham Copse RH16 . . . . . . 50 F4
Pinehurst RH15 . . . . 73 A1
Pinehurst Wlk TN34 . . . . . . 160 B7
Pines The
 2 Brighton BN2 . . . . 189 C4
 Hastings TN34 . . . . 160 B7
 Haywards Heath RH16 . . . . 51 B4
 Hove BN3 . . . . 163 E6
Pine Tree Cl
 Hurstpierpoint BN6 . . . . 97 B5
 Newhaven BN9 . . . . 179 C7
Pine Tree Rd TN21 . . . . 82 A6
Pine Trees BN6 . . . . 97 D4
Pine Trees Ct BN6 . . . . 97 D4
Pine Way BN27 . . . . 152 A7
Pine Way Cl RH19 . . . . 10 E7
Pine Wlk TN20 . . . . 78 D8
Pinewood 5 BN1 . . . . 142 E3
Pinewood Chase TN6 . . . . . . 25 D3
Pinewood Cl
 Brighton BN1 . . . . 142 D2
 Eastbourne BN23 . . . . 173 D2
 Seaford BN25 . . . . 180 F4
Pinewood Ct RH16 . . . . 50 D2

Pinewood Rd TN2 . . . . 8 D5
Pinewoods TN39 . . . . 156 E4
Pinewoods Ct TN39 . . . . . . 156 E4
Pinewood Way
 Haywards Heath RH16 . . . . 50 D2
 St Leonards TN38 . . . . 135 E3
Pinfold 4 RH16 . . . . 50 D6
Pinfold Cl BN2 . . . . 165 E6
Pinton Hill TN5 . . . . 31 B3
Pinwell Rd BN7 . . . . 190 B1
Pipe Pas BN7 . . . . 190 A2
Pipers Cl
 Bexhill TN40 . . . . 157 C5
 Hove BN3 . . . . 141 C3
 Wadhurst TN5 . . . . 30 A4
Pipers Field TN34 . . . . 78 D4
Piper's Gate TN22 . . . . 78 D4
Pipers Yd TN20 . . . . 40 C3
Pipit Mdw TN22 . . . . 78 D5
Pippin Cl BN27 . . . . 131 B5
Pitcairn Ave BN23 . . . . 175 B2
Pit La BN6 . . . . 97 A5
Pitreavie Dr BN27 . . . . 152 A8
Pitt Ct BN6 . . . . 97 A5
Pitt Dr BN25 . . . . 181 A5
Pitt Gdns BN2 . . . . 165 D7
Place La BN25 . . . . 180 E3
Plainfields Ave BN1 . . . . 143 A7
Plaistow Cl BN2 . . . . 164 F6
Plashett Park Gates
 TN22 . . . . 102 F3
Plat The TN31 . . . . 67 B6
Platt The
 Dormansland RH7 . . . . 2 A8
 Frant TN3 . . . . 17 B1
 Haywards Heath RH16 . . . . 51 B5
PLAYDEN 93 C8
Playden Cl 1 BN2 . . . . 164 E4
Playden Gdns TN34 . . . . . . 160 B8
Playden La TN31 . . . . 70 C3
Pleasant Row 25 TN34 . . . . 160 B4
Pleasant View Cotts TN6 . . 25 E4
Pleasant View Rd TN6 . . . . . 25 F4
Plemont Gdns TN39 . . . . . . 157 A6
Pleyden Rise TN39 . . . . 155 F4
Plough La TN37 . . . . 136 B5
Plover Cl BN23 . . . . 174 C2
Plover Ct
 Hailsham BN27 . . . . 152 D7
 St Leonards TN38 . . . . 135 E3
Plumey Feather Cotts
 TN3 . . . . 14 E3
PLUMPTON 121 E8
Plumpton Bostall BN6,
 BN7 . . . . 121 E6
Plumpton Cl
 Bexhill TN40 . . . . 157 C6
 Eastbourne BN23 . . . . 174 A4
Plumpton Coll BN6 . . . . 121 D8
Plumpton Cross BN7 . . . . . . 99 E3
Plumpton Crossways BN7,
 BN8 . . . . 74 E1
PLUMPTON GREEN 99 E6
Plumpton La BN7 . . . . 99 E3
Plumpton Prim Sch BN7 . . 99 F5
Plumpton Race Course
 BN7 . . . . 99 E4
Plumpton Rd
 Brighton BN2 . . . . 164 D6
 North Chailey BN8 . . . . 75 A5
Plumpton Sta BN7 . . . . 99 E5
Plum Tree Cotts TN18 . . . . . . 45 E8
Plymouth Ave BN2 . . . . 143 F1
Plymouth Ct BN23 . . . . 185 F8
Plynlimmon Rd TN34 . . . . . 160 A4
Pocock's Rd BN21 . . . . 184 D5
Poels Ct RH19 . . . . 1 E2
POLEGATE 173 B5
Polegate By-pass BN26 . . . 172 F7
Polegate Prim Sch BN26 173 A7
Polegate Sta BN26 . . . . 173 A4
Polegate Windmill ★
 BN26 . . . . 173 A5
Polesden Rd TN2 . . . . 8 D2
Polley Cl TN2 . . . . 9 D7
Pollington Pl TN6 . . . . 25 F2
Pomper La BN6 . . . . 72 A2
Pond Cl TN31 . . . . 90 B5
Pondcroft Rd RH16 . . . . 51 B7
Pondside RH16 . . . . 50 C3
Pondsyde Ct BN25 . . . . 180 F4
Pond Way RH19 . . . . 2 B1
Ponswood Rd TN38 . . . . . . 136 B2
Pont Cl TN21 . . . . 83 C6
PONTS GREEN 110 B4
Pook Reed Cl TN21 . . . . 81 F6
Pook Reed La TN21 . . . . 81 F6
Pool Pas BN1 . . . . 189 B1
Pool Valley BN2 . . . . 189 B1
Popes Ct BN2 . . . . 143 B1
Popes Row Cotts TN17 . . . . 20 F2
Poplar Ave BN3 . . . . 141 E3
Poplar Cl
 Bexhill TN39 . . . . 157 A7
 Brighton BN1 . . . . 142 F2
 Hove BN3 . . . . 141 E4
Poplar Mews 12 RH16 . . . . . 50 C2
Poplars Cl RH15 . . . . 72 C3
Poplars The BN6 . . . . 98 A3
Poplar Wlk BN22 . . . . 173 D3
Poppinghole La TN32 . . . . . 87 E8
Popps La TN39 . . . . 156 C3
Poppyfield TN31 . . . . 70 C1
Porters Way BN26 . . . . 173 B6
Portfield Ave BN1 . . . . 143 A6
Portfield Cl TN40 . . . . 157 D5

Port Hall Ave BN1 . . . . 163 E8
Port Hall Mews BN1 . . . . . . 163 E8
Port Hall Pl BN1 . . . . 163 E8
Port Hall Rd BN1 . . . . 163 E8
Port Hall St BN1 . . . . 163 E8
Portland Ave BN3 . . . . 162 E7
Portland Bsns Pk BN3 . . . . 162 E8
Portland Cl BN27 . . . . 129 A1
Portland Cotts 11 TN34 . . . 159 F8
Portland Ho 5 RH19 . . . . 10 F3
Portland La BN3 . . . . 162 D7
Portland Mews 19 BN2 . . . 164 C4
Portland Pl
 18 Brighton BN2 . . . . 164 C4
 13 Hastings TN34 . . . . . . 159 F8
Portland Rd
 Burgess Hill RH15 . . . . 72 F3
 East Grinstead RH19 . . . . . 10 F8
 Hove BN3 . . . . 162 E7
Portland Rd Trad Est
 BN3 . . . . 162 D8
Portland Sq TN21 . . . . 82 D7
Portland St BN1 . . . . 189 A2
Portlands The BN23 . . . . . . 185 G7
Portland Terr
 16 Hastings TN34 . . . . . . 159 F8
 Newhaven BN9 . . . . 168 D2
Portland Villas
 16 Hastings TN34 . . . . . . 159 F8
 Hove BN3 . . . . 162 D7
Port Rd BN22 . . . . 174 A1
Portsdown Way BN20 . . . . . 173 B2
Portside BN2 . . . . 164 F3
Portslade Com Coll
 BN41 . . . . 141 A1
Portslade Com Coll (Lower)
 BN41 . . . . 141 A3
Portslade Inf Sch BN41 . . . 162 B3
Portslade Sta BN3 . . . . 162 C8
Portsmouth La RH16 . . . . . . 50 F8
Portsmouth Wood RH16 . . . 50 F8
Portsmouth Wood Cl
 RH16 . . . . 50 F8
Portsmouth Wood Dr
 RH16 . . . . 50 F8
Port View BN22 . . . . 168 E2
Posey Cotts BN27 . . . . 131 B5
Possingworth Cl TN21 . . . . . 80 F8
Post Horn Cl RH18 . . . . 12 B1
Post Horn La RH18 . . . . 12 B2
Post Office Pas 17 TN34 . . 160 A4
Post Office Sq TN1 . . . . 8 A3
Potato La BN8 . . . . 124 F5
POTMAN'S HEATH 49 E4
Potman's La TN33, TN39 . 133 F4
Pottens Mill La TN21 . . . . . . 59 F4
Potteries Cotts BN27 . . . . . 128 D3
Potteries The TN22 . . . . 78 D4
Potters Field BN8 . . . . 124 D6
POTTER'S GREEN 56 C3
Potters La RH15 . . . . 72 F1
Potter's La BN7 . . . . 190 A1
Pottery Cl TN31 . . . . 90 A2
Pottery Cotts BN6 . . . . 74 A1
Pottery La TN31 . . . . 90 A2
Pottingfield Rd TN31 . . . . . . 93 A6
Potts Marsh Ind Est
 BN24 . . . . 174 F4
Pouchlands Dr BN8 . . . . . . 100 C7
Pound Cl BN23 . . . . 185 F6
Pound Cnr BN8 . . . . 101 D4
POUNDFIELD 26 A2
Poundfield Farm TN6 . . . . . . 26 B2
Poundfield Rd
 Crowborough TN6 . . . . 26 B2
 Sandhurst TN18 . . . . 47 B5
POUNDFORD 58 B5
POUNDGATE 37 A6
Pound Gate BN6 . . . . 97 D3
POUND GREEN 56 D4
Pound La
 Alfriston BN26 . . . . 171 A7
 Framefield TN22 . . . . 79 E7
 Laughton BN8 . . . . 126 C7
POUNDSBRIDGE 6 D8
Poundsbridge Hill TN11,
 TN3 . . . . 6 D7
Pound The RH15 . . . . 72 F4
POUNSLEY 80 B8
Poveys Cl RH15 . . . . 72 D3
Powdermill Cl TN4 . . . . 8 C8
Powdermill La
 Battle TN33 . . . . 112 C1
 Goatham Green TN31, TN33 89 D3
Powder Mill La TN4 . . . . 8 B8
Powell Gdns BN9 . . . . 168 D1
Powell Rd BN8 . . . . 76 D7
Powis Gr BN1 . . . . 189 A3
Powis Rd BN1 . . . . 163 E6
Powis Sq BN1 . . . . 163 E6
Powis Villas BN1 . . . . 189 A3
Poynings Cl BN25 . . . . 181 C2
Poynings Dr BN3 . . . . 141 F3
Poynter Rd BN3 . . . . 163 A8
Pratt's Folly La TN6 . . . . 25 E1
Prescott Gdns RH15 . . . . . . 73 A3
PRESTON 142 F1
Preston Cir BN1 . . . . 189 B4
Preston Dro BN1 . . . . 142 F2
Preston Gr TN22 . . . . 79 B6
Preston Grange BN1 . . . . . . 142 E1
Preston Manor Mus ★
 BN1 . . . . 142 E1
Preston Mans 3 BN1 . . . . . 163 F8
Preston Park Ave BN1 . . . . 142 F1
Preston Park Sta BN1 . . . . 142 E1
Preston Rd
 Bexhill TN39 . . . . 157 B7

Preston Rd continued
 Brighton BN1 . . . . 163 F8
Preston St BN1 . . . . 163 E5
Preston Village Mews
 BN1 . . . . 142 E1
Prestonville Ct 2 BN1 . . . . 163 E7
Prestonville Rd BN1 . . . . . . 189 A4
Prideaux Ct BN21 . . . . 184 F5
Prideaux Rd BN21 . . . . 184 E5
Pride View BN24 . . . . 174 B5
Primrose Acre BN27 . . . . . . 127 B3
Primrose Cl
 Burgess Hill RH15 . . . . 72 D4
 Eastbourne BN23 . . . . 174 B3
Primrose Hill
 Bexhill TN39 . . . . 156 F6
 Fairlight Cove TN35 . . . . . 138 F5
Primrose La RH16 . . . . 12 A1
Primrose Way BN27 . . . . . . 127 B3
Prince Albert St BN1 . . . . . 189 B2
Prince Charles Cl BN42 . . . 141 A1
Prince Charles Rd BN7 . . . 190 C4
Prince Edward's Rd BN7 123 B1
Prince of Wales Ct BN3 . . . 162 F6
Prince Regent's Cl BN2 . . . 164 E4
Prince Regent's Ct 2
 BN2 . . . . 164 E4
Princes Ave BN3 . . . . 163 A6
Princes Cl
 Seaford BN25 . . . . 180 E5
 Uckfield TN22 . . . . 78 A7
Princes Cres BN3 . . . . 163 A6
Prince's Cres BN2 . . . . 189 C5
Princes Ct 6 BN3 . . . . 163 A6
Princes Field BN26 . . . . 150 B3
Prince's Ho BN1 . . . . 189 B2
Prince's Pl BN1 . . . . 189 B2
Princes Rd BN23 . . . . 185 E7
Prince's Rd
 Brighton BN2 . . . . 164 B8
 St Leonards TN37 . . . . . . 159 D7
Princess Ct RH16 . . . . 50 F6
Princess Dr BN25 . . . . 180 D5
Princes Sq BN3 . . . . 163 A6
Princess Sq TN38 . . . . 136 A4
Princess Royal Hospl RH16,
 RH17 . . . . 51 A3
Prince's St
 Brighton BN2 . . . . 189 B3
 Royal Tunbridge Wells TN2 . . 8 C3
Prince's Terr BN2 . . . . 164 E4
Prince William Par BN23 185 F6
Principal Cl TN39 . . . . 155 F5
Prinkle La BN27 . . . . 109 C1
Prinsep Rd BN3 . . . . 163 A8
Prior's Way TN8 . . . . 4 A6
Priory Ave TN34 . . . . 136 E1
Priory Cl
 Hastings TN34 . . . . 136 E1
 Pevensey Bay BN24 . . . . . 175 D5
Priory Cres BN7 . . . . 190 A1
Priory Ct
 Bexhill TN40 . . . . 157 C5
 Brighton BN1 . . . . 163 F8
 1 Eastbourne BN20 . . . . 184 F1
 7 Haywards Heath RH16 . . 50 E3
 Lewes BN7 . . . . 190 B2
Priory Flats BN7 . . . . 190 A1
Priory Ho BN7 . . . . 190 B1
Priory Hts BN20 . . . . 184 A5
Priory La BN23 . . . . 174 E3
Priory Meadow Sh Ctr 19
 TN34 . . . . 159 F8
Priory Orch 8 BN23 . . . . . . 174 E1
Priory Rd
 Burgess Hill RH15 . . . . 73 A1
 Eastbourne BN23 . . . . 174 E2
 Forest Row RH18 . . . . 11 D2
 Hassocks BN6 . . . . 97 E5
 Hastings TN34 . . . . 160 B5
Priory Sch BN7 . . . . 190 C1
Priory St
 Hastings TN34 . . . . 159 F7
 Lewes BN7 . . . . 190 A1
Priory The
 Brighton BN1 . . . . 142 D5
 2 Hove BN3 . . . . 163 B5
Priory View TN34 . . . . 160 A5
Priory Way RH16 . . . . 50 F4
Promenade BN10 . . . . 178 C6
Promenade The BN24 . . . . 175 D4
Prospect Cotts
 Burwash TN19 . . . . 62 B6
 Crowborough TN6 . . . . 25 E3
 Lamberhurst TN3 . . . . 20 A3
Prospect Gdns 21 BN21 . 184 D4
Prospect Pl TN34 . . . . 159 E7
Prospect Rd
 Heathfield TN21 . . . . 82 B6
 Royal Tunbridge Wells, Camden
  Park TN2 . . . . 8 C3
 Royal Tunbridge Wells TN4 . . 7 F8
Prospect Terr TN21 . . . . 82 A7
Provence Ho BN23 . . . . 174 F1
Providence Cotts
 Crowborough TN6 . . . . 25 D4
 Groombridge TN3 . . . . 15 C7
Providence Pl BN1 . . . . 189 B4
Prowting Mead TN39 . . . . . 156 C3
Pudding Cake La TN32 . . . . 78 C7
Pulborough Ave BN22 . . . . 173 E2
Pulborough Cl BN2 . . . . 164 F7
Pump Ho The BN3 . . . . 162 D8
Pump La TN22 . . . . 79 D4
Pump Terr TN11 . . . . 8 B4
PUNNETT'S TOWN 83 C5
Punnetts Town Prim Sch
 TN21 . . . . 83 B6
Purbeck Cl BN23 . . . . 174 C4

Purbeck Ho BN2 . . . . 189 C2
Putlands Cres TN39 . . . . . . 157 A8
Pyecombe St BN45 . . . . . . 119 A6

Q

QUABROOK 12 C1
Quadrangle The BN8 . . . . . 105 C5
Quadrant The
 Eastbourne BN21 . . . . 184 E4
 Keymer BN6 . . . . 98 A4
Quail Ct BN27 . . . . 152 D7
Quakers La RH16 . . . . 51 A5
QUAKER'S PLATT 2 A8
Quantock Cl
 Eastbourne BN23 . . . . 174 D3
 Royal Tunbridge Wells TN2 . . 8 D5
Quantock Gdns TN34 . . . . . 160 B7
Quarry Bank Rd BN1 . . . . . 143 B6
Quarry Cl RH15 . . . . 73 D3
Quarry Cotts TN5 . . . . 29 D7
Quarry Cres TN34 . . . . 160 A5
Quarry Hill
 Haywards Heath RH16 . . . . 50 C6
 St Leonards TN38 . . . . 159 B7
Quarry Ho TN38 . . . . 159 B6
Quarry La BN25 . . . . 181 A5
Quarry Rd
 Hastings TN34 . . . . 160 A5
 Newhaven BN9 . . . . 179 D5
 Royal Tunbridge Wells TN1 . . 8 B5
Quarry Rise RH19 . . . . 2 A3
Quarry Terr TN34 . . . . 136 F1
Quarry View 1 TN6 . . . . 37 F8
Quay Ct BN43 . . . . 161 B6
Quayside Bldgs BN41 . . . . 162 D6
Quay The 5 BN43 . . . . 161 A6
Quay Units BN10 . . . . 178 D7
Quebec Cl
 Bexhill TN39 . . . . 157 C5
 Eastbourne BN23 . . . . 185 F7
Quebec Mans TN38 . . . . . . 159 A8
Quebec Rd TN38 . . . . 136 A4
Quebec St BN2 . . . . 189 C3
Queen Alexandra Ave
 BN3 . . . . 142 A3
Queen Anne's Cl BN7 . . . . 190 A2
Queen Caroline Cl BN3 . . . 142 A3
Queen Elizabeth Ave
 RH15 . . . . 73 A2
Queen Elizabeth Cl TN33 112 F5
Queen Mary Ave BN3 . . . . . 142 A3
Queens App TN22 . . . . 55 D1
Queen's Ave 3 TN34 . . . . . 159 F7
Queensbury Mews BN1 . . 163 E5
Queens Cotts TN5 . . . . 29 E6
Queens Cres RH15 . . . . 73 A2
Queens Cres BN23 . . . . 185 E7
Queens Ct 8 TN39 . . . . 157 B3
Queen's Ct RH16 . . . . 50 F6
Queensdown Sch Rd BN1,
 BN2 . . . . 143 D2
Queens Dr
 Hassocks BN6 . . . . 97 F4
 Maresfield TN22 . . . . 54 F4
Queen's Gdns
 Brighton BN1 . . . . 189 B3
 Eastbourne BN21 . . . . 185 B3
 Hove BN3 . . . . 163 C5
 Royal Tunbridge Wells TN4 . . 8 B6
Queensmount TN20 . . . . . . 58 B7
Queens Par 8 TN34 . . . . . . 159 F8
Queen's Par
 Eastbourne BN22 . . . . 173 F1
 Hove BN3 . . . . 141 E2
Queens Park Gdns BN25 180 C4
Queens Park Mews BN2 . 164 C6
Queen's Park Prim Sch
 BN2 . . . . 164 C5
Queen's Park Rd BN2 . . . . 164 C6
Queen's Park Rise BN2 . . . 164 C6
Queen's Park Terr BN2 . . . 164 C6
Queen's Pl
 Brighton BN1 . . . . 189 B4
 Hove BN3 . . . . 163 C6
Queen Sq BN1 . . . . 189 A2
Queens Rd
 Crowborough TN6 . . . . 25 F1
 Haywards Heath RH16 . . . . 50 E6
 Herstmonceux BN27 . . . . 130 E5
 Southwick BN42 . . . . 140 E1
Queen's Rd
 Brighton BN1 . . . . 189 A3
 Eastbourne BN23 . . . . 185 D7
 East Grinstead RH19 . . . . . . 1 E1
 Hastings TN34 . . . . 159 F8
 Lewes BN7 . . . . 190 B4
 Royal Tunbridge Wells TN4 . . 8 B6
Queens Sq TN34 . . . . 159 F8
Queen St TN18 . . . . 47 B5
Queensway
 Brighton BN2 . . . . 164 D6
 East Grinstead RH19 . . . . . . 1 E1
 Seaford BN25 . . . . 181 A6
 St Leonards TN37, TN38 . 135 E5
Queen's Wlk RH19 . . . . 1 E1
Queen Victoria Ave BN3 . 142 A3
Queen Victoria Hospl The
 RH19 . . . . 1 F3
Querneby Cl BN43 . . . . 161 D7
Quickbourne Cotts TN31 . 67 D8
Quickbourne La TN31 . . . . 67 C7
Quinnell Dr BN27 . . . . 129 B2
Quintin Cl BN27 . . . . 152 A5
Quintins The BN27 . . . . 152 C8

R

Radcliffe Cl TN37 . . . . . . 136 C3
Radinden Dr BN3 . . . . 142 D1
Radinden Manor Rd
BN3 . . . . 163 D8
Radnor Ho RH16 . . . . 50 D6
Radnor Mews TN38 . . . . . 135 E2
Rafati Way TN40 . . . . 157 D6
Ragged Dog La TN21 . . . . 81 B3
Raglan Ct
Brighton BN1 . . . . 189 A2
Pevensey Bay BN24 . . . . . 175 C3
Railway App
East Grinstead RH19 . . . . 1 E1
Newhaven BN9 . . . . 179 D7
Railway Cotts
Cowden TN8 . . . . 4 D8
Horsted Keynes RH17 . . . . . 33 A8
Ripe BN8 . . . . 149 A6
St Leonards TN38 . . . . . . 158 F6
Railway La BN7 . . . . 190 B2
Railway Land Nature
Reserve ★ BN7 . . . . 190 C1
Railway Rd BN9 . . . . 179 D7
Railway St BN1 . . . . 189 A3
Railway View TN6 . . . . . . 38 C8
Rainey Ct BN21 . . . . 185 B3
Raleigh Cl BN23 . . . . 185 E7
Ramsay Way BN23 . . . . . 185 F7
RAMSLYE 7 D1
Ramslye Rd TN4 . . . . 16 E8
Ranalah Est BN9 . . . . 179 D8
Randiddles Cl BN6 . . . . 97 B4
Randolph Ho TN39 . . . . . 156 E5
Randolph La TN31 . . . . . . 70 B3
Ranelagh Ct BN23 . . . . . . 185 E6
Ranelagh Villas BN3 . . . . 163 B8
Rangemore Dr BN21 . . . . . 184 D6
Rankine Rd TN2 . . . . 8 D7
Ranmore Cl TN34 . . . . . . 136 E6
Rannoch Rd TN6 . . . . 25 D2
Rannoch Road W TN6 . . . . 25 D2
Ranscombe Hill BN8 . . . . 147 A6
Ransombe La BN8 . . . . . . 147 D6
Ranworth Rd BN23 . . . . . 174 B4
Raphael Rd BN3 . . . . 162 F7
Rapson's Rd BN20 . . . . . . 173 A3
Rastrick Cl RH15 . . . . 72 F1
Ratton Dr BN20 . . . . 184 B7
Ratton Gdn BN20 . . . . . . 184 B7
Ratton Rd BN21 . . . . 184 E4
Ratton Sch BN21 . . . . . . 184 C7
Raven Ct
Battle TN33 . . . . 112 F4
St Leonards TN38 . . . . . . 135 E3
Ravensbourne Ct BN2 . . . 165 D8
Ravens Cl TN39 . . . . 156 C3
Ravens Croft BN20 . . . . . 188 F8
Ravens Ct BN20 . . . . 188 F8
Ravenside Ret & L Pk
TN40 . . . . 158 A4
Ravenswood BN6 . . . . 97 E4
Ravenswood Ave TN2 . . . . . 8 D6
Ravenswood Dr BN2 . . . . 165 F6
Ravenswood Rd RH15 . . . . 73 B3
Ravine Cl TN34 . . . . 160 A7
Rayford Cl BN10 . . . . 178 C7
Rayford Ct
2 Bexhill TN40 . . . . . . 157 D4
15 Seaford BN25 . . . . . 180 E2
Raymond Cl BN25 . . . . . . 181 A5
Rayner Cl TN6 . . . . 25 F3
Raystede Ctr for Animal
Welfare ★ BN8 . . . . 103 D1
Readers La TN31 . . . . 69 F5
Reading Rd BN2 . . . . 164 F4
Reba Ct BN2 . . . . 177 D4
Rectory Cl
Burwash TN19 . . . . 62 B6
Eastbourne BN20 . . . . . . 184 D3
East Hoathly BN8 . . . . . . 105 A5
Hove BN3 . . . . 162 D7
Newhaven BN9 . . . . 179 C6
Shoreham-by-S BN43 . . . 161 D7
St Leonards TN38 . . . . . . 136 B2
Rectory Ct 15 BN43 . . . . 161 C8
Rectory Field TN7 . . . . . . 13 E4
Rectory La
Beckley TN31 . . . . 67 F4
Rye TN31 . . . . 93 C8
Winchelsea TN36 . . . . . . 117 E7
Rectory Pk TN35 . . . . . . 116 E1
Rectory Rd
Newhaven BN9 . . . . 168 E2
Shoreham-by-S BN43 . . . 161 D7
Rectory Way TN40 . . . . . 157 D5
Red Barn Mews TN33 . . . 112 D4
Redbridge La TN6 . . . . 37 D5
Redbrook La TN22 . . . . . . 56 D4
Redcross St BN1 . . . . 189 B3
Red Dyke Cotts BN24 . . . 173 F6
Redford Cl BN23 . . . . 174 E1
Redford Ct TN39 . . . . 156 F4
Redgarth Ct RH19 . . . . 1 B3
Redgeland Rise TN38 . . . 135 F2
Redgill La BN8 . . . . 53 B1
Redhill Cl BN1 . . . . 142 C5
Redhill Dr BN1 . . . . 142 C5
Red Lake Prim Sch
TN35 . . . . 160 D8
Red Lake Terr TN35 . . . . 160 D8
Redleaf Cl TN3 . . . . 8 D6
Red Lion Mobile Home Pk
TN33 . . . . 132 E2
Redman King Ho BN20 . . 184 F2

Redmayne Dr TN34 . . . . . 159 E7
Red Oak TN18 . . . . 45 E8
Red Oast Cotts TN5 . . . . . 32 C3
Redoubt Rd BN22 . . . . . . 185 C4
Redoubt The ★ BN22 . . . . 185 C4
Redshank Ct BN27 . . . . . 152 D7
Redvers Rd BN2 . . . . 143 D1
Redward Bsns Pk BN23 . . 185 B7
Redwell Ave TN39 . . . . . . 157 B8
Redwood Dr RH16 . . . . . . 50 D3
Reed Ct BN7 . . . . 190 B4
Reedham Rd BN23 . . . . . 174 B4
Reed Ho BN8 . . . . 100 F1
Reed Pond Wlk RH16 . . . . 51 A4
Reedswood Rd
Broad Oak TN31 . . . . 90 B4
St Leonards TN38 . . . . . . 158 E8
Reeves Ct TN3 . . . . 6 B5
Reeves Hill BN3 . . . . 143 D5
Reeves Terr TN5 . . . . 31 E1
Refectory Rd BN1 . . . . . . 144 B7
Regal Dr 10 RH19 . . . . . . 10 F8
Regency Cl
Brighton BN1 . . . . 142 D3
12 Eastbourne BN20 . . . 185 A1
Regency Gdns TN38 . . . . 159 A8
Regency Hall 21 TN2 . . . . . 8 A2
Regency Ho TN2 . . . . 8 B2
Regency Mews
15 Brighton BN1 . . . . . . 163 E5
11 Eastbourne BN20 . . . 185 A1
Regency Rd BN1 . . . . 189 A2
Regency Sq BN1 . . . . 163 E5
Regent Arc BN1 . . . . 189 A3
Regent Bsns Pk RH15 . . . . 72 E2
Regent Hill BN1 . . . . 189 A2
Regent Pl
Heathfield TN21 . . . . 82 A8
Royal Tunbridge Wells TN2 . . 8 D3
St Leonards TN37 . . . . . . 135 F7
Regent Row BN1 . . . . 189 A2
Regents Cl BN25 . . . . 180 E5
Regents Pl TN31 . . . . 184 D8
Regent Sq TN31 . . . . 93 C6
Regent St BN1 . . . . 189 B2
Regina Ct TN4 . . . . 7 F4
Reginald Rd TN39 . . . . . . 157 B4
Regnum Cl BN22 . . . . 173 E4
Reigate Rd BN1 . . . . 142 D1
Renascent Ho 18 BN21 . . 185 B3
Renfields RH16 . . . . 50 C3
Renown Cl TN40 . . . . 157 D6
Resting Oak Hill BN8 . . . 100 F3
Reynolds Dr TN40 . . . . . . 157 E5
Reynolds La TN4 . . . . 7 F7
Reynolds Rd
Eastbourne BN23 . . . . . . 174 E1
Hove BN3 . . . . 162 F7
Reynoldstown La BN26 . . 172 F6
Ribbetts Cotts BN6 . . . . . 97 A5
Ribbetts Ho BN6 . . . . 97 A5
Riccards La TN33 . . . . 88 A2
Rich Ind Est BN9 . . . . 168 E1
Richborough Cl TN34 . . . 136 D4
Rich Ho BN3 . . . . 162 F7
Richardson Ct 5 BN3 . . . 162 F7
Richardson Rd
Hove BN3 . . . . 162 F7
Royal Tunbridge Wells TN4 . . 8 A5
Richborough Cl TN34 . . . 136 D4
Richmead Gdns TN20 . . . . 40 B2
Richmond Ave TN39 . . . . 156 F3
Richmond Cl TN39 . . . . . 157 A3
Richmond Ct
9 Hove BN3 . . . . 163 E7
Seaford BN25 . . . . 180 E3
Richmond Gdns 2 BN2 . . 189 C3
Richmond Gr TN39 . . . . . 157 A2
Richmond Hts 12 BN2 . . . 189 C3
Richmond Mews BN25 . . 180 E3
Richmond Par BN2 . . . . . 189 C3
Richmond Pl
Brighton BN2 . . . . 189 B3
Eastbourne BN21 . . . . . . 184 F4
Royal Tunbridge Wells TN2 . . 8 B1
Richmond Rd
Bexhill TN39 . . . . 157 A3
Brighton BN2 . . . . 164 B8
Pevensey Bay BN24 . . . . 175 D5
Seaford BN25 . . . . 180 E3
Richmond Sq RH19 . . . . . . 1 D2
Richmond St
Brighton BN2 . . . . 189 C3
Hastings TN35 . . . . 160 C6
Richmond Terr
Brighton BN2 . . . . 189 C4
2 Seaford BN25 . . . . . . 180 E3
Richmond Way RH19 . . . . 10 F8
RICKNEY 153 D2
Riddens Cl BN7 . . . . 99 E5
Riddens La BN7 . . . . 99 E6
Riddens The BN7 . . . . 99 E5
Riddlesdale Ave TN4 . . . . . 8 A6
Riders Bolt TN39 . . . . . . 156 E5
Ride The BN1 . . . . 142 F1
Ridge Cl
Nutley TN22 . . . . 35 C5
Portslade-by-S BN41 . . . . 141 A4
Ridge Rd BN1 . . . . 144 C7
Ridgeside Ave BN1 . . . . . 142 E5
Ridge The
Groombridge TN3 . . . . . . 15 A6

Ridge The continued
St Leonards TN34, TN37 . 136 D6
Winchelsea Beach TN36 . . 118 C6
Ridge View BN1 . . . . 143 E5
Ridgeway
East Grinstead RH19 . . . . 10 E7
Hurst Green TN19 . . . . . . 45 A3
Pembury TN2 . . . . 9 D7
Southwick BN41, BN42 . . 140 F1
The Moor TN18 . . . . 45 E8
Ridge Way RH17 . . . . 51 B2
Ridgeway Cl
Heathfield TN21 . . . . 82 A8
Southwick BN42 . . . . 140 F1
Ridgewaye The TN4 . . . . . . 8 A8
Ridgeway Gdns BN2 . . . . 165 E7
Ridgeway
Burgess Hill RH15 . . . . . . 73 B4
Friston BN20 . . . . 183 B1
Herstmonceux BN27 . . . . 130 E6
Seaford BN25 . . . . 180 F4
RIDGEWOOD 78 C4
RIDGEWOOD Ave BN2 . . . 166 C3
Ridgewood Ave TN22 . . . . 78 D4
Ridgewood Gdns
Bexhill TN40 . . . . 157 F4
Hastings TN34 . . . . 136 E5
Ridgewood Ind Pk TN22 . . 78 E4
Ridge W The TN37 . . . . . 136 A7
Ridgway Cl BN2 . . . . 165 D8
Ridgway Paddock BN7 . . 145 E6
Ridgway The BN2 . . . . . . 165 D8
Ridings The
Bexhill TN39 . . . . 156 F8
Burgess Hill RH15 . . . . . . 73 C2
Newick BN8 . . . . 76 C7
Ovingdean BN2 . . . . 165 C4
Royal Tunbridge Wells TN2 . . 8 A6
Seaford BN25 . . . . 180 F5
St Leonards TN37 . . . . . . 136 C5
Telscombe Cliffs BN10 . . . 167 B2
Rigden Rd BN3 . . . . 142 C1
Riley Rd BN2 . . . . 143 C1
Rill Wlk RH19 . . . . 2 B1
Ringle Gn TN18 . . . . 47 C5
RINGLES CROSS 55 C2
Ringles Cross TN22 . . . . . 55 D2
RINGMER 124 C6
Ringmer Bsns Pk BN8 . . . 124 C6
Ringmer Cl BN1 . . . . 143 E4
Ringmer Com Coll BN8 . . 124 E6
Ringmer Dr BN1 . . . . 143 F4
Ringmer Pool ★ BN8 . . . . 124 E6
Ringmer Prim Sch BN8 . . 124 E5
Ringmer Rd
Brighton BN1 . . . . 143 E4
Newhaven BN9 . . . . 179 B6
Seaford BN25 . . . . 180 E2
Ringmer Way BN23 . . . . . 174 A4
Ringwood Cl BN22 . . . . . 185 B5
Ringwood Ct 6 BN22 . . . 185 C5
Ringwood Rd
Bexhill TN39 . . . . 157 C7
Eastbourne BN22 . . . . . . 185 B5
RIPE 126 D1
Ripe La BN8 . . . . 126 E2
Ripley Chase BN21 . . . . . 184 E3
Ripsley Cl BN23 . . . . 174 E2
Risden La TN18 . . . . 46 D7
RISEDEN 29 B1
Riseden Rd TN5 . . . . 29 C1
Rise Pk Gdns BN23 . . . . . 174 E2
Rise The
East Grinstead RH19 . . . . 10 F8
Haywards Heath RH16 . . . 51 B8
Horam TN21 . . . . 106 F7
Portslade-by-S BN41 . . . . 140 F2
Risings The BN25 . . . . . . 180 F4
Rising The BN23 . . . . 174 E2
Rissom Ct TN35 . . . . 142 E2
Ritz Blgs TN1 . . . . 8 A3
Riverbourne Rd 10 BN22 185 B4
Riverbridge Cotts TN33 . . 113 B4
Riverdale BN2 . . . . 190 A3
Riverhall Hill TN5 . . . . . . 28 E8
Riverhall La TN5 . . . . 28 F8
River La BN26 . . . . 171 A3
Riverside
Forest Row RH18 . . . . 11 E3
Hadlow Down TN22 . . . . . 57 D1
Southwick BN42 . . . . 161 A4
Riverside Bsns Ctr BN43 . 161 A7
Riverside Gdns TN6 . . . . . 38 C8
Riverside Ho BN2 . . . . . . 179 D6
Riverside Ind Est BN7 . . . 190 B3
Riverside N BN9 . . . . 179 D7
River Way TN22 . . . . 78 C6
Rixons Cl RH17 . . . . 33 C5
Rixons Orch RH17 . . . . . . 33 C5
RNLI Lifeboat Mus ★
BN21 . . . . 185 A1
Robert Lodge BN2 . . . . . 164 F4
ROBERTSBRIDGE 64 B4
Robertsbridge Com Coll
TN32 . . . . 63 F4
Robertsbridge Sta TN32 . . 64 A4
Robert's Hill TN36 . . . . . 117 E8
Robertson Pas TN34 . . . . 159 F7
Robertson Rd BN1 . . . . . 142 D1
Robertsons Hill TN34 . . . 160 B6
Robertson St TN34 . . . . . 159 F7
Robertson Terr 1 TN34 . . 159 F7
Roberts Row BN1 . . . . . . 68 C5
Robert St BN1 . . . . 189 B3
Robert Tressell Cl TN34 . . 136 E1
Robert Tressell Workshops
7 TN34 . . . . 159 F8
Robian Dr TN22 . . . . 55 A4

Robin Cl
Eastbourne BN23 . . . . . . 174 C2
1 East Grinstead RH19 . . . 1 F2
Robin Ct TN39 . . . . 157 A3
Robin Davis Cl BN2 . . . . . 143 E1
Robin Dene BN2 . . . . 164 E4
Robin Hill TN39 . . . . 156 D4
Robinia Lodge BN1 . . . . . 142 E2
Robin Post La BN26 . . . . 151 B1
Robin Rd RH15 . . . . 72 C2
Robin Rise RH16 . . . . 50 F3
Robinson Rd BN9 . . . . . . 179 C8
Robinsons Ct BN22 . . . . . 185 C6
Robins Ct BN27 . . . . 127 B3
Robins Reach BN27 . . . . . 127 B3
Robins Row BN41 . . . . . . 141 A1
Roborough Cl BN21 . . . . . 185 A4
Robsack Ave BN23 . . . . . 185 F8
Robsack Wood Com Sch
TN38 . . . . 135 E2
Rochdale Ho TN1 . . . . 8 C5
Rochdale Rd TN1 . . . . 8 C6
Rochester Cl
Eastbourne BN20 . . . . . . 188 C8
5 Hove BN3 . . . . 163 D6
Rochester Ct 4 BN3 . . . . 163 D6
Rochester Gdns BN3 . . . . 163 D6
Rochester Ho TN6 . . . . . . 26 C1
Rochester St 4 TN37 . . . 136 B2
Rochester St BN3 . . . . . . 164 D5
Rochester Way TN6 . . . . . 26 B1
Rochford Way BN25 . . . . 180 B6
Rochmans Way TN6 . . . . . 38 A8
Rockall Ave BN23 . . . . . . 185 F8
Rockall Dr BN27 . . . . 129 A2
Rock-a-Nore Par TN34 . . 160 B4
Rock-a-Nore Rd TN34 . . 160 B3
Rock Channel TN31 . . . . . 93 C5
Rock Channel Quay TN31 . 93 C5
Rock Cl
Hastings TN35 . . . . 160 D8
12 Southwick BN42 . . . . 161 E7
Rock Cotts TN3 . . . . 17 B1
Rockdene Cl RH19 . . . . 2 A1
Rock Gr BN2 . . . . 164 E4
Rock Hall Cotts TN22 . . . . 78 D8
Rockhurst Dr BN20 . . . . . 184 B6
Rockington Way TN6 . . . . 38 B8
Rock La TN35 . . . . 137 D7
Rocklands Cotts BN27 . . 131 B5
Rocklands La TN35 . . . . . 160 C5
Rockmead Rd TN35 . . . . 138 F4
Rock Pl BN2 . . . . 189 C1
ROCKROBIN 29 D6
Rock's Hill TN35 . . . . 114 E7
Rocks La TN22 . . . . 55 F7
ROCKS PARK 78 B8
Rocks Park Prim Sch
TN22 . . . . 78 B8
Rocks Park Rd TN22 . . . . . 78 B7
Rock St BN2 . . . . 164 E4
Rocks The RH19 . . . . 11 C6
Rock Villa Rd TN1 . . . . 8 A4
Rocky La RH16 . . . . 50 D1
Roderick Ave BN10 . . . . . 178 C8
Roderick Avenue N
BN10 . . . . 167 C2
Roderick Ct BN10 . . . . . . 178 C8
RODMELL 167 D8
Rodmell Ave BN2 . . . . . . 166 D1
Rodmell CE Prim Sch
BN7 . . . . 146 E1
Rodmell Ct 5 BN25 . . . . 180 C4
Rodmell Pl BN1 . . . . 143 A6
Rodmell Rd
Royal Tunbridge Wells TN2 . . 8 A2
Seaford BN25 . . . . 181 B2
Rodmill Dr BN21 . . . . . . 184 D6
Rodmill Rd BN21 . . . . . . 184 D5
Rodney Cl BN23 . . . . 185 F7
Rodwell Ho TN6 . . . . 26 C1
Roebuck St 18 TN34 . . . . 160 B4
Roedale Cl 1 BN1 . . . . . . 143 B1
Roedale Rd BN1 . . . . 143 B1
ROEDEAN 165 B4
Roedean Cl
Bexhill TN39 . . . . 157 A5
Seaford BN25 . . . . 181 A4
Roedean Cres BN2 . . . . . 165 A4
Roedean Ct BN2 . . . . 164 F4
Roedean Hts BN2 . . . . . . 165 A4
Roedean Path BN2 . . . . . 165 A3
Roedean Rd
Brighton BN2 . . . . 164 F4
Royal Tunbridge Wells TN2 . . 8 A3
Roedean Sch BN2 . . . . . . 165 C3
Roedean Terr BN2 . . . . . 165 B3
Roedean Vale BN2 . . . . . 165 B3
Roedean Way BN2 . . . . . 165 B3
Roeheath BN8 . . . . 75 F4
Roffrey Ave BN22 . . . . . . 173 D1
Rolfe Dr RH15 . . . . 73 D3
Romaine Cl RH15 . . . . . . 73 D5
Roman Cl BN25 . . . . 180 B6
Roman Cres BN42 . . . . . 161 E6
Roman Croft BN21 . . . . . 184 E4
Roman Ct RH15 . . . . 73 A3
Roman Rd
Hove BN3 . . . . 162 D6
Southwick BN42 . . . . 161 E6
Romans Way BN24 . . . . . 174 E4
Roman Way
Southwick BN42 . . . . 161 E6
Uckfield TN22 . . . . 78 E7
Romany Cl BN41 . . . . 162 B8
ROMFORD 9 F7
Romford Rd TN2 . . . . 9 F7

Romney Cl BN25 . . . . 181 C4
Romney Ct 8 TN40 . . . . . 157 D4
Romney Rd
Polegate BN26 . . . . 173 B7
Rottingdean BN2 . . . . . . 166 A1
Romney St BN22 . . . . 185 C5
Romsey Cl BN1 . . . . 143 C2
Rookery Cl
Brighton BN1 . . . . 142 E1
Newhaven BN9 . . . . 168 E2
Rookery La
Rushlake Green TN21 . . . . 83 E2
Winchelsea TN36 . . . . . . 117 F7
Rookery The BN23 . . . . . 174 C4
Rookery Way
Haywards Heath RH16 . . . 50 E1
Newhaven BN9 . . . . 168 E2
Seaford BN25 . . . . 180 B5
Rookhurst Rd TN40 . . . . . 157 F5
Rookley Cl TN2 . . . . 8 D2
Rookwood Ct TN22 . . . . . 78 E8
Roopers TN3 . . . . 7 A7
Roosevelt Ct TN38 . . . . . 136 B3
Roper's Gate TN2 . . . . 7 E1
Rope Walk Sh Ctr 6
TN31 . . . . 93 C5
Rope Wlk
Hailsham BN27 . . . . 152 B8
Rye TN31 . . . . 93 C6
Rope Wlk The TN18 . . . . . 47 B5
Rosary Ct RH15 . . . . 73 B2
Rosebarn Ct RH15 . . . . . . 73 C1
Rosebery Ave
Eastbourne BN22 . . . . . . 173 E1
Woodingdean BN2 . . . . . 165 C8
Rose Cotts
Danehill RH17 . . . . 34 A4
Forest Row RH18 . . . . 11 E3
Rose Ct BN6 . . . . 97 E4
Rosedale Pl BN22 . . . . . . 173 D3
Rosedene Cl BN2 . . . . . . 165 E6
Rosefield Cotts TN32 . . . . 65 F1
Rose Gr BN27 . . . . 127 B3
ROSE HILL 102 F6
Rose Hill BN2 . . . . 189 B4
Rose Hill Cl BN1 . . . . 189 B4
Rose Hill Ct BN1 . . . . 189 B4
Rosehill Gdns TN6 . . . . . . 26 C1
Rose Hill Sch TN4 . . . . 7 E5
Rose Hill Terr BN1 . . . . . 189 B4
Rosehill Wlk TN1 . . . . 8 A3
Roseland Ct 2 BN22 . . . . 185 C5
ROSELANDS 185 B5
Roselands
Bexhill TN39 . . . . 156 F6
Sedlescombe TN33 . . . . . 88 E1
Roselands Ave
Eastbourne BN22 . . . . . . 185 C5
Wellbrook TN20 . . . . 39 F1
Roselands Cl BN22 . . . . . 185 C5
Roselands Inf Sch BN22 . . 185 B5
Roseleigh Gdns RH17 . . . . 51 F3
Rosemary Cl
Haywards Heath RH16 . . . 50 B6
Peacehaven BN10 . . . . . . 167 C1
Rosemary Dr BN43 . . . . . 140 C5
Rosemary Gdns TN19 . . . . 62 B7
Rosemary La
Guestling Green TN35 . . . 138 D6
Stonecrouch TN5 . . . . 32 A5
Rosemount
Lower Dicker BN8, BN27 . 128 A7
Muddles Green BN8 . . . . 127 F7
Rosemount Cl BN25 . . . . 180 A6
ROSER'S CROSS 80 C7
Rosetti Rd BN24 . . . . 175 D4
Roseveare Rd BN22 . . . . . 185 C6
Rose Walk Cl BN9 . . . . . . 179 C9
Rose Walk The BN9 . . . . . 179 C7
Rose Wlk
Burgess Hill RH15 . . . . . . 73 C7
Seaford BN25 . . . . 180 F4
Rossdale TN2 . . . . 8 D5
Rossington Cl BN21 . . . . 184 D5
Rosslyn Ave BN43 . . . . . 161 A7
Rotary Lodge BN1 . . . . . 143 E6
Rotary Point BN41 . . . . . 141 A1
Rothbury Rd BN1 . . . . . . 162 D7
Rother Ave BN24 . . . . . . 173 F5
Rother Cl
Burwash TN19 . . . . 62 B6
Crowborough TN6 . . . . . . 38 A7
Rother Ct TN39 . . . . 157 B6
ROTHERFIELD 39 E7
Rotherfield Ave
Bexhill TN40 . . . . 157 D4
Eastbourne BN23 . . . . . . 174 A4
Hastings TN34 . . . . 160 B5
Rotherfield Cl BN1 . . . . . 143 B4
Rotherfield Cres BN1 . . . 143 B5
Rotherfield Cty Prim Sch
TN6 . . . . 39 B8
Rotherfield La TN20 . . . . . 39 F1
Rotherfield Rd TN6 . . . . . 38 E8
Rotherhill Rd TN6 . . . . . . 38 A7
Rother Ho TN21 . . . . 82 A8
Rotherhurst La TN6 . . . . . 39 B6
Rother Ironworks The 5
TN31 . . . . 93 C5
Rothermead TN20 . . . . . . 39 F1
Rother Rd BN25 . . . . 181 A2
Rother Valley Rly ★ TN32 . 64 C3
Rotherview TN32 . . . . 64 C5
Rother View
Burwash TN19 . . . . 62 B7

Rother View continued
Etchingham TN19 . . . . 44 C1
Rothley Chase RH16 . . . . 50 F4
Rothsay Ct TN38 . . . . 159 B7
Rothsay Rd TN38 . . . . 159 B7
Rothwell Ct BN9 . . . . 179 A7
Rotten Row BN7 . . . . 190 A1
ROTTINGDEAN 177 A6
Rottingdean Pl BN2 . . . . 165 F4
Rotunda Rd BN23 . . . . . . 185 D8
Rotyngs The BN2 . . . . 165 F2
Rough Brow BN25 . . . . . . 181 A4
Rough Field RH19 . . . . 1 D4
Rough The BN8 . . . . 76 C7
Roundacres Way TN40 . . 157 E6
Roundel The TN37 . . . . . . 136 D5
Roundhay Ave BN10 . . . . 178 E6
ROUND HILL 164 B8
Round Hill Cres BN2 . . . . 164 B8
Roundhill Rd TN2 . . . . 8 D1
Round Hill Rd **2** BN2 . . . . 164 B8
Round Hill St **3** BN2 . . . . 164 B8
Roundhouse Cotts TN21 . . 82 D7
Roundway
Brighton BN1 . . . . 143 E5
Haywards Heath RH16 . . . 50 C1
Roundwood La RH16 . . . . 50 F8
Roundwood Rd TN37 . . . 136 B5
Rowan Ave
Eastbourne BN22 . . . . . . 173 D3
Hove BN3 . . . . 141 E1
Rowan Cl
Haywards Heath RH16 . . . 51 B4
Heathfield TN21 . . . . 82 A5
Portslade-by-S BN41 . . . 141 A1
Seaford BN25 . . . . 181 C3
St Leonards TN37 . . . . . 136 D6
Rowan Ct
Brighton BN1 . . . . 142 E1
Polegate BN26 . . . . 173 A6
Rowanden Ct BN2 . . . . . . 177 C4
Rowan Gdns TN40 . . . . . . 157 F6
Rowan Ho
6 Brighton BN2 . . . . . . 189 C4
Royal Tunbridge Wells TN4 . . 7 E4
Rowan's Ct BN7 . . . . 190 A2
Rowans The
Burgess Hill RH15 . . . . . . 72 D4
Hurstpierpoint BN6 . . . . . 97 A7
Rowan Tree Rd TN2 . . . . . . 7 E1
Rowan Way BN2 . . . . 165 E4
Rowbarns TN33 . . . . 112 C6
Rowe Ave BN10 . . . . 178 B7
Rowe Avenue N BN10 . . 178 B8
Rowsley Rd BN20 . . . . . . 188 D7
Royal Alexandra Children's
Hospl BN2 . . . . 164 C4
Royal Chase TN4 . . . . 7 F4
Royal Cres BN2 . . . . 164 C4
Royal Crescent Mans 10
BN2 . . . . 164 C4
Royal Crescent Mews 8
BN2 . . . . 164 C4
Royal Ct TN34 . . . . 136 F1
Royal Dr BN25 . . . . 180 E6
Royal George Ct RH15 . . 72 F3
Royal George Par BN43 . 140 C1
Royal George Rd RH15 . . 72 E3
Royal Hippodrome★ **23**
BN21 . . . . 185 B3
Royal Mews TN38 . . . . . . 159 A6
Royal Military Rd TN36 . . 118 A8
Royal Oak La TN22 . . . . . . 56 B8
Royal Par BN22 . . . . 185 D5
Royal Pavilion★ BN1 . . . 189 B2
Royal Sovereign View
BN23 . . . . 185 F6
Royal Sussex Cres BN20 . 184 B5
Royal Sussex Sct BN7 . . . 190 B1
Royal Sussex Cty Hospl
BN2 . . . . 164 D4
Royal Terr **4** TN37 . . . . . 159 C7
ROYAL TUNBRIDGE
WELLS 8 D3
Royal Victoria Pl TN1 . . . .8 B4
Royal Victoria Place Sh Ctr
TN1 . . . . .8 B4
Royles Cl BN2 . . . . 166 A2
Royston Cl BN20 . . . . 183 A1
Royston Gdns TN40 . . . . 157 F6
Rubislaw **3** BN31 . . . . . . 184 F4
Rudge Ho **2** RH19 . . . . 1 F1
Rudyard Cl BN2 . . . . 165 E8
Rudyard Kipling Prim Sch
BN2 . . . . 165 E7
Rudyard Rd BN2 . . . . 165 E8
Rue De Bayeux TN33 . . . 112 D5
Ruffet Ct TN2 . . . . 7 E1
Rufus Cl BN7 . . . . 190 A2
Rugby Cl BN25 . . . . 181 B4
Rugby Ct **5** BN2 . . . . 164 E4
Rugby Pl BN2 . . . . 164 E4
Rugby Rd BN1 . . . . 143 A1
Rumbolds La RH16 . . . . . . 50 D2
Rumsey Ct TN6 . . . . 25 F1
Rusbridge La BN7 . . . . . . 190 C2
Rush Ct **4** BN2 . . . . 185 B3
Rushers Cross TN20 . . . . . 40 E5
RUSHER'S CROSS 40 E6
Rushes The RH16 . . . . 51 C4
Rushetts TN3 . . . . 6 F4
Rushey Cl BN2 . . . . 124 E5
Rushlake Cl BN1 . . . . 143 E5
Rushlake Cres BN21 . . . . 184 D6
RUSHLAKE GREEN 83 D2

Rushlake Rd BN1 . . . . 143 E5
Rushlye Cl TN3 . . . . 17 F5
Rushmere Rise TN38 . . . . 135 E1
Rushwood Cl RH16 . . . . . . 51 B4
RUSHY GREEN 124 E5
Ruskin Pl BN3 . . . . 162 F7
Ruskin Rd
Eastbourne BN20 . . . . . . 173 B1
Hove BN3 . . . . 162 F8
Rusper Ho **16** BN21 . . . . . 184 E4
Rusper Rd
Brighton BN1 . . . . 143 D6
Eastbourne BN20 . . . . . . 184 B6
Ruspers RH15 . . . . 73 D2
Russell Cotts **5** BN21 . . 184 E4
Russell Cres **1** BN1 . . . . 189 A4
Russell Ct **5** TN34 . . . . . 160 A3
Russell Mews **14** BN1 . . 163 E5
Russell Pl BN1 . . . . 189 A2
Russell Rd BN1 . . . . 189 A2
Russell Row BN7 . . . . 190 A4
RUSSELL'S GREEN 133 A3
Russell Sq BN1 . . . . 189 A2
Russell St TN34 . . . . 159 F8
Russet Cl BN26 . . . . 173 C6
Russett Way BN27 . . . . . . 131 B5
RUSTHALL 7 C4
Rusthall Grange TN4 . . . . . 7 C4
Rusthall High St TN4 . . . . . 7 C4
Rusthall Pk TN4 . . . . 7 D4
Rusthall Rd TN4 . . . . 7 D4
Rustic Cl
Rustic Cl BN10 . . . . 167 B1
Rustic Pk BN10 . . . . 167 B2
Rustic Rd BN10 . . . . 167 B2
Rustington Ct BN20 . . . . 188 F8
Rustington Rd BN1 . . . . . 143 A5
Rustlings Cl RH16 . . . . 51 B5
Rustwick TN4 . . . . 7 D4
Rutherfords Bsns Pk
TN33 . . . . 113 B7
Rutland Cl BN21 . . . . 184 D6
Rutland Ct
3 Eastbourne BN23 . . . 174 E1
Hove BN3 . . . . 162 F6
Rutland Gdns BN3 . . . . . 162 F7
Rutland Rd BN3 . . . . 163 A7
Rutley Cl TN32 . . . . 64 C5
Ruxley Ct BN20 . . . . 174 D2
Rydal Cl TN4 . . . . 7 E5
Rydal Dr TN4 . . . . 7 E5
Rydal Way BN23 . . . . 174 C4
Ryde Ct BN3 . . . . 141 D1
Ryde Rd BN2 . . . . 164 D7
Ryders TN3 . . . . 7 A3
RYE 93 B6
Rye Art Gall★ TN31 . . . . . 93 C5
Rye Cl
Polegate BN26 . . . . 173 C7
Saltdean BN2 . . . . 166 F2
Seaford BN25 . . . . 181 C4
Ryecroft
12 Brighton BN2 . . . . . . 164 F5
Haywards Heath RH16 . . . 50 E3
Ryefield Cl BN21 . . . . 184 C7
RYE FOREIGN 69 E1
RYE HARBOUR 93 F2
Rye Harbour National Nature
Reserve★ TN36 . . . . 93 C2
Rye Ind Pk TN31 . . . . 93 D4
Ryelands Dr BN2 . . . . 143 D3
Rye Rd
Four Throws TN18 . . . . . . 46 D8
Hastings TN35 . . . . 137 D5
Iden TN30 . . . . 70 A8
Peasmarsh TN31 . . . . 69 E2
Rye St TN31 . . . . 93 B6
Rylstone Rd BN22 . . . . . . 185 C4
Rymers Cl TN2 . . . . 8 D7
Rymill Rd TN38 . . . . 136 A3
Ryst Wood Rd RH18 . . . . . 12 B1

S

Sackville Cl
East Grinstead RH19 . . . . . 1 C3
Lewes BN7 . . . . 190 A1
Sackville Coll★ RH19 . . . . 1 F1
Sackville Ct
Bexhill TN40 . . . . 157 D5
3 East Grinstead RH19 . . 10 F8
Sackville Gdns
East Grinstead RH19 . . . . . 1 C3
Hove BN3 . . . . 162 F6
Sackville La RH19 . . . . 1 C3
Sackville Rd
Bexhill TN39 . . . . 157 B3
Eastbourne BN22 . . . . . . 173 F2
Hailsham BN27 . . . . 152 C6
Hove BN3 . . . . 163 A7
Sackville Sch RH19 . . . . . . 2 A1
Sackville Trad Est BN3 . . 163 B8
Sacred Heart Cath Prim Sch
TN35 . . . . 160 B5
Sacred Heart Sch TN5 . . . 29 D5
Saddlers Cl
Saddlers Cl RH15 . . . . 73 D1
Saddler's Ct **5** TN38 . . . 159 B6
Sadlers Way BN8 . . . . . . 124 D4
Sadler Way BN2 . . . . 164 F6
Saffreys Ct TN38 . . . . 159 B7
Saffron Cl BN43 . . . . 140 C1
Saffron Gate BN3 . . . . . . 163 C7
Saffron Gdns BN26 . . . . . 170 F3
Saffrons Ct BN21 . . . . . . 184 E2
Saffrons Mead **9** BN20 . 184 E2
Saffrons Pk BN20 . . . . . . 184 E1
Saffrons Rd BN21 . . . . . . 184 F2

Saffrons The RH15 . . . . . . 72 F5
St Agnes Rd RH19 . . . . 1 E2
St Aidan's Ct **9** BN22 . . . 185 C5
St Andrews CE Inf Sch
BN22 . . . . 185 D6
St Andrew's CE Prim Sch
BN3 . . . . 163 B7
St Andrews Cl BN27 . . . . 129 A1
St Andrew's Ct BN9 . . . . 179 B7
St Andrew's Dr BN25 . . . 180 B6
St Andrew's La BN7 . . . . 190 B2
St Andrews Rd RH15 . . . . 73 C4
St Andrew's Rd
Bexhill TN40 . . . . 157 C5
Brighton BN1 . . . . 143 A1
Portslade-by-S BN41 . . . 162 C7
St Andrews Sch BN20 . . . 188 D7
St Andrew's Sq 6 TN34 . 159 F8
St Andrew's Villas TN34 . 160 A4
ST ANNES 123 A1
St Anne's Cl TN40 . . . . . . 157 D5
St Anne's Cres **3** BN7 . . 123 B1
St Anne's Ct
5 Brighton BN1 . . . . . . 189 A4
7 Brighton, Kemp Town
BN2 . . . . 164 C4
St Anne's Gdns BN6 . . . . . 98 A3
St Annes Gn TN19 . . . . 62 A6
St Anne's Ho **6** BN1 . . . . 189 A4
St Annes Rd BN20 . . . . . . 173 B3
St Anne's Rd BN21 . . . . . 184 F4
St Anne's Terr **6** BN7 . . 123 B1
St Annes Well Ho 6
BN3 . . . . 163 D6
St Ann's Ct
Hove BN3 . . . . 163 D7
Pevensey Bay BN24 . . . . 175 D4
St Anns Mans **5** BN1 . . . 163 E7
St Anthonys BN8 . . . . 124 E6
St Anthony's Ave BN23 . 185 E8
ST ANTHONY'S HILL . . . 185 C8
St Aubyns BN3 . . . . 163 B6
St Aubyn's Cres BN41 . . 162 B7
St Aubyn's Gdns **13** BN3 . 163 A6
St Aubyns Mans BN3 . . . 163 A5
St Aubyn's Mead BN2 . . 166 A1
St Aubyn's Rd
Eastbourne BN22 . . . . . . 185 B3
Portslade-by-S, Aldrington
BN41 . . . . 162 C7
Portslade-by-S, Fishersgate
BN41 . . . . 162 A7
St Aubyns S BN3 . . . . 163 A5
St Aubyn's St BN2 . . . . . 165 F1
St Augustine's CE Prim Sch
RH17 . . . . 51 F3
St Augustines Cl RH17 . . 51 F3
St Augustine's Cl TN39 . 156 F3
St Augustine's RC Prim Sch
TN4 . . . . 8 A7
St Barnabas CE Prim Sch
TN1 . . . . 8 B5
St Barnabas' Cl TN1 . . . . . 8 B5
St Bartholomew's CE Prim
Sch BN1 . . . . 189 B4
St Bedes Prep Sch BN20 188 E7
St Bedes Sch BN27 . . . . . 151 A4
St Bernadette's RC Prim Sch
BN1 . . . . 142 E2
St Boswells Cl BN27 . . . . 152 A8
St Brelades BN21 . . . . . . 185 B2
St Catherine's Cl TN37 . . 159 D8
St Catherine's Ct RH19 . . . 1 D2
St Catherine's Terr 1
BN3 . . . . 163 B5
St Christopher's Rd BN6 . 97 A6
St Christopher's Sch
BN3 . . . . 163 A6
St Clements Caves★
TN34 . . . . 160 A4
St Clement's Ct BN21 . . . 184 D6
St Clements Pl **1** TN38 . 159 C6
St Crispians BN25 . . . . . . 180 D3
St Crispians Ct BN25 . . . 180 D3
St Cuthmans BN2 . . . . . . 164 F6
St David's Ave TN40 . . . . 157 C5
St Davids Cl BN22 . . . . . . 173 D4
St David's Ct BN10 . . . . . 178 B8
St David's Rd TN4 . . . . 8 B6
St Denys BN21 . . . . 184 E4
St Dominic Cl TN38 . . . . . 159 A8
St Edmund's Rd RH16 . . . 50 F3
St Edward's Cl RH19 . . . . . 1 C1
St Elizabeth's BN25 . . . . 180 F4
St Francis Chase TN39 . . 157 A5
St Francis Cl RH16 . . . . . . 50 F2
St Georges Ct
11 Bexhill TN40 . . . . . . 157 D3
East Grinstead RH19 . . . . . 1 C3
Royal Tunbridge Wells TN4 . . 8 A5
St George's Ho BN6 . . . . . 97 B5
St George's La BN6 . . . . . . 97 B5
St George's Mews BN1 . . 189 B3
St Georges Mount 14
TN37 . . . . 159 C7
St George's Pk 3 TN2 . . 16 F8
St George's Pl
Brighton BN1 . . . . 189 B3
Hurstpierpoint BN6 . . . . . 97 B5
St George's Rd
Bexhill TN40 . . . . 157 C5
Brighton BN2 . . . . 164 D4
Eastbourne BN22 . . . . . . 185 B4
Hastings TN34 . . . . 160 A5
St George's Terr **5** BN2 . 164 C4
St Giles CE Prim Sch
RH17 . . . . 33 C6

St Giles Cl
Shoreham-by-S BN43 . . . 161 B8
Winchelsea TN36 . . . . . . 117 C7
St Gregory Cl BN20 . . . . . 188 E8
St Gregory's Cath Comp Sch
TN4 . . . . 8 A7
St Helena La
St Helena La BN7 . . . . 74 D1
St Helena's Ct **1** BN21 . 184 E4
ST HELEN'S 137 A5
St Helen's Ave TN34 . . . . 136 E3
St Helen's Cres
Hastings TN34 . . . . 136 E2
Hove BN3 . . . . 141 D3
St Helen's Ct TN34 . . . . . 136 E2
St Helen's Down TN34 . . 160 E4
St Helen's Dr BN3 . . . . . . 141 D3
St Helen's Park Rd TN34 . 136 E3
St Helen's Rd
Brighton BN2 . . . . 164 D7
Hastings TN34 . . . . 136 D2
St Helens's Wood Rd
TN34 . . . . 136 E5
St Helen's Wood Nature
Reserve★ TN34 . . . . 136 E4
St Heliers Ave BN3 . . . . . 162 E7
Saint Hill Gn RH19 . . . . . . 10 C4
Saint Hill Manor★ RH19 . 10 C4
Saint Hill Rd RH19 . . . . . . 10 C5
St James BN24 . . . . 176 D8
St James' Ave TN40 . . . . 157 D6
St James CE Inf Sch TN2 . 8 C4
St James CE Jun Sch TN2 . 8 C4
St James' Cl TN40 . . . . . . 157 C7
St James' Cres TN40 . . . . 157 D7
St James Ct RH19 . . . . 1 E1
St James' Ho **13** BN2 . . . 189 C2
St James La TN22 . . . . 35 C4
St James' Pk TN1 . . . . 8 C5
St James Rd
Eastbourne BN22 . . . . . . 185 C4
East Grinstead RH19 . . . . . 1 D1
St James' Rd
Bexhill TN40 . . . . 157 C6
Royal Tunbridge Wells TN1 . . 8 C5
St James' Ave BN2 . . . . . 189 C2
St James' Ct TN1 . . . . 8 B4
St James' Pl BN2 . . . . 189 B2
St James' Rd TN34 . . . . . 136 F1
St James's St Mews BN2 189 C2
St James's St BN2 . . . . . . 189 C2
St James St BN7 . . . . 190 A1
St James Wlk BN9 . . . . . . 75 E1
St John Bank BN8 . . . . . . 100 D8
ST JOHN'S
Crowborough 25 D4
Royal Tunbridge Wells . . . 8 A5
St John's Ave RH15 . . . . . 72 F4
St John's CE Prim Sch
TN6 . . . . 25 C4
St John's Cl
Crowborough TN6 . . . . . . 25 E3
East Grinstead RH19 . . . . . 1 E2
South Chailey BN8 . . . . . 100 D7
St John's Coll BN2 . . . . . 164 D5
ST JOHN'S COMMON . . . 72 E4
St Johns Ct
Burgess Hill RH15 . . . . . . 73 A3
Polegate BN26 . . . . 173 A6
St John's Dr BN24 . . . . . . 174 E6
St John's Hill BN7 . . . . . . 190 A4
St John's Ho BN26 . . . . . 188 F8
St Johns Meads CE Prim Sch
BN20 . . . . 188 D7
St John's Mount **8** BN2 . 189 C2
St John's Pk TN4 . . . . 8 A8
St John's Pl
Brighton BN2 . . . . 189 C2
23 Brighton BN2 . . . . . 163 C6
St Johns Rd RH15 . . . . . . 73 A3
St John's Rd
Bexhill TN40 . . . . 157 D6
Crowborough TN6 . . . . . . 25 D4
Eastbourne BN20 . . . . . . 188 F8
East Grinstead RH19 . . . . . 1 E2
Haywards Heath RH16 . . . 50 E2
Hove BN3 . . . . 163 C5
Polegate BN26 . . . . 173 A6
Royal Tunbridge Wells TN4 . . 8 A6
Seaford BN25 . . . . 180 E2
St Leonards TN37 . . . . . 159 C7
St Johns Sch BN25 . . . . . 180 E6
St Johns St BN7 . . . . 190 B2
St John's Terr BN7 . . . . . 190 B2
St John the Baptist RC Sch
BN2 . . . . 164 C6
St Josephs Bsns Pk 2
BN3 . . . . 163 A8
St Joseph's Cl BN3 . . . . . 163 A8
St Joseph's RC Prim Sch
Brighton BN2 . . . . 143 C1
Haywards Heath RH16 . . . 50 E4
St Joseph's Trad Est 3
BN3 . . . . 163 A8
St Josephs Way RH16 . . . 50 E4
St Julian **5** BN3 . . . . 141 A3
St Julians Cl BN43 . . . . . 161 D7
St Julian's La BN43 . . . . . 161 D7
St Keyna Ave BN3 . . . . . . 162 D6
St Kilda Mans **5** BN21 . 184 F3
St Kitts **3** TN39 . . . . 157 A2
St Kitts Dr BN23 . . . . 185 G7
St Laurence Cl BN10 . . . 167 A1
St Lawrence CE Prim Sch
BN6 . . . . 97 A6
St Lawrence Mews BN23 175 A1
St Lawrence Pl BN23 . . . 175 A1
St Lawrence Rd TN39 . . . 157 B7

St Lawrence Way
Eastbourne BN23 . . . . . . 175 A1
Hurstpierpoint BN6 . . . . . 97 A7
ST LEONARDS 159 A7
St Leonard's Ave BN3 . . 162 C7
St Leonards CE Prim Sch
TN38 . . . . 159 A7
St Leonards Cl BN9 . . . . 168 F2
St Leonards Ct TN38 . . . 159 A6
St Leonard's Gdns BN3 . 162 D7
ST LEONARD'S GREEN . . 136 A1
St Leonards Mayfield Sch
TN20 . . . . 40 A3
St Leonards Pk RH19 . . . . 1 E1
St Leonard's Pl BN20 . . . 184 C3
St Leonards Rd
Bexhill TN40 . . . . 157 C3
Newhaven BN9 . . . . 168 F2
St Leonard's Rd
9 Brighton BN2 . . . . . . 164 C8
Eastbourne BN21 . . . . . . 185 A3
Hove BN3 . . . . 162 C7
St Leonards Terr BN26 . . 172 F7
St Leonards Warrior Square
Sta TN38 . . . . 159 C7
St Louie Cl BN42 . . . . 162 A8
St Lucia **1** TN39 . . . . 157 A2
St Lucia Wlk **8** BN23 . . . 185 F8
St Luke's CE Inf Sch TN4 . 8 C7
St Lukes Ct
Burgess Hill RH15 . . . . . . 73 A3
Newhaven BN9 . . . . 179 C6
St Luke's Inf Sch BN2 . . 164 C6
St Luke's Jun Sch BN2 . . 164 C6
St Luke's La BN9 . . . . 179 C7
St Luke's Rd
Brighton BN2 . . . . 164 C6
Royal Tunbridge Wells TN4 . . 8 B6
St Luke's Terr BN2 . . . . . 164 C6
St Margarets BN22 . . . . . 185 A1
St Margaret's Ave RH19 . . . 1 F1
St Margarets CE Prim Sch
BN2 . . . . 177 A6
St Margarets Cres TN39 . 156 B8
St Margaret's Pl BN1 . . . 189 A2
St Margaret's Rd
East Grinstead RH19 . . . . . 1 F3
St Leonards TN37 . . . . . 159 D7
St Margaret's Rise BN25 . 180 A6
St Margarets Terr 8
TN31 . . . . 93 B5
St Margaret's Terr TN37 . 159 D7
St Mark's CE Prim Sch
Brighton BN2 . . . . 164 E5
Hadlow Down TN22 . . . . . 57 C5
Royal Tunbridge Wells TN4 . . 7 D1
St Marks St TN39 . . . . . . 156 D5
St Marks Field TN22 . . . . . 57 B5
St Mark's Mews **13** BN2 . 164 E4
St Mark's Rd TN2 . . . . 16 F7
St Mark's St BN2 . . . . . . 164 E4
St Martins TN33 . . . . 112 D5
St Martins CE Prim Sch
BN2 . . . . 164 C8
St Martins Cres BN9 . . . . 168 D1
St Martin's Ct **6** BN2 . . . 189 C5
St Martin's Flats **6** BN2 . 164 C7
St Martins Ho BN8 . . . . . 124 E6
St Martin's La BN7 . . . . . 190 A1
St Martins Pl BN2 . . . . . . 164 C7
St Martins Rd BN22 . . . . 173 D3
St Martin's St BN2 . . . . . 189 C5
St Mary in the Castle Arts
Ctr★ **10** TN34 . . . . 160 A3
St Mary-in-the-Fields
TN20 . . . . 40 B2
St Mary Magdalene Cath
Prim Sch TN40 . . . . 157 F6
St Mary Magdalene St
BN2 . . . . 189 C5
St Mary Magdalen RC Prim
Sch BN1 . . . . 163 B5
St Marys TN21 . . . . 80 E7
St Marys Ave BN27 . . . . . 152 C7
St Marys Cath Prim Sch
Crowborough TN6 . . . . . . 26 A2
Portslade-by-S BN41 . . . 162 B7
St Mary's CE Sch RH19 . . 1 D2
St Mary's Cl
Cackle Street TN31 . . . . . 90 A2
Eastbourne BN22 . . . . . . 173 B2
Seaford BN25 . . . . 180 E4
Ticehurst TN5 . . . . 31 D1
St Mary's Cnr **3** BN21 . . 184 D3
St Marys Cotts **18** TN38 . 159 C7
St Mary's Cotts
Battle TN33 . . . . 112 E3
Bexhill TN39 . . . . 156 F3
4 Eastbourne BN20 . . 184 D3
St Mary's Ct
2 Eastbourne BN21 . . . 184 D3
8 St Leonards TN37 . . 159 C7
St Mary's Farmhouse
TN33 . . . . 112 E3
St Marys Garth TN22 . . . . 56 C4
St Mary's Gdns TN33 . . . 112 E3
St Mary's La
Bexhill TN39 . . . . 156 F8
Speldhurst TN3 . . . . 7 A8
Ticehurst TN5 . . . . 31 D1
St Marys Mead TN22 . . . . 56 B3
St Marys Pl **3** BN43 . . . . 161 A6
St Mary's Pl BN2 . . . . 189 C2
St Mary's Rd
Burgess Hill RH15 . . . . . . 72 F4
Eastbourne BN21 . . . . . . 184 D4
Hastings TN34 . . . . 160 A5

St Mary's Sch
  Bexhill TN40 . . . . 157 E6
  Maynard's Green TN21 . . . . . 82 A1
St Marys Specl Sch TN36 . . 82 A1
St Mary's Sq 17 BN2 . . . . . . 164 D4
St Mary Star of the Sea RC
  Prim Sch TN37 . . . . 159 D8
St Mary's Terr
  Battle TN33 . . . . 112 F3
  Hastings TN34 . . . . 160 A5
St Mary's Villas TN33 . . . . . . 112 E3
St Mary's Wlk BN27 . . . . 152 C7
St Mary the Virgin CE Prim
  Sch TN7 . . . . 13 D4
St Matthews Ct BN2 . . . . . . 136 C1
St Matthew's Dr TN38 . . . . 136 C1
St Matthew's Gdns BN1 . . 136 B1
St Matthews Prim Sch TN4 . 8 B8
St Matthew's Rd TN38 . . . . 136 B1
St Mellion Cl BN27 . . . . 151 F8
St Michaels CE Prim Sch
  TN31 . . . . 70 C2
St Michaels Cl
  Crowborough TN6 . . . . 38 B8
  Stone Cross BN24 . . . . . . 174 A6
St Michael's Pl
  Brighton BN1 . . . . 163 E6
  8 Hastings TN34 . . . . . . 159 E7
St Michaels Prim Sch
  TN7 . . . . 14 B5
St Michaels Rd TN19 . . . . . . 1 E2
St Michael's Rd
  Portslade-by-S BN41 . . . . . 162 B7
  Royal Tunbridge Wells TN4 . . 8 B7
St Michaels Terr BN7 . . . . . 190 B4
St Nicholas' CE Jun Sch
  BN41 . . . . 162 B8
St Nicholas Ct RH16 . . . . . . 51 A6
St Nicholas La BN7 . . . . . . 190 B2
St Nicholas Lodge BN1 . . 189 A2
St Nicholas Pl 2 BN43 . . 161 A6
St Nicholas Rd
  Brighton BN1 . . . . 189 A3
  Portslade-by-S BN41 . . . . . 162 B7
St Nicolas Cl BN24 . . . . . . 175 B6
St Nicolas & St Mary CE Fst
  & Mid Sch BN43 . . . . 161 A8
St Olive's Cl TN21 . . . . 81 C7
St Pancras Cath Prim Sch
  BN7 . . . . 123 B1
St Pancras Gdns BN7 . . . . 146 B8
St Pancras Gn BN7 . . . . . . 145 E5
St Pancras Rd BN7 . . . . . . 146 B8
St Patrick's Cres TN40 . . . 157 C5
St Patrick's Rd BN3 . . . . . 163 A7
St Pauls CE Jun Sch TN4 . . 7 B4
St Pauls CE Prim Sch TN4 . . 7 B4
St Paul's CE Prim Sch
  BN1 . . . . 189 A3
St Pauls Cl BN22 . . . . 173 D3
St Paul's Cl RH16 . . . . 50 F5
St Paul's Ct
  Rusthall TN4 . . . . 7 C4
  St Leonards TN37 . . . . . . 159 D8
St Paul's Pl TN37 . . . . 159 D8
St Paul's RC Coll RH15 . . . 72 D5
St Paul's Rd TN37 . . . . 136 C1
St Paul's St
  Brighton BN2 . . . . 189 C5
  Rusthall TN4 . . . . 7 C4
St Peter & St Paul CE Prim
  Sch TN40 . . . . 157 C4
St Peter's Ave BN10 . . . . . 178 A8
St Peters CE Prim Sch TN2 . 8 C3
St Peter's CE Prim Sch
  BN8 . . . . 75 E4
St Peter's Cl
  Hove BN3 . . . . 141 F2
  Seaford BN25 . . . . 180 E5
St Peter's Com Inf Sch
  BN41 . . . . 162 B7
St Peter's Cres TN40 . . . . . 157 D5
St Peters Ho BN1 . . . . 189 B3
St Peters Mead TN6 . . . . . . 39 A7
St Peter's Mews TN40 . . . 157 D5
St Peter's Pl BN7 . . . . 190 A2
St Peter's Pl BN1, BN2 . . . 189 B3
St Peter's RC Prim Sch
  BN43 . . . . 161 A8
St Peters RC Sch RH19 . . . 1 C1
St Peters Rd RH15 . . . . 73 A4
St Peter's Rd
  Portslade-by-S BN41 . . . . . 162 B7
  Seaford BN25 . . . . 180 E5
  St Leonards TN37 . . . . . . 159 C8
St Peters Row TN3 . . . . . . 6 A5
St Peter's St
  Brighton BN1 . . . . 189 B4
  Royal Tunbridge Wells TN2 . . 8 C3
St Philip's Ave BN22 . . . . 185 B5
St Philips Ct TN2 . . . . 8 D6
St Philips Mews 3 BN3 . . 162 F7
St Philips Pl BN2 . . . . 185 B5
St Philip's RC Prim Sch
  TN22 . . . . 78 C5
St Richards Cath Coll
  TN40 . . . . 157 E4
St Richard's Ct BN41 . . . . 162 D1
St Richard's Flats BN41 . . 162 B7
St Richards Ho TN38 . . . . 159 C7
St Richards Rd TN6 . . . . . . 38 A7
St Richard's Rd BN41 . . . . 162 B7
St Saviours TN22 . . . . 78 D6
St Saviours Ct 1 BN1 . . . 164 B8
St Saviour's Rd TN38 . . . . 158 F1
Saints Hill TN11 . . . . 6 A8
SAINT'S HILL 6 A8
St Stephens Ct TN1 . . . . . 8 B5

St Swithun's Cl RH19 . . . . . . 1 F1
St Swithun's La BN7 . . . . 190 A1
St Swithun's Terr BN7 . . . 190 A1
St Thomas 5 TN39 . . . . . . 157 A2
St Thomas a Becket Cath Jun
  Sch BN21 . . . . 184 F5
St Thomas a Becket Inf Sch
  BN21 . . . . 184 F5
St Thomas Ct BN7 . . . . . . 190 C2
St Thomas of Canterbury Ct
  TN20 . . . . 40 A2
St Thomas's Rd TN34 . . . 160 A5
St Thomas's St TN36 . . . . 117 F7
St Vincent's Ct BN2 . . . . . 165 A3
St Vincents Flats TN37 . . 136 B4
St Vincents Pl BN20 . . . . 184 E1
St Vincents Rd TN38 . . . . 158 F7
St Wilfred's Ct 5 RH16 . . 50 E4
St Wilfred's Pl BN25 . . . . 181 B3
St Wilfrid's CE Prim Sch
  RH16 . . . . 50 F3
St Wilfrids Cl RH15 . . . . . . 73 B4
St Wilfrid's Ct BN27 . . . . 152 B8
St Wilfrids Flat's BN2 . . . 164 C7
St Wilfrid's Gn BN27 . . . 152 C8
St Wilfrid's RC Prim Sch
  RH15 . . . . 72 F2
St Wilfrids Rd RH15 . . . . . 73 B4
St Wilfrid's Way RH16 . . . 50 E4
Salcey Cl TN38 . . . . 135 E2
SALEHURST 64 D5
Salehurst CE Prim Sch
  TN32 . . . . 64 B4
Salehurst Gdns TN38 . . . . 135 D2
Salehurst Rd BN21 . . . . . . 184 C4
Salisbury Cl BN22 . . . . . . 173 C2
Salisbury Ct
  19 Hove BN3 . . . . 163 C6
  Seaford BN25 . . . . 180 E4
Salisbury Rd
  Bexhill TN40 . . . . 157 B8
  Eastbourne BN20 . . . . . . 188 C8
  Hove BN3 . . . . 163 C6
  Langton Green TN3 . . . . 6 F3
  Royal Tunbridge Wells TN4 . . 8 C8
  Seaford BN25 . . . . 180 E3
  St Leonards TN37 . . . . . 136 C1
Salisbury Terr TN21 . . . . . 81 B8
Salisbury Yd TN37 . . . . . . 136 C1
Sally Ct 3 BN22 . . . . 185 B3
Salomons Mus* TN3 . . . . . 7 D8
Salomons Rd TN4 . . . . 7 C4
Saltcote La TN31 . . . . 93 C7
Saltcote Mews TN31 . . . . . 93 C7
SALTDEAN 177 D6
Saltdean Cl TN39 . . . . 156 E3
Saltdean Dr BN2 . . . . 166 B1
Saltdean Park Rd BN2 . . . 166 C1
Saltdean Prim Sch BN2 . . 166 C2
Saltdean Vale BN2 . . . . . . 166 D2
Saltdean Way TN39 . . . . . 156 D3
Salters La TN34 . . . . 160 B4
Saltwood Rd BN25 . . . . . . 181 C4
Salvador Ct BN23 . . . . 185 F7
Salvadori Ct TN2 . . . . 9 D6
Salvington Cres TN39 . . . 156 F4
Samoa Way BN3 . . . . 175 B2
Sancroft Rd BN20 . . . . . . 184 B3
Sanctuary The BN20 . . . . 184 B4
Sandbanks Cl BN27 . . . . 152 A5
Sandbanks Gdns BN27 . . 152 B6
Sandbanks Gr BN27 . . . . 152 B6
Sandbanks Way BN27 . . 152 A6
Sandbrook BN6 . . . . 97 F3
Sanders Ho BN3 . . . . 162 E8
Sanderstead 1 BN2 . . . . 164 F5
Sandfield Rd TN11 . . . . . . 6 A7
Sandford Mews BN23 . . . 174 D3
Sandgate Cl BN25 . . . . . . 181 C5
Sandgate Rd BN1 . . . . 143 A2
Sandhawes Hill RH19 . . . 2 A4
Sandhill La
  Churches Green BN27 . . 109 B6
  Crowborough TN6 . . . . . . 26 E7
Sand Hill La BN8, TN22 . . 104 B8
SANDHURST 47 C6
Sandhurst Ave
  Pembury TN2 . . . . 9 E6
  Woodingdean BN2 . . . . . 144 D1
Sandhurst Cl
  Royal Tunbridge Wells TN2 . . 8 C6
  Sandhurst Cross TN18 . . 47 A4
SANDHURST CROSS 46 F4
Sandhurst Gdns TN34 . . . 136 F6
Sandhurst Ho TN2 . . . . . . 8 D5
Sandhurst La TN39 . . . . . 156 B6
Sandhurst Mews BN23 . . 174 E1
Sandhurst Pk TN2 . . . . . . 8 C6
Sandhurst Prim Sch TN18 . 47 C5
Sandhurst Rd TN2 . . . . . . 8 D6
Sandhurst Vineyards*
  TN18 . . . . 47 E5
San Diego Way BN23 . . . 175 B1
Sandore Cl BN25 . . . . 181 A4
Sandore Rd BN25 . . . . . . 181 A4
Sandown Cl
  Eastbourne BN23 . . . . . . 174 B4
  Royal Tunbridge Wells TN2 . . 8 F6
Sandown Ct BN3 . . . . 141 D1
Sandown Gr TN2 . . . . 8 F6
Sandown Ho TN6 . . . . 25 F3
Sandown Pk TN2 . . . . 8 F6
Sandown Prim Sch
  TN34 . . . . 160 C8
Sandown Rd
  Brighton BN2 . . . . 164 D7
  Hastings TN35 . . . . 160 C7
  Southwick BN42 . . . . 161 E8

Sandown Way TN40 . . . . 157 E6
Sandpiper Wlk BN23 . . . 174 C2
Sandpit Cotts BN6 . . . . . . 99 C2
Sand Rd TN3 . . . . 20 A4
Sandridge TN6 . . . . 25 F1
Sandringham Cl
  East Grinstead RH19 . . . 11 A8
  Hove BN3 . . . . 142 A3
  Seaford BN25 . . . . 181 A6
Sandringham Dr BN3 . . . 142 A3
Sandringham Hts TN38 . 135 D3
Sandringham Lodge 17
  BN3 . . . . 163 C6
Sandringham Mews TN4 . . 8 A5
Sandrock Hall TN34 . . . . . 136 F5
Sandrock Hill TN33, TN38 . 135 A4
Sandrock Ho TN2 . . . . 8 D4
Sandrock Pk TN34 . . . . . 136 F5
Sandrock Rd TN2 . . . . 8 C4
Sandrocks Way RH16 . . . 50 E2
Sandwich TN38 . . . . 158 F8
Sandwich St BN22 . . . . . 185 C6
Sandy Cl TN37 . . . . 136 B5
SANDY CROSS 82 B5
Sandy Cross Cotts TN21 . . 82 A5
Sandy Cross La TN21 . . . 82 B5
Sandy La
  Chelwood Gate RH17 . . . 34 C8
  Coleman's Hatch TN7 . . . 23 D6
  East Grinstead RH19 . . . 1 F1
  Framefield TN22 . . . . . . 79 A7
  Horam TN21 . . . . 81 E2
  Nutley TN22 . . . . 50 E2
San Feliu Ct RH19 . . . . . . 2 B2
San Jose Cl TN35 . . . . . . 160 C6
San Juan Ct BN3 . . . . 185 G2
Sanshaw Ct BN21 . . . . . 184 E3
Santa Cruz Dr BN23 . . . 185 F7
Santer Ho BN18 . . . . 45 E8
Santos Wharf BN23 . . . . 185 F8
Sanyhils Ave BN1 . . . . . . 142 F7
Saunders Cl
  Hastings TN34 . . . . 160 A5
  Uckfield TN22 . . . . 78 A8
Saunders Hill BN1 . . . . . 143 D7
Saunders Park Ho 2
  BN2 . . . . 164 C8
Saunders Park Rise BN2 . 143 C1
Saunders Park View
  BN2 . . . . 143 C1
Saunders Rd TN4 . . . . 7 E1
Savill Rd RH19 . . . . 51 A8
Sawyard Cotts TN22 . . . . 53 C5
Sawyers Cl RH15 . . . . 73 D1
Saxby Cl BN23 . . . . 174 E1
Saxby Rd
  Bexhill TN39 . . . . 157 A5
  Burgess Hill RH15 . . . . . 72 D4
Saxonbury 16 BN2 . . . . . . 189 C3
Saxonbury Cl TN6 . . . . . . 25 F2
Saxon Cl BN2 . . . . 166 C2
Saxon Ct
  Hove BN3 . . . . 162 D6
  Pevensey Bay BN24 . . . . . 175 D5
  St Leonards TN37 . . . . . 159 C8
Saxon Gd BN21 . . . . 184 E4
Saxonhurst Ct TN37 . . . . 136 B4
Saxon La BN25 . . . . 180 E2
Saxon Mount Specl Sch
  TN38 . . . . 158 E7
Saxon Pl BN21 . . . . 184 C6
Saxon Rd
  Hastings TN35 . . . . 160 D7
  Hove BN3 . . . . 162 D6
  Newhaven BN9 . . . . 179 C7
Saxon Rise TN40 . . . . 157 E4
Saxons TN39 . . . . 156 F3
Saxon St TN37 . . . . 159 C6
Saxonwood Rd TN33 . . . 112 C5
Sayerland La BN26 . . . . . 173 A4
Sayerland Rd BN26 . . . . 173 A8
Sayers The 5 RH19 . . . . 1 C1
Scamps Hill RH16 . . . . . . 51 C6
Scanlon Cl BN20 . . . . 173 A3
Scarborough Rd BN1 . . . 142 D1
Scarletts Cl TN22 . . . . . . 78 B7
Sceptre BN1 . . . . 142 E2
Schofield Way BN23 . . . . 185 F7
School Cl
  Burgess Hill RH15 . . . . . 72 F2
  1 Southwick BN42 . . . . 161 E6
School Cotts
  East Chiltington BN7 . . . 100 A3
  Maresfield TN22 . . . . 55 B4
School Field BN8 . . . . . . 101 E5
School Hill
  Barcombe Cross BN8 . . 101 E4
  Lamberhurst TN3 . . . . . . 20 B6
  Old Heathfield TN21 . . . 82 D7
  Winchelsea TN36 . . . . . 117 E8
School La
  Ashurst Wood RH19 . . . 11 E6
  Blackboys TN22 . . . . 80 A6
  Crowborough, St John's
   TN6 . . . . 25 D4
  Crowborough TN6 . . . . . 25 F1
  Danehill RH17 . . . . 34 B5
  Forest Row RH18 . . . . . . 11 F2
  Hadlow Down TN22 . . . 57 B5
  Lindfield RH16 . . . . 51 B7
  Nutley TN22 . . . . 35 C5
  Peasmarsh TN31 . . . . . . 69 B2
  Polegate BN26 . . . . 173 A4
  Pyecombe BN45 . . . . 119 C6
  Saltdean BN2 . . . . 166 C2
School Path BN8 . . . . . . 101 D4
School Pl TN40 . . . . 158 A5

School Rd
  Hastings TN35 . . . . 160 C7
  Hove BN3 . . . . 162 F8
School Rise
  Brighton BN2 . . . . 164 E6
  Royal Tunbridge Wells TN2 . . 7 F1
School Terr TN32 . . . . . . 64 C5
Schwerte Way 5 TN37 . 159 E7
Science Park Rd BN1 . . . 144 B7
Science Park Sq BN1 . . . 144 B6
Scotland St BN2 . . . . 189 C3
Scotney Castle* TN3 . . . . 20 D3
Scotney Castle Gdn & Est*
  . . . . 20 D3
Scotsford Cl TN21 . . . . . 59 F1
Scotsford Hill TN20 . . . . 40 E1
Scotsford Rd TN21 . . . . . 59 F2
Scott Rd BN3 . . . . 162 F7
Scotts Acre TN31 . . . . . . 94 E2
Scotts Way TN2 . . . . 16 E8
Scrace Hill Terr RH16 . . . 73 F8
Scraper's Hill BN8 . . . . . 128 A8
Scrase Lodge RH15 . . . . 73 D3
Scutes Ct TN34 . . . . 160 A7
Sea Cotts 5 BN25 . . . . . 180 F2
Sea Ct BN24 . . . . 175 D4
Seabeach La BN22 . . . . . 185 C5
Seabourne Rd TN40 . . . 158 A6
Seacliffe BN10 . . . . 177 F3
Seacotts 5 BN25 . . . . . . 180 F2
Seafield Cl BN25 . . . . . . 181 B5
Seafield Rd BN3 . . . . 163 B6
SEAFORD 180 C2
Seaford Ave BN3 . . . . . . 161 B6
Seaford Ct 1 BN25 . . . . 180 E2
Seaford Head Com Coll
  BN25 . . . . 180 F2
Seaford Head Nature
  Reserve* BN25 . . . . 181 E1
Seaford Head Pool
  BN25 . . . . 181 A2
Seaford Mus of Local
  History* BN25 . . . . 180 E4
Seaford Prim Sch BN25 . 180 E4
Seaford Rd
  Eastbourne BN22 . . . . . 185 C5
  Friston BN20 . . . . 182 E1
  Hove BN3 . . . . 162 C6
  Newhaven BN9 . . . . 179 F8
Seaford Sta BN25 . . . . . . 180 E3
Seagrave Cl BN25 . . . . . 180 A6
Seagrove Way BN25 . . . 180 F5
Seahaven Swim & Fitness Ctr
  BN9 . . . . 179 D7
Sea Ho 14 BN42 . . . . . . 161 E7
Sea Houses Sq 24 BN22 . 185 B3
Sea Rd
  Bexhill TN40 . . . . 157 D3
  Camber TN31 . . . . 94 F2
  Fairlight Cove TN35 . . . 139 A5
  Pevensey Bay BN24 . . . 175 D5
  St Leonards TN38 . . . . . 158 F6
  Winchelsea Beach TN36 . 118 B7
Searle Ave BN10 . . . . . . 178 A6
Sea-Saw Way BN2 . . . . . 164 F7
Seaside BN22, BN23 . . . 185 C5
Seaside Pas TN38 . . . . . 158 F6
Seaside Rd
  Eastbourne BN21 . . . . . 185 B3
  St Leonards TN38 . . . . 158 F6
Seaside Rdbt BN23 . . . . 185 D7
Seaside Way BN38 . . . . . 158 F6
Sea Spray Ave BN43 . . . 161 B6
Seattle Dr BN23 . . . . 175 A1
Seaview Ave BN10 . . . . . 178 A6
Seaview Cotts TN36 . . . 116 E5
Seaview Est BN42 . . . . . . 161 F7
Seaview Ho BN9 . . . . 179 D6
Seaview Rd
  Newhaven BN9 . . . . 168 F1
  Peacehaven BN10 . . . . 178 E6
  Woodingdean BN2 . . . . 165 B8
Seaview Terr
  Icklesham TN36 . . . . . . 116 E5
  2 Rye TN31 . . . . 93 C5
Sea View Way BN2 . . . . 144 D1
Seaville Dr
  Eastbourne BN23 . . . . . 185 D8
  Pevensey Bay BN24 . . . 175 D5
Second Ave
  Bexhill TN40 . . . . 157 F5
  Camber TN31 . . . . 94 F2
  Hove BN3 . . . . 163 C6
  Newhaven BN9 . . . . 179 C6
Second Rd BN10 . . . . . . 178 A7
Sedgebrook Gdns TN34 . 136 E2
Sedges The TN38 . . . . . . 135 E1
Sedgewick Rd TN40 . . . 157 C6
SEDLESCOMBE 88 D7
Sedlescombe CE Prim Sch
  TN33 . . . . 88 E1
Sedlescombe Gdns TN38 136 B2
Sedlescombe Organic
  Vineyard* TN32 . . . . . 88 D5
Sedlescombe Road N
  TN37 . . . . 136 B4
Sedlescombe Road S
  TN38 . . . . 136 B1
Sefton Chase TN6 . . . . . 26 A3
Sefton Rd BN41 . . . . 140 F3
Sefton Way TN6 . . . . 26 A3
Segrave Cl BN7 . . . . 123 B2
Selba Dr BN2 . . . . 143 E3
Selborne Pl BN3 . . . . . . 163 C7
Selborne Rd BN3 . . . . . . 163 C6
Selby Cl TN22 . . . . 78 D5
Selby Ct RH16 . . . . 50 E3
Selby Gdns BN22 . . . . . . 78 D5

Selby Rd
  Eastbourne BN21 . . . . . 184 D5
  Uckfield TN22 . . . . 78 D6
Selby Rise TN22 . . . . 78 D5
Selham Cl BN1 . . . . 143 D6
Selham Dr BN1 . . . . 143 D6
Selham Pl BN1 . . . . 143 D6
Selhurst Rd BN2 . . . . 165 E6
Sellbourne Pk TN3 . . . . . 17 C4
SELMESTON 149 D2
Selmeston Cl BN1 . . . . . 136 D1
Selmeston Ct 2 BN25 . . 180 C4
Selmestone Pl BN2 . . . . 164 F6
Selmeston Ho 8 BN21 . 184 D4
Selmeston Rd BN21 . . . 184 C7
Selsey Cl BN1 . . . . 143 E6
Selsfield Cl BN21 . . . . . . 184 D6
Selsfield Dr BN2 . . . . 143 D3
Selwyn Dr BN21 . . . . 184 E4
Selwyn Ho 10 BN21 . . . 184 E4
Selwyn Park Ct 9 BN21 . 184 E4
Selwyn Rd BN21 . . . . . . 184 E4
Semley Lodge BN6 . . . . . 97 C3
Semley Rd
  Brighton BN1 . . . . 143 A1
  Hassocks BN6 . . . . 97 C3
Sempstead La TN31, TN32 . 66 C4
Senlac Ct TN33 . . . . 112 D5
Senlac Gdns TN33 . . . . . 112 E4
Senlac Gn TN22 . . . . 78 E8
Senlac Pl TN3 . . . . 15 C7
Senlac Rd BN9 . . . . 179 D7
Senlac Way TN37 . . . . . . 136 C5
Sergison Cl RH16 . . . . . . 50 C5
Sergison Rd RH16 . . . . . 50 D5
Sessingham La BN26 . . 150 E6
Setfords Field BN8 . . . . . 75 E1
Sett The BN41 . . . . 141 B2
Sevelands Cl BN2 . . . . . . 164 F7
Seven Acre Cl TN37 . . . 136 A5
Seven Dials BN1 . . . . . . 189 A4
Sevenfields RH15 . . . . . . 72 C4
Sevenoaks Rd BN23 . . . 174 D2
Seven Sisters Canoe Ctr*
  BN25 . . . . 181 F4
Seven Sisters Ctry Pk*
  BN25 . . . . 182 A2
Seven Sisters Rd BN22 . . 173 C3
Seven Sisters Sheep Ctr*
  BN20 . . . . 187 B7
Seven Sisters Visitor Ctr*
  BN25 . . . . 181 F4
Seville St BN2 . . . . 164 C7
Sewell Ave TN40 . . . . . . 157 C5
Seymour Cotts TN6 . . . . 27 D1
Seymour Ho 5 BN2 . . . . 164 D4
Seymour Sq 3 BN2 . . . . 164 D4
Seymour St 4 BN2 . . . . 164 D4
Seymour Villas TN34 . . . 160 A7
Shaftesbury Ct TN22 . . . 78 C8
Shaftesbury Pl BN1 . . . . 164 A8
Shaftesbury Rd
  Brighton BN1 . . . . 189 B5
  Royal Tunbridge Wells TN4 . . 8 A5
Shakespeare St BN3 . . . 163 A8
Shakespeare Wlk BN23 . 174 D2
Shalesbrook La RH18 . . . 11 F1
Shalfleet Cl BN23 . . . . . . 174 B3
Shandon Cl TN2 . . . . 8 C4
Shands BN6 . . . . 97 F3
Shanklin Cl BN23 . . . . . . 174 B4
Shanklin Ct
  11 Brighton BN2 . . . . . 164 C8
  Hove BN3 . . . . 141 D1
Shanklin Rd BN2 . . . . . . 164 C8
Shannon Cl BN10 . . . . . . 167 B1
Shannon Way BN23 . . . . 185 F8
SHARPSBRIDGE 77 C6
Sharp's Cnr TN21 . . . . . 106 E8
Sharpthorne Cres BN41 . 141 C1
Sharpthorne Ct BN1 . . . 189 B4
Sharrow Cl RH16 . . . . . . 50 E5
Shawcross Ho 5 BN1 . . 142 E2
Shawfield TN6 . . . . 26 B2
Shaws Cnr TN31 . . . . . . 67 B7
Shaw The TN2 . . . . 8 C2
Shedden Ct TN21 . . . . . 82 A8
Sheddingdean Bsns Ctr
  RH15 . . . . 72 F5
Sheddingdean Cl RH15 . . 73 A4
Sheddingdean Com Prim Sch
  RH15 . . . . 73 A5
Sheddingdean Ct RH15 . . 72 F4
Sheddingdean
  Neighbourhood Ctr
   RH15 . . . . 73 A5
Sheen Rd BN22 . . . . 185 B4
Sheepbell Cl BN41 . . . . . 141 B3
Sheepcote La
  Chalvington BN27 . . . . 150 C8
  Golden Cross BN27 . . . 127 D3
Sheepfair BN7 . . . . 123 A2
Sheepfold The BN10 . . . 167 C1
Sheep Pen La 3 BN25 . . 181 A3
Sheep Plain TN6 . . . . . . 37 D8
Sheepsetting La TN21 . . 81 E7
Sheepstreet La TN19, TN5 . 43 E5
Sheepwash La TN22 . . . 80 C8
Sheep Wlk BN2 . . . . 165 F1
Sheerwater Cres TN34 . 136 D4
Sheerwater Terr TN34 . . 136 D4
Sheffield Ct BN1 . . . . 189 B4
SHEFFIELD GREEN 53 C7
Sheffield Mews RH16 . . . 50 D5
Sheffield Mill La TN22 . . 53 C8

Sheffield Park Gdn★
TN22 . . . . 53 D5
Sheffield Park Sta★ TN22 . 53 A4
Sheffield Pk Way BN23 . . 174 A4
Sheila Child Cl TN40 . . . 157 C6
Sheiling Rd TN6 . . . . 25 E3
Shelldale Ave BN41 . . . . 162 B7
Shelldale Cres BN41 . . . 162 B7
Shelldale Rd BN41 . . . . . 162 B8
Shelley Cl BN7 . . . . 123 B1
Shelley Ct 4 RH16 . . . . . . 50 D5
Shelley Pk 4 TN21 . . . . . . 82 A7
Shelley Rd
  East Grinstead RH19 . . . . . . 1 D1
  Hove BN3 . . . . 162 F7
  Ringmer BN8 . . . . 124 D5
Shelley Wlk 3 BN23 . . . . 174 E2
Shelley Wood RH15 . . . . . 72 D4
SHELLIES GREEN 138 C8
Shell La 9 TN34 . . . . 160 A3
Shenfield Way BN1 . . . . . 143 B3
Shenstone RH16 . . . . 51 B8
Shepham Ave BN2 . . . . . 166 D2
Shepham La BN26 . . . . . 173 C8
Shepherd Ind Est BN7 . . 190 B3
Shepherds Cl
  Eastbourne BN22 . . . . . . 173 F3
  Piddinghoe BN9 . . . . 168 B2
  Ringmer BN8 . . . . 124 E5
Shepherd's Hill TN39 . . . 156 D4
Shepherds Cot BN10 . . . 167 D2
Shepherds Croft BN1 . . . 142 C4
Shepherds Ct TN35 . . . . 138 E4
Shepherdsgrove La
  Dormansland RH19 . . . . 2 F5
  Holtye RH19 . . . . 3 A4
Shepherds Mead RH15 . . . 72 F4
Shepherd St 3 TN38 . . . 159 C6
Shepherds Way
  Ringmer BN8 . . . . 124 E5
  South Chailey BN8 . . . . . 100 C7
  Uckfield TN22 . . . . 78 C5
Shepherd's Way TN35 . . 138 E4
Shepherds Wlk
  Crowborough TN6 . . . . 26 C1
  Hassocks BN6 . . . . 97 F5
  Royal Tunbridge Wells TN2 . . 8 D4
Sheppard Way BN41 . . . 141 A3
Sheppeys RH16 . . . . 50 D2
Sheppey Wlk BN27 . . . . 129 A3
Shepway Par BN25 . . . . 180 E3
Shepway The BN25 . . . . 181 B4
Sheraton Cl BN21 . . . . . 184 F2
Sherborne Ct 5 BN21 . . 184 D4
Sherbourne Cl
  Hove BN3 . . . . 141 D3
  Royal Tunbridge Wells TN2 . . 8 D2
Sherbourne Rd BN3 . . . . 141 D3
Sherbourne Way BN3 . . . 141 D3
Sheridan Ho BN3 . . . . . . 163 D6
Sheridan Mans BN3 . . . . 163 A8
Sheridan Pl
  Baldslow TN37 . . . . 136 A6
  East Grinstead RH19 . . . . . . 1 C1
Sheridan Terr BN3 . . . . . 163 A8
Sheriff's La TN6 . . . . 39 D7
Sheringham Cl TN34 . . . . 65 E2
Sherrington Rd BN2 . . . . 165 F8
SHERWOOD 8 E6
Sherwood Cl TN34 . . . . . 136 F1
Sherwood Dr RH16 . . . . . 50 C5
Sherwood Gn BN27 . . . . 152 B6
Sherwood Park Prim Sch
  TN2 . . . . 8 D6
Sherwood Pl TN3 . . . . 6 E3
Sherwood Rd
  Royal Tunbridge Wells TN2 . . 8 E5
  Seaford BN25 . . . . 180 F4
Sherwood Rise BN25 . . . 180 F4
Sherwood Way TN2 . . . . . 8 D6
Shinewater Ct BN23 . . . . 174 B3
Shinewater La BN23 . . . . 174 B4
Shinewater Prim Sch
  BN23 . . . . 174 B4
Shinewater Rdbt BN23 . . 174 B3
Shingle Ct TN38 . . . . . . 135 E7
Shingle Rd BN43 . . . . . . 161 A6
Shining Cliff TN34 . . . . . 136 F4
Shipley La TN39 . . . . 156 D3
Shipley Mill Cl BN24 . . . 174 B5
Shipley Rd BN2 . . . . 165 E7
Ship St
  Brighton BN1 . . . . 189 A2
  East Grinstead RH19 . . . . . 10 E8
  Newhaven BN9 . . . . 179 D5
Ship Street Gdns BN1 . . 189 A2
Shipwreck & Coastal
  Heritage Ctr★ TN34 . . . 160 B3
Shipyard La TN31 . . . . 93 C5
Shirlea View TN33 . . . . . 112 E4
Shirley Ave BN3 . . . . 142 B2
Shirley Cl BN43 . . . . 161 D8
Shirley Dr
  Hove BN3 . . . . 142 C2
  St Leonards TN37 . . . . . 136 B4
Shirley Gdns TN4 . . . . 7 C5
Shirley Gr TN4 . . . . 7 C5
Shirley Mews BN3 . . . . . 163 B7
Shirley Rd BN3 . . . . 163 C8
Shirleys BN6 . . . . 98 E2
Shirley St BN3 . . . . 163 B7
SHOREHAM BEACH 161 A6
Shoreham Beach Com Fst
  Sch BN43 . . . . 161 A6

Shoreham By-pass BN41,
  BN43 . . . . 140 D2
Shoreham Coll BN43 . . . 161 D7
SHORTBRIDGE 77 E8
Short Brow BN25 . . . . . . 181 A4
Short Brow Cl BN22 . . . . 173 B3
Shortdean Pl BN21 . . . . 184 D4
SHORTGATE 104 B3
Shortgate La
  Laughton BN8 . . . . 126 B8
  Shortgate BN8 . . . . 104 B2
Shortgate Rd BN8 . . . . . 143 F4
Shortlands Cl BN22 . . . . 173 C1
Shorts Cl RH16 . . . . 50 E3
Shotters RH15 . . . . 72 E1
Shovelstrode La RH19 . . . 11 D8
SHOVER'S GREEN 30 C1
Showfields Rd TN2 . . . . . . 7 F1
Shropshire Ct BN20 . . . . 184 B7
Shrub La TN19 . . . . 62 C7
Shrublands Ct TN2 . . . . . . 8 C4
Shrublands The TN39 . . . 156 E3
Sicklehatch La TN21 . . . . 82 B2
Sidcup Cl BN23 . . . . 174 D2
Sidehill Dr BN41 . . . . . . 140 F2
Sidehills BN8 . . . . 101 D4
SIDLEY 157 A7
Sidley Gn TN39 . . . . 157 C7
Sidley Prim Sch TN39 . . 157 C7
Sidley Rd BN22 . . . . 185 C5
Sidley St TN39 . . . . 157 C7
Sidney Cl TN2 . . . . 16 F8
Sidney Tidy Ho 5 BN2 . . 164 C6
Silchester Ct TN38 . . . . 159 C7
Sillwood Cl 19 BN1 . . . . 163 E5
Sillwood Hall 20 BN1 . . 163 E5
Sillwood Pl 17 BN1 . . . . 163 E5
Sillwood Rd BN1 . . . . . . 163 E5
Sillwood St BN1 . . . . 163 E5
Sillwood Terr 22 BN1 . . 163 E5
Silva Cl TN40 . . . . 158 A6
Silvan Rd TN38 . . . . 135 E4
Silver Bank Cotts TN19 . . 64 B8
Silver Birches
  Brighton BN2 . . . . 142 E1
  Haywards Heath RH16 . . . 51 A4
Silver Ct RH19 . . . . 1 B2
Silverdale BN6 . . . . 98 B3
Silverdale Ave BN3 . . . . 163 D7
Silverdale Ct BN27 . . . . 152 B6
Silverdale La
  Royal Tunbridge Wells TN4 . . 8 B6
  Sandhurst Cross TN18 . . . 46 F5
Silverdale Prim Sch
  TN38 . . . . 136 B3
Silverdale Rd
  Burgess Hill RH15 . . . . . . 73 B2
  Eastbourne BN20 . . . . . 184 F1
  Hove BN3 . . . . 163 D7
  Royal Tunbridge Wells TN4 . . 8 B6
Silverden Cotts TN18 . . . 46 F4
SILVERHILL 136 C3
SILVER HILL 64 B8
Silver Hill TN19 . . . . 45 B1
Silverhill Ave TN37 . . . . 136 C4
SILVERHILL PARK 136 C4
Silverlands Rd 1 TN37 . . 136 C2
Silver Strand E 8 BN3 . . 175 A1
Silver Strand W BN23 . . 175 A1
Silvester Rd TN40 . . . . . 157 C5
Silwood Cl TN2 . . . . 8 E7
Simmonds Ct TN4 . . . . . . 7 B4
Simons Cl TN6 . . . . 26 A1
Sinclair Wlk BN1 . . . . . . 189 B4
Singleton Mill Rd BN24 . 174 C5
Singleton Rd BN1 . . . . . 143 A6
Singleton Way RH15 . . . . 73 C1
Singleton Wlk TN40 . . . . 158 B6
Sinnock Sq 17 TN34 . . . 160 B4
Sion Wlk 8 TN1 . . . . 8 A2
Sir David's Pk TN4 . . . . . . 7 E8
Sir Henry Fermor Prim Sch
  TN6 . . . . 26 A2
Six Bells Mews TN31 . . . 67 C5
Skinner's La TN33 . . . . . 133 D8
Skinners Sch The TN4 . . . 8 A6
SKIPPERS HILL 58 B8
Skippers Hill Manor Sch
  TN20 . . . . 58 B7
Skyline View BN10 . . . . 167 D1
Slade The
  Hastings TN35 . . . . 160 B3
  Lamberhurst TN3 . . . . . . 20 A3
Sleeches Cross TN5 . . . . 17 B2
Sleepers Stile Rd TN5 . . 19 B1
Slider's La
  Fletching TN22 . . . . 53 A7
  Furner's Green TN22 . . . . 34 B1
  Scaynes Hill TN22 . . . . . . 52 F6
Slides The TN38 . . . . . . 135 F3
Slimbridge Rd RH15 . . . . 72 F3
Slindon Ave BN10 . . . . . 178 D6
Slindon Cres BN23 . . . . 174 E1
Slinfold Cl BN2 . . . . 164 D5
Sliverick's La TN33 . . . . 109 F7
Sloane Ct 4 BN2 . . . . . . 164 C5
Sloe La BN26 . . . . 171 A3
Slonk Hill Rd BN43 . . . . 140 A1
Sloop La RH17 . . . . 52 D5
Slugwash La
  Scaynes Hill RH17 . . . . . . 51 D1
  Wivelsfield RH17 . . . . 74 B7
Small Acre BN27 . . . . . . 127 B3
Smeatons La TN36 . . . . 118 B5
Smeeds Cl RH19 . . . . 2 A3
Smith Cl TN33 . . . . 133 B5
Smithlands La BN8 . . . . 106 A3
Smithy's Cl TN37 . . . . . 136 C5

Smithy The
  Best Beech Hill TN5 . . . . . 29 A3
  Uckfield TN22 . . . . 78 B6
Smolletts RH19 . . . . 10 C8
Smuggler's Adventure★ 11
  TN35 . . . . 160 A4
Smugglers Cl BN26 . . . . 170 F3
Smugglers La TN6 . . . . . 25 D5
Smugglers Way TN35 . . . 138 F4
Snape La TN5 . . . . 29 D1
Snape View TN5 . . . . 29 F4
Snatt's Rd TN22 . . . . 55 C1
Snednore BN7 . . . . 145 F5
Snipe Cl TN2 . . . . 9 E8
Snowdon Cl BN23 . . . . . 174 D3
Snowdrop La RH16 . . . . . 51 C4
Snowflakes La RH16 . . . . 51 D6
Soames Ct RH15 . . . . 72 F4
Solomons Cl BN23 . . . . 175 B2
Solomon's La TN32 . . . . . 87 C4
Solway BN27 . . . . 129 A2
Solway Ave BN1 . . . . . . 142 F7
Somerhill Ave BN3 . . . . 163 D7
Somerhill Ct 10 BN3 . . . 163 D7
Somerhill Jun Sch BN3 . 163 D6
Somerhill Lodge BN3 . . . 163 D6
Somerhill Rd BN3 . . . . . 163 D6
Somerset Ct
  Eastbourne BN23 . . . . . 174 E1
  3 Hove BN3 . . . . 163 C7
Somerset Point 1 BN2 . . 164 C4
Somerset Rd TN4 . . . . 8 A6
Somerset St BN2 . . . . . . 164 C5
Somerset Villas TN3 . . . . 15 C7
Somerville Ct BN3 . . . . . 185 E7
Somerville Gdns TN4 . . . . 7 A4
Sompting Cl BN2 . . . . . . 164 F7
Sompting Ct
  Brighton BN2 . . . . 164 F7
  3 Shoreham-by-S BN43 . 161 B8
Sorlings Reach 6 BN43 . 161 B6
Sorrel Cl BN23 . . . . 174 C3
Sorrel Dr BN23 . . . . 174 C3
Southall Ave BN2 . . . . . 143 D2
Southampton Cl 16
  BN23 . . . . 185 F8
Southampton St BN2 . . . 189 C3
South Ave
  Brighton BN2 . . . . 164 C5
  Eastbourne BN20 . . . . . 184 B5
  Hurstpierpoint BN6 . . . . . 97 A5
South Bank BN6 . . . . 97 E3
Southborough CE Prim Sch
  & Tunbridge Wells
  Language U TN4 . . . . 7 F8
Southbourne Rd BN22 . . 185 C6
South Brooks Rd TN29 . . 96 F2
SOUTH CHAILEY 100 D7
South Cl
  Beachlands BN24 . . . . . 175 F6
  Burgess Hill RH15 . . . . . . 72 E3
  Hailsham BN27 . . . . 152 B6
South Cliff
  Bexhill TN39 . . . . 156 F2
  13 Eastbourne BN20 . . . 185 A1
South Cliff Ave
  Bexhill TN39 . . . . 156 E2
  Eastbourne BN20 . . . . . 184 F1
South Cliffe BN7 . . . . . . 190 C2
South Cliff Twr BN20 . . . 188 F8
South Coast Rd
  Peacehaven BN10 . . . . . 178 D6
  Telscombe Cliffs BN2,
  BN10 . . . . 177 E4
Southcourt Ave TN39 . . . 156 F2
South Ct
  Lewes BN7 . . . . 190 C2
  Royal Tunbridge Wells TN4 . . 8 A6
Southdown Ave
  Brighton BN1 . . . . 143 A1
  Eastbourne BN20 . . . . . 173 A3
  Hastings TN34 . . . . 160 B7
  Lewes BN7 . . . . 146 A8
  Peacehaven BN10 . . . . . 178 E6
  Portslade-by-S BN41 . . . 162 C8
Southdown Cl
  Haywards Heath RH16 . . . 50 D2
  Newhaven BN9 . . . . 179 B6
Southdown Cotts BN20 . . 173 B3
Southdown Ct
  3 Hailsham BN27 . . . . . 152 C7
  Polegate BN26 . . . . 172 F6
Southdown Ho
  7 Eastbourne BN20 . . . . 184 F1
  9 Eastbourne BN20 . . . . 185 A1
Southdown Jun Sch
  BN9 . . . . 179 C2
Southdown Mews BN2 . . 164 C5
Southdown Pl
  Brighton BN1 . . . . 143 A1
  Lewes BN7 . . . . 190 C3
Southdown Rd
  Brighton BN1 . . . . 143 A1
  Eastbourne BN20 . . . . . 184 C7
  Newhaven BN9 . . . . 179 B6
  Portslade-by-S BN41 . . . 141 A2
  Seaford BN25 . . . . 181 A2
  Southwick BN42 . . . . . . 161 E7
South Downs Bsns Pk
  BN7 . . . . 190 C3
South Downs Com Specl Sch
  BN20 . . . . 184 B4
South Downs Ct TN22 . . 166 C2
South Downs Rd BN7 . . . 190 B3
South Dr RH15 . . . . 72 E3
SOUTHEASE 167 E7

Southease 18 BN2 . . . . . 164 F5
Southease Sta BN8 . . . . 168 A7
Southerden Cl BN27 . . . 152 C7
Southern Ave BN26 . . . . 173 B6
SOUTHERN CROSS 162 A8
Southern Cross BN41 . . 162 B8
Southern Rd BN22 . . . . . 173 F2
Southern Ring Rd BN1 . . 144 B6
Southfield BN26 . . . . . . 172 F5
Southfield Rd TN4 . . . . . . 8 A6
Southfields
  Speldhurst TN3 . . . . 7 A7
  Turner's Green TN5 . . . . . 29 F6
Southfields Ct 9 BN21 . . 184 F3
Southfields Rd BN21 . . . 184 F3
Southfields Way TN4 . . . . 8 B8
Southgate TN4 . . . . 7 F3
SOUTH HEIGHTON 168 E2
South La
  Newhaven BN9 . . . . 179 D7
  Wood's Corner TN21 . . . . 84 E2
Southlands RH19 . . . . . . 10 E7
Southlands Ave TN39 . . . 157 A4
Southlands Ct
  5 Haywards Heath RH16 . . 50 E6
  1 Shoreham-by-S BN43 . 161 B8
Southlands Hospl BN43 . 140 A1
Southlands Rd TN39 . . . 157 A7
South Lodge 9 BN2 . . . . 164 F5
South Lodge Cl RH15 . . . 72 F4
South Lynn Dr BN21 . . . 184 F4
SOUTH MALLING 146 B7
South Malling CE Prim Sch
  BN7 . . . . 190 C4
Southmead Cl TN20 . . . . 40 D3
Southmount BN1 . . . . . . 143 B1
Southon Cl BN41 . . . . . . 140 F3
SOUTHOVER 146 B7
Southover CE Prim Sch
  BN7 . . . . 190 A1
Southover High St BN7 . . 190 A1
Southover Manor Ho
  BN7 . . . . 190 A1
Southover Pl BN2 . . . . . 189 C4
Southover Rd BN7 . . . . . 190 A1
Southover St BN2 . . . . . 189 C3
South Pl BN7 . . . . 190 B2
South Point 9 BN43 . . . . 161 A4
South Rd
  Brighton BN1 . . . . 142 E1
  Hailsham BN27 . . . . 152 B6
  Haywards Heath RH16 . . . 50 E4
  Newhaven BN9 . . . . 179 D7
  Wivelsfield Green RH17 . . 74 D4
South Rd Mews BN1 . . . 142 E1
Southridge Rd TN6 . . . . . 37 E8
Southridge Rise TN6 . . . . 37 E8
South Rough BN8 . . . . . . 76 C7
South Side TN21 . . . . 59 E1
South St
  Brighton BN1 . . . . 189 A2
  Crowborough TN6 . . . . . . 25 F1
  Ditchling BN6 . . . . 98 D3
  Eastbourne BN21 . . . . . 185 A2
  East Hoathly BN8 . . . . . 104 F4
  Falmer BN1 . . . . 144 C6
  Lewes BN7 . . . . 190 C2
  Mayfield TN20 . . . . 40 D3
  Portslade-by-S BN41 . . . 141 A1
  Rotherfield TN6 . . . . 39 B7
  Seaford BN25 . . . . 180 E2
  St Leonards TN37 . . . . . 159 C7
SOUTH STREET 75 E1
South Terr
  Broad Oak TN21 . . . . 59 E1
  Hastings TN34 . . . . 159 F8
  Westfield TN35 . . . . 114 E3
South Undercliff TN31 . . . 93 C5
Southview RH17 . . . . 51 F3
South View
  Ditchling BN6 . . . . 98 E5
  11 Eastbourne BN21 . . . 184 E4
  Hastings TN34 . . . . 160 B4
  Newhaven BN9 . . . . 168 E2
Southview Cl
  Crowborough TN6 . . . . . . 25 E1
  Shoreham-by-S BN43 . . . 161 C7
  Southwick BN42 . . . . . . 140 E1
South View Cl TN19 . . . . 44 F3
Southview Dr TN22 . . . . . 78 C8
Southview Rd
  Peacehaven BN10 . . . . . 178 C8
  Southwick BN42 . . . . . . 161 E8
South View Rd
  Crowborough TN6 . . . . . . 25 E1
  Royal Tunbridge Wells TN4 . . 8 B8
  Turner's Green TN5 . . . . . 29 F6
Southwater Cl BN2 . . . . 164 D6
Southwater Rd TN37 . . . 159 C8
Southway RH15 . . . . 72 D3
South Way
  Lewes BN7 . . . . 123 A1
  Newhaven BN9 . . . . 179 D7
  Seaford BN25 . . . . 181 C1
Southway Jun Sch RH15 . 72 D3
Southwick Cl RH19 . . . . . 1 D2
Southwick Ho RH19 . . . . 1 D2
Southwick Sq BN42 . . . . 161 E7
Southwick St BN42 . . . . 161 E8
Southwick Sta BN42 . . . 161 E7
Southwood Ave TN4 . . . . 8 A6
Southwood Cl TN38 . . . . 136 A1
South Woodlands BN1 . . 142 E5
Southwood Rd TN6 . . . . . 25 E1
Sovereign Bsns Pk RH15 . 72 E2
Sovereign Cl
  Hastings TN34 . . . . 160 A8

Sovereign Cl continued
  Seaford BN25 . . . . 181 A5
Sovereign Ct
  Bexhill TN40 . . . . 157 E5
  Brighton BN2 . . . . 165 A3
  Eastbourne BN22 . . . . . 185 C5
Sovereign Ctr
  Burgess Hill RH15 . . . . . . 72 E2
  Eastbourne BN22 . . . . . 185 E6
Sovereign Ho TN38 . . . . 159 A6
Sovereign Mews TN38 . . 159 A6
Spa Ct 11 BN3 . . . . 163 B5
Spa Ind Pk★ TN2 . . . . 8 E8
Spaldings The TN38 . . . . 135 E1
Spanish Ct RH15 . . . . 73 B4
Sparke Gdns TN33 . . . . 133 A6
SPARROW'S GREEN 29 F5
Sparrows Green Rd TN5 . 29 F5
Sparrows The BN10 . . . . 167 D1
Sparrow Way RH15 . . . . . 72 D3
Spatham La BN6 . . . . 98 F4
Spa Valley Rly★ TN3 . . . . 15 D7
Spears Wlk BN2 . . . . . . 165 D8
Speckled Wood TN35 . . 160 C7
SPELDHURST 7 B7
Speldhurst CE Prim Sch
  TN3 . . . . 7 A7
Speldhurst Hill TN3 . . . . . 7 B8
Speldhurst Rd
  Langton Green TN3 . . . . . . 6 F4
  Royal Tunbridge Wells TN3,
  TN4 . . . . 7 E8
Spencer Ave BN3 . . . . . 141 D3
Spencer Mews 6 TN1 . . . . 8 A2
Spencer Rd BN21 . . . . . 185 A2
Spences Ct BN7 . . . . . . 190 C3
Spences Field BN7 . . . . 190 C3
Spences La BN7 . . . . . . 190 C3
Spicers Cl RH15 . . . . 72 F5
Spindlewood Ctry Holiday Pk
  TN35 . . . . 160 C6
Spindlewood Dr TN39 . . 156 C4
Spinnals Gr BN42 . . . . . 161 D7
Spinney Cl BN6 . . . . 97 C5
Spinneys The
  Heathfield TN21 . . . . 82 B6
  Lewes BN7 . . . . 190 C1
Spinney The
  Battle TN33 . . . . 112 F3
  Bexhill TN39 . . . . 156 D3
  Burgess Hill RH15 . . . . . . 73 B5
  Golden Cross BN27 . . . . 127 B3
  Hassocks BN6 . . . . 97 F5
  Hastings TN34 . . . . 136 E1
  Haywards Heath, Franklands
  Village RH16 . . . . 50 F3
  Haywards Heath RH16 . . . 50 D8
  Hove BN3 . . . . 142 C3
  Robertsbridge TN32 . . . . 63 F3
Spire Tunbridge Wells Hospl
  TN3 . . . . 6 B3
Spital Rd BN7 . . . . 123 B1
SPITHURST 101 F7
Spithurst Rd BN8 . . . . . 101 E6
SPLAYNE'S GREEN 54 A5
Spode La TN8 . . . . 4 A7
Sponden La TN18 . . . . . . 47 A7
Sportcentre Rd BN1 . . . 144 A6
Spotted Cow La TN22 . . . 56 E5
Spout Hill TN6 . . . . 27 D1
Spray Hill TN3 . . . . 20 B4
Spray's La TN33, TN35 . . 114 B4
Spray Water Sports Ctr
  BN22 . . . . 185 D5
Springate Rd BN42 . . . . 161 F8
Spring Barn Farm Pk★
  BN7 . . . . 146 A6
Spring Cl BN20 . . . . 173 B1
Spring Copse RH19 . . . . . 1 D3
Springett Almshouses
  TN18 . . . . 45 E8
Springett Ave BN8 . . . . 124 D5
Springett Cotts BN8 . . . 124 D5
Springfield RH19 . . . . 1 D4
Springfield Ave BN10 . . 177 F4
Springfield Cl
  Crowborough TN6 . . . . . . 26 B2
  Westham BN24 . . . . 174 F6
Springfield Cotts
  Cackle Street TN31 . . . . . 90 A2
  Rotherfield TN6 . . . . 39 B8
Springfield Rd
  Bexhill TN40 . . . . 157 C6
  Brighton BN1 . . . . 164 A8
  11 Eastbourne BN22 . . . 185 B4
  Groombridge TN3 . . . . . . 15 C7
  St Leonards TN38 . . . . . 136 B1
Springfields TN5 . . . . 31 E1
Springfields Farm Ind Est
  RH17 . . . . 73 F5
Springfield Valley TN38 . 136 B1
Spring Gdns
  Brighton BN1 . . . . 189 B2
  Glynde BN8 . . . . 147 F5
  Lewes BN7 . . . . 190 B2
  Rusthall TN4 . . . . 7 B4
  6 Southwick BN42 . . . . 161 E2
Springhead TN2 . . . . 8 D5
Springhead Way TN6 . . . 37 E8
Spring Hill
  Northiam TN31 . . . . 67 B7
  Saint's Hill TN11, TN3 . . . 6 A7
Spring La
  Bexhill TN39 . . . . 156 C5
  Burwash TN19 . . . . 61 F6
  Clayton BN6 . . . . 119 E8
  Poundford TN20 . . . . 58 A5
Spring Lodge Cl BN23 . . 174 E2

Spring Mdw RH18....... 11 F1
Spring Pk TN21......... 82 A8
Springside Wlk TN38... 135 F1
Spring St
  Brighton BN1......... 163 E5
  St Leonards TN37..... 136 C1
Spring Stps TN36...... 117 F8
Springview Apartments
  TN2.................. 8 D6
Spring Way RH19....... 2 A4
Springwood Rd TN21... 82 A8
Spruce Cl BN22........ 173 D2
Spruce Ho TN4......... 7 E4
Spruce Pl RH19........ 2 A3
Spur Rd BN26.......... 173 B5
Spurway Pk BN26....... 173 B5
Squab La BN27......... 130 A5
Square The
  Beachlands BN24..... 175 F6
  Brighton BN1........ 142 E6
  Cowden TN8.......... 4 B6
Square The BN27....... 152 A7
Square The TN5........ 30 A4
Squires Farm Ind Est
  TN22................ 79 D1
Squirrel Cl
  Bexhill TN39........ 156 F6
  St Leonards TN38.... 135 F3
Squirrels Drey BN27... 127 B3
Squirrel Way TN2...... 8 E5
Squirrel Wlk BN27..... 127 B3
Stable Ctyd TN22...... 23 A1
Stabledene Way TN2.... 9 D6
Stablefield TN35...... 114 E4
Stable Mews TN7....... 136 C5
Stables La 9 BN21..... 185 A3
Stables The
  Ponts Green TN33.... 110 D2
  The Moor TN18....... 45 E8
Stables Theatre & Art Gall
  The TN35............ 160 B4
Stacey's Cnr TN21..... 85 A5
Stafford Ct
  Brighton BN2........ 189 C2
  2 Eastbourne BN23... 174 E1
Stafford Ho 10 BN21... 184 F3
Stafford House........ 98 A3
Stafford Jun Sch BN22. 185 A6
Stafford Rd
  Brighton BN1........ 163 E8
  Royal Tunbridge Wells TN2.. 8 E4
  Seaford BN25........ 180 F3
Stafford Way BN6...... 98 A3
Stag Rd TN2........... 8 D8
Stainsby St 1 TN37.... 159 C7
Stalkers La BN8....... 105 E5
Stamford 6 RH16...... 50 D6
Stamford Bldgs BN8.... 148 E5
Stamford Ct TN35...... 160 D6
Stamford Lodge 2 BN1. 142 E2
Stanam Rd TN2......... 9 E6
STANDARD HILL........ 132 F6
Standard Hill TN33.... 132 F6
Standard Hill Cl TN33. 132 F6
Standean Cl BN1....... 143 D6
Standen Cl RH19....... 1 A4
Standen House* RH19.. 10 D4
Standen Mews TN22.... 57 C5
Standen St
  Royal Tunbridge Wells TN4.. 8 A5
  Standen Street TN17. 47 E8
STANDEN STREET....... 47 D8
Stanford Ave
  Brighton BN1........ 143 A1
  Hassocks BN6........ 97 E4
Stanford Cl
  Hassocks BN6........ 97 E4
  Hove BN3............ 142 C1
Stanford Ct 1 BN1.... 163 F8
Stanford Inf Sch BN1.. 163 E8
Stanford Jun Sch BN1.. 163 F8
Stanford Rd BN1....... 163 F8
Stanford Terr BN6..... 97 E4
Stanhope Pl 1 TN38... 159 C6
Stanhope Rd TN1....... 8 C5
Stanier Rd TN38....... 135 F5
Stanley Ave BN41...... 140 F3
Stanley Avenue S BN41. 140 F3
Stanley Ct 3 BN23.... 164 C8
Stanley Rd
  Brighton BN1........ 189 B4
  2 Eastbourne BN22... 185 B4
  Hastings TN34....... 159 E8
  Peacehaven BN10..... 167 B1
  Portslade-by-S BN41. 162 A8
  Royal Tunbridge Wells TN1.. 8 B5
Stanley St BN2........ 189 C3
Stanmer BN1.......... 143 F8
Stanmer Ave BN2...... 166 D3
Stanmer Ct BN1....... 143 A2
Stanmer Dr BN22...... 173 D1
Stanmer Ho BN1....... 143 B2
Stanmer Park Rd BN1.. 143 B2
Stanmer St BN1....... 143 B2
Stanmer Villas BN1... 143 B2
Stansfield Rd BN7.... 123 B2
Stanstead Cres BN2... 165 F6
Stansted Rd BN22..... 185 A4
STAPLECROSS......... 65 E2
Staplecross Methodist Prim
  Sch TN32............ 65 E2
Staplefield Dr BN2.... 143 F3
Stapley Ct BN3....... 162 D8
Stapley Rd BN3....... 141 D1
Starboard Ct BN2..... 164 F3
Starborough Cotts RH7.. 1 F7
Starfield TN6........ 25 E1
Star Ho TN3.......... 20 B5

Star La
  Alfriston BN26...... 171 A3
  Blackboys TN22...... 80 B6
  Mayfield TN20....... 40 B2
Starling Cl TN21..... 72 C3
Star Mews TN20....... 40 B2
Star Rd 6 BN41...... 184 E4
Starr's Cotts 10 TN34. 160 B4
STARR'S GREEN....... 112 F3
Starr's Green La TN33. 113 A3
Starrs Mead TN33..... 113 A3
Starvecrow La TN31... 91 D6
Starwell Cl TN34..... 136 D3
Station App
  Battle TN33......... 112 E3
  Eastbourne BN22..... 173 F1
  Etchingham TN19..... 44 C1
  Falmer BN1.......... 144 B6
  Hassocks BN6........ 97 F4
  Hastings TN34....... 159 E8
  Heathfield TN21..... 82 A7
  Horsted Keynes RH17. 33 A3
  Hove BN3............ 163 B8
  Mayfield TN20....... 39 F2
  Rye TN31............ 93 B6
  Seaford BN25........ 180 E3
  St Leonards TN37.... 159 C7
Station Approach E BN6. 97 E4
Station Approach W BN6. 97 E4
Station Cl
  Plumpton Green BN7.. 99 E5
  Town Row TN6........ 27 D1
Station Cotts
  Crowhurst TN33...... 135 A6
  Hassocks BN6........ 97 E4
  Winchelsea TN36..... 92 D1
Station Mews TN32.... 64 A3
Station Par 11 BN21.. 184 F3
Station Rd
  Arlington BN26...... 150 B2
  Bexhill TN40........ 157 C4
  Brighton BN1........ 142 D3
  Burgess Hill RH15... 73 B2
  Crowhurst TN33...... 134 F5
  East Grinstead RH19. 1 D1
  Forest Row RH18..... 11 F3
  Groombridge TN3..... 15 C7
  Hailsham BN27....... 152 C6
  18 Hastings TN34.... 159 F8
  Heathfield TN21..... 82 A7
  Hellingly BN27...... 129 A5
  Horsted Keynes RH17. 33 C5
  Hurst Green TN19.... 45 A4
  Isfield TN22........ 102 D8
  Lewes BN7........... 190 B1
  Mayfield TN20....... 40 A2
  Newhaven BN9........ 168 F1
  North Chailey BN8... 75 F7
  Northiam TN31....... 67 B8
  Plumpton Green BN7.. 99 E6
  Polegate BN26....... 173 A6
  Portslade-by-S BN3, BN41 162 C7
  Robertsbridge TN32.. 64 B4
  Rockrobin TN5....... 29 C6
  Seaford BN25........ 180 B5
  Sharpthorne RH19.... 21 A6
  7 Southwick BN42.... 161 E7
  Stonegate TN5....... 42 E5
  Town Row TN6........ 27 C1
  Winchelsea TN36..... 92 E1
  Withyham TN7........ 14 B5
Station Road Ind Est
  BN27................ 152 C6
Station St
  Brighton BN1........ 189 B3
  8 Eastbourne BN21... 185 A3
  Lewes BN7........... 190 B2
Staveley Rd BN20..... 188 E8
STEEL CROSS......... 26 B3
Steellands Rise TN5.. 31 F1
Steep Hill TN31...... 89 E2
Steep Rd TN6......... 38 D3
Steine Gdns BN2...... 189 B2
Steine St BN2........ 189 B1
Stennings The RH19... 1 C3
Stephens Cl BN2...... 124 D5
Stephenson Dr RH19... 10 F7
Stephens Rd BN1...... 143 B2
Stephen's Rd TN4..... 8 B6
Stepney Dr BN1....... 189 B4
Stevens Cl TN39...... 157 C7
Stevens Ct BN3....... 162 E7
Stevenson Cl BN23.... 174 E3
Stevenson Rd
  Brighton BN2........ 164 C5
  1 St Leonards TN37.. 136 B3
Stewards Inn La BN7.. 190 A1
Stewart Rd TN4....... 8 C7
Steyne Cl 4 BN25.... 180 F2
Steyne Ct 18 BN25.... 180 E2
Steyne Rd BN25....... 180 E2
Steyne The BN25...... 180 E2
Steyning Ave
  Hove BN3............ 141 F3
  Peacehaven BN10..... 178 C4
Steyning Cl BN25..... 181 C2
Steyning Ct 7 BN3.... 163 B7
Steyning Rd
  Rottingdean BN2..... 166 A1
  Seaford BN25........ 181 C2
Stildon Mews RH19.... 1 C3
Stiles The BN27...... 152 C7
Stirling Ave BN25.... 181 C4
Stirling Ct
  Burgess Hill RH15... 73 C4
  Seaford BN25........ 181 C3
Stirling Ct 5 BN3.... 163 C7

Stirling Ct Rd RH15.. 73 C4
Stirling Pl BN1...... 163 A6
Stirling Rd TN38..... 135 F5
Stirling Way RH19.... 2 B3
Stock Dale TN35...... 138 F4
Stockland Green Rd TN3. 7 B8
Stockland La TN22.... 57 B6
Stockleigh Ct 15 TN38. 159 C7
Stockleigh Rd TN38... 159 C7
Stocks Mdw TN33...... 133 B5
Stockwell Ct
  Burgess Heath RH15.. 72 F3
  1 Haywards Heath RH16. 50 E3
Stockwell Rd RH19.... 10 E6
Stoddards La TN31.... 67 F6
Stoke Brunswick Sch
  RH19................ 11 E7
Stoke Cl BN25........ 181 B3
Stoke Manor Cl BN25.. 181 B3
Stokes Ho 6 TN39.... 157 A4
Stonebeach Rise TN38. 135 F7
STONE BRIDGE........ 29 E6
Stonebridge La TN22.. 79 D5
Stonecott BN7........ 37 F8
Stone Cotts TN3...... 19 F4
Stonecroft BN3....... 141 B4
STONE CROSS
  Crowborough......... 37 F6
  Eastbourne.......... 174 C6
Stone Cross TN20..... 39 F2
STONE CROSS......... 6 A2
Stone Cross BN24..... 174 B5
Stonecross Rd BN2.... 143 F4
Stone Cross CP Sch
  BN24................ 174 A5
Stone Cross Rd
  Crowborough TN6..... 38 A7
  Wadhurst TN5........ 30 A4
Stone Cross Windmill*
  BN24................ 174 B5
STONECROUCH........ 31 F6
Stone Ct La TN2...... 9 E8
Stonedene Cl RH18.... 12 B2
Stonefield Pl 2 TN34. 159 F8
Stonefield Rd TN34... 159 F8
Stonefield Way RH15.. 72 F5
STONEGATE.......... 42 F6
Stonegate CE Prim Sch
  TN5................. 42 F5
Stonegate Cl BN23.... 174 A4
Stonegate Ct TN5..... 30 C1
Stonegate Sta TN5.... 42 D3
Stonegate Way TN21... 82 B8
Stoneham Rd BN3...... 190 A4
Stoneham Rd BN3...... 162 F7
Stonehaven Ct 5 TN40. 157 D3
Stonehill BN8, TN21.. 106 C3
Stonehouse Dr
  Hastings, Beauport Park TN33,
  TN38................ 113 F1
  St Leonards TN38.... 136 A2
Stonehurst Ct 10 BN2. 164 C6
Stonehurst La TN20, TN22. 57 D7
Stoneleigh BN1....... 142 F6
Stoneleigh Cl
  Brighton BN1........ 142 F6
  East Grinstead RH19. 1 F1
Stonelink Cl TN37.... 135 F7
Stonepark Dr RH18.... 12 A2
Stone Pit La TN18.... 47 E5
Stonepound Crossroads
  BN6................. 97 D3
Stonepound Rd BN6.... 97 E4
Stonepound Ridge BN6. 97 D4
STONEQUARRY........ 2 A3
Stone Quarry Rd RH17. 34 D7
Stone Row TN3........ 6 B5
Stone Row Cotts TN3.. 6 D1
Stonery Cl BN41...... 141 A2
Stonery Rd BN41...... 141 A2
Stone St
  Brighton BN1........ 163 E5
  12 Hastings TN34.... 159 F8
  Royal Tunbridge Wells TN1. 8 B4
Stonestile La TN35... 136 F8
Stonewall Park Rd TN3. 6 F3
Stonewood Cl
  Royal Tunbridge Wells TN4. 8 A8
  Seaford BN25........ 181 C4
Stone Works Cotts TN31. 93 F3
Stoney La
  Hailsham BN27....... 152 C7
  Shoreham-by-S BN43.. 161 C8
Stoneywish Nature Reserve*
  BN6................. 98 E3
Storrington Cl BN3... 141 D2
Stour Cl BN24........ 173 F5
Straight Half Mile TN22. 55 B3
Strand TN31.......... 93 B5
Strand Ct 1 TN31.... 93 B5
Strand Hill TN36..... 117 F7
Strand Mdw TN19..... 62 B7
Strand The BN2....... 165 A3
Stratford St TN1..... 8 C5
Strathenden Ct 16 BN25. 180 F2
Strathfield RH16..... 50 F4
Strawberry Cl TN2.... 16 E7
Strawberry Fields TN31. 67 A7
Strawlands BN7....... 99 E6
Stream La
  Fairlight Cove TN35. 139 A5
  Sedlescombe TN33.... 88 C2
  The Moor TN18....... 46 A7
Stream La Cotts TN18. 46 A7
Stream Pit La TN18... 47 B5
Stream Pk RH19....... 1 A3
Streamside TN34..... 136 E3

STREAT............. 99 C3
Streat Bostall BN6... 121 C6
Streatfield Gdns TN21. 81 F8
Streatfield Ho TN22.. 78 C8
Streatfield Rd
  Heathfield TN21..... 81 F8
  Uckfield TN22....... 78 B7
Streat Forge BN7..... 99 D3
Streat La BN6........ 99 C4
Streele La TN22...... 56 D1
Streele View TN22.... 78 E8
Street End La TN21... 59 E1
Streetlands TN33..... 88 E1
Street The
  Framefield TN22..... 79 B6
  Kingston near Lewes BN7. 145 A5
  Litlington BN26..... 182 A8
  Muddles Green BN8... 127 E8
  Sedlescombe TN33.... 88 C1
  Selmeston BN26...... 149 C3
  West Firle BN8...... 148 B3
  Westmeston BN6...... 120 F8
  Wilmington BN26..... 171 F6
Stretton Ct 6 BN3... 162 F7
Stringer Way BN1..... 142 F3
Stringwalk The BN27.. 152 C7
Stroma Gdns BN27.... 128 F2
Strome Ho TN39...... 157 C7
Strongs Pas 5 TN34.. 160 B4
Strood Gate RH17.... 74 C5
Strood Rd TN37...... 136 C2
Stroudley Rd BN1..... 189 B4
Stuart Ave BN24..... 184 C6
Stuart Cl TN2....... 16 F8
Stuart Way RH19..... 10 F7
Stubb La TN31....... 90 D2
Stud Cotts BN27..... 151 A8
Studdens La BN27.... 108 D1
STUNTS GREEN....... 130 D7
Sturdee Ct BN23..... 185 F7
Sturton Pl BN27..... 152 B7
Styles Field BN7.... 190 B2
Sudeley Pl BN2...... 164 D4
Sudeley St BN2...... 164 D4
Sudeley Terr 6 BN2.. 164 D4
Suffolk Cl BN22..... 185 C4
Suffolk Mews 1 TN1.. 8 A4
Suffolk Rd TN39..... 157 C7
Suffolk St BN3...... 162 F8
Sugar La RH17....... 33 C4
Sugworth Cl RH16.... 50 D7
Sullington Cl BN2... 143 F4
Sullington Way BN43. 161 A8
Sumach Cl BN22..... 173 E2
Summer Cl BN41..... 162 A7
Summer Ct BN20..... 188 D7
Summerdale Rd BN3.. 141 D2
Summerdown Cl BN20. 183 C1
Summerdown La BN20. 183 C1
Summerdown Rd BN20. 184 D3
Summerfields Ave BN27. 152 A4
Summerfields Wood Nature
  Reserve* TN34..... 159 D8
Summer Hayes BN9... 179 C8
Summerheath Rd BN27. 152 B8
SUMMER HILL....... 152 A4
Summer Hill TN38... 159 A8
Summerhill Cl RH16.. 50 F7
Summerhill Dr RH16.. 51 A7
Summerhill Grange RH16. 50 F7
Summerhill La RH16.. 50 F7
Summer Hill Rd TN39. 156 F7
Summerlands Rd BN22. 173 C2
Summersdeane BN42.. 140 F1
Summervale Rd TN4.. 7 E1
Sunhill Cl TN2...... 9 C6
Sun La TN34........ 160 A3
Sunningdale Cl
  10 Bexhill TN40.... 157 E4
  Hailsham BN27...... 129 A1
  Seaford BN25....... 181 A2
Sunningdale Dr TN38. 158 F7
Sunninghill Ave BN3. 141 F2
Sunninghill Cl BN3.. 141 E2
Sunnybank TN5...... 32 E3
Sunnybank Cl TN20.. 40 B2
Sunnybrooke Cl TN2.. 78 D7
Sunnycroft RH17.... 51 E2
Sunnydale Ave BN1.. 143 A6
Sunnydale Cl BN1... 143 A6
SUNNYSIDE......... 7 C4
Sunnyside Cvn Pk BN25. 180 B4
Sunnyside Rd TN4... 7 C4
Sunnywood Ct RH16.. 50 D3
Sunnywood Dr RH16.. 50 D3
Sunset Ave BN27.... 127 C3
Sunset Cl
  Beachlands BN24.... 175 F6
  Peacehaven BN10.... 167 B1
Sun St BN7......... 190 A2
Sunstar La BN26.... 172 E6
Sunte Ave RH16..... 50 F7
Sunte Cl RH16...... 50 F7
Sunview Ave BN10... 178 D6
Surrenden Cl BN1... 142 F4
Surrenden Cres BN1. 142 E4
Surrenden Holt BN1. 142 E3
Surrenden Lodge BN1. 142 F2
Surrenden Pk BN1... 143 A4
Surrenden Rd BN1... 142 F3
Surrey Cl
  Royal Tunbridge Wells
  TN2................ 16 F8
  Seaford BN25....... 180 D4
Surrey Ho 12 BN2... 164 D4
Surrey Rd BN25..... 180 C4

Surrey St BN1...... 189 A3
Susans Cl BN8...... 105 A5
Susan's Rd BN21.... 185 A3
Sussex Ave BN27.... 152 B8
Sussex Cl
  Bexhill TN39....... 156 F5
  Hailsham BN27...... 152 A8
  Royal Tunbridge Wells TN2. 8 C1
Sussex Cotts RH19.. 21 A6
Sussex Ct
  Eastbourne BN22.... 185 B5
  2 Haywards Heath RH16. 50 E3
  3 Hove BN3......... 163 C6
  4 Shoreham-by-S BN43. 161 A6
Sussex Cty Cricket Gd
  BN3................ 163 C7
Sussex Downs Coll (Cliffe
  Bldg) BN7.......... 190 B1
Sussex Downs Coll
  (Eastbourne Campus)
  BN21............... 184 E7
Sussex Downs Coll
  (Newhaven Campus)
  BN9................ 179 C8
Sussex Downs Coll
  (Southover Bldg) BN7. 190 B1
Sussex Eye Hospl BN2. 164 D4
Sussex Farm Mus & Nature
  Trails* TN21...... 106 E7
Sussex Gdns
  East Dean BN20..... 183 C1
  Haywards Heath RH17. 51 B3
Sussex Ho
  6 Eastbourne BN21.. 185 A4
  Telscombe Cliffs BN10. 177 F3
Sussex House Bsns Pk
  BN3................ 162 F8
Sussex Hts 13 BN1.. 163 E5
Sussex Mews
  4 Brighton BN2..... 164 E4
  19 Royal Tunbridge Wells
  TN2................ 8 A2
Sussex Pl BN2...... 189 C3
Sussex Rd
  Haywards Heath RH16. 50 E3
  Hove BN3........... 163 B5
  St Leonards TN38... 159 A6
Sussex Sq
  Brighton BN2....... 164 E4
  17 Haywards Heath RH16. 50 E4
Sussex Sq Mews 15 BN2. 164 E4
Sussex St BN2...... 189 C3
Sussex Terr BN2.... 189 C3
Sussex View BN3.... 163 D7
Sussex Way
  Burgess Hill RH15.. 72 E5
  Telscombe Cliffs BN10. 177 F3
Sussex Wharf BN43.. 161 B6
Sutherland Ave TN39. 157 A4
Sutherland Cl 1 TN39. 157 A4
Sutherland Rd
  Brighton BN2....... 164 C5
  Royal Tunbridge Wells TN1. 8 B3
SUTTON............ 181 B4
Sutton Ave
  Peacehaven BN10.... 178 B7
  Seaford BN25....... 181 A3
Sutton Cl BN2...... 144 E1
Sutton Cotts BN7... 146 B3
Sutton Croft La 6 BN25. 180 E3
Sutton Dro BN25.... 180 F4
Sutton Mews BN25... 181 A4
Sutton Par BN25.... 181 A4
Sutton Park Rd BN25. 180 C3
Sutton Pl TN40..... 157 E4
Sutton Rd
  Eastbourne BN21.... 185 A3
  Seaford BN25....... 181 A3
Suttons Ind Pk TN36. 118 A7
Suttons The
  Camber TN31........ 95 A1
  St Leonards TN38... 135 F2
Sutton Tye RH16.... 50 F6
Sutton Wall BN7.... 146 D4
Suva Rd RH19....... 1 C3
Swaine's Pas 6 TN34. 160 B4
Swaines Way TN21... 82 A6
Swainham La TN38... 135 B4
Swainsthorpe Cl RH16. 50 F3
Swale Cl BN24...... 174 A5
Swallow Bank TN38.. 135 F2
Swallow Cl BN23.... 174 C2
Swallow Ct TN22.... 78 D5
Swallow Dr
  Battle TN33........ 112 F4
  Royal Tunbridge Wells TN2. 8 F6
Swallow Rest RH15.. 72 C3
Swallows The BN10.. 167 B1
Swan Ave 9 TN34... 160 A4
Swanborough Cotts BN7. 146 A4
Swanborough Dr BN2. 164 F7
Swanborough Dro BN7. 145 D2
Swanborough Hollow
  BN7............... 146 A4
Swanborough Pl BN27. 164 F7
Swan Bsns Ctr BN27. 152 D6
Swan Cl BN8........ 100 E7
Swan Ct BN8........ 100 E7
Swanley Cl BN23.... 174 D2
Swann Cl RH15...... 73 D3
Swannee Cl BN10.... 167 D1
Swan Rd BN27....... 152 D6
Swansbrook La TN21. 106 E2
Swans Ghyll RH18... 11 E3

Swan Terr TN34........160 A4
Swaylands Ave TN6.......37 F7
Sweda Ct 13 BN2........164 D4
Sweeps Hill Cl TN2.......9 D7
SWEETHAWS...........37 C6
Sweethaws La TN6......37 C6
Sweetings La TN3, TN5...19 D1
Sweetlands BN6.........98 B5
Swife La TN21..........60 D5
Swift Cl
  Burgess Hill RH15.......72 D3
  Crowborough TN6.......25 D1
  Uckfield TN22..........78 D5
SWIFTSDEN............44 F6
Swiftsden Cotts TN19.....44 F6
Swinburne Ave TN34....129 C5
Swingate Cross BN27....129 C5
Swissland Hill RH19, RH7...1 E7
Swynford Dr 1 TN38.....136 A5
Sybron Way TN6.........38 D8
Sycamore Cl
  Bexhill TN39..........156 C4
  Eastbourne BN22.......173 D3
  Heathfield TN21........82 B6
  Hove BN41............141 C3
  Seaford BN25.........181 C3
  St Leonards TN38......136 A1
  Woodingdean BN2......165 E8
Sycamore Cotts TN2......9 C6
Sycamore Ct
  Brighton BN2.........164 D8
  Uckfield TN22.........78 D8
Sycamore Dr
  East Grinstead RH19......2 A1
  Hailsham BN27........152 B5
Sycamores The
  Peacehaven BN10......167 D1
  St Leonards TN37......159 C8
Sydenham Ct TN40......157 D3
Sydney Cl TN38........136 B3
Sydney Little Rd TN38...135 D4
Sydney Rd
  Eastbourne BN22......185 B4
  Haywards Heath RH16....50 E6
Sydney St BN1.........189 B3
Sylvan Cl RH16..........51 B4
Sylvester Way BN3......141 C3
Symbister Rd BN41......162 C7
Syresham Gdns RH16....50 F4

T

Tackleway TN34........160 B4
Taddington Ho 2 BN22..185 C4
Taddington Rd 1 BN22..185 C4
Tainter's Brook TN22.....78 E8
Talbot Cres BN1........143 D6
Talbot Pk TN2...........8 D5
Talbot Rd TN18..........45 F8
Talbot Terr BN7........190 A2
Talland Par 5 BN2......180 E2
Tall Ash Dr TN37.......136 C4
Tall Oaks RH16.........51 B5
Tall Timbers BN27......127 B4
Tamarack Cl BN22......173 D2
Tamar Cl BN24.........174 A5
Tamarisk Gdns TN40....157 E5
Tamerisk Stps 24 TN34..160 B4
Tamplin Terr BN2.......189 C3
Tamworth Rd BN3......162 F7
Tanbridge Rd BN23.....174 F2
Tandridge Rd BN2.......162 E6
Tangier La TN1.........17 B6
Tanglewood Coppice
  TN39...............156 E3
Tangmere Cl TN39......156 E3
Tangmere Rd BN1......143 A6
Tanhouse La TN31.......68 F2
Tanneries The BN27.....129 F4
Tanners' Brook BN7.....190 B1
Tanners Cross 1 RH16...50 C2
Tanners Field RH17......74 A5
Tanners Way TN6........26 A1
Tanyard TN18...........47 B5
Tanyard Ave RH19.......11 A8
Tanyard Cotts
  Battle TN33...........112 E3
  Buxted TN22...........56 C1
Tanyard La
  Chelwood Common RH17,
  TN22................34 C4
  Winchelsea TN36.......117 F8
Tan Yd Cotts TN36......117 F8
Tapsell's La TN5.........29 D5
Tarland Ho TN2..........8 D3
Tarner Rd BN2.........189 C3
Tarragon Way BN43.....140 C1
Tarring Cl BN9.........168 D2
TARRING NEVILLE.......168 D4
Tas Combe Way BN20...173 B2
Tasmania Way BN23.....175 A2
Tate Cres RH15.........72 F5
Taunton Cl BN2........144 A1
Taunton Pl BN2.........144 A1
Taunton Rd BN2........143 F1
Taunton Way TN2......144 A1
Tavistock 8 BN21......185 A2
Tavistock Down BN1....143 C2

Taylor Cl TN38.........135 F4
Taylor Ct 1 TN2.........8 C7
Taylor St TN4...........8 A8
Tea Garden La TN3.......7 C2

Teal Ct
  Hailsham BN27........152 D7
  St Leonards TN38......135 E3
TEASLEY MEAD..........5 C4
Teasley Mead TN3........5 C4
Tedder Rd TN4...........8 B7
Tedder Terr TN35.......137 D5
Teg Cl BN41...........141 C2
Teise Cl TN2............8 D2
Teknol Ho RH15.........72 E2
Telegraph St 12 BN2....164 C4
Telford Rd TN38.......136 A5
Telham Cl TN34........137 A5
Telham La TN33........112 E1
TELSCOMBE...........167 B3
Telscombe Cl BN10.....167 D2
TELSCOMBE CLIFFS....177 F4
Telscombe Cliffs Prim Sch
  BN10...............178 A8
Telscombe Cliffs Way
  BN10...............178 A8
Telscombe Pk BN10....167 C2
Telscombe Rd
  Eastbourne BN23......174 F2
  Peacehaven BN10......167 D2
Temple Gdns BN1......163 E6
Temple Gr RH15........72 D4
Temple Hts 14 BN1.....163 E6
Temple St BN1.........163 E6
Temple Way TN1.........8 C7
Tenantry Down Rd BN2.164 E8
Tenantry Rd BN2.......164 D8
Tennis Cl BN27........152 B7
Tennis Rd BN2.........162 E6
Tennyson Ct
  5 Haywards Heath RH16..50 D5
  3 Hove BN3..........163 A7
Tennyson Rise RH19.....10 C8
Tennyson Wlk BN23....174 E3
Tenterden Ct BN23.....174 D2
Tenterden Rise TN34....136 E2
Terminus Ave TN39.....157 A3
Terminus Pl
  7 Brighton BN1.......189 A4
  6 Hailsham BN27......152 C7
Terminus Rd
  Bexhill TN39..........157 B3
  Blackboys TN22........80 A6
  Brighton BN1.........189 A4
  Eastbourne BN21......185 A3
  Framefield TN22........79 F6
Terminus St BN1.......189 A3
Terrace Rd TN37.......159 C7
Terraces The B BN2....189 C1
Tescombe Grange BN10.177 F3
Tetley Mews 1 TN2......8 D5
Teynham Ho BN2.......177 C4
Thackeray Cl BN2......174 E3
Thakeham Cl TN40.....158 A6
Thalia Ho TN40........157 B4
Thames Cl BN2.........189 C2
Thanet Way TN34......136 E2
Thatchers Cl RH15......73 D1
Thatchings The BN26...173 A5
Theaklen Dr TN38......136 B2
Theobald Ho 1 BN1....189 B3
Theobalds Gn TN21.....82 A5
Theobalds Rd RH15.....73 D6
Theodore Cl TN2.........8 D7
Third Ave
  Bexhill TN40.........157 F6
  Hove BN3............163 B6
  Newhaven BN9.......179 C6
Third Rd BN10.........178 A7
Third St TN5............6 F3
Thirlmere Rd TN4........7 E5
Thomas Brassey Cl TN37.136 B5
Thomas Peacocke Com Coll
  TN31................93 B6
Thomas St
  Lewes BN7...........190 C3
  Royal Tunbridge Wells TN4...8 B1
Thomas Turner Dr BN8..105 A3
Thompson Rd
  Brighton BN1.........143 C1
  Newhaven BN9.......168 F2
Thornbank Cres TN39...156 F3
Thornbush Cres BN41...141 B3
Thorn Cotts TN35......116 A4
Thorndean Rd BN2.....143 D3
Thornden Ct TN17......49 A8
Thornden La TN17......49 A8
Thorne Cres TN39......133 E1
Thornfield Gdns TN2.....8 F5
Thornhill Ave BN1......143 A7
Thornhill Cl BN3......141 E2
Thornhill Rise BN41....141 A4
Thornhill Way BN41....141 A3
Thornhurst RH15........73 C1
Thornsdale 5 BN2......189 C3
Thorns The TN35......138 A8
Thornton Ct 5 BN22...185 B3
Thorntree Cl TN21......81 F7
Thornwell Rd BN26....171 F7
Thornwood Cl BN22....173 E2
Thorny Cl TN21........82 A7
THREE CUPS CORNER...83 F5
Three Gables TN22......35 C4
THREE LEG CROSS......31 D3
Three Leg Cross Rd TN5..31 D3
THREE OAKS..........115 E2
Three Oaks La TN5......29 D7
Three Oaks Sta TN35...115 D2
Toronto Terr
  Brighton BN2.........164 C6
  Lewes BN7...........190 A2
Thunders Hill BN27....128 A7
Thurrock Cl BN20......173 B4
Thyme Cl BN43........140 C1
Thyssel La TN31........67 B6
Tibbs Mill La TN22, TN6..37 E2

TICEHURST...........31 E2
Ticehurst Ave TN39....155 F5
Ticehurst Cl
  Bexhill TN39.........155 F4
  Hastings TN35........160 C7
Ticehurst Cl TN38......159 B7
Ticehurst & Flimwell CE
  Prim Sch TN5.........31 F1
Ticehurst Rd BN2......164 F5
Tichborne Cotts RH16...51 C6
Tichborne St BN1......189 B3
Tickerage La TN22......79 F6
TIDEBROOK...........41 A8
Tidebrook Cotts TN5, TN20..40 F7
Tidebrook Gdns BN23...174 F2
Tide Mills Way BN25...180 B5
Tideswell Rd BN21......185 A3
Tideway Sch BN9......179 B6
Tidy St BN1...........189 B3
Tilbury Pl BN2.........189 C3
Tilbury Way BN2.......189 C3
Tile Barn Cl TN22......102 D8
Tilebarn Ct RH16........50 E2
Tile Barn Rd BN8.......135 F4
Tilehurst Dr BN27.....152 A8
Tilekiln La TN35.......160 E8
Tilers Cl RH15..........73 D3
Tilford Ct 1 TN40.....157 F4
Tilgate Cl
  Brighton BN2.........164 D1
  Eastbourne BN21.....184 D7
Tilgate Dr TN39.......156 D3
Tilley La BN27.........131 E6
Tilling Green Inf Sch
  TN31................93 A5
Tillingham Ave TN31....93 B6
Tillingham Cl BN24....174 A5
Tillingham Ct TN31.....93 A5
Tillingham La TN31.....92 A6
Tillingham View TN31...90 B5
Tillingham Way BN24..174 A5
Tillington BN2.........164 F7
Tillington Terr TN35...160 C6
Tillstone Cl BN2.......143 D2
Tillstone St BN2.......189 C2
TILSMORE.............81 F7
Tilsmore Ct BN2.......164 F5
Tilsmore Cnr TN21......81 F7
Tilsmore Rd TN21.......81 F7
Timberlaine Rd BN24..175 C4
Timberley Gdns TN22...78 E4
Timberley Rd BN22....173 D1
Timbers Ct BN27......152 C8
Timbers The RH19.......1 C2
Timberyard La BN7....190 C2
Timber Yd Cotts BN7...190 C2
Tindal Ct RH15.........73 D3
Tinkers La TN5.........31 E3
Tinker's La TN22........57 E3
Tintagel Ct BN3.......163 A8
Tintern Cl
  Brighton BN1.........143 B1
  Eastbourne BN22......173 E3
Tisbury Rd BN3.......163 C6
Titchfield Cl RH15.......73 D1
Tithe Barn Field TN36..116 F5
Titian Rd BN3.........162 F7
Tiverton Dr TN40......157 E5
Tivoli BN1............142 E2
Tivoli Cres BN1........142 D1
Tivoli Crescent N BN1..142 D2
Tivoli Pl BN1..........142 D2
Tivoli Rd BN1.........142 D2
Tobago BN1...........157 A2
Tobias Sch of Art RH19..10 E6
Tolkien Rd BN23......174 F2
Tollgate
  Lindfield RH16.........51 B8
  Peacehaven BN10......167 B1
Tollgate Gdns BN23....185 D7
Tollgate Jun Sch BN23..185 D7
Tollgate Lock TN31.....93 B4
Tollgate Pl RH19.......10 F8
Tollgates TN33.........112 B4
Tollgates The TN32......65 E1
Toll La
  Dodd's Hill TN22.......35 F1
  Fairwarp TN22.........36 A1
Tollwood Pk TN6........26 B1
Tollwood Rd TN6........38 B8
Toll Wood Rd TN21....106 F7
Tompset's Bank RH18...11 F1
Tomtits La TN18........11 E1
Tonbridge Rd TN2.......9 A7
Tongdean Ave BN3.....142 C3
Tongdean La BN1......142 C4
Tongdean Pl BN3......142 C3
Tongdean Rd BN3.....142 C3
Tongdean Rise BN1....142 C4
Top Cross Rd TN40....158 A7
Top Dr TN22...........55 A6
Top Hill Cl BN41......140 F7
Top Rd RH15...........21 B5
Torcross Cl BN2.......143 E1
Torfield Cl TN34......160 B4
Torfield Ct BN21......184 E4
Torfield Ho TN34......160 B4
Torfield Rd BN21......184 E4
Torfield Specl Sch TN34.160 B5

Tott Hill BN6...........97 B5
Tottington Way BN43...140 B1
Tott Yew Rd BN20.....173 A4
Tovey Cl BN21.........184 D6
Tower Cl
  Beachlands BN24......175 F7
  East Grinstead RH19.....1 E2
Tower Ct
  East Grinstead RH19.....1 E2
  Uckfield TN22..........55 D1
Towergate BN1.........142 E2
Tower Ho
  Brighton BN1.........142 E2
  Burgess Hill RH15......73 B2
Tower Mill Pl BN26....173 A5
Tower Rd
  Brighton BN2.........164 C6
  St Leonards TN37......136 C1
Tower Ride TN22........55 D1
Tower Road W TN37,
  TN38...............159 B8
Towerscroft Ave TN37..136 C1
Tower St
  Heathfield TN21........82 B8
  Rye TN31.............93 C6
Tower View TN22.......78 D8
Town Hill TN3..........20 A4
Townlands Rd TN5......29 F4
TOWN LITTLEWORTH....76 C1
Town Place Farm Cotts
  RH17................52 C7
TOWN ROW............27 C2
Town Wall 2 TN31.......93 B5
Tozer Ct BN41.........162 B7
Traders Pas 6 TN31.....93 B5
Trafalgar Cl
  Peacehaven BN10......167 C1
  1 St Leonards TN37....135 F7
Trafalgar Cotts 8 TN34.160 B4
Trafalgar Gate BN2....164 F3
Trafalgar Ho 8 TN40...157 D3
Trafalgar La BN1......189 B3
Trafalgar Mews 9 BN22.185 C4
Trafalgar Pl BN1......189 B3
Trafalgar Rd BN41.....162 B8
Trafalgar St BN1......189 B3
Trafalgar Terr BN1.....189 B3
Trafalgar View BN1....189 B3
Tram Rd TN31..........94 A2
Transit Rd BN9........179 D7
Travellers La TN35.....160 C8
Treasure Island Adventure
  Pk★ BN2.............185 C4
Treasury of Mechanical
  Music★ 9 TN31.......93 B5
Trebilco Cl TN2..........8 D7
Treblers Rd TN6........38 E6
Tredcroft Rd BN3......142 C2
Treemaines Rd BN23...174 F2
Treemans Rd (Lewes Rd)
  RH17................33 B2
Treetops Cl BN2.......165 E8
Tremola Ave BN2......166 C2
Trenches Rd TN6........25 F1
Trevelyan Pl RH16......50 E5
Trevor Gdns BN8......147 F6
Treyford Cl BN2.......144 E1
Triangle Ho 4 RH16....50 F3
Triangle Rd RH16......50 E3
Triangle The BN20.....173 B3
Triangle Way RH15.....72 D5
Trickland Cotts TN22...53 C5
Trinity Cl TN2..........8 D4
Trinity Cotts TN31......71 F2
Trinity Ct BN6.........97 B5
Trinity Field BN8......124 E6
Trinity Mews 3 TN34...159 E7
Trinity Pl BN21........185 B2
Trinity Rd BN6.........97 A6
Trinity St
  Brighton BN2.........189 C4
  10 Hastings TN34.....159 E7
Trinity Theatre & Arts Ctr★
  3 TN1................8 A4
Trinity Trees BN21.....185 A2
Trinity Villas 2 TN34...159 E7
Tristan Gdns TN4........7 D4
Trojans Plat TN36......117 E7
TROLLILOES...........108 D2
Troon Cl BN25.........180 A6
Troon Ct RH16.........50 E4
Trossachs Cl BN23.....174 D3
Troy Cl TN6............26 A1
Trujillo Ct BN23.......185 G8
Truleigh Cl BN2........165 F7
Truleigh Dr BN41......141 A4
Truleigh Way BN43....140 A1
Truman Dr TN37.......135 F6
Trumpet La BN27......109 C2
Trumpkins BN6.........97 A5
Tubwell La
  Crowborough TN6......38 D7
  Horam TN21...........81 F2
Tudor Ave TN38.......159 A7
Tudor Cl
  East Grinstead RH19....10 F8
  Hove BN3............141 F2
  Rottingdean BN2......166 A4
  Seaford BN25.........180 D4
Tudor Ct
  Bexhill TN39.........156 F4
  Royal Tunbridge Wells TN2...7 E1
Tudor Gdns RH15.......72 F4
Tudor Rose Pk BN10...178 F6
Tudor Wlk TN22........79 B5
Tugwell Rd BN22......173 F2
Tumulus Rd BN2......166 C3

Tunbridge Wells Adult Ed Ctr
  10 TN1..............8 B4
Tunbridge Wells Girls Gram
  Sch TN4.............8 A6
Tunbridge Wells Gram Sch
  TN4................8 A7
Tunbridge Wells High Sch
  TN2................8 F5
Tunbridge Wells Mus★
  TN1................8 B4
Tunbridge Wells Rd
  Argos Hill TN20, TN6....39 E5
  Mark Cross TN3, TN6....28 A5
Tunbridge Wells Sports Ctr
  TN4................8 A7
Tunbridge Wells Sta TN1..8 A3
Tunbridge Wells Trade Pk
  TN2................8 D8
Tunbridge Wells West Sta★
  TN2................7 F1
Tunnel Rd TN1..........8 B4
Tuppen Ho BN7.......145 E5
Tuppenney Cl TN35....160 C7
Turkey Cock La 2 TN3..93 C6
Turkey La RH15........73 B3
Turkey Rd TN39.......156 E7
Turley Cotts TN3........7 A8
Turnberry Cl TN38.....158 F7
Turnberry Ct 14 RH16..50 E4
Turnberry Dr BN27....152 A8
Turner Cl
  Bexhill TN40.........157 E5
  Eastbourne BN23.....174 D1
Turner Ct RH19.........2 A3
Turner Dumbrell Workshops
  BN6................98 D4
Turner Ho 3 BN41.....162 C7
Turners Cotts TN31.....68 C5
TURNER'S GREEN
  Heathfield............83 F4
  Wadhurst............29 F6
Turners Green La TN5...29 F6
Turners Green Rd TN5...29 F6
Turner's Hill Rd RH19...10 B6
Turners Mill Cl RH16....50 D7
Turners Mill Rd RH16...50 D6
Turners Way RH15......72 F5
Turnpike Cl
  Broyle Side BN8......125 A8
  Peacehaven BN10......167 C1
Turnpike Piece BN1....144 B6
Turret Ct RH19..........1 C3
Turton Cl BN2.........164 D5
Tuscan Ct BN10.......177 F3
Tutts Barn Ct BN21....184 F5
Tutts Barn La BN22....185 A5
Tuxford Rd TN4.........7 B5
Tweedsmuir BN23.....174 C3
TWELVE OAKS.........85 E5
Twineham Cl BN2......164 F7
Twineham Rd BN21....184 D7
Twitten Cl 2 BN42.....161 E7
Twitten The
  Bexhill TN39.........156 D4
  Burgess Hill RH15......73 B4
  Crowborough TN6......25 E1
  Ditchling BN6..........98 D3
  Southwick BN42......161 E7
Twyford Cres TN37....136 C4
Twyford Rd BN1.......143 E6
Twyfords TN6..........25 E1
Twyhurst Ct RH19.......1 D3
Twysden Cotts TN18....47 A4
Tye Cl BN2............177 D4
Tyedean Rd BN10.....177 F4
Tye Hill Rd BN26......151 A4
Tye View BN10........167 A1
Tyhurst TN22..........78 C6
Tyler's Gn RH16, RH17..50 B4
Tylers La TN22..........35 E1
Tyndale Ave TN39.....156 C3
Tyson Pl 9 BN2........189 C2

U

UCKFIELD............78 D7
Uckfield Cl BN2.......164 F6
Uckfield Com Hospl TN22.78 D6
Uckfield Com Tech Coll
  TN22...............78 D8
Uckfield Rd
  Poundgate TN6........37 B7
  Upper Wellingham BN8..124 B7
Uckfield Sta TN22.......78 C6
Uckham La TN33......112 E6
Udiam Cotts TN32......65 C5
UDIMORE.............91 D2
Udimore Rd TN31.......91 C3
Undercliff TN38.......159 B6
Undercliff Terr 7 TN38.159 C6
Underdown Rd BN2....161 E8
Underhill TN22.........55 B5
Underhill La
  Clayton BN6.........119 E8
  Westmeston BN6......120 C8
Under Rd BN27........130 D3
Underwood Rise TN2....7 F1
Unicorn Ho 1 TN34....160 A4
Union Cl BN21.........129 B3
Union Rd BN2.........189 C4
Union Sq 22 TN2.......8 A2
Union St
  Brighton BN1.........189 B2
  11 St Leonards TN38...159 C7
Union Street TN5........32 B3

UNION STREET 32 B3
Univ of Brighton
  Brighton BN1 .... 189 B2
  Eastbourne BN20 ...... 188 D8
  Falmer BN1 .... 144 B6
Univ of Brighton (Cockcroft/ watts Annexes) BN2 ... 143 D2
Univ of Brighton (St Peter's Ho) BN2 .... 189 B3
Univ of Sussex BN1 .... 144 A7
Updown Hill RH16 ...... 50 C2
Upland Rd BN20 .... 184 C3
Uplands Cl
  Bexhill TN39 .... 156 F6
  Uckfield TN22 .... 55 C1
Uplands Com Tech Coll TN5 .... 30 A4
Uplands Dr TN22 .... 55 D1
Uplands Pk TN21 .... 59 E1
Uplands Rd BN1 .... 143 C2
Uplands The TN38 ...... 159 B7
Upper Abbey Rd BN2 .... 164 C4
Upper Ave BN21 .... 185 A4
Upper Bedford St BN2 .. 189 C1
Upper Belgrave Rd BN25 . 180 F5
Upper Bevendean Ave BN2 .... 143 E1
Upper Broomgrove Rd TN34 .... 160 B7
Upper Carlisle Rd BN20 . 188 D8
Upper Chalvington Pl BN2 .... 164 E5
Upper Church Rd TN37 .. 136 B4
Upper Chyngton Gdns BN25 .... 181 B4
Upper Cl RH18 .... 11 F2
Upper Clarence Rd TN37 . 136 C2
Upper Cumberland Wlk TN1 .... 8 B1
UPPER DICKER 151 A8
Upper Dr The BN3 ...... 163 D8
Upper Duke's Dr BN20 .. 188 C7
Upper Dunstan Rd TN4 ... 8 B6
Upper Gardner St BN1 .. 189 B3
Upper Glen Rd TN37 .... 136 A5
Upper Gloucester Rd BN1 .... 189 A3
Upper Greenwoods La TN21 .... 83 C6
Upper Grosvenor Rd TN1, TN4 .... 8 B6
Upper Hamilton Rd BN1 . 189 A3
UPPER HARTFIELD 13 A2
Upper Hollingdean Rd BN1 .... 143 B1
UPPER HORSEBRIDGE 129 B3
Upper Horsebridge Rd BN27 .... 129 A3
Upper King's Dr BN20 .. 173 B1
Upper Lake TN33 .... 112 E4
Upper Lewes Rd BN2 .... 189 C4
Upper Lodges BN1 ...... 143 D8
Upper Market St [5] BN3 . 163 D5
Upper Maze Hill TN38 .. 159 B7
Upper Nellington TN3 ... 7 B4
Upper North St BN1 .... 189 A2
Upper Park Pl [7] BN2 .. 189 C2
Upper Park Rd TN37 .... 136 C1
Upper Platts TN5 ...... 31 F1
Upper Profit TN3 ...... 7 A3
Upper Ratton Dr BN20 .. 184 B8
Upper Rock Gdns BN2 ... 189 C2
Upper Roedale Cotts BN1 .... 143 B4
Upper St James's St BN2 .... 189 C1
Upper St Johns Rd RH15 . 73 A4
Upper Sea Rd TN40 ..... 157 D4
Upper Sherwood Rd BN25 .... 181 A4
Upper Shoreham Rd BN43 .... 140 B1
Upper South Rd TN37 ... 136 C1
Upper Sq RH18 .... 11 F3
Upper St
  East Dean BN20 ...... 187 B8
  Rusthall TN4 .... 7 D4
Upper Stables RH16 .... 50 C3
Upper Station Rd TN21 .. 82 A7
Upper Stephens TN3 .... 7 A3
Upper Stoneham BN8 ... 123 F4
Upper Sudeley St [7] BN2 .... 164 D4
UPPERTON 184 F5
Upperton Gdns BN21 ... 184 F3
Upperton La BN21 ...... 184 F3
Upperton Rd BN21 ..... 184 E4
Upper Valley Rd BN9 ... 179 B6
UPPER WELLINGTON 124 B8
Upper Wellington Rd [5] BN2 .... 164 C7
Upper Winfield Ave BN1 . 142 F6
Upper Wish Hill BN20 .. 184 B8
Upton Ave BN42 .... 140 E1
Upton Quarry TN3 ..... 6 F3
Upwick Rd BN20 .... 184 C3
Ursa Ct [14] BN2 ...... 164 C8

V
Vale Ave
  Brighton BN1 .... 142 E7
  Royal Tunbridge Wells TN1 .. 8 A3
Valebridge Cl RH15 .... 73 C6
Valebridge Dr RH15 .... 73 C5

Valebridge Rd RH15 .... 73 C6
Vale Cl BN25 .... 181 B4
Vale Ct BN41 .... 162 B7
Vale Gdns BN41 .... 162 B7
Valence Rd BN7 .... 123 B1
Vale Rd
  Battle TN33 .... 112 B5
  Haywards Heath RH16 . 50 E2
  Mayfield TN20 .... 40 B2
  Portslade-by-S BN41 . 162 C7
  Royal Tunbridge Wells TN1 .. 8 A3
  Saltdean BN2 .... 166 D3
  Seaford BN25 .... 181 A4
  St Leonards TN37 .... 136 C2
Valerie Cl BN41 .... 141 C2
Vale The BN2 .... 165 E5
Vale View Rd TN21 ..... 82 B6
Vallance Cl RH15 ...... 72 E4
Vallance Ct [7] BN3 ... 163 A6
Vallance Gdns BN3 ..... 163 A6
Vallance Rd BN3 .... 163 A6
Vallensdean Cotts BN41 . 141 C2
Valley Cl
  Brighton BN1 .... 142 C4
  Newhaven BN9 .... 179 B8
Valley Dene BN9 .... 179 B7
Valley Dr
  Brighton BN1 .... 142 C4
  Seaford BN25 .... 181 A5
Valley Rd
  Crowborough TN6 ..... 25 F1
  Lewes BN7 .... 146 A8
  Newhaven BN9 .... 179 A7
  Peacehaven BN10 .... 167 C2
  Portslade-by-S BN41 . 141 A2
  Rusthall TN4 .... 7 D4
Valley Rise BN25 ...... 180 F4
Valley Side Rd TN35 ... 160 C7
Valley View TN22 ...... 53 A8
Valley View Cl TN6 .... 25 F1
Val Mascal TN38 .... 136 A1
Val Prinseps Rd BN24 .. 175 C4
Valverde Ho [13] BN3 .. 163 C7
Van Alen Bldg The BN2 .. 189 C1
Van Alen Mews BN2 ..... 189 C1
Vanbrugh Ct [21] BN3 .. 163 C6
Vancouver Rd BN23 ..... 175 B2
Vantage Wlk TN38 ...... 136 B1
Varndean Cl BN1 .... 142 E3
Varndean Coll BN1 ..... 142 F3
Varndean Dr BN1 .... 142 E3
Varndean Gdns BN1 ..... 142 E3
Varndean Holt BN1 ..... 142 F3
Varndean Rd BN1 .... 142 E3
Varndean Sch BN1 ...... 143 A3
Vega Cl BN27 .... 152 D7
Ventnor Cl BN23 .... 174 B4
Ventnor Villas BN3 .... 163 B6
Venture Cl TN40 .... 157 F4
Verbania Way RH19 ..... 2 B1
Verdant Cl BN2 .... 159 D8
Vere Rd BN1 .... 189 B5
Vermont Rd TN4 .... 7 C4
Vermont Way TN37 ...... 135 F6
Verner Ho [7] BN3 ..... 163 B5
Vernon Ave
  Peacehaven BN10 .... 178 D6
  Woodingdean BN2 .... 165 C8
Vernon Cl
  Eastbourne BN23 ..... 185 E7
  New Town TN22 .... 78 D6
Vernon Ct [3] BN3 ..... 163 E6
Vernon Gdns [4] BN1 ... 163 E6
Vernon Lodge [9] BN21 . 185 A4
Vernon Rd
  Royal Tunbridge Wells TN1 .. 8 C6
  Uckfield TN22 .... 78 D6
Vernons Rd BN8 .... 76 C7
Vernon Terr BN3 .... 163 E7
Veronica Way BN2 ...... 189 C1
Verrall's Wlk BN7 ..... 190 A1
Vert La BN8 .... 127 B8
Verulam Pl TN37 .... 159 E7
Viaduct Rd BN1 .... 189 B4
Vian Ave BN23 .... 185 F7
Vicarage Cl
  Newhaven BN9 .... 168 D2
  Ringmer BN8 .... 124 D5
  Seaford BN25 .... 180 F3
Vicarage Dr BN20 ...... 184 D3
Vicarage Field BN27 ... 152 C8
Vicarage La
  Burwash Common TN19 . 61 A3
  Eastbourne BN20 ..... 184 D3
  Hailsham BN27 .... 152 C8
  Hellingly BN27 ...... 129 A6
  Rottingdean BN2 ..... 165 F1
  Scaynes Hill RH17 ... 51 F3
  Westfield TN35 ...... 114 D3
Vicarage Rd
  Burwash Common TN19 . 61 A3
  Eastbourne BN20 ..... 184 D3
  Hailsham BN27 .... 152 C7
  Hastings TN34 .... 160 A5
Vicarage Terr BN2 ..... 165 F1
Vicarage Way
  Hurst Green TN19 .... 45 A3
  Ringmer BN8 .... 124 D5
Viceroy Lodge [10] BN3 . 163 A6
Victor Cl BN25 .... 180 E5
Victoria Ave
  Burgess Hill RH15 ... 72 E3
  Hastings TN35 .... 160 C8

Victoria Ave continued
  Peacehaven BN10 .... 178 C7
Victoria Bsns Ctr RH15 .. 72 E2
Victoria Cl
  Burgess Hill RH15 ... 72 F2
  Polegate BN26 .... 172 F7
Victoria Cotts
  High Cross TN6 ...... 39 C6
  [9] Hove BN3 .... 163 B5
  St Leonards TN37 .... 136 A5
  Stone Cross BN24 .... 174 B7
Victoria Ct
  [6] Hove BN3 .... 163 C6
  Portslade-by-S BN41 . 162 C8
  St Leonards TN38 .... 159 B6
Victoria Dr BN20, BN21 . 184 C5
Victoria Gdns
  Burgess Hill RH15 ... 72 F2
  Eastbourne BN20 ..... 184 C4
Victoria General Hospl BN7 .... 123 A4
Victoria Gr [7] BN3 ... 163 C6
Victoria Ind Est RH15 .. 72 E2
Victoria Mans BN21 .... 185 B2
Victoria Mews BN2 ..... 165 F1
Victoria Park Gdns BN41 . 162 C8
Victoria Pl [6] BN1 ... 163 E6
Victoria Rd
  Bexhill TN39 .... 157 B4
  Brighton BN1 .... 163 E6
  Burgess Hill RH15 ... 72 E2
  Crowborough TN6 ..... 38 C8
  Eastbourne BN20 ..... 184 C5
  Hailsham BN27 .... 152 C7
  Haywards Heath RH16 . 51 A3
  Mayfield TN20 .... 40 A3
  Polegate BN26 .... 172 F7
  Portslade-by-S BN41 . 162 C8
  Royal Tunbridge Wells TN1 .. 8 B4
  Southwick BN42 ...... 161 D7
  St Leonards TN37 .... 159 D7
  Windmill Hill BN27 .. 131 B5
Victoria Road Trad Est BN41 .... 162 C8
Victoria St BN1 .... 163 E6
Victoria Terr
  Burwash TN19 .... 62 A6
  [6] Hove BN3 .... 163 B5
Victoria Way
  Burgess Hill RH15 ... 72 F2
  East Grinstead RH19 . 10 F7
  Winchelsea Beach TN36 . 118 A5
Victory Mews BN2 ...... 165 A3
View Bank TN35 .... 160 D6
View Rd BN10 .... 178 C8
Views Path RH16 .... 51 B4
Views Wood Path TN22 .. 55 D1
View Terr RH7 .... 2 A8
Viking Cl BN25 .... 180 B6
Viking Way BN23 .... 185 F8
Village Barn The BN1 .. 142 E7
Village Cl
  Bexhill TN39 .... 156 C4
  Portslade-by-S BN41 . 141 B2
Village Mews BN39 ..... 156 C4
Village The
  Alfriston, Alciston BN26 .. 170 D8
  Eastbourne BN20 ..... 188 D8
Village Way BN1 .... 144 C6
Village Wks BN8 .... 105 A5
Villa Rd TN37 .... 159 D7
Villiers Cl BN26 ...... 165 E8
Villiers Ct BN1 .... 189 B3
Vincent Cl BN23 .... 185 F7
Vine Cotts TN6 .... 38 C7
Vine Farm Cotts BN8 ... 104 A5
Vinehall Cl TN34 ...... 137 A5
Vinehall Rd TN32 ...... 87 E5
Vinehall Rd TN32 ...... 87 E5
VINEHALL STREET 87 E6
Vine Pl BN1 .... 189 A3
Vineries The
  Burgess Hill RH15 ... 73 D3
  Eastbourne BN23 ..... 174 D2
  Hove BN3 .... 163 E6
VINE'S CROSS 107 D8
Vines Cross Rd
  Brighton BN2 .... 164 F7
  Horam TN21 .... 107 B7
Vineyard La TN5 .... 31 C2
Vintry The
  Eastbourne BN21 ..... 184 C7
  Nutley TN22 .... 35 C4
Virgin's Croft TN33 ... 112 D6
Virgin's La TN33 ...... 112 D6
Visage [17] BN3 .... 163 D7
Volks Electric Rly★ BN1, BN2 .... 164 C4
Vue Gris Nez TN36 ..... 118 B5

W
Wade Cl BN23 .... 185 F7
Wade Rd RH18 .... 11 F2
WADHURST 30 A4
Wadhurst Bsns Pk TN5 .. 29 B7
Wadhurst CE Prim Sch TN5 .... 29 F5
Wadhurst Cl
  Eastbourne BN22 ..... 173 F2
  St Leonards TN38 .... 136 B5
Wadhurst La TN33 ..... 111 E6
Wadhurst Rd
  Frant TN3 .... 17 D1
  Mark Cross TN6 ...... 28 C3

Wadhurst Rise BN2 ..... 164 F5
Wadhurst Sta TN5 ..... 29 C6
Wadlands Brook Rd RH19 .. 1 D5
Wagg Cl RH19 .... 2 A1
Waghorns La TN22 ..... 57 C6
Wainwright Cl TN38 ... 135 D3
Wainwright Rd TN39 ... 157 B4
Waite Cl BN7 .... 190 B3
Waites La TN35 .... 138 E5
Wakefield Rd BN2 ..... 189 C5
Wakehams Cl TN39 ..... 157 C7
Waldegrave Ct BN22 ... 166 D3
Waldegrave Rd BN1 .... 143 A1
Waldegrave St [4] TN34 . 159 F8
Waldene Cl TN34 ...... 136 F2
Walden Terr TN33 ..... 112 E4
WALDRON 80 F3
Waldron Ave BN1 ...... 143 D6
Waldron Cl BN22 ...... 184 D8
Waldron Ct TN21 ...... 82 B8
WALDRON DOWN 80 D8
Waldron Pl BN1 .... 143 D6
Waldron Rd BN1 .... 105 A5
Waldron Thorns TN21 .. 82 A7
Waldshut Rd BN7 ...... 123 A3
Walesbeech Rd BN2 .... 177 D4
Wales Farm Cotts BN7 .. 121 C7
Walhatch Cl RH18 ..... 11 F2
Walker Cl BN23 .... 185 F7
Walks The TN5 .... 15 C8
Wallace Cl TN2 .... 17 A8
Wallands Cres BN7 .... 190 A2
WALLANDS PARK 123 B1
Wallands Park Rise [9] .. 123 B1
Wallands Prim Sch BN7 . 123 A2
Walled Gdn The TN22 .. 55 D4
Wallers TN3 .... 7 A8
Wall Hill Rd RH18, RH19 . 11 E5
Wallingham Twrs [4] TN40 .... 157 F4
Wallis Ave BN23 ...... 185 E7
Wallis Cl TN6 .... 26 A1
Wallis Field TN3 ..... 15 B6
Wallis Ho RH19 .... 1 E1
Wallis Pl BN23 .... 185 E8
Wallis Way RH15 ...... 72 E4
Wallsend Rd BN24 ..... 175 C6
Walmer Cl BN2 .... 144 B1
Walmer Cres BN2 ...... 144 B1
Walmer Rd BN25 .... 181 C4
Walnut Cl
  Brighton BN1 .... 142 E3
  Heathfield TN21 ..... 82 B6
Walnut Ct BN26 .... 173 A6
Walnut Pk TN6 .... 51 B4
Walnut Tree Wlk BN20 .. 184 B8
Walnut Way TN4 .... 8 D8
Walnut Wlk BN26 ...... 173 A6
Walpole Rd BN2 .... 164 D5
Walpole Terr BN2 ..... 164 D5
Walpole Wlk BN23 ..... 174 E3
Walshes Rd TN6 .... 38 B7
Walsingham Cl BN22 ... 173 D3
Walsingham Rd BN3 ... 162 F6
Walter May Ho [14] BN2 . 164 F5
WALTER'S GREEN 5 E6
Walters Green Rd TN11 . 5 E6
Walton Bank BN1 ..... 143 E5
Walton Cl
  Eastbourne BN23 ..... 174 E3
  St Leonards TN37 .... 136 C5
Walton Pk TN39 .... 156 F4
Walwers La BN7 .... 190 B2
Wanderdown Cl BN2 ... 165 E4
Wanderdown Dr BN2 ... 165 E4
Wanderdown Rd BN2 ... 165 E4
Wanderdown Way BN2 .. 165 E4
WANNOCK 172 E4
Wannock Ave BN20 .... 172 F3
Wannock Cl TN40 ..... 158 A6
Wannock Dr BN26 ..... 172 F3
Wannock Gdns BN26 ... 172 F3
Wannock La BN20, BN26 . 172 F3
Wannock Rd
  Eastbourne BN22 ..... 185 D5
  Polegate BN26 .... 172 F5
Warberry Pk Gdns TN4 .. 7 E4
WARBLETON 83 A1
Warbleton Cl BN2 .... 164 E5
Warburton Cl
  Eastbourne BN21 ..... 184 C8
  East Grinstead RH19 . 11 A8
  Uckfield TN22 .... 78 D8
Ward Cl TN5 .... 29 E5
Warden Ct RH17 .... 50 A6
Warden Park Sch RH17 . 50 A5
Wardsbrook Rd TN5 .... 43 D7
Ward's La TN5 .... 30 E4
Ward Way TN39 .... 157 A6
Ware Ct RH15 .... 73 D3
Wareham Ho [3] RH19 .. 11 A8
Warelands TN5 .... 72 F1
Warenne Rd BN3 ...... 141 C4
Wares Field TN22 .... 78 D4
Wares Rd TN22 .... 78 D4
Warleigh Rd BN1 ..... 189 B5
Warmdene Ave BN1 .... 142 F6
Warmdene Cl BN1 ..... 142 F6
Warmdene Rd BN1 ..... 142 F6
Warmdene Way BN1 .... 142 F6
War Meml Hos BN20 ... 184 C6
War Meml Hospl TN6 ... 25 E1
Warminster Rd BN24 .. 175 D5
Warner Cl RH15 ...... 73 A3
Warnham Ct BN3 ...... 163 C5
Warnham Gdns TN38 ... 156 E2
Warnham Rise BN1 .... 143 A5

WARREN 188 C8
Warren Ave BN2 ...... 165 C8
Warren Cl
  Crowborough TN6 ..... 25 E2
  Eastbourne BN20 ..... 188 C8
  Friston BN20 .... 183 B1
  Lewes BN7 .... 146 B8
  Roser's Cross TN11 .. 81 A6
  St Leonards TN38 .... 158 B8
  Woodingdean BN2 .... 165 B8
Warren Cnr TN21 ...... 81 A8
Warren Cotts
  Mayfield TN20 .... 40 C3
  North Chailey BN8 ... 75 F7
Warren Ct
  [9] Crowborough TN6 . 25 F3
  Southwick BN42 ...... 140 E1
Warren Dr BN7 .... 146 A8
Warren Farm La TN3 ... 16 B4
Warren Gdn TN6 ...... 25 E2
Warren Hill BN20 ..... 184 A1
Warren La
  Friston BN20 .... 183 B1
  North Chailey BN8 ... 75 E8
  Roser's Cross TN11 .. 81 A7
Warren Lodge BN10 .... 167 A1
Warren Rd
  Crowborough TN6 ..... 25 C1
  Fairlight TN35 ...... 138 C8
  Woodingdean BN2 .... 165 B8
Warren Ridge
  Crowborough TN6 ..... 25 D2
  Frant TN3 .... 17 C3
Warren Rise BN2 ...... 165 B8
Warren The
  Burgess Hill RH15 ... 73 C1
  Mayfield TN20 .... 40 C2
  Ticehurst TN5 .... 31 E1
Warren Way
  North Chailey BN8 ... 75 F8
  Telscombe Cliffs BN10 . 167 A1
  Woodingdean BN2 .... 165 D8
Warrenwood BN8 .... 53 A1
Warren Wood TN6 ..... 25 D1
Warrior Cl BN41 ...... 141 B2
Warrior Ct TN37 ...... 159 D7
Warrior Gdns TN37 ... 159 D7
Warrior Ho BN20 ..... 188 E8
Warrior Sq
  [6] Eastbourne BN22 . 185 C4
  St Leonards TN37 .... 159 D7
Warrs Hill La
  North Chailey BN8 ... 75 E8
  Scaynes Hill BN8 .... 52 E1
WARTLING 154 D7
Wartling Cl TN38 .... 135 F3
Wartling Dr TN39 .... 155 F5
Wartling Rd
  Eastbourne BN22 ..... 185 D6
  Wartling BN27 .... 131 C2
Warwick Cl BN27 ..... 129 C3
Warwick Ct
  [4] Eastbourne BN23 . 174 E1
  [8] Hove BN3 .... 163 E7
Warwick Mount [2] BN2 . 164 C4
Warwick Pk TN2 ...... 8 B1
Warwick Pl TN38 ..... 135 E2
Warwick Rd
  Bexhill TN39 .... 156 F5
  [4] Royal Tunbridge Wells TN1 .... 8 A2
  Seaford BN25 .... 180 E3
Washington Ave TN37 .. 135 F6
Washington Rd RH16 .. 51 A5
Washington St BN2 ... 189 C4
Washwell La TN5 ..... 29 F3
Wassall La TN17 ..... 48 E7
Watchbell La TN31 ... 93 C5
Watchbell St TN31 ... 93 C5
Waterbury Hill RH17 .. 33 B5
Waterdown Rd TN4 .... 7 E1
Waterdyke Ave BN42 .. 161 E7
Waterfield TN2 ...... 17 A7
Waterford Cl BN10 ... 167 C2
Waterfrets Cotts TN3 .. 6 F5
Waterfront BN2 ...... 164 F3
Waterfront The BN23 .. 185 G8
Watergate BN39 ..... 157 B8
Watergate La BN7 .... 190 A1
Waterhall Rd BN1 .... 142 C6
Waterloo Cl [2] TN37 . 135 F7
Waterloo Ho [9] BN3 .. 163 D5
Waterloo Pas [15] TN34 . 160 B4
Waterloo Pl
  [1] Brighton BN1 .... 189 C3
  [13] Hastings TN34 .. 160 B4
  Lewes BN7 .... 190 B2
Waterloo Sq BN26 .... 171 A3
Waterloo St BN3 ..... 163 D5
Watermen's Cl TN34 .. 136 F3
Watermill Cl
  Bexhill TN39 .... 157 B7
  Polegate BN26 .... 173 A5
Watermill Dr TN38 .... 135 D3
Watermill La
  Bexhill TN39 .... 134 B2
  Clayhill TN31 .... 67 D2
  Icklesham TN35, TN36 . 116 C3
Watermill La Cotts TN35 . 138 C8
Water Mint Cl TN38 .. 135 E1
Waters Cotts TN5 .... 30 A4
Waters Edge [13] BN43 . 161 A6
Waterside
  Crowborough TN6 ..... 25 F2
  East Grinstead RH19 . 2 B1

Waterside Cl TN35 ... **160** C7
Waterside Ctr BN7 ... **190** A3
Waterworks Cl RH18 ... **11** F3
Waterworks Cotts
Friston BN20 ... **183** A1
1 Hastings TN34 ... **159** F8
Hove BN3 ... **142** A2
Waterworks Rd
Eastbourne BN22 ... **185** A4
1 Hastings TN38 ... **136** F1
Watling Cl 5 BN42 ... **161** E7
Watling Ct 8 BN42 ... **161** E7
Watling Rd BN42 ... **161** E7
Wattle's Wish TN33 ... **112** C6
Watts Cl TN5 ... **29** F4
Watts La BN21 ... **184** E4
Watts Lodge RH15 ... **73** D3
Watts' Pal La TN31 ... **89** D7
Waverley Cres BN1 ... **143** C1
Waverley Ct
4 Hastings TN34 ... **159** E7
7 Seaford BN25 ... **180** F2
Waverley Dr TN2 ... **8** F6
Waverley Gdns BN24 ... **175** D5
Wayfaring Down BN26 ... **172** D3
Wayfield Ave BN3 ... **141** F1
Wayfield Cl BN3 ... **141** F1
Wayford Cl BN23 ... **174** D2
Wayland Ave BN1 ... **142** C3
Wayland Hts BN1 ... **142** C4
Wayside
Brighton BN1 ... **142** D6
Friston BN20 ... **183** B1
Wayside Wlk TN21 ... **81** F6
Weald Ave BN3 ... **162** F8
Weald Cl
Barcombe Cross BN8 ... **101** E4
Lewes BN7 ... **190** A3
Wealden Cl TN6 ... **25** F3
Wealden Cotts TN19 ... **61** C3
Wealden Ho TN21 ... **82** A8
Wealden Ind Est TN6 ... **38** C8
Wealden Pk BN22 ... **173** C1
Wealden View TN19 ... **62** B7
Wealden Way
Bexhill TN39 ... **156** C6
Haywards Heath RH16 ... **50** D4
Weald Rd RH15 ... **72** E3
Weald Rise RH16 ... **50** E1
Weald The RH19 ... **1** F4
Weald View
Barcombe Cross BN8 ... **101** E4
Staplecross TN32 ... **65** E2
Turner's Green TN5 ... **29** F6
Wealdview Rd TN21 ... **81** F7
Weare Rd TN4 ... **8** C8
Weatherby Cl BN21 ... **184** C8
Weavers Cl RH15 ... **73** D1
Weavers La BN26 ... **170** F3
Weavers Mead 6 RH16 ... **50** C2
Weavers Rock La TN21 ... **82** C5
Wedderburn Rd BN20 ... **173** B1
Week La BN8 ... **124** D2
Weirwood Resr Nature Reserve★ RH19 ... **10** D1
Welbeck Ave
Hove BN3 ... **162** E6
Royal Tunbridge Wells TN4 ... **8** C8
St Leonards TN38 ... **159** A7
Welbeck Cl
Burgess Hill RH15 ... **73** D4
Eastbourne BN22 ... **173** D3
Welbeck Ct
Hove BN3 ... **162** E6
9 Seaford BN25 ... **180** E3
Welbeck Dr RH15 ... **73** D5
Welbeck Mans BN3 ... **162** E6
Welesmere Rd BN2 ... **166** A3
Welkin (Brighton Univ) BN20 ... **184** E1
Welkin The RH16 ... **51** B8
Welland Cl TN6 ... **38** A8
WELLBROOK ... **39** E1
Wellcombe Cres BN20 ... **188** D7
Wellend Villas 2 BN1 ... **163** F8
Weller Rd TN4 ... **7** C4
Wellesley Cl
Bexhill TN39 ... **156** D3
Crowborough TN6 ... **25** D1
Wellesley Ct 19 TN34 ... **160** B4
Wellesley Rd 7 BN21 ... **185** A3
Wellfield RH19 ... **11** C7
Wellgreen La BN7 ... **145** F5
Wellhouse La RH15 ... **98** C7
Wellhouse Pl BN7 ... **190** A2
Wellingham La BN8 ... **124** A7
Wellington Cl 3 BN23 ... **175** A1
Wellington Ct
Brighton BN2 ... **165** A3
4 Eastbourne BN22 ... **185** C5
Wellington Gdns TN33 ... **112** C5
Wellington Ho
17 Hastings TN34 ... **159** F8
Portslade-by-S BN41 ... **162** C6
Wellingtonia Ct 8 BN1 ... **142** E3
Wellington Lodge BN27 ... **152** B8
Wellington Mews TN34 ... **159** F8
Wellington Pk 1 BN25 ... **181** A3
Wellington Pl
6 Hastings TN34 ... **159** F7
Sparrow's Green TN5 ... **29** F5
Wellington Quay BN23 ... **175** A1
Wellington Rd
Brighton BN2 ... **189** C4
Hastings TN34 ... **160** A4

Wellington Rd *continued*
Newhaven BN9 ... **168** F2
Peacehaven BN10 ... **178** E6
Portslade-by-S BN41 ... **162** B6
Wellington Sq TN34 ... **159** F8
Wellington St
Brighton BN2 ... **164** C7
Lewes BN7 ... **190** B2
Wellington Terr 14 TN34 **159** F8
Wellington Town Rd RH19 . **1** D2
Wellington Way 12 BN23 **175** A1
Wellis Ct TN38 ... **159** A8
Wellis Gdns TN38 ... **159** A8
Wellplace Cotts TN36 ... **116** F5
Wellsbourne 8 BN2 ... **164** F5
Wellsbourne Rd BN24 ... **174** A5
Wells Chase BN7 ... **99** E6
Wells Cl
Eastbourne BN20 ... **188** C8
Plumpton Green BN7 ... **99** E6
Royal Tunbridge Wells TN1 ... **8** A3
Wells Ho TN4 ... **7** F4
Wells Lea RH19 ... **1** D3
Wells Mdw RH19 ... **1** D3
Wellsmead Pk BN20 ... **188** D8
Wellswood RH16 ... **50** F3
Welsley Mews TN6 ... **25** F2
Welton Rise TN37 ... **136** B6
Wendale Dr BN10 ... **167** D2
Wendover Grange 3 BN3 ... **163** A6
Wenham Gdns BN8 ... **104** C5
Wenthill Cl BN20 ... **187** B8
Went Hill Gdns BN22 ... **173** B3
Went Hill Pk BN25 ... **181** A3
Went La BN20 ... **183** C1
Went Way BN20 ... **187** B8
Wentworth Cl
Bexhill TN40 ... **157** F5
Hailsham BN27 ... **129** A1
Wentworth Ct BN23 ... **185** E6
Wentworth St BN2 ... **189** C1
Wentworth Way TN38 ... **158** F8
Wessex Pl BN20 ... **184** C5
West Ascent TN38 ... **159** B6
Westaway Dr TN39 ... **157** A4
West Beach Ct BN25 ... **180** B4
West Beeches Rd TN6 ... **26** B2
WEST BLATCHINGTON ... **141** F1
West Blatchington Inf Sch BN3 ... **141** E4
West Blatchington Jun Sch BN3 ... **141** E4
West Blatchington Windmill★ BN3 ... **141** F2
Westbourne Ct TN39 ... **156** C2
Westbourne Gdns BN3 ... **163** A7
Westbourne Gr BN3 ... **163** A7
Westbourne Pl BN3 ... **163** A6
Westbourne St BN3 ... **163** A7
Westbourne Villas BN3 ... **162** F6
Westbrook
Forest Row RH18 ... **11** E3
Saltdean BN2 ... **166** C2
Westbrook La TN35 ... **114** E5
Westbrook Terr TN2 ... **8** D1
Westbrook Way BN42 ... **161** F7
West Cl
Alfriston BN26 ... **170** F3
Polegate BN26 ... **173** B7
Westcliff Man BN20 ... **188** F8
Westcombe 1 BN1 ... **163** E7
West Comm RH16 ... **50** F6
West Comm Dr RH16 ... **51** A7
Westcourt BN27 ... **152** B7
Westcourt Dr TN39 ... **156** F3
Westcroft BN7 ... **99** E1
WESTDEAN ... **182** B4
Westdean Ave BN9 ... **179** A5
West Dean Rise BN25 ... **181** A4
WESTDENE ... **142** C5
Westdene Cl TN37 ... **136** C6
Westdene Dr BN1 ... **142** C5
Westdene Prim Sch BN1 **142** C5
Westdown Ho 4 BN21 ... **185** A2
Westdown La TN19 ... **61** A3
Westdown Pk TN19 ... **61** A3
Westdown Rd BN25 ... **180** D4
West Down Rd TN39 ... **157** A5
West Dr BN2 ... **164** C6
West End BN27 ... **130** E6
Westergate Bsns Ctr BN2 ... **143** E4
Westergate Rd BN2 ... **143** E4
Westerham Rd BN23 ... **174** D1
Westerings The 4 TN21 ... **82** A6
Westerleigh Cl TN38 ... **159** A8
Western Ave
Battle TN33 ... **112** D5
Polegate BN26 ... **173** B7
Western Concourse BN2 **164** F3
Western Ct BN9 ... **179** C6
Western Espl BN41 ... **162** D6
Western Gdns TN6 ... **38** D8
Western Rd
Bexhill TN40 ... **157** C3
Burgess Hill RH15 ... **72** E3
Crowborough TN6 ... **38** C7
Eastbourne BN22 ... **185** B4
Hailsham BN27 ... **152** A8
Haywards Heath RH16 ... **50** F4
Hove BN1, BN3 ... **163** E5
Lewes BN7 ... **123** B1
Newhaven BN9 ... **179** C6
Newick BN8 ... **76** C7
Pevensey Bay BN24 ... **175** D4
Royal Tunbridge Wells TN1 ... **8** C5
St Leonards TN37 ... **159** C7

Western Rd *continued*
Turner's Green TN5 ... **29** F6
Western Road Cty Sch BN7 ... **196** A1
Western St BN1 ... **163** D5
Western Terr 21 BN1 ... **163** E5
WESTFIELD ... **114** F4
Westfield Ave BN2 ... **166** D3
Westfield Avenue N BN2 **166** D3
Westfield Avenue S BN2 **166** D3
Westfield Cl
Brighton BN1 ... **143** A4
Five Ashes TN20 ... **58** B6
Polegate BN26 ... **173** A7
Westfield Cres BN1 ... **143** A5
Westfield Ct BN26 ... **173** A7
Westfield La TN35, TN37 . **136** C8
Westfield Prim Sch TN35 ... **114** E4
Westfield Rd BN21 ... **184** D6
Westfield Rise BN2 ... **166** E3
WEST FIRLE ... **148** C3
West Furlong Ct BN6 ... **97** A5
West Furlong La BN6 ... **97** A5
West Gate BN7 ... **99** E6
Westgate St BN7 ... **190** A2
WESTHAM ... **174** E5
Westham 13 BN2 ... **164** F5
Westham Cl TN39 ... **156** E3
Westham Dr BN24 ... **175** F6
WEST HILL ... **137** B1
West Hill
Dormans Park RH19 ... **1** E6
East Grinstead RH19 ... **10** D8
West Hill Arc 3 TN34 ... **160** A3
West Hill Cliff Rly★ TN34 ... **160** A4
West Hill Ct
Eastbourne BN21 ... **184** E4
4 St Leonards TN38 ... **159** B6
Westhill Dr RH15 ... **72** E3
West Hill Mews TN38 ... **158** F6
West Hill Pl BN1 ... **189** A3
West Hill Rd
Brighton BN1 ... **189** A3
St Leonards TN38 ... **159** A6
West Hill St BN1 ... **189** A4
West Ho 15 BN21 ... **185** A2
West Hoathly Rd RH19 ... **10** D4
West Hove Inf & Jun Schs BN3 ... **162** F7
West La RH19 ... **10** D8
Westland Ct BN41 ... **162** A7
Westlands Rd RH16 ... **51** B5
West Leigh RH19 ... **10** E7
Westlords BN21 ... **184** C8
West Mallion RH16 ... **50** F3
WEST MARINA ... **158** F5
Westmeston Ave BN2 ... **166** B2
Westminster Cl BN22 ... **173** D4
Westminster Cres TN34 . **160** A8
Westmoreland Cl TN38 ... **135** F3
Westmoreland Ct TN22 ... **78** C5
Westmorland Ct
16 Brighton BN1 ... **163** E7
Eastbourne BN20 ... **184** B7
Westmount 3 BN2 ... **164** C6
Westmount Cl BN42 ... **161** D8
West Par TN39 ... **157** B2
West Park Cres RH15 ... **72** D4
West Park Nature Reserve★ TN22 ... **78** A7
Westpoint BN8 ... **76** C7
West Point 8 BN43 ... **161** A6
West Quay BN9 ... **179** D6
West Rd
Kilndown TN17 ... **20** F3
Portslade-by-S BN41 ... **162** A7
West Rise Com Inf Sch BN23 ... **174** C2
West Rise Jun Sch BN23 **174** C2
West St La TN21 ... **81** F2
West St Leonards Prim Sch TN38 ... **158** F8
West St Leonards Sta TN38 ... **158** F7
West St
Alfriston BN26 ... **170** F3
Brighton BN1 ... **189** A2
Burgess Hill RH15 ... **72** E4
Ditchling BN6 ... **98** D3
Dormansland RH7 ... **2** A8
Eastbourne BN21 ... **184** F2
East Grinstead RH19 ... **10** E8
Hastings TN34 ... **160** A3
Lewes BN7 ... **190** B2
Mayfield TN20 ... **40** A2
Portslade-by-S BN41 ... **162** C7
Rottingdean BN2 ... **165** F1
Rye TN31 ... **93** C5
Seaford BN25 ... **180** E2
West Terr
Eastbourne BN21 ... **184** F2
Herstmonceux BN27 ... **130** E6
West Undercliff TN31 ... **93** A5
West View
Hastings TN34 ... **160** B6
Hove BN3 ... **163** C8
Lindfield RH16 ... **51** B6
Seaford BN25 ... **180** E2
Uckfield TN22 ... **55** D1
West View Cotts RH16 ... **51** B6
West View Ct 17 BN25 ... **180** E2
West View Gdns RH19 ... **10** E8
West View Terr BN9 ... **168** D2
Westville Rd TN39 ... **157** A4
Westway TN2 ... **9** D7
West Way BN3 ... **141** D2

Westway Cl BN41 ... **140** E4
Westway Gdns BN41 ... **140** E4
Westwood Rd TN4 ... **7** C5
Wharf Rd
Eastbourne BN21 ... **184** F3
Hove BN3 ... **162** D6
WHATLINGTON ... **88** A1
Whatlington Rd TN33 ... **112** E7
Whatlington Way TN38 ... **135** D2
Wheatfield Ct TN37 ... **136** C5
Wheatfield Way BN2 ... **143** F3
Wheatland Cl BN10 ... **167** B2
Wheatsheaf Cl RH15 ... **72** E5
Wheatsheaf Gdns BN7 ... **190** C3
Wheatsheaf La RH17 ... **50** A6
Wheeler Ct RH16 ... **50** F2
Wheelers La TN22 ... **57** D6
Wheelers La Cotts TN22 ... **57** D5
Wheel Farm Bsns Pk TN35 ... **114** D4
Wheel La TN35 ... **114** D3
Wheelwright Cl BN22 ... **173** D4
Wheelwright La RH15 ... **73** D1
Whichelo Pl BN2 ... **164** C6
Whiffens Cl BN27 ... **152** A6
Whincroft Pk TN6 ... **37** D8
Whippingham Rd BN2 ... **164** C7
Whippingham St BN2 ... **164** C8
Whipping Post La BN2 ... **165** F1
Whistler Ct BN1 ... **142** F1
Whitbread Cl BN23 ... **174** B4
Whiteacres Cl TN31 ... **89** A5
Whitebeam Ct 9 RH16 ... **50** C2
Whitebeam Mews 8 RH16 ... **50** C2
White Bear Pas 3 TN1 ... **8** A2
Whitebread La TN31 ... **67** E8
White Chimneys TN6 ... **26** A1
Whitecross St BN1 ... **189** B3
White Ct BN26 ... **170** F2
Whitefield Rd TN4 ... **8** A6
Whitefriars Rd TN34 ... **160** A5
Whitegate Cl TN4 ... **8** A8
Whitegates Cl BN8 ... **100** E7
Whitegates La TN5 ... **29** D8
Whitegates Pk TN35 ... **114** D2
WHITEHAWK ... **164** E5
Whitehawk Cl BN2 ... **164** E5
Whitehawk Cres BN2 ... **164** D5
Whitehawk Hill Rd BN2 ... **164** D5
Whitehawk Prim Sch BN2 ... **164** E6
Whitehawk Rd BN2 ... **164** F5
Whitehawk Way BN2 ... **164** F6
WHITEHILL ... **37** F8
White Hill BN7 ... **190** A2
White Hill Ave TN39 ... **156** E4
Whitehill Cl
Crowborough TN6 ... **25** F1
Eastbourne BN20 ... **184** B5
Whitehill Ct TN39 ... **156** E5
White Hill Dr TN39 ... **156** E4
Whitehill Inf Sch TN6 ... **26** A1
Whitehill Rd TN6 ... **37** F8
Whitehouse Ave TN39 ... **157** B7
Whitehouse La TN21 ... **81** B4
White House Prim Sch BN27 ... **152** B8
White Lodge
Hove BN3 ... **163** C8
Royal Tunbridge Wells TN1 ... **8** C4
Whitelot Cl BN42 ... **140** E2
Whitelot Way BN42 ... **140** E2
WHITE POST ... **5** D7
White Rock TN34, TN37 ... **159** E7
White Rock Gdns 7 TN34 ... **159** E7
White Rock Grounds★ TN34 ... **159** E7
Whiterock Pl BN42 ... **161** E7
White Rock Rd TN34, TN37 ... **159** E7
White Rock Theatre★ TN34 ... **159** E7
Whitesand Dr TN31 ... **94** E3
White's Cl BN6 ... **97** A7
WHITESMITH ... **127** B8
Whitesmith BN8 ... **105** B1
Whitesmith La BN8 ... **105** B1
White St BN2 ... **189** C2
Whitethorn Dr BN1 ... **142** B4
White Way
Alfriston BN26 ... **170** F1
Lewes BN7 ... **146** B1
Whiteway Cl BN25 ... **180** E6
Whiteway La BN2 ... **166** A2
Whiteways Cotts BN7 ... **146** C2
Whitfeld La BN8 ... **123** C6
Whitley Rd BN22 ... **185** B5
Whittingehame Gdns BN1 ... **142** F3
Whittington Coll (Almshouses) RH19 ... **1** A4
Whittington's Way TN34 . **160** B8
Whittle Dr BN23 ... **174** A1
Whittlewood Cl TN38 ... **135** E2
Whitworth Rd TN37 ... **136** B7
Whybourne Crest TN2 ... **8** D1
WHYDOWN ... **156** B8
Whydown Hill TN33 ... **113** E6
Whydown Rd TN39 ... **156** B7
Wickens Ct 2 RH16 ... **50** C2
Wickets The RH15 ... **72** F5
Wick Hall BN3 ... **163** D6
Wickham Ave TN39 ... **157** B3
Wickham Cl RH16 ... **50** E7
Wickham Dr BN6 ... **97** C5
Wickham Gdns TN4 ... **7** D5

Wickham Hill BN6 ... **97** C4
Wickham La BN7, BN8 ... **100** E3
Wickham Rock La TN36 ... **117** C5
Wickham Way RH16 ... **50** E7
Wickhurst Cl BN41 ... **140** F2
Wickhurst Rd BN41 ... **141** A2
Wickhurst Rise BN41 ... **140** F3
Wicklands Ave BN2 ... **166** D1
Wick St BN26 ... **150** E6
WICKSTREET ... **150** D6
Widbury TN3 ... **6** F3
Widdicombe Way BN2 ... **143** E2
Wigmore Cl BN1 ... **143** B1
Wilbury Ave BN3 ... **163** C8
Wilbury Cres BN3 ... **163** D7
Wilbury Gdns BN3 ... **163** C8
Wilbury Gr BN3 ... **163** C6
Wilbury Grange 9 BN3 ... **163** C6
Wilbury Lodge 13 BN3 ... **163** C6
Wilbury Mans BN3 ... **163** D8
Wilbury Rd BN3 ... **163** C6
Wilbury Villas BN3 ... **163** C7
Wilby Ave BN42 ... **140** E1
Wilderness Gdns TN31 ... **67** B7
Wilderness La TN22 ... **57** C3
Wilderness Pk TN6 ... **25** E2
Wilderness Rd BN6 ... **97** A6
Wilderness Rise RH19 ... **2** A6
Wilderness The RH16 ... **51** B8
Wilderness Wood Visitor Ctr★ TN22 ... **57** D4
Wilderwick Rd RH19 ... **2** A5
Wild Park Cl BN2 ... **143** E3
Wild Park Nature Trail★ BN2 ... **143** D5
Wildwood BN23 ... **174** C4
Wilfrid Rd BN3 ... **141** D1
Wiliamson Cott Homes BN3 ... **163** A7
Wilkinson Cl BN2 ... **165** F3
Wilkinson Way BN25 ... **180** E4
Wilkins Way TN40 ... **157** F6
Willard Cl BN22 ... **185** A6
WILLARD'S HILL ... **63** C5
Willard Way RH19 ... **1** A3
Wille Cotts BN7 ... **190** C2
Willetts Cotts TN3 ... **5** C4
Willetts Field BN8 ... **127** E8
Willetts La TN3 ... **5** C4
William Allen La RH16 ... **51** B6
William Parker Sports Coll TN34 ... **136** D4
William Rd TN38 ... **158** E7
William St Trad Est BN41 ... **162** A7
Williams Ct 7 BN23 ... **174** E1
Williams Rd BN43 ... **161** C8
William St
Brighton BN2 ... **189** B2
Portslade-by-S BN41 ... **162** B7
Royal Tunbridge Wells TN4 ... **8** A5
William Sutton Ho BN1 ... **189** B2
Williams Way TN6 ... **26** A2
Willicombe Ho TN2 ... **8** D4
Willicombe Pk TN2 ... **8** D4
WILLINGDON ... **173** A1
Willingdon Ave
Bexhill TN39 ... **157** A4
St Leonards TN38 ... **136** A5
Willingdon Cl
Eastbourne BN20 ... **173** B1
St Leonards TN38 ... **136** A5
Willingdon Com Sch BN20 ... **172** F4
Willingdon Ct BN20 ... **173** B3
Willingdon Dro BN23 ... **174** B2
Willingdon La BN26 ... **183** C7
Willingdon Park Dr BN22 ... **173** D2
Willingdon Prim Sch BN20 ... **173** A3
Willingdon Rd
Brighton BN2 ... **143** E1
Eastbourne BN20, BN21 ... **184** C6
Willingdon Way
Eastbourne BN22 ... **173** B2
St Leonards TN38 ... **136** A5
Willingford La TN19 ... **61** C2
Willoughby Cres BN22 ... **185** C6
Willow Ave BN27 ... **129** B1
Willow Bank TN32 ... **64** B3
Willowbed Wlk TN34 ... **136** E5
Willowbrook Way BN6 ... **98** A3
Willow Cl
East Grinstead RH19 ... **1** D3
Etchingham TN19 ... **63** B8
Heathfield TN21 ... **82** B8
Woodingdean BN2 ... **165** E8
Willow Ct
4 Hove BN3 ... **163** D7
Polegate BN26 ... **173** A6
Willowdowne Cl BN26 ... **173** A5
Willow Dr
Bexhill TN39 ... **156** C5
Polegate BN26 ... **173** A5
Seaford BN25 ... **181** C3
Willow End TN34 ... **136** F4
Willow Est BN9 ... **179** E8
Willowfield Rd BN22 ... **185** B4
Willowfield Sq 7 BN22 ... **185** B3
Willow Gdns BN6 ... **97** A7
Willow Ho BN6 ... **97** E5
Willow La TN36 ... **118** B6
Willow Lodge TN4 ... **7** E4
Willowmead TN6 ... **37** E8
Willow Mead 8 RH19 ... **10** F8
Willow Mews
19 Eastbourne BN22 ... **185** B3

Willow Mews continued
Robertsbridge TN32..... 64 B3
Willow Pk RH16........ 51 B4
Willows Cl TN22........ 78 D8
Willows Mobile Home Pk The
BN27.................. 129 A3
Willows Rise TN22....... 79 B5
Willows The
Barcombe Cross BN8.... 101 E5
2 Brighton BN2........ 189 C5
Burgess Hill RH15...... 73 B5
Hassocks BN6.......... 97 E4
St Leonards TN37...... 136 A6
Willow Stream Cl TN35.. 115 E3
Willow Tree Rd TN2......7 F1
Willow Wlk
Eastbourne BN22....... 173 D2
Newhaven BN9......... 179 C8
Royal Tunbridge Wells TN2... 8 E8
Wilman Rd TN4..........8 B7
WILMINGTON.......... 171 F5
Wilmington Cl
Brighton BN1.......... 143 A5
Hassocks BN6.......... 97 F4
Wilmington Gdns BN1.. 185 A1
WILMINGTON GREEN.. 171 E7
Wilmington Par BN1... 142 F5
Wilmington Rd
Hastings TN34......... 160 A7
Newhaven BN9......... 179 B6
Seaford BN25.......... 180 D4
Wilmington Sq BN21... 185 A1
Wilmington Way
Brighton BN1.......... 143 A5
Haywards Heath RH16... 51 A5
Wilmot Ct 6 BN43..... 161 C8
Wilmot Rd BN43........ 161 C8
Wilson Ave BN2........ 164 F6
Wilson Gr TN22........ 78 A7
Wilson's Cross BN27... 131 F7
Wilton 1 RH16......... 50 D5
Wilton Ave TN22....... 173 F2
Wilton Ho TN38........ 158 F6
Wilton Rd TN40........ 157 C3
Wiltshire Ct BN23..... 174 E1
Wiltshire Ho 16 BN2... 189 C2
Wiltshire Way TN2...... 8 D7
Winceby Cl TN39....... 156 E2
Winchcombe Rd BN22.. 185 A4
WINCHELSEA.......... 117 E7
WINCHELSEA BEACH.. 118 A5
Winchelsea Beach Holiday
Village TN36.......... 118 A4
Winchelsea Cl BN25... 181 C5
Winchelsea Court Hall Mus★
TN36................. 117 E7
Winchelsea La
Cock Marling TN31, TN36... 92 C1
Hastings TN35......... 137 E5
Winchelsea Rd
Eastbourne BN22...... 185 D6
Guestling Green TN35... 137 F7
Hastings TN35......... 160 D8
Rye TN31.............. 93 B5
Winchelsea St Thomas CE
Prim TN36............ 117 F7
Winchelsea Sta TN36... 92 D1
Winchester Ho BN22... 173 E3
Winchester St BN1..... 189 B5
Winchester Way BN22.. 173 C2
Wincombe Rd BN1..... 142 D1
Windermere Cres BN22. 185 C5
Windermere Ct 9 BN2.. 164 C6
Windermere Rd RH16... 50 F4
Windgrove Cotts TN33. 112 D6
Windgrove Ho TN33.... 112 D6
Winding St 21 TN34... 160 B4
Windlesham Ave BN1.. 163 E6
Windlesham Cl
Crowborough TN6...... 25 F1
Portslade-by-S BN41... 141 A1
Windlesham Ct 14 BN1.. 163 E7
Windlesham Gdns BN1,
BN3.................. 163 E7
Windlesham Hall 18 BN1 163 E6
Windlesham Ho 15 BN1. 163 E6
Windlesham Mans 17
BN3.................. 163 E7
Windlesham Rd BN1.... 163 E6
Windlesham Sch BN1... 163 E8
Windmill Ave BN6...... 97 F3
Windmill Cl
Eastbourne BN21....... 184 D6
Heathfield TN21........ 82 B8
Hove BN3.............. 141 F2

Windmill Ct
Royal Tunbridge Wells TN2... 8 C3
Winchelsea Beach TN36. 118 B6
Windmill Dr
Bexhill TN39.......... 157 B6
Brighton BN1.......... 142 C6
Burgess Hill RH15...... 73 A4
Windmill Gn BN24..... 174 C5
WINDMILL HILL....... 131 B6
Windmill La
Ashurst Wood RH19..... 11 C7
Cousley Wood TN5...... 30 C8
Durgates TN5.......... 29 E4
East Grinstead RH19.... 1 D3
Friston BN20.......... 183 A1
Windmill Par BN42.... 140 E1
Windmill Pl BN26..... 173 A5
Windmill Rd
Polegate BN26......... 173 A6
Southwick BN42....... 140 E1
St Leonards TN38...... 136 B2
Windmills Jun Sch The
BN6.................. 98 A3
Windmill St
Brighton BN2.......... 189 C3
Royal Tunbridge Wells TN2... 8 C3
Windmill Terr 20 BN2.. 189 C3
Windmill View BN1.... 143 B7
Windmill Way TN36.... 118 B2
Windover Cres BN7.... 123 A2
Windover Way BN22... 173 B3
Windsor Bsns Units TN6. 38 C8
Windsor Cl
Eastbourne BN23...... 174 C3
Haywards Heath RH16... 50 E2
Hove BN3.............. 142 A3
Seaford BN25.......... 180 B6
Windsor Ct
Brighton BN1.......... 189 A2
Brighton, Withdean BN1. 142 D3
Crowborough TN6...... 38 C8
8 Eastbourne BN23.... 185 B3
Polegate BN26......... 173 A7
Windsor Lodge 5 BN3. 163 B6
Windsor Pl
Crowborough TN6...... 38 C8
East Grinstead RH19.... 11 A8
Hastings TN34......... 136 E2
Windsor Rd
Bexhill TN39.......... 157 B4
Crowborough TN6...... 38 C8
Hailsham BN27......... 152 B6
St Leonards TN37...... 136 B3
Windsor St BN1........ 189 A2
Windsor Way
Polegate BN26......... 173 A7
Winchelsea Beach TN36. 118 A5
Windward Quay 10 BN23 185 F8
Wineham Way TN40.... 157 F4
Winfield Ave BN1...... 142 F6
Winfield Cl
Brighton BN1.......... 142 F5
Portslade-by-S BN41... 141 A3
Wingate Cl TN38....... 136 A1
Wingle Tye Rd RH15... 98 A8
Wingrove BN26........ 173 A3
Winkfield Ct RH16..... 50 D5
Winkhurst Way RH15... 73 D1
Winkney Rd BN22...... 173 F3
Winnals Pk RH16....... 50 D5
Winscote Cl TN6....... 25 D1
Winston BN27.......... 152 B7
Winston Cres BN23.... 185 D7
Winston Dr TN39....... 156 B3
Winstone Scott Ave TN3...6 E4
Winterbourne Cl
Hastings TN34......... 159 D8
Lewes BN7............. 146 A8
Winterbourne Hollow
BN7.................. 146 B8
Winterbourne La
BN7.................. 146 A8
Winterbourne Mews
BN7.................. 146 B8
Winter Gdn★ 17 BN21. 185 A1
Winterton Way BN43... 161 B6
Winton Ave BN2....... 166 C3
Winton St BN26........ 171 A4
Wisden Ave RH15...... 72 E5
Wiseacre TN3.......... 20 A3
Wish Ct BN3........... 162 E8
Wish Hill BN20........ 173 B1
**Wishing Tree Cl TN38.. 135 F2
Wishing Tree La TN38.. 135 F1
Wishing Tree Rd TN38.. 135 F2
Wishing Tree Road N**
TN38................. 136 A4

Wish Rd
Eastbourne BN21....... 185 A2
Hove BN3.............. 162 E6
Wish St TN31.......... 93 B5
Wish Twr★ BN21....... 185 A1
Wish Ward TN31....... 93 B5
Wiston Ct 12 BN43.... 161 C8
Wiston Rd BN2......... 164 F6
Wiston Way BN2....... 164 F7
WITHDEAN............ 142 F4
Withdean Ave BN1... 142 D2
Withdean Cl BN1...... 142 D3
Withdean Court Ave
BN1.................. 142 D3
Withdean Cres BN1.... 142 E3
Withdean Ct 7 BN1.... 142 E3
Withdean Hall 9 BN1.. 142 E3
Withdean Rd BN1...... 142 D3
Withdean Rise BN1.... 142 D3
**Withdean Stad (Brighton &
Hove Albion FC)** BN1. 142 D3
Witherenden Rd TN20.. 41 A1
Withy Bush RH15...... 72 E5
WITHYHAM........... 14 A3
Withyham Rd
Bexhill TN39.......... 156 C2
Groombridge TN3...... 15 B7
Wittersham La TN31... 70 B5
Wittersham Rd
Iden TN31............. 70 B7
Potman's Heath TN17, TN30 49 D4
Wittersham Rd Sta★
TN17................. 49 D6
Wittersham Rise TN38.. 135 E2
WIVELSFIELD.......... 73 F6
WIVELSFIELD GREEN.. 74 C4
Wivelsfield Prim Sch
RH17................. 73 F6
Wivelsfield Rd
Haywards Heath RH16... 50 E2
Saltdean BN2.......... 166 C3
Wivelsfield Sta RH15... 73 C4
Woburn Cl BN27....... 129 A1
Woburn Pl BN1........ 143 F5
Woburn Way BN22.... 173 D3
Wode Rd TN33......... 133 A3
Wolfe Cl TN6.......... 38 A8
Wolseley Rd
Brighton BN1.......... 143 D6
Portslade-by-S BN41... 162 A8
Royal Tunbridge Wells TN4.. 8 A5
Wolstead Lodge 3 RH16. 50 F3
Wolstonbury Cl BN6.... 97 B4
Wolstonbury Ct RH15.. 73 B2
Wolstonbury Rd BN3... 163 E7
Wolstonbury Way RH15. 73 B2
Wolverstone Dr BN1... 143 C2
Woodbanke La 5 RH16. 50 C2
Woodbourne Ave BN1.. 143 A4
Woodbrook TN34...... 136 F2
Woodbury Ave RH19...2 B1
Woodbury Cl
East Grinstead RH19.... 11 B8
2 Royal Tunbridge Wells
TN4................. 8 A5
Woodbury Park Gdns TN4..8 B5
Woodbury Park Rd TN4...8 B5
Woodcombe TN34..... 136 F4
Woodcote Ho 3 RH16.. 50 C2
Woodcote Rd RH18.... 11 F2
Woodcrest Rd RH15.... 72 F1
Woodcroft RH15....... 72 F5
Woodcroft Dr BN21.... 184 C7
Woodcutters RH17..... 51 F3
Woodgate Mdw BN7... 99 E7
Woodgate Rd BN22.... 185 C5
Woodhams TN33....... 112 D5
Woodhill Pk TN2....... 9 C6
Woodhouse Cl BN3.... 162 E7
Woodhouse Rd BN3.... 162 E7
Woodingdean Bsns Pk
BN2.................. 144 D1
Woodingdean Prim Sch
BN2.................. 165 C8
Wood La BN27......... 131 D2
Woodland Ave
Burgess Hill RH15...... 73 C4
Eastbourne BN22...... 173 C1
Hove BN3.............. 142 B3
Woodland Cl
Burgess Hill RH15...... 73 C4
Hove BN3.............. 142 B2
Royal Tunbridge Wells TN4.. 8 C7
Woodland Cres RH15... 73 C4
Woodland Ct BN3...... 142 B4

Woodland Dr BN3..... 142 B3
Woodland Mews TN21.. 82 B6
Woodland Par BN3.... 142 B3
Woodland Rd TN4...... 8 C7
Woodland Rise TN40... 157 E4
Woodlands
Bexhill TN39.......... 156 D6
Hove BN3.............. 142 C2
Pembury TN2...........9 F7
Woodlands Cl
Hailsham BN27........ 129 C2
Heathfield TN21....... 82 B5
Peacehaven BN10...... 167 B1
Peasmarsh TN31....... 69 C2
Uckfield TN22......... 78 D8
Woodlands Rd
East Grinstead RH19.... 2 A4
Haywards Heath RH16... 50 F4
Woodlands The
Brighton BN1.......... 142 E5
Hastings TN34......... 136 E5
Woodlands Way TN34.. 136 E6
Woodland Vale Rd TN37,
TN38................. 159 C8
Woodland Way
Brighton BN1.......... 142 F4
Crowborough TN6..... 37 F8
Crowhurst TN33....... 134 F4
Fairlight Cove TN35.... 138 E4
Heathfield TN21....... 82 B6
Woodland Wlk BN2.... 165 D4
Woodleigh Rd RH15... 73 C4
**WOODMANS GREEN... 88 A3
Woodmans Oak TN33.. 88 A3
Woodpecker Cres RH15. 72 D3
Woodpecker Dr BN27.. 152 A8
Woodpecker La BN27.. 127 B3
Woodpecker Rd BN23.. 174 B2
Woodpecker Way**
Golden Cross BN27.... 127 B3
Uckfield TN22......... 78 D5
Wood Ride RH16....... 50 D3
Woodridge Cl RH16.... 51 A3
Woodruff Ave BN3..... 142 C2
WOOD'S CORNER...... 84 E3
Woodsgate Ave TN40.. 157 C6
Woodsgate Pk TN39... 157 B6
Woodsgate Way TN2....9 B6
Woods Gd RH17....... 74 B4
WOOD'S GREEN....... 29 F8
Woods Green Cotts TN5. 29 F7
Woods Hill Cl RH19.... 11 D6
Woods Hill La RH19.... 11 D6
Woods Ho BN3........ 163 A8
Woodside
Broad Oak TN31....... 90 B5
Crowborough TN6..... 25 E2
Kilndown TN17........ 20 F2
Woodside Ave BN1.... 142 D2
Woodside Cl TN2.......9 E6
Woodside Lodge BN1.. 142 D2
Woodside Rd
Pembury TN2...........9 E6
Rusthall TN4...........7 D4
Woodside Terr TN37... 151 F4
Woodside Way BN27... 152 A4
Woodsland Cl BN6..... 97 F4
Woodsland Rd BN6.... 97 F4
Wood's Pas 4 TN34... 160 B4
Woodspring Cl TN37... 136 B5
Wood St
East Grinstead RH19.... 1 D1
Royal Tunbridge Wells TN1.. 8 B4
Woodstock RH19....... 1 C2
Woodstock Rd TN39... 156 C6
Woodview Cl BN1...... 143 D6
Woodville Ct 9 TN39.. 157 B3
Woodville Rd TN39.... 157 B3
Woodward Cl BN23.... 185 E7
Woodwards Cl RH15... 73 B1
WOOLBRIDGE.......... 39 E2
Woolven Cl RH15...... 72 E1
Worcester Ct
5 Eastbourne BN23... 174 E1
1 Hove BN3.......... 163 E6
Worcester Villas BN3.. 162 C7
Worcester Way BN27.. 131 B5
Wordsworth Dr BN23.. 174 E2
Wordsworth Rise 6 RH19. 1 C1
Wordsworth St BN3.... 163 A7
Workhouse La
Icklesham TN36....... 116 F5
Westfield TN35........ 114 E3
WORLD'S END......... 73 D4
Worsham Ct TN39..... 156 C4
Worsham La TN40..... 157 F7
Worsted La RH19...... 11 B8

Wil–Zio 221

Wray Cl RH19.......... 11 D6
Wren Cl
Burgess Hill RH15...... 72 D3
Heathfield TN21....... 82 A7
Wren Ct
Battle TN33........... 112 F4
St Leonards TN38...... 135 E3
Wrentham Ho RH15.... 73 B3
Wrestwood Ave BN22.. 173 C1
Wrestwood Cl TN40... 157 D6
Wrestwood Rd TN40... 157 D6
Wrotham Cl
Eastbourne BN23...... 174 D1
Hastings TN34......... 136 E5
Wroxham Rd BN23.... 174 B4
Wyatts La RH17....... 33 D5
Wyberlye Rd RH15.... 73 A4
Wybourne Rise TN2... 17 B8
WYCH CROSS......... 22 E5
Wychperry Rd RH16... 50 D5
Wychurst Gdns TN40.. 157 D6
Wyck Ct BN41......... 162 A7
Wykeham Ct TN34..... 159 E8
Wykeham Rd TN34.... 159 E8
Wykeham Terr BN1.... 189 A2
Wykeham Way RH15... 73 C2
Wynberg Cotts TN4.... 39 C6
Wyndham St BN2...... 189 C1
Wynnes Mews BN3.... 163 A7
Wynnstay RH15........ 73 B2
Wyshe The BN45...... 119 C6
Wythwood RH16....... 50 E1
Wyvern Way RH15.... 73 C3

Y

Yardley St BN1........ 189 B5
Yarrow Rd BN7........ 123 B2
Yates Cl TN31......... 95 A2
Yeomans BN8.......... 125 A7
Yeowart Bsns Ctr TN22. 78 C7
Yesterdays World Mus★
TN33................. 112 D4
Yew Ct 1 RH19.........1 D2
Yew La RH19...........1 B3
Yew Tree Cl
Broyle Side BN8....... 124 F7
Hastings TN34......... 136 E6
Heathfield TN21....... 82 A6
Yew Tree Cotts
Burgess Hill RH15...... 73 B3
Groombridge TN3...... 15 F8
Yewtree La TN6........ 39 E8
Yew Tree Rd TN4.......8 B8
Yielding's Cl BN21.... 184 D5
York Ave
East Grinstead RH19.... 11 A8
Hove BN3.............. 163 E6
York Bldgs 5 TN34... 159 F7
York Ct 13 BN3........ 163 E7
York Gdns 4 TN34.... 159 F7
York Gr BN1........... 189 A4
York Hill BN1......... 189 B4
York Ho BN41......... 162 B8
Yorklands BN3......... 142 B4
York Mans E 13 BN3.. 163 E6
York Mans W 12 BN3.. 163 E6
York Pl
Brighton BN1.......... 189 B3
Hove BN3.............. 163 E6
York Rd
Bexhill TN40.......... 158 A5
Burgess Hill RH15...... 72 D2
Eastbourne BN21...... 184 F2
Hove BN1, BN3........ 163 E6
Peacehaven BN10...... 178 E6
Royal Tunbridge Wells TN1.. 8 A4
St Leonards TN37..... 136 C4
Yorkshire Ct BN20.... 184 B7
York Villas BN1....... 189 A4
Youl Grange BN20.... 184 D1
Youngsmere Cl BN1... 143 B6
Ypres Tower Mus★ TN31.. 93 C5
Yvonne Robertson Ho
TN40................. 157 D5

Z

Zion Gdns BN1........ 189 A2

Addresses

Name and Address	Telephone	Page	Grid reference

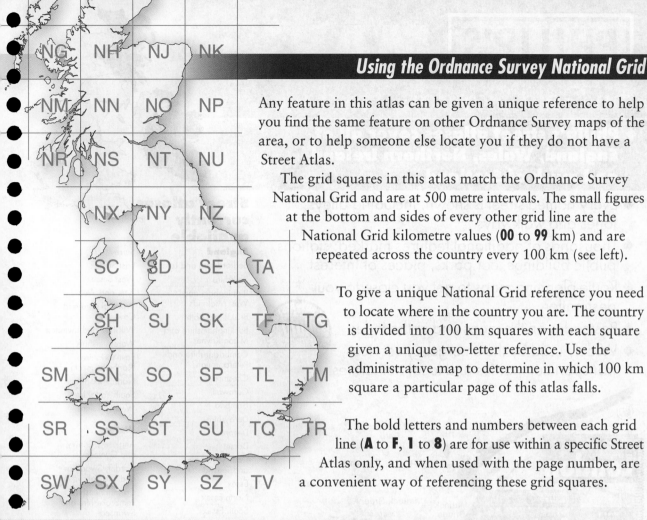

Any feature in this atlas can be given a unique reference to help you find the same feature on other Ordnance Survey maps of the area, or to help someone else locate you if they do not have a Street Atlas.

The grid squares in this atlas match the Ordnance Survey National Grid and are at 500 metre intervals. The small figures at the bottom and sides of every other grid line are the National Grid kilometre values (**00** to **99** km) and are repeated across the country every 100 km (see left).

To give a unique National Grid reference you need to locate where in the country you are. The country is divided into 100 km squares with each square given a unique two-letter reference. Use the administrative map to determine in which 100 km square a particular page of this atlas falls.

The bold letters and numbers between each grid line (**A** to **F**, **1** to **8**) are for use within a specific Street Atlas only, and when used with the page number, are a convenient way of referencing these grid squares.

Example   The railway bridge over DARLEY GREEN RD in grid square B1

Step 1: Identify the two-letter reference, in this example the page is in **SP**

Step 2: Identify the 1 km square in which the railway bridge falls. Use the figures in the southwest corner of this square: Eastings **17**, Northings **74**. This gives a unique reference: **SP 17 74**, accurate to 1 km.

Step 3: To give a more precise reference accurate to 100 m you need to estimate how many tenths along and how many tenths up this 1 km square the feature is (to help with this the 1 km square is divided into four 500 m squares). This makes the bridge about **8** tenths along and about **1** tenth up from the southwest corner.

This gives a unique reference: **SP 178 741**, accurate to 100 m.

Eastings (read from left to right along the bottom) come before Northings (read from bottom to top). If you have trouble remembering say to yourself "Along the hall, THEN up the stairs"!

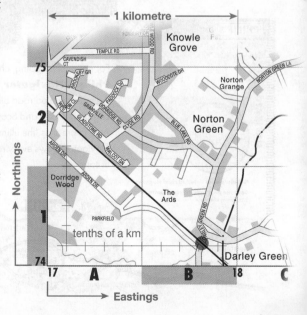

PHILIP'S MAPS

the Gold Standard for drivers

◆ **Philip's street atlases cover all of England, Wales, Northern Ireland and much of Scotland**

- ◆ Every named street is shown, including alleys, lanes and walkways
- ◆ Thousands of additional features marked: stations, public buildings, car parks, places of interest
- ◆ Route-planning maps to get you close to your destination
- ◆ Postcodes on the maps and in the index
- ◆ Widely used by the emergency services, transport companies and local authorities

PHILIP'S
STREET ATLAS
London

More **streets**
More lanes and alleys
More **named build**
More house numbers
More **clear routes**

'Absolutely fabulou
www.london-taxi.co.uk

'Must buy' Evening Standa

PHILIP'S
STREET ATLAS
Greater Manchester
Bolton, Bury, Manchester, Oldham, Rochdale

Salford, Stockport, Tameside, Trafford, Wigan

PHILIP'S
STREET ATLAS
Dorset
Bournemouth and Poole
Christchurch, Dorchester, Weymouth

PHILIP'S
STREET ATLAS
Co Armagh Co Down
Armagh, Banger, Craigavon, Downpatrick, Newry, Newtownards

Includes route-planning map

PHILIP'S
NEW EDITION
NAVIGATOR Britain

'The reigning champion of road atlases'
The Sunday Times

With speed cameras
from PocketGPSWorld.com

Britain's most detailed road mapping
Spot the best breakfast competition
in our survey of motorway services

For national mapping, choose **Philip's Navigator Britain** the most detailed road atlas available of England, Wales and Scotland. Hailed by Auto Express as 'the ultimate road atlas', Navigator shows every road and lane in Britain.

Street atlases currently available

England

Bedfordshire and Luton	Surrey
Berkshire	East Sussex
Birmingham and West Midlands	West Sussex
Bristol and Bath	Tyne and Wear
Buckinghamshire and Milton Keynes	Warwickshire and Coventry
Cambridgeshire and Peterborough	Wiltshire and Swindon
Cheshire	Worcestershire
Cornwall	East Yorkshire Northern Lincolnshire
Cumbria	North Yorkshire
Derbyshire	South Yorkshire
Devon	West Yorkshire
Dorset	
County Durham and Teesside	**Wales**
Essex	Anglesey, Conwy and Gwynedd
North Essex	Cardiff, Swansea and The Valleys
South Essex	Carmarthenshire, Pembrokeshire and Swansea
Gloucestershire and Bristol	Ceredigion and South Gwynedd
Hampshire	
North Hampshire	Denbighshire, Flintshire, Wrexham
South Hampshire	Herefordshire Monmouthshire
Herefordshire Monmouthshire	Powys
Hertfordshire	
Isle of Wight	**Scotland**
Kent	Aberdeenshire
East Kent	Ayrshire
West Kent	Dumfries and Galloway
Lancashire	Edinburgh and East Central Scotland
Leicestershire and Rutland	Fife and Tayside
Lincolnshire	Glasgow and West Central Scotland
Liverpool and Merseyside	Inverness and Moray
London	Lanarkshire
Greater Manchester	Scottish Borders
Norfolk	
Northamptonshire	**Northern Ireland**
Northumberland	County Antrim and County Londonderry
Nottinghamshire	County Armagh and County Down
Oxfordshire	
Shropshire	Belfast
Somerset	County Tyrone and County Fermanagh
Staffordshire	
Suffolk	

Philip's maps and atlases are available from bookshops, motorway services and petrol stations.

For further details visit
www.philips-maps.co.uk